The Last Impresario

ALSO BY HARLOW ROBINSON

SERGEI PROKOFIEV: A BIOGRAPHY

HARLOW ROBINSON

The Last Impresario

■ THE LIFE, TIMES, AND LEGACY OF ■

SOL HUROK

VIKING

VIKING
Published by the Penguin Group
Penguin Books USA Inc., 375 Hudson Street,
New York, New York 10014, U.S.A.
Penguin Books Ltd, 27 Wrights Lane, London W8 5TZ, England
Penguin Books Australia Ltd, Ringwood, Victoria, Australia
Penguin Books Canada Ltd, 10 Alcorn Avenue,
Toronto, Ontario, Canada M4V 3B2
Penguin Books (N.Z.) Ltd, 182–190 Wairau Road,
Auckland 10, New Zealand

Penguin Books Ltd, Registered Offices:
Harmondsworth, Middlesex, England

First published in 1994 by Viking Penguin,
a division of Penguin Books USA Inc.

1   3   5   7   9   10   8   6   4   2

Grateful acknowledgment is made for permission to reprint excerpts from the following copyrighted works:
Beyond Frontiers by Vladimir Ashkenazy with Jasper Parrott. Reprinted with the permission of Atheneum Publishers, an imprint of Macmillan Publishing Company and Collins, an imprint of HarperCollins Publishers Limited. Copyright © 1985 by Jasper Parrott.
Letters written by Irving Deakin to Sol Hurok. By permission of Natasha Deakin.
Impresario by Sol Hurok and Ruth Goode. Copyright © 1946 and renewed 1973 by Sol Hurok and Ruth Goode. Reprinted by permission of Random House, Inc.
Letters and other writings by Sol Hurok from the private archives of Ruth Hurok Lief and Arthur Lief.
My Many Years by Arthur Rubinstein. Copyright © 1980 by Arthur Rubinstein. Reprinted by permission of Alfred A. Knopf, Inc.

LIBRARY OF CONGRESS CATALOGING IN PUBLICATION DATA
Robinson, Harlow
The last impresario: the life, times, and legacy of Sol Hurok/Harlow Robinson.
p.   cm.
Includes bibliographical references and index.
ISBN 0-670-82529-8
1. Hurok, Sol, 1888–1974.   2. Impresarios—Biography.   I. Title.
ML429.H87R6   1994
780'.92—dc20
[B]   93–22138

Printed in the United States of America · Set in Adobe Simoncini Garamond
Designed by Francesca Belanger

For Ruth and Arthur Lief

■   ■   ■

"Every crowd has a silver lining."—*P. T. Barnum*

"When you are skinning your customers you should leave some skin on to grow again so that you can skin them again."
—*Nikita Khrushchev*

CONTENTS

■ ■ ■

PART III

Photographs follow page 202.

ACKNOWLEDGMENTS

■ ■ ■

MANY PEOPLE HAVE HELPED ME in the process of researching and writing this book. I am grateful first of all to Herbert Glass, who asked me to write an article on Hurok, which soon led to this project; and to Amanda Vaill, who supported and guided the work in its delicate early stages. Thanks also to those who knew and/or worked with Hurok and who agreed to be interviewed: Genrietta Belyaeva, Van Cliburn, Alexandra Danilova, Agnes de Mille, Nina Dorliak, Natalia Dudinskaya, Martin Feinstein, Betty Ferrell, Max Gershunoff, Bob Gardner, Patrick Hayes, Peter Hyams, Edward Ivanyan, Lillian Libman, Tatiana Riabouchinska Lichine, Arthur Lief, Ruth Hurok Lief, Igor Moiseyev, Larissa Netto, Rudolf Nureyev, Sergei Obratsov, Edward Perper, Nela Rubinstein, Konstantin Sergeyev, Wayne Shilkret, Alexander Slobodyanik, Isaac Stern, Anna Straus, Galina Ulanova, Lee Walter, Herbert Wasserman, and Rita Zaitseva.

Without the incomparable collection and staff of the Performing Arts Library of the New York Public Library at Lincoln Center (whose establishment Hurok's fund-raising efforts helped to make possible), I would not have been able to undertake this biography. I am especially indebted to the staff of the Dance Collection.

For unstinting encouragement, advice, and prodding along the way, I am deeply grateful to my dear friends Kate Amend and Johanna Demetrakas. Joseph Roddy kindly shared with me materials from his personal archives. Ellen Scaruffi brought to my attention letters in the Bakhmeteff Collection of the Columbia University Library. Dennis Anderson and Aleksei Mikhalev offered valuable commentary on early drafts of the manuscript. My editor at Viking, Edward Iwanicki, provided expert assistance in assembling all the pieces and ensuring they made sense. My agent, Maxine Groffsky, enthusiastically supported this book from its inception and made it possible for me to write it.

But I owe my greatest debts of gratitude to Ruth and Arthur Lief, who not only shared with me their kindness, encouragement, personal memories, and observations, but also their private archives and photographs; and finally, to Robert Holley, who throughout the entire process remained a steadfast and loving companion, editor, and guide, putting up for the most part cheerfully with all manner of disruptions and inconveniences and helping to keep me (again for the most part) sane.

All translations from Russian sources (both texts and interviews) are mine unless indicated.

Albany, New York
April 1993

INTRODUCTION
Going Backstage
■ ■ ■

"This work, it's my vacation."—*Sol Hurok*

DURING THE SIX YEARS I was working on this biography, two revolutions took place: one in the former Soviet Union, and one in the world of the performing arts in the United States. Although Sol Hurok was no longer alive to see them, his life touched on both.

I began this project in the spring of 1987, when it was becoming increasingly clear that something remarkable was going on in what we now have to refer to as the former USSR. One of the clearest signs of a new, more open spirit in Moscow was the revival of Soviet-American cultural exchange, which had fallen into sad disrepair by late 1979 after several highly publicized defections by Soviet performers on tour in the United States.

The most embarrassing for the easily offended Soviet government had been the defection of soloist Alexander Godunov from the Bolshoi Ballet in late August 1979. His dramatic request for political asylum in the United States, followed by American officials' questioning of his ballerina wife aboard a Moscow-bound jet on the runway at Kennedy Airport, had greatly heightened tensions between Moscow and Washington. A few weeks later, two more Bolshoi dancers, Leonid and Valentina Kozlova, had also requested and received political asylum in Los Angeles during the company's performances there. Three months later, in late December 1979, the badly frayed "thin thread" of Soviet-American cultural exchange snapped when the Soviet army invaded Afghanistan, provoking President Carter to retaliate by canceling American participation in the upcoming 1980 Moscow Olympics. After these unfortunate events, Soviet-American cultural relations entered the deep freeze for the next six years, until Mikhail Gorbachev came to power in early 1985.

For all these reasons, the Bolshoi Ballet's American tour in spring and summer of 1987, its first since 1979 and the first under Gorbachev, assumed special political and cultural significance. By then, relations between Moscow and Washington were thawing rapidly, leading to the remarkable series of disarmament agreements signed by Gorbachev and Reagan. Gorbachev's Gorby-mania trip to the United States in December 1987, followed by Reagan's visit to Moscow in May 1988—when the two leaders strolled casually across Red Square, the heart of what Reagan had once denounced as the "evil empire"—would effectively bring an end to the Cold War. No one (least of all Sovietologists, trained to believe in the impregnability of the Soviet system) imagined at the time, of course, that within a few years, the Communist party would fall from power all across Eastern Europe and even in the USSR itself, leading to a new world order.

In connection with the Bolshoi Ballet's appearance at the Dorothy Chandler Pavilion in Los Angeles, I was asked by Herbert Glass, the editor of *Performing Arts*, to write an article about Sol Hurok and his pioneering role in bringing Soviet attractions (including the Bolshoi) to the United States. At the time my knowledge of Hurok's work was rather superficial. I did remember seeing the Moiseyev Ensemble under the "S. Hurok Presents" label at the Felt Forum at Madison Square Garden as a college student in 1970, soon after I had spent a summer studying Russian in Leningrad—an experience that would change my life. By then, Hurok was in the twilight of his career and had already sold his firm to a corporate conglomerate.

In the course of researching that article in 1987, I came to learn much more about Hurok and to see what a huge contribution he had made not only to Soviet-American cultural exchange, but also to the development of the performing arts in the United States. I came to see that what we now think of as "serious" American dance had its beginnings in the various soloists and companies Hurok presented in New York and—even more important—in small towns and cities all across America. Many Americans living far from Manhattan owed their first experience of live dance, music, and theater to Hurok and his organization. Who knows how many future dancers, actors, violinists, and pianists in western Pennsylvania or the Texas Panhandle first found their calling because of seeing an attraction presented under the seemingly ubiquitous "S. Hurok Presents" banner?

I also came to understand that although Hurok enjoyed making, having, and—most of all—spending money, profit was never his primary motivation. A born salesman and promoter, he could probably have made much more money in other fields. He did what he did because he loved it and because he was no less needy of applause and public acclamation than any of his star performers. When he died in 1974, he was the last large-scale independent commercial presenter of high culture in the United States; since his death, no one has come forward to replace him. Since the early 1980s, financial support for the arts in America from all sources, both private and public, has declined drastically. Some of the nation's most prestigious companies have been forced to sharply cut back their scale and range of activities; others have had to cease operation altogether.

Even if Hurok's reasons for presenting dance, music, and theater on a larger scale than any other individual American impresario had ever attempted were in large part selfish, the consequences of his work enriched and improved the lives of many people. He was a shining example of enlightened capitalist self-interest, managing to get rich and still do good. Hurok was convinced that the arts were an essential part of human existence and that to live on the earth without them was hardly even worthwhile. He was an important force behind the establishment of the National Endowment for the Arts and an insistent advocate (especially in his later years) of government subsidy for dance and opera companies; nothing enraged him more than to see the arts treated as a frill. The message he delivered to members of Congress at hearings on creating the NEA on the eve of John Kennedy's assassination in 1963 sounds very relevant today, when a new Democratic administration is moving toward a renewed appreciation of the role of education and the arts in building a healthy and productive society:

> I am an American who was not born in this country but sought to be an American out of my love for this land and its great dream of freedom and democracy. I have dedicated my life to the belief that the arts are a major part of any life and that to be without them is to starve, no matter what other wealth one may achieve.
>
> The country is ready. The people's leisure time is growing steadily and where else but in the arts can it find the cure for its hunger for things beyond those materials? The arts cannot support themselves. The Government must help. It is time.

When Sol Hurok finally died on March 5, 1974, at the age (give or take a few years in the usual show business fashion) of eighty-five, he did so in the same way he had lived: with style and in a blaze of publicity. A heart attack took him quickly, after lunch with guitarist Andrés Segovia and before a meeting with banker David Rockefeller. Hurok's funeral, held a few days later on the stage of Carnegie Hall, where he had so often presented his "attractions," drew a full house of celebrities from the worlds of music, dance, opera, film, politics, and international diplomacy. Like almost all the events with which he was associated, it was a newsworthy social and cultural happening, covered on front pages from New York to Nome.

Appropriately enough, Hurok died very close to the spot in lower Manhattan where he had first entered the United States as a nearly kopeckless immigrant from Ukraine in 1906. In the intervening years, as he grew from the rustic Solomon Izrailevich Gurkov to the legendary S. Hurok, ascending from obscurity to fame, he endured many hardships, reversals, and triumphs. He became a virtuoso at catering to the whims of temperamental and talented performers and offering them up with unmatched gusto and panache to an impressionable American audience whose income and desire for high-class entertainment were shooting up as fast as the skyscrapers in Manhattan. His logo, "S. Hurok Presents"—which headlined marquees and posters and programs featuring many of the greatest names in high-culture show business—became synonymous with excellence, excitement, and hoopla.

Among the artists and ensembles who appeared under Hurok's name and aegis were dancers like Anna Pavlova, Isadora Duncan, Martha Graham, Agnes de Mille, and Leonide Massine; singers like Fyodor Chaliapin, Marian Anderson, and Galina Vishnevskaya; musicians like Isaac Stern, David Oistrakh, Mstislav Rostropovich, Arthur Rubinstein, and Van Cliburn; and ensembles like the Moiseyev Folk Dance Ensemble, the Bolshoi Ballet, the Kirov Ballet, the Royal Ballet, American Ballet Theatre, and the Moscow Art Theatre. Many of them owed their careers to Hurok, who had often taken risks on performers rejected by other, less imaginative managers. His renown as a presenter of high-profile and high-octane high-culture events was so great that his name even entered the popular American lexicon. To be "the Hurok" in a given field meant to be the best, the most prominent, the shrewdest.

As many of his detractors and admirers liked to point out, there was something of an earlier American showman, P. T. Barnum, in Hurok's persuasive, larger-than-life personality. Among other qualities, the two men shared a genius for advertising and public relations, a fondness (even obsession) for telling tall tales about themselves and their performers, a passion for self-invention, and an insatiable thirst for applause and self-aggrandizement. Like Barnum, Hurok was as much—or more—of a celebrity than any one of the artists that he liked to call his "children."

Though he gained fame through presenting tony musicians and dancers, Hurok himself could neither read music nor dance. What he did have was what the Russians call *nyukh* (a good nose for things), an almost infallible sense of an artist's potential public appeal, the vaulting ambition typical of so many Eastern European immigrants, and a keen business sense. He also had a unique combination of New York street smarts and Jewish-Slavic stamina. If Barnum's favorite maxim was the cynical and ultimately depressing "There's a sucker born every minute," Hurok's was the more subtle and ironic "When people don't want to come, nothing will stop them."

Hurok accomplished many things in his long lifetime, but perhaps his two most important and enduring achievements were introducing American audiences to ballet and bringing Soviet/Russian attractions to the United States after the death of Josef Stalin.

Almost single-handedly at first, Hurok began acquainting America with ballet in the 1920s and 1930s. He presented Anna Pavlova and then the Monte Carlo Ballet Russe in New York—and on tour—in communities all across the country, introducing ballerinas to remote and rugged places where no toe shoe had ever tread before. Hurok never hid his preference for the Russian ballet and dance tradition, which he advocated enthusiastically and tirelessly—most spectacularly, perhaps, when he imported in rapid succession the Moiseyev Folk Dance Ensemble, the Bolshoi Ballet, and the Kirov Ballet from the hitherto sealed USSR in the late 1950s and early 1960s. Their robust, energetic style was also embraced by the American audience, including that one-time arbiter of middle-class taste, Ed Sullivan, who put the Moiseyev on television at the end of the McCarthy era just as the Beatles were about to transform the entertainment landscape.

If it is true, as *New Yorker* critic Arlene Croce recently observed, that "Americans who have a passing acquaintance with ballet think of it as Russian," then Hurok is the main reason why. In this sense, his legacy is still very alive and influential today.

As an architect and practitioner of Soviet-American cultural exchange, Hurok was unequaled. In their choreographic, cultural, and political significance, his commercially successful presentations of the Moiseyev in 1958 and the Bolshoi Ballet in 1959 still rank among the great entertainment coups of the century. Both were defining events of the entire post-Stalinist Cold War era. Even now, as the vivid longtime reality of Soviet-American confrontation fades with each passing day, Hurok's contribution to better understanding between two governments capable of blowing each other to nuclear bits remains unassailable and remarkable. By bringing Soviet artists to the West and American artists to the USSR from the mid-1950s through the mid-1970s, Hurok added an important measure of continuity and humanity to the fragile superpower relationship.

By exposing each side to the other, he also helped to put into motion the process of cultural and social liberalization that eventually brought down the Berlin Wall and the entire Soviet system. Once eyes on both sides of the Iron Curtain were opened to the fact that their supposed enemies were people too, with their own songs and dances, there was no closing them again. Even at the height of the Cuban Missile Crisis, the moment at which the world came closer than ever to nuclear war, the Bolshoi Ballet was dancing across the United States under the "S. Hurok Presents" banner.

Nowhere is Hurok's central role in cultural exchange remembered more warmly than in Russia, where he is still regarded by both audiences and performers as a kind of Prince Charming of the arts who awoke them after decades of Stalinist slumber. Indeed, his name is almost more familiar there today than it is in America, whose collective historical memory seems to grow shorter with each passing year. In early 1990, after Mikhail Gorbachev had been in power for nearly five years and *glasnost* had already lost most of its luster for Soviet citizens, the magazine *Muzykal'naia zhizn' (Musical Life)* published a translation of my article on Hurok, commenting, "Today, as we look back at the many decades of the rather complicated and contradictory history of Soviet-American cultural relations (which fortunately have now entered a much more favorable phase), it would be wrong to overlook the businessman and devoted knight of music and choreography who did so much so to prevent the thin thread of mutually beneficial contacts from breaking."

Hurok's persistent and long-term efforts to import Soviet performers into the United States (he had been working toward this goal in Moscow since the 1920s) also brought him to the attention of the U.S. government, whose intelligence community felt deeply ambivalent about cultural exchange. Especially after World War II, the FBI and CIA believed that the importation of Soviet performers (especially large ensembles) was a security risk and assumed that spies were lurking among the ballerinas and violinists. There is no question (as former Soviet officials are today more than willing to admit) that some low-level surveillance was happening during American tours by Soviet performing artists, who were almost always accompanied by official escorts with vague duties.

Similarly, Hurok and other Americans involved in cultural exchange in the USSR often shared their observations with State

Department officials in Washington after returning from Moscow. Their experience was very valuable at a time when very few Americans were traveling to Russia. Because he spoke both Russian and English, and because of his diplomatic contacts in both countries, Hurok was a valuable source of information to bureaucrats on both sides of the Iron Curtain. Like virtually all regular travelers to the USSR during the Cold War era, he was monitored by intelligence organs on both sides, but there is no evidence that he ever engaged in serious espionage.

Nevertheless, the CIA still refuses to release its files on Hurok. The agency turned down my request to examine the material on the grounds (as stated in a letter to me) that the files (1) "apply to material which is properly classified pursuant to an Executive order in the interest of national defense or foreign policy"; (2) "apply to the Director's statutory obligations to protect from disclosure intelligence sources and methods, as well as the organization, functions, names, official titles, salaries or numbers of personnel by the Agency, in accord with the National Security Act of 1947 and the CIA Act of 1949, respectively"; and (3) "apply to information release of which would constitute an unwarranted invasion of the personal privacy of other individuals."

In light of the new post-ideological relations between Moscow and Washington, such knee-jerk precautions involving an entertainment personality who did nothing more suspicious than make friends and do business in the USSR at the height of the Cold War appear excessive. It turns out that our own CIA is having no less trouble adjusting to the post-Soviet era than are former members of the Communist party or the KGB.

Shortly after my article appeared in *Performing Arts* in August 1987, I was telephoned by a woman who said she wanted to tell me that she liked what I had written about her father. The caller was Sol Hurok's daughter and only child, Ruth Hurok Lief. She asked if we could meet (I was living in Los Angeles then) at the Westwood Hotel, where she and her husband, who lived in New York, were staying. They happened to be out "on the coast" visiting her son, the film director Peter Hyams, and his family. We agreed on a time and met for afternoon tea.

Talking to Ruth and her husband, Arthur Lief, a conductor who knew and had worked for Hurok for twenty years, suddenly brought Sol Hurok to life in a whole new way. Their stories of his extravagant behavior, old-country humor, and frequently insensitive treatment of both relatives and associates brought depth and reality to the one-dimensional, even propagandistic portraits (most of them created by Hurok himself) I had come across in my research. They encouraged me to write a book about this man they had loved and, at times, hated.

Over the next few years, I met many times with Ruth and Arthur at their spacious, elegant apartment overlooking the Museum of Natural History. Its walls are covered with signed photos of the great stars Hurok presented and knew: Pavlova, Stern, Shostakovich, Rostropovich. Here, they shared with me their memories of his generosity—and of his sometimes cruel insensitivity and egomania. Because Hurok couldn't write, because so much of his personality resided in what he said and how he said it, and because he belonged so completely to the Yiddish–Eastern European tradition of storytelling, the affectionate help Ruth and Arthur gave me in recreating the way he spoke and moved and reacted was vital to this book.

But I soon came to understand that even Hurok's daughter knew surprisingly little about many aspects of her father's life and past. Eager to jettison the facts of his humble origins, and intent on creating an impressive and attractive persona, Hurok had actively obscured many facts about his personal history—even from Ruth. As I sought out more people who had known and worked with him, his conscious obscuring of the record became part of a clear behavioral pattern. He held people at a strictly controlled distance, fiercely guarding his emotional privacy even as he lived nonstop in the public eye.

Several of Hurok's associates and artists have observed that one of his greatest phobias was having members of the audience come backstage and "see the ballerinas sweat." He hated to have the image of effortless beauty that had been created onstage defiled. Better to have the public leave the theater believing, in the words of the song from *A Chorus Line*, that "everything is beautiful at the ballet." No need to pry into the ugly, even sordid backstage reality of smudged makeup, professional jealousies, cigarettes, and body odor.

Toward those who sought to write about him and his life Hurok adopted a similar attitude of benevolent obstructionism. When he was shooting a feature film about Hurok's life (*Tonight We Sing*) in 1953, director Mitchell Leisen and his crew were repeatedly frustrated because Hurok refused to tell them anything "real" about himself or his past. Hurok refused to let them—or anyone else— into the backstage of his life.

As Hurok's biographer, I experienced the same frustration Leisen felt. It was a daunting challenge to try to peel away the many layers of protective public relations armor. Hurok was remarkably successful at misleading and misinforming even those who believed they knew him well. Almost never did he forget that he wasn't just Sol Hurok; he was an institution, he was "S. Hurok Presents." And one of the greatest of all his created attractions was S. Hurok himself.

When I finally had the opportunity to travel in the spring of 1992 to Pogar, the dusty town on the border of Russia and Ukraine where Hurok was born at the end of the tsarist era, I came to understand much better the reasons behind Hurok's stubborn reluctance to reveal much of the emotional truth of his life. My Pogar host, the director of the town's thriving music school, drove me a few miles out of town, past white clouds of blooming cherry trees. We turned down a rutted lane and emerged onto an open field.

It was here, he explained to me, that all of the Jewish inhabitants of Pogar had been shot in a mass execution by the occupying Nazi army in the autumn of 1941. All that marked the spot now were plain stones in the grass and a small monument erected by the Soviet government that paid vague tribute to the "Communists, partisans and peaceful residents of the region" who had been shot here by the "German-Fascist invaders."

As Hurok knew all too well, if he, a Jew, had remained in Pogar instead of seeking a better life in America, this is the fate that would have awaited him. No wonder he was uncomfortable with reality.

Part 1

■ CHAPTER ONE ■

A Pogar of the Mind

"Er zogt nor tsvey mol in yor a lign: vinter un zumer."
("He only tells lies twice a year: winter and summer.")
—*Yiddish proverb*

SOL HUROK LOVED to tell stories. His favorite was his own. Since facts never constrained him, and since a dynamic rags-to-riches saga was also good for business, this master of self-aggrandizement provided the edifying story of his extravagant life with countless and increasingly colorful variations over the years. The tale grew taller and taller. A compulsive and shameless booster, he deftly navigated his self-portrait from the spoken word to countless newspaper accounts to two ghostwritten volumes and finally to the silver screen. There, under his careful supervision, Hurok's life story attained its glamorous and improbable apogee: the feature film *Tonight We Sing*. But then, he and Hollywood were meant for each other. Wary of the truth and eager to please, both vastly preferred fantasy to reality.

Eventually the Hurok chronicles—in both biographical and autobiographical form—achieved something like the status of a folk tale or a saint's life. Transmitted primarily by oral tradition—from the subject's own mouth—with elaborate ornamentation and improvisation, they were intended to propel the listener to inspiration, admiration, and ticket purchases. "With Hurok," according to the pianist Van Cliburn, one of his most famous and successful artists, "there was no such thing as a twice-told tale. He had favorites and wanted to hear them over and over." In the telling of these picaresque tales, Hurok, performing with delicious gusto as both narrator and hero, scored his greatest artistic triumph. He succeeded at nothing less than inventing a compelling and outsize fictional character: S. Hurok.

One of his old friends said it well. "Hurok is the only man I know who can talk about himself in the third person and sound absolutely natural."

Nor did it hurt that the circumstances of Hurok's life furnished the basic ingredients of the American dream: humble boyhood in the oppressed Old Country, voyaging adolescence to the land of liberty, enterprising youth in opportunity-rich America, prosperous and useful adulthood. No matter that some of the details got fudged in the process; enough of the necessary raw material existed to spin a captivating yarn. What wasn't there could be invented. And conveniently, most of those who could produce the facts had been left far behind.

"I don't think he was capable of the truth," dancer and choreographer Agnes de Mille, who knew Hurok for most of his professional life, said of him. "He could say the most incredible things about himself and other people."

Another long-time friend and client, violinist Isaac Stern, took a somewhat more charitable view of Hurok's tendency toward self-fictionalization. "The main thing—the wonderful thing—about the way he invented stories was that he really believed in them. That's just part of what made him tick."

One fact of Hurok's early life has never been in doubt: his birthplace. It was Pogar, a "town of no importance" boasting about five thousand inhabitants "including pigs and cows and horses" on the Sudost River, a tributary of the River Desna, in Ukraine. Or was it Ukraine?

So frequently have the frontiers in this part of the world shifted that determining where Ukraine (which means "borderland") stops and where Russia, Poland, or Belorussia begin has never been easy. Today, Pogar sits on the extreme southern edge of Russia, only a few miles from the northern border of what is the newly independent country of Ukraine. This is a flat and fertile land, blazing hot in summer and cold in winter, for many centuries the captive bread-basket of the Russian—and, later, Soviet—empire. The nearest large city is Bryansk. Not far away is Trubchevsk, the ancient town from which ill-fated Prince Igor (the hero of a medieval epic poem and of Alexander Borodin's opera *Prince Igor*) set out to fight the Polovtsians. Moscow lies about three hundred miles to the north-east, and Chernobyl about three hundred miles to the southwest. (Soon after the accident at the nuclear power plant in Chernobyl in 1986, the residents of Pogar began receiving a monthly bonus of thirty rubles from the government because they were living in a ra-diated zone.) It was in this region that Russian civilization first de-veloped.

Owing to its exposed location on an unprotected flat plain at the edge of southeastern Europe, Hurok's hometown has not en-joyed an especially happy history. Invasions and warfare have long been fixtures of life here. Apparently founded by Slavs in the eighth or ninth century B.C. (before the adoption of Christianity in 988) in a land then known as Rus, the settlement was mentioned for the first time in 1155 in the Hypatius Chronicle under the name Radogoshch. Radogoshch was a Slavic pagan god who favored trade, a fact that reflected the town's early identity as a trading cen-ter located on a strategic river route leading to the Black Sea. It re-tained this name until the early seventeenth century, through the course of numerous wars.

Ravaged by the Mongol Tartars in the 1230s, then claimed in turn by Lithuania, Russia, Poland, and then Russia again, Radogoshch (on the territory of what had come to be known as Ukraine) was burned down four times in the sixteenth century alone, as the Russian and Polish armies fought to capture it. In the mid-1600s, this incendiary legacy even inspired the town fathers (then Poles) to change its name from Radogoshch to Pogar—meaning "a burned place." When Ukraine was united with Russia in 1654, Pogar came under Russian control. Like many towns that had formerly been under Lithuanian or Polish control, however, Pogar received special consideration from Russian tsar Alexei under the so-called Magdeburg Law, which granted a certain degree of self-government. The tsar also decreed that Pogar could hold three large trade fairs annually—a tradition which has existed until the present day. Because of the predominance of trade in the local economy, serfdom was less firmly established here than elsewhere in the Russian Empire.

As time went on, Russian rule over Ukraine became more oppressive, even brutal. Within the Russian Empire, Pogar remained a Ukrainian town (within Chernigov Province) until shortly after the 1917 Bolshevik Revolution. In June 1918, it became a part of the Russian Republic of the new USSR, along with a large part of northern Ukraine. Since then, it has fallen under Russian (rather than Ukrainian) jurisdiction.

What all of this means is that Hurok grew up in a relatively cosmopolitan environment and with a confused national identity. Because Pogar was what was known as a "free town," it attracted people of many nationalities. Himself a Jew in an area with a large and thriving Jewish community, Hurok came of age in close contact with Russians, Poles, Ukrainians, Belorussians, and probably Lithuanians. Out of the approximately five thousand people in Pogar at the beginning of the twentieth century, about five hundred, or ten percent, were Jews. The Jewish community had its own bathhouse and primary school, as well as a synagogue.

Linguistically, Pogar was a veritable Babel. Indeed, linguists have long been intrigued by the Pogar dialect because of its unique combination of Russian, Ukrainian, and Belorussian words and expressions. To be a successful businessman, as Hurok's father reportedly was, one had to know at least a little Yiddish, Russian, Polish, Ukrainian, and Belorussian. Children often paid a price for this multicultural confusion, however. Like Hurok, who would later add English (at least he called it English) to this casserole of tongues, they ended up knowing many languages poorly. Violinist Isaac Stern liked to joke that "Hurok knows six languages—and all of them are Yiddish."

Both in *Impresario*, his unreliable ghostwritten public relations autobiography published in 1946, and in the countless interviews he granted so willingly to print and broadcast journalists, Hurok described his East European childhood as provincial, but not unhappy. Provincial it certainly was. "The first time an automobile came into Pogar," Hurok once joked, "the peasants were convinced the Devil was sitting inside." In the 1880s, when Hurok claimed to be born, the good people of Pogar had to travel more than twenty miles by horse to the nearest railroad station; it was nearly a hundred miles to the city of Gomel, and farther yet to the Ukrainian capitals of Kharkov or Kiev, or to the Belorussian capital of Minsk.

In Pogar, life revolved around agriculture and commerce. Serfdom had been abolished in the Russian Empire in 1861, but much of the land was still owned by wealthy aristocrats. The rich soil produced good crops of tobacco, and from the late seventeenth century, Pogar had been famous for its trade fairs, jammed with traveling minstrels and merchants plying their colorful wares. Especially on holidays, the local market "overflowed with food, with smoked meats and wooden tubs of fresh caviar, pressed caviar, red caviar, with fish and herring by the barrels." The smells, noise, and hurly-burly of market days must have come back to Hurok in later years when he played the part of the bear trainer in one of his favorite ballets, Stravinsky's *Petrushka*, set amid exactly such a scene.

Like most of the Jews in Pogar, Hurok's father, Izrail, made his living in retail. With the help of his wife, Sima, he ran a sort of general store out of a small booth on the central town square, selling hardware and other items. (Pogar was particularly famous for various types of metal containers, some of which were used for making home-brewed alcoholic beverages.) Hurok later claimed that his father was "not the shrewdest of businessmen" and let himself be cheated by the townsfolk, much to the dismay of his sons. They eventually instituted a more scientific accounting system than the easily erased chalk calculations of customers' debts maintained by their father. Just how prosperous Hurok's father was is open (like so many things in Hurok's family history) to question. In a 1973 interview with Bill Moyers, Hurok claimed that his parents "were well-to-do people." Only four years earlier, however, he told a different reporter exactly the opposite. "Hurok says he can write his autobiography in one sentence: 'I was born hungry.'" According to Hurok's only surviving close relative in Russia, his niece Rita Zaitseva of Moscow, his parents were "fairly well off," but never rich.

Hungry or not, Hurok claimed to have absorbed some basic business skills from his father. "My father was a wise man," he once recalled. "When a frost hits tobacco, the crop is ruined for that year. There were times when this happened to him, yet it never seemed to bother him. I asked him how he managed to seem so unconcerned. He smiled and said, 'My son, remember: When you make money, spend a little less; when you lose money, spend a little more.' " Hurok's first understanding of the need to give the customer what he wants also came from childhood. "I saw how my father treated customers. Don't fight. Don't argue. Agree to what you must today. Tomorrow is another day."

For Hurok, this Pogar philosophy would become a Manhattan credo. The customer always knows best. Give him what he wants. Tell him what he wants to hear.

Characteristically, Hurok omitted from *Impresario* and most interviews numerous essentials about his childhood—his precise birth date, information about his mother and siblings, and the fact that his real last name was not Hurok, but Gurkov. (Hurok and his family members were often teasingly called "*gurok,*" the word for "cucumber" in the local dialect.) He also minimized his Jewish heritage. The obfuscation of the circumstances of his early life became a habit with Hurok after he came to America in 1906. Like so many other immigrants, he wanted to make a fresh start, to distance himself from a culture, life, and people he had left behind. And later, when Hurok had become an institution—"S. Hurok Presents"—and his very name had become synonymous with glamor, when he had climbed to the WASP-laden ranks of the Beautiful People, revelations about poor relations smelling of garlic and jabbering in Yiddish back in Pogar could have proved socially embarrassing and even commercially damaging. This helps to explain why Hurok sanctioned such a highly spurious version of his early life in the 1953 20th Century-Fox feature *Tonight We Sing*. In a remarkable memo to Darryl Zanuck, Hurok, credited as the film's "Technical Advisor," demanded "the complete deletion of all Jewish dialect, which can only result in a cheap vaudeville atmosphere."

When Hurok would talk with Isaac Stern, who was also born in Ukraine, about his childhood there, the violinist noticed that he would discuss only "fanciful things, never anything of substance or anything involving real feelings."

Most sources give Solomon Izrailevich Gurkov's date of birth as April 9, 1888. His official certificate of marriage to Tamara ("Mary") Shapiro, dated March 28, 1908, in Brooklyn, does not confirm this date, however. It states Hurok's age as twenty-one. Even if Hurok had given his age as of his upcoming birthday, it should have been twenty, not twenty-one, if he had in fact been born in 1888. But then many who knew Hurok well, including his stepson Edward Perper, believed he reduced his age—like so many other show business personalities—by as much as five years. When his grandson Peter Hyams once asked Hurok if he was really born in 1888 (the date also given on his U.S. passport), he replied, "No. Is mistake." But he declined to elaborate on what was the correct date.

Attempting to downplay his Jewish origins, Hurok in later years often substituted "Alexandrovich" for his patronymic "Izrailevich." Never noted for strong familial attachments, Hurok displayed few tender sentiments toward his mother. In *Impresario* she fails to receive even a single mention, perhaps because he wanted people to think that, like some mythological hero, he didn't need a mother to make his grand entrance into the world. Nor did his conversations with his daughter, Ruth Hurok Lief, ever touch upon his parents. In an interview with the *New York Times* less than a year before he died, suddenly sentimental, Hurok did reveal that his nephew in Leningrad had recently sent him the first photograph of his mother that he had ever seen.

"It's given me a new lease on life," he said then. "I have the photo right by my bed. She died more than fifty years ago. It's marvelous the way her eyes look at me all the time. She was such a smart woman, and I had such great affection and love for her as a youngster. I talk to her, and she helps me so much to be not alone anymore."

Hurok was equally reticent on the subject of his siblings. According to his niece, Hurok's mother bore no less than nineteen children—thirteen sons and six daughters. Only nine survived to adulthood, however: five sons and four daughters. Hurok was the third oldest of the sons. In a 1941 interview with *Cue* magazine, Hurok spoke of a sister who was still living in Pogar. When he began traveling regularly to the Soviet Union in the 1920s and 1930s, he also reestablished contact with an older brother, Asher, who had stayed behind and eventually became a teacher in Leningrad. Often when Hurok arrived in Moscow he would call Asher, who would come from Leningrad to see him, frequently with his son, Hurok's nephew. According to Hurok's Soviet interpreter and secretary, the brothers would spend long evenings waxing nostalgic about how they lived back in Pogar. In almost Gogolian fashion, they would celebrate the *pirozhki* and other country delicacies their dear departed mother used to prepare. Although he bought Asher many gifts, especially in the 1960s and 1970s, including a new car, and pulled strings to help him get a better apartment in Leningrad, Hurok never brought his brother to the United States, even though he wanted to come. Asher died in Leningrad in 1973 at age ninety-four, about a year before Hurok.

To Ruth, his only child, Hurok never spoke even of the existence of an uncle or aunt or cousins back in the old country. He never spoke with her of his own family background, or of her grandparents.

My own 1992 trip to Pogar failed to turn up much more information on Hurok's family. Because the few Jews remaining in the town were executed by the invading German army in October 1941, there is no one left in Pogar now who could provide any information. (Hurok's niece Rita Zaitseva survived only because she had gone to Moscow to study.) Even the young town historian had been unable to find any documentation on the Gurkov clan.

In his own accounts of his Pogar childhood, especially those intended for popular consumption, Hurok scrupulously avoided facts. Instead, he created a fairy-tale atmosphere, one drawn from the pretty world of tsarist Russia as embodied in his favorite ballets—*The Nutcracker, Sleeping Beauty, Swan Lake*. Reading *Impresario*, one can almost forget that Hurok was a Jew living in a society and in an era marred by virulent outbreaks of anti-Semitism. One can almost forget that Jews were forced to live an often humiliating existence and that cruelty and brutality on the part of local police, tsarist soldiers, and government authorities were an accepted part of daily life. One can almost forget that because of their ethnic origins and religious beliefs, Hurok and his family were considered social outcasts by the ruling Russians. Although he mentions perfunctorily that Pogar had seven churches and "our one synagogue," Hurok rhapsodizes at much greater length over the romantic delights of Christian customs. The holidays of Easter and Christmas, essential to the exotic image of Russia on which Hurok's attractions so successfully capitalized, instilled in him a special, if largely bogus, lyricism. If Hurok didn't have a fairy-tale childhood, he would invent one.

"Christmas was the high and happy time, the gaudy frosting on the cake of the year. The tinselly trees, the presents, the visiting back and forth from house to house, from town to town, from farm to village, the eating and drinking."

As a Jew in the reactionary and racist environment that prevailed in the Russian Empire in the wake of the assassination of Tsar Alexander II in 1881, Hurok belonged to a threatened minority. Denied most of the educational, legal, economic, and social opportunities available to the ruling Russians, Jews were forced to live in crowded urban settlements. Frequently they became the target of vicious attacks and mob violence. Although Pogar was spared, the widespread pogroms of 1881 and again in 1903–1905 made life for the Jews in Russia and Ukraine nearly unbearable and stimulated many to emigrate to America. As Irving Howe laments in *World of Our Fathers*, "Neither stability nor peace, well-being nor equality, was possible for the Jews of Russia."

How much pain Hurok felt as a Jewish boy in a threatening anti-Semitic world, he was never quick to reveal. But he had to learn early how to survive in a hostile environment and how to deal with many kinds of people, skills that would come in handy in the impresario's trade. He learned how to conceal his feelings and the facts of his origin, lest they be used against him. He learned how to create a more beautiful world in his imagination.

Like many Russian Jews of his generation, Hurok gravitated toward the socialist movement that was growing rapidly throughout the Russian Empire at the end of the nineteenth century. By age fourteen, Hurok claimed, he was already attending revolutionary meetings and had become "an inconspicuous figure in the little revolutionary movement of Pogar." In 1904, when on business for his father in the industrial city of Ekaterinoslav, some of Hurok's political friends took him to hear "a stocky man with a long beard, a bushel of hair, flowing mustache, dressed as a merchant. . . . What he said seared the mind with words of flame." Some months later, Hurok discovered he had been listening to the great Russian writer and political activist Maxim Gorky. The excitement and danger of Russian political life that Hurok directly experienced in the early years of the twentieth century stayed with him for the rest of his life. He remained fascinated with politics and retained his early socialist-liberal sentiments to the end.

But politics ceded to music in Hurok's youthful enthusiasms. "To be born in Russia is to be born singing," he said more than once. And truly, small towns like Pogar boasted a vital musical culture as a part of normal daily life. (Even now, the most important building on the main square of Pogar is the local music school.) Singing often accompanied work, while dancing and playing instruments were the principal means of relaxation. Everyone participated—not just those with special ability or training. To his eternal frustration, Hurok demonstrated absolutely no musical aptitude, but he still started playing the balalaika at the tender age of eight. "There was not a worse balalaika player in Pogar, perhaps not in all the Ukraine, but still I played." Eventually he tried to play "six or seven instruments," but was "bad at all of them."

"If I'd studied the piano when I was a boy," Hurok told a reporter in later years, "I wouldn't be doing what I am now. I'd be a poor pianist."

A self-confessed "bad boy" indifferent to school, he would also sneak out late at night to join in singing around a bonfire and listen with pleasure to the village maidens singing on their way to the fields. Schoolwork paled in comparison to music and dancing.

"There was music at night, there was music in the morning. The people sang and danced," he observed, adopting a self-conscious literary tone, in his second public-relations autobiography, *S. Hurok Presents*, published in 1953. "The village lake, over which the setting sun loved to linger, gave onto a little stream, hardly more than a brook. The tiny brook sang on its journey, and the rivulets danced on to the Desna; from there into the Sozh on its way to Gomel, down the Dnieper past the ancient city of Kiev, en route to the Black Sea. And in all the towns and villages it passed, I knew the people were singing and dancing."

And thus an impresario was born. Or at least it made a good story to believe so.

Soon, even the rustic delights of life in Pogar began to bore the ambitious Solomon Izrailevich. Trips with his father to the busy commercial city of Nizhny-Novogord (later called Gorky) on the Volga, and most of all to Moscow, filled the thirteen-year-old with visions of a more exciting world. "Before those domes and steeples, the great squares and the busy bustling streets—all of them paved, too!—I lost all heart for Pogar." Hurok's father did not take him to the opera or the ballet, but even so, there was no keeping him in the village after he had seen the wider world and its endless beckoning possibilities.

Meanwhile, the Russian Empire was bursting at the seams. By early 1905, the failures of the Russian fleet in the Russo-Japanese War, the worst student strikes the country had ever seen, the rise of various Marxist factions dedicated to overthrowing the tsarist regime, frequent assassinations and bombings, and nearly constant peasant disturbances in the countryside had created a dangerous atmosphere of pervasive and volatile instability. Soldiers patrolled the streets of St. Petersburg. Newspapers ceased publication. The railroads went on strike. Grand Duke Sergei, second cousin and brother-in-law of tsar Nicholas II, was shot by the terrorist organization "Will of the People."

By October, when the Revolution of 1905 reached its peak, a nationwide strike brought the economy and transportation system to a virtual standstill, paralyzing the country. The tsar was forced to make some concessions. Most important among them was the establishment of a Duma, a sort of parliament that would have the power to legislate; for the first time, the absolute power of Russian autocracy—bestowed upon the tsar directly from God—would be legally regulated. The three-hundred-year-old Romanov dynasty had become a constitutional monarchy, at least in theory. It was only the first in a series of mishandled concessions that would lead to the Bolshevik Revolution of 1917, an event that would drastically change life in Pogar and in every village, town, and city throughout the sprawling Russian Empire.

1905 was also a bad year for Russian Jews. The "Black Hundreds," notorious proto-fascist squads of right-wing extremists, repeatedly beat and even killed Jews, liberals, and intellectuals. Jewish settlements were raided and sacked. In response, thousands decided to leave for America, where many other Eastern European Jews had already taken refuge in an enormous wave of immigration. In 1906 alone, 153,748 Jews arrived in America.

In describing his own decision to leave Pogar and Russia, Hurok never mentioned the increasing persecution of Jews, although it surely affected his family and community. He presented his motivations as ambition and boredom: "Back in Pogar I announced that I could no longer stay at home." Taking a thousand rubles from his father, who thought he was sending him to learn the hardware business in the big city of Kharkov, Hurok set off. The exact sum he had when he went out into the world varied wildly depending on Hurok's mood when he told the story. "When I was about twelve," recalled Hurok's grandson Peter Hyams many years later with a smile, "he told me he came over with twenty dollars in his pocket. When I was twenty-two, he told me he had come over with no money. When I was twenty-seven, he told me he came over *owing* America about fifty dollars. So who knows?" If Hurok's resources did in fact amount to one thousand rubles, that was a lot of money in 1906, considering that as late as 1913, per capita income in the Russian Empire barely exceeded a hundred rubles.

When he left Pogar, Hurok was seventeen, although his age was also subject to variation—usually reduction—in different versions of the tale.

"My intention was not to come to America," he told Bill Moyers sixty-six years later. But at the railroad station he met an old friend, Shafran, who announced that he was on his way to America. On the spur of the moment, Hurok decided to join him, using the money his father had given him. Here the numerous versions of the tale diverge. Either he spent a week in Kharkov and then "returned to another small town near Pogar to visit a sweetheart" before leaving for the United States, or he left right away with Shafran, who promised that his brother in Brooklyn would find them jobs and homes. It is also possible that the "sweetheart"—most likely his future wife, Tamara (Mary) Shapiro—accompanied him to America.

Hurok fails to mention one important fact in his various romanticized accounts of his departure from Pogar. His oldest brother, Shmerul, had already made his way from the Old Country to America. Why Hurok later concealed the fact that he had a brother living in the United States (who apparently never returned to Russia, even for a visit) is not entirely clear. Although virtually nothing is known about Shmerul, Hurok's daughter Ruth claimed that Shmerul settled in Philadelphia, where he later ran into trouble that eventually landed him in prison. If this is true, it might explain Hurok's failure to acknowledge his existence: If the high-class public knew that the great S. Hurok had such an unsavory character for a brother, it might not be good for ticket sales.

Like most of the immigrants flowing out of Ukraine and Russia in 1906, Hurok had to spend almost all his capital just getting to New York. He followed a by now well-worn, though still dangerous, route across Russia, Poland, and Central Europe to the port city of Hamburg. There, German-Jewish organizations came to the aid of Jewish refugees and helped them continue on their way to America. Hurok's first stop was Brest-Litovsk, on the Polish border, where one could buy illegal emigration from smugglers for a fee—in his case (he said) 350 rubles. From Brest-Litovsk he traveled "huddled on the hard benches of a third-class train," only to be turned back at the Austro-Hungarian frontier. The smugglers then tried another route, via the German border. Like thousands of others, Hurok had to ford a stream in the dead of night, carrying his belongings over his head.

"When we stepped ashore we stood dripping on the inhospitable soil of the Kaiser." But it was still more hospitable than the soil of Tsar Nicholas II.

After enduring delousing steam baths and rough health examinations in the border town of Mislevitch, Hurok was shipped on to Hamburg. There he spent three weeks in a barrack, "sleeping in our clothes on the hard wooden floor, our scanty possessions for a pillow." Another Jewish emigrant has left this record of his days of waiting in Hamburg:

> Two weeks within high brick walls, several hundred of us herded in half a dozen compartments . . . sleeping in rows . . . with roll-calls morning and night . . . with never a sign of the free world beyond our barred windows . . . and in

our ears the unfamiliar voice of the invisible ocean, which drew and repelled us at the same time.

Cheating was rampant, the emigrant Jews being an easy target for unscrupulous agents eager to sell tickets to the wrong destinations. To survive required shrewdness and cunning.

But at last, full of teenage energy, Hurok found himself on a ferry boat, surrounded by hundreds of frightened and hopeful people bearing similar backgrounds and dreams, all now heading across the Hamburg harbor toward an unprepossessing "broad-beamed tub" called the *Graf Wildersee.*

In years to come, he would make his transatlantic crossings in considerably higher style.

■ CHAPTER TWO ■

"This Is No Village"

"With S. Hurok comes easier the tear than the laugh."
—Sol Hurok

HOW FITTING that Sol Hurok's feet first touched American soil at Castle Garden. Or at least that's what he told people.

An islet in New York Harbor near the west side of the Battery, Castle Garden was originally built in 1807 as a fort to repel British invasion. In the 1820s, however, the threat of war fading, city authorities converted it into a place of public entertainment on a grand scale. Over the next several decades it hosted many spectacular events heavy with Hurokian hoopla, from concerts to fireworks to balloon ascensions to the first demonstration in 1840 of Samuel F. B. Morse's "wireless telegraph."

But surely the most celebrated attraction ever held on this dramatic site was the American concert debut of Jenny Lind, the "Swedish Nightingale," who sang at Castle Garden before a crowd of more than six thousand on September 11, 1850. P. T. Barnum, Hurok's impresarial model, arranged the historic appearance. He also made sure everyone knew about it.

Only five years after Lind's concert, Castle Garden was put to more practical—if no less dramatic—use. From 1855 until 1890 it served as the immigrant landing station, receiving and processing more than eight million new arrivals to America. The conditions left

■ 17 ■

something to be desired. Several investigations conducted in the 1880s revealed that "immigrants were forced to sleep on hard floors, some were made to pay twice for shipment of their baggage, and others were cheated by money-changers who hung about the Battery like leeches." Partly in reaction to these findings, Castle Garden was closed in 1890. It reopened in 1896 in a more fishy incarnation: the New York Aquarium. Control of immigration now passed from New York City to the federal government, which in 1892 opened a much more ambitious and well-planned processing center on Ellis Island, a three-and-a-half-acre sandbar in the middle of New York Harbor.

So when impresario-to-be Solomon Gurkov steamed in on the *Graf Wildersee* in May 1906, his first stop would not have been Castle Garden—its appropriately rich entertainment history notwithstanding. He must first have landed, like the millions of others who would become the foundation of his audience, at Ellis Island. Castle Garden might have been his second stop; after processing at Ellis Island, immigrants were usually landed at the Barge Office nearby. From there, they made their way across a causeway to the Battery, up Manhattan, and out into the New World.

Hurok never mentioned stopping at Ellis Island. No doubt he did not want his public to think of the indignities he might have suffered there—at the very least, humiliating interviews and coldly impersonal medical examinations conducted by bored officials amid mobs of frightened Russians, Italians, Poles, and Ukrainians. He hated to display vulnerability, even in situations that required it. As Hurok reminded Darryl Zanuck when 20th Century-Fox was preparing to shoot *Tonight We Sing*, "It's important that there be established definitely at the beginning of the story that it is the story of a successful man." Exhibiting too many moments of doubt and difficulty in the impresario's past could hurt at the box office.

And yet at that moment on Ellis Island, thousands of miles from home and weary after more than three cramped weeks in steerage, Hurok, deny it as he might, was not the resplendently bald and luxuriously caped King of Ballet. He was (as a photograph taken at the time makes clear) a five-and-a-half-foot-tall teenager from Pogar, with unruly hair, greenish-brown eyes, prominent ears, and a broad, solid face.

Not that this restless young man would have found the idea of jettisoning the past uncongenial. For him, as for most of the Eastern European Jews flooding into America at the turn of the century, what they had left behind held little sentimental value. How romantic could one be about a past of pogroms, oppression, and racial slurs? And judging by Hurok's later love for costumes and theatrical artifice, the prospect of re-creating himself in another land would have stimulated rather than frightened him. Re-creation: Wasn't that what the dancers and singers and actors he soon came to adore did for a living?

Whatever his feelings, he never expressed regret about receiving a jaunty new surname as part of the admission procedure. As happened with so many Slavic immigrants to America, when Solomon Izrailevich Gurkov spoke his mouthful of a name in his heavy Russian accent, the customs official either got it wrong or decided to simplify it. Gurkov? Let's make that Hurok. So, in a moment and for all time, Gurkov became Hurok. Hurok—less obviously ethnic and, with its first syllable accented, somehow stronger. Hurok. Almost like an exclamation or battle cry. In those early years, in a frenzy of Americanization, he also sometimes used "Sam" as his first name. That is how it appears on his American marriage certificate.

After making his way through the bureaucratic procedures, struggling with a new language that he never came to master, Hurok emerged on the streets of Manhattan clutching "two heavy hampers of clothes, a goose-feather pillow," and three rubles. That was all that remained of the money his father had given him for that little trip to Kharkov. Exactly what happened next is a little fuzzy. In subsequent accounts, depending on his mood when asked, Hurok cited a wide variety of relatives and friends who awaited him. Sometimes it was the brother of his traveling companion Shafran in Brooklyn. Sometimes it was his own uncle. And sometimes, much more rarely, it was what appears to be the truth: a brother in Philadelphia and his girlfriend's sister in Brownsville. Only his age—it varied from fourteen to eighteen—caused Hurok more memory problems than the identity of those he knew when he came to the United States.

First stop was Brownsville, in Brooklyn, where Tamara (Mary) Shapiro, Hurok's "sweetheart," had a married sister. If, as seems likely, Tamara had accompanied Hurok from Pogar, he left her here with her sister and her family and then departed for Philadelphia. Having exchanged his three rubles for $1.50, he borrowed the enormous sum of $1.25 and, after a meal of sardines and beer, spent all his money on train fare: "I had 10 cents left for carfare from Broad Street station and I walked to save the dime."

Hurok claimed to have chosen the City of Brotherly Love not out of love for his own brother, whose existence there he most often attempted to conceal, but out of a more abstract admiration for the fraternal and patriotic ideals of Benjamin Franklin. Reading a translation of *Poor Richard's Almanack* back in Pogar had supposedly instilled in him a longing to dwell in Philadelphia. "Wasn't it, after all, the city of Independence Hall, the Liberty Bell, and especially Benjamin Franklin?" Or: "There, I knew, was a freedom, a liberty of spirit that could not be equalled." While inspirational, this version of how he came to end up in Philadelphia seems highly implausible. First of all, many of those who knew Hurok have claimed that he never did learn how to read—even in Russian. Second, that a translation of *Poor Richard's Almanack* would have found its way to Pogar around 1900 seems as unlikely as finding Cossacks in Kalamazoo.

Characteristically, Hurok's highly selective memory of his short sojourn in Philadelphia, from spring to fall of 1906, focused on economic rather than domestic accomplishments. Living at "my relatives' house," he went through "eighteen different jobs in six months." He started by peddling door-to-door, using pantomime to communicate. As he told the *Herald Tribune* forty-five years later, "I started my job on a Monday morning, and right away I learned something about America—Monday is a cleaning and washing day. The first customer to see my pantomime act was a housewife leaning out of a second-story window—while she watched, she shook her dusty mop all over me and my basket!" Another woman dumped water on him. Some even set the dogs on him.

"I got into tragic frame of mind," said Hurok nearly forty years later. "The country of freedom of speech and assembling, it did not look so beautiful. I sat down under big tree and cried. With S. Hurok comes easier the tear than the laugh. I cried and I cried. Then I said, 'That is no way to look at life. Get up, S. Hurok.' " And no sooner had he risen from his weeping, like Lazarus from the dead, than "a nice old lady stopped me . . . and bought all my towels for $1." He had realized a hundred percent profit on his first sale in America. "Go, my boy," said the little old lady with biblical magnanimity, "and be happy."

"Nice old ladies" would often come to the rescue in Hurok's life—and even more often in his stories.

With his friends already predicting that he would become a "beeg, beeg businessman," Hurok moved on to cannery worker, pie baker, ice-cream maker, bottle washer, hardware store clerk, and a brief stint as a streetcar conductor. (Harry Cohn, head of Columbia Pictures, three years older than Hurok and from a similar Jewish immigrant background, began his meteoric rise to fame as a trolley conductor in the Bronx.) Because of his faulty knowledge of the city and his less than crystal-clear pronunciation of the stops, "People were always getting off at the wrong street. The company fired me but not before I learned to handle excited women." This skill would come in handy backstage in later years.

But it was while bundling the Sunday edition of the Philadelphia *Press* that Hurok got the first real glimpse of his future. Late Saturday night, after Hurok and some other "shabby boys" had finished their work, Linton Martin, a reporter and later a music critic for the paper, would invite them home and play classical music on the piano. On the first evening, Hurok claims, Martin played the "Liebestod" from Wagner's opera *Tristan und Isolde*, and his life was never the same again. After the concert, Martin's mother would serve breakfast (or beer and cheese, the menu varying almost each time the story was told). In any case, this was the first time Hurok "heard serious music and appreciated it." In later years, he remembered how enthusiastically he and his untutored co-workers had responded to this supposedly elite and difficult music. He claimed it led him to believe that the masses would come to concerts if the tickets were sold at reasonable prices.

Despite Martin's kindness, the restless Hurok went back to the hardware business. By November, six months after arriving in Philadelphia, he had accumulated enough capital to buy a new $8 suit and a train ticket to New York "to see some friends from home." Gotham bewitched him. "I went down to Brooklyn Bridge, to Park Row, where the newspaper offices were. I watched the editions being thrown on the newsstands, heard the newsboys shouting, drank in the bustle, the rattling trolleys, the tinny music of a barrel organ and said to myself, 'This is no village.' I returned to Philadelphia, settled my affairs and hurried back to New York."

Even Benjamin Franklin's democratic ideals could not compete with such glamor and such endless possibilities.

Hurok's first job in New York was as stock boy at Charlie Weiland's wholesale hardware firm on Chambers Street. He supplemented his weekly salary of $7 with $5 more he earned by selling Rogers silver on Sundays and evenings. Other evenings he studied English—not very successfully—at the Educational Alliance. All his life, he spoke with a thick Yiddish-Russo-Ukrainian accent, dropping articles by the basketful and manhandling vocabulary and idioms with reckless aplomb. "Packing" was "pecking," "discussed" was "disgusted," and "You're out of your mind" was "You're off your mind."

In some interviews in later years, Hurok claimed to have lived during this time "on the floor of a New York rooming house for $4 a month." As a gentleman of sixty, he even "startled" the prim British ballerina Margot Fonteyn on one of her visits to New York by pointing out "a cheap slum rooming house where he once lived."

If, as seems unlikely, Hurok did in fact live in Manhattan after returning from Philadelphia, it could not have been for long. On March 28, 1908, he married his sweetheart, Tamara Shapiro, and they began (or rather, continued) living together at 1555 St. Marks Avenue in Brooklyn. On the marriage certificate, Hurok gave his first name as "Sam," his age as twenty-one, his place of birth as Russia, and his profession as "salesman." Tamara gave her age as twenty. Unable to write in Roman script, she signed her name (in its Americanized version, "Mary Shapiro") in Cyrillic. Hurok signed himself "Sam Hurok."

It does not appear that the couple had a large wedding. In later years, uncomfortable with his humble beginnings, Hurok actively obscured the facts of his relationship with Tamara. Even their only child and daughter, Ruth Hurok Lief, born in Brownsville on February 21, 1911, three years after their marriage, has never been sure if her parents married in Russia or in America. In *Impresario* and other accounts of his early life, Hurok does not mention if Tamara accompanied him in steerage; in fact, he hardly mentions her at all.

This is what he says: "By now"—this was about 1911—"I was married for the first time—my sweetheart from the town near Pogar had followed me to America. I was a man with a position in the community."

Since he eventually remarried, and since Tamara proved psychologically incapable of shedding her burdensome Old Country past, Hurok later minimized her role in his life as much as possible. He also told different people—even different members of his immediate family—different versions of his marital history. To Simon Semenoff, a dancer who eventually became one of his artistic advisers, Hurok allegedly said, "My first wife I never liked. We got married and there was no love."

If he felt ambivalent about Tamara and marriage, Hurok held no such reservations about Brownsville. By 1905, about fifty thousand newly immigrated Jews lived there, creating a lively and colorful community where they "could live as in the Old Country, without any rush or excessive worries." Populated primarily by workers, its famous Pitkin Avenue a hotbed of socialist political activity, Brownsville was an exotic island, described in a newspaper account of the time as "a land of sweatshops and whirring sewing machines, of strange Russian baths, of innumerable dirty and tiny shops, of cows which are milked directly into the pitchers and pails of customers at eventide, of anarchists, of Jew dancing schools, and of a peasant market." Later, as a successful impresario, Hurok recalled it as "a steaming microcosm of culture," although "no garden spot to the eye."

Socialism occupied a special place in the teeming life of Brownsville. Most of the Jews who immigrated to the United States from Eastern Europe around 1900 were socialists, having joined the movement back in the Old Country as a gesture of protest against sclerotic autocratic regimes and in the hopes of changing an oppressive atmosphere of intolerance, elitism, and anti-Semitism. When they arrived in the New World, they clung to these political convictions almost more tenaciously than to their religious ones. "It was not uncommon for a Jewish worker to read an anti-religious Yiddish newspaper, vote Socialist, join a socialist union, and yet attend the synagogue weekly, or even daily, and observe most of the Jewish law," one historian of Jewish life in America has observed.

Some of the most committed Jewish socialists ended up in

Brownsville, whose crowded streets became high-decibel forums for political rallies and endless debate. As the years passed, however, most of these "Old Country socialists" abandoned hard-core socialism under the influence of prosperity and the realities of American political life. Those who remained in Eastern urban centers, particularly New York, drifted closer and closer to the Democratic party. By the 1930s, they had begun to support Democratic candidates.

Hurok's political evolution closely followed this classic pattern. In his early years in Brownsville, he plunged into the heady socialist scene with gusto and enthusiasm, contributing eagerly to the discussions, meetings, and fund-raising campaigns. He relished the rhetorical fray, as he later recalled. "In meeting rooms above the crowded stores the air shook with furiously happy argument, spiced with the odors from the delicatessen downstairs—a peculiarly fortunate arrangement considering how intellectual activity always sharpens the appetite. And the argument continued through the adjournment for a hot pastrami sandwich with dill pickle and unnumbered glasses of tea."

"Hurok's politics were politics of the heart—emotional, not analytical," Isaac Stern remembered. "He came out of the same milieu as the prominent Jewish labor leaders such as David Dubinsky. They all liked music at least to a degree, and they all had the same background—the background of the oppressed. They didn't think in complicated intellectual terms, but it was always us against them."

At first Hurok worked behind the scenes, but as time went on, his bold promotional schemes captured more and more attention in the community and the newspapers. From the beginning, he used music to raise political funds and consciousness. When a socialist candidate ran for the New York State Assembly from his Twenty-third District, Hurok, proud of his new American citizenship, organized musical attractions for the campaign rallies and benefit concerts to raise money. On Sundays, Hurok "would hawk silverware to afford the concert tickets he needed to size up artists who might help his political candidates." His artists ranged from "popular artists of the day, when I could persuade them," to unknown but hopeful kids from the neighborhood.

Despite their relative isolation in the ghettos of Brownsville and the Lower East Side, the new Jewish immigrants almost immediately began responding to the cultural freedom and social mobility of American life. They could now partake of the wider life of the society in which they lived, something they had never been allowed to do in the villages of Russia and Eastern Europe, as Irving Howe observed: "The fixed rituals that had bound the east European Jews broke down under the weight of American freedom. The patterns of social existence had to be remade each day." These patterns included entertainment.

With his intuitive sense for identifying, developing, and then satisfying an audience, Hurok realized that the tightly knit Brownsville community was a ripe market waiting to be developed. Like him, most of its members grew up in Old Country towns where music and dancing was a way of life—and something they missed here in Brownsville. Hurok would supply that and more, capitalizing on the immigrants' political passions in the process. He would make good and make money.

New York offered much more than the cosy clamor of Brownsville, of course. Soon enough, the lights of Manhattan began to lure Hurok, especially since the wonders of modern transport had now made getting there as easy as walking to the corner. Subway trains began running under the East River between Brooklyn and Manhattan in 1908, while two new bridges—the Williamsburg and the Manhattan—had joined their older colleague, the already venerable Brooklyn Bridge, by 1909. New York was booming. Between 1890 and 1910 immigrants flowed in like water, doubling the city's population to nearly five million crowded people. America was emerging as a world power, with seemingly inexhaustible resources and energy. For the young man from Pogar, not yet twenty, the future vibrated with potential and excitement.

The New York music-theater scene reflected the city's naive optimism. At the turn of the century, nearly a hundred legitimate theaters presented an increasingly commercial repertoire to the growing ranks of the middle class. On April 12, 1905, just a few days after Hurok's seventeenth birthday and almost exactly one year before he arrived at Ellis Island, the Hippodrome, an extravagant entertainment palace boasting fifty-two hundred seats, opened with a massive show featuring "600 persons and 150 horses and other animals." Stretching the entire length of the block on Sixth Avenue between 43rd and 44th streets, the Hippodrome became the ultimate showcase for popular taste during its brilliant but sadly brief existence in that innocent era before movies. For Hurok, it would become both an inspiration and a goad. Over at Times Square, Oscar Hammerstein's lucrative Victoria Theater, one of the great vaudeville houses, also flourished. Hurok later confessed to standing star-struck in the Victoria's lobby, "raptly gazing at the pictures of the famous artists." By hanging around the Victoria and other theaters, the ballet critic Arnold Haskell wrote years later in admiration, the future impresario "picked up more knowledge of concert crowd psychology than most managers kid themselves they know."

As a Jew back in Russia, Hurok would not even have been allowed to enter such public places of amusement.

Nearby, two temples of high culture drew a more genteel crowd. The elegant Metropolitan Opera House, built originally by the Vanderbilts as a sort of private music club for themselves and their upper-crusty comrades, had been presenting the great opera stars of Europe in its acoustically superior home on Broadway at 39th Street since 1883. But the opera scene was changing. In late 1906, about the time Hurok settled in Brownsville, the hyperkinetic Hammerstein had fulfilled his long-standing ambition of competing head-to-head with the venerable Met. He had opened his celebrated, though doomed, Manhattan Opera House five blocks away, on 34th Street between Eighth and Ninth. It would live for only a few magnificent seasons, long enough for Hurok (he claimed) to sneak in and be tossed out on more than one occasion.

"Hurok told me more than once," wrote Irving Kolodin, "of the evenings when, as a shabbily dressed young man with stardust in his eyes, he stood in the lobby of the Manhattan Opera House with a standing-room ticket, worshipping from afar at the shrine of Hammerstein, resplendent in top hat and diamond stick-pin. If Hurok came to be acclaimed eventually as the last of the impresarios, it was in no small measure because of what he absorbed from the example of such great ones as Oscar Hammerstein."

In later years, Hurok would also learn the same bitter lesson Hammerstein did: Despite its many charms, opera rarely paid for itself.

Hammerstein was only one of many influences in Hurok's early opera education. One of his most important early encounters with the medium—and, he always claimed, one of the seminal artistic experiences of his life—came on November 20, 1907, not long after his arrival in the United States, in the cheap seats in the top gallery of the Met. Fyodor Chaliapin, then thirty-four years old, was making his American and Met debut in the title role of Boito's *Mefistofele*. Many considered this strapping Russian *muzhik* from Kazan the greatest bass in the world. Hurok admits he had never seen him perform in Russia, and it seems unlikely—though not impossible—that he had heard any of his recordings. Only three had appeared by 1907, and few people owned the machines on which to play them. So Hurok came to hear Chaliapin on the strength of word of mouth. Brownsville had plenty of that.

Conveying exactly what he found so moving and artistically original in Chaliapin's performances proved beyond Hurok's descriptive and analytical powers. The basso from the Volga always exerted a huge emotional impact even on the untutored members of his audiences, and Hurok was no exception. When Chaliapin performed, he didn't just sing notes—he created a character. When he was finally ready to go onstage, after extensive research and preparation, Chaliapin's metamorphosis was so total as to terrify his costars. (In the colorful, if specious, version of their first encounter that Hurok sanctioned for *Tonight We Sing*, Chaliapin's Petersburg performance in *Boris Godunov* left the young man from Pogar nearly bug-eyed and breathless enough to require medical attention. Perhaps his New York Mefistofele produced something like the same reaction.)

But Hurok's fascination with Chaliapin also arose from a deep personal identification. Like Hurok, Chaliapin had come from a humble Russian upbringing, and yet he had managed to scale the greatest artistic and social heights. He had created himself; he had become a star. To see the son of a drunken peasant appear on the Met stage before the Manhattan elite, having already conquered the great aristocratic opera houses of Imperial Russia and Europe, must have served Hurok as proof that his own ambitious dreams of grandeur could come true. If Chaliapin could do it, why not he?

Almost unanimously, the New York critics failed to share Hurok's ecstatic enthusiasm. Chaliapin's bare-chested sensuality and his physical, earthy presence offended their Puritan sensibilities; his raw, powerful vocalism insulted their delicate ears. They found no more compliments for his other performances at the Met that season: as Basilio in *The Barber of Seville*, as Mephistopheles in *Faust*, and as Leporello in a *Don Giovanni* conducted by Gustav Mahler. (Mahler, too, found little favor with Manhattan's taste makers, who in their inexperience preferred more conventional and undemanding talents.)

After his "short and far from happy stay," the mercurial and overbearing Chaliapin pronounced America sadly lacking in cultural awareness. "I pity Americans," he said, "because they have no light, no song in their lives. They are but children in everything pertaining to art." Hurok later claimed that he felt exactly the same way after arriving in the United States. "Despite the impact of the sumptuousness of the bright new world that greeted me on my arrival in America, I found a people who neither sang nor danced. . . . I could not understand it. I was dismayed by it."

The two men reacted differently to this culture gap. Chaliapin, nearing the peak of his career, chose to flee America's musically barren shores, but Hurok, just starting out, undertook to develop them for his hero's triumphant return.

For the time being, Hurok admired Chaliapin from a distance. (In the wish-fulfilling *Tonight We Sing*, however, Hurok finagles a backstage interview the very first time he sees him perform.) But his life had been changed. For one thing, whatever the critics and patricians might have said, the fans that surrounded Hurok as he sat in the heavens of the Met adored this wild and woolly Russian. They didn't care what the critics or the Vanderbilts thought. And if Hurok had one real talent, it was how to read an audience; he respected the public's judgment on artists. When a performer made that mysterious emotional connection with the faces and hearts in the hall—when he *projected*—Hurok noticed. Chaliapin projected. Damn the critics. People would pay to hear him.

Bringing Chaliapin back to America now became Hurok's most cherished goal—even obsession. When he exited the Met after one of Chaliapin's Met performances during the 1907–1908 season, impressed by his idol's artistry and transfigured by the sound of thousands of hands clapping, he shared his dream with a companion. They stood across the street from an office building that then housed Brown's Chop House. "Some day I'm going to manage artists like Chaliapin, maybe even Chaliapin himself," he proclaimed with the determination of Moses on the Mount. "And I'll have my office in that building."

Whether Hurok in fact spoke these prophetic words, only the now demolished walls of the Old Met might tell. In any case, it made great copy in later years—after it had come true.

Meanwhile, back in Brownsville, Tamara quietly kept house in a two-bedroom apartment on Dean Street. In 1911, she gave birth to their first and only child, a daughter they named Ruth. This joyous and tender event apparently impressed Hurok less than Chaliapin's Met appearances, however, for he doesn't mention it in either of his published "autobiographies." Nor did he ever speak of Ruth's birth or girlhood to the countless interviewers who questioned him about his early life in America. Increasingly, Tamara and now Ruth were left to themselves as Hurok poured all of his considerable energy into political and impresarial activities. Often away, he spent more and more time across the water in Manhattan. For emotional and familial support Tamara turned to her sister, friends, and neighbors, rarely accompanying her husband on his forays beyond the Old Country cocoon of Brownsville.

Ruth remembers that her mother dressed in traditional peasant style, always with a shawl. "She looked like an old bubbie. She was a young beautiful woman but she wore a shawl." Not exactly the right sort of escort for Hurok's evenings out—even in the Family Circle at the Met.

But if Hurok felt uncomfortable with Tamara's apparent inability to adapt to American ways, he never failed to provide financially for her and their daughter. Tamara never had to work her entire life, and Ruth never lacked for material comforts. For Hurok, it was far easier to express affection monetarily than emotionally.

By 1911, Hurok had achieved local celebrity as a supplier of musical talent—primarily homegrown—to Brownsville's clubs and labor organizations, mainly for political benefits. He had also established his first contact with the professional music world. Through the Wolfson Musical Bureau, one of the leading agencies of the day,

Hurok began arranging for Brownsville appearances by lesser-known professional artists. But he was feeling restless, his insatiable drive for greater recognition driving him on to bigger things and world-class talent.

Then his roving eye fell on another rising Russian star—violinist Efrem Zimbalist. Born in Rostov in 1890, Zimbalist streaked through the St. Petersburg Conservatory, graduating with the Gold Medal and the Rubinstein Prize after studying with Leopold Auer, who turned out violin virtuosos faster than a baker did bread. Notoriously stingy with praise, the conservatory director Alexander Glazunov called Zimbalist "a colossal talent." At seventeen Zimbalist tossed off the Brahms Concerto with the Berlin Philharmonic. At twenty-one he made his American debut with the Boston Symphony, giving the American premiere of Glazunov's melancholy Concerto on October 27, 1911, under Max Fiedler. He became an instant sensation, the wunderkind from Russia, "one of the most worthy of the violinists now before the public."

Any impresario worth his salt knows to strike while the talent is hot. So Hurok chose this moment to make his first move toward the big time. He resolved to bring Zimbalist to Brownsville.

It helped that Zimbalist was a green and apparently unpretentious youngster and, like Hurok—and almost everybody else in Brownsville—a Jew. At the start of Zimbalist's second American season, a reporter from the *New York Times* described him as "in appearance and manner but a boy" and quoted him as saying buoyantly, "I love America and I am sure that some day I will make my home here." (He did, joining the faculty of the Curtis Institute in Philadelphia in 1928.) In his first season in New York, he had given highly publicized performances of the Glazunov and Tchaikovsky concertos with the Philharmonic Society and several acclaimed recitals at Carnegie Hall and the Met, earning glowing notices.

So exciting and important was his first face-to-face meeting with Zimbalist that Hurok provided several versions of how it happened. The earlier variant, which appeared in newspaper stories in the 1920s and 1930s, sounded like something straight out of Hollywood—which is perhaps where Hurok got it. In 1912, while he was working in an automobile showroom (or as an errand boy for an automobile company), one of the many jobs that appear and disappear in accounts of Hurok's early life in New York, "Destiny, in the person of Efrem Zimbalist, walked in. Hurok suggested to the violinist that he be allowed to book him for a workingmen's concert; the artist agreed, the concert was a success and an impresario was launched on a career."

Or, according to the *New York Times* of April 22, 1923: "Within half an hour, Zimbalist convinced the general manager that the automobile game was not nearly as delightful as the music business. Mr. Hurok dropped mechanical engineering and became an impresario."

And they all lived happily ever after.

But *Impresario* contains none of this. There, the story sounds marginally more plausible. Collecting all his considerable chutzpah, Hurok hunted down Zimbalist's manager, Loudon Charlton. He explained that he wanted his client to play at the New Palm Garden in Brownsville for a Socialist party benefit—and at a cut rate of $500, no less. To Hurok's surprise, the gentleman didn't throw him out— perhaps because he saw the publicity value in such a pro bono appearance and realized that Zimbalist was facing stiff competition from the growing wave of European violinists (Ysaÿe, Kreisler, Elman) now flooding the American market. And after all, though he had scored some impressive initial successes, Zimbalist was only starting out. Charlton gave Hurok Zimbalist's address and told him to go talk to him directly.

For what it's worth, this is how Hurok later described *that* meeting:

> This was a moment for me. For the first time I sat and talked, face to face, as manager to artist, with a Big Name. . . . Zimbalist was a delicate-featured young man with curly black hair and a gentle, open face. He listened to me with sympathetic courtesy. When I left him I had a contract in my pocket. The contract specified $750 for the concert—it was not good business for an artist to cut his fee—but Zimbalist had agreed to deduct $250 and call it a personal donation to the Socialist Party.

The concert succeeded both artistically and financially. Hurok cleared $1,600, a tidy sum in the years before World War I.

Zimbalist must also have been pleased with the results, for he

now agreed to let Hurok present him in Carnegie Hall. This event—
Hurok's first attraction in the prestigious venue that would become
his second home—took place on Sunday evening, April 27, 1913,
under the auspices of the newborn Van Hugo Musical Society. Its
name had been created by Hurok and an erstwhile partner, a certain
Goldberg, from the first two letters of their names joined with the
prefix to Beethoven's. (Later, however, Hurok vehemently denied
that he ever had worked with a partner, and even said that the name
Van Hugo came from the combination of Beethoven and Victor
Hugo.) Their venture succeeded brilliantly, the house so packed
that there were "two hundred fifty fervent Zimbalist admirers on
the stage." The *New York Times* called it "one of the largest audiences in the history of Carnegie Hall." Its uncredited reviewer dismissed most of the music on the program, a potpourri of "more or
less trivial selections" by Kreisler, Tchaikovsky, Zimbalist, and
Chopin as "evidently chosen to make a popular appeal," but lauded
the "nobility of Mr. Zimbalist's tone and style."

Hurok liked to depict Zimbalist's benefit performances for him
as a special favor, but in fact the big name participated in at least
two other large benefit concerts in his first two New York seasons.
In April 1912, he gave a recital at the Hippodrome celebrating the
fifteenth anniversary of a socialist newspaper, the *Jewish Daily Forward*. In November, he played Beethoven's "Kreutzer" Sonata at
Sarah Adler's Novelty Theatre in Brooklyn as part of a testimonial
performance given in recognition of the work of Prince Kropotkin.
A socialist and anarchist imprisoned in Russia and abroad for his
political activities, Prince Peter Kropotkin (1842–1921) advocated a
communal society. That Zimbalist supported him suggests that
Hurok probably did not have such a difficult time persuading him
to play for a socialist cause.

His success with Zimbalist gave Hurok many things. A well-
publicized and glamorous entry into the big-time musical arena. A
boost to his already large ego. Connections in the big-time musical
world. Confidence that he could work with "name" artists. Faith in
his instincts. Knowledge that he could count on a firm audience
base of Jewish immigrants who wanted and loved music. Proof that
politics and music was a potent mixture. An escape from the nurturing, but ultimately limited, world of Brownsville. As he would tell a

journalist thirty years later, "After that I got going full speed ahead in the culture line."

What better moment, then, to go after even bigger game: Chaliapin. Ever since seeing him at the Met in 1907, Hurok had been sending his operatic hero letters, bravely offering his services as manager for American engagements. He had received no replies. Now, in the flush of success, Hurok splurged and sent Chaliapin a cable. This time the basso responded in kind. "MEET ME GRAND HOTEL PARIS CHALIAPIN."

Hurok swooned. He had been acknowledged by one of the biggest of the big names. He could no more turn down this cryptic invitation than a diva would her first *Aida*. In a gesture reminiscent of his prodigal flight from Pogar, Hurok told his long-suffering wife and newborn daughter he was going to California, withdrew the small savings he had been accumulating for capital, and set sail on the S. S. *Lafayette*. The *Titanic* had sunk just a few months before.

This time he traveled "not third, but second class as befitted a rising impresario."

■ CHAPTER THREE ■

Hip-Hip-Hooray

"Papa was different from all other papas."—*Ruth Hurok Lief*

FYODOR CHALIAPIN LURED HUROK to Paris as a practical joke. Famous for his frightening laugh, roguish tricks, and sudden rages, Chaliapin liked nothing better than to have a good time at other people's expense—especially when they wanted something from him. And they often did. Why not tease this American upstart who aspired to manage the greatest bass in the world? Why not see if he would drop everything and sail the ocean in response to a cabled summons? It would be amusing.

In *Tonight We Sing*, Chaliapin (played by Ezio Pinza as an explosively difficult star) invites Hurok (David Wayne) to Paris for no more noble reason than to win a bet with his faithful and long-suffering servant Nikolai. No evidence exists to support this explanation, but it would not have been out of character.

Over the years, Hurok wrote and spoke extensively of Chaliapin as one of his most intimate friends. That Chaliapin did not include Hurok in his autobiographical writings and had little to say about him elsewhere indicates, however, that on his side the feelings were less intense—something like cat to mouse or Don Giovanni to Leporello, in fact. In *My Many Years*, pianist Arthur Rubinstein describes the "shabby treatment" Chaliapin once gave

Hurok in his presence in New York in the early 1920s, long after they had supposedly become soulmates.

> A short fattish man was shown in whom Feodor introduced to me saying, "He's my agent here, a shrewd little man, a Russian Jew. Beware of him." The man smiled and sat himself comfortably in a chair near the window without being asked to have even a miserable cup of coffee.

For both personal and professional reasons, Hurok needed to believe that he and Chaliapin were bosom buddies. As time went on, exaggerating his intimacy with famous people became a way to attract other artists to his roster, a highly successful marketing technique—and a potent means of self-delusion.

When Hurok made this first transatlantic pilgrimage to the big name in (apparently) 1912, Chaliapin was living in high style in the cultural capital of the world. He had his own apartment, but, according to Chaliapin's son Fyodor, his father and Hurok "could have met at the Grand Hotel," as Hurok always claimed. This sophisticated and romantic backdrop certainly made for a better story, a fact not lost on the makers of *Tonight We Sing*. In the film, the two meet amid the luxurious surroundings of Chaliapin's hotel suite.

In the "literary" version of the story reproduced in *Impresario*, Hurok appeared at the Grand Hotel only to find his hero out. He didn't waste the evening, though; he dined with the Belgian violinist Eugène Ysaÿe, whom he had met recently in New York. Perhaps they discussed plans for Ysaÿe to perform in New York. Returning to the Grand Hotel, Hurok was at last received into the artist's inner sanctum and, in his far-from-perfect Russian, presented his grandiose plans for an American career to the big name himself.

"I will never go to the United States again," Chaliapin replied, beginning to laugh. He explained that the New York critics had mortally offended him, and he had summoned Hurok across the ocean only out of curiosity to see "the man who had the effrontery to write to me for four years."

"Paris is a beautiful city," Chaliapin tells a crestfallen Hurok in *Tonight We Sing*. "You can see the Eiffel Tower, the Louvre—me." The joke was on Hurok.

But becoming the brunt of bets, waiting for years for a change in mood, even self-debasement were small prices to pay for the honor of managing this big name.

As consolation for Hurok's journey, Chaliapin supposedly invited Hurok to dine with him and the French composer Jules Massenet, to whom he playfully presented Hurok as "my American manager." (Massenet had recently written the title role in *Don Quichotte* for Chaliapin, who sang the premiere in Monte Carlo in February 1910—although in *Impresario* Hurok incorrectly claims that this premiere came "later" than their 1912 meeting.) Entranced by the august company, Hurok sat by "modest and unnoticed" as the collaborators sang and drank until dawn. The mere opportunity to "bathe in the radiance of men whose gifts were wine to me that night, and would be bread and butter to me on nights to come" more than compensated him for his transatlantic crossing, he claimed.

Appealing though it may be, the story strains credibility. Hurok did not understand French at that time, and Massenet does not seem to have known Russian. Frail and emaciated, the composer had reached the age of seventy in May 1912 and had been seriously ill for some time. If we are to believe one of his biographers, he was in no condition for drinking bouts. "When the evening arrived he somehow screwed up the strength necessary to get into his carriage, to walk through the dazzling lobbies of the Opera where the lights glinted dully on his parchment skin, and to lean thankfully on the sill of his box. Then it was back to bed and the frustrating inaction of the rue de Vaugirard." Indeed, Massenet died in August 1912—right about the time of his supposed night of creative carousing with Chaliapin.

On this night and on nights to come, Chaliapin and Hurok must have made an odd pair. One, a foot taller than the other, broad-shouldered, rugged, and athletic; the other, short, round and already balding. A Volga peasant and a Ukrainian Jew. But Hurok served as a constant balm to the temperamental giant's huge ego, and they could communicate in Russian (or a close approximation thereof). He could help Chaliapin break through the culture and language barrier that he complained had separated him from the "natives of the great country, America" on his first visit in 1907–1908.

Eventually. But first Chaliapin would have to be flattered, cajoled, and catered to. He would have to be wooed and courted like a comely and willful bride.

Poorer but more star-struck than ever, Hurok made the long trip back to Brownsville, where he plunged into intense political activity.

Between 1912 and 1916, socialism in the United States reached the peak of its influence, due in no small part to the efforts of Jewish immigrant activists. The Jews elaborated upon the socialism they had brought with them from Russia, using it not only as a tool to protest and improve working conditions in New York's burgeoning garment industry, but also as a means of self-definition. From the beginning, Jewish social radicalism was intertwined with cultural romanticism. The Jewish unions and socialist organizations on Manhattan's Lower East Side and in Brownsville became much more than political entities; they became centers of Jewish cultural life, sponsoring concerts and lectures and readings. Yiddish was the language of currency.

A people with no past and only an uncertain future, the immigrant Jews embraced socialism's utopian design with understandable urgency and passion. Stressing the creation of an ideal society based on cooperation between all classes and races, socialism taught that narrow-minded nationalism would wane because the world would be better for all. Uprooted and homeless, the Jews turned to socialism in an attempt to "bleach away their past and become men without, or above, a country." For Hurok, and for thousands of other Jewish immigrants, socialism provided the opportunity to "improvise their own myths," to create a new image of themselves and of mankind.

Working in the socialist movement also gave the immigrants useful career training, teaching them pragmatic skills that would help them survive in the inhospitable capitalist world beyond the ghetto. This was surely the case for Hurok, who got his start as a presenter of talent and events within the boiling caldron of Brownsville's socialist community.

Not long after he returned from Paris, the neighborhood Socialist party organization to which Hurok belonged could not pay the rent on its small and crowded meeting room on Pitkin Avenue.

Hurok came up with an enterprising solution, as Marx Lewis, a fellow party member, later recalled:

> He proposed that instead of renting, and worrying about raising the funds needed, the branch, with the aid of other groups, mainly trade unions, buy a building, and suggested that it negotiate for the purchase of Palm Gardens (or the New Palm Gardens) at 219 Sackman St., one of the area's largest buildings. The idea that this large building, entailing an expenditure of many tens of thousands of dollars, could be bought with the meager means of the branch, or even with the meager means of the small unions which existed then, seemed fantastic, an impossible dream. Hurok was authorized to see what could be done.
>
> He made the dream come true. Through concerts which he arranged and the drives he launched the building was purchased and became the Brownsville Labor Lyceum, the center of large undertakings for many organizations in no way connected with the Socialist and labor movement. He made it self-sustaining, and profitable.

When the building suffered extensive fire damage a few years later, Hurok came up with another idea to raise the $18,000 needed to repair and expand it. He and the Socialist party leaders succeeded in selling 180 promissory notes at $100 each to likely supporters. Few of the purchasers ever demanded to be repaid, but those who did were satisfied.

As manager of the Labor Lyceum, Hurok organized all sorts of large-scale events—banquets, rallies, concerts, lectures, debates, balls. The proceeds went to orphanages, political campaigns, and funds for striking garment workers. Not all of the concerts took place at the Labor Lyceum—some were held in the spanking new Brooklyn Academy of Music. Built in a fashionable neighborhood of imposing new brownstones near both Atlantic Avenue and subway connections to Manhattan, this state-of-the-art twenty-two-hundred-seat palace had opened on November 14, 1908, with a festive production of *Faust* starring Geraldine Farrar and Enrico Caruso.

In 1915, Marx Lewis moved to Albany as secretary to socialist Abraham Shiplacoff, Brownsville's new representative in the state assembly. Hurok had played an instrumental role in Shiplacoff's election campaign and now wielded considerable power in local party affairs. On one occasion, recalled Marx Lewis, he helped to "discipline" a party member judged by the leadership to be a "dreamer" and dissident. "A good strategist," even an autocrat, Hurok never tolerated in fellow managers or subordinates the prima donna behavior he endlessly indulged in artists. This would be a key to his later success.

If Hurok had wanted to, he could have become a fine politico, but despite his talent for the trade, it remained only a sideline—and a means to an end. Always full of energy and rarely requiring more than five or six hours of sleep a night, he was gradually putting what he was learning about managing and presenting artists for political causes to more commercial use. With Europe now at war and American industry booming, Hurok drew on his growing reputation and connections to begin presenting a profitable series of classical concerts at low prices—" 'Music for the Masses' was the way I thought of the venture."

At first, the concerts were held in the Madison Square Garden built by Stanford White in 1890 on Madison Avenue between 26th and 27th streets. This was the second of the four Madison Square Gardens; many consider it the greatest, both because of its lavish design and because of its quirky history. (One of the most celebrated events to occur in this "palace of pleasure" was the shooting of White by a millionaire crazed by jealousy over the architect's involvement with his wife.) When it opened, the Garden had the largest auditorium then in existence (eight thousand seats) and presented a wide range of attractions, from operatic concerts to wakes to prize fights to Wild West Shows to the Barnum & Bailey circus. But the fanciful Garden never turned a profit and had already become a "white elephant with a past" by the time Hurok began presenting classical artists there around the time of World War I. Its owner, New York Life Insurance Company, finally tore down the structure in 1925, and a new Madison Square Garden was built uptown, on Eighth Avenue between 49th and 50th streets.

The declining status of the Garden led Hurok to look for another venue in which to produce his large-scale events. His eye fell on the Hippodrome. Its special mystique, more central location, and larger seating capacity—more than big enough to accommodate the entire population of Pogar—enticed him uptown. "The Hippodrome was the place I had dreamed about. . . . The Hippodrome was to be the temple in which simple people would enter into the mysteries of great music performed by great musicians."

In other, more Hurokian terms, he longed to be where the action was.

In 1914, failing and tawdry after a mere decade in business, the National Amusement Institution of America (the Hippodrome also went under this more pretentious title) was in transition. It had recently passed into new hands. Charles Dillingham (1868–1934), the respected and highly successful wizard behind New York's Globe Theatre, had taken it over with visions of spectacle and profits dancing in his head. Nicknamed "Good Time Charlie Dillingham" for his suave and imperturbable character, he planned to stage stylishly eclectic revues that would restore this gargantuan arena to its former status as New York's premier dispenser of quality variety-style entertainment. Under his administration, the Hippodrome aimed at a somewhat more elevated target on the cultural spectrum, without, of course, becoming more refined than its diverse and mostly untutored audience. Bring on the elephants, violinists, sopranos, ballerinas, lions, and marching bands!

One of the first things Dillingham did at the Hippodrome was deodorize. Since the area immediately below the auditorium had served as home for the numerous pachyderms, horses, monkeys, canines, and other beasts that appeared in the shows, the entire institution smelled like a barnyard. In his quest to create a more tasteful ambience, Good Time Charlie set about immediately "to purchase vast quantities of disinfectants, seal the building up and subject it to a fumigating process for several days."

When the freshly deodorized theater reopened for the first time under Dillingham's management on September 30, 1915, with an extravagant and ebullient revue called (what else) "Hip-Hip-

Hooray," even the sober critic of the *New York Times* decreed that the new owner "has done his work with his head full of ideas and his pockets full of money. What counts is the scenic endeavor, the color, the splendor and the novelty. Here we have the same old thing done handsomely—spectacle, interspersed with dashes of circus, musical comedy and vaudeville, with the emphasis on the spectacle." For lovers of dance, the show offered both an ice ballet imported from Berlin and the red, white, and blue "Ballet of the States." Musical accompaniment was provided by John Philip Sousa and his band, Hippodrome regulars.

Ticket prices were competitive. The best seats in the house cost $1.50 in the evening and $1 at matinees, while fifteen hundred rush seats were set aside for each performance at a mere $.50. This compared to a range of $1 to $2.50 for general seating—$15 to $18 for boxes—for pianist Josef Hofmann's performance with Walter Damrosch and the Symphony Society of New York at Aeolian Hall. Three blocks down Sixth Avenue, customers were paying $.75 for a "Grill Luncheon" and $1.50 for dinner at the fancy Café des Beaux-Arts. A single room (without bath) at the Hotel Ansonia was fetching $2 a day, and a large bottle of Listerine at Saks, $.52.

Dillingham's magnificent style, marketing expertise, and success in catering to the mass audience through a clever mélange of high-brow and low-brow attractions dazzled and awed Hurok. Hurok retained enough of his characteristic chutzpah, however, to suggest to his hero a series of Sunday recitals at the Hippodrome by established European artists, using the model he had already developed at the Labor Lyceum, the Brooklyn Academy, and Carnegie Hall. They signed a contract for what Hurok liked to call "Music for the Masses" in—apparently—1915.

Although later, characteristically, he gave him little credit, Hurok learned a lot from Dillingham. Like how to create public excitement and how to master the science of public relations. To think big. To assemble programs. And through Dillingham, he came to meet many leading artists, including, of course, Anna Pavlova.

It was, indeed, the Hippodrome that brought the great Russian classical ballerina and Hurok together. Then in her mid-thirties, Pavlova began appearing at this vast amusement hall around the same time Hurok started presenting there. On January 10, 1916, for example, she danced two crowd pleasers—Riccardo Drigo's *Pas de deux* and Fritz Kreisler's *The Dragon Fly*—as she shared billing with a Japanese soprano, an Italian tenor and bass, and John Philip Sousa leading his band in excerpts from Gilbert and Sullivan's *Pinafore*. In this massive proletarian arena, one found little of the aristocratic bon ton that reigned in the Imperial theaters of Tsarist Russia where Pavlova, considered by many to be the greatest dancer of her time, had begun her career.

Chances are that Hurok saw this performance; he claims to have seen every Pavlova appearance at the Hippodrome. For the moment, however, selling "Music for the Masses" took precedence even over the artist he would later worship as "The Swan."

The series for which Hurok subcontracted with Dillingham included recitals by such leading European artists as opera stars Alma Gluck (she had married Efrem Zimbalist in 1914), Ernestine Schumann-Heink, and Titta Ruffo; and violinists Zimbalist, Mischa Elman, and Eugène Ysaÿe. All of them reportedly received the modest flat fee of $500.

In advertising the concerts, Hurok tried something new and ingenious: appealing to New York's large ethnic communities. Of the $6,000 Hurok spent on each Sunday event, $1,800 went for advertising—not in the big dailies, but in the many foreign-language newspapers read by the hundreds of thousands of recent immigrants from Russia, Poland, Germany, and Italy. The ads included addresses of neighborhood box offices and detailed instructions (in Yiddish, Russian, whatever) on how to get to the Hippodrome.

"There was a drug store in Harlem and a drug store in Brooklyn, a jewelry store in the Bronx. In Brownsville there were seats at Levinson's Music Store, 1737 Pitkin Avenue, and on East Broadway it was Katz's Music Store at Number 183." As Ed Sullivan would later remark, "Hurok's ticket booths were shoeshine stores, bakery shops, spaghetti restaurants."

Like Hurok, many of the non-English-speaking immigrants had come to know and love music back in the old country, and he was betting that they would pay to hear it at prices they could afford—from $.50 to $2. Blocks of half-priced tickets were also made available to trade unions and other organizations.

He was right. They did come, as he proudly remembered years later.

"They came by trolley, by El, walked the correct number of blocks, turned to the right or the left, and they got there. They carried in their hands the fragment of crumpled newspaper in Russian or Yiddish, in Italian or German or Spanish, and they followed the directions like a precept from the Bible. For thousands of them it was the first time they had been on Broadway, the first time, indeed, that they had seen the busy heart of the city which was their home."

For Hurok, watching his new audience waiting for tickets in a line three blocks long was, he claimed, a dream come true. "In many ways, this was the most satisfying part of my whole career, because we got hundreds of thousands of people who would never have listened to classical music any other way to come to those concerts." Immigrants like himself, unable to communicate in English, they were hungry for culture and self-improvement and eager to partake of the leisure of an open society in which anyone could go to the theater. And they could see foreign performers who (both literally and figuratively) spoke their language.

For impresario, audience, and even for most of the artists, these concerts were a shared and thrilling exercise in upward mobility.

When necessary, Hurok resorted to snobbism to fill the Hipp's more than six thousand seats. An announced recital by the Belgian violinist Ysaÿe having failed to produce a suitable advance sale, he took advantage of the presence of the Belgian prince and princess in the United States to devise a provocative full-page ad:

EXCELLENCIES THE PRINCE AND PRINCESS OF BELGIUM

[in barely visible print] have been asked whether they

WILL ATTEND THE CONCERT OF YSAYE,
WORLD'S GREATEST VIOLINIST.

The recital sold out, although the royal party did not appear.

Nurtured by creative publicity, and satisfying the robust demand among all ethnic groups (including Jews, of course) and social classes for relatively high-class entertainment, the "Music for the Masses" formula proved successful and durable as an adjunct to variety. In each season from 1915 to 1923, when the series ended,

Hurok claims to have cleared $40,000. The *Morning Telegraph* even started writing about what it called the "Hurok audience."

The time had come for Hurok to take the decisive move beyond Brownsville and the Labor Lyceum. It was 1916. Already balding, he was (probably) thirty years old, had been in America for ten years, and still spoke a broken English that would never be fixed. The success of the first "Music for the Masses" recitals behind him, he finally left his various part-time jobs in retail and embroidery and went full-time into the presenting business. Under the resurrected name of the Van Hugo Musical Society, he opened his first professional offices at 220 West 42nd Street in Manhattan.

As usual, his timing was perfect. European artists fleeing war-torn Europe and Russia were flooding the American market, whose numbers and hunger for entertainment continued to grow at a rapid pace. As scores of European musicians fled World War I, wrote Henry T. Finck in *The Nation*, "America, by the strange and tragic course of events, has become the world's centre of orchestral music, with New York as the headquarters. . . . So many first-class artists have been driven to these shores by the European war that the minor ones have found the going harder than ever before." Finck calculated that 127 singers, 67 pianists, and 39 violinists had appeared in Manhattan in the 1915–16 season, a vast increase over former years. Many concert halls saw their bookings double.

While it seems that he never learned to write or speak English well, Hurok was an inquisitive character who always kept abreast of current events and trends. He could see that these newly arriving artists would need both managers and audiences. He would fill the gap. Many of the immigrating artists enjoyed solid reputations in Europe but remained almost unknown to the still unsophisticated American public. Over the coming decades, in the wake of World War I, the Russian Revolution, Hitler's rise to power, and finally World War II, Hurok would specialize in finding and packaging the best of the talent that was fleeing Europe. With this unending talent supply he would then satisfy the growing American demand for cultural respectability. He would capitalize on the desire of newly wealthy and prosperous Americans to secure social advancement through art—European art, especially music.

Hurok saw the moment and seized it. In a real sense, he and

the popular market for high culture in the United States grew up together.

Even in 1916, on the eve of their country's entry into the Great War, American audiences still had a lot to learn about classical music. Only twenty-five years had passed since Tchaikovsky, the first major composer to visit the United States, conducted at the grand opening of Carnegie Hall. One could still count on two hands the number of American symphony orchestras, most led by German musicians. For most Americans, as one social historian has pointed out, "art—particularly music—still connoted effeminacy and consequently fell largely under the jurisdiction of women."

American audiences had even more to learn about dance. Austrian dancer Fanny Elssler had scored a huge success on tour in the early 1840s, but at the end of the nineteenth century, the United States still had not developed any sustained ballet tradition. Indeed, no homegrown companies emerged until 1883, when dancers were imported to form a corps de ballet for the Metropolitan Opera House. Ballet was looked on as a silly and inferior medium, and those who liked it as "cranks, eccentrics and sissies."

Such considerations failed to deter Otto Kahn, chairman of the Board of the Metropolitan Opera. Ignoring dire warnings from many in the music business, including the Met's anti-ballet director Giulio Gatti-Casazza, he brought producer-impresario extraordinaire Sergei Diaghilev (1872–1929) and his Ballets Russes to America in 1916. By then, however, Kahn was already experienced in the dance field. It was under his sponsorship that Anna Pavlova had first danced in the United States in 1910, one year after she appeared with the Ballets Russes during its first Paris season.

For that New York premiere in 1910, Pavlova had danced *Coppelia* at the Met, partnered by the dashing Mikhail Mordkin. Because dance was still considered unworthy of receiving major billing, they were permitted to go on only at eleven P.M.—following a complete performance of Massenet's opera *Werther.* Pavlova and Mordkin then spent six months touring with *Legend of Aziade* and *Giselle* in a number of American cities, under the management of Max Rabinoff and G. P. Centanini. In their attempts to overcome the public perception of ballet as an elitist, difficult art, the promoters resorted to phrases like "an art new to America" and, less felicitously, "the interpretation of the ponderous messages of the great composers." But in presenting Pavlova and Mordkin, they had paved the way for Diaghilev—and, ultimately, for Hurok.

Over the following years, Pavlova fell out with Diaghilev and struck out on her own. She enjoyed particular success in America, where she gained a large and enthusiastic following. Pavlova was reportedly in the audience when Diaghilev's Ballets Russes opened its first American engagement on January 17, 1916, at the Century Theater, near Columbus Circle. The historic program included *The Firebird* (in which Pavlova had never danced because she did not like Stravinsky's "avant-garde" music), *La Princesse enchantée*, *The Midnight Sun*, and *Scheherazade*. After this evening, American dance would never be the same again.

Not surprisingly, most of those who sat in Kahn's packed theater found the urbane, subtle style of the Ballets Russes alien and difficult. They were used to watching stars, especially Pavlova, dance separate circus-style numbers. They had little experience of longer ballets, the ensemble aesthetic, or of the complete blending of visual, choreographic, and musical elements that was unique and essential to this company's identity.

To Leonide Massine, one of his leading dancers, Diaghilev expressed disappointment over the reception. It bothered him that "Americans still seemed to think of ballet as light entertainment to be enjoyed after a hard day at the office," and he remained "far from convinced that ballet would ever be taken seriously in America." Nor did it help when Diaghilev was summoned before a New York City judge to reply to a police department complaint that *L'Après-midi d'un Faune*, a ballet set to a score by Debussy and given for the first time on January 18, was obscene. Even so, the critics for the most part raved, and Kahn reportedly made money on the engagement.

From New York, the Ballets Russes went on an extended tour across the United States, then returned for performances at the Metropolitan Opera. There they were joined by one of the company's greatest artists, Vaslav Nijinsky, who had been interned in Budapest as a Russian national when World War I broke out and had only recently been released. After lengthy and difficult financial negotiations with Diaghilev, and despite complaints from Met subscribers that they would rather see opera, Nijinsky finally danced for the first time in New York on April 12, 1916, in *Le Spectre de la Rose* and Stravinsky's *Petrushka.* Many newspaper accounts dwelt on his "effeminacy"—a quality macho America tended to define in a narrow sense—but used words like "unforgettable" and "sensational" to describe his performances.

When all the accounts were settled, Kahn claimed to have made a tidy bundle on the Ballets Russes in America in 1916. He told Diaghilev he had taken in a thousand British pounds nightly, two hundred over the break-even point of eight hundred. Eager to capitalize on this apparently robust audience demand, Kahn arranged for a return tour the following autumn. This time, however, Nijinsky would lead the company and Diaghilev would remain in Europe.

Things did not go so well the second time around. Lacking the administrative brilliance of his creator and former lover, Nijinsky and the company foundered financially during their Manhattan Opera House engagement in October 1916 and subsequent fifty-six-city cross-country tour. At many stops, they danced before half-empty houses. In New York alone, Kahn reportedly lost $300,000. And now that the novelty was wearing off, audiences tired of making the effort to understand and appreciate the frankly elitist art of the Ballets Russes. A Dayton engineer exclaimed angrily about Nijinsky, "How I'd like to take a sock at that guy! Why doesn't he *work* for a living?"

Kahn, a German Jewish immigrant and independently wealthy banker, said he had no regrets about the financial losses he sustained. A visionary philanthropist, he saw his presentation of the company as an educational mission. According to the frequently nasty Romola Nijinsky, a Hungarian dancer whose marriage to Nijinsky led to his bitter break with his former lover Diaghilev, Kahn was also hoping to use his patronage of ballet to climb into high society.

"With so many glowing notices and the comprehension of the superlative quality of the Diaghileff Ballet Russe which was offered by a nucleus of public and critics, he had, in truth, accomplished his objective," writes ballet historian Nesta Macdonald. "A start had been made."

If Hurok attended any of the performances by the Ballets Russes in 1916 or 1917, they must not have made a big impression on him. He made no mention of them in his (supposed) writings or interviews. As a Russian-Ukrainian Jew from humble beginnings, he would not have been afforded easy access either to the grand—and often intolerably snobbish—aristocrat Diaghilev or to the members of his company. They sought out New York's social elite. Nor would the highly refined style of the Ballets Russes likely have appealed to Hurok's broad, crowd-pleasing taste at the time. He had virtually no experience of serious ballet.

Pavlova was another matter. Her performances at the Hippodrome, almost simultaneous with the Ballets Russes' American tour, sent Hurok into ecstasy. Significantly, Pavlova had left Diaghilev's company after a few seasons, having come to realize that she and Diaghilev held incompatible ideas about the future of dance. Although they had both developed in and around the ballet company at the Imperial Mariinsky Theater in St. Petersburg, the ballerina and the impresario had evolved in different directions. For Pavlova, the emphasis had to be on the personality of the individual dancer—namely, herself. She always had to be the dominating figure, the center of attention, and she enjoyed bringing her art to the widest possible public. An unapologetic elitist, Diaghilev regarded the wider public with disdain, even contempt. For him, dancers were only one part of a whole artistic enterprise, only one feature on a larger canvas ultimately controlled by the choreographer.

Charles Dillingham had less lofty ambitions. For his second season at the Hippodrome, he put together another completely new extravaganza, and one of the most famous productions ever mounted there—the "Big Show." It opened on August 31, 1916, about six weeks before the Ballets Russes began their second American season ten blocks south at the Manhattan Opera House.

"Slightly confused, but effective and impressive," ranging in content from a baseball game played by elephants to a four-hundred-man minstrel show, this gung-ho revue had a little bit of everything, including the first extended engagement by *prima ballerina* Pavlova on the vast Hippodrome stage. With her partner Alexander Volinine, she danced excerpts from Tchaikovsky's *Sleeping*

Beauty, using the original choreography created in 1890 by Marius Petipa for the Mariinsky Theater. From Léon Bakst, one of the leading designers for Sergei Diaghilev's Ballets Russes, Dillingham commissioned lavish new sets and costumes.

Lions, elephants, and patriotic hoopla notwithstanding, Pavlova seems to have managed to retain her dignity in this cameo appearance. Dancing the ballet's "Vision" scene "in a palace courtyard setting resplendent with fountains and multi-hued gardens," and backed up by two hundred "strictly Broadway chorus girls" whom she had personally trained, Pavlova earned critical raves. On Heywood Broun, sports editor and baseball correspondent for the New York *Tribune*, she produced a most favorable impression— even if his exposure to ballet was limited and he tended to think of it in track-and-field terms:

> For the first time, beauty has invaded the mammoth playhouse. . . . It is interesting and at times enchanting, but it is not a thing of joy in its entirety. . . . It lacks coherence. Pavlova, however, delighted the audience. This great dancer had not all the fire which she once possessed, but her art flames as brightly as ever. It is a pleasure to watch Pavlova dance, since you can applaud her without being told when. Then, too, we have always admired her art because she is the only toe dancer in the world who has not fat legs.

After a few weeks, Dillingham decided that the cerebral "Vision" scene conveyed too little fairy-tale flavor and ordered Bakst's costumes sewn over with sequins. When even this alteration failed to please the "Big Show" audience, most of whom had never seen a ballerina perform, Pavlova reverted to dancing her usual program of divertissements—at the grueling pace of two shows daily for five months.

By the time of these appearances in the "Big Show" in 1916, Pavlova was no stranger to American balletomanes, of course. They had come to know her first through her performances in New York and other American cities in 1910. The warm reception Pavlova had received in America on this first tour even led her to seek temporary refuge in the United States in 1914 when she left Russia, never to return. Pavlova's star power and popular appeal soon brought her to the attention of Hollywood. Acclaimed for her leading role in the Universal "photo-play" *The Blind Girl of Portici*, she spent all the money she earned in order to buy her own opera-ballet company: the Boston Grand Opera Company. That venture lasted a scant nine months, however. In need of money and eager to dance for a wide public, she accepted the somewhat déclassé engagement at the Hippodrome, right under the nose of her former Ballets Russes colleagues and in front of Hurok's adoring eyes.

Many writers tried to describe Pavlova's ethereal essence during her early appearances in America. Indiana journalist Frank Odell's portrait is better than many:

> Her height was slightly below average. She said that her weight never rose above 108 pounds, although she consumed gallons of cod liver oil in an effort to fatten a little. Her hair was thick and black. Her eyes were dark, set wide below a high forehead. The nose was large, the mouth too wide to be pretty, the cheek bones high and prominent. . . . Her complexion was smooth, the skin dead white. . . . The arms were adequately muscled and tapered attractively to delicate, small-boned wrists and hands. . . . The waist was small. Her uncorsetted figure . . . seemed almost boyish in litheness and spare muscularity.

This was the Pavlova who cast her spell on Hurok. Every night of her five-month run in the "Big Show," he later claimed, he stood at the back of the house to "watch and worship from afar." One night, Dillingham invited him to come backstage and meet his idol in the flesh. What supposedly followed later inspired the members of Hurok's public relations staff to some of their purplest prose. In this touching wish-fulfillment scene, Hurok plays the noble smitten cygnet to Pavlova's womanly swan. In fact, he was more of a frog prince. Back in Russia, where the world of ballet belonged to the monarchy and aristocracy, such a meeting would have occurred only in fairy tales.

The words that I would say to Anna Pavlova when I met her were ready on my tongue. I had polished and rehearsed them during the thousand times I had met her face to face in imagination. I had practiced my speech in Russian, and I had practiced it in English, and I had never made up my mind in which language my flowery eloquence would be most effective.

Eloquence would have eluded Hurok in either language, since his English was still rudimentary at best, and his Russian, mixed with Ukrainian and Yiddish, remained remote indeed from the refined Petersburg language Pavlova commanded.

She sat before her dressing table, a plain little red robe thrown over her shoulders. Dillingham's voice, presenting me, came from a million miles away.

English or Russian, Russian or English? Which should I speak? I was pilloried by the dilemma. I stood dumb, silent, stupid, blanketed by a fog in which Russian words and English words ran together and became Sanskrit and ancient Greek.

She was smiling. She put out her hand to me and, like an automaton, I bent over it. When I straightened she was speaking to Dillingham.

"Let your friend come too," she said. "It will be gay, three of us."

So I had met Pavlova, and been invited by her to supper, and I had not said a single word.

In *Impresario*, Hurok goes on to describe the ensuing supper at Palisades Park with childlike delight—how Pavlova ate with such appetite and gusto, how she laughed and smiled, how with Dillingham they rode the roller coaster and giggled in front of the fun-house mirrors, how he and she danced a fox-trot.

"After that," reported Hurok, "I was a frequent visitor in her dressing room at the Hippodrome, and there were many suppers together. Her partners, Alexander Volinine and Ivan Clustine, were often with us, and we had many happy evenings."

How much of this is true, and how much the product of Hurok's drive to establish himself as confidant and companion to the stars, is unfortunately impossible to determine. What is sure, however, is that he and his Hollywood collaborators later came up with a very different version of the first meeting between Hurok and Pavlova for the film *Tonight We Sing*.

Here, he sees Pavlova (played by Tamara Toumanova) dance on the very evening of his own wedding night to his childhood sweetheart (played by the very young Anne Bancroft). After Pavlova's performance of *The Dying Swan*, Hurok feels compelled to tell the ballerina that she is too good for the lowly Hippodrome. Abandoning his hapless but ever-patient bride, he stands concealed backstage, watching as the suddenly temperamental Pavlova refuses to see Dillingham. Hardly has the spurned manager withdrawn, however, before Hurok charms his way into Pavlova's dressing room, where he pours out his admiration and desire to present her.

"You need someone to advise you," he tells her. "A man who appreciates your genius. In my hands, madame, you will receive the treatment of a goddess."

Flattered, Pavlova does not exactly discourage this young upstart—who also speaks perfect, unaccented English. Hurok leaves with hope for the future.

Meanwhile, he has completely forgotten his lovely new bride, who has tired of waiting for him and gone home on her own. Initially heartbroken by his careless neglect, she melts when Hurok despairs of making his mark as an impresario. Their romantic reconciliation is sealed by the arrival of a telegram; Chaliapin is summoning Hurok to Paris. Ever understanding, his new wife encourages him to go.

"You're not the type of man to give up a dream," she urges, in the best Hollywood tradition.

But the reality of Hurok's married life when he encountered Pavlova at the Hippodrome in 1916 had little in common with this celluloid fantasy. According to his daughter Ruth and other sources, he never took Tamara to performances in Manhattan. In fact, as his professional and political activities intensified, he spent almost no time with his wife at all—either in theaters or at home. He rarely appeared for dinner. Most nights, he would come home at three A.M.

after the Lyceum or the Hippodrome and restaurants with his cronies. Tamara and Ruth were quickly getting used to life without Father.

By now, Ruth was old enough to understand and remember what was going on around her. She began to realize that her father was a special person who lived in a whirl of activity and excitement, that he enjoyed an increasingly glamorous existence very different from the traditional, quiet life she led with her mother:

Even in those early days in Brooklyn, Papa was different from all other papas. He had a flair, a style. It was quite unusual in that era to see any papa walking down the street with a beautiful coat, a fedora hat, and a cane. All my little friends, of course including myself, the proud little daughter, used to wait on the street to see this elegant man walking home. All my little friends, and we were no more than four or five, said, "Ruthie, is he an actor? He looks different! He doesn't look like my father!"

"No," another child said, "he doesn't look like my father! He's wonderful! Exciting!"

My heart palpitated when I saw him come along the street. I couldn't wait to run up to him, grab him and kiss him, when he'd pick me up and take me piggyback up the stairs to our apartment. My friends would follow; they were so in awe of this man.

And then, as it was until the very end of his days, the little boy in him would come out, and he would begin to play with us, imitate Chaplin, imitate other actors, tell us stories, and we all sat around with our mouths open.

Finally, they would leave and I would go into my room and he sat with me. Always we'd have an apple together and I'd look at him. . . .

He would ask me what I did during the day, and he would tell me about what was happening at the Labor Lyceum. Perhaps he felt he could confide in me, because my mother couldn't really understand. She didn't know his world of glamour and sophistication. She was a sweet, gentle, prim, simple woman who made my clothes and fixed my lunch when I came home from school. . . .

There were a lot of Italian weddings then, and I remember when I was very tiny, maybe two or three, they would take me to them and put me in the office on the couch and I would go to sleep. Then I'd wake up and I remember seeing barrels of peanuts—they ate a lot of peanuts. These Italian weddings would go on until late. Then they would pick me up and take me home. . . . I couldn't quite believe that this extraordinary figure, this glamorous figure, was my father, in that humble immigrant section of Brooklyn.

Ruth wrote these reminiscences many years later, as an adult and mother, and they show a strong desire to romanticize what she has admitted was far from an entirely happy childhood. Believing that her little friends "were so in awe of this man" helped her, perhaps, to deal with the emotional scars left by her father's indifference. From an early age, Ruth was aware that she and her mother meant little to her father, who seemed embarrassed to acknowledge their existence and who clearly preferred his business to spending time with them. This awareness led her to feel bitter and ambivalent toward Hurok in later years, a fact she has never attempted to conceal. Throughout his life, Hurok tried to compensate financially for his physical and emotional absence from his daughter's life. Even when he was not earning very much, in his early days at the Labor Lyceum, he would take Ruth and Tamara to Hoffman's Restaurant on Pitkin Avenue. "Everyone sat at his table and . . . he always picked up the check." But money can never fill the emotional void left by an inattentive parent.

Being Hurok's daughter wasn't easy. Parenting held little interest for him, and he was noticeably uncomfortable and awkward around small children (except for his grandchildren at the very end of his life). As he and Tamara drew further apart, Ruth received less and less of the constant nurturing, encouragement, and attention any child craves. Increasingly, he came to associate both Tamara and Ruth with the Old World of Pogar, a world he wanted to leave behind in his obsessive quest for a new persona amid the bright lights of Broadway. Success meant so much more to Hurok than family life. His chosen role as "papa" to his artists was all the fatherhood he would ever want or need.

Facing the difficult truth of her father's indifference has led

Ruth to remember one childhood incident with special tenderness and clarity:

> I was walking with my mother and father, I might have been four or five, on the great Champs-Élysées of Brooklyn—Pitkin Avenue—when suddenly I thought I was with them and suddenly I found myself alone; I panicked and I ran. I ran and ran, and cried and cried. Suddenly I was alone and there were no parents. I don't remember how long I ran, but suddenly a policeman found me and took me to the police station and there I wailed and howled, and suddenly my father and mother burst into the police station and my father, with tears in his eyes, grabbed me and hugged me.
>
> "We thought we lost you," he said, "but you see, we're here," and he held me in his arms.
>
> I always remembered those tears in his eyes when he found me.

Or could those tears have been the product of a neglected daughter's wishful thinking?

■ CHAPTER FOUR ■

Poi-son-ality

"We Russians are not a happy people."—*Anna Pavlova*

FOR EUROPE, World War I meant suffering, death, and the destruction of aristocratic culture. To America it brought prosperity and a new national confidence. Even the far from intellectual Hurok later reflected on this irony in a ghostwritten commentary published in *Variety* in 1943, during the darkest days of the second world war—the one the first was to have made impossible. Between 1914 and 1918, musical life boomed in the United States, as Hurok (or more likely, a more literate member of his staff) recalled.

> Wherever you turned you were faced with feverish activity. The Metropolitan Opera House was in ferment . . . and Boston boasted an opera of its own. There were three symphony orchestras in New York City plus the French orchestra on a good will tour. The ballet world was being dazzled by the first visit of Diaghilev's Russian Ballet. The immortal Pavlowa seemed to be everywhere at the same time. Isadora Duncan was at her zenith.
> I was adding my bit to the excitement with weekly concerts in the now departed Hippodrome, inveigling ticket buyers from the Bronx and Brooklyn to make those rare trips to Times Square to hear and see Pavlowa, Chaliapin,

■ 56 ■

Ruffo, Tetrazzini and Schumann-Heink at popular prices. . . . Thousands of people saw the theater district for the first time. Concert-goers got the habit. And impresarios were made.

It was all exciting and new. You had the feeling of being in on the birth of a new era of music. And it was. Victrola records began to cover the globe. Radio went on a vitamin diet and grew into a network. Man became intoxicated with his own mechanical genius. But he also developed a laziness which constituted a threat to the box office.

In person, Hurok would not have expressed these ideas with such literary refinement. Words like "inveigling," "ferment," and "zenith" no more belonged in his rustic vocabulary than a ballerina in a brothel. He would have said "net-woik," not "network." But whoever wrote these paragraphs was right about what was happening in cultural life in America during and immediately following World War I: A new era was beginning, and Hurok would be one of its bravest pioneers.

Suddenly thrust into international political and military prominence, the United States had by default assumed the role of defender of Western—that is, European—civilization.

Meanwhile, back in the Old World, proletarian ideologies were replacing monarchies and an ancient system of noble privilege and patronage was teetering on its rotting foundations. The bloody, chaotic Russian revolutions of 1917 only accelerated the collapse of the European balance of power and set the stage for a new polarization in East-West relations. Hurok's native Ukraine had sunk into anarchy, overrun by disorganized armies of Germans, Bolsheviks, White Russians, and Poles. Kiev changed hands five times in less than a year. The glorious Imperial theaters, now nationalized, more often housed political rallies than ballet or opera. Millions of Slavic refugees fled the disintegrating Tsarist empire for America's safer shores and booming industries.

Now as never before, New York became a world capital. To a city previously dismissed as a cultural backwater flocked scores of dispossessed composers, artists, dancers, and musicians, eager to make a new life in a young and innocent society spared the destruction and horror of the worst warfare man had ever known. In the words of one of the new arrivals, Polish-born pianist Arthur Rubinstein, Manhattan "seemed to be living through a joyful bacchanal."

But Rubinstein and his colleagues also encountered some painful realities in the New World. In a city awash in big names and possessed of a pure and brutal capitalist economy, no free lunch awaited. Competition was fierce. Speaking only of pianists, audiences could choose between such greats as Josef Hofmann, Benno Moiseiwitsch, Mischa Levitzki, Ossip Gabrilowitsch, and even composer-pianists like Sergei Rachmaninoff and Sergei Prokofiev, both newly arrived from Russia. There was no shortage of violinists, either. At a Carnegie Hall recital in early 1918, America finally heard Leopold Auer, the remarkable pedagogue who had trained so many future stars at the St. Petersburg Conservatory. Auer's pupils had proceeded him—Mischa Elman, Hurok's erstwhile artist Efrem Zimbalist, and, of course, the incomparable Jascha Heifetz. Heifetz's American debut in Carnegie Hall on October 27, 1917, undertaken after an arduous journey across Siberia and the Pacific, as one historian of violin playing has observed, "cast a spell of utter amazement over every professional listener" and "effectively barred the rise of any competitor for a good decade."

Amid this abundance of riches, the buyer called the shots in post–World War I New York concert life. As concert manager R. E. Johnson told Rubinstein, his slightly overwhelmed client, "There are too many goddamn pianists in this city and the managers are clamoring for Hofmann and Rachmaninoff. Here only the box office talks."

Not long after the signing of the Armistice ending World War I, Hurok presented his first important dance "attraction." The Isadora Duncan Dancers (the troupe did not include Isadora herself), affectionately dubbed the "Isadorables" by the intrigued American press, appeared under Hurok's auspices in Carnegie Hall in May and June 1919 for a total of six well-attended and critically acclaimed performances. Subsequently Hurok organized an extensive and successful cross-country tour for the troupe during the 1919–20 season.

The "Isadorables" had been trained in Europe by the American-born modern dance pioneer Isadora Duncan (1877–1927). Acclaimed abroad for her free-form dancing, which rejected tutus and the formality of ballet in favor of loose tunics and improvised "natural" movement, Isadora had encountered more obstacles in the United States. Her dream was to establish a dance school in America, but her tours of 1909, 1911, and 1917 failed to stir significant interest in the project. Instead, she created schools first in Berlin and later in Paris, where she taught six girls—Anna, Lysel, Gretel, Theresa, Erica, and Irma—who eventually became known as the Isadora Duncan Dancers.

Isadora viewed her "children" as an extension of her own creative identity and expected them to wait patiently out of sight until she needed their services. As they grew older and more self-confident, it was inevitable that strains would develop in the relationship. Their independent performances under Hurok's management at Carnegie Hall were proposed and worked out by Duncan's brother Augustin, who often found himself in an uncomfortable position between his sister and her protégées. By this time, Duncan had sought refuge in France, having left America a few months earlier, exhausted by her only partially successful efforts to achieve her educational and artistic goals. "My struggles to establish a permanent school here have been to no avail. I feel utterly disheartened and much too discouraged to continue," she told Irma. "Perhaps in France, where I have certain properties left, I may be able to raise some money and return in the fall."

In their independent performances under Hurok's management, the "Isadorables" danced Isadora's pieces, taking turns in her roles. They had already appeared with Isadora in her performances at the Metropolitan Opera House in 1917, and independently with pianist George Copeland at the Neighborhood Playhouse and at the Century Theater in New York in early spring 1918. It was their Hurok-sponsored Carnegie Hall dates in the spring of 1919, however, that finally captured the attention of the critics and the ladies' magazines.

The New York *Evening Sun* reported that the Isadorables' performances attracted "an audience of amazingly large size which thundered and thirsted for more." Wrote journalist Sigmund

Spaeth, "It may truthfully be claimed that no dancing in the world today has more of truth and sincerity in its appeal than has the dancing of these six adopted daughters of Isadora Duncan." During the run at Carnegie Hall, the Duncan Dancers also participated in a high-society "Garden Fete" at the Long Island estate of Mr. and Mrs. George D. Pratt, to benefit the Italian War Relief of America. Then they went on a tour of army camps, further endearing themselves to a patriotic public.

By taking on the "Isadorables," Hurok became identified with one of the most innovative and exciting dance attractions of the time, and overnight became known as a specialist in the field. His reputation started to attract other dancers looking for help in arranging tours. Without telling her "children" and thereby worsening their already strained relations, Isadora herself approached Hurok through her secretary, Norman Harle, and her brother Augustin in late 1920, to investigate the possibility of a solo American tour. By now, Isadora had developed a reputation as a difficult and undependable artist who caused problems for managers. Despite Hurok's obvious interest, Augustin did not encourage her in a letter to Harle:

Nov. 25, 1920

My dear Mr. Harle:

. . . I had occasion to see Mr. Hurok the other day and he asked me to write you the following and to give you his address in case you cared to write to him. He expresses a willingness to arrange some appearances in this country, with or without the girls, after the first of January. Even as late as March running into April and May provided the negotiation was completed by Christmas time.

Orchestra is only possible for New York (Metropolitan); piano on the road. Isadora could get a large fee, possibly $2,000 a performance, if she appeared with piano. But even $1,000 is unlikely if orchestra is insisted upon, outside of New York. In the latter case Hurok would not guarantee but only share on percentage. However, I advise you to write to him direct and leave me out of the negotiation. Do not ask less than $2,000 guarantee with piano.

You can get it. Turn that into francs at the present rate of exchange and realize what that would mean. H. also offers a tour of the Orient. My advice is that you deal with him direct and not any representative, as they do *not* represent him.

My own opinion is that Isadora should not come to this country. The conditions are worse than ever before and I do not believe she would fulfill her contract. No one else in the business is more hopeful than I am on that point and therefore she could not make advantageous terms. For instance, payment in advance and steamer fares paid—entirely out of the question. She would be forced to stand all the risk of failure to carry out the bookings, as confidence in the likelihood of fulfilling a contract once made, is down to Zero.

Very truly yours,
Augustin Duncan

For the moment, Isadora stayed in Europe, although she and Hurok would eventually work together. Four years later, he would bring her to the United States for the most sensational and scandal-plagued tour of her long and vivid career.

As Augustin Duncan's letter indicates, Hurok was already acquiring a reputation for unpredictable independence: "deal with him direct and not any representative, as they do *not* represent him," August Duncan warned. Increasingly, Hurok was entering into temporary partnerships with large managing concerns in order to present individual artists with whom he had cultivated special relationships. This way, he could take advantage of a larger agency's facilities without paying for expensive overhead, operating as a kind of free-lance impresario. He enjoyed particular success, of course, in working with Russian-speaking artists, with whom he could establish a special linguistic and cultural rapport.

One of those was Michel Fokine, presented by Hurok during the same (1919–20) season as the "Isadorables."

Among the most gifted choreographers ever produced by the Russian Imperial ballet tradition, Fokine (1880–1942) created early successes at the Mariinsky Theater in St. Petersburg with *The Dying*

Swan, destined to become Pavlova's trademark, and *Chopiniana* (later reworked as *Les Sylphides*, also featuring Pavlova). But Fokine did his greatest work for Diaghilev, who engaged him as principal choreographer for the Ballets Russes in Paris in 1909. For this company he produced, among other revolutionary masterpieces, *Le Pavillon d'Armide* (with Pavlova), the *Polovtsian Dances*, *The Firebird*, *Le Spectre de la rose*, and *Petrushka*. After his relationship with the Ballets Russes soured because of Diaghilev's desire to promote the choreography of his lover and protégé Nijinsky, Fokine worked for a variety of enterprises in Europe and Russia, including the Anna Pavlova Ballet Company in Berlin.

Like so many Russian artists of his generation, Fokine elected to leave his homeland permanently after the Bolshevik Revolution, fleeing starvation and runaway inflation. Homeless and in need of a job, Fokine spent some time working in Scandinavia before accepting an offer from Morris Gest (1881–1942), one of the leading American theatrical agents of the time—as well as an early model for Hurok. In the autumn of 1919, Fokine brought his family to New York and set to work on staging the bacchanal for *Aphrodite*, "a spectacular musical play whose chief attraction was that one of the participating young ladies was to appear nude." Fokine seemed to have little idea of what awaited him. When he arrived on November 7, he "declared" to a *New York Times* reporter "that the latest dances of the tango and jazz type have no place in art."

When Gest presented Fokine at the Metropolitan Opera House on December 30, he drew what one critic claimed was the Met's largest audience of the decade for a dance performance, as well as flattering comparisons with the New York appearances of Pavlova and Mordkin a decade earlier. The program featured Fokine's ballerina wife Vera Fokina in *The Dying Swan* and *Salome*, Michel in *Bacchus*, and the pair in *Spectre de la rose*, Spanish dances, and choreographed Russian folk songs. The Fokines repeated the same sort of divertissements at the Hippodrome on January 18, 1920. Another appearance at the Met was also scheduled for February 10—this time under the "exclusive management" of "S. Hurok Musical Bureau, 220 W. 42nd St."

There is no precise documentation on how Hurok and Fokine found each other, but given Hurok's high profile in the tightly knit (even claustrophobic) Russian émigré community, it is hardly surprising that they did. As so often happens with dancers, however, illness and injury disrupted Hurok's carefully laid plans for their first collaboration. Just before the scheduled February 10 performance, Fokine suffered an injury and was unable to dance. So Vera Fokina bravely went on to give an entire evening of dances alone, performing seven numbers with conductor Arnold Volpe and his orchestra, and one, Beethoven's "Moonlight" Sonata, in free Duncanesque style, to solo piano accompaniment. So warm was the audience reception that she encored with the *Dying Swan* and some Polish, gypsy, and Russian folk dances. By filling in for her husband, Vera not only saved the show; she also made history, becoming the first and only ballerina ever to give a solo performance at the Met.

In his self-congratulatory and frequently inaccurate memoirs, Hurok characteristically takes all the credit for suggesting to Fokina that she go on alone. "There was all the publicity, all the advertising, and the rent of the Metropolitan Opera House had to be paid." And so the wily impresario came to the rescue, protecting his investment and his grateful artists. Exactly what happened we will never know, but it seems likely that Vera and Michel Fokine, veteran performers, probably had something to do with the decision.

Hurok did not make himself so indispensable to the Fokines that they would refuse to work with other managers. The following season, Morris Gest, not Hurok, presented them at the Met in another notable performance that was again marred by injury. Having aggravated an earlier leg strain, Michel was forced to limp and hop through the world premiere of a new ballet he had choreographed, *The Dream of the Marquise.*

For the Hippodrome, where the Fokines also appeared under Hurok's management in 1920, Michel choreographed *Thunderbird*, a one-act ballet with a story by Vera based on an Aztec legend and using music by a hodgepodge of Russian composers. Part of an extravagant new revue called *Get Together*, it ran for 397 performances. The Fokines' new creation pleased the critics, largely ignorant of dance, nearly as much as did a new ball-catching animal act, Jacko the Crow and the Three Bobs.

Initially, Fokine had not planned to stay in America. His relationship with the Ballets Russes effectively ended, however, he gradually settled in New York, with occasional trips to work in Europe. He and his family moved into a large house near the Hudson River, living "in an atmosphere of nostalgic gloom, a sort of Chopinesque twilight." It was quite a comedown for the genius behind *Les Sylphides* and *The Firebird*. Accustomed to working with the world's best dancers and companies, Fokine suddenly found himself stranded in a country that still regarded ballet as a frivolous and even suspect occupation and that lacked a tradition of serious dance performance.

Even with the backing of Hurok's energy, ambition, and increasingly sophisticated publicity machine, Fokine and his wife failed to make it big in America. Deprived of his former status, embittered by circumstances beyond his control, and unable to capture the public imagination, Michel stagnated in New York. He devoted himself primarily to teaching in his new ballet school. He did continue to choreograph for such later enterprises as the Ziegfeld Follies, the Rene Blum company, and Colonel de Basil's Ballets Russes de Monte Carlo, where he and Hurok would again cross paths. But Fokine, like Russian composer Sergei Rachmaninoff (who settled in the United States in 1918), belonged too completely to the exclusive, aristocratic Old World and seemed temperamentally incapable of adapting to the New.

As would become obvious only ten years later, the opportunity was ripe to create a new American dance tradition, but this great choreographer, as Hurok's public relations agent so delicately put it, "muffed the big chance."

Fokine's close friend and collaborator Anna Pavlova, on the other hand, did not shy away from the rough-and-ready egalitarian atmosphere of the Roaring Twenties. In fact, this swan with nerves of steel spent much of that decade eagerly crisscrossing the globe, bringing ballet to audiences who had never seen it before. No shrinking violet, as she is often wrongly portrayed, Pavlova craved adventure, new sights, and the adoration of her fans, for whom she happily endured conditions more primitive and taxing than any of today's touring rock stars would possibly tolerate.

After her long, successful, and lucrative ($8,500 a week) run at the Hippodrome ended in January 1917, Pavlova and her company had danced around Latin America for two years, performing to often frantic mobs in bullfighting rings and opera houses. They lived hand-to-mouth, arranging bookings as they went. She returned to Europe after the war, making guest appearances in Spain and France before alighting briefly at Ivy House, the home near London that she and her husband Victor Dandré had purchased in 1912.

But Pavlova could not bear to stay in one place for long. Soon Fortune Gallo (1878–1970) lured her back to the United States for an extended tour that opened at the Manhattan Opera House in March 1921. Born in Italy, Gallo was an opera impresario who had immigrated to the United States in 1895. In 1909, he had formed the San Carlo Opera Company, which had become very successful by presenting touring performances at reasonable prices. Outfoxed in his passion for Pavlova by his better-established competition, Hurok nonetheless subcontracted with Gallo to manage the tour's New England portion, and used it as an opportunity to further ingratiate himself with the greatest ballerina of the era. As with Chaliapin, Hurok played the adoring myrmidon to Pavlova's regal artiste.

"In Boston I began to talk about the following season," he claims in *Impresario*. "I met her in Detroit, went to Indianapolis and Chicago with her. After Chicago I had a signed contract for the next year in my pocket, and I was a happy man." However it really came about (Pavlova never talked about it), Hurok did in fact now become her American manager. Beginning in 1921–22, he presented the "Incomparable" (as she was known) annually on exhausting six-month tours until 1925.

The frog had won the princess.

"Hurok was in love with Anna Pavlova, and I don't blame him," Agnes de Mille has said. "So was I. I saw her throughout my youth, and I adored her. She was hypnotizing. Nobody I have ever seen on stage had that power—Maria Callas, perhaps, to some degree. She could absolutely *bewitch* the audience. And convey a sense of time stopping, of nothing else in the world mattering. By the time Hurok started presenting her, she was the biggest dancing star in the universe."

Pavlova was, in fact, the first dancer to become world famous. In recorded interviews about his collaboration with Pavlova,

Hurok stressed her phenomenal ability to connect with the audience—a quality he would seek in all his artists in years to come. "She had *poi-son-ality*," he would say in his awkward English, with its missing suffixes and adverbs. "She was very poetic inclined. She would electrify an audience even she didn't dance: her eyes, her voice. Pavlova did more to popularize the ballet than any other individual in the world."

Professionally, Hurok and Pavlova had a great deal more in common than might appear on the surface. They were both strongly democratic by nature and wanted to bring "elite" art—in this case ballet—to the widest possible audience. They both believed in the importance of "stars," and much less in the idea of an artistic ensemble in which all members were equal. Their aesthetic (if one can call it that) directly contradicted the philosophy Diaghilev implemented in his work with the Ballets Russes, one later carried on by Balanchine at the New York City Ballet.

Both Hurok and Pavlova possessed rather conventional taste. They tended to follow the audience rather than to lead it. Not for them Diaghilev's credo that "the longer a work of genius remains hidden from the enthusiasms of the multitude the more complete and more intact will it remain for the lovers of true art." Pavlova—and certainly Hurok—wanted to be loved, not respected. "I want to dance for everybody in the world," she said. "Dancing is my gift and my life. . . . God gave me this gift to bring delight to others. That is why I was born. I am haunted by the need to dance." And Hurok was only too happy to help, serving as altar boy to this terpsichorean priestess, arranging the tedious details of touring, lavishing unending praise on her art and person.

That these two populists worked well together, therefore, comes as no surprise. But was work the only thing they shared? Were they lovers, as has often been rumored—at least by Hurok and his agents?

Breaching the fat wall of hoopla that surrounds the Hurok-Pavlova relationship is no easy matter. Reticent and mysterious, Pavlova was unfailingly discreet and even secretive about matters of the heart. She loved no one nearly as much as ballet and left no record of intimacy with her American impresario. For his part, until the day he died Hurok loved to boast of his special closeness to Pavlova, while remaining shrewdly vague as to the details.

Rudolf Nureyev recalled that whenever he was asked if he and Pavlova had been lovers, Hurok "smiled, and you could see a happy grin on his face, but then he would always deny everything." Being linked romantically to one of the greatest ballerinas ever, Hurok knew, could only help business.

That a deeply spiritual, frequently prudish, and rigorously circumspect woman like Pavlova would ever have entered into a sexual liaison with a squat, ill-spoken, and nearly illiterate Jewish immigrant like Hurok seems highly improbable. Although it does appear that as a young ballerina she was not above entering into affairs with critics and other prominent figures who could help advance her career, none of Pavlova's numerous biographers has ever provided evidence of romantic involvement between her and Hurok. By the time she came to know Hurok, however, Pavlova did not need to resort to such devices. Nor was Hurok noted for his sex appeal. "He never was a great success with the ladies, you know," his associate Lillian Libman once remarked, "although he liked to have people think he was."

Whatever the truth, there were unexpected and striking similarities in their personalities. Like Hurok, Pavlova sought to obscure the facts of her apparently humble origins and avoided discussing her early life: "Her face clouded if the subject was raised." Both the exact date of her birth and the identity of her father still remain in question. It was often rumored that she was illegitimate and/or the daughter of a wealthy Jew, although the ballerina maintained officially that her father was Matvey Pavlovich Pavlov, a Russian peasant and reserve soldier. In *Impresario*, Hurok claimed Pavlova once told him she was a Jew "and made me promise not to tell while she lived."

But Hurok understood even better than she that being revealed as a Jew could do severe damage to the image of noble Russian spirituality Pavlova had so successfully cultivated in the West. Her secrets were safe with him. Indeed, what brought them together was a mutual need (born of personal identity and commercial realities) to re-create themselves and their past. Codependents in compulsive self-creation, they could use each other as blank slates on which to write new lives. Both dramatic and self-deluding, they could invent each other and their relationship as they went along, engaging in an elaborate psychic pas de deux.

For both Pavlova and Hurok, the illusion of the stage far surpassed reality. No living human could possibly compare with the marvelous characters they constructed in their minds.

Not surprisingly, then, they both found it difficult to form lasting romantic relationships with the opposite sex. Just as Hurok sought to conceal the circumstances of his marital life with Tamara, so did Pavlova never completely explain the nature of her liaison with Victor Dandré. A former member of the St. Petersburg city council, Dandré had been traveling and living with Pavlova in London since 1912, serving as her manager. Their relationship "struck many people as more like a business partnership than a marriage," and it seems they were never legally married. Realizing that such an ambiguous and, by puritanical American standards, highly immoral state of affairs could endanger Pavlova's popularity, Hurok fed American newspapers a story in 1925 that Pavlova and Dandré had married seventeen years before. In that more gullible era, the editors and their public bought it.

The North American tours Pavlova made under Hurok's management would have exhausted a teenager, let alone a veteran ballerina past forty. Usually they required thousands of miles of grueling train travel for six or seven months of one-night stands, with eight performances a week in large cities and small towns. During her last North American tour in the 1924–25 season, she and her company, often accompanied by Hurok, gave 238 performances in 77 towns in 26 weeks. "Often it meant that we had to get into an express after our performance," she told *Dance* magazine, "snatch what rest we could despite the bumping and the noise, and arrive at our next destination only just in time to get changed, and appear on the stage again."

In Jackson, Mississippi, then a town of about fifteen thousand souls, this delicate product of the Mariinsky danced on a rickety improvised stage in an old garage that had been converted into a movie theater. In Fresno, the hall went dark because of a fire in the next block, but the performance went on, illuminated by car headlights hooked up to a generator. In Nashville, Madame had to dress in the organ loft and her audience sat in pews. Such rustic conditions apparently invigorated Pavlova, who, like a character out of Chekhov, burned with the desire to bring culture to what Hurok loftily called "the common folk."

"Never mind, Hurokchik," she supposedly told him after a leaky roof in Montgomery forced her to pirouette in a puddle. "These are the people who need us, and it gives me more joy to dance for them than at the Metropolitan Opera House."

And Hurok *didn't* mind, especially since he and his ballerina were doing quite handsomely at the box office. Estimates of what Hurok earned on these tours vary wildly, anywhere from $25,000 to $1 million, but despite the considerable cost of touring a company of as many as forty-five people, there seems little doubt that both of them emerged richer from the collaboration.

And more famous.

The 1921–22 season was a turning point for Hurok. He had realized one of his greatest ambitions, to present Pavlova, and was now, at the age of thirty-three, about to achieve another—to present Chaliapin.

Like Fokine and Pavlova, Chaliapin was brought to Hurok by the Russian Revolution. In his memoirs, Chaliapin claims that just before World War I, he had signed a contract to sing in America in 1915, but that the outbreak of fighting in Europe made traveling abroad impossible. Spared military service because of his age (forty-one), he remained in Russia throughout the war, the Russian Revolution, and the Civil War, continuing to perform even as the Imperial theaters passed into the hands of the new Bolshevik government.

"Little by little life became more and more difficult," he would write later. "It was as hard for me to get milk and bread—the bare necessities—as for the humblest workingman to provide food for his family. I was glad to sing for the reward of a bag of flour, a ham, some sugar. Sometimes, even, I received a little money, which had already become of very little value."

But he never stopped singing.

"All these seven years of horrible revolution the voice of music was never stilled. Perhaps this was because Russians cannot live without music. What had been art under the tsars remained art under the Soviet. As for me, who had never played any part in politics but had consecrated my life to art, I was looked upon as a '*bayan*,' our ancient Slavonic word for bard or singer."

Despite his supposed lack of interest in politics, the wily

Chaliapin did manage during those difficult years of war and revolution to become acquainted with many prominent Bolshevik leaders. Through his close friendship with the writer Maxim Gorky, a great favorite of the new Soviet elite, the basso claimed to have met Lenin, Trotsky, Zinovyev, Kamenev, and Stalin. Chaliapin admitted later that he did not know them well, but his friend Ivan Bunin, an émigré Russian writer, noted in his diary that the singer had addressed both Lenin and Trotsky by the familiar pronoun ("thou"). One must view Chaliapin's claims of intimacy with the Soviet ruling elite with considerable caution, however, since he was no less adept than Hurok at twisting the truth in retrospect to suit his artistic or personal purposes.

"Around his dining-room table," writes Chaliapin's biographer Victor Borovsky,

> where previously Stasov, Rimsky-Korsakov, Korovin, Stanislavsky and Rachmaninov had been sitting, there lounged new guests whom he would later "hate to remember": commissars of all ranks and sizes in leather jackets; members of the secret police, now the Cheka, headed by Dzerzhinsky; newly fledged officers of the new Red Army; and some others whose names Chaliapin forgot. One had to welcome them with a smile and some vodka at all hours of the day or night; they came without warning, announcing their arrival by a loud knock on the door—the same knock as their men used when they burst in to make searches and confiscate the last remnants of silver or paintings which they fancied.

Hurok would later benefit from Chaliapin's close Kremlin connections.

Another of Chaliapin's influential friends was the newly appointed People's Commissar of Enlightenment, Anatoly Lunacharsky (1875–1933). Highly cultured and a valued defender of artists' rights, Lunacharsky and his Ministry of Culture began to operate as a kind of collective manager for Soviet performers who were invited abroad.

In July 1921, Lunacharsky told Chaliapin that he had received a letter from an American impresario offering a contract for a lucrative tour in the United States. Although Lunacharsky did not mention Hurok by name, the proposal obviously came from him.

> I have received a very serious contract for you from a firm with the intriguing name "The Incomparable Pavlowa." [Lunacharsky must have been confusing the promotion for Pavlowa on Hurok's stationery with the name of his firm.] Most likely you will sign it. The fee is enviable. According to the calculations of the People's Finance Committee, you will receive 57.5 million in our currency for each performance. So that's how much we're robbing you by paying you only five million per performance.

Hurok's letter arrived at just the right moment. Before the 1917 revolution, as a soloist with the Russian Imperial theaters, Chaliapin had never needed a manager. In Russia, all his appearances were covered under his relationship with the Mariinsky and other state-subsidized theaters. As for his relatively infrequent foreign performances, he carried out any negotiations himself, directly with the foreign impresario or with the management of the opera houses, whether in Milan or Monte Carlo. (This is how he had arranged his appearances under Diaghilev's auspices in Paris and London.) If there were any details to be worked out, Chaliapin relied on his friend and personal secretary Isai Dvorishchin to take care of them. Under these conditions, there was no need for him to engage an impresario to manage his career and set up bookings.

But World War I, the Russian Revolution, and the subsequent civil war in the new USSR radically changed that situation. With his country cut off from the rest of the world and travel both dangerous and hard to arrange, Chaliapin stopped performing abroad after 1914 for seven long years. Meanwhile, life in Russia was becoming more difficult and chaotic for everyone, including writers, musicians, and artists. Looking for relief from isolation and privation, Chaliapin had been contemplating leaving the USSR for some time: "The day came when it seemed to me an absolute necessity to get out of Russia and see if I had been forgotten." The arrival of Hurok's letter gave him the pretext he needed. Through

Lunacharsky, Chaliapin obtained permission, a passport, and space on a government train taking some officials to Riga, Latvia, then the capital of an independent country.

"And so, in August, 1921," he later wrote, "I left my country in a coat, vest, and trousers that bore absolutely no relation to one another, taking with me only my theatrical costumes, my make-up, and my worn and patched dress suit for concerts."

After giving an acclaimed concert in Riga, Chaliapin was inundated with more offers from managers all over the world. One of Hurok's most serious competitors was the American Francis C. Coppicus, who had worked as secretary to Giulio Gatti-Casazza, the Italian-born general manager of the Metropolitan Opera, before becoming a high-powered concert manager. Never one to fight battles he couldn't win, Hurok decided in this case to join forces. He and Coppicus's well-established Metropolitan Musical Bureau made a joint offer (by telegram), and Chaliapin accepted. The singer would receive a fee of $3,000 for each concert. After a quick trip to Finland to visit his daughter, and after tumultuously received concerts in England, including one at London's Royal Albert Hall in London, the singer Hurok had been plotting to represent for the last fifteen years was on his way to New York.

In a letter to his oldest daughter, Irina, written on board ship as he sailed to America, Chaliapin expressed deep suspicion and even hostility toward all the Western managers (without citing any by name) who were trying to "exploit" and "blackmail" him. He was especially offended that he had to sign a document provided by U.S. Immigration stating that he would not be asking for money from anyone in the United States. He worried that he would be thereby prevented from giving benefit concerts whose profits would go to famine relief in the USSR.

> Oh my Irina, if only you knew what sneaks and liars live in Europe and America. Of course they all call themselves by that noble-sounding name of "businessmen." If somebody snatches something away, for example, then that means they've "done some business"—a fine expression. It's not like "stealing" but still manages very nicely to retain the same meaning. In any case, I'll find out after arriving in America what it's all about.

At the pier, Hurok was among a crowd Chaliapin later described vaguely as "a number of Russians" who had come to meet him. Nor did the basso later recall (as Hurok did) carousing that evening with his eager manager at the Castle Cave Restaurant. When departing New York fifteen years earlier, it seems, Chaliapin had praised this establishment as "the best thing in New York." His endorsement had led to a boom in business, so the restaurant's owner, a man named Bardush, was waiting in his Packard to whisk the basso off for a thank-you feast "beginning with Bardush's famous oysters prepared over charcoal—of which Chaliapin ate three or four dozen—and continuing with enormous steaks."

Whether from overeating or some other cause, Chaliapin almost immediately came down with a cold that vastly complicated the concert and opera appearances Hurok had scheduled for him. Postponed three times, his debut recital finally took place on November 13, 1921, at the Manhattan Opera House. Even then, Chaliapin agreed to go on only after a special personal appeal from his "dear old friend" Anna Pavlova, who had appeared—also under Hurok's management—in the same theater just two nights before. Characteristically, Hurok later took the credit for bringing her backstage to soothe the ailing artist.

> She flung her slender arms around his massive shoulders and tears poured from her eyes—and from his.
> "All right, Aniuta, all right," he said. "But let someone go out and tell them I have a cold—otherwise I cannot."

After the announcement of his indisposition, Chaliapin sang a recital of songs and operatic extracts by Glinka, Glazunov, Schumann, Grieg, Schubert, Mussorgsky, Gounod, and Beethoven that Hurok later called "pitiful," although Richard Aldrich of the *New York Times* reacted charitably to the concert by the temperamental star he described as "a great blond." What especially impressed the critic was the atmosphere in the theater, however:

> The Manhattan Opera House was crowded, with an audience largely composed of his countrymen and women in New York, but showing also a considerable number of people prominent in the musical world, operatic and oth-

ers. The house was charged with enthusiasm, ready to welcome and applaud at every opportunity, and the welcome, which burst in a storm at the singer's appearance, was such as apparently to impress him deeply.

Such a warm reception did a great deal to soften the resentment the egotistical Chaliapin still felt over the rude reception he had encountered on his first foray into the United States in 1907. "I was ill, yet the audience understood and applauded me!" he wrote later.

But Chaliapin's cold and laryngitis lingered, forcing the cancellation of concerts at Carnegie Hall and the Hippodrome. Packed off to a rest home in rural New Jersey to recuperate, he returned, recovered, to sing for a huge audience at the Hippodrome on Sunday afternoon, November 27. Facing a "continuous and often overwhelming roar of enthusiasm from 5,000 compatriots," he tore full voice through a Russian program of Rimsky-Korsakov, Dargomyzhsky, and others.

That same afternoon, twenty-five thousand New Yorkers attended ten high-profile musical events. Culture was booming.

The crowning event of Chaliapin's return to New York came two weeks later at the Metropolitan Opera. On December 10 (not November 21 as stated in *Impresario*), "acclaimed from his first entrance to the end with great enthusiasm," he sang the title role in *Boris Godunov*. Even the fact that Chaliapin sang in Russian and the rest of the cast in Italian, as had been the practice at the Met for the last nine seasons, failed to ruin the strong dramatic impact of his performance.

By the time of Chaliapin's next *Boris* four days later, word-of-mouth had spread so rapidly that the theater was assailed by what the *New York Times* called one of its "most excited and turbulent throngs ever." That December 14 performance ranks unquestionably as one of the greatest and most rambunctious nights in Met history.

A man in an orchestra chair was seized with a fit and carried through the aisle. Later another $11 spectator arose with loud remarks as to opera here and in Russia, which led to his ejection. . . . Several hundred persons stormed the police lines to buy his one vacant seat. . . . For the first time on record the lines that had formed from noon onward to standing admission reached four abreast around the block. It was estimated that the audience which got in hardly exceeded the thousands turned away.

Inside, the crowd responded to their hero's usual intense performance with a "deafening din" that lasted for fifteen minutes. What amazed the audience and the critics was the singer's ability to enter fully into the tortured character of the doomed and guilty Tsar Boris, to literally become him, using his voice as only one weapon in his arsenal of dramatic effects. When Chaliapin sang this role, he brought alive not only an individual, but a whole era and atmosphere. For the many Russians in the house, the strength of his portrayal was almost too much to bear.

Chaliapin's triumph at the Met came at a time when that very conservative institution was beginning to reflect new social realities. The old aristocratic families that had long supported and monopolized the opera were being challenged by a rising tide of democratization reflected in the diversity of the crowd—which included many recent immigrants—that jammed in to hear *Boris*. Just a month before Chaliapin's first Met performance, a *New York Times* story on the upcoming opera season noted that the list of boxholders showed "some changes in what was formerly called the 'Golden Horseshoe,' a name almost as obsolete now as the expression '400,' owing to the growing dimensions of society and the changes that come with time. . . . There are several newcomers in the parterre row, and mourning has eliminated at least five families which have been identified with the Opera House for several decades."

Jews, long denied the right to own boxes, were also appearing at the Met in larger numbers. The wealthy Jewish banker and arts promoter Otto Kahn had received a box in 1917, after serving as chairman of the Met's board of directors for ten years.

As a result of these changes, the Met audience now included more real opera fans and fewer socialites interested solely in making an appearance. This change helps to explain why Chaliapin received a much more enthusiastic reception in 1921 than in 1907.

Overwhelmed, even confused by the force and enormity of the public response, Chaliapin felt (correctly) that he had reached an important new stage in his career. Now he was confident that he could make it in the West. Originally he had planned to return to Russia by late December, but instead he stayed for another month.

"I only realised this," he wrote a few years later. "On that evening I had indeed been crowned as an artist, at the Metropolitan Opera House!"

And Hurok, applauding harder than anyone, had been crowned an impresario.

In later years, after Chaliapin was safely dead and buried, Hurok loved to tell of the times they spent hanging around New York together. One of the impresario's favorite photographs shows them, disheveled, sharing food around a table with some street bums in the Bowery—proof, it would seem, not only of their friendship, but also of their shared proletarian sympathies.

As usual, however, the reality doesn't match the public relations fantasy. Far from a spontaneous encounter, the episode was a planned stunt. Chaliapin and Hurok donned their oldest clothes one night and descended to the Bowery "for a taste of flop-house luxury. They slept—not well—and were awakened in the morning by a cherub-faced derelict (extreme right in the photo, eating an apple) who urged them to hurry and share the free meal that was being served downstairs by 'some gent who wants to take our picture.' "

Hurok also loved to talk about going to Turkish baths with Chaliapin, where they could reenact elaborate Russian bathhouse rituals—which always included plenty of philosophizing.

"And once, when we were drying off," Hurok told two reporters years later, "he said to me: 'Talk about democracy—look right where you are this very instant. There are no limousines, no chauffeurs—everybody uses the same soap—even eats the same food at the same table—and here everybody is also *nude*! I tell you, only in a Turkish bath, Hurok, do you find the *true* democracy!' "

As men who had grown up poor in a highly stratified society and who had received little formal education, both Chaliapin and Hurok loved to rhapsodize about equality and self-government. But, in fact, they both came increasingly to pander to the elite classes who could afford the sophisticated art they presented. And deep down, these two egotists did not really believe they were equal to everyone else. They were superior and special.

Chaliapin certainly didn't treat Hurok like an equal, as numerous witnesses have stated. One was the singer's old friend Arthur Rubinstein. In his memoirs, Rubinstein recalls enjoying a regal breakfast with Chaliapin in his New York hotel suite in the fall of 1921. When Hurok arrived, Chaliapin treated him with what was to Rubinstein startling condescension. Apparently taking no offense at this sort of behavior, Hurok sat patiently in the corner as Chaliapin asked Rubinstein to play the piano arrangement of *Petrushka* that Stravinsky had written for him:

> I opened the lid of his piano and started banging out joyously the "Dance Russe." Chaliapin, who knew and loved the piece, did not allow me to stop until I had played most of it. Then he hugged me enthusiastically. "You are great, you are great!" he screamed. "Sol," he said to his agent, using the familiar "thou," "you heard something good, eh? . . . This fellow knows nothing about music," he said to me loudly.

About music Hurok really did know little, but he did know a thing or two about talent, and even more about what he always called "projection." And he knew after listening to Rubinstein that he had both.

A few days after this scene in Chaliapin's hotel suite, Rubinstein's agent, R. E. Johnson, called in the pianist. Johnson had not been very successful in marketing Rubinstein, no doubt because he had been sending him off to second-rate engagements in second-rate cities.

"A feller called Hurok, a smart cookie, came to see me," Johnson told Rubinstein.

> He's running some concerts at the Hippodrome, ha, ha; that damn place has five thousand seats, so he can offer expensive artists at cheaper prices. Now he wants you to take part in a concert with Titta Ruffo, who will be the

star. He wants you to fill up the program with a few piano pieces. I asked for five hundred dollars but that s.o.b. brought it down to three hundred and I think you should accept it. It's good for you to be heard by a big audience.

And accept it Rubinstein did, with gratifying results. Unimpressed by Ruffo, who was not in good voice, the huge Hippodrome crowd lavished on the thirty-four-year-old pianist the kind of ovations he was used to receiving in Buenos Aires or Madrid but had yet to encounter in the United States. For the moment, the relationship between the pianist and manager went no further, but Hurok would play a decisive role in Rubinstein's career in years to come, having found him, as he would so many of his artists, through the recommendation of one of his stars.

Rubinstein's friend Chaliapin spent the early winter of 1922 expanding his American reputation with concerts in New York, Montreal, Boston, Chicago, Cleveland, and Philadelphia. In a letter, he dubbed the exhausting tour a "cantata caravan." Traveling on American trains annoyed him, since the sleeping berths were designed for people "of medium height, but that's too short for me, so I have to sleep sort of bent over, and the hell with them!"

Significantly, Chaliapin left no written record of Hurok in any of his numerous recollections of his appearances in the United States in 1921–22. He did find the time, however, to write about theatrical manager Morris Gest, whom he had met after his first New York recital and who spent time with him at the New Jersey rest home. What he said of Gest, born in Russia but educated in the Boston public schools, would soon be said of Hurok, seven years his junior:

Further acquaintance with him made me realise one of the finest things about America—the richness of the soil that forms the basis for the country's social life and relations. This soil is so fertile that any plant, northern or tropical, may grow in it. Here was an example for, in this fertile soil, this man with the tired face, wide-brimmed soft hat, and La Valliere tie had grown from a gamin selling newspapers in the streets into a theatrical power capable of bringing across the ocean interesting Russian productions, not alone for money, but to show a special form of art.

A very quick learner, Hurok would take more than a few pages from this respected manager's book—including the addition of an elegant cane to his wardrobe. With the passage of time (and without the benefit of a Boston education), he would even out-Gest Morris Gest.

After fulfilling his very successful American engagements under Hurok's auspices, Chaliapin returned briefly to Russia. He stayed in Petrograd only long enough to sing his last performance (a benefit) in a Russian theater. Appropriately, it was in the lead role in *Boris Godunov*. Shortly afterward, he left the USSR with his second wife, their daughters, and his stepdaughter, never to return.

Hurok, meanwhile, was taking his first trip to Europe in ten years. Ecstatic over presenting his operatic hero (in conjunction with Metropolitan Music Bureau, a detail he tended to forget later on) and Pavlova successfully in a single season, he set off—in what would become an annual ritual—to the Old World "in search of talent for the next season." These would not be easy acts to follow.

This time, as a serious impresario, he traveled on the liner *Majestic*—first class.

CHAPTER FIVE

"Mi Laik Amerika"

"My husband was a Russian, and all Russians break furniture when they are drunk."—*Isadora Duncan*

BY THE TIME HUROK, "in a roseate haze," sailed off to Europe in what seems to have been the spring of 1922, he was spending very little time at home in Brooklyn. His absence confused and hurt his daughter, Ruth, then eleven, who later reproached him for leaving her just when she needed him most. She also remembered that her mother, Tamara, Hurok's Old Country wife, accepted the situation with sad resignation, remaining quietly in their apartment, the rent for which he continued to pay.

As his achievements grew and he began to become known more and more, there was a rift between Mama and Papa. She couldn't understand him or keep up with his world of glamor and achievement. And so they separated. I never realized until much later on in my life what a great void this was for me. There were not the nightly visits anymore, the kisses, the wonderful excitement of seeing him at night, no matter what time. Mother was bewildered, unhappy, and I, busy with school and my friends, didn't quite realize what impact this had on me. He always called me, and as I grew older we met for lunch or we met for dinner and still, always, that wonderful flutter in me and the thrill of seeing Papa sitting in the McAlpin Hotel, the Astor Hotel, or the St. Regis, sitting opposite me and telling me about his work.

Whenever Ruth would meet with her father, her mother—envious of their relationship—would make her feel guilty about leaving her behind.

His disrupted domestic situation apparently caused Hurok few sleepless nights. In *Impresario*, he minimizes the impact of his new condition of singleness, remarking offhandedly that by the mid-1920s, "I had got myself divorced . . . and I had no family." (The existence of a teenaged daughter who adored him had somehow slipped his mind.) But exactly what sort of "divorce," if any, Hurok obtained at this point is far from clear. What we do know is the following.

Years later, in 1941, Hurok and Tamara received a legally binding divorce in Reno, Nevada. According to that "Findings and Decree" dated September 16, 1941, they had "for some time past lived separate and apart and now do and hereafter intend to live separate and apart from each other." (By 1941, Hurok had also been living with another woman for a number of years—but more on that later.) This document also states that Hurok had secured an earlier divorce from Tamara "under the laws of the State of Cuernavaca, Mexico," but that she questioned its validity. Under the terms of the 1941 divorce, they agreed to live separately "regardless of the validity or invalidity" of the Mexican divorce, and Hurok agreed to pay her a $10,000 fee as well as a weekly support payment of $75. It has been impossible for me to determine whether Hurok obtained the Mexican divorce mentioned here in the mid-1920s, as he claims in his memoirs, or at some later point. All this evidence leaves little doubt, though, that Tamara was not the one who originally sought to terminate the marriage.

Whatever the actual legal status of their relationship, Hurok always provided financially for Tamara and Ruth, even before they obtained the binding 1941 divorce. He saw to it that they lived comfortably and never lacked for any essentials. With the genuine affection of a husband and father he was more stingy.

Both before and after the separation, Hurok's relations with his wife and daughter often showed a tension between his fierce striving for status and a consciousness of his lowly origins. When she was about ten years old, Ruth went to the Metropolitan Opera for the first time, with her mother and father. During the intermission, her mother gave her an orange to eat, since, "like all Jewish mothers, she thought I never ate enough." When Hurok walked in to find her eating a piece of fruit in the sacred temple of elite culture, he "almost fainted" and mercilessly scolded his cowed wife. "How dare you bring an orange to the Metropolitan!" he said.

When Ruth was a little older, Hurok sent her to a dancing school in Manhattan and to an expensive performing arts summer camp, where she danced and acted. He would come—alone—to visit Ruth there, but did not encourage her to pursue her obvious interest in an artistic career. His attitude of "you'll never be good enough to have a career" made her feel inadequate and unloved.

The motivations behind Hurok's behavior toward his wife and daughter were brutally pragmatic. As he moved up in the world in the early 1920s, hobnobbing with the opera stars and glamorous ballerinas, it became painfully obvious to him that Tamara—whose appearance, demeanor, and attitudes still reeked of Pogar—simply wouldn't do as a partner. While far from admirable, his conduct was hardly unique in the context of the history of how Eastern European immigrants adapted to life in America. In his book *An Empire of Their Own: How the Jews Invented Hollywood*, Neal Gabler documents a very similar process among the studio magnates, many of whom also rose from the humblest of immigrant origins, and whose burning ambitions for economic and social success closely resembled Hurok's. As they became more wealthy and more socially prominent, these tycoons often jettisoned spouses they had wed in more rustic surroundings and who now proved incapable of keeping up.

"Those who couldn't adjust were often replaced, and in the end divorce among the top Hollywood Jews was usually less a product of sexual temptation than of inadequate social performance," Gabler writes. "For the husbands, their wives could no longer be provincial Jewish mamas any more than their cars could be jalopies or their homes shacks. They had an image to maintain."

▪   ▪   ▪

Judging by the cosmeticized description provided (many years after the fact) in *Impresario*, Hurok spent much of his "first trip in style" to Europe on the *Majestic* in 1922 not only maintaining, but building his image. This included flirting with attractive fellow passengers. Whatever the truth of his marital situation, he clearly liked to think of himself as an eligible single man, dashing about the decks like some show-business Errol Flynn.

His eye settled on a "tall, good-looking brunette, a buyer making her annual trip to Paris for a Fifth Avenue store." (He never gave her name.) The dining-room steward had set them up. Nurtured by starry nights on the open ocean, their romance bloomed (because of his short stature, Hurok usually fixed upon tall objects of affection) and they subsequently traveled, he claimed, through Paris, Berlin, Frankfurt, and London. Back in New York, he even introduced the woman to his daughter, Ruth, which led to "a big scene" with Tamara. Perhaps because he was still legally married to Tamara, Hurok's relationship with this mysterious brunette buyer eventually ended, although she apparently remained very fond of him to the end of her life. When Hurok died, she came to his funeral and told Ruth that she had never forgotten him, and even that she regretted not marrying him.

In his own heavily doctored literary account of this failed romance produced many years later for his "memoirs," Hurok adopted a strangely hostile attitude toward the "brunette" and her colleagues. Not unlike Hurok himself, these chic department store buyers regularly made smart transatlantic crossings in search of snappy new European merchandise to sell to the folks back home in the States. Perhaps Hurok's hostility arose from the fact that he could see himself in these sophisticated pilgrims of retail. Their uncertain status and transparent attempts at social climbing, so like his own, disturbed him, as a long passage in *Impresario* reveals. The paragraphs are remarkable for their emotional pain and candor amid endless pages of public relations insincerity.

> They wore a sleek armor of knowing everything about everything, and indeed they did know almost everything. They knew how to travel and how to drive a shrewd busi-

ness bargain; they held their own at the bridge table and the bar. But the one thing they did not know was how to be happy.

Under their Daché hats and Schiaparelli frocks, inside the shell of sophistication, they were scared little girls, easily flattered because so little secure in themselves, and to me, at least, their painful uncertainties, the scent of their inner fearfulness were perceptible even through their Chanel Number Five.

Significantly, Hurok's favorite cologne, the only one he used, was also Chanel Number Five.

What provoked Hurok's attack on "these scared little girls" was their cultural insecurity and transparent attempts at social climbing—traits he displayed quite often himself. It clearly angered him that no matter how well the career girls might dress, or how much money they might accumulate, they would always be on the outside looking in. He feared to share their fate. The highborn, or those with talent, would never completely accept them—or him.

"They gazed with longing at the glamour boys of the theatre, the concert, the literary world whom they met on these trips, but the glamour boys, with the inherent snobbery of the talented for the merely business-successful, passed them by. . . . I was curious about these girls, and more than a little sorry for them."

And more than a little sorry for himself?

In London, Hurok visited Pavlova. She was resting at her country home, Ivy House, in Golders Green. Here she taught elementary classes to promising young students, surrounding herself with children in whom she instilled her principles of discipline and dedication. Here she dug and planted flowers in the garden. Here she looked over the lawn at the pond, where "two stately swans move gracefully. . . . Of my pets the swans are, of course, my favourites because I so love to dance *The Dying Swan*. . . . They are very fond of me, principally because, the gluttons, I feed them cakes and crackers."

Pavlova was also preparing for a upcoming tour of the Orient Hurok had arranged for the 1922–23 season. It would take her to

Japan, China, India, and Egypt, further fueling her exotic and elusive image.

From London, Hurok went on (with or without his brunette buyer) to Paris and Berlin, both swarming with dispossessed Russian performers and artists of all political persuasions. On this first trip as an established American impresario, with some impressive credits to his name, he worked at building a network of contacts among what he condescendingly labeled "the little people." These included "anonymous friends, the small-time promoters, the newspaper critics, the hotel managers, the headwaiters and café proprietors who came to know my pleasure in good wines and good food as well as good entertainment."

Here, for once, Hurok was telling the truth. As the years passed, he came to rely more and more heavily on tips from his vast collection of acquaintances, from the box office manager at Moscow's Bolshoi to the doorman at London's Savoy. These were his eyes and ears. They kept him close to the public pulse and helped him beat the competition in signing up new talent for the vast American market.

Ever the concerned, generous, and gracious host, he was also a master at using food to get what he wanted—information, deals. Restaurants were his conference rooms, meals his meetings. Few could outdine him. In later years, his regular table at the Russian Tea Room in New York, right next door to Carnegie Hall, became his real office, its tablecloth covered with caviar and contracts.

"It took years to lay my wires, and many good dinners and many bottles of vintage wine in many cafés," he bragged. "A large capacity for eating and drinking is an essential item in the equipment of an impresario."

For the time being, the talent he wined and dined was almost exclusively European. Newcomers to the world of high culture, Americans tended to equate quality with foreignness. Music, musicians, and ballerinas had to be imported to be good. Always eager to satisfy the public demand, Hurok responded by scouring the continent for up-and-coming Old World artists: "It was on the originality, the quality, the variety of my importations from Europe that I was to make my name in the next fifteen years."

Later on, Hurok would be criticized in the United States for his excessive reliance on imported talent. Some observers felt he made it difficult for performers native to America to emerge and succeed by fostering a snobbish condescension toward them. He would always answer, with circular reasoning, that he was just giving the audience what it wanted.

And Hurok did make some important exceptions to the rule that European was better. One of them was Isadora Duncan. She had been trying to interest Hurok in presenting her in the United States at least since 1920, in the wake of his successful presentation of her disciples, the Duncan Dancers. In 1922, he finally agreed. He would not regret the decision, for Duncan would bring him more publicity and attention, at least for a short time, than Chaliapin and Pavlova combined.

It seems that it was Anna Pavlova who urged Hurok to take on Duncan. Often perceived as polar opposites in both life and art (the swan and the slut, as it were), these two fiercely independent women, only four years apart in age, in fact had great respect for each other. Pavlova had already been dancing with the Imperial ballet for five years when Duncan, a scandalous free spirit who ran about the stage in a shocking white tunic and sandals to music by Beethoven and Wagner, made her first visit to St. Petersburg in 1904. Seeing Isadora display her style of "natural movement," so radically different from the constricted formality of the Russian ballet tradition, may well have pushed Fokine to create his reformist choreography for Pavlova. One of Duncan's adopted daughters, Marie-Therese Duncan, also remembers receiving compliments and candy from Pavlova after a performance by the Duncan Dancers in St. Petersburg in 1908. Marie-Therese even believes that Pavlova came to adopt a softer, less classical arm technique in The Dying Swan under the influence of Isadora's free-form dancing.

Clearly, Pavlova and Duncan were keenly aware of each other, even though they developed in very different artistic directions. Both loners and "stars" with democratic ideals, they yearned, along with Chaliapin and Hurok, to reach "the people" through their art.

Not surprisingly, Isadora's "anti-technique" proved distasteful to Diaghilev and George Balanchine—more distasteful, even, than Pavlova's grandstanding. "I thought she was awful," Balanchine said of Isadora's performance in Russia in 1920. "I don't understand it when people say she was a great dancer. To me it was absolutely unbelievable—a drunken, fat woman who for hours was rolling around like a pig."

Given their shared populism and anti-elitism, then, it does not strain credibility to think that Pavlova would, as Hurok claimed, have encouraged him to bring Isadora back to the United States. At the time, Duncan was living in Russia. Discouraged by her inability to establish a school in Europe or America, she had moved there in 1921, pledging idealistically to "work for the future of the Russian Republic and its children." Almost immediately upon arriving in Moscow, she met Sergei Yesenin, a twenty-six-year-old Russian poet, blond, talented, and with an irresistible "beautiful-depraved face." He became her first husband (though far from her first lover) in the spring of 1922.

Despite her opposition to marriage on philosophical grounds, Duncan even wedded Yesenin in order to make it easier for them to cohabitate on their upcoming trip to Europe and America. She remembered the puritanical outrage Soviet writer Maxim Gorky encountered when he toured the United States in 1906 with a female companion not his wife.

The agreement for Duncan's American tour had emerged from an exchange of telegrams. It began in the spring of 1922, before Hurok's trip to Europe.

S. Hurok 220 W. 42nd St. New York
Propose tournee twelve weeks or more myself Irma great Russian poet Essenin [Yesenin] and twenty pupils minimum four performances a week guarantee twelve hundred dollars per performances you paying all theatre expenses including voyages large towns orchestra small towns piano.
Isadora Duncan
18/IV 1922

Isadora Duncan
Prechistenka 20 Moscow
New York
Offer you for fifty performances forty thousand dollars

net I pay all expenses steamship from Riga railroad fares here theatres advertising orchestra in New York Boston Chicago pianist other cities tour begins October cable acceptance forward photos publicity programs

Hurok

Isadora accepted Hurok's terms, even though they stipulated only $800 instead of $1,200 per performance. In the end, she and Yesenin went alone, since the Soviet government refused to give the students permission to travel abroad.

With Pavlova headed for the Orient, Hurok returned to New York from his European trip ready to put all his energy into this new cross-cultural attraction.

When "Mr. and Mrs. Yesenin" steamed into New York harbor on October 1, 1922, Hurok was waiting at the pier. Things did not begin well. Enflamed by rampant anti-Bolshevik sentiment, immigration officials detained Isadora on board the S.S. *Paris* overnight to question her concerning "opinions which Miss Duncan is said to have expressed from time to time concerning the Russian Soviet government." Government officials also maintained that Isadora had forfeited her American citizenship by marrying an alien and was therefore subject to the procedures used for any foreigner.

Even Hurok fell under suspicion for sponsoring Duncan and her husband. Immigration officials searched and questioned him after he visited Isadora on board ship—all of which provided a marvelous opportunity for preconcert publicity. Loudly indignant, Hurok claimed he had been "obliged to remove every stitch of clothing, while sharp eyes peered into every pocket, and hands felt of the linings of my suit and topcoat. When I was permitted to put my clothes on again I felt that every shred of my Constitutional rights as a citizen had been trampled. I was ready to fight the whole Department of Labor."

Instead, he took his revenge in the press. A large feature article appeared in *Musical America* on the day, not coincidentally, of Isadora's first performance at Carnegie Hall:

Mr. Hurok protested vigorously against the treatment he said he was subjected to on leaving the *Paris* after a visit to

Miss Duncan's cabin. An immigration official, he said, threatened him with force if he failed to go to an office on the dock. There, the manager said, he was stripped of his clothes, apparently in an effort to discover "invisible writing." Mr. Hurok is an American citizen. He declared he would either make a complaint to Washington or prefer a charge of assault against the inspector.

Yesenin—whom Isadora grandly labeled the "Walt Whitman of Russia"—and his wife were finally released, but only after her trunks and clothing were searched and a number of their Russian books confiscated "for translation." Once on dry land, they continued to attract reporters eager to chronicle each move of this exotic and Bohemian couple.

Hurok, of course, did nothing to discourage the journalists' prurient interest. As he said often over the years, when his artists were on the front page, it saved him money on publicity. Twenty-four years later in *Impresario* he and his press agent Gerald Goode also provided what Gordon McVay, author of the meticulously researched *Isadora and Esenin*, has called their own "fanciful" account of Isadora's dramatic grand entrance into Manhattan:

> When the ferry docked, a crowd was waiting. Isadora stepped off and, grandly gesturing the taxicabs aside, she set forth on foot to the Waldorf-Astoria. In her red-leather Russian boots and Russian caracul hat, with her startling red hair and her long cape flying, she marched from the Battery up Broadway, up Fifth Avenue, a triumphal parade of one, with me, Modeste Altschuler the Russian Symphony Orchestra conductor, and even young Essenine panting behind her free-striding, heroic, figure.

Dramatic, but apparently invented, at least compared to Yesenin's considerably more sober version of events, written less than a year later as part of "The Iron Mirgorod," his sketch of America. The poet makes no mention of any uptown procession. "When we got into our car," he wrote, "I said to the journalists: 'Mi laik Amerika . . .' Ten minutes later we were at our hotel."

Nor does Hurok's colorful description of Yesenin upon his landing in New York as "the tall Russian youth in the peasant smock" exactly square with the facts. At five feet six inches, Yesenin was no taller than Hurok, and he adored Western styles and clothing. The New York *Herald* found his dress "no different from that of an ordinary American business man, being a plain gray tweed."

However they were dressed, and however they made their way to the Waldorf-Astoria, Isadora and Yesenin had captured the public imagination. Ticket sales for Duncan's appearance at Carnegie Hall on October 7, 1922, went from sluggish to brisk. When that day came, three thousand people showed up to see this "woman from Mars" perform her interpretations of Tchaikovsky's Sixth Symphony and *Marche Slave*. Here, and throughout the American tour that followed, "critical" reaction focused more on the dancer's unorthodox personal life and political views than on a serious analysis of her art.

"In every pose and gesture," wrote the reviewer from the New York *Tribune*, "in the emotional gamut reflected by eloquent facial play, Miss Duncan portrayed the hopes, fears, disillusionments and sufferings of the Russian nation." Isadora also had an uncontrollable fondness for closing her appearances with inflammatory speeches in praise of Bolshevism. In the conservative Republican climate of Warren Harding's scandal-ridden administration, she might as well have been advocating devil worship.

"I have given my hand to Russia," she announced to her Carnegie Hall audience, "and I tell you to do the same. I tell you to love Russia, for Russia has everything that America lacks, just as America has everything that Russia lacks. The day when Russia and America understand each other will mark the dawn of a new epoch for humanity."

Prophetic words, but profoundly disturbing for a New York audience of 1922.

In Boston, Isadora ran into more serious trouble. Her liberated behavior during her recitals at staid Symphony Hall made the Brahmins livid. Exactly what happened is, like so many facts surrounding Hurok and Isadora, difficult to determine with complete precision. It seems Yesenin started things. A ferocious drinker, he enjoyed a relationship with his wife that was turbulent even without the extraordinary pressures of touring as a male escort to a celebrity in a country where he did not speak the language. In an act of taunting defiance, he threw a red flag out of a Symphony Hall window while shouting "Long live Bolshevism." Already offended, the audience responded coldly to Isadora's performances on October 20 (all Wagner) and October 21 (all Tchaikovsky)—so coldly that she started preaching to them.

"This is red! So am I! It is the color of life and vigor. You were once wild here. Don't let them tame you!" she cried, waving a red silk scarf over her head.

Some members of the audience cheered, but others got up to leave.

According to one account, she also "tore off her flimsy red tunic." Hurok, who was not present, quotes Sergei Kournakoff, his company manager for Isadora's tour, as saying that she went on to bare one of her breasts, declaring theatrically, "This—this is beauty!"

Boston's Mayor Curley forbade Duncan to appear again on any of the city's stages. Hurok rushed to the scene, where he set up a press conference at which Isadora expounded on the repressive consequences of puritanism and the salutary effects of nudity. Meanwhile, she and Yesenin engaged in almost nightly drunken brawls in a country that had outlawed alcohol. Isadora later blamed the deterioration of her husband's mental and physical health, accelerating as the tour progressed, on his consumption of dangerous bootleg liquor.

The "Banned in Boston" label pursued Duncan wherever she appeared. In Chicago, she defied Hurok's instruction to avoid curtain speeches at all costs, and proclaimed, "My manager tells me that if I make more speeches the tour is dead. Very well, the tour is dead. I will go back to Moscow where there is vodka, music, poetry, and dancing. . . . Oh, yes, and Freedom!"

Denounced by evangelists (as a "Bolshevik hussy who doesn't wear enough clothes to pad a crutch") and community leaders, Isadora nevertheless continued to receive engagements. Traveling with her accompanist, Max Rabinovitch, she performed to large and often rowdy crowds in Indianapolis, Louisville, Kansas City, St. Louis, Memphis, Detroit, Cleveland, Baltimore, Philadelphia, Toledo, and Brooklyn. All along the way, she and her husband denounced American moral hypocrisy, praised Soviet Russia, and fought like cats and dogs.

On Christmas night, Duncan failed to complete a performance at the Brooklyn Academy of Music after Rabinovitch, insulted by a remark she had made, left her alone on stage and/or she became disoriented after drinking a bottle of etherized champagne. Later, Hurok also claimed that her costume had slipped from one shoulder, exposing a breast. Accounts of the performance in the *New York Times* and the New York *Tribune* omit any mention of this incident, however.

The atmosphere of scandal surrounding Isadora grew even thicker when her husband Yesenin became involved in a scandal of his own in early 1923. Invited to a literary evening at the Bronx home of the well-known Yiddish writer Mani Leib, this very gifted and insatiably egotistical poet apparently became enraged when his wife, as usual, received all the attention. In Hurok's typically cinematic version of events, a very drunk Yesenin tore Isadora's dress off her shoulder, tried to jump out the window, ran out onto the Grand Concourse where he encountered a policeman who brought him back to the apartment, and then called Mani Leib "yid" when the frightened guests tied him up with rope. It does not seem that Hurok was present.

McVay's version sounds more plausible. He agrees that Yesenin was drunk and abusive toward Isadora, but claims the poet said the shocking word *yid* while reading from his play *The Land of Scoundrels.* Not surprisingly, and probably with Hurok's help, the story of Yesenin's anti-Semitism immediately hit the newspapers, elaborately embroidered. The Jewish writers present, however, did not take the incident very seriously. They apparently realized that Yesenin was a very disturbed personality, and that, unfortunately, the "Great Russian" nationalism which he espoused had always included an undercurrent of anti-Semitism.

Exhausted and looking like "a hunted animal," Isadora gave the farewell performance of her tour in a half-filled Carnegie Hall on Monday evening, January 15, 1923. It featured her interpretations of Wagner, some Brahms waltzes, Schubert's *Marche Militaire*, and concluded defiantly with the Communist hymn "The Internationale." On February 3, she and Yesenin sailed for Cherbourg on (ironically enough) the liner *George Washington*.

To the reporters who gathered see her off, she vowed—correctly—that she would never return to the United States, and declared that Americans had no understanding of art or beauty. Responding in kind, the Department of Labor decreed that Isadora had permanently lost her American citizenship and could regain it only by petition.

Duncan's scandal-plagued final American tour may have ruined Isadora, but it made money for both her and Hurok. "The lurid headlines which trumpeted her march across the country caused mayoral apoplexy and occasional cancellations, but they also assured long lines at the box offices where she did appear," he said later. More important, the tour further strengthened Hurok's reputation, particularly as a presenter of dance events, and gave his agency an extraordinary amount of free publicity. It also gave him significantly greater financial security and resources. It was, in fact, in February 1923, just after Duncan's farewell performance, that Hurok officially chartered his operation as "S. Hurok, Inc.," on authorized capital of $50,000.

But besides producing monetary rewards, his presentation and "defense" of this outspoken champion of the Russian Revolution and her husband, one of the founders of Soviet Russian literature, also helped to endear him to the Soviet cultural establishment, which would prove both useful and profitable in years to come.

Finally, Isadora's last American tour produced important artistic results. By presenting her at this moment in time, Hurok helped to influence the development of modern American dance. He showed audiences a startling alternative to the dominant, highly disciplined Pavlova tradition, a new style ultimately better suited to America's informal, democratic temperament. Charles Frohman, manager of Duncan's unsuccessful 1908 American tour, had terminated her contract because he "considered her art over the heads of the public"; in fact, just the opposite was true. A self-proclaimed "enemy of the ballet," Isadora made dance less intimidating and more accessible to the common man.

Duncan's work profoundly affected the young American and Russian choreographers who saw it. Agnes de Mille and Martha

Graham learned a great deal from her emotional approach, and Isadora's use of significant symphonic scores paved the way for the later experiments of Leonide Massine.

In the aftermath of the Russian Revolution, the United States pursued a policy of active hostility toward the new Soviet Union and its Communist regime. President Wilson sent American troops to fight on the side of the anti-Communist White Russians in the Russian civil war and refused to grant diplomatic recognition to the Soviet government. Wilson's successors Harding, Coolidge, and Hoover continued to ignore the USSR and fanned the sort of public anti-Communist hysteria that surrounded Isadora Duncan's tour. Members of the fledgling American Communist party were arrested and even deported to Russia, their constitutional rights violated. Socialist representatives (one of whom Hurok had helped to elect back in his Brownsville days) were expelled from the New York Assembly. In this polarized and intolerant environment, Hurok's earlier socialist activities must surely have caused him some anxiety.

But American audiences did not share their government's animosity toward things Soviet. Perhaps the diplomatic chill merely piqued their curiosity about this alien, idealistic new society and its people. (That phenomenon would recur during the Cold War that followed World War II.) Or perhaps they discovered that they and the Russians, both inhabitants of vast, relatively underdeveloped countries outside the mainstream of European civilization, had more in common than they had thought. In any case, the increasing number of Russian performers who, along with Pavlova and Chaliapin, appeared in the United States in the early 1920s generated large and enthusiastic crowds.

One of the most successful of these Russian artists was Nikita Balieff (1877–1936).

"A big burly man with a vast genial moon-face," Balieff brought his cabaret-style revue *La Chauve-Souris* (*The Bat*) to New York in February 1922. Its popularity with American audiences surpassed even his great previous successes in Paris and London. The satirical revue featured seven actors formerly associated with Konstantin Stanislavsky's Moscow Art Theatre, where it had originated as an in-house joke. Consisting of "short burlesques, and small, often mimed, sketches based on old ballads, folksongs, prints, engravings, the woodenness of a toy soldier or the delicacy of a china shepherdess," *La Chauve-Souris* became the musical and social sensation of the 1921–22 season. One of its numbers, the "Parade of the Wooden Soldiers," even became a Broadway classic.

The show enjoyed a long run, altered the course of the American musical, and turned Balieff into an instant celebrity. Soon everybody who was anybody was turning up at the 49th Street Theatre to see it. Ralph Barton even created a famous curtain for *La Chauve-Souris* showing Balieff's back as he faced a typical star-studded audience, with caricatures (among many others) of Al Jolson, Irving Berlin, Giulio Gatti-Casazza, Randolph Hearst, Alexander Woollcott, Lillian Gish, Jascha Heifetz, Eugene O'Neill, Sergei Rachmaninoff, Ring Lardner, and the show's increasingly prominent producer, Morris Gest.

Although Hurok would have us believe he was by now a prominent personality on the New York entertainment scene, his face is absent. Several of his artists did make the curtain, however: Pavlova, Chaliapin, and the Fokines.

For the next season, Gest, working with his longtime partner F. Ray Comstock, produced an even more prestigious Russian attraction with even better results. On January 8, 1923, he fulfilled a longtime ambition when Konstantin Stanislavsky's Moscow Art Theatre (MAT) opened at Jolson's Fifty-Ninth Street Theatre with Alexei Tolstoy's *Tsar Fyodor Ivanovich*. Maxim Gorky's *The Lower Depths*, two plays by Chekhov (*The Cherry Orchard* and *The Three Sisters*), and a production combining scenes from Dostoevsky's *The Brothers Karamazov* and Turgenev's *A Provincial Lady* followed over the next twelve weeks.

The first eight weeks of the Moscow Art Theatre's engagement had been sold out even before it opened. The box-office receipts were the largest ever recorded for any dramatic company performing on Broadway in any language, including English. Over the next sixteen months, the MAT gave 380 performances of thirteen productions in twelve American cities.

Such popular acclaim notwithstanding, some critics, used to light entertainment like the *Ziegfeld Follies*—then at their deliciously frivolous height—did not welcome the intellectual demands made by the MAT. One observed sourly that the MAT appealed to "the elite and bon-ton." But many others, such as Robert Burns Mantle, "the dean of the Dramatic Critics," praised the company and its productions to the skies. "No dramatic importation within this generation's memory has created the stir the Muscovites caused, nor the comment," Mantle wrote.

For his part, the reticent Stanislavsky was overwhelmed by the reception he and his company encountered in the United States:

> We have never had such a success in Moscow or anywhere else. . . . No one seems to have had any idea what our theatre or actors are capable of. I am writing all this . . . not in self-glorification, but just to give you an idea at what an embryonic state stage art is here and how eagerly they snatch up everything good that is brought to America.

The MAT and what became known rightly or wrongly in the United States as the "Stanislavsky Method" also exerted a huge influence on the development of modern American theater. During the two seasons it toured, Stanislavsky's company helped to inspire a new approach to acting, based on an actor's psychological understanding of a character's behavior and motivations. Eventually, it revolutionized the dramatic—and cinematic—professions. American theater people suddenly discovered they had a great deal to learn from their Russian colleagues.

While in New York, Stanislavsky spent time with some of the many Russian musicians who were performing there. Sergei Rachmaninoff came to see *A Provincial Lady*. On March 13, 1923, Chaliapin, whose approach to opera Stanislavsky considered a model for students, came to see *The Lower Depths*. The entire MAT company returned the favor on March 25 by attending his recital at the Met.

Morris Gest, the manager who had lured Stanislavsky to the United States, was ecstatic to have a hit on his hands. But then this shrewd producer had carefully orchestrated the engagement, planting an article in the *New York Times Book Review* in the autumn and providing the press with plenty of photo opportunities. (In Berlin, where the MAT played before coming to New York, Gest even provided photographers with stand-ins for Stanislavsky's wife and daughter, who had been delayed in Riga.) Gest's ingenuity and industry impressed everyone, including the members of the MAT, unused to such naked—but undeniably successful—commercialism.

Although he doesn't mention them in his "autobiographies," Hurok must have seen *La Chauve-Souris* and the MAT in New York between 1922 and 1924. Even more certain is that he was soon trying to imitate Gest's success with Russian theatrical attractions.

Hurok's first such attempt was *Seeniaya Ptitza*. A Russian cabaret-style revue directly modeled on *La Chauve-Souris*, *Seeniaya Ptitza* (an awkward transliteration of the Russian words for "Bluebird") had developed in the burgeoning postrevolutionary Russian émigré community in Berlin. It was headlined by comedian and conferencier Yascha Yushny. Wendell Phillips Dodge first imported the ensemble to New York, where it opened on December 28, 1924, at the Frolic Theatre, "direct from 1680 successful performances in Moscow, Berlin, Vienna, London."

Inevitably, however, critics compared *Seeniaya Ptitza* to *La Chauve-Souris* and judged the new arrival an entertaining but still pale imitation of the original. Stark Young did find praise for several of the show's numbers: Madame Valery's rendition of a forlorn street performer, and the chorus of Volga boatmen, which seemed "to express profoundly the thing that most of all draws us to the Russian quality in art."

This was also the sort of schmaltzy, nostalgic entertainment Hurok adored. Inspired by the opportunity to run head-to-head against *La Chauve-Souris*, he took over the faltering *Seeniaya Ptitza* just a few weeks into its New York run. He supervised an overhaul of the show, changed its name to *Bluebird: 2nd Edition*, and announced the opening of an "Entire New Bill" on January 29. But even with several new numbers (a tea-drinking scene, some popular ditties, and a certain Mme. Yurieva dancing the ubiquitous *Dying Swan*), better reviews, and a less clumsy name, the venture failed to thrive. There simply wasn't room for two Russian cabaret-style revues on Broadway—especially when one enjoyed both a long head start and the support of the theater world and high society.

Not surprisingly, Hurok makes no mention in his memoirs of his early failure with *Bluebird*, an ensemble he would bring back to

New York more successfully and in somewhat different form seven years later.

Hurok never could beat his early rival and model Morris Gest at the theatrical game. But he surely learned a great deal from watching this well-connected (Gest's wife was the daughter of actor-manager and playwright David Belasco, one of the most important personalities of the American stage) Broadway veteran manage both *La Chauve-Souris* and the Moscow Art Theatre. Oliver Sayler's eye-witness description of Gest in action makes it clear that Hurok, always quick to imitate and then outdo the competition, later used many of Gest's public relations techniques. Gest was also the source of many of the pieces of impresarial wisdom Hurok loved to dispense in later years, claiming them as his own inventions.

At the center of Gest's operation was image making. The way he made the MAT a success, Sayler wrote,

> would fill a text-book on publicity, propaganda and public relations: by enlisting the interest of patrons and sponsors in the walks of society, art, letters and the stage itself; by cooperation with the magazines and newspapers in providing a mass of information so that he who ran might read and be unable to plead ignorance; by the publication of books and pamphlets and translations of the entire repertory; by printing a program that visualized the action step by step for those who knew no Russian; by capitalizing on the visitors' idiosyncrasies, such as the ban on applause and on the interruptions of latecomers. . . . In short, Gest got the Moscow Art Theatre talked about, and he kept it talked about until it became "the thing to see."

Gest and Hurok also shared similar personal backgrounds and emotional motivations. Both humbly born in remote areas of the Russian Empire (Gest in Vilna, Lithuania, and Hurok in a Ukrainian village), both burned to show the world they had made it. Assuming that it is true, the following account of a legendary meeting between Stanislavsky and Gest provides a vivid example.

> "Do you know why I brought the Moscow Art Theatre to America?" they say Gest demanded of the venerable

player, throwing wide his arms and tossing his big, suf-
fused eyes on high. "Do you think it was for money, or
fame, or anything like that? No, it was because my dear
old father and mother, back there in Russia, would see in
the newspaper that their son, their Morris in far-away
America, had the power to bring the most famous actors
in the world on a journey of five thousand miles. . . ."

The suave, slightly impatient Stanislavsky is said to have
interrupted him: "My dear Mr. Gest, I am exceedingly
sorry, but I fear that we can not do business on the basis
of your father and mother."

Like Gest, and like all the Russian Jews who had fled the Tsar's
empire seeking prosperity in the New World, Hurok yearned not
only to belong, but to excel, to rise above his origins in a dramatic
fulfillment of the immigrant's dream. More egotistical than Gest,
however, and possessed of considerably less education and family
feeling, he never spoke of wanting to impress or gladden his aging
parents back in Pogar. He had more immediate goals. He wanted to
impress the folks right here in America.

CHAPTER SIX

"My Blue Period"

"Shakespeare was interested in fine literature. Likewise S. Hurok and fine music. As the Bard said, anyone that doesn't like good music is something wrong with his brains."

—*Sol Hurok*

HUROK, WHO VALUED PUBLICITY much more than money, worshiped the *New York Times*. Whenever his name appeared in its gray, tasteful pages, he received as much—or more—pleasure as from savoring a gourmet meal or pinching a buxom behind.

Over the years, he and his public relations staff became adroit at flattering and cajoling the *Times*'s critics, editors, and owners, gaining extensive coverage of Hurok attractions and activities in the process. But then Adolf S. Ochs, the paper's publisher, himself something of a outsider (he was born thirty years before Hurok into a Jewish family in Tennessee), admired this immigrant's chutzpah. He also shared his desire to improve the cultural life of their rapidly expanding metropolis.

On Sunday, April 22, 1923, the *New York Times Magazine* ran the first of what would be many features on Hurok's work as an impresario. It was now hard to ignore any booking agent whose stable of artists included celebrity performers as disparate and well-respected as Fyodor Chaliapin, Mischa Elman, Anna Pavlova, Isadora Duncan, Eugène Ysaÿe, Austrian-American contralto

Ernestine Schumann-Heink (known for her roles in Wagner's operas), and Austrian pianist-composer Artur Schnabel. The boy from Pogar was newsworthy. He had made it.

Lengthy but unattributed, the highly complimentary piece led the reader to believe that Hurok spoke perfect Oxford English. It also contained more than its share of inaccuracies and exaggerations. One was the claim that Hurok had arrived in the United States "fifteen years ago, when just half his present age"—which would mean 1908, two years later than the actual date. Another was the assertion that it was Efrem Zimbalist who convinced him to become an impresario after the young violinist happened to wander into the automobile company Hurok was managing. There were some notable omissions, too. His early socialist activities in Brooklyn received no mention, not surprising considering the prevailing mood of virulent anti-communism.

And yet Hurok focused less on his ever-changing life story in this interview than on the need to develop a larger audience for the arts—especially for serious music—in the United States. Displaying a sharp professional command, he bemoaned the lack of suitable concert halls for musical attractions and the small number of concertgoers even in a city as large as New York.

"You will be surprised when I tell you that but 60,000 persons go to the highest type of attractions during the entire season," he confided to the *Times'* readers.

> You see the same faces at the Carnegie Hall attractions as you see at the Sunday night concerts at the Hippodrome or the special programs at the Metropolitan Opera House. If you look at the mailing lists of these three auditoriums you will see the same names on each. . . .
>
> Music must be popularized. People must be educated to the appreciation of music. . . . Music should be taught as a necessary element in our lives. Classes should be conducted in public schools, just as faithfully as geography, history, botany and anatomy are taught. Music is as important to the future life of the child as these subjects are, for it is the greatest thing in our life. It brings happiness to the family, the community and the nation.

As an example, Hurok told how he watched married couples arrive at his attractions "in a bad humor." No sooner had the music begun than they were snuggling up and making up. Even better, the exalted influence of high art could carry over into real life, propelling patrons to extravagant purchases. "And you can bet that husband has forgotten what the difference was about, and that wife will get her fur coat."

Admitting that "the longing to hear music of the highest type has not been developed" in the United States, Hurok rhapsodized about the huge untapped market America offered to performers of international stature. They could "complete the usual concert tour of the Old World in four months," but even seven years would be insufficient to hit the 915 cities on the vast and potentially lucrative American circuit.

What the country needed, Hurok said, was more attention paid to the arts. America could even learn a thing or two from the Russian government, which had been providing subsidies for artistic institutions and educations for generations. And that's why we hear so much about Russian art, music, and ballet, he said. "The foundation for the love of better things was built in the hearts of the concert fans through years of proper education."

Hurok's interview (actually it reads like a prepared press release or sermon) concluded with a calculated reference to the national pastime. All that was missing was apple pie.

> Baseball is the national game in America. The papers are full of it. Everyone understands it. Office boys and show girls can tell you how many homers Babe Ruth slammed out last season and tell the batting average of Ty Cobb. I am not advocating that batons and violins be substituted for bats and mitts in the hands of young America, but I do so earnestly pray that the leaders of education and the great publications will, as they so easily can, help to promote the art which brings so much real happiness to every one.

Not that Hurok was speaking out of prely altruistic motives. If Americans were to receive better instruction in arts appreciation, they would, of course, be more likely to pay for the entertainment services his agency provided. As he said more than once, "A manager does not make an artist. What he makes is an audience."

Ever mindful of his image, however, Hurok took care not to come across as an unpatriotic egghead. Even though there is no evidence that he had ever attended a baseball game or that he ever developed any real interest in the sport (indeed, he showed little interest in any organized athletics), he carefully created the impression that he passionately followed the American pastime. Insulting baseball fans would not help at the box office, after all.

"Tell me," he asked the reporter in a concluding flourish, "was Christy Mathewson really such a great pitcher? I couldn't read the sporting slang when he was in his heyday."

By the end of the 1922–23 season, the recently incorporated offices of "S. Hurok, Inc., Manager Distinguished Artists and Concert Tours" in Suite 714–717 of Aeolian Hall on 42nd Street just west of Fifth Avenue were a busy place. Artists called in for instructions. Hurok's secretaries—on whom he always relied heavily for literary and administrative support—worked busily at writing his advertising copy, press releases, and correspondence. He would sign the letters "S. Hurok," underlining his name backward from the *k,* as if emphasizing its importance. Some of those letters were written in Russian—like a particularly flowery and unctuous one extending congratulations to Russian conductor Serge Koussevitzky, who had just arrived in America to take up his new post with the Boston Symphony.

Another one of the numerous projects then occupying the manager's attention was a bold, but ultimately unsuccessful attempt to bring the former Mariinsky Imperial Ballet to New York. Since he hated nothing more than to admit failure, Hurok omitted any mention of this first overture in his later autobiographies. Letters written by dancer-choreographer Michel Fokine, as well as newspaper accounts of the time, however, reveal that Hurok did come to a tentative agreement with Soviet cultural officials in June 1923 to collaborate on a tour of the company for the following winter. Clearly, Hurok was hoping to cash in on the current fad for Russian attractions in New York.

The *New York Times* of June 29 quoted Ivan Vasilevich Ekskuzovich, then manager of the former Mariinsky Imperial Ballet and Opera, as reporting that "authorization had just been received for an American tour." By now, the Mariinsky had a new official title. In early 1918, not long after the 1917 Bolshevik Revolution and the establishment of the Soviet government, the Mariinsky and almost all other former Imperial theaters had been renamed. (The title *Mariinsky* had originally been bestowed in 1860 in honor of a royal patron named Maria.) At first, briefly, Soviet officials called this most prestigious and refined of all Tsarist cultural institutions the State Mariinsky. Then, in 1920, that label was changed to the Petrograd State Academic Theater of Opera and Ballet, reflecting a desire to downplay the theater's aristocratic origins and the fact that St. Petersburg's name had been changed to the less German-sounding Petrograd at the beginning of World War I. (The city was called Petrograd until early 1924, when its name was changed to Leningrad in honor of Vladimir Lenin, only to change back to the original St. Petersburg in 1991.)

In order to cope with such a long name, most Russians just shortened it to one of those acronyms that rapidly became such a fixture of Soviet life in the 1920s: GATOB. But even this name wasn't fated to stick too long. Soon after the mayor of Leningrad, Sergei Kirov, was assassinated (on Stalin's orders) in 1934, the theater became the Kirov Opera and Ballet Theater in his honor. This name lasted almost sixty years, until 1991, when it, too, was rejected—because of its association with the now-discredited Soviet Communist party. As this book goes to press, the theater is again calling itself the Mariinsky (except on tours abroad, where, to avoid confusion, it still often bears the label Kirov!).

But to return to Ekskuzovich and Hurok and 1923: According to Ekskuzovich, performances of this first-ever Mariinsky tour would begin in early December and would feature two hundred artists, "a selection of its unparalleled costumes and decorations," and an unbelievably ambitious repertoire of ten operas and ten ballets, "all entirely Russian." Chaliapin had been invited to become musical director for the venture, the "first time in history that a full Russian ballet has appeared on a foreign stage with its own costumes and decorations."

Having witnessed the phenomenal success of Diaghilev's Ballets Russes—many of whose members had come from the Mariinsky—throughout Europe in the years immediately following World War I,

Ekskuzovich had good reason to believe that the public response would justify the enormous expenses involved.

As Chaliapin's manager (actually co-manager, with Metropolitan Musical Bureau) and champion, it was inevitable that Hurok would become involved. Ekskuzovich reported the two managers were scheduled to meet in Berlin the following week to sign a contract.

Encouraged by the American enthusiasm for Russian theater, music, and ballet, Ekskuzovich predicted a bright future for the Petrograd company in the United States. "If America likes our work, we propose to establish a permanent ballet in New York with seventy of our best performers. Perhaps in other cities also. We have enough props to run five theatres in America."

But not everyone thought it would be so easy. In a letter to his Petrograd friend and colleague Pavel Goncharov, an artist and designer who worked in the company and had participated in the 1910 Ballets Russes season in Paris, Fokine voiced some doubts about the proposed tour. He also warned Goncharov to beware of American managers.

> I read in the papers that Ekskuzovich is entering into an agreement with Hurok. (He's my former manager. I have worked a great deal with him and know him very well.) If that is all true, then I wish the Petrograd Ballet the best of luck abroad. (I hope that you'll be taking part in it as well.) But I want to call your attention to the fact that you should be very careful in drawing up the conditions of the agreement with the Americans. They swindled me but good, and so I have some experience, for which I paid dearly. When choosing the repertoire you must also take American tastes into consideration, and what the audience is like. In this regard the Moscow Art Theatre made some mistakes. And so, I await your response with great interest: is it true that the company is coming?

Alas, it wasn't true. Embroiled in a difficult and ever-changing political situation, deprived of sufficient food and materials, suffering countless defections as performers and artists emigrated, the Petrograd Opera and Ballet never did make it to New York. Such an ambitious undertaking lay beyond its vastly reduced resources and capabilities. Running any cultural institution in the USSR, let alone one this size, during the 1920s took heroism and a sense of martyrdom, as Ekskuzovich told American reporters: "Though bullets flew in streets outside, though stage or dressing rooms were in arctic cold through lack of fuel, the Petrograd State Theatre carried on its business as usual." But a trip to America, a country with which the USSR still had no official diplomatic relations, was too much to ask.

Hurok would finally succeed in bringing this celebrated, long-suffering company to New York. But by then it would be 1961. Thirty-eight years would have passed, Petrograd would have become Leningrad, the troupe would have yet another name (the Kirov), and the Soviet Union would be a very different place.

After the deal with Ekskuzovich fell through, Hurok and Chaliapin came up with another idea. They had good reason to feel confident, for both were now considerably wealthier as a result of their partnership. In September 1923, just before embarking for another season in America, Chaliapin wrote to Gorky's wife from Paris, "Roaming around America, I feel like I am doing hard labor—my pile of American gold is so heavy that this summer I didn't have to go to Russia, or even to move in any particular direction. I just stayed and rested up in one spot—at the seashore."

So Chaliapin and Hurok decided to collaborate on a different venture, only slightly less ambitious: the Russian Opera Company. The company already existed—its ninety-three members had made their way from Russia to Tokyo, where they had been stranded during the Russian Revolution, and then across the Pacific to the United States. They performed a large repertory of Russian opera and would make a perfect vehicle for Chaliapin in roles such as Boris Godunov. With them, the singer could also fulfill his ambition of being his own "stage manager," controlling most aspects of direction and production.

During the 1924–25 season, the Russian Opera Company made an extensive American tour, earning generally positive reviews but little money. Expenses were prohibitive. In Chicago, Chaliapin received $3,500 a performance, three performances a week, during a four-week run of *Boris Godunov*—the opera's first American performances sung entirely in Russian. Costs rose still further as a result of the singer's legendary fanaticism for detail. Chaliapin demanded extra rehearsal time and would hold up performances in order to correct problems with the scenery. When Hurok asked him why all this was necessary, he (allegedly) replied with considerable impatience, "Salomon, an artist who does not insist on perfection is no artist!"

By the end of the engagement, Hurok had won over the city's critics (including Claudia Cassidy, who had only recently begun her very long and, some would say, very destructive career in Chicago) with the lavish parties for which he was gradually becoming famous—but he had lost $60,000. He then sent the company to Mexico (apparently without Chaliapin), where they engaged in the sort of incessant backstage feuding he would see much more of in his coming years as manager of Russian dance companies. One faction of the troupe sued Hurok, he claimed, for the salary they lost when the other faction abruptly left Mexico before completing the tour. "Believe it or not, I paid them off," he said later.

But Hurok loved the role of generous dispenser of funds, contracts, and entertainment. It made him feel like a *grand seigneur,* magnanimous, important, appreciated, and—most importantly—in control. Even Chaliapin's fabled ability to consume four dozen roasted oysters and two big steaks at a single sitting did not disturb him. It made good copy.

Chaliapin's own writings, however, make it clear that he had ambivalent feelings about Hurok—and about all the American managers who sought to enrich themselves through him and his singing—and about being in a country that had outlawed the sale and consumption of liquor. In letters to Russian friends, he referred to "all these bloodsucking impresarios" and complained that the American way of working was as different from the Russian "as an apple from a dill pickle. It's hard, oh so hard."

Philadelphia was "a big, but boring" city "populated, like most American cities, by hypocritical people, and, despite 'liberty,' with no freedom to be found—everything is prohibited, and they've thought up such strict and ridiculous laws that all you can do is throw up your hands—but there is the dollar!!! O, that powerful coin is buying up everything, both retail and wholesale." Chaliapin found the American people "egotistical and extremely uncultured," and their nearly complete lack of familiarity with opera shocked and dismayed him.

He did not mind spending the money he earned, however, and boasted in letters to his children of the astronomical fees he was receiving from the gullible American consumer.

Even as he became more successful, or at least more famous, Hurok still retained ties to the Brownsville community that had first nurtured him. Always happy to play the role of paternalistic benefactor to those less wealthy or successful than he, he used his influence to help struggling (and forever indebted) friends and acquaintances.

In late 1923, for example, he made it possible for two Russian musicians—a married couple—to immigrate to the United States as artists with their four-year-old son. The husband, a flutist, was the brother of Charles Koot, Hurok's "close buddy" in Brownsville.

American immigration policy had changed drastically in the seventeen years since Hurok sailed into New York harbor. Each year from 1900 to 1915, nearly one million immigrants entered the United States. Only temporarily inhibited by World War I, this massive flood brought one million more Europeans to America in 1921. By then, however, amid an atmosphere of revived nationalism, numerous voices were calling for restrictions on the flow. New legislation was passed placing quotas on the number to be accepted from each country, with preference shown the supposedly more easily assimilated immigrants from northwestern Europe. Suddenly it became much more difficult for Poles, Russians, and other Eastern Europeans to leave their homelands to find a better life in the New World—as Hurok had done. America was growing up, becoming less hospitable and more suspicious of strangers.

So when Charles Koot's relatives, the Gershunoffs, wanted to leave Russia for the United States, they had to find a loophole. Since they were musicians, they could enter as practicing artists if a manager would sponsor them. Hurok agreed. He (or, more likely, a member of his staff) wrote a letter to Mr. and Mrs. Gershunoff in Southampton (dated December 10, 1923) on his official stationery, accepting them as his artists for the 1924–25 season:

"It is understood that I am to arrange your concerts on a percentage basis and receive Twenty (20%) percent of the gross receipts as my compensation. You are to pay all expenses such as advertising, printing, railroad fares, etc."

According to the Gershunoffs' son, Max, his parents never performed under Hurok's management after they arrived in the United States. "Ironically, after they had come here, everyone went their own way, because they all were really floundering, including Mr. Hurok." Even more ironically, nearly forty years later, Hurok hired Max, also a musician, to work in his agency, where Max eventually became a vice president. At the time he was hired, however, neither Max nor Hurok was aware of the connection between them. Max's parents had never told him how they got to America, and Hurok had forgotten the incident—or more likely, he had only signed the letter as a favor to his friend Charles Koot back in 1923, without even knowing Gershunoff's name.

When it all became clear, Max told Hurok about their special relationship. " 'You know, Charles Koot was my uncle, and you are the one who brought my parents to this country,' I told him. 'I guess I owe the fact that I was born in America to you.'

"And he said, 'Oh, my.' "

It was generous (if theatrical) gestures like these that would lead his artists and friends to call him "Papa Hurok."

"My Blue Period" is what Hurok later called the mid-1920s. Never one to hoard his earnings, he had by late 1925 managed to spend on the Russian Opera Company and other attractions virtually all of the substantial sum he had made on Chaliapin, Pavlova (who made her last American tour in the 1924–25 season), Duncan, and his other artists. This pattern would repeat itself many times through Hurok's career, bust following boom with an almost predictable regularity. For him, money was never an end in itself, but only a means to an end: It allowed him to live well, to lure more artists to his agency, and to present them with the necessary élan. Saving was not in his nature. Impresarios spent.

On travel, for one thing. In an attempt to compete with the numerous independent managers who crowded the musical scene in the 1920s (Wolfson Musical Bureau, Loudon Charlton, Arthur Judson Concert Management, R. E. Johnson, Daniel Mayer, Mischa

Elman Concert Direction), Hurok made annual summer trips to Europe in search of new talent. He always went in style. On July 4, 1925, for example, he sailed on the luxury liner *Leviathan*, bound for a conference of his stars in Paris at which they would discuss plans and strategy for the coming season. He stayed abroad for a month. In the summer of 1926 he made another trip to Europe that included an extended stay in Paris and the first of many trips to the Soviet Union. Between 1926 and 1937, in fact, he would visit Russia eight times.

Expanding in all directions, Hurok now had the Manhattan Opera House under lease and planned to keep it open "every week during the season," presenting a number of imported "musical novelties, in addition to giving Sunday night operatic concerts." He had also formed the "S. Hurok Amusement Corporation" in order to lease two more New York theaters.

By late 1925 these huge financial obligations had made Hurok's situation so precarious that he was facing bankruptcy and was forced, against his principles, to enter into a partnership with a bank in order to launch yet another operatic venture starring Chaliapin. Now working for a larger artists' management agency called Universal Artists, headquartered at 1440 Broadway, Hurok announced that Chaliapin "would himself invest in the company a large amount of money he has made in this country." The rest would be guaranteed by the National City Bank. The new company, reported the *New York Times*, would attempt to present young American singers, "as Mr. Chaliapin wishes to show his appreciation of what America has done for him since he arrived here penniless in 1923."

"Penniless" was a bit of an exaggeration, and 1923 an inaccuracy. He had arrived in 1921, a stellar career already established.

For the first production of their first (1926–27) season, Chaliapin and his troupe (which included Spanish soprano Elvira de Hidalgo, later one of Maria Callas's teachers) chose *The Barber of Seville*. The bass took the relatively minor character role of Don Basilio, one that showed off his acting skills to particular advantage and one he had been giving with great pleasure for thirty years. Midway through the tour, which was plagued by technical problems and poorly equipped theaters, Chaliapin caught a cold and returned to New York. Stranded in St. Louis, the company and orchestra had to be paid. By the end of the tour, the National City Bank had lost $120,000 on its investment, and Hurok had learned the hard way that producing fully staged opera on the run—even in Italian—was a losing proposition.

In *Tonight We Sing*, this ill-fated tour receives a considerably more fanciful treatment. Temporarily estranged from Hurok because another manager has been wooing him, Chaliapin comes to the rescue like some sort of fairy godmother, suddenly producing a suitcase overflowing with money. (He has been led to this magnanimous gesture because the new manager insulted him by sending domestic champagne and salty caviar, a faux pas the likes of which Hurok would never have committed.) Saved from bankruptcy and reunited with his wife—whom he had offended by forgetting their wedding anniversary and splurging on a silver swan brooch for Pavlova—Hurok mounts a new full season of grand opera at popular prices. A triumphant scene from *Faust*, with Chaliapin (played by Ezio Pinza) in the title role, follows. This sequence deeply offended Chaliapin's children, who felt it debased and trivialized their father and implied a more intimate relationship between their father and Hurok than in fact existed.

As is natural between artist and impresario, there had always been serious conflicts between Hurok and Chaliapin, but a particularly violent one arose in early 1927, while Chaliapin was touring the United States. Chaliapin was accompanied on this tour by a female companion from Russia, Maria Valentinova Petzold, even though he was still legally married to another woman, Iola Tornaghi. Tornaghi had been his wife since 1898, she had borne his children, and they had lived together for many years in Moscow.

At the time, American public opinion, and the American press, could get very indignant and puritanical over instances of marital infidelity involving public figures. These outraged moral attitudes had been very much in evidence twenty years earlier, in 1906, in the case of another prominent Russian, the writer Maxim Gorky. Like Chaliapin, Gorky had toured the United States in the company of a Russian female companion while still legally married to another woman. When this fact was revealed in the press, a huge scandal ensued, and Gorky was nearly hounded out of the country. Even Mark Twain refused to preside over a banquet in the writer's honor.

Remembering this incident, which had occurred exactly when he had first arrived in America, Hurok now decided to take advantage of Chaliapin's ambiguous marital status, apparently seeing a possible solution to his growing money problems. In a letter to his daughter Irina written on April 23, 1927, Chaliapin claimed that he had been blackmailed by Hurok, who in collaboration with an unnamed "Jewish female journalist" in New York had threatened to make the facts of his infidelity public.

> They wanted to do the same thing to me that they did to Gorky, but I have avoided that for the moment by paying some money. This little affair has cost me about $10,000. I have tried to ask mother to divorce me—but she has refused, out of some deep feeling of arrogance. Now I'm afraid that the time will come when I'll no longer be able to get work or money because of this, and will no longer be in a position to support all of you, because it is IM-POS-SI-BLE to earn as much in Europe.

As part of this scheme of petty blackmail, Hurok also tried to convince Chaliapin to accept less than the amount they had agreed upon for his appearances.

Hurok's behavior infuriated and alienated Chaliapin and led to a permanent break in their relations. Chaliapin's daughter Tatiana later said her father was so disgusted with Hurok's dirty tactics that he told her "never to shake that man's hand." After 1927, Hurok never again presented Chaliapin in America or anywhere else, and the relationship between them became distant and even hostile. (In an apparent attempt to discredit him, Hurok would later accuse Chaliapin of fraternizing with the Nazi leadership.) Eventually, having obtained a divorce from Tornaghi, the singer toured the United States again, but under other management. Most likely because he was loath to lose the prestige and coverage connected with being Chaliapin's manager, however, Hurok continued to leave the impression in the press that they were still somehow linked right up until the time of Chaliapin's death in 1938.

Lest Hurok appear the undisputed villain in this unsavory tale, one should not forget that he had also endured his share of abuse and trickery from Chaliapin over the years, beginning from the moment when he was lured to Paris just for a laugh and lasting through every booming threat of cancellation and indisposition. Both of these aggressive and scheming men liked to have money and the upper hand in any professional relationship. It is hardly surprising that their stormy and manipulative "friendship" ended badly.

During these stressful years, Hurok had other headaches to deal with besides Chaliapin and his floundering company. He also had two new attractions on his hands: the dancer Loie Fuller and the Habima Jewish Theatre from Moscow.

Born in Fullersburg, Illinois, in 1862, Marie Louise Fuller had, like Isadora Duncan, gone to Europe to become a celebrated and frequently scandalous creator of modern dance. Possessed of even less formal dance training than Duncan, Fuller started out as an actress. She even toured for a time with Buffalo Bill before finding stardom in 1890 as a dancer with her *Serpentine Dance*, which relied for its impact on elaborate costumes (some of them transparent) and sophisticated lighting effects. What she lacked in technique she made up for with personality and theatricality, conquering Paris and London as she swirled and twirled through flashy numbers like *Fire Dance*, *The Butterfly*, and *Dance of Joy*.

Some critics have even credited "La Loie" with contributing to the development of the art nouveau style—"its curlicues and colors, its badge of a peacock's tail, its running glazes and its irrepressible movement." One of the most famous of all pieces of art nouveau sculpture is a bronze statuette (1900) by Raoul Francois Larche called "Loie Fuller, the Dancer." As a dancer and performance artist, Fuller has influenced a number of American choreographers, most obviously Alwin Nikolais, whose works most often revolve around lighting, fabrics, and stage design.

A lesbian whose Bohemian existence raised more than a few eyebrows in puritanical Prohibition-era America, "the lady with the scarf" was long past her prime by the time Hurok undertook to present her. He claims in *S. Hurok Presents* that it was Fuller's energetic and insistent agent who persuaded him to bring the dancer and her "students"—the Loie Fuller Dancers—on tour to the United States in late 1926. According to Hurok, Fuller invited him to the Royal Palace in Bucharest to discuss the tour with the dancer and her longtime confidante, Queen Marie of Rumania. The queen was about to leave for a royal trip to America, and the performances were to coincide with her visit. Since the proposal had glamorous diplomatic overtones, Hurok agreed, even though he would receive little publicity or credit.

But he got more than he bargained for. (Or then again, perhaps he got just what he wanted.) Political controversy and scandalous rumors pursued Marie's American tour from start to finish. Protestors used the queen's presence as an opportunity to expose oppressive conditions in Rumania, while continual questions were raised as to the nature of her "intimacy" with Fuller. Some newspapers reported that the two women were actually trying to raise money for a film project (*The Lily of Life*) on which they had collaborated.

The controversy finally crystallized around a gala held on October 24, 1926, at the Metropolitan Opera House and managed by Hurok. The program featured "Dance Scenes from *The Lily of Life*, a Fairy Tale by Her Majesty Queen Marie," danced by "The Ballets of Loie Fuller with eighty Members of the New York Symphony Orchestra." Because of the controversy and threatened disturbances, now hitting the front page daily, many members of the audience canceled their $100 reservations for boxes and bought less expensive seats in the orchestra instead. In the end, the boxes were filled, but with spectators paying less than full price.

Both in New York and during the cross-country tour that followed, Fuller's performances received little attention, overwhelmed by the "personal interest" aspects of the story. One journalist dismissed her as "an interpretative dancer" who was "widely known some years ago." Another described her as "a tired, sick little woman in black, seeming very old."

Dogged by gossip and criticism, and concerned over the prestige of her country and office, the queen finally asked Fuller to leave her entourage at Denver. Little more than a year later, the dancer died in Paris, still largely unappreciated (like Isadora Duncan) in her own country.

While he admits that the Fuller tour was "not one of my proudest achievements," Hurok glosses over the controversy in his relentlessly upbeat *S. Hurok Presents: A Memoir of the Dance World*.

Being associated with a reactionary Rumanian queen would not necessarily help business. But it made perfect sense that he should have
played a role in creating one of the great public relations events of
the celebrity-conscious Roaring Twenties, an incident that brought
together "the world's first ultra-modern publicity machine and the
world's first ultra-modern queen." His experience with Fuller and
Queen Marie surely reinforced his conviction that scandal could sell
tickets, provided that the social elite were not scared off. It also
showed him that the naive American public, ever richer but still culturally underdeveloped, was desperate for personalities and larger-
than-life stars to glorify and love, whether they be ethereal
ballerinas, temperamental basses, Eastern European monarchs,
matinee idols, or valiant transatlantic aviators.

For all that, Hurok's next new major attraction caught his eye
less through star quality than long-term commercial potential and
personal interest.

The Habima Jewish Theatre had evolved out of a small group
of Jewish players who performed first in Bialystok and Warsaw, and
then in many small cities throughout Poland, Lithuania, Hungary,
Austria, and Bohemia, in the early years of the twentieth century.
The members of the troupe came from the same sort of background
as Hurok himself. In 1912, the company set up a theater in Moscow
eventually closed by tsarist officials. After the Russian Revolution
the ensemble revived in the new hurly-burly atmosphere, even attracting the attention of Stanislavsky and his Moscow Art Theatre,
where Habima eventually became one of four affiliated studio theaters. In 1922, under the artistic control of Stanislavsky's student
Yevgeny Vakhtangov, one of the most important figures in early Soviet theatrical life, Habima—which means "tribune" in Hebrew—
presented its most famous production, *The Dybbuk*, written by
Solomon Rappaport.

More folklore than drama, set in the oppressive world of a
Hassidic sect, *The Dybbuk*, performed in a Russian-Lithuanian dia-
lect based on Hebrew, tells the eternal story of star-crossed lovers.
Leah is the daughter of a wealthy man, while her sweetheart
Channon is an impoverished student. Forbidden to marry Leah,
Channon dies, but his spirit (dybbuk) inhabits her body. Holy men
succeed in exorcising the dybbuk, but Leah dies.

The play's theme—and language—were ones Hurok could understand well from his own Pogar upbringing. "It told of the monstrous injustice of life, of the poor and the rich, of the despair of the former and the smugness of the latter, and of love triumphant over death," said Vakhtangov's assistant Yuri Zavadsky. Produced in a frequently grotesque style of "ecstatic stylization," or "mystic expressionism," with the actors' faces painted and the ten elders costumed in identical grease-stained black robes, *The Dybbuk* conveyed a vivid, disturbing picture of life in a devout, closed community.

Hurok saw the entire Habima repertoire, including *The Dybbuk*, in Paris in the summer of 1926, during the ensemble's touring engagement at the Théâtre Madeleine. The house was full of American producers, including Morris Gest and Lee Shubert. They didn't much care for the shabby clothes and dirty beards, and told Hurok American audiences would not want to see the Habima. Eager to prove them wrong and hoping to establish himself as a theatrical—and not just concert—impresario, he decided to bring them to New York anyway. By late August 1926, he had announced that the Habima would be appearing for eight weeks by special permission of the Soviet government.

As had happened with so many touring Russian performers in the past, the Habima encountered many obstacles in receiving permission to come to America. Delayed several times, they finally docked in New York on December 6, only to be carted off to Ellis Island by anxious Immigration officials. Hurok had to post a $500 bond for each of the company's forty members before they were released and allowed to go ashore.

One week later, Habima opened with *The Dybbuk* at the Mansfield Theater. According to Hurok, only thirty-nine paying customers, at $10 a head, showed up, despite a carefully planned publicity campaign. But the critics, especially young Brooks Atkinson of the *New York Times*, lavished praise on the company's theatricality. Comparing this *Dybbuk* favorably to one staged the previous season by the Neighborhood Playhouse, he wrote that "our stage may learn a good deal from it in the orchestration of producing."

Predictably, the city's Jewish community, always one of the strongest pillars of the Hurok audience, embraced Habima. The Zionist Council of Greater New York even organized a reception for the company at Mecca Temple on the Upper West Side. Eventually, in 1931, what was left of the company would settle in Israel and later become the country's national theater.

The support of New York's large Jewish community notwithstanding, Hurok lost (he said) $55,000 on the Habima engagement. The company was too specialized, highbrow, and avant-garde to make the same kind of broad commercial and artistic impact in New York as had the Moscow Art Theatre or *Chauve-Souris*. Its American tour did not bring Hurok the recognition he seemed to crave as a theatrical impresario. Significantly, this would be his last attempt to compete head-to-head with Morris Gest in this realm.

Henceforth, he would put his energy into music and, increasingly, into a field where he would have much less competition: dance. Neither music nor dance rely as heavily as does the theater on verbal skills, which were not Hurok's strong suit.

Habima did bring Hurok some highly favorable publicity. In a lengthy advance piece on the company in the *New York Times Magazine*, H. I. Brock produced several paragraphs that the impresario would never tire of quoting until the day he died. Hurok "has indeed probably done more than any other one man toward the building up of the country-wide American audience of more or less discriminating music lovers," Brock wrote grandly.

> Not only has he brought the artists over, he has sent them on tour all over the country. Not only has he sent the imported artists to the country beyond the Hudson; he has organized concerts like those in the old Madison Square Garden and at the Hippodrome which have brought the outlying parts of the city to the artist.
>
> It might fairly be posed as a question whether the phonograph or S. Hurok had most to do with creating the great body of American music fans who jam the Metropolitan and all our concert halls every season—who constitute the largest body of appreciators of any one art on this continent—even though they are not always as adept as they think they are.

With the newspapers printing such lavish tributes, Hurok was fast acquiring the larger-than-life status he would use to such great effect in the years to come. He was beginning to rival his artists as a star in his own right. Perhaps he couldn't coax a tune from a single instrument, but Hurok played publicity like a born virtuoso.

■ CHAPTER SEVEN ■

Fifty Cents and a Park Bench

"Money is like manure, of very little use except to be spread."—*Francis Bacon*

EVERY IMPRESARIO WORTH THE NAME must go bankrupt at least once. It's a rite of passage, like losing your virginity or falling in love. Going bankrupt builds character, provides emotional stimulation—and makes good copy. Nor was it difficult to do in the era before nonprofit guarantees, foundation grants, and subsidized performing arts centers, when risk was the name of the game. Making money on the presentation of "high" culture was never easy in America, where it carried the stigma of something foreign and sissified, but the volatile business environment of the 1920s (so similar to that of the 1980s) created additional challenges. Competition among the many independent impresarios was fierce, and the possibilities for failure (and sometimes, success) were endless. The growing popularity of radio, phonograph, and films (about to go to sound) were beginning to cut into the audience for live entertainment. And under the laissez-faire policies of Republican presidents Harding, Coolidge, and Hoover, huge fortunes could be made and lost in a matter of days.

Hurok went bust for the first time in late 1925 after losing heavily on Chaliapin's opera company and the Habima Theatre. He was nearly $200,000 in debt. Characteristically, he later presented

■ 119 ■

this development as yet another romantic and not entirely unpleasant adventure, proof of his endurance and ability to land on his feet after reversals that would ruin a lesser man. Which, to give him his due, it was.

When people like Hurok crashed, joked his acquaintance and artist Jan Peerce, they "ended on their bottoms higher than most people ever rose."

According to the transcript of hearings held at U.S. District Court No. 39815 (southern district of New York), and to the findings of a 1938 investigation of Hurok's finances conducted by Bankers Trust Company, an involuntary petition in bankruptcy was filed in New York for both Hurok and S. Hurok, Inc., in October 1925. It showed assets of $76,000 and liabilities of $184,000. At the same time, Hurok filed a voluntary petition for bankruptcy showing liabilities of $188,000 and no assets. The bankruptcy hearings also revealed that Hurok had been lent over the last few years a total of $33,000 by a lawyer named Jacob Berman. The two had become business partners beginning in 1923, when all the S. Hurok, Inc., contracts and stock were transferred to Berman's control. (In later years, however, Hurok always vehemently denied he ever worked with a partner.) During the summer of 1925, Hurok cashed in his life insurance policy as collateral for his debt to Berman. It was the only way he could meet artists' payments. When asked by the investigators why he lent so much money to Hurok, Berman, who admitted he did not know Hurok well, replied that it was because he "inspires confidence."

By October 1925, S. Hurok, Inc., owed money to several artists, including Anna Pavlova. Hurok also owed money to Chaliapin and violinist Mischa Elman, with whom he had personal contracts. (With Chaliapin he worked on a guarantee basis, with Elman on commission.) Of these three, only Chaliapin remained—although only briefly—with Hurok after his bankruptcy. As part of the bankruptcy settlement, Hurok went to work for Universal Artists, an artists' agency that employed his former secretary Mae Frohman. Chaliapin came with Hurok to Universal Artists as part of the deal, although their relations broke off in early 1927 as a result of Hurok's attempt to blackmail him (see chapter 6). In addition, Hurok had to agree to part with his car (a Studebaker) and chauffeur.

But the 1925 bankruptcy did not discourage Hurok or drive

him out of the business. The case was discharged in November 1926 and by 1927, after taking shelter for a while at Universal Artists, he was able to find enough investors to allow him to charter a new company, Hurok Attractions, Inc., with an authorized capital of $10,000 on one hundred shares of $100 each.

In his oral and literary reminiscences, however, Hurok was sure to get maximum mileage out of his bankruptcy experience. When it struck, he was living in the fashionable Ansonia Hotel at the corner of Broadway and 73rd Street, a lavish seventeen-story French beaux arts–style palace opened in 1899. "One of the most opulent hostelries in town," as he immodestly described it, topped by cupolas and railings offsetting a Parisian-style mansard roof, the Ansonia enjoyed special favor with musicians owing to thick soundproofed walls and its proximity to Carnegie Hall and the Metropolitan Opera House. Many stars resided, practiced, and threw temperamental tantrums here: Enrico Caruso, Leopold Auer, Chaliapin, Mischa Elman, Geraldine Farrar, Igor Stravinsky, and Arturo Toscanini. Hurok thrived on the celebrity-rich atmosphere. "I had spent thousands of dollars at the Ansonia, had housed most of my artists there."

But none of this spared him the indignity of eviction. The way he told the story, one evening he returned to the Ansonia from a day of stargazing only to find that his key no longer opened the door to his room. When Hurok complained to the desk clerk, he was told that because he owed $500 on his bill, the board of directors had decided to ask him to leave the establishment. Even an appeal to the Russian manager didn't help.

Thrown out into the street, Hurok gave no thought, apparently, of returning to Brooklyn to his wife and fifteen-year-old daughter. He had moved to Manhattan to stay, and would rather sleep *en plein air* in Central Park than retreat to ignominious exile in the outer boroughs. In the self-serving and highly dramatized account of his eviction and homelessness that later appeared in *Impresario*, Hurok strove to portray his predicament in the most noble, pastoral, and literary terms:

> I was broke, and I was alone. But oddly enough I was not
> sad. The nights I spent in Central Park I did not spend de-
> bating the comparative advantages of jumping out of a

window. I spent them enjoying the fresh air and the peace of the city after midnight.

Nor did I think of going to my friends. I remembered what Tolstoy had said when he was very ill. "Don't publish any more bulletins about my illness," he told the doctors. "What good do they do? My friends will be saddened, my enemies cheered."

I kept my troubles to myself, kept my clothes in order as best I could, kept my office and my secretary at 55 West 42nd Street, and kept my ear to the ground for a chance to get started again.

Judging by his comments in similar situations in later years, Hurok would in fact have been much more likely to mumble something like "The bes-tirds, the bes-tirds, the ungrateful bes-tirds" and leave it at that. But this sort of language was rather too colorful and provincial for the respectable published memoir of America's premier presenter of high culture.

In later years, Hurok never tired of drawing on his alleged sojourn in Central Park—which his daughter Ruth insists was a complete fabrication, just another fanciful chapter in his self-created legend—for inspirational sermons to the pampered younger generation. What was a little camping out to a man who had survived pogroms, steerage, Brownsville, and Chaliapin? "I had a chance to take stock that night in Central Park," he told the New York *Herald Tribune* in 1951. "Everything had been coming in too easy, but now again I had a chance to learn how hard life can be. Next morning I tightened my belt, spent my last 50 cents on a shave and some breakfast—and then I began coming to life again.

"And that suggests a little experiment: Why not take some of the young people of today who don't know how hard life can be, and just start them out with one 50-cent piece and a park bench? . . . When you start at the bottom, you know, there is only one direction to go—UP!"

Opera had busted Hurok. Now it saved him. Not full-scale staged opera, with all these expensive costumes and sets and stagehands and endless rehearsals, but just the essentials: a concert hall, singers, and an orchestra. Bankruptcy notwithstanding, he persuaded Lee Shubert, oldest of the three Shubert brothers, who between them already controlled more than a hundred theaters in New York, to rent him the Century Theatre.

There, on October 9, 1927, Hurok presented what must have been a lengthy Sunday afternoon program featuring orchestral selections and a concert version of Tchaikovsky's opera *Eugene Onegin*. To his surprise, it turned a profit of $2,500, due both to the continuing popularity of Russian attractions and to the large size of New York's music-loving Russian community. (Still a novelty in New York, *Onegin* had received its American stage premiere at the Met only in 1920, sung in Italian.) On subsequent Sundays, he presented concert versions of *Samson and Delilah* (starring the "sumptuous, Junoesque" Hungarian contralto Margarete Matzenauer in the title role), Meyerbeer's *Les Huguenots*, Tchaikovsky's *Queen of Spades*, Anton Rubinstein's *Demon*, Strauss's *Die Fledermaus*, Wagner's *Tannhäuser*, and a program of excerpts from ballets danced by the Fokine Ballet under the direction of his longtime artist, Michel Fokine.

Encouraged, Hurok next ventured into concert performances of Wagner operas, starring the distinguished German soprano Johanna Gadski, now in the twilight of her long career. Like so many of Hurok's artists, Gadski (1872–1932) came complete with a controversial reputation that helped save him money on publicity. Since 1900 a regular at the Metropolitan Opera, where she sang 296 performances in 25 roles, Gadski, like many other German artists, had become in 1917 the victim of the anti-German hysteria that swept the United States on the eve of the country's entry into World War I. Among other things, she and her husband were accused of hosting a party at which one of the guests sang a ditty praising the German sinking of the *Lusitania*. Eventually, after her husband was charged with espionage and deported as an undesirable alien, she left America to return to Berlin.

But Gadski still retained numerous admirers in New York, one of whom, Geraldine Hall, offered to give Hurok the financial backing to bring her back to the United States. And so, with the usual media fanfare, Hurok presented her in a Sunday-evening series at the Jolson Theatre—which he had received rent-free after being asked by the Shuberts to vacate the Century Theatre to make room for Max Reinhardt. (Reinhardt, an Austrian actor, manager, and producer, had founded the Salzburg Festival and was regarded as one of the most influential theater people of his time. He had produced an acclaimed season of plays in New York in 1927–28.) Gadski's performances in her signature Wagnerian roles of Brunnhilde and Isolde in the spring of 1929 proved popular with the public and critics, who had now forgotten—at least for the moment—their former Teutonophobia.

Gadski was so popular, in fact, that Hurok decided to create what he called the German Grand Opera Company for the next (1929–30) season. During the summer, Hurok scoured Germany for new singers, scenery, and costumes. The new Company featured Gadski and a group of German artists who had originally been brought to the United States the year before by George Blumenthal, Oscar Hammerstein's secretary. With continued support from Gadski's patron Geraldine Hall, the German Grand Opera Company toured Philadelphia, Baltimore, Washington, Cleveland, Pittsburgh, Milwaukee, Chicago, Indianapolis, St. Paul, and Cincinnati, presenting Wagner's *Ring* cycle, *The Flying Dutchman*, and Mozart's *Don Giovanni*. Even the loss of the two performers engaged to sing the central role of Mime in the *Ring* failed to stop the show. In Milwaukee, Hurok simply told the local manager that the stage was too narrow for Mime's scenes, which take place in a cave. Apparently neither he nor the audience objected to the abridged version.

With Gadski—whom he described as "an old-fashioned German *hausfrau*"—and her colleagues Hurok also shared some pleasant offstage moments. Some occurred at her house outside Berlin, amid "knockwurst and sauerbraten and good Moselle wine." After one particularly memorable birthday party that lasted nearly until dawn, Hurok claimed (with his usual tendency for theatrical self-romanticization) he was seduced by a certain "Wagnerian lady" who "carried me off Walkure-fashion to the Hotel Adler, but she was less the Brunnhilde type than the Isolde."

But Hurok's relationship with Gadski was not quite so *gemütlich* as he liked to portray it in later years. He resigned as manager of the German Grand Opera Company in April 1930, at the end of its second season, after which time Gadski continued to tour (until her death in an auto accident in 1932) under the management of

J. J. Vincent. A year after resigning, Hurok sued the singer for $1,700. "Hurok asserts the money is owed to him for commissions on concerts he arranged for the singer in 1930 and from which she received $27,000," reported the *New York Times*. "He said she paid him only $1000, although he was to have received 10 per cent, or $2700, for his services." Hurok loved opera, but he didn't mind money, either. And he would not tolerate getting less than what he believed to be his fair share.

Significantly, the German Grand Opera was also Hurok's last large operatic venture. Due to changes in tax laws, an increasingly diversified entertainment scene, and a growing interest in dance, opera's appeal for the small social elite which had traditionally supported it was weakening. The "golden age" of opera was over, and Hurok, ever mindful of changing trends, began to shift his focus toward the ultimately more profitable areas of soloists and ballet.

It is a perfect symbol of how much more "real" backstage life was for Hurok than his own private life that he failed to describe in his autobiography an important romantic encounter that occurred on one of his trips to Europe around the same time he was supposedly schmoozing with Gadski and her friends. This was his first meeting with his future wife, Emma.

According to most versions of the story, Hurok first saw Emma in 1929, when she was performing in Europe (most likely in Berlin) as a singer in a new version of Yascha Yushny's variety show *The Bluebird*—the same attraction Hurok had presented in an earlier incarnation in New York in 1924. By the time Hurok first saw her, the extravagant Emma had gone through the Russian Revolution, a good deal of money, and two husbands. Born Emma Rybkina into a large and prosperous Jewish family in St. Petersburg, she had shared a bench with Jascha Heifetz while studying the piano at the St. Petersburg Conservatory. Her first husband, a prominent banker and lawyer, gave her his name (Perper), financial security, and three sons. But like so many members of the Russian upper class, the family fled Russia in 1918, going first to Finland and then to Germany, where Emma's husband died in 1920.

Soon afterward, alone in a foreign country and with three young sons to support, Emma met and married Osip Runich, a popular Russian silent-film star who had left the Soviet Union in 1919. Famous for his portrayal of Nicolas Rostov in a 1915 version of Tolstoy's *War and Peace*, he had also played opposite the great Russian femme fatale Vera Kholodnaya. But he had a much more difficult time finding work in the Berlin studios, which were overrun by Russian refugee actors. Seductive and glamorous, he succeeded in persuading Emma to squander most of her first husband's fortune on various impractical schemes revolving around him. Eventually they ended up in Riga, then the capital of independent Latvia, where Emma did some performing with some former members of the Moscow Art Theatre who were living there. She also toured around Europe as a member of Yushny's show.

In *The Bluebird*, Emma sang melancholy Russian folk and gypsy songs, draped over the piano in yards of silk and enveloped in clouds of cigarette smoke and Slavic ennui. Her act and regal demeanor captivated many who saw her, including Hurok. "That was her hold on him," Nela Rubinstein, wife of pianist Arthur Rubinstein, said years later. "Hurok always visualized Emma as his beautiful *artiste*. He used to melt away the moment she would sing—especially the gypsy song *'Ochi chernye'* ['Black Eyes']."

"She played the piano and sang, like Liberace, dressed in fantastic costumes," said Simon Semenoff, a Russian dancer who knew Emma in Riga. "But she was a very cultured and educated lady. And very beautiful. I remember we were always at the beach, where we would see her and her three kids—Eddie, George, and Victor. Hurok really fell for her when he met her. 'My first wife I never liked even though I married her,' he told me. 'There was no love. With Emma—with Madame Hurok, with Mrs. Perper—I really fell in love.' "

It's not difficult to see why he would have been attracted to Emma's talent, cultured background, glamorous past, dramatic personality, and melodramatic hauteur. Unlike his first wife, Tamara, who feared and worshiped him, Emma treated Hurok with a certain distance and condescension that excited him both emotionally and sexually. As many friends have observed, she knew how to tease him and make him jealous so that he would desire her more than ever. Also unlike Tamara, Emma knew and felt comfortable with the world of classical culture; she had grown up with it and never hesitated to make her strong opinions known to Hurok, who received them as gospel. By wooing and eventually winning this diffident and often difficult Russian intellectual, Hurok (consciously or unconsciously) strove to a higher social and cultural standing. Even with friends and associates, he loved to refer to her as "Madame Hurok," or Emma Borisovna—formal terms of address conveying respect and status. Only a few years earlier, back in the highly stratified world of Russian prerevolutionary society, he would hardly have been able even to approach such a person, let alone become her life's companion.

What attracted Emma to Hurok is less clear. Emma's son Edward, whom Hurok later hired (like his brother George) to work in his organization, could never quite understand why his sophisticated, well-educated mother took up with this rough-hewn and provincial merchant's son who had never even learned to speak proper Russian. They seemed ill matched. And yet, according to Edward, Hurok did "have a lot of charm. He knew how to charm people and get around them. He would smother them with candies and champagne and parties. My mother was on the rebound from Runich, with three sons to support. He was always so good at lavishing attention on people and making them feel appreciated. And they did share their familiarity with the artistic world, in which they had many friends in common."

According to dancer Alexandra Danilova, who knew both parties for many years, Emma decided to marry Hurok for a meal ticket—"in order to improve her position. After all, everybody knew him. Everybody. Everybody wanted him so they could go to America or somewhere else. He was simply the best-known impresario at the time."

In pursuing Emma, who suffered no shortage of admirers, Hurok relied on his enormous stock of energy, persistence, and self-confidence. "I don't know myself why I married him," she confided some years later to Anna Straus, her daughter-in-law. "But you know what he's like when he wants something. When he wants something, he gets it. Don't ask me how, I don't know. All of a sudden, here was this man, and the next thing I know, I'm marrying him. I don't know why. Don't even ask me why."

A woman given to theatricality in every gesture, Emma found

in Hurok, who worshiped "personality," an unfailing foil and admirer. Their relationship was full of elaborate dramatic rituals that amused their friends and relatives and gave their domestic existence an operatic flavor. "She never understood money very well," recalled Anna Straus.

> But she knew beauty, and money could buy that. Her clothes didn't have to be expensive, but when she put them on, it became an entrance. I saw her together with Marilyn Monroe, with Marlene Dietrich, with so many actresses who could make grand entrances. Emma could make an entrance right there along with them.
>
> She wasn't tall, but she had this walk, and a look in her eyes, and her hands—she always talked with her hands, and the cigarette holders. If it was hot, she would hold a fan, a glorious fan that she knew just how to open and close and fan herself, and she had beautiful veins. There were many women with more beautiful bodies and all that. But she had beautiful legs and feet. She would be lying on her bed in negligees and feathers and everything, and Hurok used to come and pick up her feet and kiss them. Right there, in front of anybody. It was just a foot that demanded to be kissed. Everybody—her sons, everybody—kissed her feet the way people usually kiss a woman's hand. And she was so used to this that she didn't even pay any attention. She had gorgeous feet and beautiful skin. And she just loved all these theatricalities.

Others who knew Emma are less complimentary. Choreographer Agnes de Mille, who first met Hurok in 1929 and saw him frequently until his death, remembers Emma as "a marvelous sad-eyed Russian woman—very, very handsome. But God knows what she used instead of a brain. She rarely spoke. She would wear these great big emeralds—not from Hurok, but from her superb past. Hurok thought she was pretty wonderful, a princess. But she treated him pretty badly, I think. And she just loved to gossip with her spiteful Russian friends."

The circumstances of Hurok's marriage to Emma remain

murky, like so many details of his private life. Semenoff believed that Emma obtained a divorce from her former husband Runich in Riga, where such things were more easily arranged. Whether or not Hurok was still officially married to his first wife, Tamara, is unclear; it is possible that he had by then secured the Mexican divorce that is referred to in his legally binding 1941 Nevada divorce from Tamara (see Chapter 5).

Anna Straus maintains that Emma and Hurok were married twice, both times in America, once by a justice of the peace and once in a Jewish ceremony. Hurok himself was vague on the topic. In *Impresario*, he chose to include his marriage to Emma as simply one item in a catalogue of events, almost as a postscript. "Many things happened to me in the Thirties, most of them wonderful. I heard Marian Anderson sing for the first time in a Paris concert hall; Arthur Rubinstein became my friend; my lovely Emma became my wife."

In later years, Emma was no more exact about the circumstances of her marriage to Hurok. According to his associate Lillian Libman, who knew them both well for many years, "I don't think even Emma herself remembered the date they were married."

Once Hurok found Emma, of course, he spent even less time and energy on his first wife, Tamara, and their daughter, Ruth. Increasingly, he focused his energy on "Madame Hurok," who came to live with him in the United States in the early 1930s. Her three sons stayed behind in Paris to finish their schooling. A few years later, Hurok brought both George and Eddie Perper to New York and into his business, where they would work for many years. Meanwhile, Tamara was continuing her quiet, self-effacing existence in Brooklyn and Ruth was graduating from high school. Hurok would occasionally take Ruth out to lunch and ask her about her life in school and at summer camp, but long periods would also go by when she would hear nothing at all from her father. Although she loved to dance, he did nothing to encourage her aspirations toward a dance career. Instead, he used to tell her that "dancers had brains in their feet" and she would be smarter to seek a "more solid profession. Maybe he didn't think I had enough talent, or maybe he just didn't want to bother."

But even more difficult for Ruth to accept than her father's indifference to her dancing was his businesslike tone in dealing with her emotional needs. Often he seemed to want to treat her like one of his clients or associates and to distance himself from any family connection or responsibility. "When I was in camp, he would send me these typewritten letters written by his secretary and signed 'Your loving father, sincerely yours, S. Hurok,' done with a rubber stamp. . . . He didn't give me the kind of love I wanted."

Such behavior brings to mind what Jack Warner, Jr., said ruefully of his father, Jack Warner, Sr. (of Warner Brothers), and the other Hollywood studio magnates whose backgrounds were so similar to Hurok's. They were, he remarked, "creatures of a drive that didn't leave them much time to be good husbands or fathers."

In 1929, perhaps at Emma's urging, Hurok brought the venerable Russian composer Alexander Glazunov to the United States. Emma had studied with him—and personally benefited from his legendary generosity—at the St. Petersburg Conservatory, where he had been an esteemed professor for thirty years and director for twenty-five. A devoted pedagogue, Glazunov (1865–1936) had encouraged many students, including such important talents as Prokofiev and Shostakovich. As a composer, he looked backward to the nineteenth-century Russian tradition of Borodin, Balakirev, and Tchaikovsky and, despite the enduring popularity of his charmingly sentimental ballets *Raymonda* and *The Seasons*, was belittled as an academic dinosaur by the musical avant-garde that emerged around the time of the Russian Revolution. Unlike most of his contemporaries, however, Glazunov elected to remain in the Soviet Union after 1917 and continued to devote his energy to the protection of the St. Petersburg (and later Leningrad) Conservatory until 1928, when he left for Europe. At the time Hurok invited him to come to the United States as a conductor and accompanist, he was an old man of sixty-five, living uncomfortably in an atmosphere of Western emigration and touring through various European countries.

As was the case with so many of the artists Hurok presented, he had been pursuing Glazunov for years. He claimed to have first met Glazunov in Berlin in 1923, at which time they signed a contract for the composer's appearance in America. Because of difficulties back home in St. Petersburg, however, Glazunov could not honor his commitment. When they met again in Paris in 1929, Hurok repeated his invitation, to which Glazunov replied with characteristic lethargy, "Mister Hurok, I'm such heavy artillery. Why would I travel so far? And would it really be worthwhile?"

But Hurok refused to give up: "I convinced Glazunov that his visit was essential for creating interest in his music, for his many students, and finally, for Russian art. With complete sincerity, I told Glazunov that I have no intention of making money on him. I was prepared to pay all the expenses and any losses on the strength of the enormous pleasure and pride it would give me to be the first person to bring Glazunov to America. He was touched by my words and agreed to come."

Hurok's true enthusiasm for the cause of Russian art and artists had a hidden commercial motive, of course. Now that he was traveling more frequently to the Soviet Union, and was even on the brink of signing agreements to bring Soviet artists to the United States, his generous treatment of Glazunov would not be lost on the cultural officials in Moscow, with whom the composer had good relations. And it surely stroked Hurok's ego that he, a humble Jew from the pale, could invite and present one of Russia's most distinguished cultural figures, a man who had known and even trained many of the great Russian artists of his remarkable generation.

Glazunov's tour in the United States included appearances with orchestras in New York, Chicago, Philadelphia, Detroit, and Boston. Since the haughty New York Philharmonic had shown no interest in engaging Glazunov as a conductor, Hurok organized a pickup orchestra composed mainly of the composer's students and rented the Metropolitan Opera House for the evening of December 4, 1929. Composer and conductor Walter Damrosch, the recently appointed musical director at NBC, gave an eloquent introductory speech in which he (not incidentally) included praise for Hurok as "the king of managers, a credit to New York." The audience stood and applauded for ten minutes when Glazunov appeared. Hurok, the dispenser of largesse, bathed in the warm glow of philanthropy.

En route to one of the composer's appearances, Hurok (who loved to tell this story and did so often) and Glazunov made a stop to see Niagara Falls. "It was winter, and Niagara was wrapped in snow and ice. Despite the cold, Glazunov walked on foot around the falls, and then said to me, full of enthusiasm, 'I've dreamt for many years of seeing Niagara, and at last my dream has come true. Now I can die in peace.' "

Hurok loved playing the role of the Fairy Godfather.

Nor did he mind a few years later when he was told by some of Glazunov's American admirers that they had been unsuccessful in trying to persuade the composer to return to the United States to celebrate his fifty years of professional activity. "If Hurok hasn't written to me about it," Glazunov reportedly told them, "then that means I don't really need to come."

For most Americans, and for most concert managers, 1929 was not a good year. The stock market crash and subsequent economic depression made an already difficult life even more so for impresarios, who always operated at a high level of risk and a low profit margin in a highly competitive marketplace and whose business was more dependent than most on vagaries in the level of disposable income.

When the economy sneezes, the arts (particularly "high culture") come down with pneumonia, since they are perceived by audiences and governments alike as dispensable frills. And unlike European countries in which the tradition of state subsidies for opera, ballet, and symphonic music had existed for centuries, the United States in 1929 was still a society new to and somewhat uncomfortable with the idea of elite culture or federal support for the arts. As Hurok had noticed when he arrived in New York twenty-three years earlier, Americans were a people "who neither sang nor danced" and who regarded such behavior as frivolous and even sinful. (He never developed much interest in or respect for art forms native to America, such as spirituals, square dancing, or jazz.) Whatever all the reasons, the Depression hit even established institutions like the Metropolitan Opera hard; by the end of the 1931–32 season, the Met had accumulated an enormous deficit of nearly $500,000 and was even considering shutting down altogether.

The economic devastation of the Depression meant the end of expecting a few wealthy patrons to support expensive elite culture. Increasingly, opera houses and symphony orchestras were forced to rely on box office income and to run their operations in a more businesslike fashion. Large corporations began to enter into close relationships with cultural institutions. In 1931, the Met began its weekly radio broadcasts; these were sponsored in turn by Lucky Strike, Listerine, and RCA, before Texaco came on board to stay in 1940. Radio brought a much larger popular audience to opera, which had traditionally been an art form (in America, at least) with rather limited appeal. In 1932, the San Francisco Opera House became the first in America to be municipally owned. Throughout the 1930s, the power of the old WASP elite that had traditionally supported culture declined, while the power of cities and immigrants—Hurok's audience—grew.

On the brink of going under, many independent concert managers now turned to mergers in order to survive. The move toward mergers had actually begun during the 1920s, with the formation of such large networks as the Community Concerts Corporation and the Civic Music Association. These organizations packaged a series of "name" performers represented by various managers but administered through a central New York office. The package was then offered to small communities (where they were often presented in high school auditoriums) unable to undertake such bookings on their own. The arrangement proved highly profitable for its founders, especially for Arthur Judson. A former music critic and creator of the Community Concerts Corporation, he represented a large group of artists controlled by seven formerly independent New York managers.

In 1930, the centralization of the concert management business went one step further. Daniel Mayer, one of the seven founding members of the Community Concerts Corporation, and his assistant, Marks Levine, set up what was called the National Broadcasting and Concert Bureau, under the aegis of the rapidly expanding National Broadcasting Company. Not long afterward, the other controlling members of Community Concerts (including Arthur Judson, who headed two of the merged agencies) responded by forming the Columbia Concerts Corporation. It operated under the auspices of NBC's rival, the Columbia Broadcasting System. Judson became the president and chief operating officer of Columbia Concerts, which also subsumed what was left of the Community Concerts Corporation and renamed it as the Community Concert Service. A few years later, NBC bought the Civic Music Association's network in order to compete with Community on a national scale.

The presentation of high culture was now controlled by two corporate giants. Between them, NBC and Columbia controlled 80 percent of the concert business in the United States.

As far as William Paley (who became the president of CBS in 1928) was concerned, he was doing the arts a favor by agreeing to create the Columbia Concerts Corporation:

> Concert attendance was very low, concert managers were going broke, the whole structure and organization of booking and producing concerts was in jeopardy. So . . . I helped merge the seven leading concert bureaus in the country into the Columbia Concerts Corporation. In one fell swoop, we represented about 125 of the best concert singers, soloists and musicians of the nation. Among them were Jascha Heifetz, Ezio Pinza, Lily Pons, Lotte Lehmann, Paul Robeson, Yehudi Menuhin, Mischa Elman, Vladimir Horowitz, Nathan Milstein and Serge Prokofieff. . . . Our purpose was to step into the breach and to save concert management during the Depression rather than any great hope for a profitable business. We did indeed sustain some losses for a while but ended up making a modest profit.

So where did all this leave Hurok, that most independent of independent managers? Due to shrewd maneuvering and well-established artistic and business contacts, in a highly unusual and favorable position. Refusing to "be merged," he entered into his own separate relationship with NBC, which allowed him to take maximum advantage of their network and resources for booking tours but to retain his own rights and label ("S. Hurok Presents") for his artists. (In August of 1930, the operation had changed its name from Hurok Attractions, Inc., to Hurok Musical Bureau, Inc., which would change back again to Hurok Attractions in 1934.) Under his special deal with NBC, Hurok also held on to his most prized possession, his well-honed publicity staff, so that he continued to promote his own artists—something he knew how to do better than anyone else in the business. Aware that New York was still the center of the cultural universe, he also retained sole control over any appearances by his artists there.

Hurok surely got the better end of the deal. In return for paying NBC a small percentage of the fees his artists received for the dates that NBC arranged for them outside New York, Hurok eventually acquired a rent-free office in stylish Rockefeller Center (which opened in late 1933); free telephone and telegraph service; and the prestige, stability, and resources of an enormous and fast-growing corporation. Even more important, he retained his distinct personal and professional identity in a field that was rapidly homogenizing. (Neither Arthur Judson at Columbia Concerts Corporation nor Daniel Mayer and Marks Levine at NBC's concert wing ever achieved anything approaching Hurok's power or stardom.) This special relationship between Hurok and the National Broadcasting and Concert Bureau (in its various incarnations) lasted for nearly thirty years, until 1957.

That's when Luben Vichey put an end to what he judged to be a highly inequitable arrangement. A one-time baritone at the Met, he became the new head of Hurok's parent organization, then called National Artists Corporation. When he had examined the relationship between Hurok and his firm, he was amazed (as he told *Variety* in 1957) by the exceedingly good terms Hurok had been able to extract back in the days of the Depression.

> He had a contract impossibly favorable to him. I do not know how it happened in the beginning, years ago. I inherited the deal. Hurok paid National no rent. All his telephone and telegraphic expense was charged against us. We booked Hurok attractions for a commission frequently as low as seven and one-half percent, although sometimes higher. We collected perhaps $100,000 a year from Hurok, but in order to satisfy and serve him, all our regular field representatives had to give Hurok acts precedence. Nor could we compete with him for big units. Hurok was one part of a big organization. We have over 100 employees, over $750,000 in annual overhead, but Hurok was the tail that wagged the dog.

Hurok's legendary negotiating skills also served him well in Moscow, where he continued to cultivate relationships with artists and cultural officials. Beginning in 1926, Hurok made nearly annual visits to the USSR (he told a Russian newspaper in New York that he made eight trips there between 1926 and 1937), although he provided few details either to American reporters at the time or in his two books of "memoirs." No doubt he wanted to keep his negotiations secret, since he was afraid of competition from other managers and he didn't want to scare off publicity-shy Soviet officials. As for his "memoirs," they were published during a period of antagonistic Soviet-American relations and before he finally succeeded—after thirty years of trying—in bringing Soviet performers to the United States in the mid-1950s. Hurok was never one to dwell on his failures.

In the early 1920s, Hurok had been using his contacts both in and outside Russia to work toward an agreement to bring on tour to America what had been the leading ballet and opera company in pre-Revolutionary Russia: The Mariinsky of St. Petersburg. Renamed the State Academic Theatre of Opera and Ballet in 1920, this legendary institution, supported since the late eighteenth century by lavish subsidies from the Tsars, had entered a turbulent new era after the 1917 Bolshevik Revolution. Its elitism and conservatism called into question by a struggling and impoverished new regime supposedly based on socialist principles, the former Mariinsky was groping, like all Soviet cultural institutions, toward a new repertoire, artistic identity, and administrative structure.

At the same time, Lenin's decision to transfer the Soviet capital from Petrograd to Moscow in 1918 had served to undermine the historic identity of "Peter" as Russia's cultural center. By the late 1920s, the Bolshoi Theatre in Moscow was receiving considerably more attention and more financial resources from the Soviet government, which remained suspicious of the aristocratic pretensions and heritage of Leningrad and its leading cultural institutions—especially the former Mariinsky. It's no accident, for example, that what is generally called "the first Soviet ballet"—*The Red Poppy,* by Reinhold Gliere—received its world premiere at the Bolshoi in 1927 and was staged in Leningrad only two seasons later. Before the Revolution, important premieres almost always took place in St. Petersburg.

By the late 1920s, Hurok also seems to have understood that it would be easier, and more politically advantageous, to arrange an American tour by the Bolshoi Ballet and/or Opera. But accomplishing that goal would take many more years than the impresario could possibly have imagined when he started working toward it.

To understand why it took Hurok, a patient and skillful Russian-speaking negotiator with a proven track record of presenting Russian artists in the United States, such a long time to reach agreement with the Soviet authorities, one must remember how often, and how rapidly, the political/cultural scene changed in the USSR in the late 1920s and early 1930s. Under Lenin, who came from a cultured middle-class background and who even confessed to a shameful weakness for music ("it makes me want to say kind stupidities"), Soviet culture enjoyed a period of relative freedom. Lenin appointed Anatoly Lunacharsky, a tolerant, well-educated liberal who had many friends among artists and writers, as his first Commissar of Enlightenment. Unfortunately, Lenin died prematurely in 1924, and within three years, Josef Stalin, a brutal party bureaucrat openly hostile to the cultural intelligentsia, had gained virtually unlimited control of the Communist party and Soviet government.

One of the more telling descriptions of Stalin in these early years comes from Chaliapin, who had met him not long before leaving Russia in the early 1920s. "From the way he spoke, which was at the same time opaque and energetic, I could see that he was not the sort of man who liked to joke. If necessary, he could softly, ever so softly, just as if he were dancing the *lezginka* with a soundless step in his soft boots, blow up the Cathedral of Christ the Saviour, the post office or the telegraph office—whatever you wish. That sort of possibility was there in his gestures, his movements, the sound of his voice, his eyes. It's not exactly that he was an evil person—he was just born that way."

Irritated by Lunacharsky's defense of such rebellious artists as Chaliapin, Dmitri Shostakovich, Sergei Prokofiev, theater director Vsevolod Meyerhold, and even Isadora Duncan, the puritanical and pathologically suspicious Stalin removed him from the post of Commissar of Enlightenment in 1929. After this time, official Soviet policy in the field of culture became both more regimented and more unpredictable, subject to Stalin's personal whims and unbridled compulsion to control all aspects of Soviet life.

Hurok's position in Moscow was not made any easier by the fact that the U.S. government had yet to recognize the Communist party and the Soviet government as the legitimate rulers of Russia. American soldiers had even fought against the Red Army in the civil war that followed the 1917 Revolutions. Only in 1933 would President Roosevelt finally extend diplomatic recognition to the USSR and appoint William Bullitt as the first American ambassador to Moscow.

And yet, despite all these obstacles, Hurok still managed to strike what sounded like an important deal in the summer of 1930. On August 2, it was announced that Hurok had signed a two-year contract "with the Soviet government" giving him the "monopoly right to engage Soviet artists for appearance in the United States and England and for American and British artists in Russia. The contract covers musicians, singers, the theatre, ballet and the circus." Hurok, reported the *New York Times*, had already signed up a number of performers for American tours, including Anastasia Abramova, a leading Bolshoi ballerina of the 1920s; a group of Ukrainian bandura players; the "young violinist, David Oistrakh," then twenty-two years old; and pianist Lev Oborin. The contract was signed "in the record time of two weeks," allegedly with the help of American singer Sergei Radamsky, who had already made several tours in Russia. Not coincidentally, the contract also called for Hurok to sponsor Radamsky's further appearances in the USSR.

Because of continuing political and cultural instability in the USSR and uncertainty in Soviet-American relations, however, the contract was never fulfilled and none of these Soviet performers came to the United States at this time. Oistrakh would make his American debut only twenty-five years later, in 1955—after Stalin's death. Despite such bitter disappointments in his negotiations with the Soviet government, Hurok continued to travel regularly to the USSR, seeing and hearing important new artists, accumulating goodwill, and biding his time. Emma often accompanied him. They would travel together to Leningrad, where she would visit her brothers who still lived there, and Hurok would spend time with his own brother, Asher.

On his 1930 summer visit to Russia (and perhaps earlier), Hurok also asked Soviet officials to let him travel to his hometown of Pogar, where his mother and numerous other relatives still lived. But under the strict restrictions on travel imposed on foreigners (especially Americans) by the Soviet government, the area around Pogar was closed and his request to go there was denied. He was allowed, however, to travel to Minsk, the capital of Belorussia, for a reunion with members of the Gurkov family there. According to Hurok's niece Rita Zaitseva (the daughter of his sister Esfir), who was seven years old at the time, he sent word for his relatives to come to Minsk, where they met and spent two days together at a hotel.

One can only imagine what transpired at this reunion, but one thing is certain: it was overshadowed by the death only a few months earlier of Hurok's father, Izrail. He had been arrested in Stalin's brutal campaign against small merchants and private farmers, part of a mammoth effort to collectivize agriculture and institute state control over every single enterprise. Being arrested had proved so traumatic to Izrail that he suffered a heart attack and died. (There were many such cases at the time.) So Hurok never did get to see his father again. Indeed, this 1930 reunion in Minsk proved to be the last time Hurok ever saw his Old Country relatives together. Although he began sending dollars to his mother Sima each month after this, his niece insists he never saw her or any of the other members of the Pogar clan again before his mother's death in 1936. He only reestablished contact with Rita after Stalin's death, when he tracked her down in Moscow.

Characteristically, Hurok did not record his impressions of this trip anywhere or share them with American journalists when he returned to New York. Most likely, he was concerned that if he honestly described the horrible poverty and suffering afflicting the Russian and Ukrainian countryside during this terrible enforced transformation to collectivized agriculture, his delicate negotiations with the powers in Moscow might suffer and he might never be allowed to travel to the USSR again. For in the summer of 1930 in the region around Pogar and Minsk, famine and misery were everywhere. Millions of peasants who resisted Stalin's policies were being sent to labor camps, and farmers were burning their own property and slaughtering their own cattle rather than surrender them to the new state farms. It is estimated that between five million and seven million people perished during the brutal collectivization drive.

It seems impossible that Hurok could not have known or seen what was happening—especially after talking to his relatives. No doubt it was wiser, and certainly less dangerous, for him to remain silent about what he saw and heard.

But two remarkable photographs provide eloquent documentation of the American impresario's visit to Minsk, at the time still a rustic urban settlement hardly worthy of the name *city*. In one, Hurok—with a prodigious stomach, resplendent in a tropical white suit with dark shirt and white tie, topped with a fedora—stands gleaming in the middle of a drab cobblestoned street. He is gingerly holding the reins of a shaggy horse harnessed to a cart bearing an indifferent local resident who is looking away from the camera. Sporting a cane, the forty-two-year-old local-boy-who-has-made-good looks knowingly into the lens, all too aware that he is slumming. This attitude comes across even more strongly in the other photo, which shows Hurok standing inside a local house. White and impeccable, he towers over a dark and smudged man who is stuffing his mouth with food as he sits hunched and alone at a table set with the best china for tea.

Hurok isn't smiling.

CHAPTER EIGHT

Ballerinas,
Baby and Otherwise

"Sol Hurok was a peasant and a midget who would never give an opinion on anything until he had been told what to say."
—Agnes de Mille

DURING THE SHORT PERIOD between September 1927 and January 1931, three artists who had played a major role both in dance history and in Hurok's life died: Isadora Duncan, Sergei Diaghilev, and Anna Pavlova. Their passing represented a turning point in the evolution of modern dance and ballet, and set the stage for Hurok to proclaim himself their legitimate managerial heir. Characteristically, he made sure to associate himself in the public mind with each one of them at the time of their deaths, shrewdly exploiting their fame and prestige for his own personal and professional aggrandizement, clearing the way for his growing Hurok Musical Bureau to solidify its control over the increasingly vital American dance scene.

Isadora died first, on September 14, 1927. Chronically short of funds, locked in a destructive relationship with her romantic Russian poet Yesenin, who eventually committed suicide in Leningrad in late 1925, she had been living from hand to mouth for the last few years. On his regular trips to Paris, Hurok happily indulged her extravagant tastes in food and young men. The last time he saw her there, claimed Hurok stagily, she made him promise he would bring her students—she called them her "children"—on tour to America, "as though she had a premonition of her own death." Not long afterward, he received word that she had died in a freak accident in Nice. As described in countless cinematic and literary accounts, she strangled when the long shawl she was wearing became entangled in the spokes of the wheel of a Bugatti sportscar as she was about to set off on a drive with her latest *roué*. According to show-business legend, her last (highly operatic) words were *"Adieu, mes amis, je vais à la gloire."*

Such theatricalities provided ample grist for Hurok's publicity mill. In *Impresario* and elsewhere, he rhapsodized on her cultural and personal legacy. "She brought sunlight and fresh air into the lives and the thinking of all of us; she cut the bonds of spirit as well as flesh." And, he emphasized between the lines, he understood her and knew her and supported her through thick and thin.

Sergei Diaghilev was another matter. With him, the founder and longtime artistic director of the enormously influential Ballets Russes who died in Venice on August 19, 1929, Hurok did not have (and did not pretend to have, since there were many available who could contest such a claim) an intimate relationship. The two men didn't even have a casual friendship. In later years Hurok told some associates that he and Diaghilev had once met by chance (in what sounds like a movie script) on a train somewhere in Europe, but he never provided any documentation of this alleged encounter. At the time of Diaghilev's death, Hurok also claimed that he was holding a contract for another American tour by the Ballets Russes de Serge Diaghilev.

Hurok and Diaghilev belonged to very different social and cultural worlds, as alien as Brownsville and Park Avenue. Diaghilev came from the snobbish St. Petersburg elite, Hurok from the Ukrainian salt of the earth. Nor did Hurok possess the sophistication or the creative conceptual talent that inhabited Diaghilev, the gift that allowed him not merely to present personalities and whip up public interest, but to combine and develop them in completely new configurations. Diaghilev was a trendsetter, Hurok a trend follower. Diaghilev created artists; Hurok popularized them. In comparing the two impresarios, ballerina Alexandra Danilova, who knew and worked with them both, remarked, "Hurok was able to choose, but he wasn't able to find or discover. Diaghilev could find and discover."

"Hurok thought in terms of stars and of how his superb publicity machine could build them up," the English dance critic Arnold Haskell (1903–1980) has written. "He was in fact the very reverse of Diaghilev, and they could never have worked together."

Despite their professional and personal dissimilarities, Hurok was asked—along with dancers Adolph Bolm, Pavlova, Leonide Massine, Ruth St. Denis, Ted Shawn, and others—by *Dance* magazine several months after Diaghilev's death to comment on the significance of his passing. Writing, as always, through a secretary and public relations staff, he stressed Diaghilev's single-mindedness.

> Diaghilev was absolutely determined in his undertakings. He was the complete master of ceremonies in all his projects. I would also say that he was absolutely the man that brought the Russian and the classic ballet to Europe in spite of obstacles from different sources. He really sacrificed a good part of his personal life in order to promote and to spread the gospel of the Russian ballet, and classic dancing particularly, not only in Europe but all over the world.

Hurok would grab that gospel (along with many of Diaghilev's dancers) and preach it from the Atlantic to the Pacific with a strictly American commercial fervor.

Not surprisingly, Pavlova's death on January 23, 1931, affected Hurok even more deeply. In keeping with the carefully managed public image of their quasi-romantic relationship, he lavished eloquent tributes on his beloved "Swan," lamenting her failure to take care of herself and even hinting that his last meeting with her (as in the case of Isadora) somehow led to her untimely passing just one week before her fiftieth birthday. As he never tired of repeating in later years, Hurok stopped in Southampton at Pavlova's request in late summer of 1930 on his way back to New York. Even after he rejected her suggestion that he sponsor an American tour by her small ensemble for the upcoming season, Pavlova insisted on seeing him off on the *Leviathan*. Her "husband" Dandré objected, fearing she would fall behind in her tight schedule. "Don't you know that I may never see him again?" she protested in a scene worthy of Hollywood. Ever solicitous, Hurok worried that she would catch cold in the damp air at the pier.

And so when a few months later Pavlova died unexpectedly of what in fact started as a chill and quickly developed into pleurisy (following the time-honored tradition of tubercular stage heroines), he felt somehow personally involved. She refused to rest, Hurok told a television reporter many years later. She was obsessed with *"woik"* and lived only to *"rehoise."* He used to tell her that she should be "carried on stage in silk tissue paper," but she would insist that she was strong and had to perform for the "simple people" in "simple surroundings." To Hurok, she represented the ideal of the self-effacing artist who sacrifices everything for the sake of art: personal life, health, happiness. "It's the small artists who complain more and want more," he said. "She never complained."

Hardworking and stoical. A manager's dream.

Not everyone felt such reverence for Pavlova and her legacy, however. Many dancers, including Nijinsky, and many balletomanes, including critic David Faulkes in a 1934 article, "The Future of the American Ballet," regretted her failure to use her enormous popularity to more significant artistic ends. "Her artistic ideals were early overwhelmed by personal vanity," wrote Faulkes. "As long as her own appearances drew ovations, she was content to surround herself with often mediocre dancers and invariably shoddy decors."

When she died, Pavlova left fourteen thousand pounds sterling, as well as about $377,000 which had been managed in the United States not by Hurok but by Otto Kahn, who had first brought her to the Metropolitan Opera House in 1910. Since she left no will, the Soviet government claimed the estate on behalf of Pavlova's elderly mother, said to be still living in Russia. Hurok came forward to support Dandré's counterclaims as her husband and business manager. Despite his efforts, most of her financial assets did return to her homeland. Most of her artistic legacy, however, remained in the West, fiercely guarded and tirelessly publicized by Hurok, the frog who got the princess, at least in his vivid imagination.

As the Roaring Twenties turned into the Troubled Thirties, the American dance scene was becoming considerably more varied and serious. What is generally considered to be the country's first native-grown modern dance company, the Denishawn Company with its Denishawn School, founded by Ruth St. Denis and Ted Shawn, had been in operation since 1915, first in Los Angeles and later in New York. Introducing students and audiences to a wide range of musical and dance styles from all over the world, from the Japanese sword dance to the Hawaiian hula to Negro spirituals, Denishawn encouraged them to regard their own American traditions as valid material for art. Shawn also struggled through his own example to promote the message that men could be taken seriously as dancers, an idea that still held little currency in the land of rugged cowboys and hard-boiled capitalists.

Many talented young dancers passed through the Denishawn laboratory, including several pioneers of the American dance movement: Martha Graham (who gave her first solo recital in New York in 1926), Doris Humphrey, and Charles Weidman. By the time Denishawn broke up in 1932, it had done an enormous amount to improve public acceptance of and interest in modern (nonclassical) dance and in dance as an expression of national culture. It helped American audiences to understand that dance was more than a few variety acts at the Hippodrome or Pavlova doing her dying swan. In this way, Denishawn paved the way for Hurok to diversify his activity in the field of dance in the early 1930s.

Another young dancer just beginning to make a name for herself—in her inimitably independent fashion—was Agnes de Mille, daughter of Hollywood film producer William C. de Mille and niece of the film director Cecil B. DeMille. In 1929, at age twenty, she was already choreographing and dancing in the Hoboken revival of *The Black Crook*, a phenomenally popular musical variety show that had run almost continuously for more than forty years after its premiere in 1866. Knowing of Hurok's sponsorship of Isadora Duncan and of his interest in dance, she bravely invited him to come see the show in hopes that he might manage a solo recital for her in New York. Always ready to check out new talent, Hurok went, and then delivered his verdict:

> He told me I didn't have very good technique. He told me that with the balance I had, I should be able to turn better.

He told me my technique was faulty—and it was. He didn't know enough to say exactly what the matter was, but he could spot that it wasn't very good. And then I asked him how much it would cost to present me in New York.

"You're very frank," he said.

"Well, that's the point, isn't it?" I said.

"About $3000," he said.

"And I'm not worth that much, am I?" I said.

And he told me to ask my family, but I didn't want to. They wouldn't have given me the money anyway. And so we parted.

De Mille and Hurok—whom she later dismissed as "a peasant and a midget who would never give an opinion on anything until he had been told what to say"—were fated to meet and tangle again. Many times.

Hurok's lack of interest in de Mille's work, she charged later, had to do less with her faulty technique than with the prevailing wisdom that American audiences were only interested in established foreign, especially European, dance and dancers. Uncertain of its cultural identity, adolescent America in 1930 still looked to Europe for "serious" art and cultural status. Young people were considered educated only after they had toured the Continent; the captains of industry built mansions modeled on European palaces and stuffed with European furniture; symphony orchestras from New York to San Francisco routinely imported conductors and players from Germany or Russia or Italy. If American performers were to make it in America, they had to make it in Europe first, as Isadora Duncan, Ruth St. Denis, Loie Fuller, and so many others had shown. Only after World War II and the collapse of the Old World would this European chauvinism begin to be seriously challenged.

De Mille's claim that in 1930 "the big managers like Hurok and Columbia and NBC wouldn't have anything to with Americans— they despised us" contains a large portion of the truth.

When asked, along with several other working managers, by the three-year-old *Dance* magazine in 1929 to evaluate the situation facing classical dancers in America ("Does Classical Dancing Pay?"), Hurok chose to divide classical dancing into "toe" and "interpretive." "Toe" dancers, he said, could "to some extent" make a living at what they did, but "interpretive" dancers could do so "only in exceptional circumstances." (The Duncan Dancers, he added, were such an exception.) This was because toe dancers, with their classical training, could, unlike interpretive dancers, be hired for movies, revues, musical comedy, and vaudeville, receiving about $50 a week—enough to "just get by." Dancing in the ballet at the Metropolitan Opera, they would receive $18 a week.

There were still very few employment opportunities for classically trained dancers, Hurok stressed. "An actress has hundreds of companies to go into; a classical dancer has only some half-dozen." But he did see the possibility for the audience to grow. "More dancing troupes, put out in one way or another, may educate the public to attend a dance recital as they now attend the recitals of solo singers or instrumentalists."

Francis Coppicus, the manager of Diaghilev's 1916 American tour for Otto Kahn and now one of Hurok's major competitors, basically agreed when he was interviewed for the same article. "There are some things in life which are always destined for limited popularity. Classical dancing is one of those. . . . The public won't pay to see concert dancing unless the dancer is very famous or has a big troupe with him or her." But Coppicus was more pessimistic about the future and advised dancers to concentrate on vaudeville or musical comedy, since he saw no likelihood of a classical concert tour. In this, of course, Coppicus proved mistaken, as he would see soon enough, when Hurok scored popular successes touring Mary Wigman and the Monte Carlo Ballet Russe.

Another significant development in the field of American dance around 1930, and one important to Hurok's business, was the slow but steady increase in the number of serious dance writers and publications. *American Dancer* started up in 1927, *Dance* magazine in 1926, and *Dance Observer* in 1933. Even more influential than the appearance of these relatively specialized journals, however, was John Martin's appointment in 1927 as dance writer, and a year later as staff dance critic, at the august *New York Times*. Well informed, witty, and fair, Martin, "the first American dance critic," did a great deal to educate the American public. Always aware of the power of the press, Hurok carefully cultivated Martin, who covered Hurok's dance attractions extensively and intelligently. Martin also conducted lecture-demonstrations on various aspects of dance at the New School in New York from 1930 to 1940. At last, there was an American journalist who could write about dance as something other than an exotic athletic feat.

Martin, then thirty-seven, wrote enthusiastically of Mary Wigman, the celebrated German dancer whom Hurok finally lured to America in late 1930, for example. By this time, Wigman (1886–1973) was well established across Europe as an avant-garde choreographer and performer. Dark and gloomy, often called "expressionistic," her dances bore forbidding titles like *Face of the Night* and *Witch Dance*, and often had her kneeling, crouching, swirling, crawling, creeping, stomping—or just lying still on the stage floor. Although she disliked explaining what her dances "meant," they seemed to deal with subconscious spiritual and psychological processes, and with abstractions rather than with personalities. In another departure from tradition, she sought to assert the primacy of movement and dance over music, usually commissioning new music for each of her dances, or even dispensing with it altogether. Regarded as a guru by the many students who swarmed to her school in Dresden, Wigman—like Isadora—strove to challenge and disturb her audiences, not just entertain them. She regarded her art as a religious experience. By no means a conventional beauty, she was able to use her imposing, heavy stature to surprising advantage.

Having heard Wigman praised by both Isadora and Pavlova, Hurok had been trying to persuade her to make an American tour under his management at least since 1927. At first she refused, citing her many responsibilities at home. But at last she relented under the force of Hurok's encouragement and persistence. He had followed her to the Alps to press his case. "I finally yielded one summer evening when I was vacationing at a lake called Wiesen in Switzerland," she wrote some years later. "It was one of those clear, star-drenched nights. I felt as if I were receiving an offer of marriage." No one could beat Hurok at charming the pants—or skirts—off artists he had determined to add to his list.

Even after she had agreed to Hurok's proposal, the prospect of performing in America scared Wigman.

> I anticipated my coming with mixed emotions. Other artists had told me that Americans were so busy building higher skyscrapers and better automobiles that they had no time or energy left for the appreciation of serious art. Still others told me, with equal irresponsibility, that Americans wanted only that kind of dancing provided by the Tiller Girls or the Rockettes.
>
> However, I remembered the type of American girls that came to my school in Dresden. They were different from the European girls who danced with such deadly seriousness and who analyzed their emotions, turned their minds so deeply inward that they lost spontaneity. The American students gave themselves to the dance freely, instinctively, yet not thoughtlessly. They had a spontaneous vitality which I adored. For it is just that quality which is needed in the directness and candor of the modern dance.

Hurok was pleasantly surprised to discover that Wigman already had numerous devoted followers in the United States, many of them "quite mad." They turned out in force for her first performance in New York at the Chanin Theater, and although the response didn't equal the scandals that had surrounded Isadora's American appearances, Wigman became an overnight sensation. As usual, of course, Hurok had engineered a shrewd advance publicity campaign, linking her to Pavlova and Duncan as one of the great dance pioneers and making the event an irresistible must-see. For help in this effort, he hired a bright young fellow who had returned from a recent trip to Germany a committed Wigman fan.

His name was Gerald Goode. Goode proved so successful in this first assignment that Hurok made him the head of his publicity department, where he produced brilliant results for the next fifteen years. Indeed, Hurok owed a great deal of his success to the loyal support of Goode and of his faithful secretary, Mae Frohman. (She had been with Hurok since the days of his bankruptcy). Between them, they wrote virtually all of the countless press releases and letters that emerged from Hurok's agency. Hurok still had trouble composing his thoughts in grammatical English and happily assigned that chore to others. According to several of Hurok's artists, Frohman also lent him money, worked endless overtime hours, and sacrificed her personal life to his business. He was a genius at motivating and inspiring the people who worked for him, making them feel (despite low pay and few benefits) like they were part of a marvelous loving family presided over by a benevolent dictator, "Papa Hurok."

Even though he admitted—through his ghost-writer Ruth Goode, Gerald's wife—that Mary Wigman was a bit highbrow for his taste ("Occasionally I wondered whether I was offering the public a form of entertainment or a course in the philosophy of Nietzsche and Schopenhauer with a glance at Sigmund Freud"), Hurok was delighted when the crowds lined up to see this large, stuffy, rather humorless woman, who must have seemed to his vaudeville-minded competitors the most unlikely of attractions.

The insatiable American appetite for "human interest stories," brilliantly exploited by Hurok and Goode, amused and exhausted Wigman, who said later that it seemed "as if all the journalists of the country were converging upon me. There were mornings when I got up expecting to find a photographer under the bed." To the many people who asked what her dances meant, she replied, "whatever you want them to mean. If I could have expressed them in words, I would have been a poet, not a dancer."

Like Nijinsky and Isadora before her, Wigman also had a brush with the law on her first American tour. A Mr. Powell Crichton of the New York Sabbath Committee issued a complaint about her Sunday performance which led a New York City police patrolman to issue a summons to the dancer and Hurok. When at the trial it became clear that Miss Wigman was "just making motions to a piano accompaniment before an audience that paid to watch the performance," the judge ruled that this did not constitute a violation of the Sabbath law and dismissed the complaint. Needless to say, neither the free publicity nor the whiff of scandal hurt business.

Wigman's 1930 American tour proved so successful both financially and artistically that Hurok brought her back the next two seasons. By the end of the second tour, she was losing patience with the endless reporters who asked her the same trivial questions. When "another publicity hyena" importuned her in the lobby of a Los Angeles hotel immediately after a cross-country train trip and asked her what she ate to preserve her figure, she snapped, " 'Raw meat.' A few hours later I received a wire from my impresario in New York: 'Congratulations. That was the best possible publicity. Signed Sol Hurok.' These hastily spoken words had been exploited as: 'Mary Wigman, the high priestess of the dance, eats raw meat.' "

For her third and last American tour in 1932–33, Wigman brought her group of twelve dancers, clones of herself. Audiences and critics were considerably less enthusiastic this time around. "Her ample presence required no reinforcement; so that these Teutonic Amazons seemed extraneous," wrote one. Hurok was more frank: "It was a dismal flop." Even so, Wigman's tours had heightened the public's consciousness of and interest in dance, both modern and classical, and could even be said to have been instrumental in the success of Martha Graham, whose highly introspective, often ugly choreographic style had a great deal in common with Wigman's. For Hurok, the risky venture of presenting Wigman proved to be another financial and public-relations triumph, and served to further solidify his reputation as America's premier dance impresario.

But any manager is only as good as his next attraction. Having laid the groundwork, Hurok followed up immediately on Wigman's success with two other imported dancers, both well known in Europe, and both recommended to him by Pavlova: Vicente Escudero from Spain and Uday Shan-Kar from India.

When Escudero, who had been scheduled to tour the United States with Pavlova in 1932, performed his program of wild gypsy dances with his partners Carmita and Carmela for the first time in America on January 17, 1932, at the Chanin Theatre in New York, he attracted "one of the most brilliant audiences of the season." This was due in part to Hurok's careful publicity campaign, which had capitalized on Escudero's popularity among "the *Vogue, Vanity Fair* and *Harper's Bazaar* set," whose stylish members had heard of him in Paris. Soon this diminutive, intense "peacock" and his "elemental art" became the toast of Manhattan. Audiences packed in, eager to experience the ferocious insolence of his *Farruca*, set to Spanish folk tunes, or the sophistication of his interpretation of the

Miller's dance from Manuel de Falla's *Three-Cornered Hat*, with its Picasso costumes. At Escudero's second sold-out performance, he was forced to give almost as many encores as regular numbers. Hurok brought him back the next year and sent him on tour to the West Coast.

Uday Shan-Kar was no less successful. He had danced extensively with Pavlova and had even introduced her to the traditions of Indian dancing. Shan-Kar created two ballets for Pavlova that were later incorporated in her *Oriental Impressions*, partnered her in *Radha Krishna*, and toured with her through Canada, Mexico, and the United States. It was Pavlova who encouraged Shan-Kar to concentrate on the dance traditions of India rather than to learn Western classical ballet. By the time he made his solo debut in New York, then, in late December 1932, Shan-Kar was well known among dance enthusiasts, including John Martin, who had written a long advance piece for the *New York Times* calling his appearance "one of the most provocative and delightful events of the dance season." For his part, Hurok was optimistic about how well Shan-Kar would do, but "I never anticipated his being a smash hit." What drew the predominantly female sold-out houses, Hurok believed, was Shan-Kar's sex appeal, enhanced by the adoring female dancers who surrounded and worshiped him like some Hindu god. He was received as a matinee idol.

With this string of commercial and artistic successes, Hurok had by the end of 1932 firmly established himself as New York's—and America's—leading presenter of dance events. Amid pervasive economic and social insecurity, with millions out of work and the national income less than half what it had been in 1929, his operation continued to grow and prosper, perhaps because—like booming Hollywood—it offered a public weary of their troubles a chance to escape into an exotic and worry-free world where life and everyone in it was beautiful. On Christmas night, only six weeks after Franklin Roosevelt had won a convincing victory over Herbert Hoover, Hurok opened an "International Dance Festival" at the New Yorker Theater. It featured performances by Mary Wigman and her group, Shan-Kar and his dancers, and Escudero, at prices ranging from $1.10 to $3.30 per ticket. Widely publicized as the biggest dance event in many seasons (and perhaps ever), the festival further solidified Hurok's credibility and reputation. He had found his niche.

But Hurok knew that it was important to diversify, and he continued to present a wide variety of nondance attractions. During the 1932–33 season he also brought on tour to the United States the Wiener Saengerknaben (The Vienna Choir Boys), which would prove very lucrative, and the Teatro dei Piccoli puppet theater from Rome, which would not.

Nor did Hurok neglect his wife. As a special present to Emma, he presented her at New York's Cort Theater in a return engagement of Yascha Yushny's variety show, *The Bluebird*. (He also made sure that both Wigman and Escudero occupied prominent boxes on opening night.) This new edition of the show, which had been touring through Europe for the last several years, relied—like the one that had been seen in New York in 1924—heavily on Russian nostalgia and color. "There are songs of the mischievous schoolroom," wrote Brooks Atkinson in a generally favorable review, "of St. Petersburg in the snowy season, of a cheese market in Holland, of gibbering gossips around a samovar. There are gypsy ballads, the glees of a Cossack chorus, and there is the regulation Volga boatmen's song, too consciously staged. There is a comic music box number, set with the gauche dolls of Switzerland. There is a spinning Boyar dance and Isa Kremer sings folk songs in several languages, including English."

Atkinson makes no mention of Emma's contribution to the show, though her name (given as Emma Runich) is listed among the principals. Even with Hurok's backing, Emma never did become a star in America, although she appeared with various similar revues in New York and on tour frequently through the 1930s. Her failure to catch on came as no surprise to the discerning Alexandra Danilova, who saw Emma perform both in Europe and in the United States. "She had a small role in the show—which was a sort of artistic salad—in the early days, but it got bigger after she met Hurok. She had always wanted to be a singer, and especially loved to do the song 'Bublichki,' about a street vendor trying to seduce passers-by into buying her rolls. She sang in a gypsy style, very tragically—always sad songs. People would clap because she was Mrs. Hurok, but she was nothing special."

By far the most significant event in Hurok's career to date as a dance impresario, and one of the most important moments in the history of American dance, was the American premiere of the Monte Carlo Ballet Russe at the St. James Theatre on December 22, 1933. By presenting this colorful and eclectic troupe, composed primarily of former members of the Ballets Russes de Serge Diaghilev, Hurok launched the process that would lead by the late 1930s to the permanent transfer of most of the Russian Imperial ballet tradition to the New World. (The Soviet ballet tradition would develop in a very different fashion.) Born in St. Petersburg, nurtured in Paris, these dancers and their theatrical culture would continue their work in New York, where their art would blend with the vitality and enthusiasm of the American scene. With their arrival, the center of the dance world shifted across the Atlantic and has stayed here ever since. Throughout the process, Hurok would serve as the high priest of popularization.

The convoluted story of the Monte Carlo Ballet Russe and its many similarly named relatives (Les Ballets Russes de Monte Carlo, Ballets Russes de Monte Carlo, Col. W. de Basil's Ballets Russes, Covent Garden Russian Ballet, Original Ballet Russe) reads like a Dostoyevski novella full of impossible names, fatal attractions, homicidal jealousies, passionate liaisons, and noisy scandals. It has inspired exposés, autobiographies, biographies, musicals (*On Your Toes*), films (*The Red Shoes*), and lawsuits. Always colorful both onstage and off, the cast of characters (dancers, choreographers, designers, musicians, composers) made great copy and almost immediately caught America's fancy. Following the glamorous, always complicated life of this histrionic troupe provided at least as much entertainment as the latest installment of the new radio soap operas of the mid-1930s—one of the most popular of which, not incidentally, was called *Back Stage Wife*.

For Hurok, who had never presented a complete ballet company before, the Monte Carlo Ballet Russe (and its successors) provided endless material for the "human interest stories" that were the fuel on which his operation ran. Managing this motley group of egos was also a useful lesson in logistics, psychology, and anarchy that prepared him for later, even more epic ventures: Sadler's Wells, the Moiseyev Dance Company, the Bolshoi, the Kirov.

Perhaps it was his trials with the Monte Carlo Ballet Russe that led Hurok to make his oft-quoted observation (which he stole from Oscar Hammerstein): "This isn't a business. It's a disease."

But where did the company come from, and how did Hurok find it?

The fairy-tale kingdom of Monte Carlo was closely associated with the first of all the Ballets Russes companies—Ballets Russes de Serge Diaghilev—almost since its beginnings on the eve of World War I. In this sun-drenched paradise on the Riviera, the company found a supportive financial and artistic atmosphere in which to prepare, rehearse, and often premiere new ballets that later went on to face more difficult audiences in Paris and London. So it seemed entirely natural when a new company composed of performers from Diaghilev's troupe coalesced there in the spring of 1932, nearly three years after his death.

This new enterprise was organized by two very different individuals. The first was René Blum, the ballet director of the Monte Carlo Opera and a former patron of the writer Marcel Proust, "a mild-mannered man of exquisite taste who, apparently, was loved by every dancer who worked for him." Blum provided the artistic leadership.

The second was Colonel Wassily de Basil. De Basil's real name was Vasily Grigorevich Voskresensky. A hard-bitten Cossack officer who had served in the tsarist army, he distinguished himself in the Persian campaign of 1916 and participated in negotiations between the anti-Communist allies and the Bolsheviks around the Caspian Sea in 1918. Like all good Cossacks (and like Hurok), de Basil made his way by playing all ends against the middle. To this new ballet venture in Monte Carlo, de Basil brought his experience working as assistant to Prince Alexis Zereteli at the L'Opera Russe a Paris in the late 1920s, his legendary military discipline, lots of promises, a certain exotic *je ne sais quoi,* and "a natural propensity for the devious and the Machiavellian." As time went on, outmaneuvering his colleagues through impossibly convoluted ruses, de Basil gained increasing control over the company and its disastrous finances. One of the very few people who could get the better of this indefatigable schemer was Hurok.

Well respected by Diaghilev's leading dancers and choreographers, the mild-mannered Blum was able to attract an impressive array of talent to the new company. George Balanchine signed on as *maître de ballet.* Serge Grigoriev agreed to become *régisseur général,* the same job he had done for Diaghilev. Boris Kochno, librettist for

Prodigal Son and many other ballets, was named artistic collaborator. French painter Christian Berard was engaged to do sets and costumes.

Never content to rest on his creative laurels, *maître de ballet* Balanchine set out immediately to discover new dancers who would set Les Ballets Russes de Monte Carlo (that was their new name) apart from Diaghilev's company. He came across three prodigies. Irina Baronova was twelve, Tamara Toumanova thirteen, and Tatiana Riabouchinska fourteen. Baronova and Toumanova had been studying with Olga Preobrajenska, and Riabouchinska with Mathilde Kschessinskaya, absorbing the wisdom and experience these two great teachers had gained as leading ballerinas at the Mariinsky Theater. Girls this age would never have been considered suitable to take leading roles at the Imperial theaters, but Balanchine had already shown himself more than willing to defy received tradition. He set about building ballets especially for them.

The first was *Cotillon*, set to music by Emmanuel Chabrier. Still considered by many as Balanchine's masterpiece, it featured Toumanova, a black-haired, dark-eyed, almost Oriental beauty, in an enigmatic tale of dark fate and youthful high spirits. Also in the cast were David Lichine (his real name was the unfashionably Jewish Liechtenstein), another young Russian-born dancer who had appeared with Pavlova; and Leon Woizikowsky, a Pole who had taken many leading roles in Diaghilev's troupe. *Cotillon* was first presented in a preview performance at the Opera de Monte Carlo on January 17, 1932, and then repeated as part of the first official performance by Les Ballets Russes de Monte Carlo on April 12, 1932. Also on the program was Balanchine's *La Concurrence*. As in all of Balanchine's work, both ballets stressed theatricality and characterization over simple technique.

Already by early summer of 1932, however, strains were showing in the relationship between de Basil and Balanchine. They disagreed over the artistic direction of the company: De Basil wanted to "peddle nostalgia" to White Russian exiles, while Balanchine envisioned a more vital aesthetic and a wider audience. But de Basil had the upper hand. Before he had the chance to resign, Balanchine was replaced with Leonide Massine, another

Diaghilev alumnus. Massine's more recent credits included staging big dance extravaganzas (his most celebrated was *Scheherazade*) between movies at New York's Roxy, and a production of *The Rite of Spring* in Philadelphia in 1930 with Leopold Stokowski, the Philadelphia Orchestra, and Martha Graham as the Chosen Maiden. At the time, then, Massine was better known than Balanchine in the United States and at the height of his powers as a dancer. De Basil's decision to go with what he perceived as the "big names" (Massine and the Diaghilev heritage) rather than with the new and adventurous (Balanchine) exhibited his conservative taste. It was a taste that his future collaborator Hurok shared.

By the time Hurok first saw Les Ballets Russes de Monte Carlo during their engagement at the Theatre des Champs-Élysées in Paris in the summer of 1932, Balanchine was already on his way out. None of this influenced Hurok's reaction. He loved what he saw and, he later claimed, immediately signed up the troupe for an American tour. He became convinced of the rightness of this decision when his PR man Gerald Goode later sent a cable from Paris, raving about Les Ballets Russes de Monte Carlo and advising him to book them as soon as possible. If a young American who had never seen the Diaghilev troupe could get this excited about ballet, Hurok reasoned, then there really must be a market.

On his annual summer excursion to Europe in 1933, Hurok saw the company again at the Alhambra Theatre in London. At one of these performances, he met the distinguished balletomane Arnold Haskell. The American impresario did not strike Haskell as much of a connoisseur; in fact he demonstrated "little knowledge of ballet." Hurok's response to Woizikowsky's restaging of Fokine's masterpiece *Carnaval* (first given by Diaghilev in 1910) was that it "was too short and trivial and 'needed some meat added to it." Haskell did admire Hurok's enthusiasm and passion, however.

As always, Hurok carefully prepared the ground for his new attraction. The newspapers cooperated nicely, running numerous advance stories about the company and even reviewing its 1933 Paris and London seasons. Soon after Franklin Roosevelt's inauguration as president on March 4, 1933, in the wake of crippling bank failures, massive unemployment, bread riots, and hunger marches, when the idea of launching a new and financially ambitious venture like the Monte Carlo Ballet Russe (this was the name under which Les Ballets Russes de Monte Carlo were presented in the United States) seemed an extravagant folly, John Martin reported that "financial conditions notwithstanding," Hurok had announced that he was committed to bringing the troupe to New York in the autumn. Perhaps Hurok, an old-time socialist, had confidence that FDR would really accomplish the idealistic Democratic goals he had articulated in his successful campaign against Hoover. Perhaps he believed that the economy was bound to improve. Perhaps he knew that audiences needed entertainment now more than ever. Whatever his reasoning, it proved right.

Martin added that he hoped the arrival of the Monte Carlo Ballet Russe would "vitalize" the indigenous dance movement, leading "American forces to the point where they will feel able to undertake production of their own. The time seems ripe." Martin was right. Within a few years, several American-based ballet companies would be in operation, including those that would eventually become the New York City Ballet and American Ballet Theatre. Many of the dancers whom Hurok brought to New York with the Monte Carlo Ballet Russe in 1933 would be involved.

In preparing for the late December opening, Hurok and his minions set about cultivating New York's business and social elite—just as Diaghilev had done so successfully in Paris and London. Gerald Goode organized a Sponsors' Committee. It was headed by a surviving member of the Russian Imperial family, the Grand Duchess Marie of Russia, and by Otto Kahn, one of Manhattan's most well connected bankers and the longtime chairman of the board of the Metropolitan Opera. (In addition to bringing Diaghilev's Ballets Russes to America in 1916, Kahn had also backed Morris Gest's presentation of the *Chauve-Souris* and the Moscow Art Theatre.)

Hurok sent out personal letters to New York's leading philanthropists asking them to support what he promised would be "the outstanding artistic event of the decade." Such groundwork lent the upcoming performances by the Monte Carlo company cachet and a place in the social pages. Two of the performances during the first week of the run were held as fashionable benefits for charitable causes favored by the city's upper crust, and Hurok's efforts lined up $10,000 in advance sales.

When at last the company arrived on December 20, 1933, on the liner *Lafayette*, seasick and anxious, Hurok was at the pier to meet them. There were sixty-four dancers, each of whom presented an individual immigration problem. Some were Soviet citizens, who always aroused the suspicion of the U.S. Immigration officials. Others had Nansen passports, issued as temporary documents by the League of Nations to stateless persons in the aftermath of World War I and the Russian Revolution.

Besides the dancers, the entourage included "eleven Mamas, four Papas, three cats and two monkeys." Hurok had incurred huge expenses in transporting the company, its costumes, and its scenery, and now he had to pay salaries. The leading dancers received $100 a month, which had to cover all their expenses. Members of the corps de ballet had to make do on even less. To save money, they lived five and six to a hotel room, playing what ballerina Alicia Markova later called the "Army Game": "One person would book into an hotel, and six others would creep up to the room, bribe the maid to bring extra towels and other necessities, and camp there for the night. Only by this means could they actually afford to stay in a hotel at all."

Hurok was not happy that the company included no established young stars, which he considered essential to its commercial success in New York. All the American public wanted, he complained to composer Nicolas Nabokov, was "big names. . . . You tell them this is the best ballet company outside of Russia, but all they want is Pavlova and Nijinsky! And where am I going to get them Pavlova and Nijinsky?" Hurok and de Basil immediately clashed over the quality of the ballerinas. According to Arnold Haskell, "the first thing" Hurok asked de Basil the day the company landed in New York was "Why don't you get rid of some of these old girls?"

But just two days later, on Friday, December 22, 1933, the Monte Carlo Ballet Russe, "the first classically trained ballet to present a season here in a generation," gave its American debut at the St. James Theatre—"old girls" and all. The glittering audience included many members of European royal families and such cultural celebrities as Rachmaninoff, conductor Leopold Stokowski, Pierre Matisse (son of the artist Henry Matisse) and the publisher Condé Nast, who had given the company lavish coverage in *Vanity Fair*.

The program included three works. Two were choreographed by Massine: *Les Présages*, a setting of Tchaikovsky's Fifth Symphony, and *Le Beau Danube*, based on music by Johann Strauss as arranged by Roger Desormiere. The other was Balanchine's *La Concurrence*. (Balanchine himself had arrived in New York two months earlier to found the School of American Ballet with Lincoln Kirstein.) On John Martin, *Le Beau Danube* and *La Concurrence* made the most favorable impression, while *Les Présages* was dismissed as overly emotional and banal. Martin's opinion was a sign of things to come: Balanchine, de Basil's misgivings notwithstanding, would have a much more successful career as a choreographer in Europe and America than Massine.

After the performance, the company and a selected group of socialites retired to the Savoy-Plaza for the first of the elegant gala ballet suppers for which Hurok would become famous. Prohibition had just been repealed, and the champagne flowed freely, consumed out of ballet slippers made expressly for the occasion. The stars of the evening were the irresistible troika of Riabouchinska, Toumanova, and Baronova—jealously guarded by their ambitious stage mothers. Soon afterward, they would become known as the "baby ballerinas," a name bestowed by Arnold Haskell. If the Monte Carlo Ballet Russe had too few familiar stars like Pavlova, and too many unsuitable "old girls," then Hurok would take matters in hand. He would focus his publicity machine on the "new girls," the three prodigies whom Balanchine had discovered and trained.

Accordingly, during the coming months he fed reporters colorful accounts of their lives in Russia and elsewhere (not unlike the ones he had made up about himself) that mixed fact and fiction with wild abandon. They also contributed to the exotic, energetic atmosphere surrounding the company. Here's an example:

> Toumanova had been born in a boxcar somewhere in Siberia en route to Shanghai and freedom. Baronova made it in a leaky skiff that was tossed across the waters to Rumania. Riabouchinska, imprisoned in her parents' Moscow home, was pointed (along with other family members) in the direction of possible escape through the

offices of a loyal servant and, with jewels sewed into clothing, made it by caravan and boat to Western Europe.

Rumors also circulated that Hurok was in love with Toumanova—just like the stories that had circulated about his "romance" with Pavlova twelve years earlier. In fact Hurok (who always had a special fondness for dark-haired ladies) did develop a closer relationship with Toumanova than with the other two "babies." She even forgave him and de Basil for luring her to America under false pretenses by telling her that Balanchine was rejoining the Monte Carlo Ballet Russe in New York.

Placing his box office hopes on the drawing power of these three innocent girls whose image he had helped to create in the mold of Hollywood starlets, Hurok went so far as to take out an insurance policy on Riabouchinska that would pay him off if she married.

The newspapers' fascination with youth and what she considered trivial gossip dismayed one of the veteran dancers in the troupe, the indomitable and feisty Alexandra Danilova. Then thirty years old, she was already considered one of the greatest dancers of the twentieth century. In Europe the reporters had asked serious questions about art, she complained, but "American reporters wanted to put their noses into everything. . . . So when the reporters would come after me, I would tell them, 'I am not blond and I am not sixteen, so you don't want to interview me,' and I would walk away."

American journalists were even less interested in the company's male dancers, who were still regarded as freakish and of dubious sexuality. Allegedly, Hurok, who prided himself on his ability to judge what the public wanted and paid rather less attention to "what was good in itself," used to go backstage and tell the men to stuff tissue paper in the front of their tights. It was important to satisfy the ladies.

Despite all the advance publicity, the performances during the first week of the engagement did not sell out. Once the socialites had come and gone, the audience dwindled down to the dancers' parents and company staff. In fact, according to Riabouchinska, "the theater was almost empty. People still didn't really know what ballet was in America." And even if the performances had sold out, the St. James had too few seats to make the run profitable. Against such odds, and with an enormous public relations budget, Hurok was losing lots of money. He and Emma, in her son's words, "were so poor they didn't have a pot to piss in."

No stranger to financial reversals, Hurok remained confident—at least publicly—in the ultimate success of his enterprise. He told the dancers not to worry. Several factors were working in his favor: the growing audience for dance; good reviews; word-of-mouth advertising; the repeal of Prohibition, which led to a more liberated social climate and a desire for entertainment; the establishment in November 1933 of diplomatic relations with the Soviet government, which led to a greatly increased interest in Russians of all kinds; and the more optimistic economic and social environment created by the policies and attitudes of Roosevelt's New Deal administration.

And there was one more thing. RCA—the parent corporation that now controlled NBC and its affiliated organizations, including the National Broadcasting and Concert Bureau under whose auspices Hurok's agency operated—had just moved into a spectacular new seventy-story skyscraper in Rockefeller Center. Hurok Attractions now moved there, too, to Room 523 at 30 Rockefeller Plaza. In the heart of midtown just off Fifth Avenue, glamorous Radio City with its lavish music hall, towering Christmas tree, and celebrity-filled skating rink would soon become one of the most famous addresses in a town where location was everything. To the rest of the nation, it would come to symbolize the pulsing heart of the American entertainment industry. To Hurok, the boy from Pogar, these ultramodern new headquarters at the very center of the cultural and public relations universe represented a big move up in the world. The King of Ballet had found a throne.

Part II

■ CHAPTER NINE ■

Holy Russia on Tour

"The gnome from moonland plays the Chopin air,
The ballerina glides out of the wings,
Like all the Aprils of forgotten Springs."

—*John Masefield, "Ballet Russe"*

THE NEW YEAR 1934 began uncertainly, with the American economy still deeply troubled and the dollar devalued. But business for the Monte Carlo Ballet Russe at the St. James Theatre was looking up.

Ever vigilant over box office receipts and up to his habitual fedora in expenses, Hurok had been asking critics and friends to explain why the troupe had not been drawing well after the first few society-sponsored performances just before Christmas. What W. J. Henderson, the influential critic for the New York *Sun*, told him was that New Yorkers expected a more traditional prewar Diaghilev-style repertoire, not abstract "avant-garde" creations like Massine's *Les Présages*. This allegorical setting of Tchaikovsky's Fifth Symphony might please more knowledgeable European audiences, Henderson and others advised, but it was too sophisticated for the less experienced Americans. Give them something simpler. Something more familiar.

Always ready, like an overindulgent parent, to please his customers, Hurok accordingly asked de Basil to bring more of the

Diaghilev classics back into the repertoire. Whether because these more familiar ballets really did have greater popular appeal or because New Yorkers—encouraged by word-of-mouth advertising—were gradually learning to like this exotic new art form on their own, attendance rose.

The improvement was so dramatic, in fact, that Hurok ran into trouble with the "stop clause" in his contract with the St. James. Since he had been understandably uncertain about how well the Ballet Russe would draw and was unwilling to take the entire risk for failure upon himself, he had signed a contract with the theater which provided for the sharing of both expenses and box office income. Under this arrangement (unlike a straightforward rental fee, which gives the presenter more freedom), the theater can prevent the attraction from leaving if ticket sales remain above a certain fixed level. That is called the "stop" point. Having fixed this point very low in order to protect himself, Hurok now found himself a hostage to rising box office receipts. Although the houses were still not full, neither were they empty enough that the theater management would let the company leave to begin the short tour that Hurok had already booked in a few eastern and midwestern cities.

The solution? Divide and conquer. Hurok and de Basil separated the company into two troupes, keeping one at the St. James and sending the other on the road. This proved a brilliant tactic, since it allowed New York to get to know the company even better and prepared the ground for the next season's much more extensive tour in the American provinces. Characteristically, Hurok also turned what could have been a problem into a public relations coup. Newspaper advertisements announced that the Ballet Russe engagement had been extended for two weeks beyond its original January 28 closing "by popular acclamation." Nothing makes a hit like saying it's a hit.

Closely following W. J. Henderson's advice, Hurok had the New York troupe (which included Baronova, Riabouchinska, Lichine, and Woizikowsky) give a single traditional program for the next few weeks at the St. James: *Les Sylphides, Petrushka*, and *Prince Igor*, all of which had been given by Diaghilev's troupe in New York in 1916 and 1917. On the road, Danilova, Toumanova, and Massine danced in *Les Sylphides*, Balanchine's *Concurrence* and *Le Beau Dan-*

ube. For these highly cultured and sophisticated dancers, who had moved in the highest circles in St. Petersburg, Paris, and London, turning pirouettes in gritty industrial towns like Reading, Pennsylvania, came as something of a shock.

"Most American audiences had never seen ballet and didn't know anything about it," Danilova remembered years later. "We could sense their astonishment from the stage. I loved dancing for these audiences; I knew that I was introducing them to ballet. By the end of that first American tour, I was longing to get back to Paris. But after New York, Paris seemed small and insignificant. From then on, I was always happy to return to America."

Eager to imitate New York's high society, and impressed by the stylish national magazines that were featuring the glamorous Ballet Russe in many articles and photo spreads ("Ballerinas in Bathing Suits"), the wealthy and influential citizens of the small towns where Danilova and her colleagues performed happily used the company as an excuse to dress up and feel elegant.

As would become very clear the next season, American socialites, both *nouveaux riches* and just plain *riches,* were hungry for the opportunity to flaunt their appreciation of culture and the better things in life. As shrewdly marketed under the marquee "S. Hurok Presents," a label that was now acquiring its own snob appeal, the ballet would prove a perfect vehicle in their relentless struggle for upward mobility and respectability. Then, too, the fairy-tale world of the dance held great appeal for a public weary of depressing economic realities. "The anguish of the Great Depression was so intensely real," writes one historian of the period, "that the public generally preferred escapism and sweetness in their entertainment and art." Hurok was happy to oblige.

But he was also careful to prepare his neophyte audiences for what they were going to see. "Good as it was, it had to be sold to them," wrote Arnold Haskell, who accompanied the troupe on that first tour. "Sol Hurok did this in an inspired fashion, not merely by advertisement but by the most skilled public relations. I know that his own great enthusiasm played a very great role in establishing ballet. He was tireless. Wherever we went newspapers were fed with material, clubs and organisations were given talks and lectures and the way was prepared not only for that season but for the future."

In the cities it visited that first season, the Monte Carlo Ballet Russe reinvigorated the social scene. The Minneapolis *Journal* breathlessly reported that the company's impending arrival in St. Paul would be "the incentive for many dinners." After the fact, the newspaper declared that the performances had stimulated "the largest attendance of out-of-town persons ever attracted to St. Paul for a similar event."

Meanwhile, back in New York, attendance had finally fallen below the "stop clause," and Hurok was free to move the company on to Chicago, where it was reunited with the road company for a hugely successful engagement at the magnificent Auditorium Theatre. The troupe's February performances in the Windy City drew an astonishing thirty thousand people and were pronounced "the most brilliant event of the winter, long after the winter is regarded as over and done." The leading ladies of Chicago society vied to honor the dancers at teas and receptions, and the impressed de Basil began speaking publicly about settling the Ballet Russe permanently in America.

With a huge hit on his hands, Hurok seized the moment. He decided to extend the American tour through April, booking additional performances in New York and elsewhere for what he was now billing as "the most glamorous spectacle in the theatre today." Encouraged by vociferous overflow audiences that turned out to see the Ballet Russe at Philadelphia's Academy of Music in early March, he even chose that city (where, he reminded every reporter in sight, he had first come to appreciate serious music) as the site of the world premiere of a new work choreographed by Leonide Massine.

What eventually became known as *Union Pacific*—which is widely regarded as the first American ballet—had been germinating in Massine's mind for some years. When on tour in the United States with Diaghilev's troupe in 1916, Massine saw some Sioux Indians perform their war dances in Washington, D.C. They inspired him to begin collaborating with Diaghilev's music director, the conductor Ernest Ansermet, on a ballet based on the legend of Pocahontas, using tribal dances, ceremonies, and rites. Nothing came of this project, but Massine never abandoned the hope of creating a ballet on American material.

In December 1933, he shared this idea with Hurok, who was

intrigued but (as usual) cautious. Shortly afterward, Hurok happened to meet the Russian émigré composer Nicolas Nabokov on a train bound for Philadelphia. (Among many other things, Nabokov had composed music for Massine's 1928 ballet *Ode*.) Hurok now suggested to Nabokov that he should talk to Massine about this American project. As it turned out, Nabokov was also friendly with the famous American poet Archibald MacLeish, who had already told the composer of his own long-standing desire to write a ballet libretto on an American subject: the race to complete the first transcontinental (Union Pacific) railroad in 1869.

And so, Nabokov brought the choreographer Massine and the poet MacLeish together with yet another friend, Gerald Murphy, an American-born connoisseur of the arts who had recently returned from a sojourn in Paris. Murphy owned a large collection of early cylinder recordings of turn-of-the-century American popular and folk music. This material, Nabokov believed, would provide a young American composer like Aaron Copland or Virgil Thomson with the appropriate musical building blocks for a railroad ballet.

When Nabokov told Hurok and "the crooked Colonel" de Basil about his idea for Massine's project, their immediate reaction was "a firm no." When they were told of the existence of this unknown record collection, however, their resistance began to soften. And when Hurok was told that MacLeish's name could surely help raise money for the new ballet, he threw caution to the winds and said: "Then . . . vai . . . not . . . try?" De Basil immediately set to work on the figures and calculated that they needed to raise $25,000.

At this point the project stalled once again. This time the obstacle was the conviction of both Hurok and de Basil, both strong believers in the importance of established "stars," that it would be a mistake to engage a young unknown "serious" American composer to do the score—"even if it was done with other people's money." Finally, MacLeish and Massine broke the deadlock by persuading Nabokov himself to write the music. The idea of a Russian-born composer producing the first "American" ballet seemed to Nabokov more than a little strange, but he finally agreed anyway.

Once all the money had been raised (most of it came from the Barnes Foundation in Philadelphia), Hurok and de Basil told Nabokov to go ahead with the score. By then it was only weeks before the scheduled premiere. Hurok found Nabokov a young orchestrator, Eddie Powell, to help in putting the pieces of American music together; they included popular tunes of the 1870s like "Oh! Susanna," "Pop Goes the Weasel" and "Yankee Doodle," as well as elements of jazz, Dixieland, and Harlem style. Albert Johnson, scenic designer for the 1934 Ziegfeld Follies, was hired to design the sets, and the up-and-coming Irene Sharaff was engaged to do the costumes.

Everyone involved in *Union Pacific* feared the worst. With the company homeless and constantly on tour in poorly equipped theaters, there was no time to prepare a new ballet. Massine taught the exhausted dancers the choreography in hotel ballrooms and lobbies, after their regular evening performances. As the date of the premiere approached, tensions rose and tempers flared. At the dress rehearsal, Nabokov asked Hurok how he liked the music.

"He looked at me with surly eyes and said, 'What d'you mean, the music? Everything about the goddam thing is lousy! Especially in the first act, you have there one sour note. Take it away!' "

And yet, contrary to all expectations, as often happens in the theater, the opening night performance on April 6, 1934, at Philadelphia's Forrest Theater, began well and turned into a triumph. The audience liked the simplicity of this straightforward "American" story of macho frontier builders and their feisty ladies. The cast and collaborators were called out for twenty curtain calls. Massine's choreography was imaginative and energetic. Especially effective was his idea of using dancers lying rigid in brown sacks as the rails and ties of the track under construction.

Union Pacific was a socialist realist fable celebrating the triumph of technology and the building of a new industrial society. Like Hurok himself, the ballet's brawling workmen were immigrants—the Irish heading West, the Chinese heading East, a few Mexicans tossed into the melting pot for good measure, and all of them finally united in their common utilitarian task. Perhaps the fact that only two of the principal dancers, Roland Guerard and Sono Osato, had been born in America (and Osato was a Japanese-American) only served to emphasize that immigration was a fundamental part of the American experience and identity. Besides Guerard as the Cameraman, and Osato, a fifteen-year-old newcomer to the troupe, as the Barman's Assistant, the cast included Massine in the role of the Barman, Toumanova as the Mexican Girl, André Eglevsky as the surveyor of the Irish Workmen, Eugenia Delarova as the Lady Gay, and David Lichine as the Surveyor of the Chinese Workmen.

A few weeks after the Philadelphia premiere, *Union Pacific* traveled to New York, where it encountered a similarly enthusiastic reception. John Martin called it "a highly amusing piece of work." He could not resist pointing out, however, how odd it was that the first American national ballet should have been produced, choreographed, composed, and danced by Russians. "To call the work strictly an American ballet is to stretch a point, for its extremely clever musical score and choreography both approach their American material from an objective angle that has nothing of the native about it," he observed. "It becomes, then, essentially a European ballet on an American theme."

In a program note, the Slavophile de Basil went so far as to proclaim that an American ballet tradition could "only be developed upon the technical and artistic foundation of Russian ballet," a point of view that infuriated the growing ranks of American dancers, composers, and choreographers. This attitude of Russian chauvinism also helps to explain why many of the founding fathers and mothers of American dance later came to view Hurok as an oppressor. At the same time, even they could not deny that *Union Pacific* clearly led the way to other more truly American ballets, notably Eugene Loring's 1938 *Billy the Kid* and Agnes de Mille's 1942 *Rodeo*. Both of these hits had music by Aaron Copland, one of those "unknown" American composers Hurok and de Basil had scorned as box office poison.

Over the next two seasons, *Union Pacific* became one of the most successful works in the Monte Carlo Ballet Russe repertoire. Even so, it brought its librettist and composer virtually no financial reward. Never imagining that this modest, slapdash project would ever enjoy a commercially profitable run, neither MacLeish nor Nabokov bothered to sign a proper contract with Hurok or de Basil. When the ballet turned out to be a hit, they found themselves utterly unprotected by copyright. Nabokov even had trouble collecting the $500 fee de Basil had orally promised to pay him for his services; it was doled out to him in grudging "homeopathic doses" over a period of months. Only years later, after the colonel's death, were Nabokov's original orchestral and piano scores returned to him.

But then Nabokov's experience was hardly unique. As one chronicler of the company has pointed out, virtually no one who worked for it "ended up without a financial grievance."

With the splashy success of *Union Pacific*, Hurok's first season of the Monte Carlo Ballet Russe came to an unexpectedly brilliant conclusion. What he had learned was that America was now ready for ballet. The golden age of opera might be over, but the new era of dance was just beginning. He mused on this development in a rambling interview ("Public Hungering for Beauty, Says Producer of Many Hits") with the Philadelphia *Evening Public Ledger*, which accorded him all the respect and affection due a hometown-boy-made-good. As almost always happened, the interviewer standardized—and neutralized—Hurok's colorful speech, making him sound oddly academic.

> Three years ago I felt there was a decided trend toward the return of beauty and the passing of ugliness. People get enough of ugliness in their daily lives with their trouble and misery at home. When they read the papers they learn of misery elsewhere, in Cuba, in France, in Austria, in Germany, or wherever there happens to be a revolt that particular day. The public cries for relief, and no wonder. For relief I then have given them something beautiful, something unusual each year. They love it.
>
> By beautiful I don't mean something so "highbrow" it is over the heads of every one. Any one can understand the dances and interpretations I bring from Europe. By unusual I mean a change. Grand opera has suffered in their country more from being a "back number" than from the depression. There is too much sameness.
>
> The people of this country, with the exception of a limited group, have grown tired of grand opera. Opera should be remodeled, reformed and reorganized from every standpoint and brought up to date. People have

grown tired of seeing some 220-pound woman of fifty trying to play the part of a twenty-three-year-old lover.

Of course Hurok wasn't the only one in 1934 who saw that dance
was destined to supplant opera and play an increasingly important
role in the performing arts in America. Ballet schools and companies, largely staffed by Russian émigré dancers, were suddenly appearing all over the country. The San Francisco Opera Ballet,
considered America's oldest ballet company, had been founded in
1933, along with the San Francisco Ballet School. Adolph Bolm, another Diaghilev alumnus who had also toured with Pavlova, became
the first chief choreographer there.

Back in New York, an even more important dance institution
was forming around George Balanchine and a young American,
Lincoln Kirstein. After being dropped from the Blum–de Basil company in favor of Massine after its first season in Monte Carlo in
1932, Balanchine had assembled Boris Kochno and some other
former members of the Monte Carlo to create Les Ballets 1933. This
company gave a short but exciting season that year in Paris and
London. Among those in the audience in Paris was Kirstein, a
twenty-six-year-old Harvard-educated connoisseur of art and dance
from a wealthy Rochester family. The experience of witnessing the
"parade of brilliant artistic successes" that Balanchine and Les Ballets 1933 presented at the Theatre des Champs-Élysées (which included masterpieces such as Tchaikovsky's *Mozartiana*, the
Brecht-Weill *Seven Deadly Sins*, and Milhaud's *Les Songes*) in June
and July changed this young man's life forever. In Balanchine,
Kirstein found his artistic idol and his mission.

> Everything he did spoke for the present, of immediacy, by
> surprise, with brilliance: for 1933. There was a magical
> transference of private caprice onto a public platform.
> Studio talk and studio planning were projected in a heroic
> dimension, far larger than life. Everything was intensified
> through the physicality of the dancing itself, through the
> power, athletics, and lyricism of ballet's language. This
> was where I wanted to live. This was what I wanted to do;
> here I was learning how it should be done.

Within months, Kirstein had managed to lure Balanchine, who found himself at loose ends and without any binding European ties, to America with the promise of financial support for a company and a school. Overcoming severe financial and administrative obstacles, Kirstein and his Harvard classmate Edward Warburg found an appropriate space at 637 Madison Avenue. There the School of American Ballet opened on January 1, 1934—even as the Monte Carlo Ballet Russe held forth nearby at the St. James Theatre. To Balanchine's credit, he insisted that the school should come before public performances or anything else, since training a new generation of American dancers for what he envisioned as an American ballet company had to be the first priority.

Unlike Hurok, who found it constitutionally impossible to think more than a few seasons ahead, Balanchine looked forward to future generations. Hurok was a presenter; Balanchine and Kirstein were creators. What they began in 1934, and nurtured through many lean years, would grow into the New York City Ballet, one of the world's great dance companies, guided by an unabashedly elite and "difficult" aesthetic that was the antithesis of Hurok's ballet populism. Despite the many years he devoted to dance and dancers, Hurok never would succeed like they did in building a permanent company.

At first, Kirstein perceived both Hurok and the first Monte Carlo Ballet Russe American tour in 1933–34 as threats to his plans for Balanchine. Later, they came to realize that "such importations could only familiarize America with an alien art, that only after considerable exposure to ballet as appreciated in Europe could this country be willing to accept any kind of indigenous effort." As time went on, the members of the various Ballet Russe companies imported by Hurok came to combine and collaborate more and more often with Balanchine's new troupe, providing important cross-fertilization and mutual inspiration.

It became increasingly clear, however, that Balanchine's company was much more adventurous and avant-garde than the backward-looking collectives overseen by de Basil, Massine, and Hurok. Balanchine, always driven to push the limits and explore the impossible, was the true heir to Diaghilev's restless and questing spirit. Fascinated by the spirit of America, he had no use for the safe Russian nostalgia sold by his less intellectual competitors.

Ballerina Alexandra Danilova knew Balanchine (they lived together in Europe and remained close after coming to America) and Hurok well. She saw them as fundamentally different in personality and taste. "Hurok always thought about selling tickets. Balanchine never did—he thought only about art. They had as little in common as champagne *Veuve Cliquot* and *Coca-Cola*. They were like a hamburger stand and a fine restaurant."

At one point in the mid-1930s, when Hurok had firmly established his reputation as a dance presenter with his increasingly successful tours of the Monte Carlo Ballet Russe, Balanchine asked Danilova to arrange a luncheon with Hurok at the Russian Tea Room, Hurok's favorite New York restaurant, snuggled up next to Carnegie Hall on 57th Street. He wanted to explore whether Hurok might provide financial support, or perhaps sponsor a tour, for his fledgling company. But the meeting, held over traditional Russian *zakuski*, did not go well, as Danilova later recalled:

> When the talk got down to business, they really couldn't understand each other. Balanchine, of course, wanted to have complete artistic control, but Hurok wanted to reserve the right to give his okay, as he did with the de Basil company. And Hurok didn't like the idea that Balanchine and Kirstein wanted to be the directors. Hurok was a simple mortal, unlike Balanchine, and it flattered him to be an artistic director, as well as the general director. But Balanchine wanted no part of that; he always insisted on having things his way artistically. Geniuses like Balanchine are always twenty-five years ahead of their time. By the time we catch up they're already far ahead of us. Kirstein understood that, but not Hurok.

In her work with the Monte Carlo Ballet Russe, Danilova had already been able to observe how Hurok liked to give advice about who should dance and which ballets should be given. After all, he had been presenting dancers for more than ten years, and fancied himself something of a ballet connoisseur. And yet for Hurok, the public remained the most discriminating judge. That was why he urged de Basil and Massine to present pretty young dancers in familiar, unchallenging works, preferably with accessible "stories." Hurok's plebeian taste, and his reverence for Pavlova as an aesthetic model and inspiration, used to make Danilova and her worldly colleagues snicker. After all, they had worked with Diaghilev.

> Everyone knew that Hurok wasn't very well educated. He would always tell us, "You know I brought over Pavlova." And we would say, "Well, so you brought her over. Big deal." He had strictly commercial taste. He loved waltzes, and things like *Gaîté Parisienne* and *Le Beau Danube*. He preferred Fokine's old-fashioned choreography to Massine's symphonies, or to Balanchine's new work.
>
> I remember that Hurok hated Balanchine's *Apollo*, danced to a score by Stravinsky, because it was choreographed partly on point and partly on flat feet. For him, ballet meant *pointe,* and nothing but *pointe.* If Balanchine's company had been under Hurok's management, he would have tried to give it as rarely as possible. Even when Balanchine did have his own company and they went on tour, local managers would try to give *Apollo* as little as possible because they thought it was difficult for the audience. They thought like Hurok. But now, of course, it is one of Balanchine's most important and popular ballets.
>
> Balanchine and Hurok just didn't get along.

The 1933–34 Monte Carlo Ballet Russe tour to America was an artistic success but a financial failure. Not surprisingly given the huge expenses, Hurok had failed even to recoup his initial $75,000 investment. Even so, he was optimistic about the future, as he told the European edition of the Chicago *Tribune* at the end of his usual European tour and talent search in August 1934. His bookings were up forty percent, and "there is no better barometer of business than the amusement field." Nor did he miss an opportunity to put in a good word for FDR and his economic policies, criticizing the few "selfish and greedy individual industrialists" who had "obstructed the Government program of reconstruction."

And in fact over the next few seasons, Hurok did begin to

make some serious money. On the strength of the popular response to the first twenty-week Ballet Russe American tour in 1933–34, he booked the company for 172 performances over five months in 92 cities in 1934–35. The next two seasons were ever bigger: six months in 112 cities in 1935–36 and eight months in 110 cities in 1936–37. The box office gross (Hurok claimed) rose from $1 million in 1934–35 to $1.3 million in 1935–36 and to $1.5 million in 1936–37. At a running cost of approximately $16,000 per week, this worked out to be a healthy profit margin.

Hurok's success with the Ballet Russe brought him new respectability and a torrent of publicity. Critics and columnists increasingly referred to him as the "heir of Morris Gest" and paid as much attention to all his comings and goings as they did to those of the Hollywood moguls whose films he like to criticize as vulgar, dirty, and a threat to civilized society.

Newspapermen especially loved to report on Hurok's annual summer talent searches, which would take him, accompanied by the fashionably dressed Emma, across Europe to Russia. Hurok himself (most likely with Emma's help) described these voyages in letters he wrote home to Irving Deakin, an English-born American arts writer and lecturer who had been giving him advice on publicity and artistic matters. Deakin (1894–1958) had good connections in the Russian ballet world, since he was married to Natasha Bolm, daughter of the dancer and choreographer Adolph Bolm, who had worked with Pavlova and Diaghilev. On July 4, 1935, Hurok wrote Deakin from Riga as he and Emma were about to leave for Russia:

> I must begin by saying that the trip with the *Normandie* did not come up to my expectations. The weather was bad, the food was in no way extraordinary, and all in all, there was no thrill. I have been kept pretty busy since my arrival in Europe. From Paris, I went on to Prague, then to Warsaw and then to Lithuania. Now I am in Riga on the point of proceeding once more to Russia. On my return from Russia I shall visit Vienna and Budapest and then go back to Paris. From Paris I contemplate going across to London where I shall wind up my business and troubles with Covent Garden. . . .

Please show Miss Frohman this letter and let her know that I have no objection to her giving you a list of bookings of the ballet in the different States, as this will help our publicity indirectly. But please keep the information you get from Miss Frohman about the bookings strictly confidential, so that our competitors may not see them. Please mail correspondence to the American Express, Paris.

Soon after Hurok returned to New York, he presided over one of the most significant events of his career to date: the first performances by the Monte Carlo Ballet Russe in New York's Metropolitan Opera House, the holiest temple of American high culture. (In the United States, the company performed under the name Monte Carlo Ballet Russe, but in London it was now called the Ballets Russes de Col. W. de Basil, reflecting René Blum's withdrawal from the enterprise.) The Met had signed a three-year contract with Hurok which allowed him to present his attractions there during the Opera's off-season weeks in early fall and late spring. He took the house "on a four-walls basis, guaranteeing to use it a certain number of days with so much to the Met per performance." This was the first arrangement of its kind in the Met's history.

Badly shaken by the Depression, which had caused growing annual deficits and had forced management to abbreviate two seasons in a row, the Met was experiencing an identity crisis as it entered a new era of greater democracy and fiscal uncertainty. With longtime backers like Otto Kahn dying off and the fifty-year-old building in disrepair, the job of general manager passed in 1935 from Giulio Gatti-Casazza to the Canadian-born Edward Johnson. The influence of the few (often anti-Semitic) wealthy families who had traditionally occupied the glittering boxes of the Diamond Horseshoe was now waning as radio vastly expanded the audience for what in America had been an almost exclusively elitist art form. The Diamond Horseshoe itself would disappear after the theater was reopened following renovations in 1940.

The Met's willingness to sign a contract with Hurok for outside attractions pointed out several things: his emergence as New York's leading presenter of music and dance, the Met's new social and financial vulnerability, and the rising prestige of ballet as an art form.

When Pavlova first danced in the United States in 1910, ballet had to be explained to American audiences as "visual opera" and "ocular opera," and the Met deigned to present her only as a late-night afterthought to a complete performance of *Werther*. Twenty-five years later, the Met management was grateful for Hurok's business and found nothing shameful in giving the theater over to a group of stateless dancers performing an entire evening of ballet in tights and tutus—with nary an opera in sight. When the Monte Carlo Ballet Russe gave its first performance at the Met on October 9, 1935, dance in America reached a new level of respectability and maturity. And Hurok had arrived.

For the company, used to dancing in fine houses like Covent Garden or the Salle Garnier in Monte Carlo, the Met was a vast improvement over the inappropriate and ill-equipped Broadway theaters into which it had been booked in New York in the past two seasons. Here, in this more spacious and more carefully maintained facility, the productions and the dancers could be seen to full advantage. The Met being the Met, the company also drew a tonier crowd that would not have darkened the door of the scruffy St. James or Majestic. Hurok shrewdly exploited the theater's clout by sending out a special mailing to its subscribers. The influential opera crowd began to discover ballet, and many of them liked what they saw. Their snobbish condescension toward dance as a frivolous, unserious art form began to change, along with their prudish attitudes toward dancers as prostitutes turning pirouettes.

The imposing aura of the Met did not prevent Hurok from engaging in his usual tricks of manufacturing controversy, raising hoopla, and manipulating the media. When David Lichine danced the role of the Faun in *L'Après-midi d'un faune* there, Hurok made sure to remind all the newspapers of the scandal that had surrounded Nijinsky's performance in this ballet in New York in 1916. Hurok even paid a woman in the audience $50 to scream when the Faun began to simulate masturbation with the Nymph's scarf at the ballet's end.

On Election Day 1936, when voters registered their approval of Roosevelt's New Deal policies by returning him to office in a landslide, Hurok presented an "election day special." It featured a luncheon (complete with vodka), a lecture and book signing by Irving Deakin, and a program of *Le Lac des cygnes* (a one-act version of Petipa's *Swan Lake*), *Scheherazade*, and *Le Beau Danube*. After the performance, election returns were announced from the Met stage. Food, entertainment, and politics—the same combination Hurok had sold back in Brownsville. And all for $3.75.

At the price of free tickets, Hurok also made sure that the audiences were stocked with friends who would applaud loudly (like he did, dashing back and forth along the back of the house) and dispense complimentary remarks at intermission. One of those upon whom he relied to "spread the gospel" was Deakin, who gladly accepted the role of propagandist, as a polite but pragmatic note he wrote to Mae Frohman makes clear:

> I should be ever so much obliged if, commencing with Tuesday . . . you will have four seats left in my name for each performance at some location where you are not selling out. . . . And in the intervals I can circulate about and drop the right sort of word here and there in the right places.

With the aid of such tactics, the Monte Carlo Ballet Russe had become an established institution by the end of its fourth North American tour in 1936–37. (In 1936, the company adopted the same name in America that it had been using in London: Col. W. de Basil's Ballets Russes.) Americans were embracing the dance as never before. Ballet historian Vincente Garcia-Marquez may not be exaggerating when he claims that the troupe, largely owing to Hurok's brilliant publicity campaign ("No City nor Community Can Afford Not to Have This Attraction Next Season"), had become "the most popular expression of entertainment available on a grand scale throughout the country after cinema and radio."

Not everyone was happy with this state of affairs. Homegrown choreographers and dancers like Martha Graham and Agnes de Mille watched in envy and frustration as the invading horde of Russians cornered the market and "swept everything else to the corners." The "craze" over the Ballet Russe especially galled the irascible de Mille, who held Hurok personally responsible for the fact that American audiences now seemed to believe that only Europeans could devise or perform ballet. She also blamed him for surrounding ballet with a circuslike atmosphere and pandering to the public weakness for technique and tricks at the expense of dramatic and psychological truth.

"Hurok knew stunts, and anything that looked like the old Russian ballet," she said. "If the audience was just going mad, and tearing the seats up, and throwing flowers and bits of their clothing, then he knew that yes, it was a success. If one did 98 *fouetté-pirouettes* on top of a billiard ball—then he thought that was something."

Not surprisingly, the dancers in the de Basil company were less critical of their American impresario. To them, the extensive American tours of the mid-1930s brought steady employment and excitement. At loose ends after Diaghilev's death, terrified at the prospect of being sent back to Stalin's Russia, they viewed Hurok as their savior and protector—his favorite role. One of the main reasons Hurok preferred to work with Russian dancers was because their vulnerable legal status gave him almost unlimited power over them. They were more passive and less assertive than Americans. Happy for the work, they bore the incredible physical and emotional demands of their nonstop schedule with stoic determination.

Traveling more than twenty thousand miles each season in an uncomfortable caravan of eleven Pullman cars, the 125 (nonunionized) performers rarely spent more than several days at a stop, catching what sleep they could on the train as it rumbled through small cities and towns like Albany, Utica, Akron, Youngstown, Terre Haute, Peoria, Davenport, Wichita, and Lincoln. In many places, they danced—like Pavlova before them—in primitively equipped high-school and college auditoriums. Everywhere, too, they were expected to mingle and socialize with the local socialites and cultural leaders, who turned out in droves and dressed to the nines to greet them. For all of this, they received very modest wages: between $35 and $40 weekly for members of the corps.

The story of these tours, wrote Arnold Haskell, who went along for the ride and sent dispatches home to the *Daily Telegraph*, was "one of deadly monotony; lack of sleep, tasteless food, inane interviews and creative frustration. One rarely realized in which town one was appearing and in any case it made not the slightest difference. Only the warming charm of Sol Hurok and his masterly organization and the comfort and warmth of railway stations and hotels made the whole thing possible and, but for a cancelled or late performance through snow or flood, the ballet was like a circus; arrived on time, gave its show and departed."

Even in this prolonged state of transience, however, the dancers—and especially their guardians—struggled to maintain their daily rituals and cultural identity. In fact, they had little contact with the realities of American life, instead retreating into the familial hothouse environment of "Holy Russia on Tour." Since Russians love scandal, intrigue, high emotions, and sentimental melodrama, there was no shortage of melancholy, showy quarrels, and self-indulgent breast-beating in what Danilova called "the most chaotic organization I have ever known." The reigning Slavic zaniness even infected aliens like dancer Paul Petroff, a Dane. One night he was stabbed in the hotel by another member of the company after returning from a night on the town with de Basil's wife, Nina. When the police arrived, Petroff refused to identify his attacker. For his part, the image-conscious Hurok paid "a small fortune" to keep the story out of the papers. A self-described lover of "temperament," Hurok tended to view such incidents as part of the impresario's territory.

Such excesses could be hard on newcomers like Vera Zorina, however, a beautiful Norwegian whose real (non-Russified) name was Eva Brigitte Hartwig. She had joined the Ballet Russe as a principal dancer in 1934 at the age of seventeen, after studying in London with Marie Rambert. According to her, Hurok used to encourage the prima ballerina behavior practiced so devastatingly by the company's senior Russian members:

The natural hauteur which most of the Russian ladies in the company possessed and practiced was carried even further with Danilova, who had a habit of cocking her head to one side and managing from that position to appraise you with sidelong, critical glances. You felt that you were being scrutinized physically and that every piece of clothing was being evaluated as to its suitability. Many years later in San Francisco . . . Sol Hurok gave me a lecture on why I should not arrive at the theater by trolley car, looking windblown, but that I should wear a hat with a veil; he cited Danilova as an example of what a star should look and behave like. He was unmoved when I pointed out that the trolley cars in San Francisco were fun and that I didn't want to spend all my money on taxicabs.

Like others, Zorina also came to see very quickly that there was a strict and inviolable hierarchy at the managerial level. At the top, like some backstage Mephistopheles, stood the crafty de Basil and his chronically neglected first wife, Nina. Below them were the company manager Grigoriev and his wife, Lubov Tchernicheva, who had enjoyed considerable success as a dancer in the Diaghilev company. Mme. Grigorieva was to be kissed each morning. Unless, that is, Hurok and Emma were traveling with the company, in which case "Mme. Hurok was given first obeisance." On a somewhat lower level was David Libidins, a singer born in Istanbul of Russian parents, who worked as tour manager. Adopting the manners and pretensions of Russian aristocrats, the company's hierarchy—including Hurok, through whose increasingly rotund body not a single drop of aristocratic blood flowed—did not mix socially with the company members, except at the huge parties given in the larger cities.

Nepotism also thrived in the company. The Grigorievs' son Vsevolod was the assistant stage manager. Hurok brought Emma's son Eddie into the fold to work with the company on the road, while his daughter, Ruth, spent a brief stint answering the phones back at the office in Rockefeller Center. The ambitious and incessantly feuding mothers of the "baby ballerinas" were also given employment: Tamara Toumanova's mother worked in the scenery department, and Baronova's in the costume shop. The jealousy that seethed between them over their daughters led to frequent altercations.

Under the terms of the three-year contract he signed with de Basil in 1935, Hurok had to cover all expenses for visas, boat tickets, and the transportation of scenery and costumes. He also had to provide musicians, wardrobe keepers, technical staff, stagehands, and insurance; promise to book at least five performances weekly; and refrain from managing "any other classic ballet of major importance, except by mutual consent." Hurok and de Basil agreed that "the Attraction is of unique and extraordinary character, enjoying a special reputation in the artistic world and cannot be duplicated." In return for his financial backing, Hurok received the important right to select the ballets given on tour out of the company's repertoire.

Hurok's love of the tried and true, combined with the exhausting routine of touring, left the company's dancers and choreographers little room or energy for creative growth. Only five new ballets were staged between 1934 and 1937, compared to seven in the single season 1933–34. Of these five, only one—Massine's *Jardin Public*—received its premiere in the United States, where Hurok supervised the company's time, and it proved a failure with both audiences and critics.

The score for *Jardin Public* was written by Vladimir Dukelsky, another Russian émigré composer with former links to Diaghilev. (He had written the score for the 1925 ballet *Zéphire et Flore*.) Now living in America under the name Vernon Duke and producing music—the 1935 *Ziegfeld Follies, Cabin in the Sky*—for Broadway, Dukelsky, eager to maintain his reputation as a "serious" composer, happily agreed to work with Massine on a new ballet for the de Basil company. The composer even suggested a subject: an adaptation of a passage from André Gide's novel *The Counterfeiters*. After financial backing was secured from Estrella Elizaga, an international socialite friendly with Dukelsky, de Basil and Hurok gave their approval and the project proceeded. As had been the case with *Union Pacific*, rehearsals of *Jardin Public* took place under the most trying conditions. The company learned the work toward the end of the 1934–35 tour in the basement grill of New York's Hotel Piccadilly.

This time, however, the results were less successful. When the new ballet, an episodic and self-conscious attempt at a ballet of social awareness using portraits of various Dostoyevskian misfits, received its premiere at the Auditorium Theatre in Chicago on March 8, 1935, it provoked little interest. The New York performances a few weeks later went no better. Even after *Jardin Public* was completely revised a year later, it still didn't catch on. Perhaps its subject—the misfortunes of the poor—was insufficiently escapist for an audience trapped in the middle of a Depression, or perhaps the score was too eclectic.

Massine had much better luck with *Symphonie Fantastique*, an enormous "choreographic symphony in five scenes" that was developed and rehearsed in London in late spring of 1936. Since Hector Berlioz had provided his own written scenario for the symphony, it was a perfect vehicle for Massine's exploration of the new genre of "symphonic ballet." With Massine himself dancing the role of the Young Musician and Toumanova as The Beloved, *Symphonie Fantastique* made a great impression at its premiere at Covent Garden on July 24, 1936. Despite Hurok's aversion to such "modern" works, he chose it on the strength of its London reception to open the de Basil's Ballets Russes season at the Metropolitan Opera House on October 29, 1936.

By the end of the 1936–37 American tour, which concluded with a widely publicized five-day return engagement at the Met in April, the personal and creative tensions that had existed from the very founding of the de Basil company had heated to the boiling point. Co-founder Blum had already departed in 1935, forming his Ballets de Monte Carlo and hiring Fokine to choreograph. Massine, meanwhile, was chafing under de Basil's tyrannical control and feeling creatively stifled by the company's emphasis on traditional repertoire and debilitating commercial tours. In the summer of 1936, he had already brought an (unsuccessful) injunction against de Basil in London to prevent the colonel from presenting his ballets in Australia with another company. Massine had already decided that he would move on when his contract with de Basil ran out in January 1938. The always wary relationship between Hurok and de Basil was also growing increasingly fractious, their three-year contract notwithstanding. Both fond of exercising complete control, they were too much alike to get along well. One of their most bitter and chronic disagreements was over billing on programs and advertisements; de Basil insisted that his name should be in type at least as big or bigger than Hurok's.

And so all of the parties involved began casting about for other possibilities. As early as December 1936, with more than a year to go on his contract with de Basil, Hurok, who prided himself on his ability to outscheme and outdeal any and all competitors, was already discussing the idea of managing another ballet company. He boasted to confidants that it would "continue and develop the work of the late Sergei Diaghileff" by using the resources of a new player on the already cluttered scene: Serge Denham. Like Hurok and de Basil, Denham (1897–1970) was an ambitious self-invented person. Born in Russia as Sergei Ivanovich Dokouchaiev, he had changed his name after emigrating to the West. (He chose Denham in tribute to Charles Denby, father of dance critic Edwin Denby, a State Department official who had helped him obtain American citizenship.) In America, Denham had made a successful career as a banker.

Denham had also gained the confidence of a wealthy ballet-loving Cincinnati industrialist, Julius Fleischmann of Fleischmann's Yeast fame. A great admirer of Massine, Fleischmann had created an artistic enterprise called World Art, Inc. (an approximate translation of the title of Diaghilev's famous journal *Mir iskusstva*), and hoped to entice the dancer-choreographer into a new ballet venture. The understanding was that Hurok would book and manage the troupe in North America and elsewhere.

Lying low, Hurok sent his minion David Libidins to propose to Massine that he become the artistic director of this new company, also to be headquartered in Monte Carlo. In building the troupe with Massine, Denham and Fleischmann and Hurok were counting on using what was left of René Blum's Ballets de Monte Carlo, now collapsing in the wake of the departure of its chief choreographer, Fokine. This scheme appealed to Massine. Eager for the greater artistic freedom the new organizers promised him, he responded favorably to their proposal. Like Hurok, however, he was still legally bound to dance and work with the de Basil company for one more season.

On May 13, 1937, Denham and Hurok finally signed a contract for the new venture. It would take effect beginning in the 1938–39 season. Before drawing up the contract, however, Denham had taken the precaution of doing a thorough check on Hurok's credit history. The assistant manager of the branch of the Chase Manhattan Bank at Rockefeller Center where Hurok kept his account had assured Denham in a memo that his future partner's financial status was "entirely satisfactory" and that S. Hurok Presents was "one of the leading organizations of its type in this country."

The agreement between Denham and Hurok included understandable uncertainty over the right to use the much-abused "de Monte Carlo" title. It also contained a pledge from Hurok to refrain from any activity "which might be detrimental to the high artistic and cultural standing of the ballet," and a promise to produce souvenir programs "in a manner compatible with the Hurok management standard." In return, Hurok received the power to select the program and to approve the cast "for each and every performance" at least thirty days in advance.

Now they had to rid themselves of de Basil. In preparation for his own impending split with the colonel, Massine brought a copyright suit against him in the summer of 1937, asserting sole ownership over the ballets he had choreographed for the company. This legal action further polarized the already strained situation, splitting the garrulous dancers into hostile factions. Histrionic in the best of times, all the participants in this Byzantine struggle played their parts to the hilt, reveling in the gossip and intrigue like fascinated courtiers whispering feverishly in the corridors of the Winter Palace. "The 'balletic' world . . . is in complete turmoil, and the air is thick with rumors and gossip," wrote Serge Denham to Irving Deakin from London on June 20, 1937. With more than a little help from Hurok, it would remain that way for some years to come.

■ CHAPTER TEN ■

Low Notes and High

"No pen or writer could give a true description of what's happening there."—*Sol Hurok on the USSR (1937)*

HUROK PASSED TWO MILESTONES IN 1938: his fiftieth birthday and the twenty-fifth anniversary of his professional debut as an impresario. The birthday boy made sure the significance of these historic occasions was not lost on the members of his industrious public relations staff, who alerted the media in a blizzard of commemorative press releases worthy of Buckingham Palace. Conveniently, these flowery announcements landed in most of the country's major newspapers just as a big Hurok attraction (most often the de Basil company) was about to hit town, creating a reverential atmosphere conducive to the purchase of tickets. In this more innocent era, editors felt less squeamish about running the standardized puff pieces that emerged in a steady stream from 30 Rockefeller Plaza; they often appeared with slight variations under a local writer's byline. The way Hurok and his workers saw it, they were just making life easier for those toiling in the rocky garden of journalism.

And Hurok did have a lot to be proud of as he passed the half-century mark. On the strength of his brilliant marketing of the de Basil company, he was now America's leading presenter of dance, famous not only in New York but in towns and cities large and small all over the United States. Having long ago outmaneuvered and out-

■ 188 ■

classed such early rivals as Fortune Gallo and Morris Gest, he had established himself as the country's most vivid performing arts manager, his name recognized from coast to coast. And he had accomplished all this without sacrificing his individuality for the sake of security, like so many of his colleagues. "Mr. Hurok is one of the last of the old-time entrepreneurs," remarked the New York *Sun*, "to whom presenting artists is a highly personal business, and not a matter of corporate activity."

By making shrewd use of the many contacts and friends he had made during twenty-five years of hustling, and by capitalizing on his new exclusive contract with the Met, Hurok had also amassed the largest and most influential mailing list in the entertainment business. An unfailingly gracious host and a shameless flatterer, he could also count on New York's trendsetters (so-called "café society") to show up at his important premieres and turn them into media events reported on the national radio and wire services. Hurok had similarly cultivated the leading critics in every city, remembering their birthdays and sending them baskets of goodies at Christmastime. Such gestures didn't always produce rave reviews, but they did grease the wheels of the publicity machine. As he often said, "There are two ways of writing a bad review." Regular gifts of caviar and chocolate, or invitations to luxurious repasts at the Russian Tea Room, Hurok's second home next to Carnegie Hall, could help a critic find the right one.

As the result of all his personal diplomacy, strategic planning, hard work, and impeccable timing, the "S. Hurok Presents" label—backed up by the prestige and financial protection afforded him through his advantageous arrangement with NBC—had become a trusted trademark and seal of approval. It could sell tickets to the theater as effectively as the trademark "General Motors" could sell cars.

Always aware of the importance of appearances, Hurok played the part of the impresario for all it was worth, competing successfully with his artists for the limelight. Though he claimed to dislike attention, he never failed to turn out meticulously outfitted for the season in elegant understated attire. He was rarely photographed without his fedora and one of his "six or eight" canes. Canes had been a standard part of his wardrobe, Hurok claimed, from the time

"I was a child of fourteen years of age. I got accustomed to go with a cane all the time. It goes with full dress, and it's better to have a gold top cane than a silver top." His favorite cane with a gold handle, Hurok said, was a gift from Pavlova. In more relaxed and unguarded moments, though, he could be seen with a new children's toy that had captured his fancy under one arm and a copy of the *Jewish Daily Forward* under the other, no cane in sight.

Fifty years had taken away Hurok's hair and his love of fine food had added some inches to his waistline, but these physical modifications only heightened the aura of self-satisfied respectability and substance that increased his leverage in difficult negotiations in Paris, London, or Moscow. When singer Marian Anderson saw Hurok for the first time in Paris in June 1935, she observed that he "was built along generous lines" and possessed "the impressive bulk befitting the grand impresario." And yet despite the fact that he never exercised (except for leisurely city strolling), Hurok enjoyed nearly perfect health. Many friends and associates have commented on how youthful the skin of his moon-shaped face was—smooth and unwrinkled—until the day he died.

Time had not appreciably changed his manner of speaking, either, which remained as heavily accented and grammatically eccentric as ever. ("As long as I am alive, I shall continue for the rest of my life.") This, too, however, he had learned to use very much to his advantage as a symbol of his populist origins, capable of inspiring identification and admiration in the democratically minded American audiences of the New Deal era.

The thousands of feature stories devoted to Hurok in this anniversary year invariably used words like "genial," "jovial," "calm," "portly," and "paternal" to describe him. Despite his obvious success in the business world, an environment not noted for turn-the-other-cheek behavior, the tenacious and if need be ruthless negotiatior Hurok had managed to develop a public image that fell somewhere between Santa Claus and your favorite uncle. Those on his staff and the theater people with whom he wrangled over salaries and profits called him shrewd, stubborn, and tyrannical, but to his public, to whom he dispensed culture, and to his artists, to whom he gave bookings and fame, he was nothing less than "Papa Hurok."

▪ ▪ ▪

To his own daughter, Ruth, however, Hurok at fifty remained as elusive and inattentive as ever. After courting and winning Emma, who had three sons of her own, his relationship with Ruth and her mother, Tamara, became if anything even more distant and awkward. Emma now accompanied him on his trips to Europe and on portions of the long de Basil tours across the United States. Often Ruth had to arrange conversations and meetings with him through his secretary, who more than once offended her by saying that her father could not see her that evening "because he would be spending it with his family." (What did that make her? she would ask herself.) After graduating from high school, Ruth spent a year studying drama and dance privately in New York, since she had been told by the instructors at summer camp that she had promise. But far from encouraging her, Hurok told her that dancing was not a very stable profession, and he urged her to do something else. The idea of having a dancer daughter who was not in the same class as Toumanova and Pavlova no doubt embarrassed and confused him.

At loose ends, Ruth then enrolled in a three-year teacher training course for certification as a teacher at the kindergarten and first-grade level. After graduation, however, she still had ambivalent feelings about teaching, which seemed to her a dull and pedestrian life compared to her father's glamorous theatrical existence. Ruth had gotten an intoxicating taste of this exotic world when he took her along with him and Emma on one of his summer trips to Paris in the early 1930s. Finally, Hurok offered his daughter a job as a receptionist in his office. For about a year, she answered the telephone, but never felt comfortable or successful in that role. When she finally concluded that she should leave "because I didn't belong there," her father was "glad to get rid of me. He didn't want me to know what was going on in the office anyway." And so Ruth did go into primary teaching after all.

In early 1937, she decided to marry an aspiring writer named Barry Hyams, who was working for the Federal Theater under the auspices of the WPA. She introduced him to her father over lunch at the Hotel Astor. Hurok seemed to like him (he was a nice smart Jewish boy) well enough, but told her he wondered how he would be able to support her on his small salary. After they were married (at the Astor), the young couple moved into the apartment in which Ruth and her mother had been living in Brooklyn.

Tamara, who had never been able to get over Hurok, had moved out to live with her sister, but not before making Ruth feel guilty by letting her know that she would have been happy (as in the Old Country) to stay and live with her daughter and son-in-law. Within a few years, Hurok offered Hyams a position with his agency, as an assistant to Gerald Goode in public relations. Although Goode apparently disliked Hyams, who would also irritate Hurok by showing up late for work, Ruth's husband remained in the Hurok office for nearly fifteen years, eventually becoming a respected PR man. Ruth was happier in this new situation, since they moved to Manhattan and her husband's work brought her closer to her father's world and its glamor. If he couldn't give Ruth love or encouragement, Hurok did see to it that she lived comfortably.

Following this pattern of nepotism, Hurok also gave work to Emma and to two of her three sons. Emma continued to perform as a cabaret singer (under the name Emma Runich) in attractions partially or completely booked by her husband, including the *Continental Varieties* headlined by the Parisian *diseuse* and *grande étoile* Lucienne Boyer. Famous from her recordings (and especially for her song *"Parlez-moi d'amour"*), Boyer was joined in this Russian-style review by Nikita Balieff, now in the twilight of a career that had started on Broadway with *La Chauve-Souris*; the concertina virtuoso Raphael; Hurok's discovery Escudero; and the singer Lydia Chaliapine, Chaliapin's daughter.

Continental Varieties opened on October 3, 1934, in the Little Theatre. Produced by Ben Franklin and Edgar Selwyn with several Hurok artists, it then moved to the Rainbow Room in Rockefeller Center—some floors upstairs from Hurok's office. But even Hurok and his crack staff could not turn it into a hit, perhaps because the supply of these eclectic assortments of Russian nostalgia viewed through the bleary lens of Parisian chic had finally outstripped the demand. Nor did the show give a boost to Emma's flagging career, although she did make a few recordings for Columbia. Her failure to make it as a singer in America may well have contributed to the difficulties that later developed in her personal relationship with Hurok.

Emma's sons, George and Edward Perper, both asked their

stepfather to give them jobs in the business in the 1930s. According to George, Hurok was not especially enthusiastic about the idea, but relented at his insistence—and then chronically underpaid him. "I knew that he underpaid me," said George some years later of his experience as company manager.

> Because it was first of all considered family, and family had to be slightly underpaid. But I did get my training. He gave me the last tour of the Vienna Choir Boys before they returned to Austria in 1937, just before the War. It was probably the hardest tour ever undertaken. The boys were in these little racks in the bus, and we had to drive from Kansas to Oregon—about six days and five nights, giving a few concerts in between. The drivers had to cross Mount Shasta in the snow, on dark roads, but we did it. I remember how one driver went outside for a minute and he fainted, he was so tired. Luckily, we had two drivers.

But despite the low salaries, long hours, and hard work, both George and Eddie remained in the Hurok office for many years. Eddie worked for his stepfather until 1966, and George until after Hurok's death. Their presence—and Barry Hyams's—only added to the superficially familial atmosphere, although those unrelated to the boss ("bossik" for short) in fact fared better both financially and professionally.

During the years that Hurok was building an American audience for ballet, he also managed to present a number of other important theatrical and musical attractions. Between 1935 and 1939, he engineered the American debuts of Michael Chekhov's Moscow Art Players and Swiss dancer Trudi Schoop, and brought the American contralto Marian Anderson back home from Europe. He also reintroduced America to Arthur Rubinstein after a lapse of fourteen years, supervised the recital debut of Jan Peerce at Town Hall, signed a ten-year rental agreement with the Met, established a concert series at Carnegie Hall, and presented Benny Goodman there. And these were only the more notable achievements. Drawing on a seemingly infinite reservoir of energy, Hurok accomplished all this while making his usual annual trips to Europe and the Soviet Union, not to mention juggling several large and unruly ballet companies riven by dissent and scandal.

Michael Chekhov and his Moscow Art Players arrived in America for the first time in early 1935. Considered one of the greatest Russian actors of his generation, Chekhov (1891–1955) had long struggled under the psychological burden of being Anton Chekhov's nephew. Chekhov studied with many of the leading figures of the early twentieth-century Russian theater, including Konstantin Stanislavsky and Yevgeny Vakhtangov, and made his reputation in leading and supporting roles at Stanislavsky's Moscow Art Theatre between 1913 and 1923. (He was particularly acclaimed as Khlestakov in Gogol's satirical play *The Inspector General*.) Eventually Chekhov came to disagree with Stanislavsky's theory and teaching methods, particularly his reliance on psychological memory at the expense of imagination in creating a role. As director of the second Moscow Art Theatre from 1924 to 1927, he put his own ideas into practice. Eventually, however, he fell afoul of the Soviet cultural bureaucrats, who branded him a "sick artist" staging "alien and reactionary" productions in the increasingly oppressive cultural environment that developed after Lenin's death. In 1928, Chekhov accepted Max Reinhardt's invitation to perform in Berlin and never returned to Russia.

For the next few years, Chekhov, like so many other Russian artistic émigrés, took on all sorts of work. He starred in German-language comedies and silent films in Berlin and set up acting studios in Paris, Latvia, and Lithuania. No doubt Hurok heard of him or even saw him on one of his trips to Europe in the late 1920s or early 1930s. In any case, by late 1934 Chekhov was conducting negotiations with Leonid Leonidov, a Russian émigré theatrical producer based in Berlin, about making a tour of the United States. Leonidov and Chekhov then made some sort of deal with Hurok. When the actor and his company—now called the Moscow Art Players—opened a four-week engagement at the Majestic Theatre on February 16, 1935, with a production of *The Inspector General*, they did so under the label of "S. Hurok Presents."

By presenting Chekhov and his troupe, Hurok was clearly attempting to assert his link to the hallowed traditions of Stanislavsky and the Moscow Art Theatre and to usurp the position of Morris

Gest, the producer who had imported them to New York in 1923. Gest had gradually faded from the scene after running up $600,000 in debts on an extravagant production of Reinhardt's *The Miracle* that he imported from Germany in 1924. He would die in 1942 at the age of sixty-one, leaving the field completely open to Hurok for the next thirty years.

By the time Chekhov came to America in 1935, he already had a devoted (if small) following there among the members of the Group Theatre. This ensemble had been formed in 1931 by a group of actors and producers devoted to Stanislavsky's theories and teachings. They greeted Chekhov enthusiastically, as a disciple of the master, and even offered him a job. New York's critics had more difficulty appreciating his work, probably because the productions he brought were performed in Russian. They included Gogol's *The Inspector General* and *Marriage*, Alexander Ostrovsky's *Poverty Is No Vice*, and two new plays by Soviet writers: Valentin Katayev's *The Primrose Path* and Mikhail Bulgakov's *Days of the Turbins*. Harold Clurman, one of the leading theater critics of the day and a founding member of the Group Theatre, complained that the New York press had "been unable to recognize" Chekhov's genius. After the New York engagement, the Moscow Art Players went on to perform in Philadelphia and Boston.

Wherever Chekhov went, the Russian émigré community lavished attention on him, as this letter from the theatrical entrepreneur Yevgeny Somov to composer Sergei Rachmaninoff indicates:

> Our dear Chekhovites have gone off on tour in Philadelphia and Boston. Unfortunately, the Russian colony both there and in Boston is not large. Despite magnificent newspaper reviews—which point out that there's no need to fear not knowing the language because one can take pleasure in the acting of these amazing artists even without understanding the text—the Americans are still attending the performances, as Mikhail Aleksandrovich writes, in rather small quantities. I'm afraid that if Hurok hasn't made any money on them he won't want to bring them back next season, and we'll be deprived of this pleasure.

Somov was right. Hurok did not bring Chekhov or his Moscow Art Players back to New York again—which must mean that he lost money and, even more importantly, saw no audience potential. Significantly, he did not even choose to describe their tour or Chekhov in his memoirs. The small audiences did not seem to bother Chekhov himself, however, who immersed himself in New York's rich cultural life, especially all the "amazing concerts. Here for the first time we heard Toscanini! We also heard Horowitz and Heifetz. And what an orchestra they have here! For us, all of this was just an enormous pleasure!" And indeed, by the mid-1930s more and more of Europe's leading musicians were seeking refuge in America.

By introducing Chekhov and America to each other, Hurok performed an important service to the future both of this influential actor-teacher and of theatrical life in the United States. During the New York run, Chekhov met the American actress Beatrice Straight, who proposed to him that he start a theater-studio at Dartington Hall, the English estate of her stepfather and mother. It was here that Chekhov refined his acting and pedagogical methods with students and instructors recruited from all over the world.

When war with Germany threatened in 1939, he relocated his Chekhov Theatre Studio to Ridgefield, Connecticut, and then opened a studio in Manhattan in 1941. Here he worked with some of the leading figures in the American theatre—Stella Adler, Bobby Lewis, Sandy Meisner. Later, in their own work as teachers, they further disseminated Chekhov's ideas about imagination, which they saw as a strong counterweight to the dominant psychological interpretation of the Stanislavsky "method" championed in America by Lee Strasberg. Chekhov eventually settled in Hollywood, where he acted in films and taught until his death in 1955. In 1945, he was even nominated for an Oscar for best supporting actor in the Austrian-accented role of Ingrid Bergman's psychoanalyst-mentor (Dr. Alex Brulor) in the Hitchcock classic *Spellbound*.

Trudi Schoop, whom Hurok imported in December 1935, did not have either Chekhov's following or intellectual credentials. Dubbed the "Charlie Chaplin of the dance," Schoop studied drama in Munich and ballet in Vienna before returning home to Zurich, where she found her calling as a comic choreographer and dancer of narrative pieces. She and her "comic ballet" gained international attention when they won fourth prize in a 1932 dance competition in Paris.

During the thirteen performances Hurok arranged at the Majestic Theatre, and on a subsequent tour, the Schoop troupe showed American audiences that there could be more to modern dance than angst and suffering. Her piece *Want Ads*, in a prologue and six short scenes, was actually a work of performance art. After various job seekers told their hard-luck stories in pantomime, each then read aloud the words of the advertisement he or she was placing. In their technique and style Schoop and her twenty-two dancers reminded critics of acrobats and clowns, and inspired the writer Edna Ferber to send Hurok an ecstatic telegram praising them as "the most amusing and the most amazingly fresh entertainment in New York." *New York Times* critic John Martin was considerably less enthusiastic, however. He dismissed Schoop in a particularly sour review as "the sort of attraction which would be endlessly delightful if one were allowed to discover it in some little provincial cafe, but seems a bit empty when subjected to the standards of a sophisticated Broadway theatre." And yet Martin's thumbs-down did not appreciably affect the popular response, for Hurok presented the company in New York and on the road for three seasons running through 1938.

Schoop went back to Switzerland in 1938, but eventually returned to settle and work—like so many of Hurok's European artists—in the United States.

On December 30, 1935, just three nights after Schoop opened at the Majestic, Hurok presented the historic American homecoming of a performer who would prove to be one of his greatest financial and artistic successes: Marian Anderson. The story of Hurok's "discovery" and management of Anderson has become one of the great entertainment tales of the twentieth century, buried under a layer of legend almost as thick as the patina that has accumulated on Chaliapin and Pavlova. Like Hurok, Anderson emerged from a life of poverty and prejudice to become one of the great cultural figures of her time, a symbol of determination and grit. Manager and artist shared the bitter experience of being outsiders in supposedly free

WASP America—Hurok as an immigrant Jew in an era of anti-Semitism, and Anderson as a black woman in an era of sexism and segregation.

They also shared their American hometown: Philadelphia. Anderson was born there in 1897 (not 1902, as has been widely reported), just a few years before Hurok arrived from Pogar and New York in search of wealth and fame. But as the daughter of struggling black parents, she had even more limited opportunities than he.

Like so many black musicians, Anderson began her career singing in the local Baptist church, where the parishioners soon recognized her talent. By the time she was thirteen, the choir director was collecting money from the congregation for a scholarship fund. But the Philadelphia music school where she went hoping to take lessons wouldn't accept her Negro money. Singing at social events and churches to pay for private lessons, she continued to impress those who heard her, including a Harlem promoter who managed to get her a date at Town Hall. Her recital there, in "the mainstream of American musical life," proved, however, a bitter and disillusioning experience. Only a "scattering of people" showed up, and the reviews were critical.

Her victory a few years later in a contest that drew three hundred contestants vying for a chance to sing with the New York Philharmonic at Lewisohn Stadium was a turning point. That performance (on August 26, 1925) received enthusiastic, if not sensational, reviews and led to more engagements, including a Carnegie Hall appearance with a choir that captured the attention of Arthur Judson. Judson managed the New York Philharmonic from 1922 to 1956 and the Philadelphia Orchestra from 1915 to 1935—in the days when managing two orchestras simultaneously was not regarded as inappropriate. Also a founder of CBS and creator of Columbia Concerts, Judson, a former violinist and music professor, was one of the most powerful and well-connected men in the music business. He took Anderson on as a client. But her new status, and her thrilling interpretations of spirituals and lieder, still didn't shield her from indignities like being made to sit in the "Jim Crow car" of the train when on tour and being denied entrance to decent hotels in the South.

Nor was Judson able to deliver many of the high-paying dates he had promised her, either because he encountered resistance from local managers or was too distracted with his other, more famous clients. He even urged Anderson to change from a contralto to a soprano, a suggestion which shook her confidence in his judgment and confirmed her in the belief that "things were not going too well." When she told him she wanted to try her luck in Europe, where numerous black performers—Josephine Baker, Paul Robeson—had encountered fewer obstacles in pursuing a career, Judson discouraged her and accused her of vanity. She went anyway.

After a disappointing initial year in London, she returned briefly to America and received a fellowship from the Julius Rosenwald Fund for six months' study in Germany. Anderson's performances in Berlin, at the time a very cosmopolitan city with less virulent racial prejudice than existed in the United States, captured the attention of the Swedish manager Helmer Enwall, who sent his friend the Finnish pianist Kosti Vehanen to hear her. Enwall and his Norwegian colleague Rule Rasmussen then brought her to Scandinavia, where audiences responded "with a mixture of open-mindedness and curiosity." A Norwegian newspaper described her as "looking very much like a chocolate bar." But her Scandinavian success had no impact on the managers back in America, who were still unable to get her the sort of bookings or fees a white singer with one-half her talent could take for granted. Judson had lined up a mere ten dates for the season, and one, in Philadelphia, was a humiliating semiprofessional engagement with the singer's honorary sorority.

So Anderson returned once again to Europe in 1933. She remained there for more than two years, building her reputation under Enwall's management (and with Vehanen as her accompanist) in Scandinavia, England, and Russia. Her earnings and audiences grew. In Helsinki, Sibelius embraced her after she sang several of his songs, and declared, "My roof is too low for you." In Leningrad and Moscow she was praised and entertained by Shostakovich, Stanislavsky, and Meyerhold, and spent her rubles (worthless outside the country) on jewels, furs, and antiques. But it was her three recitals at the Salle Gaveau in Paris in the spring of 1935 that finally brought her the sort of attention she had been waiting for. They also brought her to Hurok.

In fact, Anderson had tried to approach Hurok a few years earlier, but he had not found time to meet with her. Now that she and her soulful, dark voice were the "toast of Europe," acclaimed even by the Parisians (these most willful and respected of listeners), he felt differently. By now surely aware from his network of informers that this was an artist he could make money on, he came to hear the last of her three recitals in June.

Some years later, he described this incident in exaggeratedly poetic terms. "In Paris one evening I was sitting at a sidewalk café on the Champs-Élysées with my wife—she had begged me to take one night off and sit in the fresh air, instead of going to the concert of a young American contralto I had never heard of before." (That he had not heard of Anderson by then seems highly unlikely, but it made for a better story.) "But something told me I should hear that voice, and so I dropped in at the concert, and after the first few notes . . . I knew. . . . After the first part of the concert, I hurried backstage and introduced myself to a young Negro woman . . . who was quite excited when she heard I was coming backstage to see her. Her name? Marian Anderson."

Arthur Rubinstein tells the story quite differently in his autobiography. He claims he told Hurok that he should present Anderson in America because she was the greatest lieder singer he had ever heard. "Hurok made a sour face. 'Colored people do not make it with the box office,' he said in his professional lingo. But he was visibly impressed by my insistence. He left for Amsterdam to hear her sing and signed a contract the same night." According to Anderson, however, her first meeting with Hurok took place not in Amsterdam, but in Paris at the Salle Gaveau recital in spring of 1935.

Indeed, Hurok was not the only impresario who came courting. Anderson's accompanist Vehanen said the Salle Gaveau recitals led to "almost too many offers for engagements. Managers came by plane from Italy, Spain, Belgium, and each of them eagerly opened the door to concerts in his country, doors that until then had seemingly been closed to her. There were enough appearances possible now to assure the managers that they would receive large percentages, although in the very beginning there had been some deficits."

What Hurok now wanted to present in America was not some new unknown talent—as he later implied—but a proven international box office draw. Sol Hurok did not "discover" Marian Anderson; he simply picked the right moment to bring her home.

Hurok opened negotiations by coming backstage at intermission to pay compliments. He then asked her if she could meet with him the next day at the office of Fritz Horowitz, the Paris manager who had arranged the concert at the Salle Gaveau. When Anderson and Vehanen appeared as requested, excited and feeling "inadequate" in the presence of this grand impresario, Hurok offered her "fifteen concerts at a certain fee, which was less than I had hoped for," said Anderson. "There was a disappointing moment, but it went quickly. I was convinced in my heart that he could do something unusual for a performer if he took a notion to do so." Informed of Hurok's offer, Judson made no attempt to match it. Judson and Anderson parted company, and she and Hurok signed the first of many contracts. (After a while, as with many of his longtime artists, she and Hurok dispensed with contracts altogether.)

Although in his memoirs Hurok claims to have come to hear Anderson "cold" at the Salle Gaveau, it is hard to believe, with his many contacts, that he did not know at the time he signed her up that she would be appearing that coming summer in Salzburg, site of one of the world's most prestigious music festivals. As it happened, Arturo Toscanini came to hear her recital and allegedly delivered a ringing endorsement of the sort that public relations people dream about: "Yours is a voice such as one hears once in a hundred years." Then at the height of his influence and popularity in the United States, Toscanini had been associated for many years with the Metropolitan Opera and the New York Philharmonic. In 1937, he would become conductor of the NBC Symphony. A blurb from such a venerated source made selling Anderson in America all that much easier.

The venue Hurok selected for Anderson's triumphant return was Town Hall, where she had flopped some years before. The difference this time, though, was that she had a well-organized marketing effort behind her, billing her as the "American Colored Contralto"—a description that apparently did not offend her. Numerous advance stories about her ecstatically received appearances in Europe preceded her arrival in New York on the *Île de France*. During the crossing, Anderson fell and broke her ankle, but she and Hurok decided to go ahead with the first concert on December 30. Refusing to make an apologetic announcement of her indisposition,

Anderson was wheeled onstage behind curtains which raised to show her standing in the bend of the piano.

For this important occasion, she chose a demanding program that would "show whatever I was capable of doing, including low notes and high." There was a group of Handel songs, a Schubert group, a Verdi aria, some Finnish songs, and finally, several Negro spirituals. In these last, especially John Payne's moving "The Crucifixion," which showed off the deep, rich timbre and extraordinary low range of Anderson's voice to best advantage, the contralto felt "as if I had come home, fully and unreservedly—not only because they were the songs I had sung from childhood but also because the program was almost finished, and I had survived."

The reviews were positive, but it was Howard Taubman of the *New York Times* who seized on the historic nature of the moment in his lead: "Let it be said at the outset: Marian Anderson has returned to her native land one of the great singers of our time." In his last paragraph, he also grappled directly with the issue of race discrimination, drawing on boxing for purposes of comparison. "If Joe Louis deserves to be an American hero for bowling over a lot of pushovers, then Marian Anderson has the right to at least a comparable standing."

Anderson continued to experience the sting of racism. In New York she had to stay at the YWCA in Harlem, and when keeping appointments with her dentist at the Essex House, she had to enter by the servants' entrance. And yet attitudes were changing in the United States, in part at the courageous personal initiative of First Lady Eleanor Roosevelt. A committed advocate of civil rights, she consistently shocked conservatives (and annoyed her more pragmatic husband) by greeting black delegations in the White House. In February 1936, less than two months after Anderson's recital at Town Hall, Eleanor Roosevelt invited her to sing at a dinner in the president's private apartments at the White House. This made Hurok's "discovery" one of the first blacks ever invited to entertain a U.S. president at his official residence.

Mrs. Roosevelt also gave the event nationwide coverage by commenting on it—in an understated and natural fashion—in one of the first of her "My Day" syndicated newspaper columns. (Curiously enough, she had sent off her inaugural column on December 30, 1935—the date of Anderson's historic Town Hall appearance.)

The townspeople of Pogar around the turn of the century

Sol Hurok around the time he arrived in the United States in 1906 *(Courtesy of Dance Collection, The New York Public Library for the Performing Arts, Astor, Lenox, and Tilden Foundations)*

Anna Pavlova
at home in Golders
Green, 1920s *(Ernst Schneider/
Courtesy of Ruth Lief)*

LEFT: Anna Pavlova, in front of her
traveling trunk *(Abbe/Courtesy of Ruth Lief)*

BELOW: Hurok (with fedora) and Fyodor
Chaliapin (standing, center) with bums at a
flophouse in the Bowery, 1921
(Courtesy of Ruth Lief)

LEFT: Hurok seeing Chaliapin off, 1920s *(Courtesy of Ruth Lief)*

Hurok and Alexander Glazunov, 1929 *(Mishkin/Courtesy of Ruth Lief)*

Left to right: Edna Purviance, Hurok, Charlie Chaplin, and an unidentified man *(Courtesy of Ruth Lief)*

Members of the Monte Carlo Ballet Russe at Grand Central Station, New York, c. 1934. Left to right: Alexander Philipoff, Irving Deakin, Olga Morosova, Colonel Vasily de Basil, Sono Osato *(Courtesy of Dance Collection, The New York Public Library for the Performing Arts, Astor, Lenox, and Tilden Foundations)*

LEFT: Hurok at a train station; the signature on the photo reads: "To my dear daughter. S. Hurok." *(Courtesy of Ruth Lief)*

BELOW: Hurok standing in the room of a house at teatime in Minsk, 1930 *(Courtesy of Dance Collection, The New York Public Library for the Performing Arts, Astor, Lenox, and Tilden Foundations)*

ABOVE: The crowd gathered to hear Marian Anderson sing (RIGHT) at her concert at the Lincoln Memorial, Easter Sunday, 1939 *(Courtesy of Ruth Lief)*

LEFT: Marian Anderson and Sol Hurok in her dressing room *(Courtesy of Ruth Lief)*

RIGHT: Hurok with Alicia Markova (left, as Juliet) and Lucia Chase (right, as the Nurse) in the Ballet Theatre production of Antony Tudor's *Romeo and Juliet*, 1943 *(Alfredo Valente/Courtesy of Ruth Lief)*

LEFT: Hurok backstage at the Met with Janet Reed of Ballet Theatre, 1944—a typical Hurok publicity photo *(Courtesy of Dance Collection, The New York Public Library for the Performing Arts, Astor, Lenox, and Tilden Foundations)*

BELOW: Hurok as the bear-trainer in the Ballet Theatre production of *Petrushka*, 1942 *(Courtesy of Dance Collection, The New York Public Library for the Performing Arts, Astor, Lenox, and Tilden Foundations)*

RIGHT: Andrés Segovia. The inscription reads: "To Mr. Hurok more freind [sic] than manager, although he is the best manager . . . Cordially. New York, 1951." *(Courtesy of Ruth Lief)*

OPPOSITE: Hurok seated before the mirror in Margot Fonteyn's dressing room *(Felix Fonteyn/ Courtesy of Dance Collection, The New York Public Library for the Performing Arts, Astor, Lenox, and Tilden Foundations)*

ABOVE: Arthur Rubinstein at the keyboard. The inscription reads: "To Sol Hurok, in fond remembrance of 12 years of a perfect collaboration—with my devoted friendship. Nov. 1, 1949." *(Courtesy of Ruth Lief)*

RIGHT: Hurok about to fly off on another trip *(Rothschild Photo/Courtesy of Dance Collection, The New York Public Library for the Performing Arts, Astor, Lenox, and Tilden Foundations)*

Hurok and his wife, Emma,
appearing for a performance
*(Louis Melancon/Courtesy of Dance
Collection, The New York Public
Library for the Performing Arts, Astor,
Lenox, and Tilden Foundations)*

BELOW LEFT: Hurok and Margot
Fonteyn at the old Met, c. 1961
(Courtesy of Ruth Lief)

BELOW: Hurok and Margot
Fonteyn in Monte Carlo
(Courtesy of Ruth Lief)

Hurok and Van Cliburn arriving in Moscow, 1960 *(Courtesy of Genrietta Belyaeva)*

LEFT: Hurok (left) with Igor Moiseyev (right) and two of the dancers in the Moiseyev Dance Company, during their first performances in New York, 1958 *(Wide World Photos, Inc./Courtesy of Dance Collection, The New York Public Library for the Performing Arts, Astor, Lenox, and Tilden Foundations)*

Dean Rusk (left), Van Cliburn (center), and Hurok *(A. Less/Courtesy of Ruth Lief)*

Dancer Vladimir Papovnik of the Ukrainian Dance Company shows his fabulous elevation by leaping above a seated Hurok. *(Wayne Shilkret/Courtesy of Dance Collection, The New York Public Library for the Performing Arts, Astor, Lenox, and Tilden Foundations)*

LEFT: Mstislav Rostropovich in 1965. The inscription (a little poem in Russian) reads: "If you are smart and sly [*yurok*]/Don't strain your mighty brain./There's no better agent, it's plain/Than our great Sol Hurok." *(Courtesy of Ruth Lief)*

BELOW: Novelist Boris Pasternak (standing at center) backstage at the Moscow Conservatory after a concert by the New York Philharmonic, 1958. Seated to Pasternak's right is the orchestra's conductor, Leonard Bernstein (smoking a cigarette), and seated to his left is Hurok. *(Courtesy of Ruth Lief)*

LEFT: Hurok (right) with Dmitri Shostakovich (left) and Kiril Kondrashin (center) in Moscow in the 1960s *(Courtesy of Ruth Lief)*

Dancer Maya Plisetskaya at her dacha *(Courtesy of Ruth Lief)*

Jacqueline Kennedy receiving the Bolshoi Ballet and Hurok (center) on the steps of the White House, autumn 1962 *(Courtesy of Ruth Lief)*

Rudolf Nureyev and
Margot Fonteyn in
rehearsal *(Frederika
Davis/Courtesy of Dance
Collection, The New York
Public Library for the Per-
forming Arts, Astor, Lenox,
and Tilden Foundations)*

RIGHT: In front of the Gosconcert
offices on Neglinnaya Street in
Moscow, early 1970s. Left to
right: Simon Semenoff, Larissa
Netto, Hurok, and Vladimir
Golovin, Deputy Director of
Gosconcert *(Courtesy of Larissa Netto)*

BELOW: Hurok backstage with
Nureyev and Pierre and Margaret
Trudeau *(Courtesy of Ruth Lief)*

WASHINGTON, February 21—My husband and I had a rare treat Wednesday night in listening to Marian Anderson, a colored contralto, who has made a great success in Europe and this country. She has sung before nearly all the crowned heads and deserves her great success, for I have rarely heard a more beautiful and moving voice or a more finished artist. She sang three Schubert songs and finished with two Negro spirituals, one of which I had never heard of before.

Mrs. Roosevelt would come to Anderson's defense even more pointedly three years later, with yet greater public relations repercussions.

Although Hurok claimed otherwise, Anderson said later that even all this free publicity did not create enough interest for Hurok to scare up the fifteen engagements he had promised her in Paris. He did arrange a successful Carnegie Hall concert, and Anderson felt that he and his associates (particularly Mae Frohman and Gerald Goode) were doing an excellent and sensitive job in promoting her. As he had done with the Monte Carlo Ballet Russe, Hurok was counting on future seasons to return the initial investment he was making, and was disregarding the advice of doomsayers, one of whom had warned him, "You won't be able to give her away."

As the 1930s progressed, the international situation grew more and more ominous. On his annual summer trips through Europe and Russia, Hurok saw disturbing signs of Germany's increasing militarization and heard anxious talk of impending war. In the spring of 1933, a massive campaign of violence directed against Jews broke out all over Germany, and in April (just a few months after Hitler was appointed chancellor), "non-Aryan" civil servants were dismissed. As a frequent visitor to Berlin, where he had many acquaintances and associates, Hurok was well informed about the rising tide of anti-Semitism. Back home in New York, he began to speak out in interviews against Hitler's policies. As early as August 1934, he told the *Jewish Daily Bulletin* and the *Jewish Daily Forward* that the boycott against trade with Germany should also extend to "all artists who have accepted engagements in Nazi Germany. It was outrageous . . . that artists should sing in Germany for Nazi audiences and then come to the United States where a good part of their audiences consisted of Jews." Hurok even named several of the offending parties: Alexander Kipnis, Frieda Leider, Laurence Melchior, and, most surprisingly, his own former buddy, Fyodor Chaliapin, all of whom, "he declared, not only sang for the Nazis, but afterwards were presented to Adolf Hitler."

It is true that Chaliapin made a tour of Germany in April 1934, appearing in Munich, Stuttgart, Frankfurt, Leipzig, Dresden, Hamburg, and Berlin. In fact, Chaliapin, who often referred disparagingly to Jews—including Hurok—in correspondence and conversation, continued to perform in Germany as late as early 1937, after the racist policies of the Nazis had become clear to everyone and many performers were refusing to appear there. But the singer's son Fyodor, who lived in Germany in 1934 and claimed to have accompanied him throughout this tour, vehemently denied that Chaliapin ever met with Hitler or, as Hurok claimed elsewhere, shook his hand.

Chaliapin's son interpreted Hurok's accusation as a vengeful attempt to discredit his father as a result of their bitter break in 1927 (see Chapter 6). Ever since then, Chaliapin's American appearances had been handled by other impresarios. When the singer came on tour to the United States in late 1932, he was presented by Coppicus and the Metropolitan Music Bureau, a division of the Columbia Concerts Corporation—the main competitor of the NBC Artists Service of which S. Hurok Attractions was a part. On Chaliapin's next (and last) American tour during the first few months of 1935, the singer was presented by Musical Art Management, an agency run by another Russian émigré, Alexander Merovitch.

Curiously, however, when Hurok inaugurated his concert series at Carnegie Hall in the 1937–38 season, he advertised "The Great and Only Chaliapin" as the first attraction. By that time, however, Chaliapin was gravely ill. Indeed, it seems possible that Hurok took advantage of Chaliapin's weakened condition to publicize the concert without securing the singer's agreement, knowing full well that his sickness would make it difficult for him to object and impossible for him to come. Nor is there any evidence that Hurok and Chaliapin had reconciled their differences. In any case, Hurok cited

Chaliapin's death on April 12, 1938, as the reason for his inability to keep the Carnegie Hall date.

If Hurok went on the record early and consistently against Nazism (by the mid-1930s he stopped importing attractions from Germany and claimed he would "not set foot in Hitler's Reich"), his attitudes toward what was happening in Stalin's Russia were considerably more complicated. Through his annual visits with Emma's family in Leningrad and his own many contacts and relatives in the USSR, Hurok had a considerably more realistic idea of what was going on there than most Americans did. They were receiving rosy portraits of Soviet life from American journalists, especially the *New York Times* correspondent Walter Duranty, but Hurok was aware of another side of Soviet reality: Stalin's persecution and imprisonment of dissidents and artists, which by the late 1930s had reached epidemic proportions. He had to know, for example, of the vicious campaign launched in early 1936 by Stalin and his cultural goons against Dmitri Shostakovich and his opera *Lady Macbeth of the Mtsensk District*, which had been successfully staged in New York in 1935.

That Hurok knew much more about how oppressive life in the USSR had become than he was admitting publicly is clear from a letter he wrote (or dictated?) to Irving Deakin on July 16, 1937, from Salzburg, only eight months before the German annexation of Austria. Hurok had just returned from an extended stay in the Soviet Union. The letter's awkward grammar and diction indicate that he had a hand in composing it.

> You probably have been mad like hell at me for not writing you sooner and for not letting you know where I am and whether dead or alive, whether I have been shot or taken to one of the concentration camps or sent out to some place where nobody would know to find me, and for no reason in the world as they do now. . . .
>
> Really, Irving, you must realize I have been on the run all the time and particularly those five weeks that I spent in Russia. Now I have the O.K. of the Government officials that I can bring over any attractions I want, including

the ballet, and practically have made all the arrangements. We shall talk about the details when I get to New York. Upon my arrival there I suppose I will have to make some decisions what attractions I am to bring from Russia and also about the ballet. . . .

After I left Paris I have been through Germany, Poland, Latvia, Esthonia [sic], Russia, Austria, and am now in Mondsee which is Austria, although it is almost unbelievable that this peaceful spot belongs to any of the countries mentioned above. . . .

Speaking confidentially—by no means for publication or to tell anybody; if you do, it might endanger many lives and would put me personally on the spot—but I can't help it, every time I speak or write to my friends I simply have got to mention it: no pen or writer could give a true description of what's happening there (you know what country I am talking of), the terrible conditions, the horrors and the fear in which these almost 300 million people live. I think it's lunacy, hysteria, the fear of loosing [sic] power and control, or it is sadism and at any rate barbarism, call it whatever you want: I am actually a nervous wreck from the horrors I have seen myself and heard about.—Mrs. Hurok went straight on to Paris and did not stop in Vienna as she was all broken up and sick of the terrible times we went through: not able to find your friends, not able to see your relatives, not to dare to go up to somebody's house or people not daring to see you in a hotel for fear that for this crime they might be removed from this splendid earth.—But I have come to the conclusion that there is no hope for this system to last; the general sentiment is 90% or more in opposition against it, including the army. War or no war: the end will be soon. All you read in the newspapers about it is not one per cent of the truth.

So, my dear Irving, you and your wife and myself and all our friends, we have got to work harder than ever and to do everything in our power to fight for the only holy thing left in our world—and that is DEMOCRACY. Personal liberty, personal freedom, freedom to sleep for six hours, to be left alone, freedom to breathe, freedom of expression, of thought and of action—when you have these, nothing else matters. Give my personal love to the Statue of Liberty. Upon my arrival I shall embrace 50 times and more the Statue of Liberty and shall kiss the soil we are living on.

Forgive me for writing that kind of a letter, but I can't help it.

In letters to presenters and in *public* statements upon his arrival back in the United States, however, Hurok hid these gloomy and apocalyptic feelings. It isn't difficult to figure out why. If he told the truth about Stalinist repression as he had seen it, Soviet officials would retaliate by canceling his hard-won agreement (now in negotiation for more than ten years) to bring the Bolshoi Ballet and other Soviet attractions to the United States for the first time. ("Now I have the O.K. of the Government officials that I can bring over any attractions I want . . .") Nor would Americans be likely to spend their money on Soviet performers if Hurok were to make public the terrible truth of what was going on in Russia.

On this occasion, as on many others, Hurok put business before honesty.

In an August 28, 1936, letter to the renowned arts patron Elizabeth Sprague Coolidge, for example, he bragged: "I am now making arrangements with the Soviet government for a number of attractions for the season of 1937–38—attractions which I believe will add another year to my long record of bringing to this country artists of real merit."

In interviews with Western newspapers in 1936 and 1937, Hurok consciously misrepresented what he had seen in the USSR by spinning glowing tales of a lively cultural life and a happy Russian people engaged in building a wonderful new society. "In Russia the theatre, the music, everything is flourishing, growing, doubling itself," he told The New York *Post* in August 1936. He also lied about how easy it was to get permission for artists to travel out of the country. "Over there they have a Central Bureau for artists. You go to the bureau as you would go to a private manager for an artist in this country. The bureau protects the artist, arranges for his passport, his expenses and all that."

In fact, this central concert and touring bureau (called *Gastrol'buro*, and later *Goskontsert*) was infamous among performers for its inefficiency, corruption, and links to the secret police. Virtually no performers were granted the right to travel abroad; those who were had to turn over almost all of their foreign earnings to the Soviet government and submit to the indignity of constant surveillance by Soviet police agents.

Hurok also praised the generous subsidies cultural organizations received from the Soviet government and insisted—despite his familiarity with overwhelming evidence to the contrary—that Soviet artists were free to create and perform as they wished.

> The Government has unlimited funds to support all artistic productions. . . . They don't care how much they spend, as long as the concert or production is perfect. . . . Of course, right after the revolution . . . everybody was jittery and all that. But now the Government tells the artists their job is to raise the cultural level of the masses. The theatre is the freest in the world, because they don't even have to think about making money, which detail restricts producers in other countries. . . . They put on all the classics over there and don't omit a line.

Not surprisingly, Hurok failed to mention that as recently as February, a negative *Pravda* review of the play *Moliere* by Mikhail Bulgakov had led it to be removed from the stage of the Moscow Art Theatre after just seven nights. Nor did he mention that *Pravda* had declared the distinguished novelist and screenwriter Boris Pilnyak (who had spent five months under contract with MGM in Hollywood in 1931) to be an "enemy of the people." Pilnyak was eventually arrested in October 1937 and shot soon afterward, like thousands of other "dissident" writers, directors, actors, musicians, and scholars.

Still apparently believing (despite the worsening international climate) that he would shortly be scoring a commercial and artistic coup by bringing Soviet performers to the United States, Hurok continued to defend and praise Soviet culture. He maintained that position even after his next visit to the USSR in the summer of

1937—his last for many years. By that time, historians estimate, Stalin's purges (the "Terror") had led to the deportation to labor camps of five million citizens and the execution of five hundred thousand. But Hurok chose to ignore the accelerating anti-cultural campaign that closed twenty Soviet theaters, denounced world-famous filmmakers like Alexander Dovzhenko and Sergei Eisenstein, shut down production on one hundred films, and made even the most celebrated artists fear for their lives. Instead, he focused in an interview with the New York Russian émigré newspaper *Novoe russkoe slovo* on his plans to bring the Bolshoi Ballet and Opera to the United States.

Hurok even had kind words for the simpleminded "song opera" *Quiet Flows the Don* by Soviet composer Ivan Dzherzhinsky. Based on a classic socialist realist novel, this musically and dramatically impoverished—but politically correct—opera had flopped when first presented in 1934. In 1936, however, it returned to the repertoire with Stalin's personal blessing. Even worse, after Stalin ordered Shostakovich's brilliant *Lady Macbeth of Mtsensk* removed from all Soviet stages in January 1936 because of its supposed obscenity and pessimism, Dzherzhinsky's slight patriotic work became the enforced model for Soviet composers to follow. (Later, in 1948, Dzherzhinsky joined in another ideological assault upon Shostakovich, who had encouraged him as a student at Leningrad Conservatory.) Apparently hoping to endear himself to the Soviet cultural establishment, Hurok told *Novoe russkoe slovo* that *Quiet Flows the Don* had "made a big impression" on him. But he made no mention of the recent *Lady Macbeth* scandal.

Hurok also admitted that he had still failed to obtain final approval from Soviet officials for a planned 1937–38 American tour by the Bolshoi. "But it's possible that next year Americans will see the latest works of the Russian theatre right here at home. Then they can judge for themselves."

By 1938, however, the Soviet domestic situation was deteriorating rapidly, and Stalin's growing xenophobia made it increasingly unlikely that he would allow Soviet performers to tour the West. Even Soviet composer Sergei Prokofiev (1891–1953), whose international stature had allowed him to travel regularly between the USSR and the United States through the 1930s, was unable to keep engagements in America planned for the 1939 season. In subsequent years, the conditions were even less auspicious for tours by Soviet soloists and ensembles, as Hitler's expansion in Europe and the Soviet-German nonaggression pact of 1939 increasingly isolated the USSR from the rest of the world.

After World War II, Hurok continued to whitewash Stalin in the hopes of getting the attractions he wanted out of Russia. In *Impresario*, published in 1946 in the warm afterglow of the victorious Soviet-American wartime alliance, he even described a meeting with Stalin ("the great man of the Soviets") in Moscow in 1936. Hurok claimed that the theatrical director Vladimir Nemirovich-Dantchenko had introduced them during the intermission at a performance of Bulgakov's very popular *Days of the Turbins*, a play about which Stalin and his cultural henchmen had very mixed feelings. (They had even banned an earlier version for its overly sympathetic portrayal of the "Whites," the early enemies of the Bolsheviks.) As usual, Hurok's account of his supposed meeting with Stalin, who is portrayed here as an avid arts patron and reasonable person, is riddled with inaccuracies. The most glaring is his assertion that he was still Chaliapin's American manager.

> In those days, before the treason trials [in fact they had begun in early 1935], Stalin was not inaccessible, especially not to artists of the music and theatre world, and their managers. He went constantly to the theatre, the ballet, the opera, and it was in the lounge next to Stanislavsky's office, reserved for high Government officials and their guests, that I stood, among a dozen Soviet celebrities, in Stalin's presence.
>
> Nemirovitch-Dantchenko presented me as Chaliapin's American manager.
>
> "What is Chaliapin doing?" Stalin asked. "Why doesn't he come to Moscow?"
>
> "I suppose," Nemirovitch-Dantchenko offered, "he needs quite a lot of money to live these days. He makes money abroad."
>
> "We'll give him money, if it is money he needs," Stalin said.

"Well, then, there's the matter of housing. He has a large family, you know." The housing shortage in Moscow was one of the favorite subjects for feature stories in the European and American press in those days.

"We'll give him a house in Moscow. We'll give him a house in the country, too. Just tell him to come home."

I gave the message to Marie Valentinovna, Madame Chaliapin, whom I met in Paris. Chaliapin was in Baden-Baden, and since this was 1936, I would not set foot in Hitler's Reich. Chaliapin did not live to accept the invitation.

Hurok implies that Chaliapin would actually have seriously considered such an invitation, which was very far from the truth. By the late 1930s, Chaliapin no longer had any interest in returning to the USSR. He knew what was happening to artists there, and he knew what had happened to his old friend, the writer Maxim Gorky, who had gone back to Russia in 1931 and was later denied permission to travel abroad. (Gorky died under suspicious circumstances outside Moscow in June 1936.) Within his family, Chaliapin made no secret of his distaste for the Soviet system. He once told his son Fyodor that he "hated the whole style of life in Soviet Russia" and would never have considered living there. "My father," Fyodor said, "was persecuted even after his departure; taxes were imposed on him, he was stripped of his title of People's Artist, he was vilified." Fortunately for Chaliapin, he had become an international star and no longer needed anything from the USSR or its leaders.

But Hurok still wanted something from the Soviet government, which made him dependent on its whims and crude tactics. Ironically, however, Hurok's work as an apologist for Stalin failed in the end to produce the results he wanted. Put off time and again by fervent promises of "next season," he would finally pry the Bolshoi out of Moscow only after the suspicious and demented Great Leader of All the Peoples was dead.

CHAPTER ELEVEN

A Whore in a Church

"I will tell the truth, the whole truth, and nothing is the truth."—*Alexandra Danilova*

THE 1937-38 SEASON was the last peaceful one for Col. W. de Basil's Ballet Russe. (The company had, for some reason, elected for its American appearances to drop the plural form of its Frenchified name in favor of the singular.) Eager to go off in new directions but bound by contract to fulfill their obligations, the troupe's various and strong-willed artists and managers united (not always happily) for a last hurrah.

First came a final set of engagements at London's Covent Garden and New York's Metropolitan Opera House (in late October), then another extensive North American tour through the winter and early spring. Ironically enough in light of the troupe's impending dissolution, the performances drew record crowds and rave reviews. In celebration of the coronation of George VI, the London season was particularly festive and included the world premieres of four ballets, three of them choreographed by David Lichine: *Francesca da Rimini*, *Les Dieux Mendiants*, and *Le Lion Amoureux*. The seemingly ubiquitous Michel Fokine, who had joined de Basil's troupe in June, choreographed the extravagantly produced *Le Coq d'Or*. It was designed by Natalia Goncharova and set to music adapted by Nicholas Tcherepnin from Rimsky-Korsakov's fairy-tale opera of the same name. Critics wrote that the company was performing at its peak.

Fokine and Massine, both ballet legends and great favorites in England, had not worked in the same troupe since Diaghilev's time. Their reunion brought back fond memories to many, among them Janet Flanner of the *New Yorker*. "At Covent Garden, the de Basil Ballets Russes opened as, and still are, a triumph. Even at the old Châtelet in Paris, when Diaghilev was alive, we never saw a first night at which both spectators and dancers were more brilliantly ebullient; at which floral tributes were more florid . . . and at which a pandemonium of applause seemed more suitable." Attendance records tumbled as ballet fans stood in line for days to get standing room tickets.

With these English accolades still ringing in the dancers' ears, Hurok opened the company at the Met on October 22, 1937. During a highly publicized ten-day engagement, New Yorkers saw the four new ballets produced in London and sixteen other popular repertory items. After a one-night stand at the Brooklyn Academy of Music, not far from Brownsville, he sent them off on a profitable four-month tour of the United States and Canada.

But even as the de Basil company was enjoying its greatest artistic and commercial season ever, chronic personal, organizational, and financial disagreements were tearing it apart. On January 30, 1938, in Oakland, Massine finally left the troupe he had led as ballet master and artistic director since 1932. (Although Massine had announced his intention to leave the preceding spring, Hurok, aware of his box office appeal, had insisted to de Basil that he join the company on most of its American tour.) With Massine's departure for the newly formed Denham-Fleischmann-Hurok company, de Basil lost a very popular principal dancer and his most productive choreographer, a major artist who had created seventeen ballets and knew inside out the dancers' strengths and weaknesses.

Not surprisingly, Massine's action led to considerable anxiety and friction. Engaged in a bitter lawsuit over ownership of the ballets he had choreographed, Massine and de Basil were "not on speaking terms" for months before he actually left. According to company member Yurek Lazowski, Massine went so far as to prohibit anyone from being in the wings when he danced, since he feared that others would try to take advantage of the unsettled legal situation by studying and stealing his roles.

Thrown into confusion, most of the dancers began to take sides and make plans. Alexandra Danilova, the partner with whom Massine was most closely identified in the public mind, had already accepted "with pleasure" his invitation to go with him to the new Denham company. To her, Massine might have been a "terrible" partner, but he was a "genius" and "a first-class dancer, very passionate, expressive, with a style of his own, in some ways more a modern dancer than a classical dancer." Perhaps he wasn't as brilliant as Balanchine, but as a choreographer the 1930s "belonged to him, and he helped prepare the way for what came after," especially in his introduction of abstract ballets and complicated footwork.

With their futures suddenly cloudy, the nomadic dancers, most of them still stateless Russians, were further disoriented by some unexpected news (made public in a *New York Times* story in March) about their manager, Hurok. Having spent the American tour in his customarily clandestine fashion, scurrying about behind the scenes, he was now trying to merge what was left of the de Basil organization into his new Massine-Denham company. This new animal would be called the Ballet Russe de Monte Carlo (here we go again). What Hurok wanted was de Basil's dancers and ballets; he had no desire to retain de Basil himself.

Hurok's new proposal to the conniving colonel also stemmed from the outcome of the long legal battle between Massine and de Basil over ownership of Massine's ballets. In late February 1938, the presiding English judge had awarded just four of the works in question to Massine and the remaining thirteen to de Basil. Hurok needed and wanted this repertoire, which had been essential to the popular success of the Russian ballet in the United States. It seems likely, therefore, that one of his major goals in opening merger negotiations with de Basil in March was to get Massine's ballets back somehow.

There was yet another hidden reason why Hurok was suddenly interested in making up with the colonel. When he had signed the original agreement with Denham and Fleischmann in May 1937 to form a new company headed by Massine, Hurok had also been told that Balanchine had agreed to become a regular collaborator. It turned out that Hurok had been misled. In December, Balanchine embarrassed and angered Hurok by informing him (in somewhat broken English) that he had never authorized "anyone whomsoever to insert my name among list of regular and permanent collaborators of ballet company and I definitely refuse to let my name be used in any manner whatsoever." Hurok blamed Denham for the misunderstanding and demanded that in the future his new partner show "more businesslike methods and less fantasy." Without Balanchine's reputation and dancers, the new company was in even greater need of de Basil's resources, which helps to explain Hurok's renewed efforts to obtain them.

Hurok eventually persuaded Denham that a merger with de Basil's troupe should be attempted. Through late March and early April, attorneys for both sides met in long sessions to hammer out a solution. The complicated negotiations ended in an all-night marathon fueled by take-out hamburgers consumed in the tony conference room of the St. Regis Hotel. On April 15, 1938, Hurok finally managed to railroad the various parties to sign an agreement. Significantly, de Basil, so often an obstacle in the past, was not present. He was traveling in Europe and, clearly unaware of what his "colleagues" were up to, had assigned a proxy to represent him at the negotiations.

What resulted was a single new company to be formed out of the de Basil and Denham companies. It would be called (what else?) the Ballet Russe de Monte Carlo. Hurok believed this would be "the finest ballet company under my wing that had ever existed, finer even than Diaghilev . . . had ever achieved." The new troupe would have Julius Fleischmann as president, Serge Denham as vice president and director, René Blum as codirector, and Massine as head of the artistic council. De Basil was demoted to a member of the board of governors. Hurok would control American tours, including his usual demand to approve the cast for "each and every performance" at least thirty days in advance and to "select the program for the respective American cities." The roster would include sixty-one dancers, at least forty-eight of whom should be "artist dancers" and at least five of whom should be "known as dancer stars two of whom shall be female and having a reputation with the American public." Denham and de Basil also promised that Massine, Serge Lifar (another former Diaghilev dancer and the artistic director of the Paris Opera ballet), and David Lichine would dance.

In return, Hurok agreed to do all publicity and to arrange a twenty-three-week tour of the United States, Canada, Mexico, and Cuba. Hurok estimated that his weekly expenses for presenting the company in nine performances weekly would be about $15,000, including a basic payment of $5,625 to Denham and de Basil. Of any income above that figure Hurok would receive one-half; the other half would be shared by Denham and de Basil.

Within a few weeks, though, Denham was already complaining to his lawyer Watson Washburn that Hurok had violated the publicity guidelines by failing to include the "Monte Carlo" trademark on some new advertising materials. "This incident only shows the danger in allowing Hurok to go his way in making publicity," Denham wrote. "I have been saying all along that Hurok should be put in his right place. . . . I am asking you to advise Mr. Hurok immediately in a very definite form that he should abandon once and forever making publicity without consulting us in advance."

But Denham's complaints were nothing compared to de Basil's. Hardly had the ink dried on the merger agreement before the colonel, on tour in Germany with his company, began to understand—with good reason—that Hurok, Denham, and their lawyers had taken advantage of his absence to pull a fast one back in New York. De Basil was also horrified to discover that under the terms of the agreement signed by his proxy, he had also given up the right to produce four of his most successful ballets: *Symphonie fantastique*, *La Boutique fantasque*, *Le Tricorne*, and Fokine's *Le Coq d'Or*. Meanwhile, the dancers and backstage administrators were fanning the fires of intrigue and bad feeling, engaging in the divisive gossip and backstabbing to which they were all hopelessly addicted.

By early June, de Basil (who had not been cast as the evil sorcerer von Rothbart in *Swan Lake* for nothing) had repudiated the merger agreement. He insisted that he would never have signed such a document if he had known what it contained. Upon the advice of his friend and legal advisers, he gave up his position as director of Col. W de Basil's Ballet Russe and allowed his battered company to be regrouped under a new name, Educational Ballets, Ltd. Pavlova's husband Victor Dandré became its chairman and director. Preparations began immediately for the hastily created troupe's scheduled opening at Covent Garden on June 20, under yet another name: Russian Ballet.

What followed was a strange and desperate competition for the London ballet-going public between the remnants of de Basil's troupe and the "new" Ballet Russe de Monte Carlo managed by Hurok. Already in London, Hurok rented the Drury Lane Theatre and got ready to open on July 12. The internecine warfare between the two companies—reminiscent of the secretive and deadly struggles for the Romanov throne that make Russian history so intricate and colorful—provided considerable entertainment for London's many balletomanes. They throbbed with excitement at the prospect of a dancing showdown, a duel *en pointe* between two scandal-prone troupes of temperamental Slavs locked in a choreographic struggle for their hearts and pounds.

The city's more hardy and dedicated dance enthusiasts took to visiting both theaters in the course of a single evening, dashing across Bow Street at intervals to catch their favorite ballerinas and ballets. Both companies relied heavily on ballets choreographed by Fokine, who was, in Arnold Haskell's words, "the outstanding figure of the present season." Despite all the turmoil, Hurok's Ballet Russe de Monte Carlo managed to stage four new ballets at the Drury Lane Theatre that summer. Massine did three of them: *Gaîté Parisienne,* Seventh Symphony to Beethoven, and *Nobilissima Visione (St. Francis)* to a commissioned score by Paul Hindemith. Serge Lifar contributed the fourth—*Icare.*

Meanwhile, at Covent Garden, de Basil's Educational Ballets (or Russian Ballet, if you prefer) managed just two new productions: Lichine's *Protée* (set to Debussy's *Danse sacrée et Danse profane*) and Fokine's *Cendrillon* (with score and financial backing by Baron Frédéric d'Erlanger).

Another of the big attractions of the Ballet Russe de Monte Carlo season was Lifar's staging of the classic *Giselle.* He also danced the leading role of Prince Albrecht, whose careless aristocratic love for a peasant girl causes her death. Three ballerinas were chosen to alternate in the role of Giselle, one of the greatest female roles in the repertoire: Toumanova, Mia Slavenska, and Alicia Markova. Markova, an English girl whose real name was Lillian Alicia Marks, had only recently joined the company at Massine's invitation. A seasoned and popular artist who had danced with

Diaghilev and then in various companies in England through the 1930s, she was given the honor of dancing Giselle on opening night, opposite Lifar.

Not everyone in the company was pleased with Markova's arrival and obvious status, however. The costume shop was staffed by longtime friends and admirers of Toumanova. They had always made costumes only for her and refused to produce any for Markova. Hurok came to her rescue when he allowed Markova to wear costumes from an earlier *Giselle*, even though they didn't match Alexandre Benois's new designs. Fortified by a few sips of brandy and consoled by Danilova (Queen of the Wilis, the nocturnal sprites who lure young men into their dance of death), Markova wiped away her tears. Onstage, the proud London audience greeted their homegrown star "with such warmth . . . that I knew that I would not disappoint them."

But Markova's problems with her new colleagues continued at curtain call. The notoriously self-absorbed Lifar, famous for upstaging his partners, refused to let her take a solo bow. Finally, after twenty-four curtain calls and ten minutes of applause and cheers from the gallery, he had to be restrained backstage by two burly stagehands as she went out alone to have her deserved moment of glory. The temperamental Lifar would continue to make life difficult for Markova (and for Hurok) a few months later in New York.

Showered with publicity, both Hurok's Ballet Russe de Monte Carlo and its competitor played to capacity audiences during what Hurok later called "a summer of summers." Despite their differences, dancers and administrative personnel from the two companies met, socialized, and traded gossip in various favorite watering holes. For Hurok, there was no place like the Savoy Grill, which he had been frequenting for years and where he was treated with affection as a member of the family (and a generous tipper). After performances, he would often repair there with his rival German Sevastianov, managing director of the Educational Ballets, "to gloat over their equally excellent box office receipts." These conversations increased Hurok's respect for Sevastianov, whom he would later hire as his promotion manager.

Hurok even claimed to be on good terms with de Basil, which is entirely possible considering their similar ability to let common business interests outweigh personal feelings. Just a few years later, they would find it possible to work together again. Supposedly they even made one more attempt to merge their companies in London that summer, but failed to reach an agreement.

Now that the deal to merge with de Basil's company had fallen apart, Hurok and Denham also renegotiated their contract. In *Impresario*, Hurok claims that the negotiating process went smoothly and "agreeably," but the letters they were exchanging tell a different story. Hurok continued to irritate Denham by pursuing an independent publicity campaign and by criticizing some of the company's ballets in the presence of officials of Covent Garden. Denying the allegations, Hurok insisted in a letter written from the Hotel Prince de Galles in Paris in mid-August that "anything I do is in the interests of the business and the direction." As long as they coincided with his own interests, that is.

In another awkwardly written letter, to his friend and confidant Irving Deakin, Hurok boasted of his part in the company's summer success in London:

> I must take credit to myself for the excellent job I made, I believe I worked a miracle here—in other words, the Ballet has been reborn and re-created. If I were any sort of prophet I should tell you this Company is going to stay (of course as long as I do). . . .
>
> The male ensemble is something that no company has ever had before in Europe or America. . . . Alicia Markova will be *the* sensation. . . . To me she is the only classical dancer since Pavlova, in fact I believe she is even better than Pavlova in *Giselle*. . . .
>
> I have arranged very close friendships with both companies, have opened the doors for them to see performances and to go back stage to see their friends. Everything has been done in a very comradely spirit. It is so much better it should have happened this way at present as had it not happened, then American public would have been deprived of seeing so many great artists and so much good material which this way they will have the chance of seeing and enjoying. In this respect of course I am happy that it has happened this way.

When all the cheering and infighting had died down and the "summer of summers" was passing into autumn, the two troupes parted company. De Basil and his dancers went off to Australia, where they enjoyed a huge success in a new market. In September, Hurok's Ballet Russe de Monte Carlo successfully completed a three-week run (this time without any competition) at Covent Garden. It included a $7,000 full-length restaging (by Nicholas Sergeyev and Massine) of *Coppelia*. Danilova, who was finding life with Denham "much more glamorous than life with de Basil," scored a great success in the starring role of the coquettish Swanilda. Then it was off to America for another exhausting tour.

Critics of Hurok have often charged that he promoted foreign artists, music, and ballet at the expense of American talent. To a certain extent this was true. He advised American dancers to adopt Russian names and remained unconvinced (even after the success of *Union Pacific*) that audiences could learn to like ballets on American themes. In a 1940 letter to Denham, for example, he dismissed the idea of a new ballet set to music by the American composer Roy Harris because "I do not think his music is of the kind that has any box office value." (He did like Gershwin, however, whose music he judged "artistically sound" and commercially viable.)

And yet Hurok had not completely ignored performers from the United States. He brought Marian Anderson to wider recognition and displayed a surprising and quirky interest in certain other Americans. Perhaps the most unlikely of them all was the "King of Swing," clarinetist and band leader Benny Goodman, whom Hurok presented in a concert at Carnegie Hall on January 16, 1938. Untypical though it might have been, this was one of Hurok's greatest successes, an event that went down in history as one of the first real "jazz concerts" and a defining moment of the Swing Era.

Despite his occasional presentation of cabaret acts like the *Continental Varieties*, Hurok had become increasingly identified with "classical" music and dance and had not demonstrated any particular interest in American art forms like jazz. For him, "serious" art was still primarily European. He does not seem to have frequented the many jazz clubs or big-band concerts that were becoming so popular in New York in the 1930s. But like his model P. T. Barnum, Hurok knew a good publicity stunt when he saw one. The chance to present a countercultural hero with a vast and vociferous following, whose cool, sexy style was born of low-class blues and black music, in an upscale hall that epitomized white, stuffy, "high-culture" values was just too delicious to pass up. He knew it would generate the same sort of slightly scandalized fascination as a marriage between a high-society belle and a sexy proletarian.

The idea (like so many that he subsequently propagandized as his own) was not Hurok's. It came from publicist Wynn Nathanson of the Tom Fizdale Agency. He promoted the popular radio variety show *Camel Caravan*, on which Goodman's band was a regular feature. Knowing of Hurok's close relationship with Carnegie Hall, he called the Hurok office to investigate the possibilities.

Just recently, in October 1937, after the hall had been without a regular subscription concert series for ten years, Hurok had inaugurated the first of his Hurok Carnegie Hall Series ("at popular prices"). It would run for many years to come. The first season included performances by the Vienna Boys Choir, Efrem Zimbalist, Kirsten Flagstad, Artur Schnabel, and Marian Anderson. By now, in fact, Carnegie Hall was regarded almost as Hurok's "home base," so it was hardly surprising that Fizdale should have brought him the Benny Goodman proposal. Hurok, his timing again flawless, immediately realized the potential of presenting a name performer at the height of his popularity, and a date was set.

The prospect of playing in one of the holiest temples of high culture at first made Goodman nervous. "Are you out of your mind?" he reportedly said to Nathanson. "What the hell would we do there?" But somehow his reservations were overcome, and the concert sold out well before January 16. To accommodate the huge demand for tickets, Hurok added seats on the stage around the band and sold standing room on the day of the performance. Newspapers and magazines ran extensive advance publicity, some of them wondering, like the *New York Times Magazine* in a long article on the day of the event, whether the respectability of Carnegie Hall would ruin the marvelous spontaneity and raffishness of Goodman's style.

That Sunday evening, the King and his musicians were asking themselves the same question. Just before the curtain went up, band member Harry James whispered, "I feel like a whore in a church." A music writer who saw them backstage described the tension.

"Benny, pale as a ghost, was instructing everybody to go on together, and the boys were pushing each other around in the wing space—about four feet square, filled with photographers, musicians, ticket holders with seats on the stage, a curly headed usher, trying to be dignified, and the press."

But the concert turned out to be a huge popular, commercial, and critical success. The opening number, "Don't Be That Way," Goodman's new arrangement of an Edgar Sampson piece that went on to become one of the King's many hits, generated thunderous applause, as did everything else on the program. "The huge audience swayed and rocked and tapped its feet in tempo," enthused one of the many journalists in attendance. Yes, Carnegie Hall could swing after all.

Because the concert was held in Carnegie Hall, and because newspapers still weren't quite sure how to cover jazz, classical music reviewers were sent to pass judgment on the event. Irving Kolodin of the New York *Sun* later recalled watching *New York Times* critic Olin Downes look "in pained incomprehension at his teen-age daughter, who was bouncing up and down in her seat with pleasure." In his review, Downes declared the performance "a social and physical phenomenon," but pussyfooted around the issue of what sort of music this was. He finally confessed to being "bored" long before its end. Downes's criticism prompted an unusual rebuttal on the paper's editorial page the following day, however. "There seems to be no middle group who like swing music a little. One either loves it to the point of distraction or one takes to the hills to get away from it. It is of no use to argue about it. . . . Let those who do not like it try to bear with it."

For Goodman and his band, the Carnegie Hall concert proved a turning point. Its widely publicized success led to more high-profile engagements and increased earnings. The recording of the concert released by Columbia Records in 1950 has sold more than a million copies in the United States and is still in print (and selling) today. Musically, Goodman later looked back on that performance as perhaps the most fulfilling of his career.

"I think the band I had at the Carnegie Hall Concert, about that time, was the best band I ever had. It was a really close-knit organization and they had just a wonderful ensemble and great soloists, and I think I got more satisfaction out of that band than any other." Soon afterward, the band began to fall out due to various personal and creative tensions, but it remains, as Goodman's biographer James Lincoln Collier writes, "the one that comes to mind when we think of Benny Goodman's music."

So the "Famous Carnegie Hall Concert" turned out to be the high-water mark in one of the great American musical careers of the twentieth century. This hot program on a cold night also did a great deal to bring jazz greater critical and social respectability. And Hurok had the good luck—and good sense—to present it, realizing a nice profit in the process.

Shortly before the reconstituted (Denham-Massine-Hurok) Ballet Russe de Monte Carlo opened at the Metropolitan Opera House on October 12, 1938, the still wary Serge Denham engaged two different banks—the Guaranty Trust Company of New York and the Bankers Trust Company—to conduct a confidential investigation of Hurok's financial and business history. It was not an easy task. After reviewing his checkered passage from the embroidery business in Jersey City to the incorporation of S. Hurok, Inc., through bankruptcy and various name changes (Hurok Attractions, Inc., to Hurok Musical Bureau, Inc., and back to Hurok Attractions), the Guaranty Trust report concluded somewhat uncertainly that "irrespective of the number of shifts in title, Mr. Hurok apparently stands well in his profession but absolutely no financial information is available."

The investigators from Bankers Trust also found it difficult to deliver a definitive diagnosis on Hurok's financial health. They cautioned that "investment in the company is somewhat limited," and that "Mr. Hurok and his companies have been the subject of a good deal of litigation." They admitted, however, that this sort of thing had to be expected in show biz. "People we talked to feel in this type of business a certain amount of litigation arising from disputes is to be expected." An understatement, to be sure.

Denham and his business partners apparently decided that Hurok's financial record, while far from spotless, was not deficient enough to cause cancellation of the American tour. It opened at the Met as scheduled—in a flurry of publicity—with *Gaîté Parisienne* and *Giselle*. As in London, war broke out among the ballerinas and their champions over who should get to dance Giselle on opening night. Massine, the company's artistic director (at least in name), had promised it to Markova for her American debut. But Lifar, who would dance Albrecht, was still annoyed with her for upstaging him at Drury Lane and had promised the role to Toumanova. When Massine insisted on Markova, Toumanova withdrew from the season in protest.

Right up until curtain time, Markova was receiving threats; one day on the street a stranger gave her a note that said: "Don't dance tomorrow night, or . . ." Markova danced anyway, although Hurok took no chances. He hired detectives and dressed them as stagehands to prevent any further incidents. The opening night went off well, with a rave from John Martin, but bad luck continued to follow Markova. During the first act of the second performance, Lifar slipped and fell on her feet, and she had to be replaced in Act II and subsequent New York performances by Mia Slavenska. Even after she recovered, she continued to be the target of animosity from other company members. Preparing to change in the middle of a *Giselle* in Boston, she discovered that someone had ripped out part of her Act II costume. It turned up later in a theater restroom.

Bad blood also flowed between Massine and Lifar. Unpredictable and hypersensitive to perceived slights, Lifar was so volatile that Hurok had dancers ready in costume backstage to go on in his place if he decided (as he often did) to throw a tantrum. One night, just before the curtain was to go up on the company's version of Act II of *Swan Lake* (Hurok called it *Lake of Swan*), Lifar blew his top. Apparently jealous, he demanded that Massine remove a variation danced by the American Roland Guerard which had been receiving big ovations at previous performances. Massine and Hurok refused.

"But, you know, if you do not do as I say, I have the right to challenge you to a duel," Lifar said to Massine.

In reply, Hurok claimed he waved his hand and said, "Don't talk such tommyrot, take an aspirin." ("Tommyrot" is not a word one can easily imagine Hurok saying.)

Lifar then presented his resignation to Hurok, who accepted it. The duel, which Hurok later claimed was to have taken place in a glade in Central Park, never occurred, and Lifar sailed for Europe on the *Champlain* a few days later, never to work with Hurok again.

Attempting to justify his behavior, Lifar also claimed that he was angry at Massine for tampering with his choreography for *Icare*. In fact, the company just wasn't big enough for the two of them.

Characteristically, Hurok took advantage of the incident to drum up more publicity for the Met season, apparently with good results. By the final week the house was selling out, with nightly receipts of $3,000 and gross earnings for the New York engagement of $83,000. According to their contract, Hurok paid Denham a flat fee for the New York performances, but they split the profits on the road. Therefore he tried to keep the company at the Met for as long as possible.

The results on tour were not nearly so good. Even in Chicago, which had always supported the Russian ballet, attendance was poor. So poor, in fact, that Hurok complained bitterly to Fleischmann that the company's performance standards had fallen drastically, to a level "far below the standards of a first-rate company," and that "the working morale among the dancers shows definite signs of decline. . . . While New York is a barometer of the sophisticated East," he explained, "Chicago is the index of the rest of the country, wherein lies the bulk of the company's audiences."

In an attempt to understand better what Chicago audiences wanted, Hurok had conducted a survey of their preferences in repertoire and dancers. Predictably, they liked familiar items like *Les Sylphides*, *Le Beau Danube*, and *Prince Igor*, and turned thumbs down on more experimental works like Massine's *Seventh Symphony* and *Bogatyri*, a confusing new ballet set to music by Borodin that dealt with the legendary knights of Kievan Russia. John Goodridge, the president and general manager of the Auditorium Theatre, agreed with Hurok's criticism of the Ballet Russe de Monte Carlo. "No amount of endowment or social background will suffice to save a rotten company," he wrote to Denham, "and that is what you are going to have unless you take the necessary steps."

To Hurok's business manager David Libidins, however, Hurok's complaints were nothing more than a ruse ("Hurok's trick No. 1001") designed to stir up trouble and strengthen his own position. In his charmingly broken English, Libidins wrote to Denham that the reviews had actually been very positive ("all notices including Chicago were raving"). He also charged that Hurok had carefully focused on the few negative remarks for his own purposes. It was actually "Hurok and his Mrs." who were creating dissension in the company, he charged; they complained to certain artists about how Denham and Fleischmann were running things. "This all is not new TO ME—this is Hurok's usual trick—first disorganize the Company and after this cut the guarantee—I saw this for years the same picture with the other attractions."

To be sure, Hurok did have a long history of carefully pitting his employees and artists against each other—without their knowing what he was doing. This left all his options open and increased his own financial and personal power. In this instance, he knew that the de Basil company was still a viable entity, and he wanted to retain the possibility of representing it or merging with it. By insisting to Denham and Fleischmann that their Ballet Russe de Monte Carlo was not performing up to snuff, he could threaten to withdraw and create another company with de Basil.

Hurok, Denham, and Fleischmann quarreled incessantly over just about everything, from billing to publicity to travel details. Denham complained that the *American Banker*, the liner on which Hurok had booked the company for its return to Europe in late March 1939, was a "slow, ten-day, one-class boat having no first class nor cabin accommodations" and did not belong to "the class which corresponds to the standing of our company." Hurok and his ghostwriters retaliated with some snobbery of their own. "The standing of the company is not enhanced or diminished by the kind of boat on which they travel. As a matter of fact for your information, Mr. and Mrs. Charles A. Lindbergh, I am reliably informed, traveled to Europe on the *American Banker*," they huffed.

If the two men's working relationship had deteriorated to the point where they were arguing over boats, things were clearly less than ideal. That there was little trust or love between Denham and his erstwhile business partner was obvious from the incessant insults they hurled at each other behind the scenes. Denham took particular delight in denigrating Hurok as "that octopus." For heightened theatrical effect, or for sheer contemptuous pleasure, Denham would mispronounce the name of the grabby, uncontrollably acquisitive aquatic creature whose behavior reminded him of his colleague. Hurok, he proclaimed, was an "oc-TAW-pus."

CHAPTER TWELVE

"She's Going to Sing if I Have to Put Up a Tent"

"I had become, whether I liked it or not, a symbol, representing my people. I had to appear."—*Marian Anderson*

IN THE YEARS FOLLOWING the historic 1935 Town Hall recital that launched her big-time American career, Hurok's "discovery" Marian Anderson, the "Negro contralto" with the voice (as the critics said) "of a race" and "of a century," continued to draw crowds and curiosity. After her first series of concerts under Hurok's management in the United States in early 1936, she returned with added luster to tour Europe and Russia. Within a few seasons, Anderson was receiving more requests for engagements in the United States than she could comfortably fulfill. Hurok's job now became "not to seek dates for Marian, but to winnow out the most attractive ones each season." To this task, Anderson later wrote, he brought a degree of sensitivity and commitment she had not noted in her former manager, Arthur Judson.

> There was dignity in all things, in the publicity that was sent out and in the auspices he approved for appearances. . . . He was building for the future. He did not accept any offer that came along, simply because it meant a quick fee. He was concerned whether a concert would be right for me. If he arranged for an appearance in a concert

course, he made sure it was one of the best. If I was billed outside of a regular concert series, he saw to it that much was made of the fact that this was to be a special attraction.

Best of all, Mr. Hurok brought a deep personal interest to my career. There was the kind of friendship that you do not look for in managers. Mr. Hurok, of course, is not just a manager. He is an impresario who takes chances whenever he believes in the artist or the ensemble.

Among the venues Hurok managed to secure for Anderson was the Philadelphia Forum, in her own hometown. The critical and financial results were so impressive that she was asked back the following season. By early 1939, Anderson was receiving up to $2,000 for an engagement and had become a familiar figure on the American cultural scene.

This success did not protect Anderson from the indignities of American discrimination against black people, however. Her appearances in many cities—and not only in the South—were still marred by the difficulties and embarrassment caused by the policies of discrimination. Some hotels refused to rent her rooms altogether, while others made her use the freight elevator. Some restaurants (even in northern Duluth!) denied her a table, while others would serve her grudgingly, making her all too aware that an exception was being made. On trains, porters and fellow passengers sometimes treated her with ill-concealed disdain, and she was frequently prohibited from entering the dining car. At stations, she had to sit in the "colored" waiting room.

In the early years, Anderson even sang in halls divided into Negro and white sections by an invisible line running vertically from the front-row orchestra to the last row of the balcony. She refused, however, to sing in halls that were "horizontally" segregated—in which black customers were allowed to sit only in the last rows of the balcony. Eventually she refused to sing in segregated halls altogether. Having overcome his initial misgivings over whether a Negro singer could "sell," Hurok, himself a former victim of racist oppression, supported Anderson's struggle with injustice. He warned local managers that if they did not find her decent hotel accommodations in the city center, they would no longer receive certain other highly profitable attractions. Such tactics usually worked.

Anderson's calm response to the insults of discrimination amazed her colleagues, especially Europeans like her Finnish accompanist Kosti Vehanen, who could never understand American racism. Drawing on her deep religious faith, she was forgiving toward those who indulged in such discriminatory behavior, often remarking that they simply didn't know any better. It was her hope that her music and nonviolent example would help to change their attitudes. Unlike her friend and fellow singer Paul Robeson, who spoke out forcefully against racial prejudice, Anderson avoided making public statements on nonmusical matters and shunned a political role. "Certainly, I have my feelings about conditions that affect my people," she told one reporter years later. "But it is not right for me to mimic someone who writes, or who speaks out against segregation. That is their forte. . . . What I had was singing, and if my career has been of some consequence, then that's my contribution."

Her very prominence as a black artist in a sadly segregated society eventually forced a political role upon Anderson, however, and made her an important symbol in the early history of the civil rights movement. Her participation in an event that was destined to become a turning point in American social history grew out of a dispute over a booking in Washington, D.C. Anderson had already given a recital in the capital in May 1938, at the Rialto Theatre, sponsored by the concert series of predominantly black Howard University. The appearance was so successful that the committee which engaged artists for the series decided to bring her back the following season, but to the much larger and more prestigious Constitution Hall. It had been opened in 1929 to serve as the site for the annual Daughters of the American Revolution Continental Congress. Soon after its dedication, the DAR made Constitution Hall—then the largest in Washington—available for public rentals. It quickly became a regular stop on tours by the leading concert artists of the day.

Charles Cohen, who headed the Howard Concert Series committee, therefore contacted Anderson's manager, Hurok, and Fred Hand, manager of Constitution Hall, asking them to set up an engagement. The date Cohen requested was April 9, 1939—Easter Sunday. Hand replied (correctly) that the hall was booked that day for a concert by the National Symphony. Cohen suggested several alternative dates, but was informed by Hand that all of them were taken by other artists. At this point, the Hurok office was told of the apparent unavailability of Constitution Hall for an Anderson engagement.

Since such heavy booking was highly unusual at Constitution Hall at that time of year, Hurok became suspicious. He instructed his associate Mae Frohman to call Hand directly and ask again about the dates. After learning that they were to be used for Anderson, Hand repeated that the hall was booked. Even more suspicious now, Hurok's publicity manager Gerald Goode then called a rival manager in New York and described the situation. To him, Goode said, it sounded a lot like discrimination "in an important hall in an important city," an issue "that affected all artists and managers, and had to be dealt with sooner or later." Goode persuaded the other manager to call Hand, too, asking for the same dates for several of his white artists. Not surprisingly, it turned out that the dates were suddenly open after all.

Morally offended and smelling a good story, Hurok (as he told Patrick Hayes, then the Washington agent for the NBC Civic Concert Service) called Hand to confront him with his duplicity. Obstinate and irritated, the manager made no apologies for his behavior. On the contrary, he shouted, "No date will ever be available for Marian Anderson in Constitution Hall!"

Hand did not try to justify his action on the basis of DAR policy, because that policy had never been exactly codified. When Constitution Hall first opened, it was available to all performers, black and white. Among the first groups to appear there was the all-black Hampton Choir from a black college in Hampton, Virginia. Black tenor Roland Hayes (no relation to Patrick) also sang there in the early 1930s. At one of his recitals, Hayes had noticed a large group of blacks seated together on one side of the orchestra. This arrangement looked to him like segregation. Hayes demanded that the audience be "properly mingled" and left the stage until his request was fulfilled. But the singer's request infuriated Hand. He "stood with his arms folded in the middle of the aisle facing the stage, and the Negro patrons remained silent in their seats, not venturing to move." Although Hayes eventually did return to the stage to give the recital, Hand was so angry over the embarrassing incident that he vowed that "in his time as manager of the hall no Negro would ever again appear."

According to Patrick Hayes, Hand soon after began inserting a "Whites Only" clause in artists' contracts. These were signed without objection by the DAR treasurer general, Sarah Corbin Robert. Some years later, the DAR tried to excuse its behavior in going along with the "Whites Only" policy as an honest attempt to conform with local regulations. In an official 1962 statement on Constitution Hall policy, the National Society Daughters of the American Revolution explained that in 1932 (after the Roland Hayes recital) the hall adopted a "Whites Only" clause for rental contracts "in conformity with the laws and customs prevailing at that time in the District of Columbia." In any case, by 1935, either by the decision of Hand or the DAR, a "Whites Only" clause was in fact appearing in Constitution Hall contracts.

Nor did the DAR ever apologize for its part in denying use of the hall to Marian Anderson. In April 1939, the NSDAR president general said in her annual report to the organization's Continental Congress that the DAR was "a consistent friend of minority groups and would change its position on the use of Constitution Hall when the Community at large has worked out its problem." As late as 1979, the organization's president general Jeanette Bayliss was still maintaining that the Anderson incident was all just a misunderstanding and had nothing to do with discrimination. The hall really had been booked for other performers on the dates that Howard University wanted for Anderson, she said.

To be sure, in 1939 segregation was still a fact of life in many parts of America. Despite the fact that a liberal Democrat occupied the White House, Washington, D.C., was no exception. In both tradition and geography, it was a sleepy southern city lying below the Mason-Dixon line and had more in common with Richmond, Virginia, and Atlanta than with Philadelphia, New York, or Boston. The Civil War had ended only seventy-four years before, and the scars it left had not yet healed. That the realities of segregation—so obvious throughout the capital's neighborhoods, educational system, and public facilities—should also be encountered in its theaters was hardly surprising. At the National Theatre, for example, blacks were allowed to perform but could not sit in the audience. At Constitution Hall, blacks were not allowed to perform but could sit in segregated sections.

Even the august Washington *Post* initially defended the DAR's position in denying Anderson a date in Constitution Hall. In a February 21, 1939, editorial, the paper adopted a narrow view of individual rights, maintaining that Hand and the DAR had "the unquestionable right" to determine who could use their hall. "The issue is to be judged not alone on what is legally right or wrong but on what is civil, just and decent policy in a society committed to the realization of democratic ideals."

As Hurok—a committed socialist/liberal Democrat—well understood, however, there was growing dissatisfaction with the status quo in race relations. President Roosevelt was less outspoken in his criticism of racism than his wife because he feared alienating the powerful southern Democratic leadership, but Hurok could see that he felt uncomfortable with segregation. FDR had even taken definite steps to include blacks in his socially responsible New Deal programs. With his usual perfect timing, Hurok instinctively knew that Hand's baldly discriminatory attitudes and adamant refusal to book Anderson at Constitution Hall had come at just the right moment, when the forces for social change were in the ascendant. Presented with the marketing opportunity of a lifetime, he wasted no time in taking advantage of it.

"Of course Hurok revelled in the publicity," Patrick Hayes remarked years later. "But this was also the right thing to do, and the dividend was fame for him."

Hurok instructed Goode to compile a file of all correspondence, to transcribe all telephone calls pertaining to the incident, and to prepare a "White Paper" and press release. A press conference was held. By late January 1939, the story was breaking on the front pages of major newspapers in the United States and abroad, carefully navigated from Hurok command central at Rockefeller Center.

Meanwhile, the Howard University Concert Series committee was trying to find another venue for Anderson's recital. They approached the school board of the District of Columbia, requesting the use of Central High, which had the city's largest high-school auditorium. On February 19, the school board turned down their request on the pedantic grounds that (1) an appearance by a Negro artist would violate the legally maintained dual (that is, segregated) school system and (2) the school auditorium could not be used for commercial purposes. The school board's antediluvian response further inflamed the controversy. A congressman stood up in the House of Representatives to demand an investigation, and many other civic, religious, and educational groups followed suit. Finally, the school board reconsidered its decision and gave permission for the concert to take place, but only with the understanding that this did not represent a policy change. This stance was unacceptable to the Howard University committee. They rightly saw that to accept such a condition would make it possible for such discrimination to be repeated in the future. In response to the committee's refusal, the school board withdrew its offer.

What had started out as a minor incident had now become a cause célèbre, and one of the first major battles in the long struggle for desegregation and civil rights. As Patrick Hayes later observed, "The issue was now larger than the DAR–Constitution Hall denial; the entire city was closed to the committee and the artist. It was now more than a concert booking. It was a moral and ethical issue, a sacred cause with repercussions reaching far beyond the city limits."

Hurok's already successful publicity campaign received a further boost on February 27, when First Lady Eleanor Roosevelt announced in one of the most famous of her widely read "My Day" newspaper columns that she was resigning her honorary membership in the DAR. She did so because of its apparently discriminatory policies in denying Anderson (who had appeared at the White House three years before) the opportunity to perform in its hall.

In her usual diplomatic fashion, Mrs. Roosevelt did not actually name the DAR, but left little doubt what—and who—she was talking about.

WASHINGTON, February 27—. . . I have been debating in my mind for some time, a question which I have had to debate with myself once or twice before in my life. Usually I have decided differently from the way in which I am deciding now. The question is, if you belong to an organization and disapprove of any action which is typical of a policy, should you resign or is it better to work for a changed point of view within the organization? In the past, when I was able to work actively in any organization to which I belonged, I have usually stayed until I had at least made a fight and had been defeated.

Even then, I have, as a rule, accepted my defeat and decided I was wrong or, perhaps, a little too far ahead of the thinking for the majority at that time. I have often found that the thing in which I was interested was done some years later. But in this case, I belong to an organization in which I can do no active work. They have taken an action which has been widely talked of in the press. To remain as a member implies approval of that action, and therefore I am resigning.

At a news conference held that same day, Mrs. Roosevelt defended her decision under intense questioning.

With support now emanating from the White House, Hurok's shrewd publicity operation reached a new level of dignified outrage. The ink was hardly dry on Eleanor Roosevelt's column before he and his speechwriters issued a public statement, characterizing Mrs. Roosevelt's resignation as "one of the most hopeful signs in these troublesome times for democracy" and a gesture that showed her "to be a woman of courage and excellent taste. I applaud her." Simultaneously, he launched a carefully orchestrated telegram campaign calling upon leading American cultural figures to follow her example. This one (dated February 27, 1939) went to Serge Koussevitzky, conductor of the Boston Symphony.

Hundreds of Leaders In all Fields Are Protesting Unamerican Behaviour of Daughters of American Revolution in Barring Marian Anderson American Negro Singer from Singing in Constitution Hall in Washington, D.C. Stop Would Appreciate Your Wired Protest At this Undemocratic Violation of the Spirit of Constitution Which Has just Caused Mrs. Franklin Delano Roosevelt to Re-

sign From the Organization Stop Your Reply to Me At 30
Rockefeller Plaza New York Is Prepaid. —S. Hurok

Below this text, on the telegram he received, Koussevitzky pen-
ciled a response: "Am joining protest against barring M.A. singing
Constitution Hall in Washington."

So did many others: New York Mayor Fiorello La Guardia,
Senator Robert Wagner, Metropolitan Opera stars Kirsten Flagstad
and Lawrence Tibbett, the entire Philadelphia Orchestra, screen
and stage stars Fredric March, Florence Eldridge, and Sylvia Sidney.
By late March, a nationwide public opinion survey showed that
sixty seven percent of those polled supported Eleanor Roosevelt's
resignation from the DAR. Perhaps surprisingly, Republicans approved of her action nearly as strongly as Democrats (sixty-three
percent to sixty-eight percent). Most southerners (fifty-seven percent) disapproved, but even many of them said that it was not so
much Anderson's right to sing as a paid performer that they objected to. They disliked the fact that the president's wife had "made
a fuss about it."

Right-wing groups reacted with predictable hostility toward
those who were denouncing the DAR, however. Shortly after Mrs.
Roosevelt announced her resignation, a provocative two-page flyer
with the headline "Communist Racial Incitement: Presenting Sol
Hurok" was circulated by the "Christian Defenders of American
Heritage," whose motto was "Anti-Communism is Christian Self-
Defense." The flyer tried to link Hurok's Russian background and
frequent trips to the Soviet Union with his defense of Anderson as
part of a hypocritical Communist plot intended to stir up "Negro
antagonism against white Americans."

The unidentified authors also accused Hurok (not without
some justification) of preferring to use Russian performers "taken
from the slave markets of the Soviet Union" because he could pay
them low wages and avoid union regulations. As a result, "huge
profits fall into the pockets of the exploiter-impresarios." Marian
Anderson was nothing more than a pawn in Hurok's business
schemes, they charged. The real perpetrator of the discrimination
here was not the DAR, but the performing arts managers who refused to give employment to "Christian AMERICAN BORN artists, con-

ductors, soloists and Instrumentalists" ("How many Christian American born musicians are there in the Ballet Russe orchestra?"). The flyer concluded with a call to arms: "If fight they must, American artists white and colored are ready—they know their common enemies—who are not within the ranks of the DAR but among the devoted friends of the Soviet Union."

This would not be the last time that Hurok would be denounced as a Red sympathizer.

At the center of this whirlwind of publicity and inflamed opinion, Anderson remained calm and philosophical. She went about her business, giving her (increasingly well-attended) recitals as scheduled and replying to all questions about the Washington controversy with her usual good-mannered fatalism: "We will always go where we are welcome." She did not criticize the DAR, Constitution Hall, or the District of Columbia School Board, letting events (and Hurok) speak for her. "I trusted the management. I knew it must be working on every possible angle, and somehow I felt I would sing in Washington." Hurok, who loved nothing better than a good (and highly publicized) challenge, was no less determined as he vowed to reporters, "She's going to sing there if I have to put up a tent. When we plan a thing, we go through with it."

As is so often the case with events that later acquire the status of legends, there are several versions of how the idea arose to have Marian Anderson perform at the Lincoln Memorial. Characteristically, Hurok later claimed credit for the scheme. According to his account in *Impresario*, he sent Gerald Goode to Washington with instructions to ask for permission to use the monument and its grounds for the concert. Goode there met up with Walter White, the "sparkplug president" of the NAACP. Together they went to the Department of the Interior, which has jurisdiction over the capital's parks. They easily persuaded the Assistant Secretary of the Interior, Oscar L. Chapman, who then sought and received permission from his boss, Interior Secretary Harold L. Ickes.

Patrick Hayes, who was present in Washington throughout most of the controversy, tells the story somewhat differently. He believes Chapman's half-Indian assistant came up with the idea of presenting Anderson at the Lincoln Memorial, probably the country's most potent symbol of racial equality. The assistant then suggested it to his boss, Chapman. Chapman in turn mentioned the plan to Charles Cohen of the Howard University Concert Series, who then raised the possibility in print. Almost immediately, progressive political and cultural figures embraced his suggestion; it could go a long way toward erasing the stigma that had settled over the nation's capital as a result of the ugly behavior of some of its leading citizens in the Marian Anderson affair. Finally, Chapman "obtained immediate consent from the White House that Miss Anderson could not only appear at the Lincoln Memorial on Easter Sunday, but also that she would appear under the sponsorship of the Roosevelt Administration."

Chapman's boss, Interior Secretary Ickes, extended the official invitation to Anderson. She accepted despite misgivings over the political implications and being subjected to relentless journalistic coverage. "I could see that my significance as an individual was small in this affair. I had become, whether I liked it or not, a symbol, representing my people. I had to appear."

The public announcement of the concert was made on March 31—just nine days before the event.

Later, Interior Secretary Ickes claimed credit for making the concert happen. In his "secret diary" entry for April 6, 1939, three days before the concert, he wrote:

> Preparations are going ahead for the Marian Anderson concert at the base of the Lincoln Memorial next Sunday afternoon, at which I will preside. Marian Anderson, a Negro contralto, is said to have the best voice of a generation. The DAR refused to give her the use of Constitution Hall, although I protested, and Mrs. Roosevelt resigned as a member. The school board would not even allow her to have a school auditorium on decent conditions, and so application was finally made to me to permit an open-air concert that would be free to all in the Mall at the base of the Lincoln Memorial. After consulting with the President, I promptly gave my consent.

In his public statement, Ickes was less expansive. He said simply: "This seems to me to be a good use of the public facilities." Never before had the Lincoln Memorial been used for a concert.

However the permission was requested, once it was granted, Hurok and the Howard University committee swung into high gear to prepare for a concert that was turning into a political and social event of Hippodrome proportions. Acutely aware that the publicity would turn his client into a huge box office draw, Hurok assumed the labor costs involved in putting on the concert at the memorial. Anderson also agreed to waive her fee. In an unprecedented and no doubt painful show of modesty and self-effacement, Hurok even allowed the programs to be printed without any mention of himself or of "S. Hurok Presents." The wording went like this: "Howard University and Associated Sponsors Present Marian Anderson at the Lincoln Memorial in Washington." Below were the opening words from Lincoln's Gettysburg Address, the same ones chiseled onto one of the interior walls of the memorial: "Fourscore and seven years ago our fathers brought forth on this continent a new nation, conceived in liberty and dedicated to the proposition that all men are created equal."

Always expert at mobilizing influential people behind his enterprises, Hurok had managed within days to assemble a most impressive group of sponsors for the concert. It was headed by Chief Justice Charles Evans Hughes and included Associate Justice Hugo Black, Secretary of the Navy Claude Swanson, conductors Walter Damrosch and Leopold Stokowski, Katharine Hepburn, and even Washington *Post* editor Felix Morley, who had apparently changed his mind about the DAR's rights. Although unable to attend because of a diplomatically arranged prior commitment in Seattle (and no doubt out of sensitivity to her husband's difficult position), Eleanor Roosevelt agreed to be an honorary sponsor.

The concert's organizers were overwhelmed with ticket requests, but it was decided to give free admission to the large area in front of the memorial steps and on either side of the Reflecting Pool. Only a few hundred seats were set up at the top of the first flight of stairs, for invited dignitaries and special guests. Special facilities were set up for the many print, radio, and newsreel journalists covering the event, which was broadcast by the Blue Network of NBC. Pathe News made a newsreel film that ran in movie theaters all over the country during the following weeks.

The concert began at five in the afternoon on Easter Sunday,

April 9, 1939. A huge crowd estimated at seventy-five thousand had gathered below the monument's white marble stairs, stretching in an unbroken mass down either side of the Reflecting Pool toward the Mall, the Washington Monument, and the Capitol. (Somehow Hurok had managed to restrain himself from hanging a banner with his logo "S. Hurok Presents.") "The weather was cool and had been somewhat cloudy," wrote Interior Secretary Ickes, "but it cleared just before the hour for the concert and remained clear throughout." In his brief introductory remarks, which he thought was "the best speech I have ever made," Ickes described the scene as a "great auditorium under the sky where all of us are free," and Anderson as an artist who proved that "genius draws no color line."

Sitting behind him were Hugo Black (a former member of the Ku Klux Klan), Treasury Secretary Morgenthau, six U.S. senators and twelve representatives, including Arthur W. Mitchell of Illinois, the first black representative since Reconstruction. The failure of Roosevelt's Vice President John Nance Garner—"a vigorous candidate for President"—even to respond to a telegram asking him to be a sponsor for the event sowed doubts about his political acumen and future. For his part, Ickes had a coldly pragmatic understanding of the potential benefits he and Roosevelt could reap among the increasingly important black electorate. "The whole setting was unique, majestic, and impressive and I could not help but feel thankful that the DAR and the school board had refused her the use of an auditorium." Hurok shared those feelings.

Icke's Assistant Secretary Oscar Chapman escorted Anderson, dressed in a fur coat with a bright orange and yellow scarf, down from the top level of the memorial to the first landing, where a forest of microphones stood ready to receive her voice. The size of the mob at first intimidated and overwhelmed her. While singing the "Star-Spangled Banner," "I felt for a moment as though I were choking. For a desperate second I thought that the words, well as I know them, would not come." But the love and goodwill she felt coming toward her from the vast audience gave her strength, and she went on to sing "America" ("My Country, 'Tis of Thee"), the aria "O, Mio Fernando" from Donizetti's opera *La Favorita*, Schubert's "Ave Maria," and, after an intermission, concluded with three spirituals: "Gospel Train," "Trampin'," and "My Soul Is An-

chored in the Lord." At the end, contrary to her custom, in response to a huge ovation that would not die down, she also said a
few words. "I am overwhelmed. I just can't talk. I can't tell you what
you have done for me today. I thank you from the bottom of my
heart again and again."

Only later would the full significance of this moment become
clear. Of course (just as Hurok knew it would) that Easter Sunday
appearance would give a tremendous boost to Marian Anderson's
performing career. It made her a virtually unassailable symbol of racial and artistic freedom and one of Hurok's most lucrative assets.

But there was more. Transmitted to millions by radio and film,
the Lincoln Memorial concert would awaken many Americans, both
black and white, to the realities of racial inequality and give the
braver among them some hope that the situation could be changed
with help from a concerned government. Just two months later, the
Roosevelts would invite Anderson to sing at the White House during the state visit of King George VI and Queen Elizabeth of England. Anderson would become an important role model for all
young black people who aspired to achieve and succeed in American society. For many black singers who dreamed of breaking into
the white elitist world of opera to pursue their ambitions, she became an inspiration and teacher. Among them would be such great
future international stars as Leontyne Price and Jessye Norman.

On a larger scale, Anderson's concert gave hope to a new generation of civil rights leaders. Perhaps most important, it became a
model for the large-scale nonviolent protests of the coming decades,
most notably the March on Washington of August 28, 1963, led by
Martin Luther King. By that time, Constitution Hall had dropped
its "Whites Only" clause and many black artists—including
Anderson—had performed there and in many other halls formerly
closed to them. But much remained to be done, as King, himself a
magnificent performer, proclaimed in his "I Have a Dream" speech
to a huge integrated throng. He spoke from the exact spot on the
steps of the Lincoln Memorial where Anderson had sung nearly
twenty-five years before, when he was a boy of ten.

That Sol Hurok, an immigrant Jew from Russia, was instrumental in presenting Anderson on that Easter Sunday on the eve of
World War II and the Holocaust was significant in another way. It

represented one of the finer moments in the often uneasy alliance between Jews and blacks in the idealistic struggle for equality in America. Unfortunately, that alliance would later weaken and even disintegrate as the cultural, social, and economic interests of these two traditionally oppressed groups would diverge. Not long afterward, the paternalistic attitude that Hurok displayed toward Anderson (and toward all his artists, for that matter) would irritate and offend many black political leaders. They would come to perceive it as condescending and humiliating and an example of Jewish economic oppression. In time, the unfortunate lack of understanding between blacks and Jews would even come to Hurok's first home in America, the Brooklyn neighborhood of Brownsville, which would be racked by violent incidents between members of these two communities.

On that Sunday afternoon in April 1939, such differences were largely forgotten in the pursuit of a common cause. One of the finest examples of Hurok's credo of "enlightened self-interest," Marian Anderson's concert on the steps of the Lincoln Memorial was really not much different from the fund-raising events he had put together twenty years earlier as a recent arrival from Pogar. It's just that the audience was bigger.

■ CHAPTER THIRTEEN ■

Force majeure

"What is in the mind of this strange character, nobody knows."—*Serge Denham on Sol Hurok*

THE NERVOUS SUMMER OF 1939 was the last Hurok would spend in Europe for several years to come. From London to Amsterdam to Paris, Germany's increasingly aggressive behavior, particularly the seizure of Czechoslovakia in March, had created a suffocating atmosphere of pervasive uncertainty that made planning for the future—in any business—a chancy exercise. And yet Hurok continued to try, preparing for the worst but hoping for the best, and succeeding as usual in keeping all his options open.

In June, he presided as manager over a profitable and highly acclaimed engagement by the Ballet Russe de Monte Carlo in Paris. Hurok's relationship with his American partners in this venture—Serge Denham and Julius Fleischmann ("Junkie" to his friends)—remained problematical, but—for the time being, at least—their mutual need outweighed their mutual enmity. Despite the unsettled European situation, and despite Denham's private complaint that he and the other American backers were "far from being enthusiastic about the cooperation with Hurok," Hurok wangled the right to present the Ballet Russe de Monte Carlo in Paris again the following year. But the contract for 1940 included this important clause: "In the event of military hostilities in Europe involving France, the parties will be free to cancel the present agreement as invalid."

The possibility of such an "event" became much more likely on August 22, when Stalin and Hitler signed their nonaggression pact, clearing the way for the Nazi army to turn its full attention to Europe. On September 1 it became inevitable, when the Germans marched into Poland, precipitating a full-scale declaration of war by the Western Allies two days later.

As the continent hurtled toward a conflagration that would transform the European balance of power and the cultural world whose attractions Hurok had long been presenting, he and Emma were resting in high Gallic style at the Grand Hotel in Evian-les-Bains (Vittel), whose stationery promised *"Tous les sports, cures, Tous les Régimes suivant Prescription Médicale."* Of robust constitution but never a sportsman, it's hard to imagine that Hurok availed himself of the athletic facilities; long walks were more his style. In a breathless missive written on August 7 to Irving Deakin, he also took care to point out (in his own mangled idiom) that he had not been idle while taking the waters. "I am here for the third week now and have not stopped working and am already leaving the end of the week for Paris and again I want to tell you that I did not get any easy summer. . . . You know that by handling a Russian Company and having some American Directors connected it is a hard job, so consequently, I did not have such a pleasant stay as you think so."

Besides dealing with quarreling dancers and disgruntled backers, Hurok had been running into problems with the Russians in continuing negotiations for presenting the Soviet Red Army Chorus in the United States. "I have negociated [sic] so long with them that I really get tired of it. I am afraid to handle this attraction at this time; you can realise how hard and dangerous it is to do business with them even when they know that the peace of this world depends on their action, and even this, look how long it takes. So we have decided to drop this matter too." In fact, the signing of the Soviet-German nonaggression pact and the subsequent invasion of the USSR once again deferred for a number of years Hurok's cherished dream of importing Soviet artists to America.

But the first immediate casualty of the declaration of war was the planned September engagement of the Ballet Russe de Monte Carlo at Covent Garden in London. England's very existence being at risk, it was hardly seemly to spend time watching ballerinas twirl in tutus. So with help and lots of advice (not all of it welcome) from Denham and Fleischmann, Hurok immediately set about trying to transport the dancers, costumes, and sets to New York, where the company was scheduled to open on October 10. This proved difficult, since most shipping companies were canceling sailings of civilian passenger vessels for fear they would be sunk by German U-boats. To make matters worse, most of the Ballet Russe de Monte Carlo dancers still held Nansen passports and were informed by the few American companies still sending ships that American citizens had to be given priority for the few available spaces. The company's American members therefore sailed first, on the *Shawnee*.

Glamorous even in flight, Hurok joined some of the scenery—and numerous other celebrities—on the liner S.S. *Washington*. It departed Southampton on September 12 crammed with 1,746 passengers. Among them were Senator Robert R. Reynolds of North Carolina, novelist Thomas Mann, violinist Fritz Kreisler, and Rose Kennedy (whose husband was then the U.S. ambassador to Britain) accompanied by three of her children, including thirteen-year-old Robert. Film actor Robert Montgomery slept in a cot in the bottom of the ship's emptied swimming pool. Room service was suspended, the passengers had to dine in three shifts, and bathing was rationed. Upon arrival in New York on September 18, reporters and photographers descended upon the star-studded liner, and Hurok did not miss the opportunity to make a public statement, obligingly translated into standard journalistic English.

What disturbed him on the trip home, he said, was that some passengers were actually defending Germany's actions.

> Whenever we talked about the war and the issues, someone would always come out strongly in favor of Hitler and Stalin, and also of Mussolini, defending their policies and recent actions. I was born in Russia and I have been in these countries many times. I believe more than ever that this is a fight to the finish and that the democracies will

win if their friends support them. I also believe that Russia is disunited and cannot be of much help to any one. They are powerless and cannot be counted on.

About the eventual victory of the European democracies Hurok was, of course, right, but he was quite mistaken concerning the role Russia would play in the struggle against fascism in the coming six years.

Leonide Massine, Ballet Russe de Monte Carlo's artistic director, had arrived in New York a few days earlier on the *Statendam* to make preparations for the New York season at the Met. The opening had now been postponed to October 26. Fearful that his regular dancers would be stranded in Europe, he began training some new ones. Hurok, meanwhile, was worrying about the repertoire for the American tour in light of the international situation, particularly the rapprochement between Stalin and Hitler. Should the word *Russe* be removed from the company's title in the wake of rising anti-Soviet sentiment? Was it wise to include *Rouge et Noir*, a new Massine ballet set to the Symphony No. 1 by Soviet composer Dmitri Shostakovich? To Denham, Hurok admitted that "he was afraid of the reaction of the public toward Soviet Russian composers and that he would wait and see how things turned out." Eventually they decided to perform it anyway.

From New York, Hurok and his staff continued to work feverishly to get the dancers and musicians they needed to America. A few had come earlier with Massine, but most made it on the *Rotterdam*, which docked the morning of October 26—the very day that the second New York season of the Ballet Russe de Monte Carlo was scheduled to open. The artists, terrified about what might await them in Europe and full of gratitude to Hurok for (once again) coming to the rescue, went cheerfully to work.

Simon Semenoff, a character dancer new to the company who would become one of Hurok's most reliable advisers over the coming years, remembered the scene melodramatically some years later. The *Rotterdam* was "the last boat to leave in 1939. We arrived in New York on a Saturday, at three in the afternoon. Hurok was waiting for us. He was wearing a long cape and a hat and he said, 'Get going, tonight you perform.'" Semenoff was so grateful to Hurok for extracting him from Europe that he subsequently agreed to act as his informant. Hurok promised Semenoff that he "would take good care" of him if he would agree to "see what goes on in the ballet and then come and tell me all about it." According to many sources, Semenoff continued to fulfill the function of "backstage tattle-tale" for many years.

Fortified by breathless news stories and the high drama of the situation, the opening-night program went well. It featured *Swan Lake*, *Gaîté Parisienne*, and Frederick Ashton's *Devil's Holiday*, his first ballet for the company. The ensuing New York Ballet Russe de Monte Carlo engagement broke Met ballet box office records. Notwithstanding the logistical problems and the growing friction between Massine and Denham, whose delusions of creative grandeur were unfortunately growing apace, the company also managed to present two significant premieres.

The first, the ground-breaking *Bacchanale*, brought together Massine and Salvador Dali in a wild surrealistic representation of the delirious fantasies of Ludwig II of Bavaria set to the Venusberg music from Wagner's *Tannhauser*. The second, *Ghost Town*, was another attempt to create an "American" ballet in the style of *Union Pacific*. Choreographed by American dancer Marc Platoff (real name Marcel LePlat) to a commissioned score by Richard Rodgers, it revolved around an old prospector spinning yarns to a group of present-day hikers. Some critics, growing increasingly restless with the Russian domination of the American dance scene, found its self-conscious frontier atmosphere far from authentic, however. To the jaundiced eyes of Edward Downes, it was "about as American as a Russian Grand Duchess in dude ranch clothes."

New York merchants responded with verve and enthusiasm to the refugee artists and their company. Bonwit-Teller put new dresses inspired by some of the dancers' costumes on display in its Fifth Avenue show windows. Another store started selling five different lipsticks, each named after a different ballet. Such exploitation of the Ballet Russe name and reputation would seem to be good for business. Principal backer Julius Fleischmann, whose marketing acumen was considerably smaller than his fortune, wasn't sure, though. He voiced concern in a memo to Denham that "we are being 'gypped' some place."

After the Met engagement, the Ballet Russe de Monte Carlo embarked on a two-month, thirty-five-performance, twenty-one-city tour that took them to such notable destinations as New London, Norwalk, Corning, and Peoria. Business on the road lagged, which led to another conflict between Hurok and Denham. Denham blamed the poor box office results on a deficient publicity campaign, while Hurok—uncharacteristically—faulted a stale repertoire overloaded with too many old ballets. Such increasingly common disputes among the company's managerial troika were symptomatic of declining mutual trust and diverging commercial and artistic goals. They also led the restless Hurok to explore—as he had so many times in the past—other options. By early 1940, he was asking about the possibility of being released from the exclusivity clause of his contract with Denham and Fleischmann. This led them to wonder what new Machiavellian moves he might now be contemplating. Would he reopen negotiations with what was left of the de Basil company, which had been touring in Australia? Or would he try to become involved with a new American company, Ballet Theatre, which had given its first performances at Center Theater at Rockefeller Center in January?

Hurok's wily habit of playing his cards close to the vest and, Sphinxlike, avoiding giving a straight answer about anything until the last possible moment, infuriated and exasperated Denham, as he wrote in early 1940 to the Ballet Russe de Monte Carlo's Paris representative Jacques (Yakov) Rubinstein:

> With regard to the future, Hurok is as dumb as a stone. One day he will tell you he is going to ship the company to Europe and bring it back next fall, the next day he will say that he is trying to arrange a South American tour and the third day he won't say anything. What is in the mind of this strange character, nobody knows.

The members of the Ballet Russe de Monte Carlo were not the only performing artists fleeing Europe in the fall of 1939. Composers, musicians, and dancers had been leaving Germany for several years, most of them bound for the United States. Now they were joined by their colleagues from Eastern Europe, Scandinavia, Holland, and

France. Their arrival further enriched American culture, already the beneficiary of the immigration of European artists that followed World War I.

One of the musicians who joined this new wave and eventually sought permanent residence in the United States was Arthur Rubinstein, the Polish-born pianist who had been making increasingly successful American tours under Hurok's management since 1937. After 1922, when Hurok first presented Rubinstein in one of his "Music for the Masses" extravaganzas at the Hippodrome (which had been demolished in August 1939), the pianist had stayed away from America for fifteen years. Although he developed a respectable and steady career through the 1920s and 1930s in Europe and South America, Rubinstein's failure to catch on with American critics and audiences in the crowded and highly competitive post–World War I market still haunted him.

An unapologetic bon vivant of vivacious temperament, Rubinstein, who lived most of the time in Paris, had an insatiable appetite for "good food, good cigars, great wines, and women" that at times undermined his accuracy at the keyboard and led critics to doubt his seriousness. Even in the mid-1930s, after he made a concerted attempt to improve his technique, and after the Paris manager Dr. Paul Schiff had brought him new success, respected American managers remained cool. The cautious Arthur Judson continued to maintain that "Rubinstein is poison for the box office." Hurok's competitor Francis Coppicus was even more insulting. "I might get him an engagement with an orchestra if he gives two recitals at Carnegie Hall, and pays for it as well as all the publicity," he said.

But Hurok, who not only admired but shared Rubinstein's flamboyance and epicurean life-style, had never lost faith in the artist's box office potential. He apparently sensed that this was a pianist who could not only play, but also project and sustain a stage persona capable of dazzling the public like the cover of a glossy fashion magazine. If we are to believe his account in *Impresario*, Hurok had been pursuing Rubinstein since 1928. Finally, in 1937, he met with Schiff and Rubinstein in Paris and offered them a twenty-concert American tour for the 1937–38 season.

It helped that Hurok and his new pianist had a certain amount in common. Both had succeeded in rising from an impoverished

Jewish ghetto in the Russian provinces (in Rubinstein's case, the Polish city of Lodz) to reinvent themselves as glamorous aristocrats of the arts. In later years, Hurok liked to portray Rubinstein as his bosom buddy and soulmate. At this 1937 Paris meeting, however, according to the pianist's memoirs published after Hurok's death, the visiting American impresario made less than an entirely favorable impression. He was only "the fat and important-looking middle-aged gentleman . . . who fourteen years before had heard me play *Petrushka* for Chaliapin one morning in New York. . . . Now, this meek little man spoke with an air of supreme authority about musical matters in the United States." Rubinstein insisted that he was quite content with his flourishing career in Europe, South America, and Australia, and doubted whether Hurok could make an American tour worth his while.

" 'Let me vorry about it,' said Hurok. 'I will guarantee you a good fee for every concert. First-class travel everywhere for two from Paris and back to Paris. All the publicity and piano transportation. Dr. Schiff and I have already agreed about your fee.' "

Wooed and flattered, the vain Rubinstein acquiesced to a tour that would begin in New York in November, 1937.

Nela Mlynarski, who had been one of the leading socialites of Poland before her marriage to Rubinstein in 1932, also claims to have played an important role in her husband's decision. Knowing of her desire to return to the United States, Hurok first convinced her that he should accept the offer. Years later, she recalled what followed:

> And then between the two of us we persuaded him to accept. He agreed, but on one condition, that he not know anything about concerts and contracts and publicity and that sort of thing. "You fix them, and I will play, and that's all I want to know." Because in those days, you know, it was a nightmare, with every artist managing, and checking accounts, and worrying about how much was spent on this or that. My husband was absolutely not like that, he couldn't stand dealing with that sort of thing. So they agreed, and he went to America. And this time, it was a real success.

Not immediately, however. While generally complimentary, most reviews of Rubinstein's first appearance on November 18, 1937, at Carnegie Hall with the New York Philharmonic under John Barbirolli paid considerably more attention to Daniel Gregory Mason's now long-forgotten Lincoln Symphony than to the pianist's performance of the Brahms B-flat piano concerto. Things improved after what the *New York Times* called Rubinstein's "galvanic" account of the Tchaikovsky Piano Concerto No. 1 with the same orchestra four days later.

But it was his solo recitals at Carnegie Hall in January 1938 that really won over the New York press and public. Most impressive of all was his pyrotechnic American premiere performance of Stravinsky's *Petrushka*, arranged for piano by the composer in 1921 and dedicated to Rubinstein. "I played it with my usual freedom, as I heard it played by an orchestra and not as a piano piece. The audience burst into an ovation, screaming and shouting bravos." Only the melancholy (and perhaps jealous) Sergei Rachmaninoff dissented. Backstage, he advised his colleague not to play "dirty stuff like *Petrushka*" in America, where "they don't like that kind of modern music." Never timid about handing out free tickets when necessary, Hurok had also taken care to see that the hall was filled to overflowing.

Despite his pleasure over the warm reception, Rubinstein, allegedly disinterested in the details of publicity, professed to be irritated by posters that advertised him as "Artur Rubinstein, Prince of Pianists."

"What is this 'Prince of Pianists' for and why did you drop the 'h'?" I shouted at Hurok.

"You play the piano and let me make the publicity," he said with an indulgent smile.

"If I had to pay for your publicity," I retorted in my most sarcastic way, "I would say: 'Hurok, God of Managers,' and not just a mean 'Prince.' "

By giving him this royal nickname and dropping the "h" in his name to restore the Polish spelling (thereby making it sound more European and aristocratic), Hurok and his publicity operation were maneuvering to exploit Rubinstein's image as one of the beautiful people, a tireless, glamorous party giver and partygoer with entrée to the most chic and exclusive Parisian salons. It was a shrewd and clever campaign. Hurok worked diligently and successfully at introducing Rubinstein to the richest and most prominent members of Manhattan high society, who, eager to be perceived as culturally informed, quickly adopted this debonair "prince" and his beautiful princess. Nela and "Artur" were more than happy to play their respective roles. The image building nicely dovetailed with the huge success of Rubinstein's recording of Tchaikovsky's First Piano Concerto. This was one of the first significant records produced after the Depression by "His Master's Voice," the English subsidiary of the Victor Company.

Though Hurok later claimed that the "receipts for the first season were not good," he had laid solid groundwork for Rubinstein's American career. It would bring both artist and manager a handsome income for the next thirty-five years. By 1953, Hurok later claimed, Rubinstein was taking in a weekly box office gross of $25,000 to $30,000 and had already earned $3 million on record sales. For Hurok, star solo performers produced the greatest profits, with their high fees and relatively low expenses. He could then reinvest these profits in his real passion: the ballet. Perhaps even more important, in Rubinstein Hurok had found an artist cut from the same cloth as he, with an equally keen appreciation of the value of theatricality in all things both public and private. They understood each other so implicitly that they didn't even bother to sign contracts after the first few years.

Similarly, it is no coincidence that Hurok never represented Rubinstein's main rival, Vladimir Horowitz, a younger (by seventeen years), less flamboyant, more introverted, and more intellectual artist whose awesome talent and discipline at one point even made Rubinstein think about abandoning his stage career for teaching. When once asked why he never tried to present Horowitz, Hurok replied, "Why would I want to take on a *mishugge* [Yiddish for a mixed-up person] like him?" But neither did Horowitz, who grew up in a respected and well-to-do Jewish family in cosmopolitan Kiev and later married Arturo Toscanini's demanding daughter, find Hurok's commercial, show-biz approach or crude circus tactics to his liking. The two men were simply too different. Some years later, Horowitz replaced Hurok with the more tweedy Arthur Judson as the manager of his leading student, Byron Janis.

Even Rubinstein at times found Hurok's plebeian musical taste dismaying. In putting together the programs for his first American tour, they had some "hot arguments" by correspondence. "His managerial flair made him feed the gallery with the most popular stuff I could dig up. Here I put my foot down and wouldn't let him interfere with my own decisions."

Like Hurok, Rubinstein understood the importance of political gestures. In September 1938, he canceled a planned tour of Italy in reaction to laws enacted there against Jews and returned a personally signed photo of Mussolini to the Italian leader. The Hurok office even issued a statement in Rubinstein's name ("the artist finds that his dignity does not permit him to go into a country where his co-religionists are being persecuted so unjustly") that found its way into the major American newspapers.

Such publicity helped make Rubinstein's second American tour, which began in January 1939, even more successful, especially with the important Jewish audience. There were so many requests from smaller cities for Hurok's new pianist that he was unable to satisfy them all. Wherever he went, Rubinstein and his wife were feted and lionized by the social elite that increasingly made up the bulk of Hurok's clientele. In the autumn of 1939, as the German army solidified its control over his homeland, Rubinstein closed up his Paris house and brought his wife and children to America, where he was scheduled for another tour. This time they would stay.

As the situation in Europe worsened throughout the rest of 1939 and the spring of 1940, the flow of refugees from Europe virtually stopped. The artists stranded across the Atlantic would have to remain there for the duration of the war. For Hurok, this situation presented a unique economic opportunity. As he pointed out to a shocked Rubinstein, who was worried about his many family members still remaining in the occupied countries, the fact that other performers could no longer make it to America cut down on the competition.

" 'Europe cannot send us pianists anymore,' Hurok said with a malicious smile, 'so we have the whole country to ourselves.' "

■   ■   ■

Most of the artists on Hurok's list were still European or Russian, and he continued to have trouble believing Americans could make it as stars of opera or ballet. But his enormous success with Marian Anderson was leading him to take a few more calculated risks on performers born and bred in the United States. Actually, he claimed that it was Anderson's own voice teacher, Giuseppe Boghetti, who helped lead him to one of them, a Jewish American tenor who would develop into one of his most durable and successful attractions: Jan Peerce.

As was the case with Anderson, Hurok "discovered" Peerce long after he had made a name for himself. Like Anderson, Peerce came to broad critical and public attention (and therefore to Hurok's) when he caught the eye—and ear—of Arturo Toscanini, one of the most powerful figures in the American musical world of the 1930s and 1940s.

In early 1938, Toscanini heard Peerce sing the role of Siegmund in a performance of Act I of Wagner's *Die Walküre* broadcast from Radio City Music Hall. By then, Peerce had already spent five years there "singing over crackling candy wrappers and missed cues" between movie features. Impressed by what a New York *Post* critic described as his "ample and easy" voice, Toscanini auditioned Peerce for the tenor part in an upcoming broadcast of Beethoven's Ninth Symphony with his recently established NBC Symphony. The audition went so well that Peerce not only got the job, but became "Toscanini's tenor." For the next fifteen years, he was a regular on the most popular classical music broadcast in American history, with a weekly Saturday evening audience estimated at twenty million or more.

Like Hurok and Rubinstein, Peerce (born Jacob Pincus Perelmuth in New York in 1904) was Jewish. His father had come to America from Russia about 1902, in the same flood of immigrants seeking a better life that had carried Hurok across the Atlantic. Peerce grew up in Manhattan, not Brooklyn, but in an exclusively Jewish neighborhood where "almost everybody was kosher." His father worked exhausting twelve-hour shifts as a presser in a sweat shop. The boy's religious upbringing was strict, and, like Marian Anderson, he began his singing career performing for his fellow parishioners—as a cantor in synagogues on the Lower East

Side. Eventually he graduated to weddings and bar mitzvahs. Then he took up the fiddle and spent the summers playing as a sideman in a small dance band at Jewish resorts in the Catskills. Even as late as 1932, Peerce considered himself primarily a violinist and dance band leader, and only occasionally sang as part of his act.

In a story worthy of Hollywood, he was finally noticed by showman Samuel L. "Roxy" Rothafel while performing as a singing violinist at a testimonial dinner for a vaudeville team at the Astor Hotel. As it happened, Rothafel had been hired by John D. Rockefeller, Jr., to oversee entertainment in the two new theaters built into the just-opened Rockefeller Center complex: the gigantic Radio City Music Hall, with sixty-two hundred seats, and the smaller RKO Roxy, with thirty-five hundred. (A proposed forty-three-hundred-seat opera house was never built.) When Roxy happened to see Peerce, he was also in the market for talent to put on the radio show *Radio City Music Hall of the Air.* And so Roxy gave Pinky Perelmuth a break. He also gave him a new, more euphonious, and much more Anglo-Saxon name: John Pierce.

This Pierce made his debut in 1933 in the spiffy RKO Roxy at Sixth Avenue and 49th Street in a stage show presented between screenings of *King Kong.* (The name RKO Roxy was changed soon after the theater opened to "Center Theater," under which name it operated until it was demolished in 1954.) But soon Pierce had been moved a few blocks uptown to the main Radio City stage, where his renditions of hit songs like "The Bluebird of Happiness" won him a large following and engagements on radio shows like *The A & P Gypsies* and *The Chevrolet Hour.* After several years of this, "Roxy" Rothafel jokingly changed John Pierce's name on the air to Jan Peerce, since it seemed closer in spirit to the Jewish original but retained a musical lilt.

After Peerce became a regular at Radio City, he and Hurok, whose office was next door on Rockefeller Plaza, started to bump into each other in the barbershop of the RCA building. "I would be having my hair cut and he would be getting boiled and basted under hot towels and he [Hurok] would ask how I was doing at Radio City Music Hall and I would say fine and he would say I should do concerts and why didn't I call him up?"

But when Peerce would call, Mae Frohman, who defended Hurok from unwanted intrusions with a bulldog's tenacity, would invariably report that he was tied up or would call right back. He never did. "I could read between the lines of the run-around she gave me: I'll look [across my desk] and see if he's here. No, [he says] he's not in."

Finally, at yet another barbershop rendezvous, Peerce (Hurok pronounced his name "John Pirs") confronted Hurok with his official inaccessibility. This time, he went back to the office and told Frohman to forward the calls. When they finally talked on the record, Hurok arranged for them to meet at Giuseppe Boghetti's studio so he could hear Peerce sing and talk to his teacher. (In *Impresario*, Hurok claims Boghetti invited him without any initiative from Peerce.)

Peerce sang a few songs, and Hurok said, "All right, Pirs, you'll be my artist."

> "Is that all there is to it?" I asked. "Shouldn't there be a contract between us?"
>
> "We shake hands," he said, "but all right, I'll send you a contract in the mail." Which he did. It was a standard contract—twenty percent for concerts and ten percent for records and radio—which we didn't change over four decades.

The problem Hurok faced in marketing Peerce was the tenor's uncertain position between light and serious art. ("The Broadway people said I belonged in opera; the opera people said I belonged in shows.") Hurok used his reputation and ability to pressure other managers (if you take Peerce, I'll give you someone you really want) to move his career more definitely in a "heavy" direction. The campaign began with a recital debut at Town Hall on November 7, 1939. Olin Downes of the *New York Times* loftily dismissed that event as "the kind of recital debut that only friends and devotees can make possible." Nonetheless, it launched Peerce on the "slow career" he and Hurok had agreed upon. A slow career, Hurok explained, was one that keeps growing from year to year and lasts for many years. A fast career starts with a big buildup and yields an immediate, but not necessarily enduring, financial payoff.

Hurok's other bit of important advice to Peerce was to avoid pricing himself out of the market for the local managers—no matter how famous he might become. (This is a warning that has been almost entirely ignored by the star performers of the 1980s and 1990s, much to the detriment of the musical scene.) Otherwise, if the manager didn't do well on the concert, he would start calling the New York office to complain about the performance, even if it had been beautifully sung. Peerce followed Hurok's advice, with excellent results. After only two years under Hurok's management, he was singing the plum role of the Duke of Mantua in *Rigoletto* at San Francisco Opera. On November 29, 1941, he made his Met debut as Alfredo in *La Traviata*. At the Met, he soon became one of the most successful American singers in the company's history and a walking advertisement for upward mobility.

Because of their shared ethnic, religious, and social origins, Hurok developed a closer relationship with Peerce than with many of his artists. When the tenor passed his Met audition with flying colors, Hurok told him to "go home, make *Kiddush* over your sweet red wine, eat some good gefilte fish with horseradish, some fresh challah with a little salt, and kiss Alice [his wife]." After particularly successful performances, Hurok loved to come backstage and share the credit, talking about "our *Rigoletto*" and remarking that "we were in our best voice." Peerce accepted such behavior with amusement, as just part of being one of Hurok's "children." But even after thirty-five years of mostly pleasant association with his one and only "serious" manager, this great American tenor still felt Hurok kept him at a safe emotional distance. Though both men were Jews, they never discussed their religion or exchanged confidences.

"I never really got close to him—nobody did—even though we spoke the same language and shared many things," Peerce wrote two years after Hurok's death. "There was a certain reserve to him, although we had beautiful rapport."

One of the highlights of the Ballet Russe de Monte Carlo's long spring season at the Met in 1940 was a revival of Stravinsky's *Petrushka*. Among its more notable features was a rare onstage appearance by Hurok in a ballet (indeed, it seems to have been the only recorded one). In a case of pure typecasting, he took the nondancing role of the bear trainer. (His business partner Julius Fleischmann, "Mr. Yeast," also appeared in the production as a supernumerary.) Although Hurok didn't elaborate on the emotional or artistic dimensions of this brief performance in his memoirs or elsewhere, he saw to it that numerous photographers and reporters captured the moment for posterity and (even more importantly) for the sake of publicity. In all the photos, an elaborately costumed Hurok looks to be enjoying himself hugely.

Whether he felt a particularly strong identification with the bear trainer's role was a matter he chose not to disclose to his admirers, but the part was, after all, not so very different from the one he played in real life. In both art and life, he was responsible for getting performers onstage to show their stuff and do their tricks, a feat that demanded both the ability to threaten credibly and a skillful control of carrot-and-stick techniques. That he rewarded his artists with small doses of money, and the bear with food was a relatively minor distinction. The basic requirements for success as a bear trainer and an impresario were, after all, similar: theatricality, the ability to manipulate and discipline others, and, most of all, a supreme self-confidence.

Originally, the Ballet Russe de Monte Carlo was scheduled to follow its Met season with appearances in Paris. But by mid-June 1940, when the company was supposed to be performing at the Théâtre de Palais Chaillot, France had been defeated and occupied by Hitler's armies. In response to these new international complications, Hurok hastily assembled a South American tour for the summer. He also persuaded Rubinstein to come along and give a series of piano recitals in the cities on the tour. Rubinstein brought his wife, joining Hurok and Emma on an exotic itinerary that took them first to Rio de Janeiro, then on to Sao Paulo, Buenos Aires, Rosario, and Montevideo.

Both on board ship and off, there were the usual jealousies, intrigues, and capers among the company members, who included Danilova, Markova, Mia Slavenska, Igor Youskevitch, and British-born dancer Freddie Franklin. Ugly arguments raged between those who hoped Hitler would occupy Russia and overthrow the Communists and others horrified by Nazi anti-Semitism. Finally, Hurok threatened to send them all back home if they continued to indulge in political discussions. In a lighter vein, Danilova and Markova flirted with the sailors, and just about everyone fell ill from the heat, humidity, various vaccinations, and unpredictable tropical diet. The titillated ballerinas were warned against the dangers of white slave trafficking and the possibility of contracting syphilis from restaurant glasses. Hurok and Rubinstein also checked out various performers at each stop, including the Buenos Aires favorite, flamenco dancer Carmen Amaya, "a woman with a wild temperament who invariably made the combs fall out of her hair." Hurok would later bring Amaya to the United States.

During this tour, Nela Rubinstein also had the opportunity to get to know Emma Hurok better, although she admitted later that "nobody knew her very well." Hurok, Nela observed,

> was always extremely polite with Emma, and always wanted everybody to pay attention to her, as she sat there with her cigarette holder. She was very exacting, and Hurok was absolutely angelic with her, even though she was always looking down on him. "Hurok, why don't you give me a ring," I remember her saying in Buenos Aires, where my husband had given me a beautiful ring. And he did. He gave her everything that she wanted, mink coats and all, and you had to be nice to her because you didn't want to hurt his feelings. He built up a picture of her in his mind that was perfect; she was the little lady. He was really in love with her, even though she never acted like his companion or partner. She never did things for him or helped him. No, she always sat on the throne, and expected him to do everything.

High expenses and poor attendance led Hurok to lose not only $22,000 on the South American tour, but also whatever confidence he had left in the commercial and artistic future of the Ballet Russe de Monte Carlo. By the time the company arrived back in New York, he had decided to launch another surprise attack in the ongoing ballet wars. This time, however, in the strangest twist yet, he was going to supply and support both sides.

For the last few months Hurok had been engaged in secretive negotiations with his old crony de Basil about getting back together. In late summer of 1940, just back from South America, he announced that he had arranged to bring de Basil back into the Hurok fold. Even odder, though, was the news that he would present de Basil's company (now called the Original Ballet Russe) in New York, where it would run head-to-head against his own Ballet Russe de Monte Carlo! So Denham's suspicions that Hurok was up to something proved more than justified.

As was always the case, this apparently startling move had been preceded by months of undercover preparation. For months now, Hurok had been complaining to Denham and his associates about the poor quality of the Ballet Russe de Monte Carlo's dancing, the lack of company discipline, poor box office receipts, and the failure of Denham's public relations staff to supply adequate printed materials and photos as stipulated in their agreement. All these problems, Hurok charged, were a "result of the fact that no one in your company is willing to assume responsibility and put it on a proper efficient working basis."

But the real problem was that Hurok could not manipulate Denham as he wished. That's why he wanted to reunite with the more vulnerable and pliant de Basil. Hurok achieved this goal by making life so difficult for Denham and Fleischmann that they eventually agreed to release him from the exclusivity clause in their contract. This left him free to take on the de Basil company and other competing dance attractions. Because Denham and Fleischmann still needed Hurok's expertise, connections, booking network, and reputation, however, they and the Ballet Russe de Monte Carlo remained with him in an increasingly dysfunctional relationship for several more seasons. They would finally part company only in late 1942.

Hurok's strategy, as *Time* reported, provided yet another example of his fondness for playing all ends against the middle and hedging his bets: "If one of the companies crumbles away, he still has the other, and the title of No. 1 impresario of the Russian Ballet." Hurok would stage his own battle of the ballets and, like an omnipotent Roman emperor, reward the winner with his largesse.

Today, when we have become used to the idea of dance companies associated with a single artistic director/choreographer (Paul

Taylor, George Balanchine, Robert Joffrey), the idea that an impresario would and could simultaneously represent several troupes of similar aesthetic orientation might seem odd. But in 1940, the American dance world was still unsophisticated and unfocused. In the absence of state support, a tradition of ballet philanthropy, dancers' unions, and strongly defined companies like those in Europe, it was left to commercial presenters like Hurok to call the shots. He, in turn, took full advantage of the fact that dancers, especially Russian ones, had virtually no legal protection or rights, and treated them like pieces of furniture to be placed where he wanted them.

The arena Hurok chose in the autumn of 1940 for the Ballet Russe de Monte Carlo vs. Original Ballet Russe dance-to-the-death shootout was the 51st Street Theater (today the Mark Hellinger), the Met being closed for renovations. After changing his plans several times, Hurok opened the Ballet Russe de Monte Carlo there on October 14 for a three-week season. He followed it up almost immediately on November 6 with an extended engagement of more than two months by the Original Ballet Russe. Just as Hurok had anticipated (his newspaper ads called it the "The No. 1 Ballet of the World"), the critics were nearly unanimous in pronouncing de Basil's company the victor.

One of the main reasons was the reunion in the de Basil company—for the last time—of the "baby ballerinas" (Riabouchinska, Toumanova, Baronova) who had conquered New York seven years earlier. Now mature artists, they retained their appeal. (In their Los Angeles performances, en route to New York, the three ballerinas even inspired Walt Disney to use them as models for the dance sequences in his new film *Fantasia*.) The de Basil repertoire was also more varied, more innovative, and more authoritatively presented. Eight of the thirty ballets were new, and David Lichine's choreography, wrote John Martin, demonstrated "strength and heartiness, humor and a good, lusty sense of the flesh and the devil."

Over at the Ballet Russe de Monte Carlo, the most interesting item in the underrehearsed repertoire was *The New Yorker*, a new ballet set to music by George Gershwin and illustrating *New Yorker* cartoons. Hurok had pushed hard for this work, which he believed would capitalize on the huge popular appeal of Gershwin's music. It failed to become a hit. Perhaps audiences and critics, increasingly mindful of "American" dance and dancers, detected an alien element in Massine's attempt to capture the American experience. Or perhaps, as Denham complained to Hurok, it had been a mistake to ask classical dancers to perform in a popular style (tap, jitterbug) unsuited to their training. (George Balanchine had handled this problem very well in his choreography for the 1936 musical comedy *On Your Toes*, however.)

With two large competing companies filled with Russian dancers and impresarios in town, life offstage became an unending drama of recriminations, revenge, and backstabbing. The relationship between Hurok and his Ballet Russe de Monte Carlo colleagues deteriorated to the level of name-calling. Upset by the debacle over *The New Yorker*, Denham accused Hurok of "lack of judgement" in choosing repertoire. They also argued about the advisability of producing a new Stravinsky ballet, with Hurok doubtful that "a score by Stravinsky would have the wide popular appeal which we would like a ballet to have."

The strife continued after the Ballet Russe left New York to go on tour, the managing partners clashing repeatedly and bitterly over casting. Denham told his lawyer that Hurok was trying to get out of his contract by waging a concerted campaign "to defame and sink our company." One of his tactics was to try to lure certain artists away from the Ballet Russe by offering them more lucrative offers with the de Basil company. By February 1941, the hostility between the Original Ballet Russe and the Ballet Russe de Monte Carlo had become so intense and litigious that local managers were afraid to book either company.

Meanwhile, Hurok was engaged in another nasty struggle, this one with his former friend Irving Deakin. It concerned the rights to Alicia Markova and her English partner Anton (Patrick) Dolin. (Dolin was also a moving force in the newly established American company, Ballet Theatre.) Deakin at the time represented the two dancers. Since Markova was currently available to Hurok only through his contract with Denham's organization, Hurok began pressuring Deakin to sign a separate contract with him for her services. Such an arrangement would make it possible for Hurok to present the popular Markova on his own and, he believed, ultimately achieve his cherished goal of "smashing" (as Deakin saw it) the Ballet Russe.

But Markova and Dolin both realized that if they signed with Hurok they would become less independent and even risk the distasteful prospect of ending up with de Basil. Being close friends and colleagues who had danced together as the Markova-Dolin Ballet in England in the mid-1930s, they staunchly resisted Hurok's overtures.

Their refusal enraged him. One night at intermission at the 51st Street Theater, Deakin and Hurok even had a shouting match in the lobby, with Hurok (as Deakin later related) "completely losing his *savoir faire* and his smiling attitude of all's right with the world." Standing within earshot of the patrons, the normally unflappable impresario went on to denounce what he called the "lousy Ballet Theatre," and even made the crude threat that if its organizers "are not careful, there's going to be only one ballet company, and that will be my ballet company. I'll see to that, and all your friends will be sitting on their ass."

After this argument, the Deakin-Hurok relationship cooled for four or five years. Hurok could not bear to lose.

But the ballet double-dealing of which Hurok had lately become so fond reached its infamous height in March 1941. That's when he abandoned the hapless de Basil company in Cuba. After their highly successful New York engagement, Hurok sent the Original Ballet Russe on tour through Canada, along the east coast of the United States, and then to Mexico. There Hurok's plotting and the financial problems that continued to plague de Basil finally caught up with the colonel and his increasingly motley crew. In Mexico City, the company's secretary called the corps dancers into his office one by one to inform them that because living costs in South America were lower, their pay was being cut from the agreed-upon scale of $180 they had been receiving in America to $108 a month. This precipitated a protest from the dancers. While sailing to Havana for their next engagement, they began threatening to strike. When the company management refused to respond to their complaints, most of the corps dancers refused to dance on opening night. The show went on, but only with the principal dancers.

Then de Basil arrived and offered to negotiate with the strikers. Hurok, meanwhile, sent his Girl Friday Mae Frohman to Cuba, but she was unable to get the various parties to come to an agreement. So Hurok—who had precipitated the trouble in the first place by ordering a pay cut—suddenly withdrew his sponsorship of the company, citing its instability and failure to fulfill contractual obligations. He also seized Baronova, one of the troupe's biggest stars, placing her under his personal management.

Hurok's representative, the unsavory German Sevastianov, was present throughout the affair and was even believed to have encouraged the protesting dancers to strike. This led many to assert that he had been acting as Hurok's hired provocateur in a carefully orchestrated campaign to weaken de Basil's position. By killing off the Original Ballet Russe, Hurok would eliminate a competitor for his latest interest, Ballet Theatre, which now seemed to be attracting better artists and more interest. Back in New York, Hurok refused to pay for the dancers' last four performances in Havana, or for their passage home. In response, the reeling colonel filed charges of sabotage against him and Sevastianov. The case was dismissed, however, because de Basil (who had a habit of missing important meetings) was in South America and could not be present for the trial.

The Cuban strike and its aftermath proved fatal to the Original Ballet Russe. Some of the stranded dancers remained in Cuba for as long as five months, while the company's stars scattered. De Basil did manage to regroup under the management of Fortune Gallo (ironically, the manager from whom Hurok had first won the right to present Anna Pavlova), but the outfit never regained its former stature. Amazingly enough, de Basil would still find it possible (or, more precisely, necessary) to collaborate with his nemesis Hurok again after World War II.

Typically, Hurok maintained his usual baby-faced innocence about the flap in Havana. It rates barely a mention in either of his books of "memoirs." In his version it was, of course, all de Basil's fault: "Because of de Basil's inability to pay salaries, he started cutting salaries, with a strike that has become a part of ballet history ensuing. . . . The mess was too involved, too complicated, and the only possible course was for me to drop the whole thing." Hurok also implied that de Basil's second wife (Olga Morosova) was making trouble by demanding leading roles intended for Baronova, which seems highly unlikely.

Even if Hurok did not himself plan the strike, he surely took advantage of it once it took place, zooming in on the faltering company like a lion for the kill. When the moment came, he did not hesitate to hit a fellow Russian and colleague when he was a down. Never mind that they had been working together for nearly a decade. The events in Cuba left Hurok, he thought, in a position of unchallenged power and authority in the American ballet world, the goal toward which he had long been working and scheming. They also left him—by Fortune Gallo's calculations—$38,500 richer: That was the amount he saved by canceling the contract with de Basil.

Within weeks, like a child with a limited attention span, Hurok had turned his attention to his latest dance attraction. He began telling local managers that "as a patriotic duty" he had decided to offer them the exciting new American company Ballet Theatre in place of the now defunct de Basil Company that he had previously booked with them for the 1941–42 season. Hurok thought he was just trading one company for another, but he would find Ballet Theatre considerably more difficult to manipulate and control than the many troupes associated with de Basil.

Not everyone was taken in by Hurok's smooth publicity and "Who, me?" explanations about what happened in Cuba, of course. Among the doubters were some of the more perceptive (and equally duplicitous) members of his own staff. Sevastianov, whose less than benign influence over Hurok seemed to be growing, certainly had no illusions about his boss's behavior and motivations. At a cocktail party held around the time of the Cuban debacle, Sevastianov shared with Fleischmann some of his feelings about Hurok. He is "absolutely void of any idealism," warned Sevastianov, and he "loves only two things—his wife and money." Which of them Hurok loved more Sevastianov didn't say.

■ CHAPTER FOURTEEN ■

The Rise and Fall of the Ballet Hurok

"Never criticize anybody; you may be managing them next year."—*Sol Hurok*

THE NEAR-MONOPOLY that Hurok had exercised over the ballet scene in the United States since the early 1930s began to break up in the early 1940s. A generation of American dancers, choreographers, and critics who had grown up with the Russian traditions of the de Basil company and the Ballet Russe de Monte Carlo were beginning to assert themselves. As they came of age, they demanded greater representation of homegrown talent, style, and content.

Young dancer-choreographers like Martha Graham (who had established her School of Contemporary Dance in 1927) and Agnes de Mille, who had been working in relative obscurity for more than a decade, were finally beginning to win greater recognition and influence. George Balanchine, an American citizen since 1939, had been incorporating what he saw as the spirit of the New World in his work for movies *(The Goldwyn Follies)* and Broadway *(Babes in Arms, The Boys from Syracuse, Cabin in the Sky)*, as well as in ballets he was creating at the Metropolitan Opera and for Ballet Caravan, a company founded by his admirer Lincoln Kirstein in 1936. The dance scene was rapidly becoming more varied and pluralistic, reflecting a new confidence in the value of American traditions.

But perhaps the most important new development for the future of American dance was the formation of Ballet Theatre. The company's first performance at the Center Theater in Rockefeller Center on January 11, 1940, represented the start of a new era. "Here at last," proclaimed the editorial page of the New York *Herald Tribune*, "is a solidly American organization that has brought together a wealth of talents from many countries and put their creations, old and new, on the stage with a freshness and intelligence that have honestly earned the enthusiastic support of its audience."

Despite its carefully cultivated "American" identity, Ballet Theatre also had Russian roots. It had grown out of the remains of the Mordkin Ballet Company. Moscow-trained dancer Mikhail Mordkin had appeared with Pavlova on her first American tour. Later, he formed his own company and even ran the Bolshoi Ballet for a time before settling in the United States in 1924. After some years of free-lancing, he reestablished the Mordkin Ballet in 1937, using students from his New York studio.

Among Mordkin's students were many talented Americans. One was Lucia Chase, a leading ballerina in the company in the late 1930s. Born into a respectable clockmaker's family in the stuffy old New England mill town of Waterbury, Connecticut, in 1897, Chase had single-mindedly pursued her dream of a career in the theater. She refused to abandon this goal even after her wealthy husband died in 1933, leaving her with two young sons. With her plain and angular Yankee features, Chase was destined to be cast in character roles, but she made up in determination, intelligence, and study what she lacked in natural gifts. She was also generous (although quietly so) with her fortune. When Mordkin needed a larger space in which to rehearse new works, Chase offered him the second floor of the stables at her family summer home in Narragansett, Rhode Island.

Initially, the Mordkin Ballet was managed in a rather desultory fashion by Mordkin's friend and neighbor, the German émigré actor turned publisher Rudolf Orthwine. But the burden of running a company of sixty-five dancers soon became too much for him. Dmitri Romanoff, another dancer in the troupe, suggested hiring as manager a young American he knew, Richard Pleasant. Born in Denver and educated at Princeton, the elegant, urbane, and somewhat pedantic Pleasant proved well suited for the job of running Mordkin's outfit. But perhaps his greatest coup was persuading Lucia Chase in 1939 to provide backing for a new, more ambitious venture to be called Ballet Theatre. It was designed to showcase the work of various choreographers, including Americans.

"Richard Pleasant thought it was time for America to have its own ballet company," Chase said some years later. "And it was Dick who thought that such a company should not have a choreographer as its head, but that many choreographers should come and work with it . . . it was [his] great wish that Ballet Theatre would always be a gallery of the dance, that it would present all the best in ballet, that it would be a great international company, but American in spirit."

The choreographers engaged in preparation for Ballet Theatre's first New York season in 1940 represented many different trends. Four were Russian (Mordkin, Michel Fokine, Adolph Bolm, Bronislava Nijiinska), three were English (Antony Tudor, Andrée Howard, Anton Dolin), two were American (Agnes de Mille and Eugene Loring) and one was Mexican (José Fernandez). As Ballet Theatre evolved, the role of Mordkin and his former company would decline, while Chase's participation in management and artistic decisions would grow.

Opening night on January 11 featured a typically eclectic program of three ballets, two by Russians and one by an American. The "opening ballet" was Fokine's perennial favorite, *Les Sylphides*. Then came *The Great American Goof*. It combined surrealist dialogue by American writer William Saroyan, a score by Henry Brant (whose previous works included *Music for a Five and Dime Store* scored for violin, piano, and kitchenware), and choreography by Eugene Loring (creator of *Billy the Kid*). The evening closed with Mordkin's *Voices of Spring*. Mordkin wasn't there to see it, though; he had left the company because he felt insulted at being demoted to the position of merely one choreographer among many.

Intent on avoiding the star mania that had characterized the Russian troupes in the 1930s, both Pleasant and Chase made frequent last-minute cast changes. They wanted to create a company that operated as a collective, without dominant dancers or choreographers.

During its first two seasons, Ballet Theatre presented twenty-four ballets to almost universal critical acclaim. But box office was poor, expenses were high, and the company was in chronic financial difficulties. Losses on the first three-week season totaled more than $200,000, and the picture did not much improve the following year. Only 20 percent of the tickets for the engagement at the Majestic Theatre in February and March 1941 were sold. By mid-March 1941, Pleasant was forced to resign because of his inability to raise the money necessary for continued operation. This set the stage for Hurok, then embroiled in the Cuban strike by members of the de Basil company, to come to the rescue once again.

Believing that the dance world revolved around him, Hurok hated nothing more than to be excluded from any promising new enterprise. And by now he understood that Ballet Theatre showed promise. Even more important, at a time when communication with Europe and the Soviet Union was virtually impossible and it was difficult to say when the situation would improve, a company based in America and run by Americans was looking more appealing. Hurok wanted to minimize his risks by disentangling from risky European obligations and focusing on domestic attractions.

Several other considerations also made the new company look like a good bet to Hurok. One was his disappointment over the quality of the work currently being offered by both the Ballet Russe de Monte Carlo and de Basil's Original Ballet Russe. Another was his belief that he could persuade several top box office attractions (Alicia Markova, Irina Baronova) to sign up with Ballet Theatre. Hurok also knew that by supporting this fledgling homegrown enterprise, he could cash in on the red-white-and-blue American patriotism that was so much in fashion at the moment. In the wake of the signing of the Soviet-German nonaggression pact, attractions featuring Russians (even anti-Soviet émigrés) had lost much of their public appeal.

At first, Hurok's interest was treated by those who had been running Ballet Theatre with something akin to horror. For them, the prospect of entering into a relationship with an impresario whose preference for "Russian" ballet was all too well known looked like making a pact with the devil himself. Knowing of Hurok's need to control any organization that he presented, and contemptuous of his pandering to the public, Richard Pleasant had been adamantly opposed to the idea of working with him. Those sentiments were shared by virtually all the members of the company's artistic staff, who considered the name Hurok "a dirty word" and feared that association with him would "contaminate Ballet Theatre's purity and business integrity."

Pleasant's unwillingness to work with Hurok was, in fact, one of the main reasons for his resignation as director and vice president of Ballet Theatre in March 1941. The company's board had come to believe that Hurok, with his vast experience of profitably presenting ballet in America, was the only one who could save the floundering enterprise, but Pleasant refused to go along. To Ballet Theatre's anxious directors, Hurok's unfortunate lack of interest in American dance and dancers was less important than his big mailing list and carefully nurtured clout with "café society." To them, his trademark name and proven ability to make money on ballet was just what the doctor ordered.

Any remaining doubt about whether Hurok should be brought on board as Ballet Theatre's presenter was removed by the efforts of one of his greatest admirers, Anton Dolin. As a popular dancer and a well-regarded company member, Dolin was able to persuade the board to engage Hurok. He also convinced them to hire Hurok's assistant German Sevastianov as business manager. As usual, Dolin had his own selfish motives for engineering this move. He had already extracted a promise from Sevastianov that he would bring Alicia Markova to the company as a headline performer and his partner.

In all fairness, Sevastianov did have impressive credentials for the job. He possessed several years of dealing with the byzantine politics of ballet companies (including his recent bravura performance as provocateur among the de Basil dancers on board ship in the Caribbean). Sevastianov's wife was also an important asset: She was Irina Baronova, one of the original "baby ballerinas" and a proven box office draw. Since going to work for Hurok as promotion manager in 1939, Sevastianov had displayed undeniable skill as "a negotiator and mediator between Hurok and those who distrusted, feared, or simply disliked the old man." Like Hurok, Sevastianov believed in the absolute superiority of Russian ballet and Russian dancers, and set to work almost immediately at making Ballet Theatre into a better-run copy of the de Basil and Ballet Russe companies.

Hurok's accession to power was also aided by Lucia Chase, a major player in the company's affairs. Despite some misgivings about Hurok's taste and tactics, she was overjoyed at the prospect of relinquishing the central role in day-to-day operations that she had been forced to assume under Pleasant. Now she could hand the management over to Sevastianov and Hurok and concentrate on her first love, dancing. Over the next few years Hurok was careful to see that she received major roles in several new ballets by Fokine and Tudor. In time, however, her feelings about what company members jokingly called the "Russian Occupation" would change.

Hurok and Sevastianov moved quickly to make public their intentions of "saving" Ballet Theatre. Ever calculating, Hurok leaked stories to the press that presented his actions as those of selfless arts lover concerned about the future of a struggling American troupe. Long before the resolution of de Basil's suit against him (charging him with provoking the dancers' strike in Cuba), Hurok told local managers that he was going to give them Ballet Theatre as a replacement for the de Basil company in 1941–42 bookings. In mid-June 1941, not long after Sevastianov had become general manager and just as Hitler's armies invaded the Soviet Union, closing off all contact with Russia for the foreseeable future, Hurok and Ballet Theatre signed a contract.

At Ballet Theatre, Hurok believed he (with Sevastianov's help) would finally get what he had wanted for so long: total artistic and managerial control, without any interfering Denhams or de Basils. And for a while, he did.

The terms of his contract obligated Hurok to pay Ballet Theatre a weekly fee, even when revenue from ticket sales did not cover that amount. What he got in return was the promise of a specified number of "international stars" and the pledge that the company would stage two major and two minor new productions each year. He also obtained right of "approval" over casting and new productions. This right gave him more power in theory than in practice; in the vast majority of cases he accepted what the Ballet Theatre artistic staff presented to him.

But then Ballet Theatre was not Hurok's only company. He was still presenting the Ballet Russe de Monte Carlo. His official and unofficial statements seemed clearly partial to Ballet Theatre, however. He told the Los Angeles *Examiner*, for example, that Ballet Theatre's corps de ballet was "the best I have seen."

Such favoritism infuriated Serge Denham, who demanded that this statement and others like it be retracted as unfair to the Ballet Russe de Monte Carlo. "While we do not consider your artistic standards or general understanding of the Ballet such as permitting you to be a critic, you are free to express your thoughts—as wrong as they may be—in your private capacity," Denham fumed in a letter to Hurok. "We cannot allow you to make public statements which are undermining our organization and causing us great injury."

The critical failure of Massine's new ballets *Labyrinth* and *Saratoga* during the Met season in the autumn of 1941 only further undermined Hurok's faith in the Ballet Russe. Now he devoted even more resources and energy to Ballet Theatre. By November 1941, he had already informed Denham he would not be renewing his option on the Ballet Russe de Monte Carlo beyond the fall 1942 season. This sequence of events makes it difficult to argue with Denham's assessment that Hurok had built up Ballet Theatre "chiefly to satisfy his personal ambition and with a view of competing with—or even destroying—the Ballet Russe de Monte Carlo." In early 1942, Denham countered by signing a contract with Columbia Artists. It would take effect after the Hurok contract ran out at the end of the Met season in October 1942.

When Columbia Artists took over the Ballet Russe de Monte Carlo from Hurok in 1942, the presenting business was in the midst of an upheaval. Both Columbia Concerts Corporation, affiliated with CBS, and the National Broadcasting and Concert Bureau (the NBC affiliate under whose auspices Hurok Attractions had operated since 1930) had just been reorganized after an investigation conducted by the Federal Communications Commission. Because they operated concert agencies, CBS and NBC were found to be engaged in both buying and selling talent. This was a violation of conflict of interest guidelines. As a result, both networks sold their controlling shares to insiders and got out of the concert business. Columbia Concerts now became Columbia Artists Management, Inc., with Arthur Judson, former head of Columbia Concerts, as president. As of January 1, 1942, NBC's National Broadcasting and Concert Bureau became the independent National Concert and Artists Corporation (NCAC), with Hurok's longtime colleague Marks Levine as head of the concert division.

With the newly created NCAC, Hurok and his company retained the same advantageous and independent relationship they had enjoyed under their former relationship with NBC. The continuing "close affiliation" of Hurok Attractions, Inc., boasted the new NCAC corporate brochure, "is numbered among our most prized possessions." Hurok was required to move his agency from Rockefeller Center, however. For his new headquarters, he chose offices "in the heart of Manhattan's artistic and social life" at 711 Fifth Avenue.

Meanwhile, during the three-week 1942 spring season at the Met, Hurok was staging another battle of the ballets. He booked his two companies in alternating repertory, giving the first week to Ballet Theatre, the second to the Ballet Russe de Monte Carlo, and mixing them during the third. In publicity and advertising, if not in aesthetic, the two troupes tended to blend together like one huge Ballet Hurok. Even the newspapers confused the companies. In repertoire, Ballet Theatre was considerably more bold. While the Ballet Russe gave no premieres, Ballet Theatre presented two that season: Tudor's landmark *Pillar of Fire* (more of that later), and Fokine's *Russian Soldier*.

Lest the company be accused of forgetting the American boys fighting in Europe and the Pacific, *Russian Soldier* capitalized on the war effort. It was set to Sergei Prokofiev's *Lt. Kije Suite*, itself fashioned from music the composer originally wrote for a 1933 Soviet film. That film was a witty attack on the folly of autocrats (specifically Tsar Paul I), but Michel Fokine's feelings of fond loyalty toward the Romanov dynasty led him to create a ballet in a very different spirit. Unable to share Prokofiev's ironic attitude toward tsars and their whims, Fokine produced a patriotic celebration of a brave nineteenth-century Russian peasant who dies while defending his motherland. It had as little in common with the spirit of the original film and music as Tolstoy does with Woody Allen.

Later, after Fokine's death (in August 1942), Hurok launched a press campaign announcing the dedication of *Russian Soldier* "to the gallant Russian soldiers of World War II." And in a baldly patriotic tribute to the Soviet defense of Stalingrad, a Soviet soldier waving the hammer and sickle was added to the peasant's heroic death scene.

Russian Soldier was also performed as part of a benefit for Russian War Relief at the Metropolitan Opera House in April 1942. The Soviet ambassador to the United States, Maksim Litvinov ("himself a balletomane," claimed the Philadelphia *Record*), attended and was photographed smiling as he chatted and shook hands with Hurok. Nor was this the only benefit wartime performance in which Hurok participated. He also provided his artists for a huge testimonial rally at Madison Square Garden on June 22: "The People of New York Pay Tribute . . . Give Help to THE PEOPLE OF RUSSIA upon the First Anniversary of the Invasion of their Homeland by a Common Enemy." New York Mayor Fiorello La Guardia was an honorary chairman for the event, which raised $250,000 for medical supplies. Hurok's efforts to help Russia during the war earned him respect and gratitude in Moscow that would help him significantly in his negotiations there in later years.

In the autumn of 1942, Hurok repeated the dual Ballet Russe–Ballet Theatre season at the Met. As long as he was in control and making money (which he was), he did not seem concerned over whether the public was able to distinguish between his attractions. "People were buying not ballet companies but repertoire in those days," he claimed nonchalantly later in *Impresario*, "and I doubt whether the public knew or cared during those seasons which company they were seeing." One even wonders if he did.

Hurok also remained convinced that the only kind of ballet American audiences would buy was Russian. Immediately upon taking over the marketing and presentation of Ballet Theatre, he was "forced" (as he said) to insert the words "Russian Ballet" in its billing. (He was also responding, no doubt, to a renewed popularity of Russian attractions in the wake of the German invasion of the USSR, the stoic Russian resistance, and the entry of the United States into the war in December 1941.) Hurok's pro-Russian bias also affected the repertoire. Between spring 1941, when Sevastianov took over the management of Ballet Theatre, and May 1943, when he had to relinquish it after being drafted into the U.S. armed forces, the company produced only one non-Russian ballet, and an English one at that: Tudor's *Pillar of Fire*.

The significant operating losses (nearly $60,000) that Ballet Theatre sustained during the 1941–42 season led Hurok to pursue his Russification policy even more single-mindedly, since he believed that what was needed was more familiar fare. In building an artistic and administrative staff, he and Sevastianov also made Russian choices. They raided the disintegrating Ballet Russe and Original Ballet Russe, helping to hasten their demise even as "American" Ballet Theatre became more Slavic. This pro-Russian campaign reached its peak in November 1942, when Hurok and Sevastianov pulled off what they thought was a major coup: luring Massine, the leading Russian choreographer, from the Ballet Russe de Monte Carlo over to Ballet Theatre.

Intent as they were on promoting Russian ballet, dancers, and choreographers, Hurok and Sevastianov regarded the work of the choreographers of Ballet Theatre's "British Wing" with considerable skepticism. Even Antony Tudor failed to excite them, at least at first. With his international reputation already established on the strength of ballets he had done for several companies in England during the 1930s, Tudor had settled in America in 1939 and was one of the original members of Ballet Theatre's artistic collective. Lucia Chase considered him an essential figure in the company. But Tudor's dense, psychoanalytic style, which focused on strong acting and ensemble and failed to provide vehicles for stars, left Hurok and Sevastianov cold.

In order to keep Chase happy, and to ensure her continued financial backing, Sevastianov did sign a contract with Tudor in 1941 for a new ballet. He delayed its completion and premiere as long as possible, however. Set to Schoenberg's *Verklärte Nacht*, it was called *Pillar of Fire*, a title Hurok and Sevastianov privately mocked in their accented English as *Pills of Fire*. But finally even Sevastianov couldn't stall any longer and had to agree to let Tudor present portions of what he had completed. Hurok and his publicity men Gerald Goode and Barry Hyams also agreed to come and pass judgment. Some years later, Tudor recalled what happened:

We had the ballet at a halfway point, and it was immaculately rehearsed, we'd spent a lot of time on it; and Mr. Hurok sat there, and at the end he said, "Would you call Mr. Sevastianov in." Gerry was supposed to be watching, but he was out in another room. And so he came in, and Mr. Hurok said, "In the future, Mr. Tudor has to have first call on all the time for his ballet." Which was rather nice. And so I got the first call, and we got the ballet on that spring, which would never have happened without Hurok's intervention.

Whether Hurok truly liked what he saw—or whether he praised Tudor only to please Chase (who was dancing the role of the Eldest Sister)—is difficult to say. Given his rather prudish and conventional ideas about dance, the ballet's psychosexual story of a young girl's indiscretion and redemption through true love, and its expressionistic choreographic style, would not seem likely to have pleased him. But he could often sense and appreciate real talent. He also appreciated hits—at least when he was paying the bills. And when *Pillar of Fire* had its premiere on April 8, 1942, at the Met, it actually turned out to be a hit. It also began a new era in dance history, one in which the rich territory of the Freudian subconscious would find greater expression in the language of classical ballet. After the opening of *Pillar of Fire*, Hurok presented Tudor with a gold watch, a warm gesture that made a deep impression on this reticent Englishman:

> Often I think of Papa Hurok as though he was a fairy godmother. He personified everything I thought of as a fairy godmother when I was a child. I thought of him as superior, somewhere up in the skies. Hurok wasn't an ignorant man in any way about the arts. He had an aura of history about him. And I never remember him interfering. I never remember him seeing a production on the stage and harping about some point. And when you needed soothing, he would do it. He had a great capacity for soothing people, and he was very gallant to all the dancers.

Toward Hurok's hit man, Sevastianov, Tudor and his colleagues had less positive feelings, however. As soon as Sevastianov became general manager, Tudor said, "My weekly salary and status in the company went down about fifty dollars a week, because all of the intruders—these new Russians they were bringing in—were suddenly important, and we weren't." Tudor was quite friendly with Hurok's secretary Mae Frohman, though, who was popular among the company's members. She came around often to see her friend, the dancer Nora Kaye.

Because of the success of *Pillar of Fire*, Tudor was commissioned to create another new work for the spring of 1943. Hurok suggested that he stage Prokofiev's new *Romeo and Juliet* (which Fokine had already turned down), but Tudor did not find the score to his liking. Instead, he decided to do a *Romeo and Juliet* using music by Frederick Delius.

But when the time came to rehearse, two weeks before the scheduled opening, the corps turned out to be unavailable, since Hurok had sent the company on tour to Canada. Tudor worked separately with Alicia Markova, cast as Juliet, but the corps didn't show up until a few days before the premiere. Nonetheless, Hurok refused to listen to Tudor's pleas for postponement; the tickets for opening night had already sold out.

During the final days before the premiere, rehearsals went on all night long. Once Hurok took Tudor and the cast out to Lindy's at five A.M. and fueled them with smoked sturgeon, raw onion rings, and rye bread. Finally Tudor came up with a compromise: the new ballet could go on, but only in unfinished form. Hurok objected, but the choreographer insisted and got his way. An announcement was made before the curtain went up that the war effort had made it impossible to complete the piece—although of course the war had nothing to do with it.

"We brought the curtain down at a crucial moment, somewhere in the middle of nowhere, which was very exciting," Tudor explained later. "Nothing like that had ever happened before. And Hurok loved it, because it was a hit. He knew that he'd lost that particular little battle with me, but he wasn't resentful in any way."

Tudor's warm feelings about Hurok were not shared by another of the original Ballet Theatre choreographers, Agnes de Mille. This representative of the "American wing" had staged one ballet for the inaugural season (*Black Ritual*) and one for the second (*Three Virgins and a Devil*). Neither had been especially successful. Sevastianov had politely rejected de Mille's latest ballet idea, which led her in 1942 to try her luck with Denham and the Ballet Russe de Monte Carlo. She caught them at the right moment. About to lose Massine to Ballet Theatre and their contract with Hurok now ending, Denham and his crew were desperately looking for new choreographers and ideas. So when the intrepid de Mille presented them with a proposal for a ballet set in Texas about a cowgirl who can't catch a man until she puts on a dress, they went for it. No one was more surprised than the choreographer herself. Perhaps Denham saw the wisdom at this patriotic moment of mounting an American ballet by an American. In any case, he agreed to stage it, square dances and all.

According to de Mille, Hurok (who was still presenting both companies until the end of the Met fall season) was delighted when he heard that Denham was taking a chance on her. ("He knew it would be a flop and he had Massine over at Ballet Theatre now," de Mille said later.) But as rehearsals progressed, word got around that the new ballet (at first called *Arizona Pastorale*, but later renamed *Rodeo*) looked promising. This made Hurok uneasy. He had to take action. Finally he sent Gerald Goode to tell David Libidins, the business manager of the Ballet Russe de Monte Carlo, that *Rodeo* would not be acceptable for the Met season because it was "cheap, vulgar, poor and unworthy."

"How do you know?" roared Libidins.
"We have seen the show rehearsal," said Goode.
"It's a goddamn lie," said Libidins. "No one from your office was there."
And he hit him in the face with a telephone book.

In the end, even Hurok's spies and lies could not prevent the premiere of *Rodeo* on October 16, 1942. Set to a proudly nationalistic score by the forty-one-year-old Aaron Copland, and with sturdy homespun choreography reflecting America's frontier personality, it became an overnight sensation. De Mille danced the leading role of the overlooked Cowgirl. She and Copland received twenty-two curtain calls on opening night, and the serious American dance scene was never the same again.

Between them, the composer and choreographer had proven that American dance forms could be successfully exploited—by Americans—within a ballet framework. They had also shown something even more important: that audiences would like it. *Rodeo* demonstrated, wrote critic George Amberg, "the artistic validity of a genre which heretofore had been tolerated rather than furthered." Once and for all, de Mille and Copland had smashed the myth that ballet had to be Russian or European to sell.

For Hurok, the huge critical and popular success of the made-in-America-by-Americans *Rodeo* came as a jolt and marked the beginning of the end of his domination of the American dance scene. "The era of Russian ballet is about over," declared critic Alfred Frankenstein. "Now It's 'Miss Jones,' Not 'Mlle. Joneskaya,' " agreed John Martin in the *New York Times Magazine*.

Rodeo's reception, crowed de Mille some years later, left the impresario "dumbfounded." Witnessing the success of a ballet he personally disliked was bad enough, but to see the Ballet Russe de Monte Carlo score a major triumph just as he was dropping them (their contract expired on October 21) made him feel cheated and overruled. De Mille's friends even claimed that he "would stand at the back of the theatre when *Rodeo* was performed and try to stop people from clapping. 'It's just vulgar—it's just night club, all this tap dancing,' he would say. 'Don't clap! Don't clap!' "

But when it became obvious that people loved the ballet so much that he could do nothing about it, Hurok changed his tactics. Now he began trying to bring de Mille into his fold as a hot commercial prospect. (Later, in *S. Hurok Presents*, he even claimed he found *Rodeo* "delightful.") Summoning her to his office, he announced that " 'You should be Hurok artist. You earned it, you deserve it, you should have it.' " Their roles were now exactly reversed from what they had been in 1929, when de Mille, just starting out as a dancer, begged him to back her and he told her she had deficient technique.

This time, de Mille had the pleasure of telling Hurok she didn't need him. She was already signed up to choreograph a Broadway show. (Neither of them knew at the time that the show would become *Oklahoma!*, one of the biggest hits in the history of the American musical.) Persistent, Hurok tried to lure her with the promise of $1,000 or $1,500 to produce three ballets a year for him. As de Mille tells it:

> "For what company?" I asked.
>
> "For whatever company I manage," he replied, and sort of smiled.
>
> "Oh, no," I said, "that's blind. Some companies are honorable, some are untrustworthy, and some are perfectly awful. How do I know what Russian company you'll be wanting to sell? If the ballets are a success, I'll have sold myself short. And if they're not a success, you'll be in the hole."
>
> And I didn't do it.

After *Oklahoma!* opened in April 1943, Hurok's interest in adding de Mille to his list only intensified. "I want you should be Hurok attraction," he told her. "You could have a good career, and I think you deserve me." But de Mille, who knew she "could have the White House after *Oklahoma!*," told him she already had an agent, at which point "he nearly levitated out the window."

> "I'm an impresario. I want to manage you."
>
> "But Mr. Hurok," I said. "I don't need a manager on Broadway. On Broadway I need a hard-nosed agent."
>
> "I can do that," he said.
>
> "I don't know if you can," I said. "This is another kind of business. You're the best in the world on concerts, but this is a totally different world, and terribly rough. There's never any talk about art on this street. They would blush if you talked about art on Broadway. This is entirely money. I haven't seen any money yet, but it's there."
>
> And so I turned him down again. And he had a permanent grudge against me from then on.

One did not get the better of Hurok without paying for it later.

■ ■ ■

The persistent operating deficit that had led the directors of Ballet Theatre to fire Richard Pleasant continued to pile up after Hurok came on board. During the 1941–42 season, total losses approached $60,000, which led to a bitter dispute between Hurok and the company's lawyers over how to cover them. In a sarcastic telegram to Sevastianov sent from Mexico City in late May 1942, Hurok fumed that Ballet Theatre was not honoring its promise to cover half of his own nearly $20,000 loss. "This is great recognition by Ballet Theatre directors for what I have done to put company over for next season stop am thoroughly disgusted have no words to tell you how I feel."

For their part, the Ballet Theatre directors claimed that Hurok had failed to get the bookings in Chicago that he had promised. In the end, they reached a compromise and Hurok received a little less than he said he was owed.

The two sides squabbled over other issues, too. Hurok's insistence on billing Ballet Theatre as a Russian company was a constant source of irritation to Harry Zuckert, Lucia Chase's friend and the president of the board. "We must insist that the name of our organization, Ballet Theatre, be given at least equal prominence in all future advertising as is given to any other words in the advertisement," he advised Hurok in April 1943. Zuckert was responding to advertisements like the one that appeared in *Variety* in early 1943. Here, at the top of a list of Hurok's attractions, was "THE GREATEST IN RUSSIAN BALLET" (in large bold type) "by Ballet Theatre" (in barely legible type).

Another bone of contention was ballerinas. Hurok was convinced that Ballet Theatre had to have what he considered "prominent outstanding artists" in order to sell. He went to great pains to woo Vera Zorina to the company. As he wrote to J. Alden Talbot, who had succeeded Sevastianov in the post of managing director in the spring of 1943, "We certainly must have her, otherwise we are in the soup." After leaving the Monte Carlo Ballet Russe in 1936, Zorina had appeared in several successful films, including *The Goldwyn Follies* and *On Your Toes*. In the end, Hurok was successful in luring her to Ballet Theatre. Her husband, George Balanchine, came with her, too. She danced the role of Terpsichore in Balanchine's revival of *Apollo* for Ballet Theatre, which had its premiere at the Met on April 25, 1943.

As the presenter of Ballet Theatre, Hurok was always looking over his shoulder at the Ballet Russe de Monte Carlo. Indeed, Charles Payne, a lawyer associated with Ballet Theatre since its beginnings, claimed that Hurok was "as concerned with weakening the Ballet Russe de Monte Carlo as with strengthening the Ballet Theatre repertoire." Despite being dropped by Hurok, the Monte Carlo somehow managed to stay alive and even to hold on to such proven box office stars as Alexandra Danilova and Igor Youskevitch. In 1944 the company scored an important coup by engaging George Balanchine as resident choreographer, a position he held for two seasons. For several years, Balanchine worked for both Ballet Theatre and the Ballet Russe de Monte Carlo simultaneously.

In New York, the Monte Carlo and Ballet Theatre often performed head-to-head. The dancers "could be seen at the Russian Tea Room giving each other daggerlike glances from opposite tables." On the road, the rivalry caused embarrassment and confusion among local managers.

In this sometimes nasty struggle, Hurok's trump card was his own stardom. In the fierce competition with Columbia Concerts, which was representing the Monte Carlo, he could use the carrot of personal appearances by himself, or a guarantee of performances by some of his other surefire attractions (such as Marian Anderson or Rubinstein). But Hurok himself was the most important asset for many local presenters. "They feel you are the most important impresario in America and that your name and presence mean more to that public interested in music and ballet than any one else," wrote Irving Deakin from Houston. (Deakin had returned to Hurok's good graces and was again working for him as a press and publicity representative.) "They are convinced you should be seen personally in this part of Texas." If Hurok would agree to come, they promised to set up a lunch with local celebrities and a radio appearance.

But even Hurok's energetic efforts were not stopping Ballet Theatre from losing money. Lucia Chase quietly contributed $132,032 to keep the company going during the 1943–44 season alone.

Her generosity was inspired in large part by the fact that artistically, Ballet Theatre continued to do vital and innovative work. An example was *Fancy Free*. The first ballet by Jerome Robbins, who had been dancing with the troupe since its birth, it became an instant hit when produced at the Met on April 18, 1944. The optimistic, very "American" story of three swaggering sailors on leave in the Big Apple was set to a brash and foot-stomping score by another newcomer destined to play an important role in American theatrical music, Leonard Bernstein. *Fancy Free*'s success proved that American ballet (in the wake of *Rodeo*) was here to stay.

Other notable new works of the wartime seasons included Balanchine's *Waltz Academy* and *The Wanderer*, Tudor's *Dim Lustre*, Lichine's *Helen of Troy*, and de Mille's *Tally-Ho*.

By the spring of 1945, the war was ending in Europe, but relations between Hurok and the directors of Ballet Theatre were beginning to resemble combat. Hurok's often crude insistence upon promoting the organization as a Russian company propelled by big-name stars was becoming increasingly unpalatable to Lucia Chase and her supporters. She was also becoming suspicious of Hurok's financial dealings. Around the same time (in April 1945), managing director J. Alden Talbot resigned and the board appointed two administrative directors in his place: Chase and Oliver Smith, designer of *Rodeo* and *Fancy Free*.

Their appointment dramatically altered the way the company was run. Under their leadership, Ballet Theatre began to follow a more definite and consistent artistic and administrative course. Having lost Sevastianov to the army several years before, Hurok now had to deal directly with Lucia Chase. Despite her distaste for management, she was a strong woman of strong convictions and showed little patience for his devious show-business tricks. In recent seasons, she had become increasingly annoyed with his habit of misleading her (for his own financial gain) as to the programming desires of the local managers, as ballet historian Charles Payne has noted:

> Hurok would report that the local manager in a Midwestern city, for example, was insisting that *Helen of Troy* with Zorina must be included in the performance and that *Undertow* must definitely not be scheduled. When the company arrived in the city, the local manager would assure Miss Chase that he had made no such demand, and she

would be convinced that Hurok had once more been caught in a lie.

By the summer of 1945, the correspondence between Hurok and Chase was growing increasingly spiky. In a colorful memo to Irving Deakin, Hurok compared her behavior to that of a "milkmaid who had drawn a full bucket of rich milk and had then deliberately placed the pail so that the cow kicked it over."

They disagreed about everything: the number of new productions being prepared for the next season, how the pair of Alicia Markova and Anton Dolin should be billed, what size type could be used for the words "Russian Ballet" in advertising copy. In his letters to Chase, Hurok resorted repeatedly to the phrase "popular appeal" to defend his requests in matters of casting, repertoire, and publicity, and complained bitterly about his inability to turn a profit on presenting the company. It didn't take long before rumors about the disagreements between Hurok and Ballet Theatre management began to surface publicly. In August, a story appeared in the Houston *Post* that Ballet Theatre would no longer be managed by Hurok. Chase wrote a letter to deny the allegation, but insiders knew that something was up.

What led to the final breach between the parties were the negotiations over a new production of Stravinsky's *Firebird* to be choreographed by Adolph Bolm and designed by Marc Chagall. Markova would dance the role of the Firebird, and Dolin the Prince. Under the terms of his agreement with the company, Hurok had consented to pay for any production expenses above $15,000, believing that the overrun would go no higher than $2,000 or so. But the total production expense actually climbed to nearly $35,000—$20,000 of which, Chase claimed, had to be covered by Hurok. As she knew, Hurok was in a vulnerable position because he had already publicized and sold tickets for the production. Cancellation would be expensive and complicated. In the end, Chase won; Hurok paid up, but only on the very morning of the *Firebird* premiere—October 24, 1945. The show went on, but the relationship between Hurok and Ballet Theatre had been damaged beyond repair.

The next few months passed in a furious volley of insults and financial statistics, with Hurok continuing to insist that he was owed a refund. But by now Chase and Smith were feeling confident that they could run the company without Hurok's promotional help (or interference). In a detailed report to the Ballet Theatre board of directors (dated December 11, 1945), they advocated terminating the relationship with Hurok on the grounds that it had become "financially and artistically intolerable." They charged him with "intimidation, smothering tactics and sabotage"; with interfering with the choice of repertoire; with insisting that Markova and Dolin dance because they were also his private clients; with blocking the careers of younger dancers; even with insisting that his own photograph appear first in the souvenir program book.

Chase and Smith not only attacked Hurok; they made their report into an impassioned patriotic defense of the homegrown ballet movement:

> We claim that this is not only a crime against Ballet Theatre but it is a crime against the dance in America. The stated disdain for the work of American dancers, choreographers and composers and the smothering of their talents in order to enrich one person through the draining of the established foreign names is stifling and extremely short-sighted. Through the presentation of native talents and proper publicity we feel that we can continue to build audiences in America, rather than operate on the theory that "the peak has been reached."

For his part, Hurok moaned and groaned and complained. He also tried—without success—to lure some members (including Jerome Robbins) of the Ballet Theatre organization away. Faced with Chase's opposition, Hurok also began criticizing some Ballet Theatre productions he had previously praised. *Fancy Free*, he now told associates, was nothing but a poor imitation of Massine's 1925 ballet *Les Matelots*. But the momentum of the times was on Chase's side, and she proved no less stubborn (and considerably more principled) than he. After months of private and public sniping, Hurok and Ballet Theatre agreed to terminate their contractual agreement as of May 11, 1946, after five years of collaboration and more than a year before it was scheduled to expire.

The split with Ballet Theatre was a turning point in Hurok's career as a presenter of dance. For the first time since the early 1930s, he was left without a single ballet company in his stable. He had discarded de Basil for the Ballet Russe de Monte Carlo, then rejected that company in favor of Ballet Theatre. But now he found himself on the outside. Coming as it did close on the heels of the American victory over Germany and Japan, Chase's moral victory over Hurok also signified the victory of American dance and dancers. The Russian era which Hurok had so energetically and effectively promoted was (for the moment, at least) at an end.

Not only would Americans now control the creative aspect of dance in the United States; they would also manage and promote it. For years Hurok had successfully played various fledgling companies (most of them satellites of Diaghilev's original Ballets Russes) against each other to further his own commercial and personal ambitions. But now—just as Balanchine was joining with another rich American, Lincoln Kirstein, to create Ballet Society and the New York City Ballet—Hurok was left high and dry. History had overtaken him. For so many years reluctant (or more accurately, unable) to commit himself to one choreographer and one aesthetic, he now found himself a victim of his own double- and triple-dealing. So intent had he been on outsmarting the competition that he had outsmarted himself. He had lost the chance to create a company of his own. There would never be a Ballet Hurok.

■ CHAPTER FIFTEEN ■

"To Hell with Ballet"

"If we sell out, we'll lose less."—*Sol Hurok*

LIKE MOST AMERICAN BUSINESSMEN, Hurok exploited the patriotic feeling inspired by World War II in his marketing and public relations campaigns. A good example was the full-page advertisement he placed in *Variety* to welcome the New Year 1943. It shrewdly combined patriotism and snobbery to suggest that any red-blooded American who didn't buy tickets for events presented by Hurok Attractions, Inc., ought to be ashamed. Next to "BUY WAR (and More) BONDS" in boldface type stood this dignified (and highly tendentious) message: "The people of a democracy deserve the best. The people of America have come to expect it. In musical and theatrical entertainment 'S. Hurok Presents' always signifies the best." Similarly, the autumn 1944 Ballet Theatre season at the Met was billed as a "Fall Victory Season."

Whether due to such advertising or to the general improvement in the business climate and a desire for escapist entertainment during a period of heightened stress, Hurok's financial situation improved significantly during the war. Protected by the NCAC safety net, wisely having focused his efforts on attractions based in America, and cleverly exploiting the pro-Russia sentiment with his many Russian artists, he saw his bookings and income rise during the early 1940s. The losses he sustained on Ballet Theatre were more than offset by the income he made on solo performers. Marian Anderson, Arthur Rubinstein, and Jan Peerce had all become steady box office attractions. And unlike ballet, they were relatively easy and inexpensive to present.

According to a report in *Variety* (July 14, 1942) on Hurok's attractions, Anderson had reached a $175,000 gross during the 1941–42 season and was commanding $2,000 per performance for the 1942–43 season. Jan Peerce was also doing well, with forty-five engagements already lined up for 1942–43 at a projected gross of over $90,000. Rubinstein was earning $1,000 for each date and was scheduled to make fifty-six appearances in 1942–43. Not far behind was the Don Cossack Choir under Serge Jaroff, riding the crest of Russian nationalism. They were scheduled for eighty-nine engagements at a projected gross income of $75,000. Other money-makers on the Hurok list included gypsy dancer Carmen Amaya (sixty-eight dates at $60,000) and monologuist Ruth Draper (twenty-five dates at $750 each). These lucrative artists helped support Hurok's expensive taste for ballet companies.

Further down the 1942–43 Hurok list was a recent addition to the stable: violinist Isaac Stern. Though at the time a newcomer, he, too, would eventually turn into a steady source of income. Stern would also become one of his manager's most trusted advisers and the patriarch of a group of Jewish musicians (especially violinists) whose imposing artistic and booking influence would come to earn them the ironic nickname the "Kosher Nostra."

Stern had come to Hurok in 1940, when he was twenty years old and just another aspiring violinist. His New York debut at Town Hall in 1937 had inspired nothing more than lukewarm reviews and suggestions that the teenager should go home and practice. In fact, Stern ended up with Hurok mainly because the violinist's first manager, Paul Stoes, managed some other attractions that Hurok wanted. In order to get the Don Cossack Choir, Hurok agreed to take on Stern. So this stubby Jewish violinist from the Ukraine (via San Francisco) who was destined to become what many critics consider the first great violin virtuoso trained exclusively in America, as well as one of the most visible and articulate artists of his generation, was initially nothing more than a pawn in big-time artist management politics.

"The question," Stern recalled with a smile many years later, "when Stoes decided to join Hurok and NBC was whether I should be given to the Hurok subsidiary or to the parent bureau under Marks Levine. I was an unknown, and neither of them was tripping over themselves to get me. There was an exchange of 'You take him,' 'No, you take him,' and finally it ended up that I went to Mr. Hurok."

The more than thirty-year difference in age between Hurok and Stern quickly led to the development of a father-son relationship. This came naturally to Hurok, who loved to adopt a paternal role even with artists older than himself. But the two also had many important things in common: Ukrainian origin (Stern was born in the town of Kreminiecz), early immigration to the United States (Stern's parents arrived in San Francisco when he was ten months old), Jewishness (including a smattering of Yiddish expressions that they used to "flavor" their conversations), fireplug physique (Stern's was a chunky five feet six inches), the Russian language (which they both spoke imperfectly), a distaste for Germany (Stern insistently refused to play there), an anecdotal sense of humor, good political instincts, gregariousness, and love of good food and wine, seemingly inexhaustible energy—and last but certainly not least, a special fondness for the violin, an instrument with a unique capacity to express the bittersweet melancholy that saturated their shared memories of life in crowded Eastern European towns like Pogar and Kreminiecz.

"I honestly don't remember if Hurok had heard me play by the time he became my manager," Stern recalled. "Chances are that he had, although I don't believe he knew at that time what I had achieved or what my potential was. But he had a very good nose for things."

By the time Stern came to Hurok, he was a seasoned performer with a few lessons from the school of hard knocks. Although his parents loved music (his mother had studied voice with Glazunov at the St. Petersburg Conservatory) and believed in their son's talent, they did not have the means to pay for his education. Fortunately, Stern so impressed a wealthy San Francisco woman that she paid for his tuition at the San Francisco Conservatory. He studied there with Naoum Blinder, another Russian Jewish violinist with ties to the rich Moscow-Odessa tradition. At age fifteen, Stern made his public debut playing the Bach D-Minor Concerto for Two Violins with Blinder and the San Francisco Symphony under Pierre Monteux. Two years later (on October 11, 1937) he made his disappointing New York debut at Town Hall.

Under Stoes's management in the late 1930s, Stern performed for whoever would hire him.

> I played seven concerts the first year, fourteen the next. I traveled in upper berths in trains. I practiced day and night. What did I know from Carnegie Hall, from arts councils, from big interviews? I worked my head off. Do they think that went for nought? I had a tough, hardening apprenticeship. It taught me the value of values.

Like Hurok, Stern loved in later life to draw on his rags-to-riches example as proof that the American dream was real.

For the first few years under Hurok's management, Stern's career continued to build, but slowly. At one time he was sufficiently uncertain about his future prospects to consider taking a job as concertmaster with the local radio orchestra. What changed things was his Carnegie Hall debut on January 12, 1943.

> When I started playing in the late 1930s, it was still the fashion to some degree to play concerti with piano accompaniment, and lots of *petits fours* at the end. Above all, one did not try to get too serious in a concert. And my Carnegie debut in 1943 shows to what extent I was still under that influence. I played a Handel Sonata, the Bach B-Minor Partita with Chaconne, the Brahms D-Minor Sonata, the whole of the Wieniawski Concerto, and a Szymanowski Concerto. I went through half of the violin literature in one afternoon! It was an endless and silly program, but it started things moving.

At this recital presented by Hurok, the fussy New York critics "discovered" Stern, and he was on his way. Even critic-composer Virgil Thomson found much to praise. Within a few years, this ebullient violinist with the big, juicy tone and abundance of quotable quips ("Playing the violin must be like making love—all or nothing") was on his way to a megacareer, and toward a certain megalomania. During a single three-week period in 1949, he gave fifteen concerts. For many years to come, he would prove to be one of Hurok's most steady and profitable artists, as well as a trusted confidant and talent scout. (He would lead Hurok to both Pinchas Zukerman and Itzhak Perlman, among others.) The similarity of their backgrounds, personalities, and ambitions also allowed Stern to get closer to the impresario than any other single person. If Hurok had a real friend, it was probably Isaac Stern.

After the first five years, they even dispensed with a contract. "We worked on a personal handshake," Stern explained.

Because of their friendship, Stern was able to talk more frankly with Hurok than almost anyone.

> I was the only one who could walk into his office and say, "You're doing wrong by this one," and "You're doing this wrong," and so on. We had a very warm and personal relationship.
>
> I remember a few years after the Carnegie Hall concert I started to tell him that I was tired of playing concerti with piano accompaniment, because it was utterly wrong musically and aesthetically wrong. And he would say, "Vawt? But is wonderful for public, and good for box office, blah, blah, blah." And I would say, "Papa"—I called him Papa—"listen to me, I want to play music."
>
> And he says, "Well, if you want to not have people come, then go ahead." But he thanked me, and we went ahead and did it.
>
> And it worked, and I think it started the whole trend away from having some pianist make a massacre of the orchestral part in a violin recital. Hurok resisted at first, but he didn't ban it. With Hurok you had to prove your point. God help you if you lost, but you had to prove your point.

Something else Stern learned from his manager was the art of setting fees.

> Hurok would push the fees up, but just a little under what the artist was really worth so that he didn't really gouge the local impresarios. You know that artists have good years and bad years financially, but in all my years I never

had a bad year professionally. That's where Hurok was very special. There were times when people he had dealt with for a long time, local managers, would have a bad time with a concert, and say they couldn't pay him, and he would tell them, "All right, pay me when you can"—and he would pay me out of his own pocket, and take the loss until they could pay. He considered it an investment in the future. He didn't look for the bottom of anyone's pockets. He always thought of the long term.

Unfortunately, Stern and other superstars of the classical music world seem to have forgotten this important lesson in more recent years. As many observers have pointed out, their fees have now become so prohibitively high (Stern now receives $45,000 for a single performance) that they effectively block entrance into the booking circuit for younger, lesser-known artists. If the manager of a local classical series wants to book Stern, there is no money left in the budget to engage anyone else.

From the very start of their thirty-five-year relationship, Stern also understood that Hurok was a natural showman and as much a star as any of the artists he presented. "He worked very hard at becoming HUROK. He had to get away from Sol to become Hurok. That was an important part of his life."

And if becoming HUROK meant that he sometimes invented things and embroidered reality, Stern simply accepted that as part of the package:

> Certainly I was aware that he would fabricate and make up stories, because sometimes he would contradict himself and trip up. But you let it go. You figured, these were the games people play. The main thing, the wonderful thing, is that after he invented his stories, he really believed in them. And what mattered was how it impinged on the work you did with him. If it helped, you didn't bother with it. That's just part of what made him tick.

Stern also had ample opportunity to observe the often turbulent relationship between the "boss" and his wife, the venerable Emma Borisovna.

I knew Emma, but there was no reason to get very close to her. She was in another world altogether. I don't think they were very happy together, but of course I wasn't there all the time. What was definite is that I rarely saw them together at public events, and that she was not his hostess. She would go only if she was in a good mood. At restaurants and parties, he was usually on his own, and you never assumed that she would be there. I could see that he was very much in love with her, though, and she was a very beautiful woman. She had the air of the grande dames of Russia, women he never could have known in the Old World. And that was a lot of her appeal for him, I think.

By the early 1940s, Hurok and Emma had been living together for several years in a large apartment in a building at 91 Central Park West. In an 1973 interview with the *New York Times*, Hurok claimed that they had been married in 1939, although others (as we have seen) believed the couple had in fact been married considerably earlier, probably in Europe in the late 1920s. What is certain is that Hurok obtained a binding legal American divorce from his first wife, Tamara, on September 16, 1941. This document superseded the contested divorce from Tamara he had received some years earlier in Mexico, and finally removed any legal ambiguities still hovering around his long-term relationship with Emma. This 1941 divorce also established a schedule of alimony payments to Tamara.

At the time, Tamara still lived near where she and Hurok had first settled when they arrived from Pogar more than thirty years earlier: 367 East Second Street in Brooklyn. She had never remarried and, according to her daughter, Ruth, never had serious male companions after Hurok left her. In body and spirit, she never left the protected and suffocating "world of our fathers" that Hurok had rejected as soon as he was able. When Tamara died some years later, Hurok told Ruth in the limousine on the way back from the funeral that her mother had been "a nice lady, but she never left Pogar."

Whenever and however Hurok and Emma were officially married, they had been presenting themselves as a married couple since the early 1930s. Despite her husband's power and connections in the entertainment world, Emma's career as a cabaret singer had not flourished in America. Increasingly, she spent most of her time at home, often in bed, with a cigarette holder in one hand and the telephone in the other. Fluent in Russian and fond of gossip, she would, in Agnes de Mille's words, "sit on the telephone and get all the scuttlebutt, often about the nasty things I was saying about Hurok behind their backs. And there was this trail of bad gossip leading from the Russian Tea Room through Emma's bed, and around and around, and always entangling me and my meanness. . . . It was a very special sort of Russian gossip."

Whether or not de Mille was in fact the focus of Emma's conversations, others confirm that Hurok's wife did love to engage in behind-the-scenes maneuvering. Believing herself superior to her husband in education, culture, and taste, she did not hesitate to provide her assessment of artists and performances, often belittling him in the process. Sprinkling cigarette ashes in all directions and addressing Hurok as "Pupsenka," an endearment that simply made him melt away, she would deliver her advice in a condescending tone that would sometimes "make him bow his head like a scolded little child," Anna Straus recalled.

Moody and given to tantrums, Emma could make her husband utterly submit to her will by sitting at the piano and tossing off a piece by Chopin and Rachmaninoff, often reciting a poem or text to go with it. "He would sit open-mouthed, just collapsed in admiration for her." At less romantic moments she would upbraid him for his ignorance, swearing, and cursing, "and he just sat there and took it all. She was very eccentric."

Hurok's frequent traveling and long absences from home took a toll on his relationship with Emma. On one occasion, several of Hurok's employees went to meet him at the airport when he returned from a particularly difficult midwinter trip to Europe. They accompanied him to his apartment, where they shared a drink in the foyer; apparently he was afraid to annoy his wife by inviting them into the living room. Even though Hurok had been abroad for weeks, Emma didn't bother to come and greet him for at least thirty minutes, until she had finished watching a favorite television show. When she finally did appear, her first question was, "You know who died while you were away?" She then proceeded to list all the people who had died over the last few weeks while he was abroad.

And yet Hurok never criticized Emma to his friends or employees. He relied on her to supervise his wardrobe, approve his ties, and warn him when he had put on too much of his favorite Chanel cologne. He also depended on her to identify encores at performances, so that when the lights came up he would know the titles for conversations in the lobby.

Although Emma was not fond of traveling (especially in later years), in the 1940s she and Hurok began dividing their time between Central Park West and a house "on the coast." Their Los Angeles residence was at 803 North Roxbury Drive in Beverly Hills, not far from where Rubinstein and his family had settled. The Rubinsteins were often invited to Hurok's house for lavish parties attended by performers and movie people. Among his other Hollywood acquaintances were Sam Goldwyn and Jules Stein, president of MCA. Like most people in Hollywood, Hurok was also interested in the movie business himself, and he had succeeded in the late 1930s and early 1940s in interesting several major studios in filming his attractions. In 1942, Warner Brothers spent $200,000 to make two shorts featuring performances by the Ballet Russe de Monte Carlo. Hurok's involvement with film projects would grow through the 1940s, culminating in his 1953 screen biography, *Tonight We Sing*.

In Los Angeles Hurok also rubbed shoulders with some of the many Russian creative artists then living there: Rachmaninoff (until his death in early 1943), Stravinsky, film composer Dmitri Tiomkin, actor Michael Chekhov, and director Gregory Ratoff. Since Los Angeles was becoming an increasingly important stop on cross-country tours (especially for ballet companies), he also spent time with local presenters. One of his favorites was his longtime colleague L. E. Behymer, Founder of the Great Western Lyceum and Concert Bureau and the most important manager on the West Coast until his death in 1947. Throughout the war, Hurok and Emma spent their summers in the sunny and comfortable climate of Beverly Hills. Their usual trips to Europe were for the moment out of the question, and no one who was anyone stayed in New York through the heat and humidity.

Southern California's remoteness and more relaxed atmosphere gave Hurok the opportunity to create "a second life," according to his longtime Los Angeles employee Betty Ferrell. "He loved it out here. He loved to go out to restaurants, where everybody paid attention to him, and he was fascinated with the movie industry."

And yet Hurok only flirted with the movie business; he never attempted to become a producer like so many other immigrant Jews. Agnes de Mille, who knew the movie business intimately through her father (producer William C. de Mille) and uncle (director Cecil B. DeMille), believed he was intimidated by the power of Hollywood. Hurok, she said, knew that he would not be a match for these "gigantic egos, colossae quite as big as he." He knew that "he had his own corner cut out" and that it was too late for him to change professions.

Like the great movie moguls, Hurok had succeeded in creating a marvelous "dream factory" that sold escapist entertainment. But his dreams were built of music and ballerinas, not celluloid and scripts. Like Samuel Goldwyn and Harry Cohn and Louis B. Mayer, Hurok had built "an empire of his own" that transcended and obliterated his Jewishness and lowly origins. But his was an empire of high culture, with an audience both more elite and more limited.

When Japan and the United States signed the official document of surrender on September 2, 1945, ending World War II on all fronts, the enforced isolation which had kept Hurok away from Europe and Russia for the last six years was at last broken. But it would take time to reestablish contact with countries devastated by war. They were now occupied with more pressing problems than the resurrection of cultural life. For the next few years, Hurok would still have to make do with homegrown—or at least American-based—attractions.

One of the more intriguing of these was the Martha Graham Company. Since giving her first solo recital in New York (at age thirty-two), Graham had gradually evolved into what many critics now consider the greatest exponent of modern dance in the United States. Working out of her Martha Graham School of Contemporary Dance, she recruited and trained a cadre of young dancers on whom she choreographed her mythic, yet distinctly American work. By 1946, she had already created more than a hundred major pieces, including the epoch-making *Appalachian Spring*. Set (like de Mille's *Rodeo*) to a plain-and-fancy score by Aaron Copland, it celebrated the simple beauty of American traditions and music. Graham herself danced in the role of a young bride setting up a new life in the American frontier at the ballet's premiere at the Library of Congress on October 30, 1944. *Appalachian Spring* further strengthened the case for serious American dance—a case already convincingly argued in *Rodeo* and *Fancy Free*. It also brought Graham into the mainstream and into the public eye.

It was most likely the critical and popular success of *Appalachian Spring*, too, that gave Hurok the idea of presenting Graham in a Broadway theater and on tour. Graham's longtime friend and occasional antagonist Agnes de Mille doubts that Hurok ever saw Graham or her company dance. According to Hurok's daughter, Ruth, her father did attend a Graham performance, but took a dim view of her art. "All they do is run around in dirty feet," he told her.

What led Hurok to present Graham, de Mille has said, was good reviews and the realization "that the Americans were sticking around, and couldn't be frozen out." Hurok still found the idea of Americana onstage alien; his only comment to de Mille about her choreography for the 1945 musical *Carousel* was that "the costumes are dirty." Even so, the huge popular success during the war years of homespun works like *Rodeo, Fancy Free, Oklahoma!*, and *Carousel* must have made an impression on him. No doubt he believed that a Graham season and tour would cash in on the robust demand for native fare.

For Graham, the two-week engagement at the Plymouth Theater (from January 21 to February 2, 1946) represented an important breakthrough to respectability after two decades of struggle and temporary venues. As Graham biographer Don McDonagh has written, "The Hurok organization had a reputation for handling only the most important names in the performing arts, and his willingness to represent Graham was not just a plum for her but another step upward in the acceptance of modern dance." Broadway actress Katharine Cornell congratulated Hurok in a telegram for engaging her sometime collaborator: "As a creative artist at once produced by America and expressing America she is without peer. My best wishes to you both."

Typically, Hurok and his press staff billed the season as "Hits from the Graham Repertory," although it also included a major new work, *Dark Meadow*, to a score by Mexican composer Carlos Chavez. Used to working with high-strung and temperamental creative artists, Hurok was nonetheless startled when Graham informed him that her precarious financial condition did not permit her the luxury of owning a telephone. This made communication difficult. On opening night, she insisted that the stage floor be stripped of a new coat of paint, and Hurok obliged. He even went so far as to sprinkle the floor with perfume just before the curtain went up.

In New York, the theater was nearly sold out for the entire engagement, but on the road audiences still proved resistant (as Hurok had so long been saying) to the idea of modern American dance. Even in Los Angeles, Graham's four dates failed to draw good houses. Universal critical acclaim notwithstanding, the first Martha Graham national tour was disappointing for both impresario and artist. Hurok lost a sizable amount of money on the venture, but decided to give it one more chance the following year. He was hoping that audiences would gradually discover the company the same way they had discovered the Russian ballet in the early 1930s. But the financial results were no better the second season, despite large and enthusiastic houses in New York. Hurok was unwilling to make a third attempt and decided to drop the Martha Graham Company from his list. Forever after, Graham held him in the utmost disdain as a mere commercial presenter.

Ever the generous patriarch, Hurok hated to be the bearer of bad news. He usually assigned that role to one of his employees. When Graham had to be told that her contract would not be renewed after the 1947 season, for instance, Hurok chose a newcomer to his office, Walter Prude, to perform the task. Prude, who had joined the agency in 1945 after returning from military service in Europe, also happened to be Agnes de Mille's new husband. "Walter always had to tell everybody the unpleasant news, while Hurok would go home," griped de Mille.

An excellent writer and a closet poet, Prude proved so adept at his first assignments (which included "holding people's coats") that he was soon promoted to more important duties, like informing employees and clients that they had been fired. Within a few years,

Prude had become an indispensable part of the operation. He was responsible for writing most of Hurok's correspondence and took care of the negotiations with some of the artists on the Hurok list. A well-educated, polite, and cultured man whose subdued WASP temperament could not have been more different from Hurok's, Prude had earlier worked in radio and as Graham's manager. Loyal and diplomatic, he would remain with the organization to the bitter end, after Hurok's death.

Another important new addition to the office was Martin Feinstein, who came to work in press and public relations in August 1946. A plain-speaking native New Yorker who had majored in music at City College and spent the war writing for *Stars and Stripes*, Feinstein was only twenty-four when he was hired by Hurok's son-in-law, Barry Hyams. Like Prude, he would spend many years in the Hurok office, gradually rising to become head of public relations and a vice president. Unlike Prude, Feinstein could spar with Hurok on a verbal level, trading Jewish anecdotes and bluffs. They were perhaps even too much alike to always get along well, as Feinstein later observed:

> I think I had more knowledge of music than anybody in the office at the time, and I was not afraid to speak back to Hurok. Somehow or other, he admired that. We had many, many arguments, many differences of opinion. There were times we had such violent arguments that we wouldn't talk to each other for two or three days. And then he would come into my office, or I would come into his office, and I'd say, "Mr. Hurok, I was very hurt by your attitude the other day." We invariably kissed and made up.

One of Feinstein's first assignments was to help engineer the publicity campaigns for two major dance attractions that Hurok was presenting in the immediate postwar seasons: de Basil's Original Ballet Russe and the Markova-Dolin Company.

To an outside observer, the idea that Hurok and the old Cossack de Basil would be able to work together again after Hurok had encouraged de Basil's dancers to mutiny in Cuba might seem bizarre. But both impresarios were sufficiently pragmatic and cold-

blooded that by 1946 they were ready to put aside their mutual ran-
cor for what appeared to be mutual financial gain.

De Basil, who had spent the war years dragging his company
around South America, came to New York in late 1945 to investigate the possibility of bringing it back to the United States. Through
New York's chatty Russian émigré grapevine it soon came to
Hurok's attention that de Basil was looking for a deal. At the time,
Hurok was experiencing increasing difficulties in his dealings with
Lucia Chase and Ballet Theatre and was therefore on the lookout to
diversify and protect himself. His utmost concern was to ensure that
he had several major ballet companies with which to fulfill his rental
agreement with the Metropolitan Opera. He was committed to
present fall and spring seasons there through 1948. With Ballet Theatre looking shaky, then, it is hardly surprising that Hurok was willing to entertain de Basil's proposals. He needed attractions to fill the
house.

So Hurok forged an agreement with de Basil for a New York
season and American tour beginning in the fall of 1946. In achieving
this feat, he enlisted the financial backing of the wealthy arts entrepreneur the Marquis George de Cuevas. Born in Chile and married
to John D. Rockefeller's granddaughter, de Cuevas was a noted ballet connoisseur and had even sponsored a season of his own company, the Ballet International, in 1944.

Hurok offered de Cuevas the title of artistic director with de
Basil's Original Ballet Russe, thereby hoping to lure him to underwrite the company's return to the United States. De Cuevas was also
promised the right to choose dancers. Afraid that the de Basil dancers would not be known to the American public, Hurok also decided to supplement the troupe with some of the established "stars"
with whom he had personal contracts: Alicia Markova, Anton
Dolin, André Eglevsky, and the American Rosella Hightower.

The Original Ballet Russe was scheduled to open at the Met on
September 29, 1946. The company had neither the resources nor
the personnel to prepare a significant new repertoire; many of the
dancers had arrived from Brazil only two days before. Nor had they
ever danced before with the group of "stars" supplied by Hurok. So
many problems and difficulties arose that a harassed Hurok came
over to Martin Feinstein's desk one day and said, "You're a bright
young man. Why are you in this business?" Feinstein looked at him

and replied, "You're a bright older man. Why are you still in this business?"

But somehow the season began as planned. It included a single new work: *Camille*, one of the first major ballets created by the young American John Taras. Set to music by Schubert, this version of the Dumas classic was designed as a vehicle for the guest artists Markova and Dolin.

Meanwhile, over at the Broadway Theatre, Ballet Theatre was opening its first post-Hurok season. The stage was set for another round of dueling ballets, providing a unique opportunity for audiences and critics to compare the old Russian (Original Ballet Russe) and new American (Ballet Theatre) traditions head-to-head. Appropriately enough, both companies presented *Giselle*. For Ballet Theatre, Dmitri Romanoff staged a new version with contributions from Balanchine and Tudor, and with Alicia Alonso and Igor Youskevitch in the leading roles. As a guest artist with de Basil's company, Dolin oversaw a production featuring himself and Markova.

When the dust had settled and the accounts were tallied, the Original Ballet Russe emerged the financial victor, taking in a reputed $50,000 weekly in the spacious Met. Ballet Theatre averaged $16,000 to $22,000 in the smaller Broadway Theatre.

Artistically, however, the verdict was nearly unanimous in favor of Ballet Theatre's repertoire and dancers. Edwin Denby called the Original Ballet Russe a "morbid spectacle" and a "ghost" of its former self. While Ballet Theatre boasted a number of important choreographers and dancers and had been developing as a company with a definite aesthetic, the de Basil company was a hodgepodge of performers and styles with little to offer but pale nostalgia. The implications were clear: American dance was the art of the future. For Hurok, still smarting from his rejection at the hands of Lucia Chase and her allies, this could not have been a happy realization.

After the Met season, the Original Ballet Russe toured major American cities. Attendance was poor, at least judging from an anxious memo Hurok sent to his touring press representative Irving Deakin on November 4, 1946, about problems in Boston. After upbraiding Deakin for failing to launch a sufficient publicity campaign ("All I found was a small announcement in the lobby of the Boston Opera House which looked like a grocery sign or delicatessen announcement from Brownsville"), he complained that "our business is falling off." Hurok also worried about competition in Los Angeles and San Francisco from Ballet Theatre, which would arrive several weeks ahead of the de Basil company. According to Feinstein, the Original Ballet Russe tour incurred losses of $80,000.

The Original Ballet Russe concluded its last—rather sad—American engagement by returning briefly to the Met in March 1947. The longtime relationship between Hurok and de Basil ended at least on a positive financial note: the twelve performances there turned a small profit of $12,972. But the company that had first brought ballet to the United States in the early 1930s and had done so much to expand the ballet audience in the New World had outlived its usefulness. De Basil and what was left of his entourage would play no further role in the development of American dance. Hurok does not seem to have made any further attempt to present them in New York or elsewhere. He had needed de Basil and his company to fill the Met for a single season, nothing more. Hurok was not sad to see them go. "When the 'Colonel' and his ragtag-bobtail band clambered aboard the ship bound for Europe," he "heaved a sigh of relief."

For the next four years, de Basil shuttled between European capitals in a mostly fruitless quest for financing and engagements. When he died on July 27, 1951, in Paris, he was still hoping to revive his enterprise. Efforts to continue the Original Ballet Russe after his death were short-lived and unsuccessful.

Like the Original Ballet Russe, the Markova-Dolin Company was used by Hurok as a stopgap attraction to fill the Met after the premature termination of his contract with Ballet Theatre. Unlike de Basil's company, however, the Markova-Dolin Company boasted two bona fide stars in its British headliners. Markova had been dancing in major roles for more than twenty years. From the time Balanchine selected her at age fourteen to star in his 1925 *Le Rossignol*, Markova (born Lillian Alicia Marks) had enjoyed an exciting and consistent career. She had starred in new works by many of the century's greatest choreographers, including (besides Balanchine) Ashton, Massine, and Tudor. She was also famous for her classical roles, especially Giselle.

Anton Dolin (born Sydney Francis Patrick Chippendall Healey-Kay) had known Markova since adolescence, when they had studied together in London under the former Mariinsky ballerina Serafina Astafieva. Like Markova, Dolin soon caught the eye of Diaghilev, who engaged him for the Ballets Russes and gave him major roles in Balanchine's *Prodigal Son* and *Le Bal*. After Diaghilev's death, Dolin ("Pat" to his friends) and Markova both joined the Vic-Wells Ballet in England. Then, in 1935, they formed their own company, the Markova-Dolin Ballet. For the next three years, they performed a repertoire of classical works in London and on tour through Great Britain. In 1938, the duo split up temporarily when Hurok (who had known both dancers personally for years) persuaded Markova to come to the United States to dance Giselle with the Ballet Russe de Monte Carlo, encountering (as we have seen) the envy of other ballerinas in the process.

Dolin and Markova were reunited in America in the early 1940s in the new Ballet Theatre. They enjoyed great favor during Hurok's tenure as the company's presenter-promoter, but left with him after his split with Lucia Chase in 1946. (By then, after some initial hesitation, they had agreed to let Hurok be their personal manager.) Now in need of a ballet company to fulfill the tour obligations vacated by Ballet Theatre, Hurok revived the old Markova-Dolin Ballet and sent it on tour to Milwaukee, Chicago, and Detroit in the spring of 1946. Besides Markova and Dolin, the troupe included André Eglevsky and a hastily selected corps dancing in standards like *Giselle, Swan Lake*, and *The Nutcracker*. John Taras served as choreographer and ballet master.

Hurok had been hoping that he could put this version of the Markova-Dolin company into the Met in autumn 1946. The disastrous artistic and financial results of this tour convinced him that such a move would be premature, however. "You should have been with us in Chicago and Detroit for the past month, what with the coal strike, the rail strike, battles to get contracts signed—and no business!—to say nothing of the interminable Chase–De Cuevas–de Basil complications," wrote Irving Deakin in late May 1946. Under the circumstances, Hurok decided instead to book de Basil's Original Ballet Russe into the Met for the 1946–47 season. He would save the Markova-Dolin company for the 1947 fall Met season and a subsequent American tour.

One of the reasons Hurok liked Markova and Dolin was that

they indulged his fondness for seeing his name in lights and billings. When they performed at the Met in September and October 1947, the duo and their company were variously advertised as "S. Hurok's Russian Ballet" and "S. Hurok Presents Alicia Markova and Anton Dolin and Their Company." Both in New York and on the road, Hurok was allowed to put his own name first—something Lucia Chase would not permit.

But the grueling life of touring under Hurok's title eventually lost its charm even for Markova and Dolin. In a note to Deakin written on the stationery of the Deshler-Wallick Hotel ("1000 Rooms, 1000 Baths") in Columbus, Ohio, on January 16, 1948, Dolin moaned, "We simply cannot go on with these frightful tours and have told Sol plainly. He I think understands." They terminated their contract with Hurok a few months later "by mutual agreement." Both Dolin and Markova returned to England to dance as guests with the up-and-coming Sadler's Wells Ballet at Covent Garden. Hurok had lost another important dance attraction.

As Hurok's sixtieth birthday approached in April 1948, he found himself in the unfamiliar and uncomfortable position of an outsider on the American dance scene. He no longer had any connection with the two most important ballet companies in the United States: Ballet Theatre and Ballet Society, the latter about to become the Balanchine-Lincoln Kirstein New York City Ballet. Both Lucia Chase and George Balanchine had rejected collaboration with Hurok because of his insistence on exerting heavy-handed control over casting, billing, and repertoire. They regarded his fondness for box office stars and the traditional Russian style as old-fashioned and suffocating. They believed the time had come for a new language in ballet. As former dancers who had grown up in the world of dance, they viewed his commercialism as crass and limiting.

Even worse, Hurok, who always prided himself on understanding what the public wanted, could see that the taste of the American critics and public was also shifting to a preference for American dancers, choreographers, and companies. The upsurge in nationalistic feeling that had followed the great American victory in World War II had led to a new cultural confidence. With much of Europe in ruins, American culture was moving beyond the imported models it had so long held in awe.

But the greatest humiliation for the impresario described just five years earlier by one anonymous critic as "capable of opening a season of ballet as easily as anyone else can open a window" was having to give up exclusive ownership of the fall and spring seasons at the Metropolitan Opera House. Hurok had signed his first three-year contract with the Met in 1935. By agreeing to present ballet in the weeks just before and just after the opera season, he had come to the theater's financial rescue. He had taken the house on a "four-walls basis" for a certain number of days and performances, with a fixed rate per performance. As the popularity of the various Ballet Russe companies grew, this arrangement had proved very lucrative, and Hurok renewed it in 1938 for a period of ten years.

That decade was now drawing to a close, and the resourceful impresario found himself unable to extend the agreement. He no longer had the ballet attractions to fill the house on a regular and profitable basis. Times—and tastes—had changed.

As reported by John Martin in the *New York Times* ("The Dance: Era's End"), Hurok had been unable to match a joint offer made to the Met management by Lucia Chase (for Ballet Theatre) and Serge Denham (for the Ballet Russe de Monte Carlo) for the 1948–49 season. Hurok's former competitors had now ganged up on him. According to *Variety*, Hurok had been paying "about $700 to $900 a performance for the Met," while the joint Ballet Theatre–Ballet Russe bid offered $1,000 a performance. Hurok was also unable to match the high number of performances—sixty-eight—offered by his competitors. This, he told John Martin, was "far in excess of the number I can consider as a matter of reasonable business practice." The last money-making season he had at the Met, Hurok complained, was in 1945.

Having lost the Original Ballet Russe and Markova-Dolin, Hurok had no suitable ballet attraction to put into the Met for the spring 1948 post-opera season, the last for which he was contracted. He had no choice but to yield to Ballet Theatre. The company concluded a separate rental agreement with the theater's management for that season and mounted a (financially disastrous) spring season.

The change in Hurok's financial potential was due in part to a change in the nature of how ballet was being funded in the United

States. Throughout his career, Hurok had operated independently, most often without backers, as a profit-making enterprise. He had always viewed ballet from a commercial perspective, as a form of popular entertainment capable of generating income. By the late 1940s, however, the expenses of presenting and touring ballet companies had risen dramatically (in part because of the rising power of unions). Profit margins had been shrinking. Ballet Theatre, for example, had never been a money-making operation and had survived mainly on the strength of Lucia Chase's large annual "loans." Eventually Chase and her lawyers decided that she should be able to receive tax deductions for these sizable sums. On May 6, 1947, they established the Ballet Theatre Foundation, Inc., as an educational foundation under New York state laws. From now on, the company would be treated as a charitable institution created to sustain itself and further the cause of ballet, but not to make money.

Ballet, in other words, after many years of being treated in the marketplace as popular entertainment, had now climbed into the world of high art already occupied by money-losing orchestras, opera companies, and museums.

In a letter to William Fields of the Playwrights Company written on December 18, 1947, Hurok agreed that "no ballet company existing today is capable of paying its way on its box office draw." He disagreed with Ballet Theatre's declaration of nonprofit status, however, calling it "not a reasonable solution."

"When you have a foundation you don't pay taxes. My idea of ballet, or any art, is that it should be good enough to support itself," he argued. As time went on, Hurok modified this position to say that the answer lay in increased government subsidies to theaters and ballet companies, like those provided in European countries. Through the 1950s and 1960s, he would become an important advocate for the creation of a national endowment to support the arts.

In the winter of 1947–48, however, Hurok had to swallow his pride and regroup. Shut out of his beloved Met, abandoned and vulnerable, he raged like a frustrated child, declaring he was "through with ballet as it's operated today." If he were to write a book about his career today, he mused, he would call it *To Hell with Ballet*. But in truth he wasn't through with ballet—just the American variety. There were other worlds to conquer.

CHAPTER SIXTEEN

Slipping Beauty to the Rescue

"Hurok was not just a man in show business. Show business was his entire life."—*Margot Fonteyn*

THE INK WAS BARELY DRY on the surrender documents ending World War II before Hurok was making plans to resume his globe-trotting talent searches. In April 1946, still smarting from his rejection at the hands of Lucia Chase and her Ballet Theatre, and disillusioned with the American dance scene, he boarded the *Queen Mary* and sailed to Europe for the first time since 1939. His first stop was London. The brave British capital was a "city of austerity," its streets and buildings still scarred from years of bombing. English national pride was soaring in the aftermath of the difficult and costly victory over Hitler. Culture and cultural organizations were reviving, and Hurok found a warm welcome among his many acquaintances in the London music and dance world.

By the time he arrived in England, Hurok had already been hearing a great deal from his various informers about the artistic and administrative growth of the Sadler's Wells Ballet. The company had been growing steadily for the last twenty years, evolving under the strong leadership of former Diaghilev dancer Ninette de Valois. It had sprouted from the tiny Academy of Choreographic Art into a full-fledged ensemble featuring the work of England's leading dancers (Alicia Markova, Anton Dolin, Robert Helpmann,

Margot Fonteyn) and choreographers (de Valois, Nicholas Sergeyev, Frederick Ashton). In February 1946, just before Hurok's arrival in London, Sadler's Wells (named after the theater in which it had performed through the 1930s) had been invited to move into the reopened and refurbished Royal Opera House at Covent Garden. It would be that prestigious theater's first resident ballet company.

This ambitious new phase in the company's history opened with a celebrated revival of its 1939 *Sleeping Beauty* on February 20, 1946, given in the presence of the British royal family. The production was choreographed by Sergeyev, who had been trained in Russia before the revolution and later worked for Diaghilev. The casting of twenty-six-year-old British-born and British-trained Margot Fonteyn as the Princess Aurora helped to make this homegrown version (with additional choreography by Ashton and de Valois) of a Russian classic into a huge critical and popular success and overnight put Sadler's Wells on the international dance map. Within days, all tickets for the first month of the run had been sold out. For the indomitable de Valois, *Sleeping Beauty* brought her company to its "final phase," poised to become Britain's National Ballet.

With his usual knack for timing, Hurok arrived just in time to catch *Sleeping Beauty* (he pronounced it *Slipping Beauty*) and cash in on the British dance boom. As his colleague Clive Barnes tells it, Hurok disembarked from the *Queen Mary*, settled into his favorite London haunt, the Savoy Hotel, dined at what he liked to call his "London H.Q.," the Savoy Grill, and then strolled over to newly remodeled Covent Garden. There he was received by the theater's general administrator, David Webster, who escorted the impresario to his seat.

Hurok had come (he claimed in the flowery prose of his advance man Irving Deakin) as Webster's guest. He was there "in a completely non-professional capacity, as a member of the audience, going for the sheer fun of going, with nary a balletic problem on my mind." But it was as impossible for Hurok to attend a ballet performance in a "non-professional capacity" as it is for a chef to eat a meal without considering its ingredients.

"The overture started," wrote Barnes. "The familiar Tchaikovsky music, the red velvet and gilt curtains, the whole opera house ambience exerted their spells. The curtains parted, and the

Sadler's Wells Ballet danced *The Sleeping Beauty.* Hurok fell in love."

It had been Hurok's dream since the 1920s to bring the great companies of Russia to America to present their grand imperial versions of the classic nineteenth-century Russian story ballets. Since that was at the moment still out of the question, with the Soviet Union rapidly retreating into a hostile anti-Western posture, he was happy—for the moment—to settle for the next best thing: the British version of the Russian original. Their intimacy with and affection for the aristocratic and monarchical traditions so essential to Tchaikovsky's story ballets gave British dancers and audiences a distinct advantage. They understood the ways of royalty upon which *Sleeping Beauty, Swan Lake,* and *Cinderella* turned. Hurok, a sucker for high-class attitude, was enthralled by the company's inborn elitism.

Always hunting for sweet young ballerinas with whom to capture the public's affection and cash, Hurok was also smitten by Margot Fonteyn. In his dance "memoirs," he recalled with ghostwritten literary self-consciousness how her "fresh youthfulness" projected "the radiant gaiety of all the fairy tale heroines of the world's literature compressed into one. . . . Here, at last, was great ballet."

To Hurok, *Sleeping Beauty* symbolized everything beautiful and inaccessible about the magical world of dance. Perhaps he identified with the prince, who awakens the slumbering maiden and brings her to dynamic life. Like him, Hurok gave life to potential beauty, providing a public arena to performers and artists longing to express themselves and thereby earning their eternal gratitude and (he hoped) affection.

In any case, the Sadler's Wells production of *Sleeping Beauty* so enchanted Hurok that on the very same evening in which he first saw it he opened (or so he claimed) negotiations with de Valois at the Savoy Grill toward bringing the company to the United States. In her account, de Valois remembers the sequence of events a bit differently. They did meet at the Savoy, she agrees, but at lunch, not a postperformance supper, and at first they "failed to make any great impression on each other." The impresario informed her that "Sadler's Wells had a queer sort of idealism about it." She took this comment (accurately) to mean that he couldn't quite understand a true ensemble company with a shared style whose members were not always—like the de Basil and Denham dancers—on the lookout for other, more lucrative engagements.

But Hurok and de Valois, both of them hardheaded and tough, eventually developed a reasonably friendly rapport based (like most of his personal relationships) on mutual respect and mutual gain. Even the fact that because of his heavy accent he pronounced her name as "Madame de Vulva" didn't seem to get in the way.

Hurok also approached Covent Garden's manager, David Webster, to discuss the possibility of a collaboration with Sadler's Wells. Like de Valois, Webster was intrigued at the prospect of touring big rich America, which was then enjoying an unprecedented postwar economic expansion. But the negotiations went slowly. Like de Valois, the cautious and deliberate Webster was no pushover. Moreover, Hurok was dealing not only with two strong-willed negotiators, but also with two powerful institutions (Sadler's Wells and Covent Garden) whose interests did not always coincide.

"What made the whole business difficult is that you were talking with two heads but one voice," Hurok remarked some years later of his early discussions with Webster and de Valois. "I ask you, what kind of dealing position is that?"

In the end it would take the three of them more than three years to get the Sadler's Wells company to America. Throughout the negotiations, the main sticking point was finding the right theater in New York.

They all agreed that the most appropriate venue for such a large, important, and elite troupe would be the Metropolitan Opera. The problem was that Hurok no longer controlled the off-season rentals there after fall 1947. So Hurok suggested the City Center Theater as an alternative. That was where the performances of the International Dance Festival to be held in connection with the celebration of Greater New York's 50th anniversary would be held in 1948. (The city's Mayor William O'Dwyer had asked Hurok to be the festival's director.) But when Webster came to New York to look the theater over, he pronounced its cramped stage and poor facilities unsuitable. He advised Hurok to wait until he could get the Met.

In order to fill City Center, Hurok instead presented the Ballet of the Paris Opera there. That company was now under the artistic direction of Serge Lifar, the same dancer-choreographer Hurok had once sent packing back to Europe after a backstage scandal with Massine in the crazy old days of the Ballet Russe. Meanwhile, he was still waiting for the right moment and venue for Sadler's Wells.

With the air and oceans now safe for travel, Hurok resumed his prewar regime: winter in New York and summer in Europe. On July 18, 1947, he wrote to Irving Deakin from Paris (where he always stayed at the Hotel Meurice), "I have seen a lot of new attractions here. I also contemplate to go to Russia and other Countries and I shall bring a lot of interesting attractions."

But Hurok's plans to travel to the USSR foundered in the rapidly worsening environment of East-West relations. With Stalin's regime reasserting and even intensifying its repressive prewar control over culture and artists, President Truman was already formulating a doctrine aimed at containing the establishment of Soviet puppet regimes. A spirit of witch-hunting anti-Communism was emerging in Washington, and the contours of the Cold War were already taking shape. In Moscow, the worsening campaign against leading cultural figures reached its climax in early 1948 with vicious official attacks on Shostakovich, Prokofiev, and other composers. The crackdown in Russia and the souring of the Soviet-American relationship would have many implications for Hurok's work in the immediate postwar years. It would further delay his hopes for importing Soviet attractions.

Even without a trip to Russia, Hurok bragged to Deakin that he had covered "a flight of 18000 miles" in his travels to and around Europe in the summer of 1947.

On his European trips in 1947 and 1948, Hurok was sighted in the company of dancers and entertainment people in Paris and London. Both cities were overrun with self-confident American "liberators" basking in the gratitude of the natives, as John Taras told Irving Deakin. "Paris is full of Americans now and one meets everyone. Denby, Tudor, Sol, Lucia, Isabelle Kemp, Nora White, Bobby Lindgren, Connie Garfield, Joy Williams all wander the streets. Truman Capote, Gore Vidal, Fritz Prokosch, Tennessee Williams are all misbehaving on the Left Bank."

When not occupied with performances and business meetings, Hurok exercised his reputation as a connoisseur of fine food and wine by pursuing gourmet meals in the finest and most expensive restaurants. Chicago *Tribune* critic Claudia Cassidy once shared a luxurious repast with him at the Hotel Meurice that included "eggs benedict, filets with truffles and fraises des bois with that thick yellow cream." Despite his fondness for such rich fare, the short and plumpish Hurok somehow managed to keep his weight in check.

When in London, Hurok continued to cultivate and negotiate with Webster and de Valois. They spent much time arguing over the appropriate repertoire to bring to America. De Valois was afraid that Americans, accustomed to lighter fare, especially the programs of short works presented by the various Ballets Russes companies, would not like long, heavy, full-evening ballets like *Sleeping Beauty* and *Swan Lake.* She wanted instead to present short modern works representative of British ballet, including her own *Checkmate* and *Job.* But Hurok continued to insist that the big Russian story ballets were exactly what the company should bring, since they represented its achievement in maintaining and developing the traditions of classical ballet. No American company was at the time staging that sort of thing. Even more important, Hurok adored these extravagant old-fashioned spectacles almost as much as seeing his name in print. Those abstract modern pieces he found alien and incomprehensible.

All these preliminary discussions at last became more than purely academic when Hurok, through the intervention of his friend Edward Johnson, general manager of the Met, finally succeeded in getting the Opera House for a few weeks in the early fall of 1949 for the American debut of the Sadler's Wells Ballet. It was a big gamble. The expenses of mounting a New York season and an American tour for a company traveling with scores of soloists, dancers, musicians, and fifty tons of scenery, costumes and props ("the biggest transatlantic haul in theatrical history") were huge. And no one really knew how the American audience would respond to long Russian ballets danced by British ballerinas. Would people sit still for an entire evening to watch a fairy tale weighed down with heavy sets, clothes, and pretensions?

But as Hurok well knew, it was a propitious time to be bringing a British attraction into New York. Britain and the United States were still basking in the warm glow of their cooperation in the Allied victory, and things English were very much "in."

Even more helpful was the recent box office and critical success of perhaps the most famous ballet movie of all time, *The Red Shoes*, a story of backstage ballet intrigue loosely based on a Hans Christian Andersen tale. Set in recent times and primarily in Monte Carlo, the film (like the earlier *On Your Toes*) portrayed the colorful characters and endless adventures of a certain ballet company—a thinly disguised version of one of the Ballet Russe troupes. (This one was called the Ballet Lermontov and was led by a snobbish and single-minded impresario obviously modeled on Sergei Diaghilev.) Nominated for five 1948 Academy Awards, including Best Picture, the film won two: for Best Art Direction and Best Music Score (by Brian Easdale). Even better for Hurok, *The Red Shoes* starred Moira Shearer, who was scheduled to dance with Sadler's Wells on their American tour. The film's cast also included another company member, the esteemed romantic dancer Robert Helpmann. And these people could speak English, which made it easier on the reporters looking for interviews.

For Margot Fonteyn, facing the army of journalists who were waiting when the company arrived by plane in New York was a new and even terrifying experience. She and her fellow dancers were ordered "to smile and show a little more leg. Skirts were at a modest mid-calf length that year, which did not make for newsworthy pictures. We looked as haughty as we could under the circumstances." Since Moira Shearer was assumed already to be a familiar commodity on the strength of *The Red Shoes*, Hurok instructed his public relations staff to concentrate their efforts on the lesser-known Fonteyn, even though the whole process made her "about as frightened as a mouse confronting a cobra." The campaign was so successful that in the end, Fonteyn's American fame would far surpass Shearer's.

When the Met engagement of Sadler's Wells opened on the unseasonably warm evening of October 9, 1949, Helpmann danced the role of the Prince opposite Fonteyn in *Sleeping Beauty*. The ballet had never before been produced in its entirety in New York. (De Valois had resisted Hurok's suggestion that she make cuts.) Round-ing out the cast were Ashton, a brilliant character dancer, as the evil Carabosse, and Beryl Grey as the Lilac Fairy. The distinguished composer Constant Lambert conducted, and Oliver Messel had designed the traditional sets and costumes. Like Fonteyn and Helpmann, all the collaborators had been working together in England for years, a fact which helped to give them a feeling of security in facing the unknown American audiences and critics.

In attempting to ensure the success of his latest attraction, Hurok as usual had taken pains to see that the house was crammed with high society and prominent politicians. The evening became a grand social and political occasion. The orchestra played the "Star-Spangled Banner" and "God Save the Queen," the boxes were draped with the American and British flags, and "almost everybody in the auditorium bore a label of some kind in the arts or public affairs." Among those in attendance were New York Mayor O'Dywer, the British ambassador to the United States, and many other notables in jewels and evening wear.

Even before the performance was over, Fonteyn's intuition— and ears—told her that something very special was happening. Her partner Helpmann later compared the loud and enthusiastic applause that greeted her first appearance onstage to "the sound of a gun." After the curtain came down, de Valois—who later called the evening the greatest triumph in the company's history—was called to the stage to make a speech. Hysterical well-wishers mobbed the stage entrance. Fonteyn then joined the rest of the cast in a caravan of chartered buses. Escorted by police cars with sirens wailing, they rode to Gracie Mansion for a reception given by the mayor. Later they went on to Reuben's to wait for the reviews.

The dean of New York dance critics, John Martin, wrote a rave for the *New York Times*. The production and the company's performance, he said, showed how important the government subsidies provided to cultural institutions by the British government were and what could happen when a resident company worked together on a regular basis.

But he saved most of his praise for Fonteyn. She was "a ballerina among ballerinas" and "just about as enchanting a dancer as has come along in a score of years." Other critics were no less taken with this slim, dark-haired artist, whose onstage passion and fire were perfectly complemented by offstage grace and diplomacy. "In retrospect, I think I won New York by smiling," Fonteyn remarked later with characteristic precision and modesty. At the same time ethereal and down-to-earth, she had a simple, unpretentious nature that immediately endeared her to the American public. What was so special about her, former *New Yorker* editor Robert Gottlieb has said, was her "loveability. Everyone just fell in love with her on the spot." The facts that her real name was the considerably less glamorous Margaret Hookham and that she had been born in a plain London suburb only seemed to endear her to the American public even more.

By the end of October, Fonteyn had become a bona fide star and Hurok had a hit on his hands. *Variety* reported on October 31 that "it was as hard to get tickets for the Sadler's Wells Ballet at the Metropolitan Opera House as it was to come by a pair for *South Pacific.*" The gross for the four-week New York season was reported to be more than $250,000. Fonteyn's picture appeared on the cover of both *Time* and *Newsweek*, something that she thought could happen "only to heads of state." Hurok claimed that he could have extended the New York run for months, but of course the beginning of the opera season made that impossible.

Besides *Sleeping Beauty*, which was the first production to sell out, the engagement included de Valois' *The Rake's Progress*, as well as the American premiere of Prokofiev's full-length *Cinderella*, choreographed by Ashton and featuring him and Helpmann in drag as Cinderella's cruel stepsisters. This was the first American production of any of Prokofiev's "Soviet" ballets and helped to prepare the way in New York for *Romeo and Juliet*. Overall, the remarkable success of the Sadler's Wells company seemed to prove that the New York audience really was ready for full-evening full-length ballets. This realization would encourage Hurok to import the big Russian companies when that would become possible a few years later.

Business was also brisk on the road in nine cities in the mid-Atlantic and midwestern states. Chicago audiences bought up all the tickets for the full-length ballets even before the company arrived. Deakin, who handled the advance publicity for the tour, wrote to Anton Dolin that Sadler's Wells had enjoyed a "really fabulous success."

Twenty years later, some time after Sadler's Wells had already become the Royal Ballet, John Martin wrote that the company's first 1949 American tour represented "the greatest opening of the popular audience that the ballet had ever known in this country, and it has persisted with our own companies." *Sleeping Beauty* "exposed the American audience for the first time to 'grand' ballet, and the reaction was comparable to that of the Paris public more than a century earlier when Meyerbeer with his *Robert le Diable* exposed them for the first time to 'grand' opera."

Irving Kolodin agreed: "Dead and gone were the days when extracts, 'versions' and snippets had sufficed. The age of 'complete' had dawned and the date of its dawning was October 9, 1949."

Even before Sadler's Wells returned to London, Hurok was already negotiating with Webster about a more extensive American tour for the following (1950–51) season. After numerous difficulties with the British cultural bureaucracy that funded Sadler's Wells, an agreement was reached that called for a New York engagement at the Met followed by the longest tour in the company's history. It would include a total of 153 performances in 32 cities in the United States and Canada. This second tour generated $2.5 million in ticket sales. The 130 members of what Hurok was now calling the "Fabulous Sadler's Wells Ballet" traveled 14,500 miles in a special train that included six baggage cars, two day-coaches, six sleeping cars, and a dining car. With Fonteyn and Shearer enjoying mounting popularity, the company played mostly to capacity audiences.

The reason that the Sadler's Wells tour was so much more successful than recent tours managed by Hurok for the de Basil company and the Ballet Russe de Monte Carlo was that this was a stable, financially secure company with an established repertoire and personnel who had worked and rehearsed together for many years. While both Webster and de Valois were willing to bend to Hurok's preferences and requests, they were firm in defending their artistic integrity. They were grateful for Hurok's obvious love for artists, for the "very human fashion" in which his office did its work, and for his success in "presenting us to every possible advantage."

At the same time, they did not allow him to interfere in the company's day-to-day affairs, and Hurok did not meddle in artistic matters as he had tried to do with de Basil, Denham, Lucia Chase, and virtually ever other ballet company he had ever presented. This arrangement worked out better on both sides. So well, in fact, that Hurok would bring Sadler's Wells (and its successor, the Royal Ballet) back to the United States every other season for the next decade, until 1960.

Hurok grew fond of many of the elegant, unfailingly well-behaved members of the Sadler's Wells company. They were very different from the scandal-prone and mercurial Russians he was more used to dealing with. But no one could hold a candle to his ideal, Margot Fonteyn. No dancer since his first love, Pavlova, had ignited in him such enthusiasm and affection. To Hurok, Fonteyn was nothing less than "the greatest *ballerina* of the western world."

Like Pavlova, Fonteyn could dance a wide range of roles, including *Giselle*, and much of the effect of her dancing resided in her acting ability. Unlike Pavlova, however, she cultivated few mannerisms and was happy to work as the member of an ensemble. She did not need to be the focus of every ballet in which she danced and could be a marvelous and unselfish partner, as she would show in later years when she encountered Rudolf Nureyev. Like Pavlova and Hurok, Fonteyn, the daughter of an engineer, had risen to stardom from relatively humble beginnings, inventing herself in the process.

In his dotage Hurok liked to imply—as he had done with Pavlova years earlier—that there were some romantic feelings between himself and Fonteyn. Such implications merely amused the ballerina, whose husband was a prominent Panamanian diplomat and politician. Fonteyn's first impression of the impresario when she met him at a party in London not long before the American tour was that he was "egg-shaped and bald with a worldly look about him. . . . He loved to make deadpan jokes and to laugh at my gullibility." When he started talking in his heavy Brooklynese, speaking of "toity thousand dollars" and reversing the sounds "t" and "th," Hurok threw Fonteyn and her class-conscious and language-conscious colleagues into hilarity. She particularly loved this example: "Melba was a greath singer. She never had anyting but thea and thoast before singing Thosca."

As time passed and their acquaintance deepened, Fonteyn believed she began to see more clearly what made the man responsible for her worldwide fame tick:

When I came to know him well, I found that Hurok reminded me of an old Russian peasant woman going off to market, basket on her arm, to pick out the best of the produce. Each year until his death at the age of eighty-five, Hurok went off to Russia to pick the best of the cultural goods that were for sale.

He was always nervous about "thicket" sales, and before curtain time could be found hovering in the back of the box office. His eyes seemed to click like cash register signs behind his glasses as he watched the crush of eager patrons.

In his latter days he implied that he had been in love with me twenty years earlier. If that was true, I was never aware of it. I think it was, rather, that he was in love with all his successes. And that was his secret. He was not just a man in show business. Show business was his entire life.

And though he was entering his seventh decade, Hurok's life in the business was far from over. Sadler's Wells had given him a new lease.

Tonight We Sing

"I know audiences feed on crap, but I cannot believe we are so lacking that we cannot dish it up to them with some trace of originality."—*Darryl Zanuck*

GIVEN HIS NEED for fantasy, glamor, and fame, it was inevitable that the public-relations-conscious Hurok would eventually seek to immortalize himself, his artists, and his career on the silver screen. This desire intensified during the early 1940s, when he and Emma were spending a substantial amount of time in their house in Beverly Hills and rubbing shoulders with Hollywood actors, producers, and directors.

Hurok had successfully negotiated film deals for several of his attractions. One of them was his beloved Tamara Toumanova. As one of the original "baby ballerinas," she had capitalized on her publicity to land roles in several Broadway shows (such as *Stars in Your Eyes*) and with various ballet companies (the Original Ballet Russe, the Ballet Russe de Monte Carlo, Ballet Theatre) through the late 1930s and early 1940s. In 1943, she made her debut as a dramatic film actress in the patriotic feature *Days of Glory*, appearing opposite Gregory Peck in his first major role. Perhaps it was her performance in that role (despite a *New York Times* review that described her as "dark and bony") that gave Hurok the idea of casting her as Pavlova in his own life story.

Hurok's desire for a film version of his life had grown after the appearance in 1946 of his highly fictionalized "autobiography," entitled *Impresario: A Memoir by S. Hurok.* Published by Random House and produced "in collaboration with Ruth Goode," the wife of Hurok's longtime public relations man Gerald Goode, the book adopted a self-conscious literary tone that had little in common with Hurok's heavily accented, folksy way of speaking. Focusing primarily on the artists he presented and scrupulously avoiding personal self-revelation, *Impresario* reads more like a press release than an autobiography. It was obviously intended more to drum up business for the attractions presented under the banner "S. Hurok Presents" than to set the record straight. The Hurok that emerges from its pages is an infinitely generous, diplomatic, and learned connoisseur of the arts who bears as little resemblance to the real man as the Metropolitan Opera to Madison Square Garden. As we have seen, these "memoirs" are also filled with misstatements and inaccuracies.

A similar process occurred in Hurok's second book, *S. Hurok Presents: A Memoir of the Dance World*, which was published by Hermitage House in late 1953. This time, Hurok is listed on the title page as the sole author, although anyone who knew him and his verbal skills understood that he could not possibly have produced such a volume.

In fact, although he receives no credit anywhere, *S. Hurok Presents* was ghostwritten by Irving Deakin, Hurok's longtime public relations agent and advance man. Deakin was a recognized authority on ballet who hosted a regular program on music and ballet for the New York radio station WQXR from 1937 to 1943. He also served briefly as general manager of the San Francisco City Ballet in the late 1940s. Born in England and possessed of an insider's knowledge of the dance world through his marriage to the daughter of Diaghilev dancer and choreographer Adolph Bolm, Deakin collaborated with Hurok in creating his second book of memoirs in the early 1950s. *S. Hurok Presents* was intended as a sequel to *Impresario* and provides more detailed information on his work with Pavlova, the Fokines, de Basil, Massine, Denham, Ballet Theatre, the Markova-Dolin Company, and Sadler's Wells.

Hurok viewed anything written, said, or filmed about himself as a public relations opportunity. Some years later, he couldn't understand why Joseph Roddy, a serious journalist who was intending to write his biography, didn't expect to receive money from him for the project. It should come as no surprise, then, that *S. Hurok Presents,* like *Impresario,* shows him in the best possible light. Presenting copious information on the roots of the Russian Imperial Ballet and its rebirth in the West, the book is more a history of dance after 1917 than an autobiography. Nor did Hurok shrink from passing off Deakin's erudite research and clean writing as his own. Even the critic who reviewed *S. Hurok Presents* for the *New York Times Book Review* accepted it without question as Hurok's literary work, although the impresario had not previously shown any ability to produce such polished high-society prose.

The book *S. Hurok Presents* had not yet appeared when Hurok launched a concerted effort to bring his life story to the screen. For the literary basis on which to construct a screenplay, he and his collaborators turned to the less scholarly *Impresario.* In fact, Hurok had been pushing to make his own bio-epic film at least since 1946, when *Impresario* was published. The project had been mentioned in a brochure announcing the appearance of the book, which was reportedly so exciting that it had already been sold to 20th Century-Fox "from the manuscript." Soon, the promotional brochure predicted, *Impresario* would become "a sure-fire picture in which many of S. Hurok's stars will appear."

In fact, however, the contract between Hurok and Fox was finally signed only on October 26, 1951, more than five years after publication of *Impresario,* and for the relatively low price of $7,000. Fox was represented in the agreement by Darryl F. Zanuck, the studio's co-founder and one of the most powerful men in Hollywood.

As part of the contract, Hurok insisted on retaining right of approval over the screenplay, which was being adapted—very freely—by Harry Kurnitz and George Oppenheimer from *Impresario.* He wanted to be sure he could control the image presented to the public. Another major player in the deal was Hurok's friend Spyros Skouras, a Hollywood producer and director, who was instrumental in pushing this rather unlikely idea through to production. Hurok and Skouras had been involved in several other projects in the past. The film's producer was another acquaintance of Hurok, George Jessel (1898–1981), jokingly called the "Toastmaster General of the USA," who had worked in show business since childhood—in vaudeville, radio, television, and film. Jessel was absent from Hollywood during most of the filming, however.

In looking for a director for the film that would ultimately be called *Tonight We Sing*, the cost-conscious Zanuck wanted to find someone who could make a "high-quality picture on a relatively small budget." For that reason, he was initially skeptical when someone suggested Mitchell Leisen (1898–1972), who had the reputation of spending lavishly. A prolific minor master who had been making mostly middlebrow features (*Death Takes a Holiday, Lady in the Dark*) since the early 1930s, Leisen had earned the nickname "King of the Pros" due to his exhaustive knowledge of all the elements of film production. For a time, he had worked as a costume designer for Cecil B. DeMille. Now past his prime, Leisen dearly wanted to direct *Tonight We Sing.* To prove he could control expenses, he drew up a detailed cost breakdown for every item on the project and won Zanuck over. (In the end, the film came in $100,000 under budget.) *Tonight We Sing* was one of Leisen's last feature films; after that, he worked increasingly in television and produced several episodes for the series *The Twilight Zone.*

In negotiating with Jessel and Fox over the screenplay, Hurok once again called on Irving Deakin, who had performed so many other valuable behind-the-scenes services in the past. He used Deakin to translate his demands about the screenplay into literary English which could be presented to his Hollywood collaborators. One of the most remarkable examples is a lengthy and very revealing memo addressed to Zanuck and apparently dictated by Hurok to Deakin on April 14, 1952, after several days of consultation with Jessel and the film's production staff in Los Angeles. In the memo, Hurok requested numerous changes in the script which he believed would "turn it into a picture that will be both artistically and financially successful."

Highest on the list of Hurok's demands was the removal of any Jewish ethnicity in the character of the impresario hero or his associates. The use of "Jewish dialect" in the script, Hurok insisted, would "only result in a cheap vaudeville atmosphere" and undermine the essential central message that "this is the story of a successful man."

Hurok's fear of appearing too Semitic contained a strong element of self-hatred. It also seemed to convey a belief that clearly identifiable Jews could not be successful in the American business or entertainment world. At the same time, Hurok had demonstrated his concern for Jews annihilated and displaced by the Nazi Holocaust. He made several highly publicized trips to Displaced Persons camps in Germany and Austria in the late 1940s and sponsored performing arts groups from the newly organized state of Israel, to which he also lent significant financial support. Extending charity to Jews was one thing: accepting the full implications of his own humble Jewish heritage and showing it in the movies, however, was quite another.

Similarly, Hurok strongly objected to the presence of "the stock figures of cigar-smoking impresarios" present in the script's original opening sequence. Such images would, he feared, detract from the image of refinement and good taste he wanted his fictionalized self to convey. Having spent years climbing the Manhattan social ladder, he wanted to appear to his wealthy friends and patrons as a man of cultivation and style, not some sort of back-room shyster.

As an alternative opening, he suggested a scene that "would establish Hurok as a successful man of position in the world of arts" by showing "a large, tastefully furnished and decorated room, a combination study and office, actually more like a large study, with Hurok surrounded by his autographed photos of the great in the world of the arts whom he has developed and presented, the testimonials made him, etc. Here he sits in conversation with, let us say, Artur [he insisted on the Polish spelling the pianist disliked] Rubinstein, relaxed, genial, expansive. They are reminiscing, and the dialogue leads logically into the material of the picture. . . ."

Hurok also objected to the characterization of Arthur Rubinstein, who was initially conceived as the only artist in the film who would play himself. In the original script, the young Hurok (having just been rejected by Chaliapin in Paris) encounters the already famous pianist on a ship sailing from Europe to New York. Desperate to hear Rubinstein play for the first-class passengers, the impoverished aspiring impresario steals a tuxedo from a stateroom. Too late, he discovers that it belongs to the pianist himself. In an act of magnanimous nobility, Rubinstein forgives the theft: "When I was a boy I borrowed my father's pants to go to a concert."

After learning of the part he was expected to play in the film, however, Rubinstein proclaimed that such an undignified role was beneath his stature and dignity. He refused to participate. "I didn't want to do it. I would prefer to go to jail," Rubinstein said some years later. He was eventually replaced by violinist Isaac Stern, playing the role of the Belgian virtuoso Eugène Ysaÿe. The incident with the stolen tux stayed in, however.

Another point of disagreement between Hurok (who is credited in the completed film as a "Technical Advisor") and the studio focused on the character of Benjamin Golder. In the original script, Golder was a Lower East Side pawnbroker with a strong Jewish dialect who became Hurok's partner. The inclusion of this character (not found in *Impresario* or in any other reminiscences) greatly offended Hurok. Speaking of himself (in Deakin's words) in the grandiose third person, Hurok fumed that he

> at no time in his career had a partner. One of the interesting features of his career, from a business point of view, is the fact that all of his accomplishments have been made entirely on his own. If it is felt absolutely necessary that some such character is required for dramatic purposes, it might be a friend who has befriended him on his arrival in America. But the use of the comic-relief stock character of the pawn-broker cannot be permitted . . . the pawn-broker connection and the partnership association must be deleted. Above all, any suggestion of accent in dialogue and speech must be entirely eliminated. Comedy must be introduced by other means than accent and dialect.

Nor did Hurok approve of what he considered to be the script's buffoonish portrayal of Chaliapin. What he found most distasteful was an entirely fictionalized sequence set at Ellis Island in which the Russian bass, detained by American customs officials, is saved by Hurok—but only after being pressured to sign a ten-year contract. "Chaliapin was a great artist with grotesque humours, but he was not a clown," Hurok told Jessel. "As it stands at present, the treatment of Chaliapin is one that is likely to give offense to many people, not the least of whom would be his immediate family, widow and children." Ever mindful of the influence of the media,

Hurok also told Jessel to omit Chaliapin's criticism of the *New York Times* for having given him bad reviews on his first trip to America: "References to *The New York Times* criticisms of Chaliapin to be changed to the New York press in general."

Despite Hurok's objections, the characterization of Chaliapin as an oversized joker overly fond of food, drink, and money remained in the finished film. Just as Hurok predicted, the surviving members of the singer's family were deeply offended when they saw it. Already alienated by Hurok's attempt to blackmail Chaliapin over his marital status and infuriated by his accusations that Chaliapin had cozied up to Hitler, they now further blamed him for what they viewed as a vicious trivialization of a great artist's career and memory.

All of Hurok's suggestions to Jessel (and Leisen) concerning the script were motivated by his immodest concern that he appear as a serious and successful person, a respected and prosperous figure on the artistic scene, as Deakin's memo spelled out:

> Recognizing that a certain fictionalization of both story and characters is necessary, it should nevertheless be pointed out that, in this case, the central figure of the picture is not one lost in historical antiquity, but a contemporary figure, very much alive, and one of major importance and prominence in the world of music and the arts. Therefore, certain incidents, situation and dialogue in the present script, which show him in an unfortunate light and which could conceivably hold him up to ridicule, should either be eliminated or changed to bring the character of Hurok as portrayed more into line with credibility.

For Hurok, credibility was synonymous with his own fantastic self-image. "I have little doubt that you will find a solution which will be the right one," he told Jessel in the memo, "and that you will show the dreamer of 1926 has become the man who, in 1952, manages and presents the world's greatest artists: thus bringing to the public the fact that, in addition to still being the dreamer and idealist, he has, with the passage of time, become a realistic idealist."

Hurok's insistence on so closely controlling the story line led to considerable frustration for Mitchell Leisen during the filming of *Tonight We Sing*. "It was very hard to get any reality into the story since Hurok wouldn't tell us much about his life," the director recalled later. "We couldn't even mention his first wife."

Another important decision to be made was, of course, the casting of the role of Hurok. According to Hurok's daughter, Ruth, Jessel initially wanted to give the part to the character actor Oscar Karlweis. When this suggestion was made to Hurok, however, he would have none of it. Speaking in his usual strong dialect, Hurok reprimanded the director. "Oscar Karlweis? Playing me? With that accent?"

In the end, the role went to thirty-nine-year-old David Wayne, already well known for his appearances on Broadway (he received a Tony in 1947 for the role of Og in *Finian's Rainbow*) and in film (*Portrait of Jenny, Adam's Rib, Stella*). He played the role of Hurok with his usual wiry, energetic intensity, but without any ethnic color. Karlweis did appear in the film after all, as the budding impresario's American friend and landlord Benjamin Golder. At Hurok's insistence, however, Golder's profession was changed from pawnbroker to antiques dealer and jeweler, lest he appear too déclassé and predatory.

The rest of the cast included Ezio Pinza (acting and singing) as Chaliapin; the Russian character actor Mikhail Rasumny as Chaliapin's long-suffering valet Nicolai; Hurok's recent discovery Roberta Peters (acting and singing) as the fictional character Elsa Valdine, an up-and-coming opera star; the handsome Byron Palmer as her boyfriend, the fictional operatic tenor Gregory Lawrence, whose singing voice was supplied by Jan Peerce; Tamara Toumanova as Pavlova; Isaac Stern as Eugène Ysaÿe; and last, but certainly not least, the twenty-two-year-old newcomer Anne Bancroft in her second film role as Hurok's adoring wife Emma.

The story line of the completed film, entitled *Tonight We Sing* and released in January 1953, contains more fantasy than fact. Indeed, it is perhaps the single most revealing piece of evidence in Hurok's lifelong struggle for respectability and self-invention. The movie opens in a strikingly non-Jewish and surprisingly picturesque Russian village in which the ten-year-old Hurok (played by John Meek) is attempting, with little success, to master the piano, violin, and finally the cello under the guidance of a kind elderly music teacher. Exasperated, the teacher finally tells his pupil that he has "all the ingredients to make a good musician except one thing: talent. Resign yourself to be a member of the audience—remember that for each one who plays, there must be thousands who listen."

The scene then switches to St. Petersburg in 1910. In real life, Hurok had left Russia four years earlier and had never even visited tsarist St. Petersburg. Our film hero is now working in a hardware store. He is fired, however, because he is caught by the manager conducting a group of friends in singing a Russian folk song while he should be minding the store. (Hurok never showed the slightest talent for either conducting or choral singing.) Out on the street, he takes consolation in his lovely girlfriend Emma, with whom he goes to the opera.

They sit in the first row of the top balcony and see Chaliapin starring in *Boris Godunov*. (Hurok never saw Chaliapin perform until both of them got to New York.) The performance, which is (unfortunately) the film's musical and visual climax, sends Hurok into a trance. Confessing to Emma that he has lost his job, he exclaims, wild-eyed, "somewhere, somehow, there must be a place for me in this world of music," and rushes backstage to commune with Chaliapin. Hiding behind the door of the singer's dressing room, Hurok overhears him complaining about his rough treatment at the hands of the New York critics. Bursting with enthusiasm, Hurok steps forward and tells the temperamental star he should return to America to sing and prove them wrong.

By the time he emerges into the night air, transfixed by his contact with greatness, Hurok has forgotten all about poor Emma. She's been waiting patiently in the alley all this time.

The film spends little time on explaining how or why Hurok traveled to America. It also completely ignores the issue of Jewish emigration from Russian oppression. Omitted, too, is any depiction of the linguistic, economic, and social difficulties Hurok encountered in his early years in Philadelphia and Brownsville. Suddenly our hero is living in the comfortable New York house of Benjamin Golder and working as a trolley car conductor. (In real life he held this job—very briefly—in Philadelphia.) Already he is presenting small performances on the side. His artists include an unnamed black soprano, obviously modeled on Marian Anderson, who does not appear in the film. She sings "Sweet and Low" at the Bronx Settlement House. "I'm betting my life on eventually bringing concerts to the people's audiences," our hero says earnestly.

No doubt in response to the virulent anti-Communist mood that was intensifying in the United States in the early 1950s, the film contains no reference to Hurok's early work for the Socialist party or any mention of his deep involvement in left-wing politics in Brownsville.

Loyal and submissive, Emma (who speaks beautiful English, unlike Hurok's real wives Tamara or Emma) has also followed Hurok to America. They are married in a simple (religiously neutral) ceremony at Golder's house. To celebrate, they go to the Hippodrome to see Pavlova perform. Eager to impress, Hurok lies to his new wife that he is now a conductor and in contact with Chaliapin. After Pavlova's performance of the dying swan, Hurok loses control and rushes backstage to pay her his tribute. Persuading the ballerina's maid to let him in to see her, he pledges his undying devotion and begs to be allowed to manage her: "In my hands, madame, you will receive the treatment of a goddess."

Meanwhile, the despondent Emma, again forgotten, has gone home alone on her wedding night. When he returns to Golder's house, Hurok apologizes to her for his behavior, admits that he is only a streetcar conductor, and wins her sympathy by calling himself "no good." Just as they have reconciled, a telegram arrives from Chaliapin in Paris summoning Hurok to come to talk to him about a possible collaboration. "You're not the type of man to give up a dream," the always encouraging (and entirely fictional) Emma tells Hurok as she urges him to take up Chaliapin's offer.

In Paris, Hurok discovers that Chaliapin has summoned him only to win a bet with his servant Nicolai. The singer has no need of Hurok's services, but gives him his young student, the fresh-faced American tenor Gregory Lawrence, to manage. When Hurok discovers that Lawrence is in fact a hotel doorman, the two become fast friends. Lawrence is particularly impressed when the proud Hurok tears up the check Chaliapin gave him to cover his travel expenses. "You have daring and integrity," Lawrence tells him, "just what a manager needs."

So the two sail back to America together, now best buddies

with a shared faith in the American dream. On board ship, they encounter the great violinist Ysaÿe; Hurok inadvertently steals his tux but ultimately wins his affection. Hurok describes his dreams of creating a "Hurok audience—working people who can't get away from work to buy tickets in advance." Ysaÿe is so impressed by his drive and ambition that he agrees to let Hurok present him at the Hippodrome. At first it appears the concert will be a flop, but at the last minute hoards of "common people" appear to fill the hall to overflowing and save the day.

Tonight We Sing also cashes in on the red-white-and-blue American patriotism so much in vogue in 1953, near the end of the Korean War. The film has Hurok presenting opera to appreciative troops during World War I and giving a lavish party to celebrate the signing of the Armistice. As part of the entertainment, his new discovery Elsa Valdine sings an excerpt from Act I ("Sempre Libera") of Verdi's *La Traviata.* Suddenly from behind the door of the elegant Manhattan apartment, the ringing tenor voice of Valdine's sweetheart Gregory Lawrence is heard. (At this point in real life, Hurok was still living with Tamara in a noisy tenement in Brooklyn and had not yet become involved with opera at all.) With Lawrence in all the splendor of his uniform, they enjoy a rapturous vocal and romantic reunion, performing a duet from *Madama Butterfly.*

But suddenly (again) festivities are interrupted by the news of the arrival of Chaliapin. He has been detained as a Bolshevik troublemaker by suspicious customs officials at Ellis Island. Having fled the violence of the Russian Revolution, he is now ready to accept Hurok's offer of management. (In fact this all transpired several years later, and no such meeting at Ellis Island ever occurred.) In an attempt to test his American patriotism, the customs official asks Chaliapin if he has ever heard of baseball hero Ty Cobb. "Haven't you ever heard of Fyodor Chaliapin?" the bass booms impatiently in reply.

Having sprung Chaliapin from captivity after extracting a ten-year contract from him, Hurok now goes on to present him in Gounod's *Faust* and other extravagant operatic productions. He and his friends celebrate Chaliapin's rave reviews by bursting into a soulful (and highly kitschy) rendition of "The Song of the Volga Boatmen" at a neighborhood restaurant.

Now delirious with success and fame, Hurok is encouraged by Emma to go after Pavlova. So obsessed is he with pleasing the ballerina that on his first wedding anniversary he buys her a swan brooch and completely forgets about his wife. This is the last straw even for the long-suffering Emma, who runs off, with Hurok now in hot pursuit, through Newark, Albany, and Atlantic City. Meanwhile, Hurok's opera company is going bankrupt and Chaliapin is being courted by a rival manager. (Not surprisingly, no mention is made of Hurok's attempt to take financial advantage of Chaliapin's marital difficulties.) But just as it looks as if all is lost, Hurok's rival manager mortally offends the touchy Russian bass by buying him domestic champagne and salty caviar. This is something that the respectful and refined Hurok would never dream of doing.

In the time-honored Hollywood tradition, the ebullient Chaliapin now saves the day by producing a suitcase full of cash to keep the company going, praising Hurok for "bringing me to this wonderful America." Emma also returns, unable to live apart from her difficult but lovable hubby. A grand finale ensues, with scenes from *Faust*.

In a brief epilogue, Hurok and Emma are riding in a horse-drawn carriage through Central Park, and he is promising to take her on the honeymoon they never had. But suddenly he hears the coachman singing—what a fine tenor voice he has! Wise and forgiving, Emma smiles, knowing they'll never take that wedding trip.

"You ought to do something about the voice," she advises him.

"Mrs. Hurok, I love you," he replies with infinite gratitude for her understanding of his impossible passion.

As this synopsis makes clear, *Tonight We Sing* misrepresents and romanticizes most aspects of Hurok's life and career. It ignores the pain and oppression Jewish immigrants like Hurok and Tamara endured both in Eastern Europe and upon arrival in America; denies the importance and extent of Hurok's socialist connections in the creation of his early career as an impresario; sentimentalizes his relationship with his major artists; and provides no real insight into the nitty-gritty details of life as a manager-impresario.

But surely the most heavily fictionalized sections of the film involve Hurok's relationship with his wife, Emma. Indeed, they embody a desperate form of wish fulfillment, providing the lonely impresario with the happy married life on screen that he never enjoyed in reality. In the process, his life story is turned into an empty Hollywood happy-ending cliché. The Hurok that emerges is a romantic hero who bears as little resemblance to the real, anecdotal McCoy as *Gone With the Wind* does to Civil War–era life in the South.

Impresario, the basic source for the movie, contains only the sketchiest of details about Hurok's romantic and married life with Tamara and Emma. Wanting to portray his private life as warm and fulfilling, and well aware of Hollywood's insatiable appetite for pretty love stories, Hurok insisted, however, that his film biography contain a strong romantic interest. In his memo to Zanuck about the first draft of the script, he complained that "the love interest between the young couple is barely evident and, it is felt, should be more fully developed." He also criticized the character of Emma as "one-dimensional" and "little more than a shadow" that needed to be fleshed out. Accordingly, the completed film creates a largely fictional narrative about the genesis of the romance between Hurok and Emma, portraying their relationship as a sweet and loving one disrupted only by his fanatical devotion to his business and artists.

As developed in *Tonight We Sing*, the character of Emma has little in common with either of Hurok's real-life wives. Of the two, she probably bears a greater resemblance to his second spouse, Emma Perper, whose first name she also bears. Like the real-life Emma, the movie Emma is associated with stylish turn-of-the-century St. Petersburg, not with the backward Ukrainian village from which Hurok and his first real-life wife, Tamara, originated. Unlike the real-life Emma, however, the movie Emma has no independent artistic career as a cabaret singer. (No reference is made to Emma Perper's checkered past as the wife of a Russian silent film star.) As played by the virginally pure Anne Bancroft, the movie Emma is beautiful, innocent, malleable, and utterly submissive to her enterprising husband.

In real life, of course, Emma Perper might have been considered beautiful, at least in her younger years, but she was anything but innocent or malleable. Her fondness for teasing and condescending to the husband she clearly considered her social and intellectual inferior was well known to family and close friends. The movie also avoids any mention of Hurok's daughter, Ruth, or of his stepchildren by Emma. As he wanted to do in real life, he simply overlooked their existence. In the movie, as in life, his real children were his artists.

For Hurok, then, *Tonight We Sing* (like his books *Impresario* and *S. Hurok Presents*) presented the welcome opportunity to re-create his life as he wished it had been. Hollywood, the dream factory, was only too willing to help him live out his fantasies.

All those involved in the creation of *Tonight We Sing* had high hopes that it would be an artistic and commercial success. In an August 1952 letter to Hurok, Tamara Toumanova described a private screening of the film she had attended at the Fox studio in Hollywood. "At Darryl's last running of the picture at the studio all of the important people from the New York office saw it and were tremendously enthused. They feel that it has great class and compare it to *Red Shoes*. . . . Unless they are all mistaken we have a great, great success ahead of us." (The portrayal of the Diaghilev-like impresario in *The Red Shoes* seems to have served both as an inspiration and a goad for Hurok in creating his own character in *Tonight We Sing*.) Toumanova also mentioned that the producers had discussed making the film a two-evening attraction because of its length (124 minutes), an idea that was eventually rejected.

Leisen was disappointed with the final version of the film because Zanuck had ordered him to cut what had originally been envisioned as its main production number, a ballet starring Toumanova set to the song "Autumn Leaves." "It really was beautiful," said Leisen, "but Zanuck took one look at it, decided the boy's underwear wasn't tight enough and he ordered it cut out, just like that." Later that same year, "Autumn Leaves" became a big hit, "and it just broke my heart to think we had filmed that beautiful number and then lost it." Because of this cut, Toumanova's screen time was greatly reduced.

Initial industry reviews after the Hollywood premiere in late January 1953 were positive. *Variety* called *Tonight We Sing* a "top-flight musical drama parading a succession of artistic talents across the screen in an interesting and human story." The gullible critic apparently took most of the action as an accurate reflection of Hurok's biography: "While the main incidents are factual, dramatic license is used to better shape the material to the screen." *Film Daily* was equally impressed, calling the direction "expert," the photography "fine," and the screenplay "simple yet affecting. . . . *Tonight We Sing* is one of the real good ones. It will go places and do things—good things."

Critics in and around New York, where the film had its star-studded premiere (attended by Hurok, Emma, and the leading actors) on February 12 at Radio City Music Hall, were less kind.

"Mr. Hurok, upon seeing the picture, may be surprised to discover that he has been made into such a dull fellow," said the *Christian Science Monitor*, "and that the concert management business has come to be so tame." In a review in the Newark *Star-Ledger* headlined "*Tonight We Sing* mixes Corn and Joy," Ann X. Smith attacked the bogus nature of the "supposed episodes from Hurok's life" and joked that David Wayne "fights a losing battle with a Russian accent." To Bosley Crowther of the *New York Times*, the film was "a rambling conglomeration of musical culture and cheap romance with a catch in its throat."

And yet there were many upon whom the film made a more favorable impression—including the undiscerning critic for the *Jewish Ledger*, who trumpeted that "Jews in America will be proud of the film. . . . Himself a very modest person [!!!], Mr. Hurok is very much interested in everything that is Jewish and lends a helping hand in Jewish affairs." In Thomasville, California, the film's run was extended beyond the original two days due to popular demand, and the *Sunday Daily News* wrote of raves "noted on cards turned in by preview audiences." Typically, Hurok capitalized on these enthusiastic reviews to drum up interest in his attractions and sought to set up screenings in cities where his artists were scheduled to appear.

As a show-biz movie turning on glamor and temperament, *Tonight We Sing* did hold an appeal for aspiring artists who dreamed of big-time success as ballerinas, soloists, or prima donnas. Among these was Van Cliburn, a young pianist from Texas who was beginning to make a name for himself in New York. One of his childhood dreams had been to be represented under the title "S. Hurok Presents," and he remembers being awestruck when he went to see the film at the Capitol Theater soon after it was released. Only six years later, Van Cliburn would himself join the constellation of stars around the greatest impresario in the land.

And yet because of its dull and patently unbelievable story line, its fear to offend, and its blandness and kitschy sentimentality, *Tonight We Sing* failed to become the big hit or classic feature for which Hurok and Fox had hoped. In insisting on controlling the portrayal of the hero and removing nearly all evidence of the real pain and struggle of his rags-to-riches life story, Hurok and his collaborators robbed the film of any emotional truth, conflict, genuine feeling, or pathos. In happy-ending his life in the grandest Hollywood style, they made it something it had never been: boring.

They also left off the last, and most important, chapters.

Part III

CHAPTER EIGHTEEN

Back to the USSR

"We send them our Jewish violinists from Odessa, and they
send us their Jewish violinists from Odessa."—*Isaac Stern on
Soviet-American cultural exchange*

ON MARCH 5, 1953, a month after the Radio City Music Hall premiere of *Tonight We Sing* and a month before he reached the customary retirement age of sixty-five, Hurok's already long career as
an impresario unexpectedly entered a dynamic new phase. Just at
the moment when he seemed to have achieved everything he could
reasonably expect, including becoming the improbably romantic
hero of a major Hollywood feature, international political events
again took a surprising turn that would invigorate his business. If
anything, the next twenty-one years—Hurok's last—would prove to
be the most important, memorable, and exciting period of his entire
career. At last he would fulfill the dream that had eluded him for
more than thirty years, becoming a sort of senior statesman of cultural exchange.

For it was on that late winter day near the end of the Korean
War that Josef Stalin, supreme ruler of the USSR since the late
1920s, died. A one-time seminarian who later converted—
fanatically—to Bolshevism, he was eight years older than Hurok.
Like Hurok, the Great Leader, born in the mountains of Georgia,
grew up in a small and shabby village (his father was a cobbler) on

the fringe of the Russian Empire. Like Hurok's English, Stalin's spoken Russian, the official language of the Soviet empire, was heavily accented. But that was not all these two public figures had in common. Like Hurok, Stalin had spent his life trying to escape a difficult, even shameful childhood and youth, harnessing his enormous ambition to the task of reinventing himself (his real name was Dzhugashvili) and his surroundings. Both men were highly secretive and enjoyed pitting their subordinates against each other as a way of maintaining control. Both men adopted a paternal stance toward the world and toward their associates as a defense against genuine emotional intimacy.

And yet the purposes to which they put their energy and imagination, and the scale of their influence, had nothing in common. The self-delusionary egotism Hurok displayed in parading around with a cloak and cane, pulling the strings behind the scenes of *Tonight We Sing* to ensure that he appeared in the most attractive light, or insisting that his name came first on billboards and programs, was one thing. The single-minded megalomania of one of the most fearsome tyrants in world history—a man who ordered the slaughter of millions of peasants and forced thousands of composers and writers and directors to praise and idealize him in endless cantatas and novels and films—was quite another. Next to Stalin, Hurok appeared as selfless as a saint and as harmless as a fly.

Nor did Stalin have any real affection for the high culture so dear to the impresario's heart. In absolute power as head of the Communist party and the Soviet government for nearly thirty years, ruthless and crude, the phobic Stalin showed interest in art and artists only as a means of exhibiting and expanding his control over all aspects of life in the country he regarded as his personal fiefdom. His xenophobia and paranoia had also greatly complicated Hurok's dogged efforts to develop Soviet-American cultural exchange. Brutally enforcing a willful and often capricious policy of nearly total political, economic, and cultural isolation from the West, Stalin had made it impossible for the impresario (despite many energetic attempts in the 1920s and 1930s) to realize his lifelong ambition of developing a commercial relationship with Moscow for the import and export of Soviet and American performing artists.

In 1930, at a time when Stalin's power was not yet firmly established in all areas, Hurok had persuaded Soviet officials to sign an agreement theoretically giving him the monopoly right to present Soviet artists in the United States and England. He also received the right to present English and American artists in the USSR. Nothing ever came of this, however, because of obstacles subsequently thrown up on the Soviet side. No other additional agreements or commitments in the area of cultural exchange had been negotiated or completed since.

Stalin's fear of Western infiltration and the resulting infection of the Soviet system was complete and uncompromising. Between 1936 and 1958, not a single American scholar or student was allowed to study in the USSR (without moving there and adopting Soviet citizenship, at least). In 1944, the Rockefeller Foundation had offered to award fellowships to Soviets for study in the United States, but the proposal went unanswered. The long nightmare of Stalin's rule was an era of cultural, educational, and social isolation and repression unequaled in modern history. Soviet composer Dmitri Shostakovich, a favorite target of Stalin's wrath, put it simply: "Stalin didn't give a damn about the West."

Although during his travels to the USSR in the 1930s Hurok had been very careful never to publicly criticize Stalin or his policies, in later years he agreed that it had been next to impossible to deal with him. "Under Stalin, it was very difficult," he told the *New York Times* in 1967. "He did not want anybody to have the Soviet Union. Sometimes I would get contracts signed in Moscow and then I would receive a cable in Paris or London or New York saying the Government had decided to cancel."

Hurok had not traveled to the USSR since 1937. That's when it had become clear that the prospects for Stalin consenting to allow Soviet performers to travel and perform abroad—especially in evil, capitalist America—were less than dim. The vicious combat on the Russian front during World War II made any further business communications impossible until after 1945. Throughout this period, however, Hurok stayed in contact with bureaucrats and artists in Moscow through his extensive network of friends and informers. He had also curried the favor of Soviet diplomats (especially Maksim Litvinov, the Soviet ambassador to the United States) stationed in America during the war. Hurok had been instrumental in organizing several highly successful benefit performances for Russian war relief, and he continued to present pro-Russian programs, such as the patriotic *Russian Soldier* (set to Prokofiev's *Lt. Kije Suite*) staged by American Ballet Theatre in 1942.

Many people in both countries had been hoping for a relaxation in American-Soviet political relations in the afterglow of their successful wartime cooperation. But such a rapprochement—which would also have made it possible for Hurok and others to make new overtures in the area of commercial cultural exchange—failed to materialize in the immediate postwar years. Instead, relations between Washington and Moscow rapidly deteriorated over such difficult issues as the fate of Eastern Europe, and the Soviet Union again retreated to a position of lonely hostility toward the West. Even a 1945 invitation by the State Department to the Red Army Chorus for an American tour failed to evoke a response from Soviet officials. By 1948, the Western Allies were airlifting supplies to blockaded Berlin, the United States and the Soviet Union had entered the Cold War, the propaganda machines were gearing up on both sides, and prospects for any kind of exchange were looking more remote than ever.

At the same time, the paranoiac Stalin was showing that he had no intentions of easing up at home, either. He initiated another round of purges of prominent cultural figures in 1946, beginning with the respected writers Anna Akhmatova and Mikhail Zoshchenko. And in early 1948, his cultural goons, led by Andrei Zhdanov, severely criticized the internationally prominent Soviet composers Sergei Prokofiev and Dmitri Shostakovich at a composers congress for writing music that was excessively dissonant and intellectual and, they scolded, insufficiently "accessible" to the Soviet mass audience.

Already ill, and shocked by the arrest and subsequent imprisonment of his first (foreign-born) wife on false charges of spying, Prokofiev never recovered from this ideological assault. For his part, Shostakovich was forced by Stalin to travel to New York as a Soviet representative to the notorious Cultural and Scientific Congress for World Peace held at the Waldorf-Astoria in the spring of 1949. Attacked by the American press as an apologist for the Soviet system, the shy and terrified Shostakovich made bland official statements and played the scherzo from his Fifth Symphony on the piano before thirty thousand people in Madison Square Garden. "I had to answer stupid questions and keep from saying too much," he remembered bitterly some years later. "And all I thought about was: How much longer do I have to live?"

But now, suddenly, Stalin was gone. Would this mean that the situation could change and improve?

When the truth of Stalin's brutal repression of Soviet cultural figures began to become more widely known in the United States in the late 1940s, it contributed to a growing mood of intolerant anti-Communism. It also helped to set the stage for the Red-hunting exploits of Senator Joseph McCarthy and his like-minded colleagues in Washington.

By the time Stalin died in 1953, the blacklist of American members of the Communist party (and other "subversive" organizations) supposedly created to screen prospective federal employees had been growing for six years. The infamous Committee on Un-American Activities of the House of Representatives (HUAC) had already succeeded in sending Alger Hiss to prison as a Communist spy. It had summoned hundreds of other private citizens (including prominent Hollywood and New York artists and intellectuals) suspected of having ties to the Soviet Union to testify about their alleged pro-Communist sympathies and activities. Aroused by a pervasive mood of spy mania, and disturbed by aggressive Soviet behavior in Korea and elsewhere, Congress had already passed the McCarran Internal Security Act and the McCarran-Walter Immigration Law. Both aimed at preventing the perceived growth of Communism in America by tightening security regulations. They also made it difficult for immigrants from Eastern and Southern Europe and Asia to enter the United States.

In May 1953, the dancer and choreographer Jerome Robbins, with whom Hurok had been associated when he managed Ballet Theatre in the early 1940s, was called before the committee and asked to talk about his brief membership in the Communist party. Robbins told how his party comrades urged him to explain the impact of dialectical materialism on his choreography for the unambiguously pro-American 1944 ballet *Fancy Free*. More pliant than some other witnesses who refused to answer the committee's questions by taking the Fifth Amendment, Robbins apologized for what he called his "great mistake" in joining the party. He also willingly gave the names of other party members.

This tense climate of intense anti-Communism must have made Hurok nervous. After all, he was a Russian émigré, a Jew, an old-time socialist, a show business personality with many connections to "infected" Broadway and Hollywood, and a cosmopolitan with a long history of traveling to Moscow. He had even negotiated with representatives of the Soviet government. The realities of McCarthyism certainly help to explain why Hurok omitted any reference to his numerous earlier trips to Russia both in *Tonight We Sing* and in his second volume of memoirs, *S. Hurok Presents*. Both appeared in 1953, a year when the entertainment industry was coming under particular scrutiny from the HUAC thought police. The final chapter of *S. Hurok Presents*, "Unborn Tomorrow," which presents Hurok's professional hopes for the future, contains no mention of any plans to visit the USSR or to import Soviet attractions to the United States. The moment was not yet ripe for such public discussions.

Stalin's death, news of a more liberal regime in Moscow, and the signing of a truce ending the Korean War less than five months later gradually led to a lessening of the anti-Communist hysteria. The highly publicized censure of McCarthy by his Senate colleagues in 1954 further eroded the power and influence of HUAC, and the possibilities for greater Soviet-American cooperation began slowly to grow.

This new spirit of détente reached a climax in Geneva in July 1955, when President Eisenhower met with Soviet Premier Nikolai Bulganin, Soviet Communist party head Nikita Khrushchev, Soviet defense Minister George Zhukov, and major Western leaders to discuss disarmament and German unification. Although it produced few substantial results on these issues, the Geneva Summit opened the way to further dialogue between the United States and the USSR. Thanks to Eisenhower's efforts, it also led to a rapid increase in the number of official and unofficial proposals for Soviet-American cultural exchange. One came from a visionary "crackpot" who suggested sending a mission to Russia "to teach the Communists how to make raspberry jam just like grandmother used to make. He said this certainly would relieve the tensions of the 'cold war.' "

Over the next thirty years, in fact, until Gorbachev and *glasnost* changed the rules of the game, cultural exchange became one of the most reliable (and certainly the most visible) avenues of Soviet-American cooperation and contact. The flow of scholars, students, exhibitions, films, and publications kept communication open between two ideologically hostile societies capable of blowing each other (and the rest of the world) up on a moment's notice.

But no aspect of cultural exchange was more glamorous, more volatile, or more visible than the tours of Soviet performing artists in the United States and by their American counterparts in the Soviet Union. Like all contacts between the two countries in these years, however, those in the arts were always subject to political pressures. They flourished or floundered depending on the current state of the relationship between Moscow and Washington. Hurok would learn that soon enough.

The first moves in this new post-Stalinist game of cultural exchange—and the raising of at least a corner of the Iron Curtain—came within a few months of the Geneva Summit. Carlton Smith, director of the American National Arts Foundation, travelled to Moscow in September to negotiate with Nikolai Mikhailov, the Soviet Minister of Culture. The Soviet side immediately proposed visits to America by a number of prominent performers, including pianist Emil Gilels, violinist David Oistrakh, ballerina Galina Ulanova, and the folk dance troupe of Igor Moiseyev. The American side proposed sending a production of Gershwin's *Porgy and Bess*, singers Marian Anderson and Leontyne Price, violinist Jascha Heifetz, Katherine Dunham and her dance troupe, and three plays produced by the Actors Studio led by Elia Kazan, Lee Strasberg, and Cheryl Crawford. As would so often be the case in years to come, however, only a few of these performers would actually go.

One of the biggest obstacles to the importation of Soviet artists to the United States was the isolationist 1952 McCarran-Walter Immigration Law, which designated certain categories of aliens—including Soviet citizens—as ineligible to receive visas or to enter the country. It also required them to be fingerprinted. One way to circumvent this legislation was to grant the visiting Soviets official status, as was done with a delegation of Russian agricultural specialists in the summer of 1955.

The first Soviet performer carried to the United States by the new "spirit of Geneva" was Odessa-born pianist Emil Gilels. On October 3, 1955, just sixteen days short of his thirty-ninth birthday, he became the first Soviet artist to appear in the United States for several decades when he performed Tchaikovsky's First Piano Concerto in Philadelphia with the Philadelphia Orchestra conducted by Eugene Ormandy. Already a frequent guest in Europe's leading concert halls, Gilels also played over the following month in New York (including performances at Carnegie Hall and with Leonard Bernstein in a special concert at the United Nations), Chicago, Cleveland, Boston, and Washington.

But the political and musical sensation created by Gilels's appearances was surpassed just a few weeks after his departure by a new Soviet arrival, violin superstar David Oistrakh. Also born in Odessa, that cradle of great soloists on the Black Sea coast, Oistrakh made his long-awaited and often-postponed American debut (originally announced by Hurok in 1930) at Carnegie Hall on November 20, 1955. The audience was so large that part of it had to be seated onstage.

"Tickets were impossible to get," fellow violinist and Odessa native Nathan Milstein, who had settled in America in 1929, later remembered with perhaps a tinge of envy. Milstein wasn't the only one who was impressed. The papers raved about Oistrakh's first recital, with a wide-ranging program featuring sonatas by Beethoven and Prokofiev and lighter pieces by Tchaikovsky, Tartini, Medtner, Ysaÿe, and Soviet composer Aram Khachaturian. Word-of-mouth spread rapidly, and when Oistrakh stepped on stage three days later for his second Carnegie apppearance, he saw an astonishing constellation of musical legends sitting in the front rows: violinists Milstein, Fritz Kreisler, Mischa Elman, Isaac Stern, Zino Francescatti, and Samuel Dushkin; violist William Primrose; conductor Pierre Monteux; and singers Elisabeth Schwarzkopf and Paul Robeson. One critic spoke for many when he pronounced him "the best violinist I have ever heard."

One of the most memorable events of Oistrakh's first American tour—and even of recent American musical history—was his performance at the American premiere of Shostakovich's Violin Concerto No. 1 with Dmitri Mitropoulos and the New York Philharmonic on December 29, 1955. Written in 1947–48 as a response to Soviet anti-Semitism but withheld by the composer until after Stalin's death, the concerto, among Shostakovich's most moving and original works, had received its world premiere just two months earlier in Leningrad, performed by Oistrakh, a close friend of the composer's. Musicologist Boris Schwarz attended the Carnegie concert and wrote later that the experience of discovering simultaneously "a great composition and a great performer" was one that those who were "privileged to be present" would never forget. The performance was broadcast on radio and recorded by Columbia Records.

By the end of his tour (which also took him to New Haven, Philadelphia, Chicago, Minneapolis, Washington, Boston, Cleveland, and Ithaca), Oistrakh had been embraced by the American music-loving public. His concerts were also helping at least some Americans realize for the first time that Soviets were people, too, with passion and creativity and a love for life that transcended ideology. The virtuosity, directness, and emotional intensity of Oistrakh's playing exerted a particularly strong appeal for American audiences. His concerts, and those of Gilels, became the central event of the 1955–56 musical season—for both artistic and political reasons.

Despite his longtime involvement with Russian artists and his many earlier attempts to bring Soviet performers to the United States, Hurok was not involved in presenting either Gilels or Oistrakh in 1955. That honor went to Columbia Artists Management, which worked with the State Department and the highly bureaucratic Soviet Ministry of Culture to organize the tours. According to an official working in the Ministry of Culture at the time, it was due to the recommendation of the Soviet Embassy in Washington that Columbia (then headed by Fred Schang and his son) was awarded the contracts for Gilels and Oistrakh. Columbia also presented cellist Mstislav Rostropovich on his first American tour in the spring of 1956. (The planned Moiseyev tour did not materialize.)

For the first few seasons after the Geneva Summit, the Soviet performers who came to America were allowed to keep about one-half of the fee paid to the Soviet side by the Western presenter, who also paid for their hotel and travel. Oistrakh was reportedly paid a total of $100,000 for his American appearances in 1955. Of this amount, he was allowed to keep $48,000—a fantastically large amount at a time when Soviet citizens had no access to foreign currency and the ruble was not freely convertible. Oistrakh spent the money on two violins: a Stradivarius and an Amati. Gilels, too, boasted that he had earned a total of about $100,000 on his first American tour.

Within a few years, however, the Central Committee of the Communist party and the Soviet Ministry of Culture—both hungry for foreign currency—instituted new and strictly enforced regulations. These required Soviet performers (with only a few exceptions for the most famous) to turn over about eighty percent of whatever fees they earned abroad to the Soviet government.

Seeing the huge popular and commercial success achieved by Oistrakh and Gilels must have both annoyed and excited Hurok. He had to be happy to see that the situation had really changed and that the Soviets were now willing to deal. But to stand by as Columbia Artists harvested the first fruits of cultural exchange must have been excrutiating for a man who was always used to being "the first." He didn't stand by for long. No stranger to fighting for what he wanted, and loath to be outmaneuvered, Hurok now harnessed all his charm and wiles to lure Soviet officials and performers to his agency. From this moment on began a fiercely competitive struggle over Soviet artists that would rage between the corporate giant Columbia and the family business S. Hurok Attractions until the day he died.

In waging his campaign to bring more Russians to America, Hurok drew on his personality and connections—and on his bottomless supply of egotism and self-assurance. At one meeting on cultural exchange issues in Washington attended by Hurok, a State Department official mentioned what he called Hurok's "competitors," referring to Columbia Artists. According to his stepson and assistant George Perper, Hurok "just looked up and said, 'I have no competitors.' They were all a bit stunned."

In an attempt to make use of the new opportunities, Hurok had already traveled to Europe in late 1955 to see the Igor Moiseyev Folk Dance Ensemble, which was making its first tour to capitalist countries. In Paris he made a point of introducing himself to Moiseyev (born in Kiev in 1906), a former Bolshoi Ballet dancer turned choreographer who in 1937 had founded the first Soviet multicultural folk dance troupe. The ensemble specialized in colorful, athletic, theatrical—and highly patriotic—versions of the Slavic, Central Asian, and Caucasian dances found in the various Soviet republics. By the time of its first European performances, the Moiseyev had already become the largest folk dance company in the world. It was also a favorite of Soviet cultural and political officials and a powerful propaganda tool in promoting a sanitized image of peaceful coexistence between the different ethnic groups of the USSR.

When Hurok met Moiseyev for the first time, the choreographer later recalled, he "told me he liked our company and he expressed the desire to bring us to America. But there were so many obstacles still on both sides that we didn't really believe that he would succeed in overcoming them." There was good reason for caution, and it would take Hurok several years and a great deal of effort to fulfill his pledge to Moiseyev.

Hurok began by carefully cultivating the Soviet officials who were making the decisions in Moscow. One of these was Edward Ivanyan, a bright young man with a remarkable gift for languages who had joined the Ministry of Culture in the summer of 1955, just at the moment when relations with the United States were opening up. Fluent in several languages, including English, he was at first assigned to Latin America, but soon became chief of the division dealing with America. In the spring of 1956, Ivanyan was sent as a representative of the Ministry of Culture to the United States with the equally young Rostropovich (the "Red Cellist," as the New York *Herald Tribune* described him) and his accompanist on Rostropovich's twelve-concert American tour.

One day Ivanyan received a phone call from the reception desk at his New York hotel informing him that a "Mr. Hurok" was downstairs and wanted to see him. When Ivanyan asked who the gentleman was, the desk clerk identified him as "our local impresario." So Ivanyan told him to send him up. When Ivanyan opened the door,

Hurok "entered with arms outstretched and said in Russian, 'Hello, my name is Solomon Izrailevich.' "

> When he learned that I didn't know who he was, he pro-
> ceeded to tell me the story of his life, how he came from
> Russia as a teenager, how he took a menial job on a ship so
> he could get to America, how he came to manage Pavlova
> and Chaliapin, and how he was married to a former singer
> from St. Petersburg who spoke beautiful Russian. His
> own Russian was good, too, but heavily accented with
> Yiddish.

As usual, Hurok timed his visit brilliantly. When they met, Ivanyan was feeling increasingly dissatisfied about the treatment the Ministry and Soviet performers were receiving from Schang and Columbia Artists. "They were stingy, and I encountered lots of difficulties in negotiating with them in Moscow." He was also unhappy about how they were handling Rostropovich's tour; the twenty-nine-year-old cellist, still unknown abroad, ultimately earned only $5,000, just enough to buy a Steinway. Eager to encourage competition and find better conditions, Ivanyan had already begun to think of investigating other possibilities just at the moment that Hurok turned up.

Personal factors also played a role. Ivanyan found Schang and his subordinates at Columbia "not very pleasant to deal with. Somehow they did not appeal to me as people—and personal appeal means a lot, after all." Hurok's ebullience, generosity, and personal passion for Russian culture, on the other hand, immediately won Ivanyan over. Throughout Ivanyan's stay in America, Hurok entertained both him and Rostropovich in his customary lavish style. Several times he took Ivanyan to his favorite restaurant, Le Pavillon, and introduced him to the other regulars there, including promoter Billy Rose, who had done in the area of popular music what Hurok had done for classical music and dance. Hurok also got Ivanyan tickets for Broadway shows, including the brand-new smash hit *My Fair Lady*. All of this was certain to make quite an impression on a young man from Moscow.

Of course, Hurok also used their meetings to express his interest in bringing other Soviet attractions to the United States. The proposal interested Ivanyan, but he was not authorized to open negotiations. So he invited Hurok to come to Moscow the following fall.

Meanwhile, in his bombshell "secret speech" to the Twentieth Congress of the Soviet Communist party, an increasingly confident Nikita Khrushchev had denounced Stalin as a cruel tyrant responsible for erecting a monstrous "cult of personality," and American performers were touring the thawing USSR for the first time since the 1930s.

The first attraction to take the Soviet stage was Everyman Opera's production of Gershwin's opera *Porgy and Bess*, which had been touring Europe under State Department auspices for several years. Robert Breen, the show's co-producer and director, had been lobbying with Soviet officials for some time and received an official invitation from the Ministry of Culture in the fall of 1955. In December, the eighty-five members of the company arrived in Leningrad, where they played to packed and wildly enthusiastic audiences before moving on to Moscow and Stalingrad.

After the State Department had declined to finance the tour on the grounds that it was politically premature, the Soviet Ministry of Culture had made a striking goodwill gesture by contributing a huge (for those times) guarantee of $35,000, plus an equivalent amount in rubles. This sudden largesse on the part of the Soviet government was surely motivated by ideological concerns. Sponsorship of an opera depicting the repression of American blacks provided a marvelous opportunity to show support for the world's economically downtrodden and allowed the Soviet people to see for themselves how unfair and hard was life under capitalism. What the Soviet officials didn't count on was how astonished their citizens would be to see the supposedly oppressed black members of the show's cast appearing at parties in minks and jewels and displaying no obvious signs of hardship.

There was no denying the genuine popular appeal of *Porgy and Bess*'s jazzy, sexy, tuneful score for Russian audiences, so long fed a bland diet of aging classics and so long starved for Western culture. (Because of its heavy reliance on the chorus and its celebration of the role of the "people," critics have often called *Porgy and Bess* the American equivalent of Modest Mussorgsky's opera *Boris Godunov*.) It also struck some Russian theater people as ironic, even amusing, that a Jewish American capitalist composer should be able to write exactly the kind of politically correct opera with true mass appeal that Soviet composers—despite endless encouragement, castigation, and subsidies—had been incapable of producing in their Communist utopia for some years now.

In an attempt to improve his bargaining position in Russia, Hurok shrewdly sent two of his most famous artists on tour there in the spring of 1956: Isaac Stern and Jan Peerce. Since the Russians claimed to have insufficient hard currency to pay their fees, Hurok reportedly subsidized their appearances out of his own pocket. Stern went first, in April. He would be the first American solo instrumentalist to play in the USSR. The violinist remembered the day he left New York for the USSR very well, because it was the same day that Mae Frohman, Hurok's longtime secretary and confidante, died.

> I arrived in New York about one A.M. on Friday morning after playing in Cuba, and was set to leave Saturday evening for London, Copenhagen, Leningrad and Moscow—on the Pan Am double decker supercruiser that made London in only eleven hours or something. I unpacked and repacked, and then I went to see Hurok and he told me Mae had died, and we sat and cried for two hours. Just sat there and cried. There was no one closer to him or anyone on whom he counted more.

Frohman's death left Hurok more isolated than ever. She had been his Girl Friday since the 1920s, and one of the few people in his office he trusted. No one would ever replace her.

But Stern went on to Russia, where he encountered "warm and wonderful audiences, but very limited personal contacts." To Peerce, about to go off on his own Russian tour, Stern gave this advice: "Don't spout off politically. Don't advise people. Don't play games with money. Don't talk to strangers. Nobody will talk to you much either. When you go into your hotel room, whether or not you are being listened to, it would be wise to behave as though you were."

Peerce also discovered that his jittery hosts were less than enthusiastic about his inclusion of some Hebrew and Yiddish songs on
one of his programs; they had pointedly failed to schedule them
anywhere on his tour. But when the Israeli ambassador (the USSR
and Israel had diplomatic relations in those early days) came backstage at intermission during his recital in Moscow's Tchaikovsky
Hall and told him that twenty percent of the audience was Jewish,
Peerce insisted on singing a Yiddish-Hebrew song as an encore. He
chose "A Plea to God." It provoked "yelling and stamping"—and
from much more than twenty percent of the crowd. At such moments, cultural exchange really made a difference, by exposing Soviet audiences to new ways of thinking, and by encouraging them to
seek greater freedom of self-expression.

In Leningrad, Peerce invited Hurok's brother Asher backstage.
Not surprisingly, the singer's interpreter-escort objected strenu-
ously; it was his his job to minimize Peerce's contacts with the local
population.

Having established his credibility and good intentions in Moscow, Hurok himself traveled there in the fall of 1956. It was his first
trip to Russia since 1937. By that time, Ivanyan had already laid the
necessary groundwork with responsible officials in the Cultural Department of the Party Central Committee. In this era of superpower
tension, these high-ranking bureaucrats made all decisions about
which Soviet performers would go abroad and which American
managers would present them.

Columbia should have competition, Ivanyan had told them, or
else a monopoly would develop that would be financially unfavor-
able to the Soviet side. By then, Hurok's operation had also been
checked out and found to be reputable. "At first they weren't impressed by all this information," said Ivanyan, "but after some time
passed the Central Committee decided to give permission to enter
into negotiations with S. Hurok Attractions. This had happened by
the time Hurok came to Moscow. And little by little—with my
help—he was able to squeeze out Columbia in presenting Soviet artists in the USA."

Since the 1920s, it had been Hurok's dream to bring the
Bolshoi Ballet to America. He made this desire known to Ivanyan
almost immediately after arriving in Moscow. But the Central Com-

mittee had already given the Ministry of Culture specific instructions that the Bolshoi could be offered only as a "second step." The first had to be Moiseyev's folk dance ensemble. "I'm not sure what their reasoning was," said Ivanyan, "but the Moiseyev was at the time very popular, on the rise, and possibly—even probably—Moiseyev seemed to have some particularly good personal connections within the Central Committee." Hurok had no choice but to agree.

Even with their connections, Moiseyev and Hurok had to work long and hard to get the company to the United States. According to Moiseyev, Hurok had to "distribute bribes" to various officials in Moscow to win them over to his side. He also had to work with unflagging persistence to penetrate the enigmatic, byzantine, and corrupt Soviet bureaucracy. "It took someone with Hurok's energy, tenacity and authority to cross over that threshold of inertia and make it happen," said Moiseyev. "For two years he came to Moscow and always came to our concerts. He would applaud loud and hard and then stand up, so that the whole hall would rise, following his example." Even before the ensemble finally went to the United States, Moiseyev had come to admire Hurok's generosity and *nyukh* ("intuition") for what would sell and how to sell it. "If he saw something he liked, he would grab on to it like a bulldog and never let go." And Hurok liked the Moiseyev.

Hurok's negotiations in Moscow were always difficult and protracted, but he was prepared (after settling into his usual suite at the elegant Hotel National at the foot of Gorky Street) to spend however much time it took to work things out. In Russia, such patience and determination are highly valued. Nor did Hurok, unlike some American impresarios who sought business in the Soviet Union, fight over nickels and dimes. "He wasn't stingy as a negotiator," said Ivanyan.

> He wouldn't agree to any extra expenses, and would always fight for better terms for himself, but whenever he was asked to do something as a favor, he would agree, after a certain amount of resistance. We had some initial disagreement over the fee for the Moiseyev ensemble, but then he agreed to take on the extra expense for excess

baggage—because the performers would always return from the United States with much heavier luggage than they had gone over with.

Hurok's delicate negotiations and agreements with the Ministry of Culture were also frequently disrupted by political events. The brutal Soviet invasion of Hungary on November 4, 1956, and the French-British-Israeli attack on Egypt the following day destabilized the international situation and soured the Soviet-American relationship in all spheres. The Soviet side continued to be troubled as well by the American law requiring that Soviet citizens traveling to the United States be fingerprinted. "Fingerprinting is only for criminals," declared the colorful Nikita Khrushchev.

Indeed, this was one of the problems that ultimately postponed the first American tour by the Moiseyev Ensemble for a year. In his negotiations with the Ministry of Culture in Moscow in the fall of 1956, Hurok had obtained an agreement to bring the company to the United States in the spring of 1957, but with the condition that the fingerprinting clause (in the McCarran-Walter Immigration Act) be deleted. This failed to happen.

There were also security questions raised on the American side about allowing the ensemble to land in the United States in Soviet planes (the UPI called them "Red jet airliners"), which were assumed to be equipped with spying devices. So Hurok returned to Moscow in June 1957 for further negotiations. This time he emerged with even more impressive pledges from the Soviet side: a tour by the Moiseyev in the spring of 1958, a ten-week engagement by the Bolshoi Ballet (including ballerina Galina Ulanova) in the spring of 1959, and appearances by David Oistrakh (now wooed from Columbia Artists) and composer Aram Khachaturian. Described in an interview with the *New York Times* in Moscow as "ebullient" at being the first American to sign the Bolshoi, he "threatened to solve the cold war himself to fulfill the contract." Under the terms of the agreement, the Soviet side agreed to pay transportation to and from New York for all its artists.

This time, perhaps because the Soviet side had come to trust Hurok more completely, the agreement stuck. Fortunately, the fingerprinting provision was repealed and the way was clear for

Hurok to import the nearly one hundred dancers of the Moiseyev company.

The picture grew even brighter as the year wore on. For the first few years after the Geneva Summit, Soviet-American cultural exchange proceeded in a rather haphazard fashion, on the basis of individual agreements. But this situation changed on January 27, 1958, when the first official "Agreement Between the United States of America and the Union of Soviet Socialist Republics on Exchanges in the Cultural, Technical and Educational Fields" was signed in Washington, D.C. Usually called the Lacy-Zarubin agreement after its negotiators and signatories (William S. B. Lacy, Eisenhower's Special Assistant on East-West Exchanges, and Georgy Z. Zarubin, Soviet ambassador to the United States), it covered a two-year period but was extended periodically after that. The desire for the agreement seems to have come more from the Soviet than the American side. Spurred by the accelerating pace of cultural exchange but wary about dealing with their chief ideological foe, formalistic party officials and bureaucrats wanted to spell out clearly what were the limits and obligations of each side.

Hurok's attentive wining and dining of Soviet cultural officials over the last few years paid him huge dividends when the Lacy-Zarubin agreement was signed. Paragraph four of Section VIII ("Exchange of Theatrical, Choral and Choreographic Groups, Symphony Orchestras and Artistic Performers") gave him and his agency unprecedented official status: "The Ministry of Culture of the Union of Soviet Socialist Republics, in accordance with an agreement with Hurok Attractions, Inc., will send the State Folk Dance Ensemble of the Union of Soviet Socialist Republics to the United States in April–May, 1958, and will consider inviting a leading American theatrical or choreographic group to the Soviet Union in 1959."

With such high-level governmental support and recognition, Hurok's ability to carry out his business in Moscow received a boost that must have left the folks at Columbia Artists reaching for their smelling salts. By being mentioned in this historic document, Hurok gained unprecedented leverage and prestige which he would exploit to brilliant effect for the next ten years.

But first he had to prove he could present the Moiseyev Ensemble.

■ CHAPTER NINETEEN ■

Creatures from Outer Space

"**I'm amazed that all your workers are fat and all your million-aires thin.**"—*Igor Moiseyev on what surprised him most about America*

THE PACE AND TEXTURE of the volatile Soviet-American relationship changed with breathtaking speed during the eventful 1957–58 concert season. Stunned disbelief was the reaction all over the world when, on October 4, 1957, the first artificial earth satellite, Sputnik I, well equipped with instruments, soared into orbit from the USSR, presenting a startling challenge to the presumed superiority of American science and technology.

As a result of the Sputnik launch, respect for the USSR—hitherto regarded as a secretive, remote, and underdeveloped nation—rose dramatically in the United States. Resources were suddenly mobilized to study the Soviet Union and Eastern Europe. A new awareness grew that the two postwar atomic superpowers would have to work together in whatever areas they could agree upon if nuclear war was to be avoided in the shrinking global village. This awareness had led directly to the signing of the first Soviet-American cultural exchange agreement in January 1958. Notwithstanding the fears expressed by Secretary of State Dulles in testimony to the Senate Foreign Relations Committee that the Bolshoi Ballet was used by the Soviet government to strengthen international communism, interest in all aspects of Russian life and culture burgeoned. Russia was the forbidden other, as terrifying and alluring as sex to a teenager. Russia was hot. Red-hot.

Now officially anointed as an agent of Soviet-American cultural exchange, and with a contract for the first American appearances by the Moiseyev Ensemble and the Bolshoi Ballet in his pocket, Hurok—who liked nothing better than free publicity—was perfectly positioned to take advantage of all the hoopla surrounding the opening of the USSR and the start of the Soviet-American space race. In fact, in yet another bit of perfect timing, he had just become a completely independent impresario for the first time since joining the concert division of NBC in 1933.

Hurok had stayed with that organization when it had been re-formed (under antitrust regulations) as the National Concerts and Artists Corporation (NCAC) in 1942. But in 1955 NCAC gained a new boss, Luben Vichey, a one-time operatic baritone. Having surveyed the company's organization and lackluster performance, Vichey came to the conclusion that Hurok ("the tail that wagged the dog") had been getting an impossibly good deal all these years. He had been paying nothing either for his office space in the NCAC headquarters at 711 Fifth Avenue or for his telephone and telegraph expenses. Even more important, NCAC had ceded to Hurok the exclusive right to book any group of more than four persons, which gave him control over some of the most lucrative and highly publicized attractions. In return, all NCAC got was a low percentage (sometimes as low as seven and a half percent) of any profit realized on the Hurok attractions it booked.

Vichey, as *Variety* reported, respected Hurok "as a great showman and a unique figure without duplicate in the American concert world," but was nonetheless "dead-against renewal of Hurok's long relationship on the old terms." These terms were, he believed, part of the reason that NCAC was losing to gigantic Columbia Artists Management in the presenting war. So Vichey now presented Hurok with several demands. One was to pay one-half of the total rent for the corporation's office space, which had recently risen to $32,000. The other was to enter into a true sharing partnership with the parent corporation.

But Hurok, more confident than ever in his ability to attract and hold artists on his own, and no doubt anticipating great financial success with his new Soviet attractions, found these terms confining. Realizing that NCAC now needed him more than he needed NCAC, he decided to withdraw from the parent corporation and set up his own offices. The split became final on October 31, 1957, when Hurok moved his agency ("Hurok Artists, Inc., S. Hurok, President") and his staff of seven a few doors up the street to new, independent headquarters at 730 Fifth Avenue.

Vichey told *Variety* that Hurok's departure "clears the way for National to be revitalized for and within its own staff." But when the dust had settled, Hurok would be the real winner, poised to take full credit for the greatest achievements of his career.

Preparations for the first American tour by the Moiseyev Folk Dance Ensemble proceeded fitfully for months in advance of its scheduled arrival in the spring of 1958. Hurok made another trip to Moscow in late February to work out final details and to discuss problems connected with upcoming tours by the Beryozka Ensemble and the Bolshoi Ballet. Telegrams and letters flew between the State Department and George Perper of the Hurok office over such issues as visas, allowing Soviet artists to travel to "closed" American cities, whether the Moiseyev Ensemble would be allowed to fly to New York in Soviet airliners, and how to find advertisers for the program books. By mid-March, more than a month before opening night, the New York *Herald Tribune* was reporting that advance sales for the Moiseyev's performances at the old Met had already reached $130,000 and that the entire engagement was likely to be sold out before it even began.

The ninety-two members of the Moiseyev Ensemble flew to New York in four groups. The advance party of nine (seven men and two women) finally landed at Idlewild Airport on April 7, 1958. Since their request to come to the United States on Soviet airliners had been denied, they traveled as commercial passengers on a regularly scheduled Scandinavian Airlines System flight. According to Earl L. Packer, a State Department representative who accompanied the troupe throughout its American tour, the arriving dancers did not express resentment "over the fact that the Customs officials expropriated Russian sausages and lemons and other fruit." The officials allowed jars of caviar and bottles of gin to pass through, however.

Hurok was at the airport to meet Moiseyev and immediately

made him feel welcome in America. "He didn't put any limits on what we needed," said Moiseyev.

> I told him I needed four rehearsals, although I knew that paying the orchestra would be expensive. At first George Perper said we couldn't have so many rehearsals, but then Hurok said to give us as many as we needed. So he created a very pleasant atmosphere. And of course he didn't make a mistake. What impressed me always about Hurok is that he understood that the beginning is very important. If you start right, the rest will go well. He knew that if you come into a country from the servants' entrance, as it were, it's terribly hard to convince people that you're first-class. To scrimp at the beginning isn't financially wise in the long run. People won't come a second time. With Hurok, everything was always first-class.

Already hyped as one of the most significant cultural and political events of the century, the Moiseyev's April 14 debut also received an unexpected boost. That very same day, the news broke on front pages all over the United States that a twenty-three-year-old American pianist had won first prize in the prestigious Tchaikovsky Competition in Moscow. His name—Van Cliburn—and every detail of his life, from birth to Shreveport to lessons with his mother to his "boyish" appearance and six-foot-four-inch frame, suddenly became familiar to every household in America. As could happen only in the era of global electronic communications, he became an instant celebrity and American folk hero. Chicago's Elvis Presley fan club even renamed itself the Van Cliburn fan club in his honor.

The pianist's popularity was no less intense in Moscow, where thousands of fans called him "Vanya" and "Vanyushka" and showered him with gifts and adoration. The excitement and intensity with which the Russian public endorsed and embraced Van Cliburn's victory in the competition demonstrated that some deep shared quality (perhaps a fondness for the emotional, even sentimental style of his playing) linked Americans and Soviets, regardless of the Cold War and the Iron Curtain. It also helped that the spiritual, gracious Cliburn behaved with exemplary Deep South diplomacy and tact. He called the Russians "my people" and told them that "I've never felt so at home anywhere in my life." That Emil Gilels, who had only recently been received so enthusiastically in the United States, was on the competition jury only added to the glowing atmosphere of cultural good feeling.

At the time, Van Cliburn's manager was William Judd of Columbia Artists. Judd must have been ecstatic to see his pianist's fee suddenly jump from $1,000 to $2,500 and RCA Victor sign him to a highly lucrative recording contract. But Cliburn's meteoric rise could not help but attract other managers, including Hurok, who made overtures toward bringing the pianist on almost immediately after he won the competition. Cliburn was flattered with Hurok's attention, for, as he admitted later, "I always knew I wanted eventually to be a Hurok artist." But these two celebrities would dance around each other for more than a year before finally coming to an agreement.

To the Moiseyev Ensemble's opening night (and to subsequent performances) at the old Met, meanwhile, Van Cliburn's Moscow victory brought yet more electricity and publicity. Warmed by the affection Russian audiences had shown for one of their own, Americans were now itching to repay Soviet performers in kind. A line formed for the two hundred standing-room tickets at ten A.M. on April 14, and by curtain time at eight P.M., every one of the old Met's thirty-six hundred seats was filled. As was always the case with important Hurok openings, the audience included a good number of politicians and dignitaries. Mikhail Menshikov, the Soviet ambassador to Washington, and Arkady Sobolev, the Soviet ambassador to the United Nations, were among those sitting in the two center parterre boxes, which were draped with the American and Soviet flags. The historic evening began in a highly patriotic style as the American orchestra under Russian conductor Samson Galperin played "The Star Spangled Banner" and the Soviet national anthem ("Unbreakable Union of Free Republics").

"The implications of the occasion were enormous with regard not only to international relations but also to artistic exchange," wrote John Martin in his review the following day, "and everybody in the distinguished audience seemed to be aware of it. Under such circumstances, there might easily be a tendency to overrate the performance itself and regret it the next day. To play safe, then, let us risk understatement and call it merely stupendous."

What most impressed Martin, and the rest of the critical army in attendance, was the daring physicality, impeccable discipline, and inexhaustible energy of the performers, who (in Moiseyev's brash choreography) displayed as much acrobatic as dancing ability. No one had ever seen anything quite like this highly theatrical and frequently comic mixture of folk sentiment, dazzling costumes, ethnic color, Broadway-style glitz, Olympic training, and balletic grace. Even kitschy offerings like "Partisans" (which required the dancers to glide about the stage like scouts on horseback) or "Yurochka" (a Belorussian number about the romantic adventures of a flirtatious youth) pleased the often finicky Mr. Martin. Like everyone else in this venerable auditorium, he seemed bowled over by the sheer power of the vitality crashing across the proscenium.

The critics weren't the only ones who were impressed. Martin Feinstein recalled standing at the back of the theater with Hurok when the head usher came up to them and said, " 'Mr. Hurok, this is the biggest attraction you've ever brought here.' And Hurok said, 'Why do you say that?' And he answered, 'Because all the ushers are watching—they never do that.' " The ushers were joined by the audience in demanding seven curtain calls and screaming their appreciation. A crowd estimated at fifteen hundred then gathered around the stage door to catch a glimpse of (and perhaps even to touch) the exotic visitors as they left the theater. That night at the Met, a new era in Soviet-American relations (and therefore in international relations) began.

The festivities continued with one of Hurok's lavish trademark parties on the roof of the St. Regis Hotel. Mingling with the dancers were guests summoned from the city's musical and theatrical elite: Marian Anderson, Fredric March, Mary Martin, Robert Sarnoff, Lily Pons, Victoria de los Angeles, Leonard Warren, Agnes de Mille, Robert Merrill, Arthur Rubinstein, Leonard Bernstein (whose *West Side Story* was the new smash hit of the Broadway season and who would tour with his New York Philharmonic in Russia the following autumn), and André Kostelanetz.

For Moiseyev and his dancers, who until a few years earlier

could hardly have dreamed of traveling outside Russia, let alone conquering skyscrapered Manhattan, the debut (as he said) "was an amazing triumph. The very next day a line went two times around the theater, and all the tickets for the rest of our tour were bought up in a single day. We became celebrities. The newspapers were full of us and the photographers followed our every footstep. Even the Americans hadn't seen anything like it. If we discovered America, then the Americans also discovered the USSR."

Using the same technique that had worked for the "baby balle-rinas" thirty-five years earlier, Feinstein followed up the spectacular opening night by planting human interest stories about individual members of the company in major publications.

When Moiseyev arrived I told him I wanted a press con-ference. "I want three or four of your most beautiful girls, I want someone who's a mother, who's left a child behind in the Soviet Union, in the care of a grandma; I want a beautiful girl who has a boyfriend she's left behind; I want someone who's a newly-wed, and so on and so forth, and I'm going with this to the editors of the women's pages."

And Hurok heard that I had scheduled this press con-ference, and said to me, "What are you talking about? They're going to ask embarrassing questions, they're go-ing to ask political questions, and so on and so forth." And I said, "No, they're not, Mr. Hurok, this is a hu-man interest story: the Russians are creatures from outer space as far as the American public and press is con-cerned. This is an unprecedented story. It's all going to be wonderful."

And I finally convinced him to let me go ahead with the press conference that I had organized. And of course, you know, all the emotional and human reaction (the mother who missed her baby, the girl who missed her boyfriend) made for wonderful publicity, and humanized the whole thing. Those were the angles.

The critical and public response to the Moiseyev's perfor-mances at the Met created such demand for tickets that by the end of the three-week Met run, scalpers were reportedly getting up to $80 for a pair of $8 tickets. Happily bowing to the pressure, Hurok announced that the company would return to New York in June for four more performances at the end of its American tour. To accommodate the crowds, the radiant impresario had returned to the successful strategy of his Hippodrome days by booking the largest hall in town: Madison Square Garden. Ticket prices would be "popular," with a $6 top.

Needless to say, Hurok's coup in engineering the Moiseyev tour and its unprecedented commercial success made some of his competitors more than a little envious. At a meeting with representatives of the State Department in Washington on May 9 to discuss cultural exchange matters, Fred Schang *père* of Columbia Artists Management expressed indignation at Hurok's new ascendancy in the field. Boasting of Columbia's size and influence, he protested what he called Hurok's "monopoly" over Soviet attractions coming to the United States. According to a memorandum on the conversation, State Department representatives "pointed out to Mr. Schang (as they had done before) that the Department did not and would not wish to discriminate in any way between impresarios but that it appeared Hurok had been more energetic and active in lining up Soviet attractions." Schang was still smarting from losing out to Hurok over the contract for the Beryozka Ensemble's tour, now scheduled for the coming autumn.

Thoroughly enjoying one of the biggest and most important hits of his entire career, Hurok lavished grateful attention on Moiseyev and his dancers, who came to regard him with respect and affection. "He simply refused to have dinner without me," the choreographer said. "Even when I would try to excuse myself, he would insist that I come eat with him. And we visited the apartments of various millionaires, and went outside New York to villas. He showed me many things I would never have seen without him." Hurok continued to wine and dine Moiseyev at several stops on the road as the company proceeded cross-country, breaking attendance records as it progressed from Montreal to Toronto, Detroit, Chicago, Los Angeles, San Francisco, St. Louis, Cleveland, Philadelphia, Boston, and Washington.

Also along for the ride was Edward Ivanyan, representing the Soviet Ministry of Culture. He called it "the most popular and interesting tour I ever witnessed." One of the few problems Ivanyan faced was dealing with the dollar-hungry dancers' request that Hurok give them cash instead of providing them with the dinner that they rarely ate. "At first Hurok was angry with them and with me, but then he agreed, and gave everybody $2.50 a day instead of dinner. And everybody was happy."

Being in America and receiving such incredible public adulation was thrilling for the Moiseyev dancers, but their life on tour was physically exhausting and stressful. Before being allowed to travel to New York, each and every member of the touring company had been (in Ivanyan's words) "checked and rechecked by the KGB and vouched for by Party officials." The party members within the ensemble oversaw this process and were held responsible for the dancers' behavior abroad. Several KGB agents also accompanied the Moiseyev—and every other troupe over the coming years. Sometimes they were permanent members of the company, sometimes not. Over time, some KGB agents became "specialists" with certain companies and would always accompany them on foreign tours as bona fide company members. "It was even funny," said Ivanyan, "because they were immediately noticeable to both sides, and had meaningless titles like Personnel Director or Director of the Raising of the Curtains."

These agents knew "absolutely everything" that went on and kept the company members in a constant state of anxiety over what might happen to them if they misbehaved. The performers had a strict curfew at the hotel and were harshly interrogated if they arrived late or failed to appear at scheduled events. They were told it "was not advisable (which meant NO, by no means)" to visit private homes, and were warned to go out only in pairs—never alone. "When they weren't dancing, they were basically supposed to stay in the hotel," Ivanyan admitted many years later. After all, they were guests in a country that until just a few years earlier had been vilified by the Soviet leadership as the evil center of world capitalism. Although the Central Committee was willing to let the Moiseyev Ensemble travel and earn valuable foreign currency for the great Soviet government, it was not prepared to relax its stifling totalitarian control over the lives of Soviet citizens while they were abroad.

The Kremlin's paranoia about America was also fueled by the presence of persistent anti-Soviet demonstrators at many of the Moiseyev's performances. At a time when contacts between the United States and the USSR were so limited, it was inevitable that various groups opposed to Soviet ideology and policy would use the company's tour as an opportunity to air their grievances. Picketers in Chicago confronted the dancers at a luncheon given in their honor with placards bearing such slogans as "Hungary—Demand Free Elections," "It Will Cost Our Freedom to Flirt with the Red Death," "Cultural Exchange—New Russian Weapon for Cold War," and "Countless Slaves Are in Anguish and You Are Entertaining the Slave Drivers." Protesters with similar complaints also appeared in Los Angeles, San Francisco, Philadelphia, and New York (during the second run).

The most serious incident occurred in Boston. Just after the final curtain came down on opening night at the Boston Garden, a member of the former Polish underground made his way onto the stage and unfurled a banner reading "Now: Moiseyev Ballet, Next: Khrushchev Bullet." Another man jumped to the stage and started to rip the banner, leading to a scuffle and police intervention. Such acts of political protest became a standard fixture on American tours by Soviet attractions and would gradually intensify over the following years to a low-level terrorism that would threaten the whole cultural exchange program and eventually reach Hurok himself.

Another unpleasant political surprise awaited Hurok when the Moiseyev Ensemble returned to New York for its final engagement at Madison Square Garden. A historic television appearance on the *Ed Sullivan Show* was also scheduled. But on June 18, just two days before the Garden opening, the American guest conductor for the Moiseyev tour, Arthur Lief—who also happened to be Hurok's son-in-law—was summoned before a subcommittee of the dreaded HUAC in New York for questioning. A story about Lief's appearance ran on the front page of the *New York Times*. The incident showed that despite dramatic improvement in Soviet-American relations, the inquisition atmosphere of the McCarthy era still lingered and powerful enemies of détente were still operative in Washington. By summoning Lief, HUAC was surely trying to get at Hurok, for the first time raising public questions about his close association with Soviet officials and about the activities of Soviet performers on tour under his auspices.

In answering the committee's questions, Lief mentioned Hurok as his employer, but did not reveal, according to the *New York Times*, "if he had discussed with Mr. Hurok whether he, Mr. Lief, was a Communist, or whether any Communists had helped him get the job. He also declined to say whether any of the more than twenty Americans in the orchestra during its American tour were Communists or whether he had attended meetings with Russian members of the company on non-musical matters."

Lief had married Hurok's daughter, Ruth, in 1953, several years after her divorce from her first husband, Barry Hyams. Hyams had worked in the Hurok publicity department until the painful divorce. When Ruth introduced her new fiancé to her father at a party, she later recalled, Hurok was less than enthusiastic. "He said, 'So you say you're a conductor. How come I've never heard of you?' And he walked away. Later he said to me, 'Couldn't you have found a rich furrier? I had to support one of your husbands, and now I'm going to have to support another one.' " But Ruth (who had a son and a daughter from her marriage to Hyams) and Lief got married anyway. In a gesture of goodwill, Hurok also added Lief to his list of artists as a conductor and he began appearing frequently with the touring Soviet companies.

When Lief was called to testify before the HUAC subcommittee in June 1958, the committee was beginning another round of questioning of show business people, a favorite target in the past. Among those summoned in the same batch with Lief were Charles Dubin, a free-lance director for NBC television; Bernard Gersten, stage manager of the Shakespeare Festival in Stratford, Connecticut; and Joseph Papp, founder and producer of the New York Shakespeare Festival and a television stage manager for CBS. Like Lief, all refused to say (invoking the First and Fifth Amendments) whether they had ever been members of the Communist party. What followed demonstrated that HUAC's power, while considerably weakened, was far from dead. Both Dubin and Papp were fired by their respective ratings-conscious networks. Nor did Ed Sullivan lose any time in reacting. He announced that he was replacing Lief—who had been scheduled to conduct for the Moiseyev's up-coming appearance on his wholesome widely watched variety program—with the ensemble's regular conductor. "I don't want him in the theatre," Sullivan, his eye on the reaction of middle America, reportedly told Hurok.

Both Lief and Ruth were understandably upset about what had happened and were particularly anxious about Hurok's reaction. If suspicion were thrown on him, his entire business could be threatened and his thirty years of working toward bringing Russian attractions to America could be wasted.

Later in the same day of Lief's appearance before the commit-tee, Hurok called him at home and asked him to come into the of-fice for a chat. When they were alone, Lief (who said later that it was one of the few times he ever remembered seeing Hurok truly anxious) told Hurok: "I did what I wanted to—I didn't involve your name in any way." But Hurok wanted to know more. As a former socialist who claimed to have been deeply moved as a child by the speeches of Maxim Gorky and who began his American career by raising money for openly socialist candidates, he still couldn't resist asking his son-in-law the fateful question. "Are you now, or have you ever been, a member of the Communist party?" Lief replied, somewhat testily, "I'll tell you the same thing I told the committee: It's none of your business." (In fact, Lief, like numerous New York intellectuals, had briefly belonged to the party, but dropped out in 1943.) Hurok let the matter drop. No other member of the Hurok organization was ever called in for questioning by the HUAC orga-nization, which was rapidly losing its clout.

In his public reaction to Lief's interrogation and removal from the *Ed Sullivan Show*, Hurok behaved very cautiously. He was obvi-ously unwilling to jeopardize either his good relationship with the State Department or the financial prospects for Soviet attractions. Through a spokesman, Hurok made no comment on the rightness or wrongness of Lief's questioning, but tried to defuse the situation by declaring that he had never been scheduled to conduct on Ed Sullivan's show anyway. Sullivan vehemently disputed that version and added that he had dropped Lief on his own initiative, without any prodding either from CBS or his program's sponsors, Eastman Kodak and Mercury dealers. The only praise Lief received came from Moscow. There, *Izvestiia* hailed him for his courage and indignantly implied that the only reason he had been summoned was because of his association with the touring Moiseyev Ensemble.

Fortunately for Hurok, the Lief affair blew over rather quickly. If anything, it generated even greater support for the Moiseyev Ensemble. It certainly did nothing to dampen public enthusiasm either for the troupe's concluding performances at Madison Square Garden or for its appearance on the *Ed Sullivan Show* on June 29. Already a pro at pleasing the American audience, Moiseyev endeared himself to millions of TV viewers by ending the performance with a presentation of the down-home "Virginia Reel" that he and his company had learned during their stay in the United States.

By the time the ensemble finally left Idlewild for Moscow on July 1, it had achieved P. T. Barnum–scale success for its first American tour, having appeared before an estimated 450,000 spectators and reportedly grossing $1.6 million. As usual, however, there is considerable uncertainty about the actual financial results. According to Edward Ivanyan, the Soviet Ministry of Culture realized a profit of $1 million and Hurok cleared $800,000. Whatever the precise figures, they were clearly impressive enough to convince both Hurok and the party Central Committee that cultural exchange paid not only ideological, but financial dividends.

With the unquestioned success of the first Moiseyev tour behind him, Hurok was that much closer to fulfilling his obsessive ambition of bringing the Bolshoi Ballet to America. But one of the conditions officials at the party Central Committee and the Ministry of Culture had set down in their negotiations was that Hurok also bring another folk dance troupe, the all-female Beryozka Ensemble, before he could get the Bolshoi.

Founded in 1948 by Nadezhda Nadezhdina, who reportedly enjoyed favor in high political circles in Moscow, the Beryozka (Russian for "birch tree") specialized in dances and scenes based on Russian themes and sources and was something of a hybrid between a folklore ensemble and a character dance troupe. Hurok opened the troupe's first (and last) American tour at the Broadway Theatre in New York on November 4. It had nothing like the impact of the Moiseyev.

More significant was Hurok's presentation of the first American tour by a twenty-one-year-old Russian pianist, Vladimir Ashkenazy, that same autumn. A product of the prestigious Central Musical School and the Moscow Conservatory, Ashkenazy had already won prizes at several important international competitions. Hurok booked him for a ten-week tour that opened in Washington on October 14, 1958, with an appearance with the National Symphony.

But the experience was not an entirely happy one for Ashkenazy, who felt overwhelmed by the pressure and responsibility suddenly placed on him. Because of the usual inefficiency and red tape in the various Soviet offices charged with issuing permission and visas for foreign travel, Ashkenazy, in a scenario faced by nearly every performer invited to tour abroad, finally received his passport and tickets only one day before the Washington concert. As he wrote some years later, he flew to the United States in a state of near-terror not unlike that experienced by Shostakovich when he went to New York in 1949:

> I worried that if I did not have success, I'd be back at the beginning again and everyone would look down at me. Also, I did not know what to expect going to a country so very different from Russia. When I had gone to Western Europe, I hadn't felt too bad, but I was really intimidated about going to America with its skyscrapers and unashamed, dynamic commercialism without being able to look to anyone I knew or could trust for moral support. . . . Imagine having to face such an important debut in a totally new and alien world after all that flying and eight hours time change—and the very next day the rehearsal and concert in a huge hall, far larger than any I had been accustomed to in Russia.

Even after a highly successful Carnegie Hall recital, Ashkenazy continued to feel so anxious and homesick that he explained to the Soviet "companion" sent along by the Ministry of Culture that he wanted to go back to Moscow early. This created suspicions about the pianist's emotional stability that would come back to haunt him later, but in the end he remained in the United States for two months. Throughout his time there, Ashkenazy complained, Hurok saved money by lodging him in third-class hotels in which he had to share a room with his "companion," whose job it was to minimize his contacts with Americans. ("Hurok knew how to be generous at the most auspicious moments," explained Jasper Parrott, Ashkenazy's manager in later years, "but he also knew how to save money on those who were not yet accustomed to a better standard of life.") Thinking that he should be diplomatic, Ashkenazy lied to music critic Harold Schonberg in an interview that he was greatly enjoying both his tour and the United States. These comments were later used against him in Moscow as proof of his anti-Soviet and irresponsible behavior abroad.

The young Ashkenazy also received much less favorable financial terms than had Oistrakh and Gilels a few years earlier. A new Soviet agency, Gosconcert (Soviet State Concert Agency), had been created in late 1957 to oversee all tours by Soviet performers abroad and by foreign performers in the USSR. At first, Gosconcert's staff only carried out the orders it received from the Ministry of Culture, but as time went on, the agency became more independent. As part of the new arrangement, Gosconcert now paid Soviet performers on tour abroad only the equivalent (at the artificially low exchange rate) in foreign currency of the standard fee they received in rubles in the USSR. The fee paid by the foreign impresario for the artist to Gosconcert was not taken into account.

On Ashkenazy's first American tour, for example, he received $114 per concert, while Hurok was paying Gosconcert between $800 and $1,000 per concert. The pianist also had to pay for his own meals and personal expenses. According to Ashkenazy, Hurok also added a few concerts to the tour which he arranged and promoted himself, but he still paid the same low fee to the pianist. To Russian artists like Ashkenazy who were successful, however, Hurok also used to give an extra cash payment of several hundred dollars "under the table" (expressly forbidden by Gosconcert) at the end of the tour, as a sort of lesson in the rewards and incentives of the capitalist system.

Unlike some of his less sensitive Soviet colleagues, who regarded Hurok with unshakable awe and gratitude for his high-level connections and for his ability to pry them out of the USSR, Ashkenazy had more ambivalent feelings:

> I didn't exactly feel affection for him but certainly respect. He had a certain sort of intuition about artists, whom to push, whom to put on his posters under the banner "Hurok Presents," and he very seldom made a mistake about who was going to be a success. He tended to make these judgements himself rather than relying on others, as so many agents and impresarios do. Most of them never risk a decision until someone else has made it first.
>
> Even with this respect, however, the relationship remained essentially commercial right until the end. I never felt that we communicated on a personal level—indeed I don't believe that he felt there was any need to do so. For him, it was always a question of an impresario and an artist, even though one could be led to believe that there was something more when he would invite us to an exclusive restaurant or to his apartment after a concert. In fact, I always felt that this was simply part of the business relationship, just the frills on top and nothing more.

During his tour, Ashkenazy also had to field embarrassing questions about an explosive new cultural scandal in Moscow. Boris Pasternak had just been awarded the Nobel Prize for his novel *Doctor Zhivago*, published in Italy in 1957 but still unpublished and officially unrecognized within the USSR. Realizing he would not be allowed to return home if he traveled to Sweden to accept the award, Pasternak ultimately renounced it and stayed in Russia, where, for the less than two years that remained to him, he was subjected to intense surveillance and political pressure. His difficult fate profoundly disturbed American intellectuals and defenders of civil liberties and further heightened tensions in the always volatile arena of Soviet-American cultural relations.

Fortunately for Ashkenazy, he (like most Soviet citizens) had not had the chance to read *Doctor Zhivago* and so was able to avoid answering the journalists' persistent queries. Just before leaving New York, the pianist and his "companion" finally managed to buy a Russian copy of the novel. They read it hungrily in turn during their long journey home through Amsterdam, not daring to bring it through Soviet customs. But Ashkenazy paid for his curiosity. When the time came for his "companion" to write up his report on the pianist's tour, he upbraided Ashkenazy for having read the forbidden novel—without mentioning, of course, that he had read it, too. "I suppose he was entitled to do such things in order to know the enemy, whereas I was not!" concluded Ashkenazy sadly.

As he had in the past, Hurok maintained a stony silence about such matters as the Pasternak affair in order not to offend Soviet officials. Even so, he continued to encounter serious difficulties in making the final arrangements for the Bolshoi Ballet tour.

As of November 1958, Hurok believed he had permission from Moscow for the tour to go ahead in the spring. Travel arrangements were made and theaters booked. Then word came that the tour had been postponed to the fall, with several excuses offered: The company wanted to prepare a new work for America, it had been doing too much touring. In January, Soviet officials approved the tour after all, only to change their minds once again in February. Partly in order to resolve the matter once and for all, Hurok went to Moscow in mid-February. Meanwhile, Soviet Deputy Premier Anastos Mikoyan was in the United States, where he had happened to see the Beryozka perform in Chicago. Favorably impressed by its reception there, and still hearing glowing reports of the Moiseyev's historic tour, Mikoyan reportedly wired the Ministry of Culture (according to a State Department report) "insisting that the Bolshoi Theater group should be sent as originally planned in the spring." So before Hurok left Moscow on March 1, he was given final approval from the ministry for the Bolshoi to come to the United States in mid-April.

By this time, Hurok had become an important source of information for American officials, whose network of contacts in Moscow was still relatively limited. In a briefing session the day before he left Moscow, Hurok told staff members of the U.S. Embassy that he knew there was a faction of Soviet officials still strongly opposed to widening cultural exchange with the United States. The pro-exchange faction was led, he said, by G. A. Zhukov, Chairman of the State Committee for Cultural Relations Abroad (its Russian acronym was VOKS), who for the moment retained the upper hand and possessed considerable influence at the highest party levels.

Hurok also reported that despite his good standing with the Ministry of Culture, which even asked his advice about which attractions would do best with the American audience, he still encountered many obstacles in dealing with lower-level bureaucrats. "Having remained in Moscow for over two weeks, he still had not completed his business and therefore he complained to Minister Mikhailov about the unnecessary red tape constantly being placed in his path by subordinates in the Ministry," Richard H. Davis of the American Embassy wrote home to the State Department. "Mikhailov had immediately summoned those concerned and in front of Mr. Hurok had ordered them to cooperate fully and to get the work done immediately. This had worked wonders."

While in Moscow, Hurok was treated to a lunch in his honor by Mikhailov and the grateful Moiseyev Ensemble. But Moiseyev's friendship with Hurok and his enthusiasm about America had raised some eyebrows among Soviet hard-liners. In a private conversation with American Embassy officials, Hurok revealed that Moiseyev had been called onto the carpet for making excessively favorable public comments about his impressions of America. Nonetheless, the choreographer "had stood his ground and had refused to dilute his remarks."

On this and on earlier trips to Moscow, Hurok had also been spending more and more time at the Bolshoi, getting to know its current ballet master (Leonid Lavrovsky, in the position since 1944), repertoire, and dancers. By this time, the Bolshoi had already taken several tours abroad, including its famous 1956 London debut which introduced Prokofiev's ballet *Romeo and Juliet* to the West. First produced at Leningrad's Kirov Ballet in 1940 with choreography by Lavrovsky and starring Galina Ulanova as Juliet, *Romeo* had come to the Bolshoi with Lavrovsky and Ulanova in the early 1940s. Already recognized as the queen of the Soviet prima ballerinas, Ulanova achieved her greatest success and renown as Juliet, despite initial disagreements with Prokofiev over the alleged "undance-ability" of the score.

Ulanova first met Hurok on one of his visits to Moscow in late 1958 or early 1959. He had already seen her perform, both at home and in London. Their first meeting in person was far from auspicious, however, since the ballerina, then forty-nine years old, was suffering from a toothache. When she appeared as instructed in the director's box to meet the legendary impresario who was supposed to be bringing the company to America, she joked later:

> I was very pale, and didn't have on any makeup or anything, with my hair in braids, and dressed very informally. Lavrovsky and a few others were there, and we had tea, and Hurok was staring at me very fixedly. Remember we lived differently then—we were more modest people, we would never have thought of asking if we could go abroad. We did as we were told. That was even more true for me, because I had come to Moscow from Leningrad. And so we had tea and Lavrovsky told Hurok about me and the roles I danced. And he looked at me rather gloomily, with mistrust.

Ulanova's age notwithstanding, Hurok decided to bring her to the United States as a headlining star.

For the repertoire for the Bolshoi's first American tour, Hurok chose several of Ulanova's favorite vehicles. They included Prokofiev's *Romeo and Juliet* and *The Stone Flower* (neither seen before in the United States), as well as *Giselle* and *Swan Lake*. The enormous success of the Sadler's Wells tours over the last decade had obviously convinced him that American audiences were no longer afraid of evening-long story ballets.

Interest in the upcoming Bolshoi Ballet tour had been building in the United States for months, especially after the sensation created by the Moiseyev. As early as January, Martin Feinstein told a New York columnist that the office had been "swamped with blank checks by ballet lovers—to fill in after we announced the scale of prices." When it was officially announced that the Bolshoi would open at the Met with *Romeo and Juliet* featuring Ulanova, the demand for tickets reached a feverish pitch. "People not only want to see it, but they will commit arson, perjury, mayhem and murder to do so," wrote John Martin in an advance piece in the *New York Times.* Hurok's employees reported receiving phone calls at home from desperate ticket seekers. Three telephone operators quit their jobs, unable to deal with the stress. One woman who worked in the Hurok office was mobbed in a public library when she made the mistake of mentioning her connections. Scalpers were getting up to $150 a ticket. The Justice Department even launched an investigation into several organizations which had been reselling tickets to their members without obtaining affidavits certifying charitable status.

As usual, Hurok gave preference to the thirty-eight thousand individuals and charitable organizations on his special mailing list, those who had been buying seats for his attractions regularly for years. Even at relatively high prices (from $2 to $15 for evenings and $2 to $10.50 for matinees), forty thousand orders were received even before the Met engagement began. This led Hurok to add five more performances in Madison Square Garden. In the end, more than a hundred thousand tickets were sold—and there were demands for nine hundred thousand more!

Such a response proved him more than right to have invested $100,000 of his own money and to have committed $350,000 in expenses in order to get the Bolshoi across the Atlantic. In most of the publicity materials for the Bolshoi engagement, Hurok shared billing as sponsor with the American National Theatre and Academy (ANTA), a service organization that had been involved with Soviet-American cultural exchange in its early stages. But Hurok assumed all of the financial risk, and both ANTA and its director, Robert Dowling, dropped out of the picture soon afterward.

When the dancers arrived, Hurok treated them with respect and affection. Ulanova was an unpretentious woman who saw herself in the tradition of the nineteenth-century peasant-ballerinas, so she was stunned when the impresario showed her and her husband (Vadim Rindin, the Bolshoi's principal designer) around their luxurious three-room suite in a midtown hotel. Its refrigerator was stocked with caviar, champagne "and other necessaries of a ballerina's life." Since Hurok had learned that Ulanova liked coffee, a prepared percolator stood on the table. There were flowers everywhere, and, the pièce de résistance, a ballet barre with full-length mirrors. "So, my dear, you can practice here if you wish," he is reported to have told her with chic understatement. It was such attention to details and grandeur that made Hurok an impresario rather than a manager. He was an important man because he worried about unimportant things.

The Bolshoi's gala opening on April 6, 1959, was the greatest night of Hurok's career, the fruition of more than thirty years of dreaming, scheming, and persistence. At last the rough-hewn Jewish boy from Pogar had succeeded in importing to the New World what many considered to be the greatest ballet company on the planet, and one of the few surviving links to the glorious tradition of Russian tsarist culture.

Although critics were far from unanimous in their verdict on *Romeo and Juliet*, the sense that this was something everyone had to see had already been established. And the cognoscenti agreed that the company's style was nothing less than a revelation, as critic Anna Kisselgoff remembered thirty-three years later: "Here was dramatic realism made marvelously bold and conveyed through a choreographic style totally different from that seen in the West." The Bolshoi's *Romeo and Juliet* also did a great deal to popularize Prokofiev's ballets (especially *Cinderella*) in the United States, where they soon entered the repertoire of virtually every major company. Besides *Romeo*, Adam's *Giselle* proved to be the most popular item in the Bolshoi repertoire.

While some critics found the repertoire too conservative, a sense of discovery was shared by all. In *Saturday Review*, Irving Kolodin called the company nothing less than "the greatest collection of dancers to appear before the New York public during the modern era (dating from the first season of the Ballet Russe de Monte Carlo in 1933)." Perhaps the biggest surprise for many was the central role played by the male dancers, who turned out to be virile, athletic, swashbuckling types very far from the limp-wristed stereotypes many Americans still had about men in tights and ballet slippers. Something else American audiences had never seen were the spectacularly high Soviet lifts in partnering.

In New York and elsewhere on the tour, members of the

Bolshoi company worked in master classes with eager American dancers, sharing their technique and aesthetic. Although under close surveillance by their ubiquitous KGB "companions," they also socialized at the many official parties and receptions given by Hurok and others. The opening night bash was held on the St. Regis roof and featured a menu of champagne, piroshki, caviar, beef Stroganoff, and chicken Hurok (a concoction of chicken with white sauce served over rice and noodles), followed by dancing to an eleven-piece orchestra.

Such largesse, motivated by Hurok's need to justify himself and play the *grand seigneur,* overwhelmed the Russian dancers, who had never witnessed such abundance and wealth. "America was for us simply another planet," said Ulanova.

> We knew so little about the outside world, and we were just amazed by the scale of the country. All those huge stores five and six floors high, with all these clothes on sale, and entire apartments on display—we just didn't have anything like that. Hurok was always sure to see that we had enough to eat. He would give us a free noon meal, with lots of choices, because he knew that the young dancers would go without food because they wanted to spend their small dollar allowances on other things. And then they would end up weak from not eating. Hurok understood that, and made sure that the dancers stayed well-fed and healthy, so that they could dance at the highest possible level, and with pleasure. He would create the best possible conditions, and expect the best from his performers in return.

One day, after it was clear that the tour was an unqualified success, Hurok took Ulanova aside for a private talk. "I have to tell you frankly that when I first met you at the Bolshoi," he said, "I thought to myself, 'My God, on whom have I staked my fortunes?' Because after all you were hardly presentable—and so old! But you know, I am experienced person and I love to take risks—and it seems that this time I was right on target." For Ulanova, the 1959 American tour was a swan song. She retired soon after and would never dance with the Bolshoi in the United States again. But the company also brought an exciting young ballerina, Maya Plisetskaya, whose very different creative personality would continue to grow in coming years. Hurok doted on both these stars, just as he had doted on Pavlova and Markova and Fonteyn.

Throughout the Bolshoi's tour, public interest in the company and its dancers ran sky-high. In most cities, policemen had to be called out to hold back the throngs of those eager to see and touch and feel real Russians. Anti-Soviet demonstrations were also frequent, but the dancers tried not to pay attention.

In order to break even on the Bolshoi tour, Hurok had to take in at least $170,000 weekly. (This break-even amount is called the "nut" in show business parlance.) His contract with the Ministry of Culture called for a guarantee to the Bolshoi of $50,000 a week (twice as much as the Moiseyev received), plus hotels and round-trip transportation between New York and London. In addition, the company got $330,000 for the filming of two performances. According to Edward Ivanyan, the Bolshoi returned to Moscow with a healthy profit of between $500,000 and $600,000. Because of his heavy expenses, Hurok did not make nearly as much profit himself on the Bolshoi as on the Moiseyev. He told Ivanyan he did little better than to break even, although Martin Feinstein claimed that the tour did produce a small return for Hurok Artists.

But money had never been Hurok's primary motivation in anything he did. Now seventy-one years old and more than comfortable financially (his attractions were estimated to have grossed over $5 million in the last few years), he saw the successful completion of the Bolshoi's first American tour as the capstone of his creative career. To him it was no less important than it would be for a ballerina to finally dance the leading role in *Giselle*, for a soprano to sing her first *Traviata*, or for a violinist to give a solo recital at Carnegie Hall. With the importation of the Moiseyev Ensemble and the Bolshoi Ballet, an era came to an end both in Hurok's life and in the young history of Soviet-American cultural relations. It would be a tough act to follow.

CHAPTER TWENTY

At the Top

"If you were with Hurok, you had to be important."
—*Galina Vishnevskaya*

EXTRACTING THE MOISEYEV ENSEMBLE and the Bolshoi Ballet from the rusty iron jaws of the Soviet bureaucracy and presenting them in America at a large profit was a feat that would have taken every last ounce of stamina, patience, and sanity from a lesser man. But nothing about Sol Hurok was lesser. Not only had he accomplished what ranked as one of the great entertainment coups of the century while retaining his legendary humor, grace, robust health, and babyish complexion, but as one of the very few independents left in a business now dominated by corporate giants, he had also pulled it off on his own, without a large support staff, and while continuing to discover and present other new dancers, singers, and instrumentalists. Still keeping his own counsel and risking his own money, he rarely turned to backers or to philanthropists. In an era when television and a growing audience for mass culture were making it increasingly difficult for the presenters of "serious" culture to turn a profit, he still ran his operation like a business—a family business, but a business nonetheless. With his instinct for publicity and marketing, he surely could have made much more money in another arena, but he continued in his seventies to take a perverse pleasure in braving the odds and indulging his passion for art, artists, and the crazy world of show people.

"When my competitors hear about the small margin of profit on which I operate," he once boasted to dance critic Anatole Chujoy, "they think that there is something wrong with me. And from a strictly business aspect they are right. I enjoy what I am doing, which is not businesslike."

Hurok's joy for what he was doing helps to explain his seemingly inexhaustible store of energy. Those who worked for "the boss" found it hard to keep up with him. They were unceremoniously awakened at all hours by his calls to check on last night's receipts, complain about next week's poor advance sale, plan publicity strategy, or discuss next year's bookings. "I tell you, he had more pep than all of us put together," remembered Betty Ferrell, who worked out of his Los Angeles office as an advance representative. "A woman would envy his skin—there wasn't a wrinkle on his face. And he had a marvelous twinkle in his eye. He was always very bright and very up to date on every subject you'd care to bring up. Politics. Finances. He knew everything. And he had a marvelous ability to communicate with people much younger than he. He could sit and talk, and he understood, and he'd argue with you. He loved to argue."

And—unlike his more sedentary competitors—he loved to search for new talent. Even during the years when he was practically commuting to Moscow negotiating contracts that required a surgeon's strength and delicacy, Hurok continued to travel all over the world scouting to expand his stable of non-Soviet performers. He was also building the reputations of his veterans. During the ten years between 1950 and 1960, as New York and the United States enjoyed an unprecedented economic and cultural boom, he engineered an amazing series of artistic and commercial successes and reached the artistic and financial peak of his long career. A list of all his achievements during that period would fill a small volume, so a few will have to suffice here.

Out of bookish Spanish guitarist Andrés Segovia, who had come to Hurok from his competitor Coppicus in 1943, he fashioned an unlikely star whose rising popularity disproved the long-held assumption that guitarists could never be taken seriously as musicians or make money on the concert circuit. For years, Hurok regularly "papered"—that is, provided free tickets for—Town Hall to fill the many empty seats for Segovia's concerts, an investment that finally paid off handsomely.

He launched a brilliant career for young soprano Roberta Peters (born Roberta Petermann and recommended to him by Jan Peerce), turning her into America's homegrown (and Jewish!) coloratura sweetheart after her dramatic last-minute debut at the Met in 1950 as Zerlina in Mozart's *Don Giovanni.*

In 1954, he sponsored and hyped a film version of *Aida* in which nineteen-year-old Sophia Loren (described in the publicity brochure as "five feet, eight inches tall, 38 bust, 24 waist, 36 hips") and the less curvacious but more vocally endowed Renata Tebaldi shared acting and singing duties.

At the Met in 1955, he helped to bring Marian Anderson's already long career to a fittingly historic climax as he presided over her debut in the role of Ulrica in Verdi's *Un Ballo in Maschera.* It was the first time a black singer had ever performed in the house.

Overcoming his distaste for television, he became the producer-consultant to NBC on several musical programs, including *Music for the Millions* and *Producer's Showcase*, both of which featured performances by his leading artists.

In theater, he renewed his activity by importing Britain's Old Vic (Hurok pronounced it "Old Wick") Company for the first time since 1946 and the 275-year-old Comédie Française from Paris for the first time ever.

But he accomplished the most with what was his first and best love: dance. Broadening his international range, he presented in rapid succession the Azuma Kabuki Dancers and Musicians from Japan, the homegrown Agnes de Mille Dance Theater (despite ongoing mutual hostility between him and its prickly leader), the Katharine Dunham Company, the Roland Petit Ballet, the Antonio Ballet Espagnol, the Polish State Folk Ballet, the Roberto Iglesias Company, the Bayanihan Philippine Dance Company, and the Georgian State Dance Company (from the Soviet republic of Georgia). He also brought the Sadler's Wells Ballet (which became the Royal Ballet in 1956) to tour America every other season, with consistently good results.

Most surprisingly, he even renewed his on-again-off-again relationship with Ballet Theatre, which took the more nationalistic name American Ballet Theatre (ABT) in 1957. For several seasons beginning in 1955, he became the company's exclusive manager—but with less artistic control than he had enjoyed in the 1940s. The resumption of Hurok's alliance with Lucia Chase was short-lived, however. The overwhelming success of his Soviet attractions eventually led him to lose interest in the chronically indebted and still shaky ABT. Both financially and organizationally, it was actually easier for Hurok to deal with the monopolistic Gosconcert. There were no lawyers and no pretensions to democracy.

No other single figure did more than Hurok to expose American audiences to the dynamic variety of the world's dance traditions. In the process he helped to nurture a public receptive to the multicultural and multiethnic styles which would become such an important part of the increasingly pluralistic and robust American contemporary dance scene. The current generation of American choreographers owes Hurok a huge debt for creating their audience.

Nor, even as an increasingly elderly and supposedly respectable gentleman, was Hurok losing his taste for discovering quirky Barnum-like attractions bound to create sensational "firsts." As Martin Feinstein once remarked, one of the most important secrets of Hurok's success was his "uncanny ability to see not only what was *there,* but what it could *become.*" He was able to dream—realistically. He could see a palace where others could only see a pile of bricks and stones.

This was surely what Hurok was doing when he decided to import the Massed Pipers and Regimental Band of the Scots Guards from Great Britain in 1955. His colleagues in the business dismissed the idea of importing a horde of men in kilts playing on squealing bagpipes as "Hurok's folly" and predicted disaster. The management of Madison Square was so apprehensive that it refused to rent the arena on a percentage basis, instead demanding a minimum of $7,500. This drove Hurok's cost per performance up to nearly $25,000. But the ten-week tour of forty-five American and Canadian cities got off to a roaring start in Washington, D.C. There, the Scots Guards played to sold-out audiences at Uline Arena and drummed up publicity by parading in front of the White House, performing their renowned Beating Retreat ceremony on the Ellipse and laying a wreath at the Tomb of the Unknown Soldier. The critics for *Musical America* praised the band's "ingrained nobility and royal swagger."

What Hurok remembered, no doubt, in bringing the Scots Guards to America was a lesson he had learned many years before with Music for the Masses at the Hippodrome: the loyalty of ethnic communities for their native culture. As Agnes de Mille put it, Americans of Scottish and English heritage living in the United States "just started crying as soon as they saw a kilt. It didn't even matter what the performers did." By the time the Scots Guards got to New York, demand for tickets was so great that Hurok added three performances at Madison Square Garden. Later, he brought the Black Watch from Scotland with similarly impressive results.

All these triumphs—along with the epoch-making Moiseyev and Bolshoi tours—had turned Hurok into a living legend. He played this role to the hilt with his theatrical cape, cane, top hat, and fractured Old Country English. Awards now poured in to the onetime trolley conductor from Pogar.

In 1955, the editorial page of the *New York Times* praised him as "a goodwill ambassador of the first order as well as a shrewd judge of American taste" for bringing the Comédie Française, the Antonio Ballet Espagnol, the Scots Guards and the Japanese Kabuki dancers in a single extravagant season.

In 1956, the National Urban League awarded Hurok and Marian Anderson silver medallions for "notable contributions to the cause of better human relations and understanding."

In 1958, he received the Capezio Award for "contributing to public awareness of the progress of dance in the United States." Previous winners had included Lincoln Kirstein, dancer-choreographer Ted Shawn, and Alexandra Danilova. In his acceptance speech, Hurok talked about an issue that he had been raising frequently over the recent years, as the economics of presenting serious culture became more perilous: the need for governmental subsidy for the arts. Despite his own success as a commercial impresario, Hurok's passion for dance and music (and his familiarity with the heavily subsidized European scene) led him to see that such aid was essential if culture was to continue to develop in the United States.

He also announced that he was donating his $1,000 prize to the Dance Department of the New York High School for the Performing Arts, birthplace of so many important artists.

But even as he became a senior statesman for culture, the granddaddy of impresarios and the doyen of dance, Hurok remained a tough businessman who demanded complete loyalty from his subordinates and often behaved ruthlessly toward those who crossed him. Every morning he would make the rounds of the office. His first words were not "Good morning," but a gruff "Have you signed any contracts?" At weekly staff meetings, he often subjected various staff members to cruel ridicule and mockery. One of his favorite targets was his stepson George Perper, an educated man and brilliant linguist whose soft-spoken demeanor was, however, no match for Hurok's streetwise aggressiveness. Annoyed with something Lillian Libman—who worked in the public relations department and was no pushover herself—said one day, Hurok intentionally knocked a full cup of coffee out of her hand, spilling it all over her fresh new suit, crudely asserting his absolute power.

Notoriously stingy with his employees (but never with his artists), Hurok also resisted giving raises even under the threat of resignation. To Ralph Parker, an old Russian hand and foreign correspondent who represented Hurok's interests in Moscow, Hurok paid the minuscule sum of $150 monthly. And despite his supposedly socialist principles, he steadfastly refused to provide his employees with a pension plan.

"He may have been a left-wing Democrat," cracked Perper, "but he was an autocrat."

At the same time, Hurok liked to cultivate a superficially familial relationship with his subordinates, keeping them off-balance so they wouldn't know whether to expect fatherly strokes or blows from the boss. Such uncertainty was a strong motivating factor. Everyone in the office also knew that there were several spies in their midst who kept "Papa Hurok" informed on internal affairs. Perhaps the most obvious informant was Simon Semenoff, a former dancer who officially consulted with Hurok on repertoire and casting. He was also one of the very few people from the New York office who traveled with Hurok on his negotiating trips to Russia. According to Gosconcert officials, Semenoff spent most of his time there drinking and carousing with dancers from the Bolshoi. Indeed, it was a source of considerable irritation to Perper, Martin Feinstein, and Walter Prude that Hurok insisted on keeping his Moscow dealings secret from them, supposedly his senior associates.

Hurok was also tough in his dealings with artists represented by other managers. If one of his own artists left for a better deal or was terminated for any reason by S. Hurok Attractions, then, in Agnes de Mille's words, "for Hurok he was dead." According to Semenoff, for example, Hurok used to "hate" Van Cliburn when he was represented by Columbia Artists. When Cliburn turned up in tails at a party Hurok gave for one of the Soviet ensembles soon after winning the Tchaikovsky Competition, Hurok even ordered Semenoff to "get rid of the bum." But as soon as Cliburn joined the Hurok agency in November 1959, having been pursued for months with champagne and caviar, the pianist suddenly became "the best boy in the world."

Once they were his, Hurok defended his artists with a ferocious loyalty. Critic Irving Kolodin served in the 1950s as a consultant to a television broadcast that was to feature several Hurok artists. When Kolodin suggested that Marian Anderson, who had already appeared on an earlier broadcast and whose voice was by then in rapid decline, should be dropped from the program to make room for other performers, "Hurok's face darkened, and he suddenly slammed shut a folder before him. 'Without Marian Anderson there is no program. Count me out.' There was a program, of course, with Miss Anderson."

To celebrate the New Year 1960, Hurok threw a lavish party at the Waldorf-Astoria for the entire Moscow State Symphony Orchestra, which had just arrived for its first American tour, led by conductors Kiril Kondrashin and Konstantin Ivanov. Also in the entourage were violinist Valery Klimov, pianist Emil Gilels, and Galina Vishnevskaya, the temperamental wife of Hurok's artist Mstislav Rostropovich and a leading soprano at the Bolshoi Opera. She was making her American debut.

Hurok's generosity and kindness at the Waldorf, Vishnevskaya wrote some years later, clashed grotesquely with the abrupt and insulting treatment she and her colleagues received during a "brain-washing session" at the Soviet Consulate in New York the next day. "They gave us a lecture on the accursed capitalists, warning us that provocations would be luring at every corner, and they instructed the orchestra members to walk only in groups of four and not to pay any attention to what was in the store windows. That was all show-off, they said. Ordinary Americans couldn't afford those things, and in general, people here were dying of hunger."

Although Hurok knew that the Soviet artists he brought to America were subjected to such humiliation at the hands of the Communist bureaucrats, he feigned ignorance. Nor did he ever discuss his feelings about the Soviet regime. Instead, he did what he could to pamper the performers while they were under his care, for which they were eternally grateful. Even though they were supposed to feed themselves on the small per diem they received while on tour (the musicians in the Moscow Symphony received $13 a day), Hurok often helped them out by secretly providing meals. That way, they could use their dollars to buy presents to bring home. If Gosconcert were to find out about his generosity, however, it would lower the artists' allowances. To get around such pettiness, Hurok told Vishnevskaya to sign restaurant checks in his name—but warned her "not to breathe a word about it in Moscow," for otherwise the Ministry of Culture would deduct it from her pay.

"With Hurok you felt protected," she said. "If he undertook to work with an artist, you could be sure that everything possible would be done for you—sometimes the impossible. He was a tourist attraction, and wherever you appeared with him in New York—be it a restaurant, an elegant store, or a splendid hotel lobby—you would be noticed and indulged, not because you had come in with a rich and famous man, but because if you were with Hurok, you had to be important."

Not long after the successful Moscow State Symphony tour, however, Soviet-American relations, which had seemed to reach an unprecedented level of warmth in late 1959 when Nikita Khrushchev became the first Soviet leader to visit the United States, took a turn for the worse. On May 1, 1960, just two weeks before a scheduled summit meeting between Eisenhower and Khrushchev in Paris, an American U-2 spy plane piloted by Gary Powers was shot down over Sverdlovsk. The incident turned the Paris summit into an opportunity for Khrushchev to denounce American aggression. It also sent shock waves throughout the world and abruptly heightened tensions between Moscow and Washington after a relatively long period of gradual improvement.

Almost immediately, Hurok flew to Washington to talk with State Department officials about the implications for his business. The 1958 Cultural Exchange Agreement had been renewed for another two-year period in 1959, but he was concerned that Soviet indignation could lead to its cancellation. By now, according to an internal State Department report, Hurok and his staff had become so confident (even arrogant) that they believed they carried "the full brunt of the cultural exchanges with the USSR, and render an immense service to this country despite the lack of understanding and cooperation from the Department of State, whom they regard as obsessed with closed areas and incapable of grasping the larger issues involved. In fact, they are convinced that it is they who do the work of the Department of State!"

Having received assurances that the American side had every intention of proceeding with cultural exchange, Hurok left as planned for Moscow on May 25, 1960, with his new darling, Van Cliburn. The pianist was booked for an extensive Soviet tour (Moscow, Kiev, Leningrad, Tbilisi, Yerevan, and Baku). Two other Hurok artists, Isaac Stern and Roberta Peters, were also at the time on tour in the USSR.

In Moscow, Hurok and Stern both had separate meetings with the freshly appointed Minister of Culture, Ekaterina Furtseva, to discuss the future. A well-connected bureaucrat from a humble background who had risen through the ranks to sit on the Presidium of the Party Central Committee, Furtseva had no previous experience in the area of culture. Surprisingly enough, she would become the strongest Minister of Culture in years and an enthusiastic advocate of the performing arts.

At her meeting with Stern, Furtseva spouted the standard party line in blaming the United States for raising international tensions, but stated uncategorically her desire to continue and expand cultural exchanges. Indeed, for the next few years both the American and Soviet governments would go to great lengths to protect cultural exchange even as they engaged in increasingly dangerous and strident ideological warfare. It was a way to maintain contact. The fact that Stern, Peters, and Cliburn were all performing to huge and enthusiastic crowds throughout the USSR surely helped Hurok's position with Furtseva. According to Hurok, Cliburn was even mobbed by 5,000 admirers when he arrived at the Moscow airport—although a State Department report put the crowd size at a more modest 150.

Hurok's conversations with Furtseva obviously went well. When he returned to New York, he was carrying a contract for another Soviet star he had been trying to get for years: pianist Sviatoslav Richter. Hurok had been attending his recitals in Moscow for several seasons and had made a pleasant impression both on the notoriously reclusive pianist and on his wife, Nina Dorliak, a singer. Charmed by his enthusiasm and goodwill, they paid little attention to his obvious lack of musical sophistication and encouraged him in his attempts to arrange an American tour for Richter. Officials at the Ministry of Culture had been less responsive. For years, they had been answering Hurok's repeated requests to allow Richter to go to the United States with evasive diplomatic excuses like "He's sick." The pianist's staunch defense of his friends Prokofiev and Shostakovich when they were under attack in the late 1940s for having written "anti-Soviet" music had won him some powerful enemies among the cultural bureaucrats. Indeed, Richter was already forty-five years old when he was finally allowed to travel to the West for the first time in May 1960, to Finland.

Soon after his tour to Finland, Richter was also granted permission to play in America in the fall of 1960. Hurok spared no expense or energy in getting him and his wife there. (The Moscow Conservatory reluctantly allowed Dorliak to go only after Richter angrily insisted.) Hurok booked a cabin specially equipped with a piano on the *Queen Mary* (Richter hated flying), met them at the dock in New York, and found a doctor to minister to his artist's complaints of dizziness. Throughout the tour of the United States, Hurok provided anything the virtuoso requested and never tried to interfere with his choice of repertoire. On Richter and Dorliak, big brash America did not make an entirely positive impression ("We preferred Europe"), but for Hurok they had only the warmest feelings.

In subsequent years, he was a frequent guest at their Moscow apartment for feasts of *bliny,* Russian crepes traditionally served at the beginning of Lent.

When Richter (the "moody pianist from the Soviet," the *New York Times* called him) arrived in America in October 1960, one of the most exciting and hotly contested presidential campaigns in U.S. history was drawing to a photo finish. Its outcome opened a new era in American politics and cultural life and would have implications for Hurok's business as well. As a lifelong supporter of the Democratic party (his favorite president was FDR), he was certainly happy when John Kennedy defeated Richard Nixon, if only by a narrow margin of only 113,000 votes. Political sentiments aside, Hurok must have felt particular affinity for this young Irish Catholic, the son of immigrants, who had battled religious and ethnic prejudice to make it to the highest elected office in the land.

Kennedy's intellect, wit, and style soon established a fresh, more urbane atmosphere in Washington, one much more to Hurok's taste than the stiff Protestant ethic of the Eisenhower administration. In his speeches and policies, Kennedy repeatedly asserted the importance of the arts as an essential element of a civilized society ("art establishes the basic human truths which must serve as the touchstone of our judgment"), hobnobbed with leading cultural figures, and bestowed the new Presidential Medal of Freedom on musicians (including Marian Anderson), writers, and intellectuals. The new president's wife also took a more sincere and active interest in cultural and artistic affairs than any first lady since Eleanor Roosevelt. Over the next few years, the unfailingly chic and well-dressed Jacqueline would often show up at Hurok opening nights in New York and Washington. She also invited his artists to the White House. Kennedy's brothers, particularly Robert, his attorney general, were also enthusiastic patrons of the arts.

These were glamorous years in America, the perfect environment for Hurok to sell his patented populist elegance. He became the provider of court entertainment for the doomed kingdom of Camelot.

In his discussions with Furtseva in Moscow, Hurok had told her he believed the focus of Soviet-American cultural exchange should shift from large ensembles to individual soloists. Even so, it was the big troupes that continued to attract the most attention. The Moiseyev Ensemble returned for a second visit to the United States in the spring of 1961, bringing a new work of questionable taste called *Back to the Monkeys* that parodied the American teenage rock 'n' roll dance craze. Negotiations were also nearing completion for the first American tour by Leningrad's Kirov Ballet in the fall of 1961. Between 1958 and 1961, 831 Soviet artists toured in the United States.

Then, suddenly, the relatively smooth course of cultural exchanged was upset by what both sides had feared since its inauguration in 1956: a defection by a Soviet artist.

His name was Rudolf Nureyev. On June 17, 1961, this twenty-three-year-old soloist with the Kirov Ballet requested political asylum after jumping into the arms of French customs officials at Le Bourget Airport in Paris just as the company was preparing to fly to London for the next stop on a European tour. Already acclaimed as the greatest Russian male dancer since Nijinsky, Nureyev had been incurring the wrath of Soviet officials for his stubbornly individualistic behavior from his earliest days within the carefully supervised Kirov collective. In Paris he had defiantly mixed with French friends and explored the city on his own, angering the accompanying Soviet police agents. They retaliated by informing him that he was unexpectedly returning to Moscow for a special performance at the Kremlin instead of traveling on to London with his colleagues. Aware of what such "special" invitations really meant, Nureyev knew that if he went back to Russia now, he would probably never be allowed to travel abroad again. He would be doomed to obscurity and even persecution. So he decided to "fly," and took his brave leap to freedom.

Nureyev's action would inspire many other Soviet artists in the coming years, others who, like him, felt stifled by the creative limitations and psychological slavery of producing art for a totalitarian state. Coming only a few years after the international furor over the persecution of author Boris Pasternak, the defection further undermined Western credibility in the Soviet system and polarized the atmosphere surrounding Soviet performers.

Luckily for Hurok, the Kirov was not under his management

when Nureyev defected. Even so, the incident, widely publicized all over the world, badly embarrassed the Soviet government and made all arrangements for tours by Soviet performers in *kapstrany* ("capitalist countries") significantly more complicated. The Ministry of Culture and Gosconcert now became more obsessed than ever with security issues. Surveillance by the KGB on tours intensified, and impresarios like Hurok became even more anxious both about possible defections and anti-Soviet provocation from protesters. "I know what will happen," Hurok told one reporter. "Someone gets a bad ice cream here and Khrushchev calls up Hurok."

Hurok's relationship with Nureyev was destined to be a complicated one. Both had struggled to fame after escaping humble beginnings in the provinces of the vast Russian (later Soviet) Empire. Oddly enough, Nureyev, an ethnic Tartar, had seen his first ballet in Ufa, the capital of Bashkiria, beyond the Urals. It was in Ufa, too, that Chaliapin had made his first appearance.

Nureyev had learned of Hurok when still a student at the Vaganova School in Leningrad. The legendary impresario "was a hero to us" because of all he had done to introduce Russian ballet and dancers to the West. Of particular interest to Nureyev was Hurok's relationship with Pavlova, another Petersburg dancer, and the implication that they had been romantically involved. Hurok and Nureyev were linked by deep psychological and historical bonds that helped them to recognize and understand each other instantly.

But after his defection, Nureyev presented Hurok with a terrible dilemma. More than conscious of Nureyev's huge talent and drawing power, Hurok ran the risk of upsetting his carefully cultivated relationship with the Soviet Ministry of Culture if he added Nureyev to his list of artists. (Back in the USSR, Nureyev had become a nonperson, his name instantly erased from Soviet ballet history.) The situation became even more complicated after Margot Fonteyn, one of Hurok's favorite ballerinas and a mainstay of the Royal Ballet's American tours, took Nureyev under her wing. She would help to arrange his sensational performance in the Royal Academy of Dancing Gala in London in November 1961. As the leading presenter of ballet in the world, Hurok could hardly ignore a dancer whom many now considered to be among the all-time best. But neither could he afford to alienate the Kremlin's easily offended sensibilities.

Nureyev's defection cast a long shadow over the Kirov's first American tour, which came just two months later. It began on September 11, 1961, at the Met, exactly one month after the construction of the Berlin Wall fixed the Iron Curtain more firmly in place. Hurok had met several times in Moscow and Leningrad with Konstantin Sergeyev (1910–92), the Kirov Ballet's chief ballet master and a veteran dancer, to decide on the appropriate repertoire. "He loved the classics, classics, classics, and only the classics," said Sergeyev. "Sometimes we had different opinions and desires about what to produce, and he would say firmly, 'That won't work.' And he had good instincts. You could trust them."

For America, Hurok and Sergeyev chose three classics closely identified with the Mariinsky tradition—*Swan Lake*, *Giselle*, and *Sleeping Beauty*—and two programs of short pieces mostly unfamiliar to American audiences. In the absence of Nureyev, the leading dancers were twenty-one-year old Natalia Makarova (as Giselle), Irina Kolpakova, and Yuri Solovev. As usual, Hurok received the company in grand style and came to every single New York performance. Nor, according to Sergeyev, was he shy about telling Sergeyev how to use his personnel:

> You know if one evening I thought a certain leading dancer was too tired to dance and I would replace her with a second-string dancer, I would hear about it from Hurok the next day. He would call me into his office and demand to know why I did that. He would work me over, and tell me what was possible and what was not. He was always especially concerned about the casting. And if there were any mistakes or oversights made, even little ones, he could be severe to the point of cruelty. He had a bad temper, and could explode and shout "Don't do that!"

Hurok would never have dared to behave in such a dictatorial fashion with the Royal Ballet's Ninette de Valois, but Sergeyev, unlike her, was new to America and totally dependent on his impresario for everything.

On the Kirov's second American tour in 1964, Hurok got into a heated dispute with the company's managing director over casting for the opening-night *Swan Lake.* Hurok wanted Makarova to dance and felt she was being slighted because of the director's favoritism toward an older ballerina, Kaleria Fedicheva. The night before the opening, the director and Hurok argued until 4 A.M., and both men threatened to cancel the engagement if they didn't get their way. In the end, they reached a compromise possible only in that schizophrenic ballet: Makarova danced the white swan (Odette) and Fedicheva the black swan (Odile).

To maintain morale, Hurok would throw regular receptions for everyone in the company, usually at the beginning, middle, and end of the tour. In 1988, not long before his death, Sergeyev recalled how important these gestures were to him and his dancers:

> These days presenters don't have the kind of appreciation and love Hurok did for performers. They're only concerned with how to get the most possible performances of the most possible productions out of them. But he loved the role of benefactor, or bearer of gifts. He would always complain to me that he would lose lots of money on the Kirov, with so many dancers and musicians and props to transport—altogether there were about two hundred personnel. But he'd say he would then make up the losses by touring a single performer—Richter, Rostropovich, Gilels. He always thought on a grand scale.

Despite all the buildup, the Kirov's first American tour in 1961 did not produce the same critical and financial success that the Bolshoi or Moiseyev had generated. Whether because of Nureyev's defection, or the lack of stars of the caliber of Ulanova and Plisetskaya, or because the novelty value of a Russian ballet company was already beginning to fade a bit, Hurok took a substantial loss on the venture. (One member of Hurok's staff, Maxim Gershunoff, has estimated it at $175,000.) The company's more elegant, less athletic style may also have appealed less to American audiences than the Bolshoi's. With Soviet officials, too, the Bolshoi, regarded as the authentic Soviet ballet company, enjoyed much greater favor than the Kirov, which carried the aristocratic and elitist taint of its hometown. Hurok would bring the Kirov to the

United States only once more, in 1964, while the Bolshoi would come regularly every few seasons.

The Bolshoi's second American tour, in the fall of 1962, happened to coincide with perhaps the most dangerous period in postwar Soviet-American relations: the Cuban Missile Crisis. Throughout October, as the threat of global nuclear warfare waxed and waned, the Bolshoi was dancing its way across the United States, presenting (among other things) the American premiere of Khachaturian's brassy ballet *Spartacus*, with Igor Moiseyev's choreography. Most Americans seemed capable of understanding that these dancers were not responsible for Khrushchev's attempt to send missiles to Cuba, and continued to turn out in large numbers to see them. (This was fortunate for Hurok, whose weekly costs for presenting the Bolshoi had risen to between $125,000 and $135,000.) Indeed, their presence at such a moment helped to remind the American people and their leaders that Russians were people, too, and that dance and music were universal languages.

Many American artists also visited the USSR that year: the New York City Ballet, the Robert Shaw Orchestra and Chorus, the Benny Goodman Orchestra, Hurok's pianists Byron Janis and Van Cliburn, and, perhaps most incredibly, eighty-year old Russian-born American composer Igor Stravinsky, whose visit was arranged and personally subsidized by Hurok. Seeing these great performers made it impossible for Soviet citizens (no matter what their government might say) to believe that all Americans were capitalist villains intent on blowing up the world.

Once the Cuban crisis had passed and Khrushchev had withdrawn his missiles, most people felt that an important change had taken place in the nature of East-West relations. What was really at stake had become clearer than ever: the survival of the human race. Just a few weeks later, not long before the Bolshoi returned to Moscow, Rose Kennedy and then Senator-elect Edward Kennedy invited twenty-five members of the troupe to their family home at Hyannisport on Cape Cod for a pre-Thanksgiving dinner. They also celebrated the thirty-seventh birthday of ballerina Maya Plisetskaya, who had emerged (following Ulanova's retirement) as the big star of the tour.

Nor were Rose and Edward the only Kennedys smitten with Plisetskaya's beauty and talent. Robert Kennedy became so intrigued with the ballerina that rumors began to circulate that they were having an affair. A few years later, when Plisetskaya toured America with a smaller group called the Stars of the Bolshoi, Hurok's "valet" Semenoff even claimed to have witnessed an acrimonious backstage struggle between Hurok and Robert Kennedy over the right to escort her to dinner after a rehearsal. When Hurok protested that Plisetskaya had to rest in preparation for the next day's performance, Kennedy reportedly replied, "Mr. Hurok, you know they are not in Russia here. They are in America. Maybe you've forgotten that they can do whatever they want."

In the end, they all went out together to a nightclub, where Kennedy and Plisetskaya danced in a close embrace, the statuesque ballerina towering over the shorter politician.

During that same Bolshoi tour in late 1962, Nureyev also came to New York to see Plisetskaya and the company dance. The Soviet officials accompanying the troupe got very nervous when this defector started sending the ballerina flowers and fraternizing with the dancers in the company. By now established as a guest artist with the Royal Ballet and credited with reviving Margot Fonteyn's career, Nureyev flaunted his freedom and unintentionally (or even intentionally) created some headaches for Hurok, who pretended that he didn't know what was going on. Hurok's dealings with Nureyev were complicated by the fact that (trying as always to play all ends against the middle), he was simultaneously making arrangements for the Royal Ballet's upcoming tour. That the company and Fonteyn would now perform in America without their headliner Nureyev was unthinkable.

So Hurok made a special trip to Moscow to explain his predicament. According to Vladimir Ashkenazy, no less an authority than Khrushchev gave his "personal agreement" to Hurok that he would be allowed to tour Nureyev "while still dealing with all the rest of the Soviet business." Although inconsistent and unpredictable, Khrushchev was still trying to liberalize the Soviet system and change the prisonlike image his country possessed abroad. In pleading his case, Hurok reportedly stressed (somewhat disingenuously) that he was only a presenter and had no control over what the Royal Ballet did. And in fact Hurok did exercise much less artistic and other control over the Royal Ballet than he did over most other dance companies he presented.

By the time Nureyev made his long-awaited debut with Fonteyn and the Royal in New York on April 25, 1963, in *Giselle*, one of Hurok's favorite ballets, he had become a major international personality. He had already become familiar to American audiences during the preceding season through brief cameo appearances on the *Bell Telephone Hour* and onstage at the Brooklyn Academy of Music (with Chicago Opera Ballet) and with American Ballet Theatre in Chicago. (None of them had been arranged by Hurok).

But these performances had only whetted the public's appetite. In anticipation of the chance to see Nureyev in a full-length role with Fonteyn, the American media went wild. Both *Time* and *Newsweek* featured his seductive, excitingly wild profile on the cover, and reporters scrambled to cover the romantic May-December partnership between the charismatic wild Tartar and the proper British ballerina. (One uninformed fan asked Nureyev if she was his mother.) Audiences went crazy over the pair. The applause went on for twenty minutes after their performance of the pas de deux from *Le Corsaire.*

Even Jackie Kennedy came to New York to see them. After the performance, the first lady expressed a desire to go backstage and pay her respects. But Hurok was so fearful of the political repercussions (the Soviets had already been successful in barring Nureyev from a number of theaters around the world) that he absolutely refused to let her go. He even locked the door to Nureyev's dressing room. To Mrs. Kennedy Hurok said that he was worried she might fall and hurt herself. She obeyed and retreated, making Nureyev furious. Hurok, ever conscious of his clout, viewed the incident as a personal victory and used to brag privately afterward that he had told the president's wife not to go backstage, "and she actually listened to me."

Soon afterward, however, Mrs. Kennedy sent a private plane to New York to bring Nureyev, Fonteyn, and several other members of the company to Washington, where she received them at the White House and introduced them to the president. Nureyev even sat in

Kennedy's chair in the Oval Office. This "enraged" Hurok. "Of course I understood him," said Nureyev some years later. "He was afraid that he might lose all the lucrative Russian engagements and Russian artists. But later, when he saw that I had incredible drawing power at the box office, his heart somehow softened, and usually when the house was sold out you could hear him singing some Russian songs."

Together, Hurok and Nureyev did a great deal to engineer the fundamental change that occurred in ballet during the 1960s, pushing it, as Arlene Croce has observed, "from minority cult to middle-class pastime." Nureyev was the first male ballet dancer to achieve the status of an icon of American popular culture. "He connected with the rebellious, hyperbolic spirit of the times, and suddenly ballet was in." Hurok and Nureyev eventually collaborated on several other highly successful ventures besides the Royal Ballet, notably Nureyev's appearances in America with the Australian Ballet and the National Ballet of Canada.

But the problem of defections refused to go away. In July 1963, after several months of delicate maneuvering at the highest levels, another Soviet performer, pianist Vladimir Ashkenazy, announced that he was staying in England with his English wife. Unlike Nureyev, Ashkenazy was a Hurok artist. His decision did not sit well with his American impresario, who summoned him to the Savoy and told him that he should return to Russia, "that all my family and friends were there and that it's very difficult in the West, difficult to live here, with so much competition and so on." Ashkenazy was disappointed with Hurok's behavior.

> I just couldn't understand why he was saying these things and painting such a black picture of the West. I still don't know why he did it. It wasn't as though he was the sort of person who would take instructions from the Russians—he was really much too powerful and they needed him too much. Besides, he knew them too well to think he would ever get me again if I did go back. He just didn't look honest about what he was saying; he looked false, downright false. . . . Nureyev defected in 1961, and, since Hurok was already touring him by the time I stayed out,

maybe he thought that he should not add another controversial figure to his plans quite so quickly. All of this influenced my attitude to him for the rest of his life. What it really came down to was that although I knew him to be
completely anti-Soviet, here he was painting a rosy picture
of the Soviet Union for me. What was it all for?

Despite his disillusionment, however, Ashkenazy remained
with Hurok "because his office had such a good name and it would
be better to be patient." He had to wait until the 1965–66 season
before Hurok arranged for him to tour the United States again.

In the autumn of 1963, Hurok brought a Russian novelty attraction
to America for its first (and last) tour. The Obratsov Russian Puppet
Theatre, created and run by Sergei Obratsov (1901–1992), had been
attracting Moscow audiences of children and adults for many years
before Hurok "discovered" it. Obratsov was a man of many talents
(artistic, dramatic, musical) who was also known in Russia for the
ability to insert sharp political satire into what were ostensibly plays
for children. As a member of the Moscow Art Theatre Musical Studio troupe imported by Hurok's competitor and model Morris
Gest, Obratsov had actually made an earlier trip to America in
1925. In more recent years, his puppet theater, lavishly subsidized
by the state and housed in an enormous and well-equipped facility on the Sadovaya Ring Road surrounding central Moscow, had
become world-famous for the quality and innovation of its
design.

The tour opened on October 2 at the Broadway Theatre in
New York and ran for nearly two months, until November 23.
Obratsov was touched and dazzled by the personal attention Hurok
lavished on him and the thirty members of the company, especially
considering the difficult and expensive technical demands of setting
up the productions. On opening night, Hurok was in his usual place
backstage getting nervous along with the actors. He only relaxed after he heard the first bursts of applause and laughter. For Obratsov,
the tour was also an exercise in nostalgia, since many Russian
émigrés whom he had once known as theatrical colleagues came to
pay their respects. Among them was Olga Baclanova, a Russian-

born stage and screen star famous in America for her role as the heartless circus performer in the cult classic film *Freaks*.

Another night, "a short man with an athletic build" came back-stage to ask Obratsov to show him how the puppets were con-structed. "I showed him," the director wrote later in his memoirs. "He thanked me and said, 'You're going next to Washington, so you must be sure to pay your respects to my brother John.' And I fig-ured out that this was Robert Kennedy, and asked, 'But will the President really come to the theater to see us?' He replied, 'Of course he will, along with Jacqueline and the children.' "

A few days later, on the next-to-the-last day of the Puppet The-atre's New York run and just before Thanksgiving, Obratsov and his wife were in a store buying Christmas cards. Suddenly they heard the words "Texas, Texas," and "murder" coming across the radio. "We didn't understand anything, but fear was written on the sales-girl's face." She explained to them that the president had been shot. "We got into a taxi and while we were driving, Kennedy died. It was during that short period of time that he became a great man. When he was wounded, he wasn't the same Kennedy he was when he died."

The following week Obratsov and his company opened in a Washington still in deep mourning after the funeral. The planned official premiere was canceled, and the expected diplomats failed to appear. Neither the president nor his family attended as Robert Kennedy had promised. For Obratsov and his troupe, it was a terri-ble and confusing moment, as it was for everyone who lived through it. They wanted to express their grief and sense of loss. "We bought big white chrysanthemums and went to Arlington Cemetery to Ken-nedy's grave, which was surrounded by a low wooden fence. One by one, in a row, we passed by with the white flowers in our hands. And we put them on the grave."

■ CHAPTER TWENTY-ONE ■

Cashing Out

"Of all the great people in the world, I have the smallest ego."—*Sol Hurok*

IF THE DEATH OF JOSEF STALIN in 1953 marked the beginning of the most financially successful and artistically sensational phase of Hurok's up-and-down career, then the assassination of John Kennedy ten years later brought it to a close. In the decade between these epochal events, Hurok, who turned seventy-five in 1963, had rarely left the public eye while engineering an amazing string of "firsts." His name and photo regularly adorned the front pages of the leading American newspapers. A national (even international) celebrity, his fame now surpassed that of most of his artists. No less than Cadillac or Rolls-Royce, the trademark "S. Hurok Presents" had come to evoke an image of reliable luxury, pleasure, and status. Virtually guaranteeing sold-out houses, it had become synonymous with the very finest in classy entertainment, representing the epitome of glamor during one of the most glamorous eras in modern American history. Hurok had made it. He had fulfilled his Brownsville dreams, far outstripping such early models as Charles Dillingham, Otto Kahn, Morris Gest, and Oscar Hammerstein in the national scope and high profile of his achievements. In the process, he had also greatly expanded the audience for "high culture," particularly ballet, which now attracted a much broader middle-class public.

But things would never be the same again either for America or for Hurok after the shooting in Dallas. Within five years, the tone of the decade would change from stylish noblesse oblige to aggressive scruffiness; Soviet-American relations would sour with the escalation of America's military involvement in Vietnam; Jewish militants would begin targeting Hurok as a collaborator with what they saw as the anti-Semitic Soviet government; the economics of presenting large touring companies would become prohibitively precarious; the soaring popularity of rock music would profoundly alter the American cultural scene; Soviet bureaucrats would attack Hurok's near-monopoly on the presentation of Soviet artists in the United States; the Metropolitan Opera House would be torn down; and the New York that he had known and loved since arriving as a teenager would be changing rapidly and inexplicably. By the time of his eightieth birthday in 1968, the world that had always been Hurok's oyster would have turned into another creature that he found increasingly difficult to understand.

Coping with such wrenching and pervasive external change might have been easier for Hurok if his private life had provided a more comfortable refuge. But he put so much energy into his public life that he really had no private life. "Hurok's success was in living vicariously other people's lives," said Isaac Stern. "So there was no time for one of his own." "His office was his family," agreed Lee Walter, who worked there throughout the 1960s. Even the more perceptive among Hurok's artists, such as puppeteer Sergei Obratsov, also sensed "some sort of family tragedy" behind the impresario's unfailingly gracious demeanor and seemingly unshakable self-confidence. "He gave the impression of not needing anything," observed Lillian Libman, "which is one of the most typical things about an ego. That was the impression he gave. But I always felt there was something a little frightened under the whole business."

Most at home greeting audiences as they arrived at the Met, shouting bravos from the back rows as the curtain came down, or counting up receipts into the early morning hours, Hurok was least at home in his own house. Although he had taken both her sons into his office and treated them well, Hurok saw his relationship with his wife Emma become increasingly difficult and strained over the years. They often quarreled, sometimes so seriously that he would move out of the apartment they had long shared at 91 Central Park West and take up residence for several weeks—even months—at a time in the St. Regis Hotel. When Emma would eventually go to fetch him there, he would jump in the car with her and go back home without even stopping to gather up his belongings or check out.

"He behaved with her sometimes like a little boy who had been told to stand in the corner," said Emma's daughter-in-law Anna Straus, who often acted as an intermediary between them in their elaborately staged games.

Even on the very rare occasions when she made an appearance at one of her husband's opening night performances or parties, Emma often belittled his populist origins and taste. Having spent her youth in pre-Revolutionary St. Petersburg, she found his fondness for Soviet attractions suspicious and vulgar. When the Bolshoi Ballet gave the American premiere of Khachaturian's *Spartacus* at the Met in 1962, Emma, covered in her usual emeralds and chinchillas, stormed out of her box after Act I. Spying Lillian Libman, who had just returned from Mexico with Hurok after negotiating for an upcoming tour by the Ballet Folklorico de Mexico, she asked, "Did you sign up the Mexicans?" Libman replied in the affirmative. "Thank God, then maybe he'll stop bringing those goddamn Communists," Emma remarked theatrically.

At home, Emma spent most of her time in bed watching television, eating chocolates, and upbraiding her husband. Although there is no convincing evidence that he sought sexual or romantic consolation elsewhere, she particularly enjoyed accusing him of having affairs with various famous women, including Marlene Dietrich. Straus believed that she invented these stories to "psych herself up, so they could kiss and make up. It was part of the whole performance that went on between them." Hurok's response to these and other excesses (including showering him with "terrible language") was passive: "He just sat there and took it all." Others who knew the couple have agreed that Hurok never lost his total admiration and love for Emma and was ready to do anything she asked.

When, around 1960, Emma indicated some lethargic interest in moving from Central Park West, Hurok wasted no time in attempting to please her. After having her driven endlessly around the fashionable neighborhoods of the Upper East Side, he finally extracted from her a preference for a large apartment at 700 Park Avenue. Proud of her good taste, she carefully supervised its decoration and they began packing and preparing. But when the day came for the final move, Emma suddenly changed her mind. Sitting in the living room surrounded by her trunks, she informed Hurok that she needed more time to get used to the idea of a new neighborhood and all the change. "I'll come next month," she said. So Hurok moved out to Park Avenue and lived there alone in anticipation of her arrival.

But when eighteen months had passed and she was still on Central Park West, he told her she had to make up her mind or remain where she was forever. She chose to stay put in the apartment on Central Park West. He continued living on Park Avenue, and they never lived together again—although they never divorced. Their separation was not rancorous: He called her daily and often visited her, sitting by her bedside. "He loved her to death," said Straus. "He loved her. But she just didn't know how to give him love back."

In a 1973 interview with the *New York Times*, Hurok claimed that even though they were separated, he and Emma were still "good friends. She's a very nice lady, very intelligent, very good-looking. We meet; we see each other; but we agreed to disagree, that's all."

Even Emma's sons, George and Eddie Perper, did not blame their stepfather for the problems in the marriage. Hurok may have enjoyed subjecting him to occasional ridicule, but he had developed a relatively close relationship with George, who had been working in the agency since 1937 and had become one of the most experienced and knowledgeable people in the New York office. "Hurok loved George Perper as much as he could love anyone," said their co-worker Libman, "but I don't think he respected him. He didn't respect his opinions about the artists." With Eddie, a born schemer who worked on the road as a company manager, Hurok had a more direct and rough-and-tumble relationship. Eddie finally left the operation in 1966, because of what he called "differences" with his boss. Numerous other sources reported that Hurok actually forced Eddie to leave after discovering that he had been using his position to receive kickbacks from suppliers.

Nor did Hurok have an intimate relationship with his only natural daughter, Ruth. Now happy in her second marriage with the conductor Arthur Lief, Ruth still regretted that her father seemed to have little time to spend with her. At times he could be brusque and thoughtless. Once when she and Lief were having lunch with Hurok and his acquaintance the actress Claire Bloom at the Plaza Hotel, Hurok called Bloom his *"tochter"* ("daughter"), an affectionate Yiddish term that he had never used with his own daughter, Ruth. "I cried when we got home," she admitted years later. On another occasion, Hurok shared with Lief his feelings about Ruth as the two men were taking a stroll along Central Park West. "She's a good daughter," he said with his heavy Pogar accent. "She never asks me for anything."

Among those who noticed the difficulty Hurok had in expressing love or affection for his family was Isaac Stern. "He always had trouble with his children. He always had trouble with emotions," he said.

Peter Hyams, Ruth's son from her first marriage, who graduated from college in the mid-1960s, was also becoming increasingly aware of the distant relationship between his mother and his grandfather. "My mother lived in constant awe of him," he recalled.

And I know that somehow he encouraged her to be in awe. He would always give us gifts and money, but it sometimes struck me as a kind of compensation. If you have money, it doesn't take a lot of effort to give it away. Time takes more effort.

He liked to create a situation in which people would be dependent on him, and then he wouldn't respect them enough. It was a kind of "Catch-22" thing. They were dependent, but he was the one who made them and kept them that way. Since my parents were never well-off, he would always give my mother money. But he would give it to her every year, doling it out in small portions so that she would always be needing something from him.

Even so, I think he needed her a lot more than she knew. The only thing I really resented about how my grandfather treated my mother was that he never put her in a position where she didn't have to worry financially. And he could have.

Hyams's relationship with Hurok changed when he landed a high-profile job fresh out of college as a television newscaster for a New York City station.

> All of a sudden I was a success, and more people knew who I was than knew who he was. And he even got a little miffed because I was more famous. And he started to ask me for advice in running his business, and I would give it to him. He was unhappy because I was making it clear to him that I didn't want to take over the agency the way he wanted me to. But at the same time, he was proud that I was making it on my own—the way he did—and doing well. I could give him objective advice. Our equality was there in terms of success, because for him, that was the bottom line. That's how he measured people. If you were successful, if you could do it, the dynamic changed.

Later, after Hyams had moved on to Hollywood to pursue a career in film, Hurok often came to visit Hyams and his new great-grandchildren there. "When I was little," Hyams said, "I was an object to him, to be pinched and patted and kissed on the forehead. With these kids he was different, he took the time, and you could see the look on his face. It was very sweet, very touching."

His grandson's work in the movies also fascinated Hurok. After all, he had spent a great deal of time in Hollywood over the years and had associated with many of the industry's most influential producers and directors, including Sam Goldwyn. Many of them had come from humble Jewish Eastern European backgrounds very similar to his own. Hyams's first film was a "real down and dirty cop movie," *Busting*, an R-rated feature starring Elliott Gould and Robert Blake. "Every other word was fuck. And one day I was sitting in my office and Grandpa called. 'Pyotr!'—he always called me Pyotr—'I saw *Busting*.' And I thought he was going to kill me because of the language and because it was so raunchy. And he said, 'Was sold out. I spoke to manager. He said was doing very good beez-nis and was going to sell out ten o'clock performance, too.' He was proud that it was sold out, though I very much doubt that he was proud of what he saw."

After he and Emma separated, the void in Hurok's life was to some extent filled by a married couple who lived in the Park Avenue apartment as his cook and servant. He also spent a lot of time with his black chauffeur, Morgan. According to Libman, Hurok had "discovered" Morgan when he was a waiter on the Pullman car of a Washington–New York train and brought him to work for him as a chauffeur and gofer. Hurok relied on Morgan for many personal services. Several reliable sources have even claimed that Morgan used to read the newspaper aloud to his boss, who was functionally illiterate.

Beyond these domestic employees, Hurok had no real close friends, with the possible exception of Stern. The violinist was also a favorite with Peter Hyams and Peter's sister Nessa. They also remember that their grandfather had a group of "cronies," including some Russian Jews, whom he had known for years and to whom he remained steadfastly loyal. These included his accountant and his longtime lawyer, Elias Lieberman, an old-time socialist who had helped to found the International Ladies' Garment Workers Union. But these men, too, regarded Hurok with a reverence bordering on awe, an attitude he both enjoyed and encouraged in those who surrounded him.

Considering his insatiable appetite for dependence and admiration, it is perhaps surprising that Hurok never bought a dog. But when George Perper once suggested the idea, Hurok dismissed it with a characteristically streetwise retort. "Yes, George, get me a dog," he said. "But find one who will eat unsold tickets."

Just a few weeks before Kennedy's assassination, Hurok was called to Washington to testify before the recently created Special Subcommittee on the Arts of the Committee on Labor and Public Welfare of the U.S. Senate. Headed by Senator Claiborne Pell of Rhode Island, the committee was hearing testimony on two proposed bills: one to establish a United States Arts Foundation and another "to provide for the establishment of a national council on the arts and a national arts foundation to assist in the growth and development of the arts in the United States."

Pell had taken the lead in the movement to set up a governmental structure to distribute financial support to the arts at the urging of his newly appointed aide, Livingston Biddle. A novelist and longtime arts patron, Biddle began his work for Pell by researching the extent to which other countries subsidized culture. The statistics he produced were graphic. In Europe, the USSR, and Canada, government spending on the arts was twenty-five times higher per capita than the modest amount ($5 million annually initially, to rise to an annual ceiling of $10 million) proposed in Senate bills numbers 165 and 1316. Indeed, the United States was virtually the only country in the Western world that did not provide some sort of subsidy to cultural organizations.

Fortunately, Pell began his campaign on Capitol Hill under a president who was much more sympathetic to this cause than any of his predecessors since FDR. Kennedy and his wife had already made a point of inviting prominent artists to the White House and affirming publicly their belief in the importance of the arts. On June 12, 1963, Kennedy raised this support to another level by issuing an executive order establishing the President's Advisory Council on the Arts. This group would include Cabinet-level officials, heads of federal agencies involved with culture, and a number of private citizens. Kennedy also became the first president to appoint a White House cultural adviser. Less than a month before his death, he told an audience at Amherst College:

> I see little of more importance to the future of our country and our civilization than full recognition of the place of the artist.
>
> If art is to nourish the roots of our culture, society must set the artist free to follow his vision wherever it takes him. I look forward to an America which will reward achievement in the arts as we reward achievement in business or statecraft.
>
> I look forward to an America which will steadily raise its standards of artistic accomplishment and which will steadily enlarge cultural opportunities for all of our citizens.

Such words were music to Hurok's ears. He had been talking about the need for government subsidy of the arts for decades. Despite his status as a commercial promoter who actually made money on presenting "high culture" and who had rarely relied on grants, foundations, or philanthropists to underwrite his very risky operation, Hurok so loved the arts, so much wanted the audience to grow, and so well understood how difficult it would be in the future to continue to present expensive attractions like the Royal Ballet or the Moiseyev Folk Ensemble (or to foster the growth of American ballet companies) that he had become a strong advocate for the establishment of a federal cultural agency. Hurok was intimately familiar with the heavily subsidized arts establishments in Europe, and especially in the Soviet Union. There, the opera and ballet companies and orchestras and theaters he imported received virtually all of their funding from the state (through the Ministry of Culture). As a result, Hurok understood both the commercial and "nonprofit" sides of the business. As one of the only surviving successful independent managers in the field, he brought a unique perspective to the discussion.

Pell and Biddle obviously appreciated Hurok's experience, for he was the only commercial presenter called before the subcommittee during its five days of testimony. In a prepared opening statement written by his staff, Hurok waxed eloquent in fine literary English. Showing his customary pro-European bias and characteristically slighting the already significant accomplishments of the New York City Ballet and American Ballet Theatre, he stressed that American ballet dancers were still unable to compete internationally because they lacked security and continuity.

"Where is our Bolshoi, or Royal Ballet?" he asked. "Ballet cannot pay for itself, as you well know, from the financial reports given you. Opera cannot pay for itself. Repertory theater cannot pay for itself."

He also praised the accomplishments of the WPA program in the 1930s in building numerous auditoriums for the performing arts, and bemoaned the rapid decline in the number of legitimate theaters and concert halls in American cities. Even the nation's capital lacked an opera house, making it necessary to present the Bolshoi Ballet and other such attractions in arenas intended for sports events. "We are discussing here the establishment of an Advisory Council on the Arts and a U.S. Arts Foundation. This is not an extraordinary step. What is extraordinary is that we have taken so long to come to it."

Hurok concluded his remarks with an immigrant's patriotic tribute to his adopted nation:

> I am an American who was not born in this country but sought to be an American out of my love for this land and its great dream of freedom and democracy. I have dedicated my life to the belief that the arts are a major part of any life and that to be without them is to starve, no matter what other wealth one may achieve.
>
> The country is ready. The people's leisure time is growing steadily and where else but in the arts can it find the cure for its hunger for things beyond the material? The arts cannot support themselves. The Government must help. It is time.

After making his prepared statement, Hurok was briefly questioned by Senator Jacob Javits, a fellow New Yorker and another member of the subcommittee. In rambling and somewhat incoherent answers, Hurok said he believed the biggest problem at the moment was the lack of suitable auditoriums in which large attractions could be accommodated. Moreover, private philanthropists could no longer produce the kind of money needed to support orchestras and other performing arts groups.

The federal and municipal governments needed to subsidize theaters, Hurok went on, because their owners "find there is probably more income or better income to build a garage space or a parking lot or build an office building or an apartment house, whatever it may be. It gives them a greater income than to have a theater there." As an example, he told how "myself and another man from the coast" had tried unsuccessfully to save the Center Theater, a historic and lavishly appointed thirty-five-hundred-seat house originally built as part of the Rockefeller Center complex. Edward Steichen had covered the curving walls of the men's lounge with photomurals depicting great moments in aviation history, and many distinguished dance and musical groups had performed on its stage. American Ballet Theatre had started out there. Hurok and his partner had offered the management a five-year contract to fill the theater for thirty-six weeks a year, but the owners decided they could make much more money on a new office building. So the theater was torn down in 1954 and replaced with an extension to the U.S. Rubber Company Building.

Almost two years passed between the day the subcommittee heard Hurok's testimony and the day Lyndon Johnson finally signed the law establishing the National Endowment for the Arts. Its creation in 1965 finally acknowledged a difficult truth that insiders had known for many years: The "serious" performing arts could not pay for themselves in the United States. Nor should they be expected to.

For Hurok, this had to be a bittersweet moment. While he had to be happy to see the establishment of the sort of necessary support he had been promoting for years, he also had to realize more fully than ever that the wonderfully crazy days when it was possible to make money on sending a troupe of dancers, musicians, props, and equipment on a whistle-stop tour across the country were gone forever. Trains didn't even run to a lot of important cities anymore. Union regulations now prohibited the sort of exhausting regime the Ballet Russe de Monte Carlo took for granted in the 1930s. The independent private managers in every city with whom Hurok had dealt for decades were dying off and no one was replacing them. The future belonged to a new animal: the tax-exempt nonprofit sector. The future belonged to performing arts centers and universities.

At the time of his angry split with Lucia Chase and Ballet Theatre in 1947, Hurok had told a reporter that the company's decision to declare nonprofit status, then an unusual move, was "not a reasonable solution. . . . My idea of ballet, or any art, is that it should be good enough to support itself." But times, and ideas, had changed.

One of the happier, and certainly most historic, of Hurok's accomplishments of the 1960s was bringing the Moscow Art Theatre on tour to the United States for the first time since 1924. He had been negotiating the visit for several years. The troupe of seventy-five, including forty-nine actors, performed through February 1965 at the City Center in New York, presenting a dramatic adaptation of Nikolai Gogol's novel *Dead Souls, The Cherry Orchard* and *Three*

Sisters by Chekhov, and *Kremlin Chimes* by Soviet playwright Nikolai Pogodin.

Both for Hurok and for the company, the engagement was rich in personal and artistic memories. When the Moscow Art Theatre had made its first celebrated tour of America in 1923–24, its co-founder and guiding spirit Konstantin Stanislavsky was still alive, and thirty-five-year-old Sol Hurok was just starting out in the business. Indeed, he had learned a great deal from watching how his early model Morris Gest managed, promoted, and sold the Moscow Art Theatre in the United States, turning it into one of the most successful and influential entertainment events of the 1920s. But Gest had rapidly faded from the scene, never having attained Hurok's personal stardom or professional longevity.

Presenting the Moscow Art Theatre in 1965, then, gave Hurok the opportunity to revisit his early days and realize one of his life-long dreams. Whether he would turn a profit on the tour seemed relatively unimportant. In an interview with the *New York Times* at the midpoint of the New York run, he admitted almost boastfully that he expected to lose between $10,000 and $50,000. With the heavy expenses involved in housing and feeding the large company and in mounting four different productions, the break-even point was a high $300,000. The house was not selling out, however, and he predicted he would take in only $250,000 to $290,000 in ticket sales. "Thank God," he said, "I can lose it! I'm happy to lose it with a winner. This is one of my duties. The fact that I'm losing won't prevent me from bringing in more things. This is a reminder of how an ensemble works and of the repertory tradition."

With critics, the Moscow Art Theatre scored a major success. Only the transparently propagandistic "Kremlin Chimes" got panned (and rightly so). In the New York *Herald Tribune*, Walter Kerr rhapsodized about the ensemble's acting, calling each performance "almost a group accomplishment."

By 1965, the MAT had become a conservative and cautious institution after decades of adapting to Soviet bureaucracy and censorship. This time around, the company did not revolutionize American drama and acting, which were now immeasurably more mature and self-assured than they had been in 1923. Nonetheless, the theater community received the MAT with the sort of reverent attention paid to a beloved grandfather. Seeing the troupe's scrupulous ensemble work, prepared slowly and lovingly in a completely subsidized theater over a period of years, also inspired the early leaders of the struggling American nonprofit resident theater movement. It gave them strength in their struggle to create something the USSR had taken for granted for years but which America had never had: repertory theaters with stable companies of actors and directors capable of developing and perfecting serious productions of new and classic plays.

When Hurok spoke in his 1963 testimony for the Subcommittee on the Arts of his sadness over the destruction of America's distinguished and beautiful old theaters, a crisis was already building that would carry off one of the greatest of them all: the Metropolitan Opera House in New York. After years of Machiavellian planning and fund-raising, a vast new performing arts complex to be called Lincoln Center was already rising out of a scruffy old neighborhood on the West Side just above Columbus Circle. Its centerpiece would be a new home for the Metropolitan Opera. The fate of the "old" Met was suddenly uncertain.

Opened in 1883, just five years before Hurok was born, this cozy, cramped, technically outmoded and un-air-conditioned faux Italian Renaissance monument was no longer practical in an era when unions demanded fifty-two weeks of employment and an edifice complex afflicted politicians. Although Hurok professed publicly to be happy about the construction of Lincoln Center, which would also house the New York Philharmonic, privately he expressed regret over the opera company's abandonment of its longtime home. How could it be otherwise? For it was there, at the corner of 39th and Broadway, that he had fallen in love with music and dance.

It was there that he had first seen Chaliapin and vowed to present him.

It was there that he had presented the de Basil Ballet Russe in 1935, his rental fees helping to get the financially strapped Met through the depths of the Depression.

It was there that he had presented the Royal Ballet in 1949, setting the stage for the American dance explosion.

It was there that he had unveiled the previously unknown treasures of Russia: the Moiseyev, the Bolshoi, the Kirov.

He knew everyone in the place, from the management bigwigs

to the little people in the box office and stage crews. He was more at home at the Met than in his apartments on Central Park West or Park Avenue.

Hurok had been monopolizing the off-season at the Met for nearly thirty years, in the process helping to support the opera company. At the same time, he had turned what had been exclusively a home for opera into the premier American venue for large dance attractions. It might have been called the Metropolitan Opera House, but in the early fall and late spring it had belonged to ballet and to Hurok.

And so it was entirely appropriate that when the curtain finally came down for the very last time at the Met, at 12:50 A.M. on May 9, 1966, Hurok was running the show. The Metropolitan Opera, which would open in September at Lincoln Center, had already bid an emotional farewell to the old house more than three weeks earlier. Its last season there had closed with an emotional gala concert featuring the company's greatest singers. A number of Hurok artists, including Roberta Peters, had been among them.

But the last performers to use the stage were dancers. Since Hurok had begun his presenting career at the Met in 1935 with one Russian ballet company (de Basil's), his choice to end it in 1966 by presenting another—the Bolshoi Ballet—was both fitting and symmetrical. Surely Hurok also knew that the chance to see what looked to be the last performances in the old Met would lure hordes of sentimental customers to the box office. Tickets for the Bolshoi engagement sold out almost as soon as they went on sale.

Demand for tickets to the final performance in the run and in the theater, held on a Sunday night, was particularly clamorous. The line for standing-room spaces formed on Thursday. Word had already leaked out that it would be more than just another Bolshoi performance. Hurok was planning something very personal and special, an extravaganza that would feature many of the stars who had appeared at the Met under his trademark. Indeed, the Met's last night turned into a celebration of him and his achievements.

The evening began with a spoken tribute to dance at the Met delivered by John Martin. He had started out in the business around the same time as his old sparring partner Hurok and had commented (not always positively) on virtually all of Hurok's attractions. The Bolshoi dancers then took the stage. Maya Plisetskaya, a huge favorite in New York, danced her version of Fokine's *Dying Swan* to special violin accompaniment by Isaac Stern so successfully that the crowd demanded that she repeat it twice. Next she was partnered by Vladimir Tikhonov in the first act of *Don Quixote*. Other divertissements followed, featuring Bolshoi headliners such as Mikhail Lavrovsky, Nina Sorokina, Natalia Bessmertnova, and, in the finale of Yuri Grigorovich's version of *The Nutcracker*, the dynamic pair of Ekaterina Maximova and Vladimir Vasiliev.

"The Bolshoi rises to an occasion like yeast," wrote Clive Barnes in the *New York Times*, "and this was an occasion."

For the grand finale, Hurok assembled a remarkable group of dancers to perform the *Polonaise* (as choreographed by Simon Semenoff) from Glinka's opera *Ivan Susanin ("A Life for the Tsar")*. Processing around the stage with members of the Bolshoi were "Red Russian, White Russian, Blue English and just plain ordinary American" dancers, all of them presented at one time or another by Hurok: Muriel Bentley, Ruthanna Boris, Hilda Butsova, Alexandra Danilova, Eugenia Delarova, Melissa Hayden, Dame Alicia Markova, Mia Slavenska, José Greco, Hugh Laing, Igor Youskevitch, Martha Graham, Antony Tudor, and others. Even Hurok's old antagonists Lucia Chase and Agnes de Mille showed up. The assemblage so clearly reflected the impresario's imprint that Barnes jokingly labeled it the Ballets Hurok—not knowing, or forgetting, perhaps, the extent to which Hurok once seriously aspired to such a title.

Nor did the party end there. The group recessed to the St. Regis Hotel for what was said to be a particularly memorable Hurokian party that lasted nearly until dawn. Moved by the significance of the occasion, even the Bolshoi dancers threw their ideological scruples to the winds and participated in a dance considered by the Kremlin to be particularly illustrative of Western bourgeois decadence and decay: the twist.

Even after all this, the old Met was still alive—or at least, still standing. Controversy raged over whether and how the building could be saved. Just six years earlier, Carnegie Hall had been saved from the wrecker's ball at the last minute, partly through the efforts

of Hurok and his artist Isaac Stern. But the situation was more complicated for Hurok this time.

Although he clearly did not want to see the old Met destroyed
and was surely flattered by rumors that it would be saved and renamed the Hurok Center, Hurok was under intense pressure from
the management of the Metropolitan Opera to remain silent. Met
general manager Rudolf Bing was counting on rental income from
the office building to be constructed on the site of the old house. It
would help pay for the much greater expenses of running the new
house. Nor did Bing relish the thought of facing competition for
off-season bookings from another venue. Knowing that Hurok
needed at least fifteen weeks a year in the new Met for the status-
conscious audience that bought tickets to his ballet subscription series, Bing threatened to freeze him out there if he worked to save
the old house. As an added incentive, he also awarded Hurok what
seemed to be an attractive contract to take a revived Metropolitan
Opera National Company on tour. (In fact, the venture only lasted
two seasons before being abandoned as an economy measure.)

In the end, Hurok was placed in a situation in which he
couldn't afford to defend his old friend. He could only stand by as
the Met finally collapsed into theatrical rubble on January 17, 1967.

With the Met's death, something in Hurok died, too. Not only
would his weekly rental in the new house rise to $60,000 from the
$25,000 he had been paying for years downtown, making his profit
margin slimmer than ever; even more important was the fact that he
and the old Met had grown up together. It had inspired him to his
career as an impresario and given him sustenance through difficult
times. He knew its every nook and cranny. Despite its better acoustics, the new Met was another creature, a cold and impersonally futuristic slab of stone and glass surrounded by a forbidding desert of
open space. It was less an opera house than a triumph of urban renewal.

Hurok and the old Met were survivors of another era, a time in
which both artists and the halls in which they performed were noted
more for personality than for convenience. Or was it just that both
belonged so firmly to the nineteenth century and its culture, now re-
ceding ever faster from view?

▪   ▪   ▪

As it turned out, the Bolshoi Ballet's final stand at the Met also brought an end to the good relations Hurok had been enjoying with the Soviet government for nearly ten years. In May 1967, not long after returning from a draining month-long stay in Moscow, he announced that the Bolshoi Opera would make its first tour to the United States in April 1968, along with its partner, the Bolshoi Ballet. With a total of 535 people, the combined companies would be the largest group of performers Hurok had ever presented at one time. He estimated that presenting the tour, which would open at the spanking-new Met, would cost him $1.5 million.

For Hurok, bringing the Bolshoi Opera to America had been a decades-old dream and a project he had been carefully negotiating in Moscow at least since 1960. Even in his announcement, however, he admitted that it had been difficult to get the contracts signed because of the tension caused in the Soviet-American relationship by the escalation of the Vietnam War. Under Lyndon Johnson, American involvement in Vietnam had grown steadily. By late 1966, the bomb tonnage dropped on North Vietnam by American planes had exceeded the total dropped in the Pacific during World War II. The number of American soldiers sent to the front was climbing toward its peak of 550,000. The Soviet government sided with the Communist regime of North Vietnam and assailed American imperialism in Indochina with increasing belligerence.

Since relatively few official avenues of contact existed between the Soviet and American governments, it was inevitable that the building hostility between Moscow and Washington would eventually affect cultural exchange. As one of the most heavily publicized aspects of the superpower relationship, visits by performing artists could easily be manipulated by politicians on both sides to demonstrate approval or dissatisfaction with the current state of international affairs. A planned tour of the USSR by an American production of *Hello, Dolly* had already been canceled on the Soviet side in 1965 in protest over the American bombing of North Vietnam.

Larissa Netto, who worked in the American Department at Gosconcert throughout the 1960s, soon got used to the fact that "all the disagreements and difficulties in the Soviet-American relationship were immediately reflected in the area of cultural exchange." That's exactly what happened, she said, in late June 1967.

While in Moscow making final arrangements for a ten-week American tour by a group of two hundred Soviet dancers and musicians scheduled to open at the Met on July 5, Hurok was summoned to an emergency meeting with the Minister of Culture, Ekaterina Furtseva. She told him that the show, called the Russian Festival of Music and Dance, would have to be postponed for several weeks. While she was vague as to the reasons, Hurok understood that the action had been taken to protest both continuing American bombing of North Vietnam and the outbreak of the Arab-Israeli war, which once again found the United States and the Soviet Union on opposite sides of an extremely complicated and dangerous conflict. Moscow's simplistic reasoning went something like this: "How can our boys and girls sing and dance happily in a country which is waging war?"

Back in New York, Hurok rented the Met for an extra two weeks and lied that the Russian Festival of Music and Dance had been postponed because some of the attractions needed to be trimmed. But on July 11, less than a week before the rescheduled opening, Hurok received more bad news in a message from the Soviet Embassy in Washington. Now the tour had been "postponed indefinitely."

Remaining diplomatic as always, Hurok told the *New York Times* that he believed the reason for the cancellation was Soviet fear that the performers would be subjected to picketing and protests by American Jews angry over Soviet support for the Arabs. "I am a Jew and I know the Jewish are very panicky sometimes. They surely had some strong feelings during the Security Council sessions. But while they get hot quickly, they get cold quickly, too. When great artists perform, they will come to see the show." But Hurok would soon discover that some Jews could stay hot for quite a while.

The cancellation of the Russian Festival of Music and Dance created a financial and clerical nightmare for the Hurok office. Orders had already been filled for $250,000 worth of tickets for the two-week Met run. Many tickets had also been sold for the numerous stops on the planned cross-country tour, and local managers had already spent considerable sums on publicity, advertising, and promotion. For Hurok's employees, it was the biggest disaster they could remember—though their boss carefully avoided public criticism of the Soviet action. "All summer long all we did was sit and write refund checks all day," said Lee Walter.

As usual, Hurok did not reveal how much money he had lost, but it was clearly a significant sum, especially since he had always made it a practice of covering the losses of local managers. For him the financial setback was not the most important thing, however. Much more painful was seeing the relationship he had been carefully cultivating with politicians and cultural bureaucrats in Moscow for more than ten years suddenly threatened by external factors beyond his control. This last-minute cancellation was the first of its kind in the post-Stalinist period. Sadly, it was far from the last.

Ironically, the very same day that the news of the postponement hit the papers, another big ballet story broke. It, too, involved Hurok, at least indirectly. On tour in San Francisco, Dame Margot Fonteyn and Rudolf Nureyev, who were dancing sensationally in *Romeo and Juliet*, were arrested in a raid on what was described as a "hippy party" in the Haight-Ashbury section. Although charges of "visiting a place where marijuana was kept" were dropped almost immediately and the dancers were released, the story created quite a stir. Annoyed by the mob of journalists, Nureyev breathed heavily on the lens of a television camera to block out the picture.

His hands more than full with bad tidings from Moscow, Hurok was at first upset when he heard of the incident. But Simon Semenoff immediately saw its public relations value. "Don't be silly," he advised Hurok. "It makes you fantastic publicity. It will sell more tickets." Hearing this, Hurok calmed down, especially when he remembered that after San Francisco he had to fill thousands of seats in the Shrine Auditorium in Los Angeles. A little free publicity wouldn't hurt there at all.

Another impresario confronted with the last-minute Soviet cancellation of a major attraction (and the refunding of $250,000 in ticket orders) might well have abandoned the idea of ever dealing with Moscow again. But Hurok refused to give up. He resisted the temptation to fire off angry protests to Moscow, instead choosing, as he had done so many times in the past, to bide his time and wait for the situation to improve. In September, he traveled again to Russia to try to put cultural exchange back on track. He was most concerned, of course, about the fate of the Bolshoi Opera and Ballet tour, already announced for April 1968. The negotiating atmosphere he encountered in Moscow was highly combative. Taking their line as always from the Ministry of Culture and the Central Committee, the officials at Gosconcert continued to say that "no major attractions can go to the U.S. while the bombing in Vietnam continues."

Hurok's position in Moscow was further complicated because Gosconcert and the Ministry of Culture were beginning to pursue a new policy of encouraging competition among American presenters for Soviet attractions. Increasingly, Hurok's virtual monopoly over the American market was coming to be viewed as harmful to the financial—and even artistic—interests of the Soviet side. Accordingly, officials at Gosconcert began to seriously encourage and entertain offers from Hurok's main competitor: Columbia Artists.

Almost squeezed out of the running for Soviet attractions since the late 1950s, Columbia now launched an aggressive campaign to add Soviet ensembles and soloists to its list. The man who traveled to Moscow to plead Columbia's case was Joseph Zovarich. A Russian-speaking Jew whose background was similar to Hurok's and who intensely resented Hurok's dominance in the field, he was a formidable and persistent opponent. During 1967, Hurok saw his previously privileged position in Moscow weakening. At Gosconcert and the Ministry of Culture, officials now made him wait for conferences and decisions much longer than they had in the past. Larissa Netto saw the events unfold:

> At the time, it began to be said around Moscow that Hurok wasn't paying Gosconcert sufficiently large fees for the attractions he was touring, and that he was also personally paying the artists extra money under the table. That was expressly forbidden by the Ministry. And so they started wanting him to raise the fees, and even accused him of deceiving them. They also complained that he was uninterested in new young artists, that he only cared about the "big whales" like the Moiseyev and the Bolshoi.
>
> For Hurok, this was a difficult and unpleasant time. He blamed "new people" in the Ministry and Gosconcert

who didn't understand art. He accused them of caring only about money. He said he didn't see anything wrong with a monopoly, that he had never done anything wrong, and that all the artists loved him. And he said he had done all he could for the soloists and troupes.

Despite the continuing support of Minister of Culture Furtseva, Hurok suddenly saw his bargaining power in Moscow decline as the struggle with Columbia intensified. Gosconcert's desire to break his monopoly may help to explain why the planned 1968 Bolshoi Opera tour was ultimately canceled. In the end, Hurok was given only a group of Bolshoi Ballet stars instead of the enormous two-company blockbuster he had been planning.

Even for the resilient Hurok, the professional setbacks he suffered in the 1967–68 season must have been difficult to bear. His mood could hardly have been improved as he surveyed the social and racial bitterness that was erupting into violence all across the United States. The back-to-back assassinations in spring 1968 of Martin Luther King and Robert Kennedy, two politicians whose work he had always admired, profoundly shocked him, as they did all Americans. He found himself engaged in acrimonious arguments with his grandson over the Vietnam War. As a loyal Democrat he supported it, since it was being waged by a Democratic president. After Johnson's decision not to run for reelection in 1968, Hurok even tried to persuade him to reconsider.

The Soviet invasion of Czechoslovakia in August made the prospect of an improvement in relations between Moscow and Washington more unlikely than ever. Only a month earlier, the sixth consecutive Agreement of Exchanges in the Scientific, Technical, Educational, Cultural, and Other Fields had been signed in Moscow, capping a decade of U.S.-USSR exchange. As a result of the Soviet action in Czechoslovakia, however, the U.S. government put all cultural contacts with the Soviet Union and Eastern Europe on hold. The outlook for East-West cultural exchange had not looked so bleak since before Stalin died.

All this bad news did not make 1968 a very auspicious year for Hurok to celebrate his eightieth birthday. It also set him to thinking about the future of his business.

By now, it had become clear to Hurok that his grandson Peter Hyams had no interest in succeeding him as head of Hurok Concerts, as he had long hoped. "Being S. Hurok's grandson was not the kind of billing I was looking forward to," Hyams said. "And I wasn't even mildly interested in the managing and producing end of that business." Nor had Hurok groomed anyone else in the office to take over for him when he retired. If anything, he had been careful not to give any of his senior associates—Martin Feinstein, Walter Prude, and George Perper—too much information about what he was up to. He made sure each one knew only one small part of the whole, so none of them could put all the pieces together without him. He guarded the power, control, and glory for himself and himself alone.

And yet Hurok knew he had to make some sort of change. Even without all the new problems in Moscow, the business of presenting, especially for an independent like Hurok, was becoming financially unviable. The costs had risen astronomically. With increased rental and union regulations, he now had to take in $400,000 on the Royal Ballet during its Met run just to break even. Ticket prices for ballet, opera, and symphony concerts were fast growing far beyond the reach of the "masses" to whom Hurok always claimed to cater. Television and the rapidly expanding recording industry were transforming the entertainment landscape, and he did not have the sums of money necessary to invest in equipment, retooling, and retraining. Even the colleges and universities that used to book his classical attractions now wanted popular ones.

"It was just becoming crazy," observed Peter Hyams. "He knew the business was no longer going to be what it was."

So Hurok began quietly exploring the possibilities of selling his operation to a large corporation. He still had a great deal to offer: a trademark with unequaled clout and recognition at the high end of the income scale, a stable of artists that included most of the finest talent in classical music and dance, and a smoothly running office staffed by forty veterans. The operation had been producing between $8 million and $10 million annual gross and a before-tax income of $1 million in recent years. In the 1968–69 season, Hurok was presenting sixty attractions in more than two thousand concert dates to nearly five million customers.

Such numbers proved attractive to, among others, the entertainment industry conglomerate Transcontinental Investing Corporation. After delicate negotiations carried out for TIC by lawyer Herbert Wasserman, who won Hurok's trust by conversing with him fluently in Yiddish, Hurok Concerts, Inc. (as the agency was now known), was sold on February 24, 1969, for an undisclosed amount of cash. According to Wasserman, the selling price was "either $1.7 or $1.8 million"—all of which went to Hurok.

Under the terms of the sale, Hurok remained for at least three years as the handsomely salaried president and chief executive of his operation, which became one of ten TIC subsidiaries. A Manhattan-based corporation which began in real estate and later expanded into banking, discotheques, recording, and music publishing, Transcontinental also agreed to inaugurate a new record label, Hurok Records, primarily for classical releases. (That part of the deal never materialized, however.) Eager to expand its activities in television, TIC was hoping to exploit Hurok's considerable experience in preparing performing arts broadcasts for the networks and films for the educational market. For Hurok, it was a very advantageous deal.

In his comments to the press, he stressed that he would continue to be in charge of his operation. "I'm not getting out. Not until I die." Just six months before Woodstock would transform the entertainment market, he also spoke enthusiastically of the new opportunities TIC's vast resources would open up.

> We need other departments—pop music, theater, and so on. I could produce four, five or six popular records and it would be easy to slip in two or three classical records. I want to do things in a bigger way, to reach a new public. We are having great trouble getting the girls and boys to classical concerts. We have a great problem with American youth. They are not following concert music as they once did. We must not ignore the youth of this country today. We have to get them and somehow cater to them. My motto is, if you can't expand you have to suspend.

Hurok's decision to sell the business to TIC took everyone in his office, including those who considered themselves his closest associates, completely by surprise. "There had been rumors," explained Lillian Libman, "but no one paid any real attention. And he didn't prepare us at all—it was just presented as a fait accompli. Nobody knew anything. It was really terrible, and created a lot of hard feelings." After the sale, Hurok tried to explain it to his employees as a move to ensure the future of the firm, since he wouldn't be around forever. "But never for a minute did any of us ever believe that he really wanted the firm to go on after him," said Lee Walter.

Even those who weren't happy about the sale, such as George Perper and Martin Feinstein, had to admit that the boss had done very well for himself. For more than fifty years now, he had built his reputation and business the hard way, risking his own money—something the corporate impresarios at Columbia Artists would never have dared to do. He had gambled all his life, and now he deserved, in the words of his grandson, "to cash out" and let others cover the risk. The good timing that had always served him so well did not desert him on this occasion, either. When he sold, he sold high, at the zenith of his career and on his own terms.

CHAPTER TWENTY-TWO

Lots Guts and Balls

"What would it mean to me to sit in Central Park or walk the dog?"—*Sol Hurok on retirement*

FOR THE 1969–70 SEASON, its first as a subsidiary of Transcontinental Investing Corporation, Hurok Concerts fielded a remarkable list of artists, simply the best in the business. Most of them colorful characters with enough "temperament" to warm Siberia, many had long ago become theatrical and musical legends. The constellation of pianists starred Hurok's longtime sidekick Arthur Rubinstein, who turned eighty-three that season. Joining him were Texas sensation Van Cliburn, Odessites Emil Gilels and Sviatoslav Richter, and Vladimir Ashkenazy. The selection of cellists also featured the biggest names around: the ethereal and doomed Jacqueline Du Pré; Gregor Piatigorsky, a towering Russian with a huge appetite for life and music; and forty-three-year-old Mstislav Rostropovich, another wildly extroverted character who would build on the legacy of Piatigorsky and Pablo Casals in popularizing the cello as a solo instrument.

As for violinists, Hurok's inventory didn't contain a single second-rank fiddler, with the possible exception of Wanda Wilkomirska. From Russia he had superstar David Oistrakh and his son Igor; Leonid Kogan; and twenty-four-year-old Viktor Tretyakov. Most of his "American violinists" had also grown from Eastern European roots. They included Isaac Stern, now a familiar public figure who had helped to save Carnegie Hall and continued to speak out for greater government support of the arts; the prickly Nathan Milstein, who refused on principle to return to the USSR which he had abandoned in the 1920s; and the fluent youngsters Itzhak Perlman and Pinchas Zukerman. Members of the next generation, they were carrying on the tradition of soulful Jewish fiddling that had first convinced Hurok of the power of music as a restless adolescent back on the dusty streets of Pogar.

Hurok had also assembled an impressive stable of thoroughbred conductors. It ranged from French prodigy Daniel Barenboim (cross-listed as a pianist) through avant-gardist Pierre Boulez to Antal Dorati, Erich Leinsdorf, Lorin Maazel, Soviets Kiril Kondrashin and Yevgeny Svetlanov, and Russian-American Igor Stravinsky. If it was guitarists you were after you could choose among three of the greatest: Julian Bream, Andrés Segovia, and John Williams. Nor were the dance attractions second-rate. Old-timers American Ballet Theatre (back in the Hurok fold despite sometimes strained relations), the Bolshoi, the Kirov, the Moiseyev, and the Royal (which had grossed $714,000 in three California cities alone during the preceding season) were joined by the relative newcomers Ballet Folklorico of Mexico (a big commercial and artistic hit), the Royal Danish Ballet, the Royal Winnipeg Ballet, and the Stuttgart Ballet.

Reflecting the economic difficulties of presenting orchestras on tour, only three (the Minnesota Orchestra, the Moscow Philharmonic, and the Stockholm Philharmonic) made the list. Hurok generally preferred either large glitzy ensembles or individual superstars, so the presence of only one chamber ensemble—the Melos Ensemble of Isaac Stern, Eugene Istomin, and Leonard Rose—does not surprise. Considering their frequency in the general musical population, singers were underrepresented, although almost all of Hurok's were at or near the top of the profession: Victoria de los Angeles, Roberta Peters, Galina Vishnevskaya, Janet Baker, Grace Bumbry, Shirley Verrett, Irina Arkhipova, Maureen Forrester, Nicolai Gedda, Peter Pears, Jan Peerce, and Jerome Hines. Marian Anderson, who turned sixty-five in 1969, had moved into the theatrical category and was available for speaking engage ments and to narrate Copland's patriotic *A Lincoln Portrait.* Among her theatrical comrades were the Comédie Française and, lest the list look too stuffy, that outrageously irreverent detonator of musical pretensions, the merciless satirist and gifted composer P.D.Q. Bach (aka Peter Schickele).

Looking at Hurok's list, it's not difficult to see why he was often accused of favoring European names and established artists at the expense of American and younger performers. In fact European and Russian attractions do dominate—especially in the field of dance. Even officials at conservative Gosconcert criticized Hurok for being interested only in big names and neglecting to notice and develop new artists. Of course as Hurok aged, the artists on his list, many of whom had been with him for years, aged along with him. But Hurok did not completely ignore the talent of tomorrow. Among others, he "discovered" singers Teresa Stratas and Carol Neblett and pianists Stephen Bishop, Garrick Ohlsson, and Alexander Slobodyanik.

Recommended to Hurok by Sviatoslav Richter, the teenage Slobodyanik was a handsome Prince Valiant look-alike when he made his first American tour in the 1968–69 season. "I was young, just starting out as a pianist really, and I had both very successful and very unsuccessful concerts in America. There were times when the critics were very hard on me. And Hurok would just tell me not to pay attention." For Slobodyanik, Hurok was a kindly figure of mythical proportions. Even so, the pianist did not share his manager's excessive fondness for the tried-and-true repertoire, his conservative (even "retrograde") musical taste, or his apparently insatiable appetite for obvious public and commercial success.

After only two seasons with Hurok, Slobodyanik was handed over by all-powerful Gosconcert to Columbia Artists, having become a pawn in the increasingly ruthless struggle between the two American firms for Soviet attractions. Despite Hurok's shortcomings, there was no comparison, Slobodyanik said later, between Columbia, which was like a "factory with a board of directors," and Hurok's agency. Hurok's agency belonged to an earlier era, with its delicate personal concern for the artist's welfare and whim. "What was so special about being with Hurok was that his relationship with the artist was always so natural."

When Hurok took on a young artist like Slobodyanik, he almost always acted upon the recommendation of one of his established artists. That's what had happened a few years earlier in the case of Itzhak Perlman, now recognized as one of the greatest violinists of his generation. While still a boy, the wunderkind Perlman had caught the attention of Isaac Stern, who undertook to press his case with Hurok. Over a long lunch in London, Stern told his longtime manager that he had found a new "fiddler" with an astonishing talent. Years later, he recalled their conversation:

> And I told him that his name was Perlman, and that he was on crutches. And Hurok said, "Crutches? Ba-ba, ba-ba, no, no, no." And I said, "Papa, you'll do as I say. His father works in a laundry. No money. He needs help. You will pay him $500 a month plus travel and accompanist and printing costs, and you won't make him play more than ten times a season for the next two seasons. And if it costs you twenty-five or thirty or forty thousand dollars you can lay it off your taxes. After two years you make your own deal, and I guarantee you're going to make a fortune." He looked at me and said, "You really mean it?" And I said, "Listen to me." That was the contract, that was the deal. You tell me somebody else who would do that.

Hurok never regretted taking Stern's advice, since Perlman turned into a very popular and profitable addition to his list. So did another Stern recommendation, Pinchas Zukerman. Together, they became the backbone of the Manhattan-based Jewish musical clique jokingly labeled the "Kosher Nostra."

In assembling and maintaining his list of artists, Hurok operated on instinct and emotion. He would only represent something he truly believed in, something first-class. Ultimately what he looked for was projection. Hurok saw and heard with the eyes and ears of the audience and could predict with remarkable accuracy who would touch the public and who wouldn't. He could see beyond pure technique to something inside. "He didn't have the musical understanding of a scholar or specialist," explained Slobodyanik.

"But he had a sixth sense for the aura surrounding an artist, the aura of success or the ability to interest an audience. And after all, most people in a concert audience don't have any special education either. Like Hurok, they just have hearts."

If at first life changed little for Hurok's artists after the sale of his agency to TIC, his employees in the office on Fifth Avenue noticed a different atmosphere almost immediately. Although "the boss" tried to carry on as though nothing had happened and pointedly ignored the TIC officials now lurking around the office, his subordinates felt a new tension in what had always been a rather familial operation. "There were people looking over Hurok's shoulder now," observed Martin Feinstein. Besides no longer knowing who they were actually accountable to, Hurok's employees had to get used to the parent corporation's attempts to quantify all aspects of what was inherently a risky and unpredictable business. TIC demanded exact projections for all expenses and income, information Hurok had never asked his people to produce before.

"Mr. Hurok used to say, 'Okay, this is what you spend here and this is what you spend there,' " explained Lee Walter, his longtime secretary. "And we spent that, because the rest was his." The idea of predicting exactly how much the firm would make each year was completely foreign to Walter and his co-workers, since so much depended on uncertainties like whether or not an attraction would catch on with the public. The spontaneity and volatility necessary for any successful show-business venture frightened and intimidated the gray men of TIC. Expenses for items like gifts for the artists suddenly came under the scrutiny of cost-conscious accountants with little appreciation of the need to stroke performers' egos. What had been an upscale mom-and-pop store was turning into an impersonal corporate asset. Many of the office's veterans, including Lillian Libman and Martin Feinstein, started casting about for opportunities elsewhere.

The already plentiful tension and insecurity only intensified in the 1969–70 season due to a new and more ominous threat. Performances by Hurok's Soviet attractions now became a favorite target for harassment by members of the Jewish Defense League, a radical group employing terrorist tactics to bring attention to one of its main causes: the persecution of the Jewish minority in the USSR.

Founded in May 1968 in New York City, the JDL was led by an angry, charming, and eloquent Queens rabbi, Meir Kahane. Initially, he and his small but tightly organized group of followers rose to notoriety and influence by capitalizing on the growing atmosphere of racial tension that was polarizing the ethnic communities of New York and other large American cities in the late 1960s.

From the very beginning, Kahane placed the alleged anti-Semitism of New York's black community high on the list of his "Jewish pride" movement's many grievances. As traditionally Jewish neighborhoods like Hurok's own Brownsville fell into steep economic and social decline and the crime rate soared, it was tempting to blame the blacks who were moving into such areas in increasing numbers. Kahane also attacked New York's liberal Republican mayor, John Lindsay, for pandering to black leaders and refusing to protect the lives and property of Jews. Whether or not Lindsay was to blame, the golden era for Jews in New York seemed surely to be passing, and thousands were fleeing to the suburbs. Many of the JDL's early recruits were teachers who had participated in the highly publicized and divisive 1968 school strike. It pitted Jewish educators and community leaders against the black school board chief of the Ocean Hill–Brownsville district.

The basic elements of the JDL credo were a Jewish separatism ("The Jew rejects any effort to melt or integrate into non-Jewish society which is foreign to Judaism") that approached chauvinism ("Jewish interests are the first in any order of Jewish priorities"). Kahane and his supporters violently rejected the American "melting pot" philosophy so dear to Hurok. They also ridiculed what they called the "Jewish Establishment," the assimilationist "liberals" like former Supreme Court Justice Arthur Goldberg who had fought a "never-ending battle to be Jewish but not *too* Jewish." Kahane accused them of forgetting their real identity and of placing their children "on the altar of empty, vapid materialism and status."

By early 1969, Kahane and the JDL, described by many as the Jewish Black Panthers, had moved from a war of words to struggle in the streets. They picketed a Brownsville black teacher who had accused Jews of controlling the teachers union, raided Manhattan radio station WBAI for broadcasting an anti-Semitic poem, even physically threatened Mayor Lindsay (whose chic "Fun City" seemed rapidly to be losing its sense of humor) when he arrived for a Board of Education meeting. The cars of JDL supporters sported bumper stickers reading "Every Jew a .22."

But Kahane's indignation was not limited to fighting the injustices suffered by Jews in New York. On December 29, 1969, he launched what would be a long and acrimonious campaign against persecution of Jews in the USSR by staging assaults on three prominent Soviet offices in New York: the news agency Tass, the tourist agency Intourist, and the national airline Aeroflot. Another group of JDL terrorists jumped aboard an Aeroflot plane just after it landed at Kennedy Airport. These brilliantly staged acts of guerrilla theater, Kahane later boasted, opened "a radical new chapter both in the saga of Soviet Jewry and in the history of the American Jewish community." They were intended to force the Soviet government to allow Jews to freely emigrate, and "to awaken the American Jew into a recognition that he had shamefully buried the Soviet Jewish problem while he himself enjoyed the freedoms of America."

Kahane's declaration of war on representatives of the USSR in the United States also spelled trouble for Hurok. By now, after ten years of front-page stories, the impresario was more closely identified with Soviet culture in the eyes of the average American than Tass, Intourist, and Aeroflot combined.

Indeed, Hurok now became the JDL's public enemy number one. To Kahane and his disciples, this refugee from the Russian Empire and former Brownsville resident symbolized almost everything that was wrong with the "liberal Jewish Establishment." He never went to synagogue and ignored Jewish dietary and other regulations. He had practiced and preached assimilation with other ethnic and religious groups almost since the first day he landed at Ellis Island. While ignoring Jewish rights, he had been a prominent supporter of black civil rights, most notably through his promotion of the career of Marian Anderson and other black performers. Despite all his globe-trotting, he had never been to Israel for fear of alienating the anti-Israeli Soviet officials with whom he did business in Moscow. And worst of all, he encouraged American recognition and acceptance of the Soviet regime (which had been harassing, arresting, and imprisoning Jews for years) by importing Soviet performing artists to the United States. In Meir Kahane's black-and-white world, Hurok was a moral outlaw "who had hit upon the exchange program as a marvelous way to make even more money than he already had."

After a lifetime spent trying to obscure, even deny, his humble Jewish origins, Hurok suddenly saw his nose being rubbed in his Pogar past. All that he thought he had left behind was now thrown in his face by a new, much more militant generation with no use for his habitual spirit of tolerance and compromise. Once a borderline radical who had begun his career by staging fund-raising concerts for socialists and looked to the Bolsheviks as saviors, Hurok now found himself accused of selling out to the evil Soviet Communists. Ironically, one of the co-founders with Kahane of the JDL, lawyer Bertram Zweibon, was himself the son of a former official in the American Communist party.

In early 1970, performances by Hurok artists and ensembles became a battleground on which small groups of JDL terrorists fought for their cause with zealous self-righteousness. Before a concert by the Moscow Philharmonic at Brooklyn College in January, JDL activists urged people to return their tickets and handed out leaflets with the message "They played music at Auschwitz, too." Just as the orchestra began to play, their comrades rushed through a back door onto the stage, singing Hebrew liberation songs and waving Israeli flags. Fights broke out and the police were called to restore order. A similar incident took place at a recital by David Oistrakh and Sviatoslav Richter at Carnegie Hall on February 1, when JDL supporters picketed out front and then ran down the aisles pursued by security guards. The next day, Hurok's office was briefly occupied by JDL demonstrators, twelve of whom were arrested.

Hurok had faced plenty of controversy around his performers in the past and knew that a little bit could be very good for business. But the JDL's violence and aggressiveness were something new and sinister. Disturbed at seeing his customers and performers harassed, and justifiably anxious over the implications for his relationship with the Soviet government, Hurok instructed an intermediary to meet with the JDL leader.

According to Kahane, when he met with Hurok's messenger at the St. Regis Hotel, he was told that "Mr. Hurok knew of the difficult situation of the JDL and would be willing to help us out—to the tune of $5000." But the offer of a financial settlement only convinced Kahane that "we were on the right track." Clearly, their well-planned guerrilla tactics were achieving the desired result of bringing unprecedented attention both to the plight of Soviet Jews and to the cowardice of American Jews in coming to the help of their less fortunate brothers and sisters. Far from bringing the disruptions of his performances to an end, then, Hurok's overture to Kahane only ensured their escalation.

All through 1970, the JDL and its supporters struck out with increasing confidence at concerts, exhibitions, and conferences featuring Soviet artists and officials. In March, twenty-eight pictures in the "USSR Photo '70" exhibit were defaced. In August, thirty-five hundred people had to be evacuated after tear gas grenades were thrown into a Chicago theater just before a performance by the Moiseyev Folk Dance Ensemble. Security at events featuring Soviet performers increased, only adding to Hurok's expenses and worries. Soviet newspapers, including the authoritative *Izvestiia*, began to grumble about the danger posed to Soviet-American relations by these "Zionist thugs" and the lack of sufficient protection for Soviet diplomats and other official visitors in the United States.

And yet in late August 1970, in the midst of this combative and volatile situation, eighty-two-year-old Hurok took the bold and perhaps surprising step of announcing (again) that he would bring the Bolshoi Opera to New York for the first time the following May. He had arranged the final details on a trip to Japan, where the company had been on tour. Boasting in an interview with the *New York Times* that he would surely lose money on bringing the 532 performers (including dancers from the Bolshoi Ballet) to the United States in what he considered to be the biggest risk of his entire career, he dropped one of his favorite maxims: "If I would be in this business for business, I wouldn't be in this business." His weekly expenses in presenting the Bolshoi Opera, he bragged with the bravado of P. T. Barnum, would total a staggering $300,000. He was undertaking the venture, he quipped, "because nobody else is as crazy as I am." Angels with money to invest in the project were more than welcome to contribute, he added, "but there are no more angels left." None except Hurok, that is.

As summer passed to autumn, JDL actions against official Soviet representatives in the United States showed no signs of abating. The Tass office was occupied and a car rammed into the fence around the Soviet Mission to the U.N. But the most serious incident in the campaign so far occurred at 3:20 A.M. on November 25, 1970, when a pipe bomb exploded in the doorway of the offices of Aeroflot and Intourist on East 49th Street. The blast was powerful enough to shatter windows and take radio station WMCA off the air for fifteen minutes. At a news conference the next day, Kahane denied JDL involvement in the bombing, but praised the perpetrators as heroes. High-ranking officials in Washington and Moscow condemned the act, and it threatened to escalate into a major international incident.

Within days of the bombing, Hurok flew to Moscow on a previously scheduled trip to make final arrangements for the upcoming Bolshoi tour. Despite the obvious anxiety and dissatisfaction of Soviet officials over the ongoing JDL anti-Soviet campaign, negotiations appeared to proceed normally. Only on December 11, the last day of Hurok's visit, did signs of trouble appear.

Just hours before Hurok was to catch his flight to London, the First Deputy Foreign Minister, Vasily Kuznetsov, met with the American ambassador in Moscow, Jacob Beam, and read him a statement from the Soviet government. Because of the failure of American officials to stop the "criminal actions" of "Zionist extremists" against Soviet citizens in the United States or to ensure that they would not be repeated, he said, it had been decided to cancel the Bolshoi Opera's planned tour. Beam tried immediately to contact Hurok to give him the bad news, but couldn't reach him. So Hurok had to hear from his old friend Ekaterina Furtseva at what he had thought would be their final upbeat meeting before his departure that all their work had once again gone for nothing.

Even for the instinctively diplomatic Hurok, seeing his lifelong dream of bringing the Bolshoi Opera go down the drain once again, only four months before the scheduled opening at the Met, was a bitter disappointment. For once, he even had trouble concealing his sadness. Alexander Slobodyanik had volunteered to accompany

Hurok to the airport. During the preceding days, they had been talking excitedly about the upcoming Bolshoi Opera tour—even about such details as "which scenery should go in which boxes." But when Slobodyanik arrived to pick up Hurok at the National Hotel, he could see immediately that something was wrong.

> He was so quiet, something I had never seen before, with hunched shoulders, wearing his usual broad-brimmed hat and dark overcoat. He gave me a little greeting, but we were already late, so we got into the car—I was sitting in back and he was in front. And I saw, to my great surprise, that suddenly he looked much older. I saw his thin neck, the sagging brim of his hat. It seemed that his head had gotten smaller, so that his hat seemed bigger and drooped lower. He was silent for a few moments, but when the car had turned around by the Hotel Moscow next to Red Square, he said, "It's all over. They just told me I can't bring the Opera." It was a catastrophe—not because he had already spent lots of money—but because it was such a personal blow. It led to many other problems and was one of the most difficult things that ever happened to him.

Since Hurok had already committed himself to pay something like $200,000 to rent the Met for the Bolshoi performances, he and TIC scrambled to try to find a suitable replacement to fill the dates. Improbably enough, the search even led to negotiations for a series of rock concerts to be set up by the great San Francisco-based rock impresario Bill Graham (of "Bill Graham Presents").

The brash and unflappable Graham, then forty years old and at the height of his career, was both surprised and flattered to get a call from Hurok's office. Although the raucous, driving performers he presented at the Fillmore and Winterland to screaming throngs of drugged-out rock fans could hardly have been more different from the sort of upscale attractions or audiences in which Hurok specialized, Graham still had great respect for what Hurok had achieved in the entertainment industry. Graham even considered him "my hero. He was *the* guy."

Graham's reverence for Hurok came in part, no doubt, from

434 • The Last Impresario

the similarity of their backgrounds. Like Hurok, Graham (whose real name was Wolfgang Grajonca) had fled repression in the Old World (he escaped Nazi Germany on foot) to start a new life in the New World. Also like Hurok, Graham rose from a poor ethnic community in one of New York's outer boroughs (the Bronx) to find wealth and fame as an impresario. In many ways, Graham was for his generation what Hurok had been to his. It was hardly surprising, then, that the prospect of meeting the granddaddy of impresarios at his offices in New York in early 1971 would excite the younger man from San Francisco. Hurok did not fail to live up to his billing as a vivid personality.

> Mr. Hurok did not look up from his desk. He had a bunch of newspaper clippings there. Being a notorious upside-down reader, I saw the clippings were about me. Before he even looked up, Mr. Hurok pointed at the paper. Then he said, "It says here, you got lots guts and balls. S'true?"
>
> That was his line. "It says here, you got lots guts and balls. S'true?"

Hurok explained how he needed to find an attraction for the Met after the Bolshoi cancellation and proposed that Graham put together a show featuring the best rock acts he could find. Graham was immediately enthusiastic, but warned that a decision would have to be made immediately, since the groups in question were booked far ahead and made "*big, big* money." When he told Hurok that the fees for the sort of high-quality rock bands they were talking about would come to $40,000 or $50,000 per week, the old man was shocked. This made even the fees for stars like Nureyev and Stern look like peanuts. But then Hurok, to use the elegant words of Graham's associate Frank Barsalona, "knew fuck-all about the rock business." They were from different worlds, as different as Tchaikovsky and Janis Joplin.

Even so, both sides were still prepared to collaborate. But then they had to resolve the question of billing. Would Hurok and Graham receive equal billing, and who would come first? They finally agreed on "Sol Hurok and Bill Graham Present," with their names printed side by side. Then Graham had to try to persuade the groups he wanted (Frank Zappa, the Byrds, the Band) to play at the Met for less than they usually earned. That's when the venture fell apart. When Graham told Jon Taplin, the Band's manager, that he could offer no more than $50,000 a week for eight shows, Taplin laughed incredulously. The Band had been making $25,000 a night for years, and he wasn't willing to make an exception—not even for the Met, and not even for Sol Hurok.

So in the end, Hurok and Bill Graham never did consummate their collaboration, and the Met remained rock-free. Unable to find an attraction to put into the theater during the weeks reserved for the Bolshoi, TIC and the Met finally agreed on a financial settlement.

For Kahane and the JDL, the cancellation of the planned 1971 Bolshoi Opera tour was their biggest victory yet. Splashed in headlines all over the world, it publicized their cause more widely than ever, making people more aware of the human rights abuses in the Soviet Union. These had already been receiving increasing attention after the publication in the West of the novels of dissident Soviet writer Alexander Solzhenitsyn, who described the USSR as one vast prison. A number of respected American newspapers commented in editorials that while they didn't condone violence and felt sorry for Hurok, neither did they condone the Soviet persecution of Jews and other minorities. For his part, Hurok never used his prominent position to criticize publicly the Soviet government for its mistreatment of Jews. His silence—so different from his outspokenness in defending Marian Anderson from discrimination thirty years earlier when it coincided with his commercial interests—disappointed some of his friends and co-workers.

Kahane later maintained that the international pressure exerted on the Kremlin by the JDL's actions against touring Soviet performers was instrumental in Moscow's decision to begin allowing Jews to emigrate to Israel. After decades in which emigration had been virtually nonexistent, fifteen thousand Soviet Jews were allowed to leave for Israel in 1971 and an increasing number in succeeding years. But this improvement came at a high price. Back in New York, Kahane's scare tactics sowed the seeds of a bitter hatred and mistrust between blacks and Jews that still afflicts many neighborhoods today and helped to poison the city's political life.

Even as Hurok was coming under attack from the JDL in New York for importing Soviet attractions, he found himself increasingly embattled in Moscow. Columbia Artists, which had also been vilified and harassed by Kahane for its dealings with the USSR, was stepping up its efforts to capture a larger number of profitable Soviet attractions. For several years already, Columbia's representative Joseph Zovarich had been making frequent trips to Moscow, where he had been undermining and challenging the special position Hurok had occupied there since the late 1950s. He had already succeeded in winning the Beryozka Ensemble away.

In putting its case to Gosconcert, Columbia stressed its willingness to take on young unknown performers, something Hurok had been slow and reluctant to do. According to former Gosconcert employee Larissa Netto, it was largely in response to the new pressure exerted by Columbia that Hurok in the late 1960s took on such new artists as Viktor Tretyakov, Alexander Slobodyanik, and singer Elena Obratsova. Columbia countered, however, by offering to sign up even less well-known performers, and to top the fees Hurok had been paying for the big ensembles. The resulting bidding war raised the amount paid per concert for the Moiseyev Ensemble (which remained through thick and thin with Hurok) above $45,000, making it harder than ever to turn a profit.

Several other factors contributed to the decline of Hurok's power and influence in Moscow. One was his age. Although he showed no signs of slowing down, Soviet officials knew that the day would come when Hurok would be gone and they would need to have other American managers with whom to deal. Another was the sale of Hurok Concerts to TIC. Ever conscious of the realities of political and economic power, bureaucrats at Gosconcert and the Ministry of Culture were no longer certain that Hurok had the authority to guarantee that his own decisions and promises would be carried out. And finally, there was Sheldon Gold.

An artists' manager since 1955, Gold came to the Hurok office in the early 1960s. Then in his early thirties, he worked in a variety of capacities, from salesman to accompanying artists on the road to booking attractions (primarily soloists). Well educated (he earned a degree in business administration from New York University), aggressive, ambitious, and outspoken, Gold soon felt restless and undervalued at Hurok Concerts. About to get married, he demanded a raise. Hurok never responded well in such situations, as many of his employees could testify, but Gold further annoyed him by presenting an ultimatum: Either he got a raise or he went to work for Hurok's arch-rival Columbia Artists. Infuriated, Hurok showed him the door. Just as he had threatened, Gold did in fact go to work for Columbia, taking with him some inside information about Hurok's dealing with Soviet attractions.

Before long, Gold was traveling to Moscow as Columbia's representative. There, according to Maxim Gershunoff, who worked closely with Soviet attractions in the Hurok office from 1960 to 1972, Gold "tried to ingratiate himself with the Soviets" by telling them stories about how Hurok was receiving extra income from touring Soviet soloists and misrepresenting his expenses and profits. When confronted with these charges in Moscow, an annoyed Hurok—who had lost hundreds of thousands of dollars on large ensembles like the Kirov Ballet and the Moscow Art Theatre over the years and had personally subsidized the tours his American artists made in the USSR—traced them down to his former employee. Back in New York, said Gershunoff, Hurok vowed that he would someday take revenge on Gold for his duplicity.

The atmosphere at Gosconcert's shabbily utilitarian offices on Neglinnaya Street, just behind the Bolshoi, grew tense as Hurok and Columbia waged what Netto described as their "mean and desperate struggle." Sometimes the competitors would arrive simultaneously in Moscow for negotiations. Hurok would always stay in the National Hotel, and the Columbia delegation (often headed by Ronald Wilford) in the art-nouveau Metropole. "It was a constant drama," said Netto, "deciding who would come to the negotiations each day, and which artists we would give to whom. It was difficult and exhausting not only for them, but also for all of us. Because we could see both sides, and we felt bad for both parties. In the end, there was a fairness to what was happening, because it really wasn't right for us to be giving everything to Hurok." While denouncing capitalism on ideological grounds, Soviet officials could be very shrewd at manipulating its Western practitioners for financial gain.

But if Netto could see the rightness of Columbia's challenge on professional grounds, on a personal level she felt much greater rapport with Hurok, with whom she had been working since 1961. There was a stark contrast between Hurok and the representatives of Columbia, she said:

> The Columbia people worked well, accurately, and paid high fees, but they were robots. Hurok was a man. With Ronald Wilford it was very straightforward: "Okay, I like that, give me that," or "No, I don't want that, thanks." It was already like a factory, mass-production style, with all their corporate divisions.
>
> If Hurok would do a tour, he'd do a month at the Met, a few weeks in Washington, San Francisco, Los Angeles, Cleveland—the big cities. But Columbia would bleed the artists dry, sending them on buses to Community Concerts all over the place: "give a concert and get on the bus, give a concert and get on the bus." In three months they would cover as many as sixty cities. It was exhausting for them. They would arrive home just dead.
>
> Hurok would only do tours on the most prestigious level. And he would take pity on the artists and quietly, on the sly, he would feed them so they could spend their per diem allowances on something else.

But it wasn't only his obvious passion for Russian culture and his attentiveness to the artists that impressed Netto and her co-workers. His wisdom and subtlety inspired and amused them, too. "He taught us all how to live, how to do our work and how to deal with people. His behavior was a model for us in how to work in this very subtle business."

Even in his dealings with hostile officials intent on undermining his monopoly, Hurok never lost his temper or raised his voice. One of the leaders of the anti-Hurok faction was the Deputy Director of Gosconcert, Vladimir Golovin. "Once Hurok came to the office, and the negotiations were very bitter and tough. Golovin was a very explosive guy," recalled Netto.

> He was walking back and forth in the office, and talking very loudly and vociferously, crudely and aggressively.

And Hurok was sitting in a low armchair, and he let his hands drop, and he was looking calmly out of the window as Golovin carried on. And finally Golovin turned to him and said, "So give me an answer then, now," in a commanding tone of voice.

And Hurok raised his head slowly and said, with his usual accent, "You know I got a call from London yesterday and they said it was raining there. I don't know how I'm going to fly there, because I forgot to bring my umbrella."

He showed us all that he had just let everything that Golovin had been carrying on about pass right over his head, and that he would never pay attention or ever reply to that sort of behavior. He was always quiet and calm, with shrewd, intelligent eyes.

Golovin was paralyzed. He wanted to add something, but Hurok just said calmly, "Well, I guess I'll go now." He said good-bye and stood up and left. Golovin just didn't know what to do.

Meanwhile, back in New York, the officers of Transcontinental Investing Corporation were having second thoughts about owning Hurok Concerts. The entertainment part of their business was doing badly, especially record sales, and they began looking around to unload assets to produce some cash. Since they already knew him from his role in negotiating the original sale in 1969, they turned once again to Herbert Wasserman, the lawyer and former officer of TIC, to negotiate the sale of what they claimed was a still-profitable Hurok Concerts.

Despite all of Hurok's well-publicized recent difficulties, his operation still possessed a certain mystique that appealed to investors. When word got around that the agency might be on the market again, an interested party soon appeared. It was Tomorrow Entertainment, Inc., a new subsidiary of General Electric formed in December 1970. Tomorrow Entertainment had been created by Thomas W. Moore, the former president of ABC, for the purpose of investing in feature film and stage productions, closed-circuit television distribution, and other entertainment projects.

When informed by TIC of the possibility of another sale,

Hurok became anxious. He was still owed a large payment from the original sale agreement. He needn't have worried. A shrewd negotiator, Wasserman succeeded in convincing General Electric to pay just over $3 million for Hurok Concerts, nearly double the sum TIC had paid to acquire the agency just two and a half years earlier. Most of this money went to Hurok. As part of the deal, which was made public on June 27, 1971, GE insisted that Wasserman become executive vice president of Hurok Concerts, the highest-ranking officer below Hurok. The officers of GE wanted to have someone they knew and trusted in control there, especially considering Hurok's advanced age and declining health. (He had been absent from the office several times in the last few years due to various medical problems.) Hurok would remain as the salaried president of Hurok Concerts and would continue to run the outfit more or less as before.

As had been the case with the sale to TIC, news of the impending sale to GE was kept secret even from the senior members of the Hurok Concerts staff. It was presented to the three vice presidents (Martin Feinstein, Walter Prude, and George Perper) as a fait accompli. That they had been kept in the dark, again passed over, and even given a new boss, created more uneasiness among them and their colleagues.

To the press, TIC explained blandly that it had decided to sell because "expansion had not occurred as originally planned." Speaking for the new owner, Tomorrow Entertainment, Moore said that he hoped "to expand the field covered by Hurok Concerts, both by going into small towns, and by entering the popular music field."

Hurok, as usual, put the most diplomatic and optimistic face on things, claiming that "our affiliation with Tomorrow Entertainment will enable our artists to appear in more places, before more people, in more ways than anyone ever dreamed of!" Specific plans included exposing Hurok's artists more widely through television, recordings, films, and the projected closed-circuit TV network. Being affiliated with a large corporation like GE would also give Hurok greater spending power (and certainly greater personal income) than he could have as an independent. "Today, there is very little room left for independent managers because of the expenses you have to carry," he explained.

But there was a serious problem with the new arrangement. The people at Tomorrow Entertainment and GE knew even less about the business of presenting Hurok's classical entertainment than their predecessors at TIC. Moore's previous experience had been limited almost exclusively to television. "Frankly, nobody, to a person, at GE had any concept of what the classical music business was about," said Wasserman in retrospect. "I don't even know if any of them had ever been to the Metropolitan Opera House before. They used to ask the most incredible questions. Once one of the GE people asked me, 'What's a gig?' When I explained that it was an engagement for an attraction, he persisted, 'Well, why do they call it that?' The mix between Hurok and GE never really worked. They just didn't understand one another."

Dissatisfaction over the sale of GE also led Martin Feinstein, Hurok's head of publicity for twenty-five years as well as one of his closest confidants and most trusted artistic advisers, to leave the firm. As of January 1, 1972, Feinstein took the position of executive director of performing arts for the newly opened John F. Kennedy Center in Washington, D.C. Hurok was very unhappy about Feinstein's departure and begged him—in tears, according to Feinstein—not to leave. But the fact that he and the two other vice presidents still didn't have a pension plan after decades of dedicated work (the most they had been able to extract from Hurok was a profit-sharing arrangement), as well as the uncertainty of the future under GE, made Feinstein feel he couldn't afford to turn down the exciting offer of running the Kennedy Center. "I felt the office was changing," said Feinstein sadly. "It was a very difficult departure for Hurok, and a very emotional one for me. If the changes hadn't taken place, I probably would have stayed."

To fill the void left by Feinstein's resignation, Hurok made two personnel changes. He surprised most observers by bringing in an outsider, Sheila Porter, to be his new director of publicity, a position many anticipated would be given to his longtime associate Lillian Libman. And after delicate negotiations conducted by Wasserman, Hurok brought Sheldon Gold back from Columbia Artists to be a vice president at Hurok Concerts. Gold requested to be released from his contract to Columbia before it expired, but Columbia refused, forcing him to sit idle there for several months before returning to his former employer.

Why Hurok brought Gold back into the fold and then made it known that he considered him his heir apparent as president of Hurok Concerts has been a source of considerable speculation. After all, Hurok had reportedly been furious with Gold for scheming against him in Moscow on Columbia's behalf. Some longtime Hurok employees, including Max Gershunoff, have suggested that the boss was actually setting Gold up by luring him back, getting even by putting him in the position where he would be responsible for the inevitable collapse of Hurok Concerts. According to this byzantine scenario worthy of the old days of de Basil and the Monte Carlo Ballet Russe, Hurok would have his revenge by knowing that Gold would be left holding the bag when the roof fell in after he was gone.

Après moi, le déluge.

CHAPTER TWENTY-THREE ■

Bombs on Balalaikas

"The people want to see me. They're not going for the performers alone."—*S. Hurok on his eighty-fifth birthday gala*

NOT LONG AFTER the sale of his agency to Tomorrow Entertainment/GE, Hurok was persuaded by Herb Wasserman to move his nearly sixty employees from the office they had occupied for more than twenty years at 730 Fifth Avenue to new quarters. They were on the twentieth floor of a thirty-four-story building at 56th Street and Sixth Avenue, near Carnegie Hall. Totally air-conditioned, wrapped in dark-tinted glass, and outfitted with sealed windows that couldn't be opened, the building was a typical example of the latest style in midtown skyscrapers. But these futuristic towers of glass with their completely controlled internal environments were also rapidly acquiring a reputation as death traps. Asphyxiated by smoke, five people had perished in fires in sealed-window skyscrapers in 1970 alone.

Another one died on January 26, 1972, when an incendiary bomb exploded in the lobby of the new offices of Hurok Concerts.

The day, a Wednesday, began normally enough. Hurok was at his desk in the large office at the far corner of the suite by shortly after nine A.M. Ten other employees had also arrived for work already. Several workmen were putting the finishing touches on the reception area.

At about 9:20, two neatly dressed white men in their twenties came in and asked the temporary receptionist, Kelly Brown, a college student, about tickets to a performance they were interested in. He went to find the information, asking them to wait. When he returned, however, they were gone. Before Brown or anyone else had time to notice the ordinary-looking briefcase they had left behind, the tiny Micronta timer inside it had counted down to zero.

Suddenly there was loud strange whooshing sound and a pink and blue explosion. Within minutes, the connecting rooms of Hurok Concerts were engulfed with suffocating smoke, flame, and heat. Because the building was hermetically sealed, the air-conditioning ducts recycled the poisonous fumes, spreading them even to the offices at the opposite end of the suite, where several employees had sought refuge. The fire was so hot that it melted typewriters and office machines.

Hurok could see thick smoke descending from the ceiling of his large corner office. Quickly grasping that he would suffocate without fresh air, he picked up a paperweight and smashed it through the heavy glass—a considerable feat for a man of nearly eighty-four. Others did the same, overcoming their rising panic to break the windows with chairs, typewriters, and pails and screaming for help. Pedestrians scattered as debris showered down to the sidewalk three hundred feet below. But secretaries Virginia Proodian, Iris Kones, and Myra Armstrong were too scared to think of breaking the windows as they huddled together in a small room a hundred feet from the fire.

"We put ourselves down on the floor and covered our faces," Armstrong recounted. "I burst into tears. Virginia said, 'It's all right; somebody will come for us.' Iris was real frightened. I can't remember what she said, but she was absolutely still after awhile."

When firemen finally arrived, they found the three with their faces buried in the thick carpet and their hair singed. Proodian and Armstrong responded to treatment at the scene, but Kones did not. She was pronounced dead of asphyxiation on arrival at Roosevelt Hospital. Ironically, twenty-seven-year-old Kones was one of the newest additions to the staff, having started work at Hurok Concerts only a few months earlier. Like most of the people in the office, she was Jewish.

When the firemen found Hurok, they at first thought he was

dead. They carried him from the building conscious, swathed in his fur coat, but badly shaken. It didn't take the "victim" long to regain his sense of publicity, however. According to Joe Lewis, former publicity director of the National Ballet of Canada (which Hurok would present in the United States for the first time in 1973–74), he refused to leave until cameramen arrived. After his picture was taken, an ambulance took Hurok to Polyclinic Hospital, where he was treated for smoke inhalation and released. Altogether, thirteen people were injured in the bombing.

Just a few minutes before the explosion at Hurok Concerts, another incendiary bomb had exploded at the offices of Columbia Artists, a few blocks away on West 57th Street. There were no injuries there, however, because the offices were on the ground floor. Most of the few employees who had already turned up for work were able to run out a back door or to escape through windows opening on the street.

Immediately after the explosions, anonymous callers told the Associated Press, NBC, and other news organizations that they had been staged to protest "the deaths and imprisonment of Soviet Jews." Pronouncing the JDL slogan "Never again," they said, "Cultural bridges of friendship will not be built over the bodies of Soviet Jews." From Jerusalem, where he had been living for several months, Meir Kahane denied any responsibility for the action, calling the perpetrators "insane." In New York, JDL vice chairman Bertram Zweibon claimed that the deed had been done by radical left-wing provocateurs attempting to discredit his organization. The New York City police commissioner denounced the JDL anyway, accusing it of having created a "rhetoric of violence" encouraging terrorist attacks in recent years.

Recuperating on Park Avenue, where he received sympathy visits from Soviet officials, Hurok lay the blame on "irresponsible criminals" and vowed that the attack would only lead him to set up "better and bigger" cultural exchanges with the USSR. "I could be better, but I'm alive," he said. "I think if the firemen had arrived five or ten minutes later, I wouldn't be here."

Over the next few days, the attack on Hurok Concerts inspired an international outpouring of sympathy for Hurok, hundreds of articles (including an outraged editorial in the *New York Times*), broadcasts, and at least one poem. It happened that Yevgeny

Yevtushenko was in town. Accustomed to responding to the latest headlines, the thirty-eight-year-old Soviet poet toured the ruined Hurok offices the day after the bombing. That same evening, he produced a three-page *poème d'occasion,* "Bombs on Balalaikas." Composed in his customary jocular, striding, egotistical style, it praises Hurok's role as a cultural ambassador, and compares the smoke-filled room in which Iris Kones died to a Nazi gas chamber.

> How many friends you have,
> Solomon Izrailevich,
> In your office
> In frames under glass!
> There, on the floor—
> Lies Stanislavsky, wounded,
> Alongside—
> Plisetskaya, half-trampled.
> There, where the damned bomb blasted,
> Next to somebody's earrings,
> Chaliapin's broken portrait roars and booms
> Its inscription in bold letters:
> "To you, Solomonchik."
> Fresh air!
> I am frightened,
> Troubled.
> I can't restrain a cry of grief:
> Why attack you, poetry and music?
> Why attack you,
> Concertinas and violins?

Yevtushenko recited this poem for the first time before an adoring audience of five thousand admirers at the Felt Forum on the Saturday night following the bombing, the same day that it was published in the Soviet government newspaper *Izvestiia.*

The saddest irony of the bombing for Hurok was to find himself now under attack on all sides. In Moscow, Soviet officials were accusing him of paying low fees and denying him the Bolshoi Opera because of Zionist extremism directed at Soviet performers on tour in the United States. In New York, American radicals were targeting him for cozying up to the Soviets. In neither place could he find safe haven. He was now paying for all those years of free publicity given to his politically sensitive Soviet attractions.

An intensive investigation of the bombing by local police and the FBI failed to produce any suspects for nearly five months. Finally, on June 16, 1972, a federal grand jury indicted three young members of the JDL for the murder of Iris Kones: Sheldon Seigel, Stuart Cohen, and Sheldon Davis. Their trial would be long and complicated, however. A thirty-three-year-old Harvard law professor named Alan Dershowitz was persuaded by a boyhood friend from Brooklyn to defend Seigel. Never having tried a case in court before, the brilliant and highly verbal Dershowitz would turn Seigel's defense into a widely publicized landmark decision on governmental wiretapping that would launch his career as a superstar attorney.

Everyone who knew and worked with Hurok saw that he was never the same again after the bombing. His health, already somewhat weakened by several recent illnesses and operations, was undermined by the shock of the experience and the inhalation of the smoke. Intent on retaining his robust public image, he was admitted to Roosevelt Hospital—under the pseudonym Henry Williams. But his hungry ego couldn't maintain the disguise for long, and he started revealing his identity to the hospital staff with exaggerated theatricality. When it turned out that the orderlies had no idea who Sol Hurok was, he found it hard to conceal his disappointment.

And yet there were many who knew and appreciated what the old man had done. Partly as a result of sympathy generated by the bombing, Hurok found himself honored and feted with even greater frequency than usual. Over the preceding five years, he had already received a pile of honors and citations from all sorts of charitable and performing arts organizations. In 1966, *Dance* magazine gave Hurok one of its prestigious annual awards for his contribution to the development of American dance. In early 1967, the Society of Stage Directors and Choreographers gave him an award and a glittering dinner ball in the Grand Ballroom of the New York Hilton in tribute to his international contributions to the performing arts. Basking in the attention, Hurok "probably covered more mileage table-hopping than a ballerina rehearsing for *Swan Lake*."

In late 1968, the American Council for Nationalities Service had presented Hurok with its Golden Door Award, given to an immigrant who had made distinguished contributions to American life and culture. (Past winners had included Samuel Goldwyn and Leopold Stokowski.) In a telegram read at the dinner, Arthur Goldberg called Hurok "a one-man United Nations" who "has contributed to the realization of one of the great purposes of the UN—to be a center for harmonizing the actions of nations in achieving international cooperation in the cultural sphere."

But the biggest and most glamorous of all the Hurok love fests was the International Diamond Jubilee Gala held on May 21, 1973, at the Metropolitan Opera House. It commemorated Hurok's eighty-fifth birthday (assuming he really was born in April, 1888) and, rather arbitrarily, the sixtieth year of his professional work as an impresario (which actually began around 1910).

The event was put together by his artists, associates, and acquaintances among the international jet set as a benefit for the Performing Arts Research Center of the New York Public Library at Lincoln Center. Dancer-choreographers Agnes de Mille and Sir Robert Helpmann acted as masters of ceremonies, serving up a program of musical and dance bons bons that featured many of Hurok's longtime artists: Jerome Hines, Isaac Stern, Shirley Verrett, Jan Peerce, Roberta Peters, Van Cliburn, Natalia Bessmertnova, and Mikhail Lavrovsky, and Margot Fonteyn dancing the Act II pas de deux from Swan Lake with Desmond Kelly. (Rudolf Nureyev was originally scheduled to perform, but the invitation was canceled after Soviet authorities threatened to withdraw their artists in protest.) Prominent critics roasted Hurok in the program, and the Met's new general manager, Schuyler Chapin, thanked him for saving the house from financial disaster more than once during the nearly forty years he had been renting most of the off-season. (In the 1972–73 season, Hurok Concerts booked the Met for ten weeks, nearly one-third the length of the opera season.)

All thirty-seven hundred of the Met's seats were sold out weeks beforehand, yielding the library fund between $175,000 and $200,000. Mrs. Henry Ford II was the gala chairman, heading a list of socialites and diplomats in attendance that included Jackie Kennedy and her husband Aristotle Onassis, Rose Kennedy and her daughter Jean Smith, Rosalind Russell, the Prince and Princess

Alfonso de Bourbon of Spain, the Marquesa de Cuevas, and the ambassadors to the United States from Spain, France, Austria, Denmark, and the USSR. President Nixon sent a letter of congratulations. New York Mayor Lindsay bestowed upon Hurok the city's Handel Medal. Always very conscious of being recognized by those with power, influence, wealth, talent, or beauty, Hurok must have been very happy. "The people want to see me," he said matter-of-factly before the event. "They're not going for the performers alone."

His only regret was that with such a strong demand for tickets, the gala probably could have sold out Madison Square Garden at $25 a seat. At the Met, the top price was $100, coughed up by more than fifteen hundred people.

"All my life I've catered to the masses," he bragged to the *New York Times* the day after the festivities. The bejeweled crowd assembled for the Diamond Jubilee, however, was by no stretch of the imagination the same sort of "simple people" just off the boat who had turned up to see his attractions at the Hippodrome sixty years earlier. Its composition reflected the upscaling in the Hurok audience that had taken place in recent decades, especially since World War II.

Hurok also insisted that the jubilee was not to be considered a retirement party, that he was as full of plans for the future as ever, and that "age is for the calendar." "I like good food, good wine, and nice women," he told Leo Lerman of *Vogue*. "I'm not planning to go any place."

His feisty comments about the future notwithstanding, those who knew Hurok could see that he no longer had the inexhaustible energy and unfailing robust health he had enjoyed for his entire life. He looked thinner and smaller as he made his way from table to table greeting those who attended the $50-a-head gala ball at the Pierre Hotel after the jubilee performance. His wife, Emma, had also been ailing for some time now and rarely left her apartment on Central Park West. On this special and highly emotional occasion, she sent him an oddly formal telegram: "Dearest Sol, I know you will receive innumerable congratulations and honors tonight and there is little that I can add except to say keep well and be happy for many years to come. Love Emma."

Representing Hurok's family at the gala were his daughter Ruth, with whom he had been developing a somewhat closer relationship in recent years, her husband Arthur Lief, and Ruth's children Peter and Nessa Hyams, both now working successfully in the film industry in Hollywood. They, too, sensed that Papa might not be around forever.

Shortly before the Diamond Jubilee, Hurok gave an extended and surprisingly self-revelatory interview to Stephen Rubin of the *New York Times*. Here he admitted to feeling lonely sometimes, rattling around his large six-room apartment on Park Avenue with its modest collection of books and paintings. "I'm so attached to people; I love people. So if I'm not doing anything one night, I call up somebody and say, come over to the house, let's have dinner, let's sit around, let's have tea. If I go to a concert, I come home, get undressed, read the newspaper or a book, and suddenly I feel that I'd like to talk to somebody, to tell somebody the bad things and the good things." The news of the recent death of his brother, Asher, at age ninety-four in Leningrad had contributed to his unusually reflective and nostalgic mood.

Hurok also commented on the JDL, and on the ongoing trial of the three young men accused of bombing his offices:

> The JDL is just a small group objecting to everything. They certainly didn't do any good as far as the Jewish question is concerned in America, in Russia, or in Israel. The Russians want our government to take a stronger stand, and I don't blame them—to stop this mugging and harassment against Russian diplomats, artists and attractions. It's a horrible thing. I almost got killed myself. I can't understand the simply terrible judiciary system we have in this country. Those people have been brought into court a number of times, they have been proven guilty, and still the trials go on.

Only ten days after the Diamond Jubilee, and more than a year after Iris Kones was carried lifeless out of Hurok's offices, the trial of two of the three young JDL members indicted in the bombing finally opened with a splash of publicity in federal district court in New York. The trial had been delayed by the shrewd and complicated strategy adopted by Alan Dershowitz in his defense of one of the accused, Sheldon Seigel.

Seigel had joined the JDL in 1969. Soon afterward he began constructing homemade bombs for the organization, several of which were used in the terrorist campaign against Soviet officials in New York. But Dershowitz found a gaping hole in the case against Seigel in the Hurok bombing. In researching and interviewing this skinny, gawky kid who had received more than his share of abuse on the tough streets of Brooklyn, Dershowitz discovered that Seigel had been successfully recruited by the New York City Police in 1971—before the Hurok bombing—to inform on the activities of the JDL.

Finally giving in to the threats and promises of police detective Santo Parola, Seigel had become the "kosher canary," providing information about the JDL's plans in exchange for a promise that he would not be prosecuted for his known participation in several pending criminal cases. But Seigel didn't tell the cops everything. He didn't say a word in advance about the Hurok and Columbia bombings, which took the police and the FBI completely by surprise. Only after being offered an absolute guarantee that he would never be revealed as the informant at any trial did Seigel identify the perpetrators in these incidents. He also admitted making the bomb that killed Iris Kones.

Seigel's role as informer made him very anxious, however. By squealing on his collaborators, he was violating the most sacred principles of the JDL, of Jewish law, and of the neighborhood he had grown up in. He was also worried that Parola would go back on his promises. Determined to protect himself, Seigel began secretly taping their conversations, most of which took place in his car.

But Seigel wasn't the only one making recordings. Dershowitz and his associates now learned that the FBI—under authorization given by Attorney General John Mitchell—had installed wiretaps in the JDL headquarters and on Seigel's home phone without receiving the required warrant. With this knowledge, Dershowitz and his associates began building a defense for Seigel based on the unconstitutionality of these illegal wiretaps. Their interpretation was upheld by the federal judge hearing the case, Arnold Bauman.

The next step was to prove that the information extracted from Seigel by Detective Parola (and recorded on Seigel's tapes) had been "tainted" by information obtained unlawfully on the FBI wiretaps. A favorable finding on this point, Dershowitz believed, would then lead the judge to rule that Seigel would not have to testify against his friends in the Hurok bombing trial. In fact Judge Bauman did not find in Dershowitz's favor, but his decision was reversed by the U.S. Court of Appeals for the Second Circuit. Just as Dershowitz had hoped, the appeals judge declared that the court could not condone lawlessness (the use of illegal wiretaps), even in the pursuit of justice. This got Seigel off the hook. Even though he had admitted to Parola that he had fashioned the bomb that almost killed Hurok, Seigel was relieved of any threat of prosecution. Nor was he required to testify against the other two JDL members. He was a free man.

With the matter of Seigel's testimony resolved, Judge Bauman reconvened the trial against the two other JDL members accused of bombing Hurok's offices: Stuart Cohen and Sheldon Davis. Partly because of Hurok's bitter comments in his *New York Times* interview, the trial had become a media circus. The courtroom was packed with curiosity seekers and vocal JDL supporters. Seigel was called to testify but refused, as anticipated. Two other members of the JDL, Richard Huss and Jeffrey Smilow, also refused to testify on religious grounds. (According to Jewish law, one Jew cannot testify against another in a secular court.) Lacking their testimony, Bauman was finally forced to dismiss the prosecution against Cohen and Davis, too. Huss and Smilow, who hadn't directly participated in the bombing, were held in contempt of court at $50,000 bail each. The case against the Hurok bombers was dropped.

Needless to say, Judge Bauman wasn't happy about the outcome. In angry comments, he accused Dershowitz and his team of "frustrating the administration of justice." He reminded the spectators that a murder had, after all, been committed. Somewhat disingenuously, Dershowitz admitted that he was "uncomfortable" about getting Seigel off on constitutional technicalities: "I sat in court for a full hour after everyone else had left. I wanted no part of the victory celebration. I could not forget Iris Kones."

Many other people couldn't forget her, either. Indeed, the bombing of Hurok's offices drastically eroded public support for the JDL, even among Jews. They couldn't understand the need to kill an innocent Jewish girl or to target an eighty-four-year-old Jewish man who had done so much to promote international peace and understanding. After the trial, the JDL rapidly lost its influence in the Jewish community.

In Dershowitz's mind, the case also raised "profound questions, both legal and moral, about the limits of government intervention to prevent and prosecute the most serious crime." This "victory for the United States Constitution" also made it that much more difficult for prosecutors to obtain guilty verdicts and made many observers start wondering if the American legal system gave the criminal more rights than the victim. For Alan Dershowitz, the Hurok bombing trial was only the first in what would be a long series of sensational cases that would keep him as much in the limelight as any Russian ballerina. Like Hurok, this streetwise lawyer had an innate sense of the theatrical and knew how to manipulate the media (not to mention judges and juries) to his own ends.

Seeing the bombing of his office and the murder of Iris Kones go unpunished deeply disturbed and depressed Hurok. He could be vengeful when he felt he had been wronged, as he had shown in his dealings with competitors and colleagues repeatedly in the past. But in this case, as in his increasingly frustrating dealings with Moscow, he was confronting huge governmental bureaucracies with minimal respect for the logo "S. Hurok Presents." He had little choice but to put the verdict behind him and carry on.

In the USSR, meanwhile, incidents of human rights violations were increasing. This situation was at its worst since the death of Stalin. Valery Panov, a principal dancer with the Kirov Ballet and one of the stars on the troupe's American tours (the last one had been in 1964), had been expelled from the company and imprisoned after applying for an exit visa to Israel. His inhumane treatment at the hands of the KGB became an international cause célèbre and further inflamed anti-Soviet feeling in the West.

Panov's plight even overshadowed the appearance of a group of dancers from the Bolshoi Ballet presented by Hurok at the Met in the summer of 1973. In a cranky review of what he dismissed as mediocre performances, Clive Barnes warned, "When the Bolshoi comes to New York—and, in the present political climate regarding

Soviet Jewry, there are many New Yorkers who would, I think, say that no Russian companies should come to New York—it had better be very good. It also ought to take care to present its best image before the New York public." Tales were also reaching America of the intensifying harassment of other dissident Soviet intellectuals and artists, including the novelist Alexander Solzhenitsyn. He would be arrested and expelled from the USSR in February 1974.

Apparently undaunted by the unpropitious climate, Hurok made another pilgrimage to Moscow in the late summer of 1973. His position with Gosconcert and the Ministry of Culture remained uncertain. Columbia continued to make inroads into his former monopoly. The firm's president, Ronald A. Wilford, had even succeeded in winning the Kirov away from Hurok and was planning to present it in the United States in the summer of 1974. (In light of the controversy surrounding Panov, this was beginning to look like a victory of dubious value.)

But Hurok had no intention of making it easy for his competitor or of giving up on his "great dream." When he returned from Russia to New York in September, he was holding a contract to present the Bolshoi Opera at the Met in the summer of 1975. Ignoring the two bitter previous cancellations of planned tours by the company, Hurok announced this news with outward enthusiasm— but most of all, with triumph at having won out over Columbia. There was something desperate and sad about the announcement, however, almost as though he were just going through the motions this time around, just to prove that he could still pull it off.

That Hurok was feeling the effects of his various recent misfortunes is confirmed by Konstantin Sergeyev's description of an encounter they had in New York around this time. Sergeyev (of the Kirov Ballet) had come to the United States to study the Balanchine repertoire of the New York City Ballet. By then, both men knew that the Kirov would be making its next tour under Columbia Artists. Even so, remembered Sergeyev, Hurok treated him with his usual hospitality.

> Hurok met me at the airport in a big fancy car. He took me to a luxurious hotel, and even paid himself for my room. And he invited me to the Russian Tea Room, where we sat a long time together over lunch and talked. I as-

sured him I would do all I could to improve his relations with Furtseva and the other officials in Moscow.

After we had said good-bye out on 57th Street, he started to walk away, and for some reason I turned to get another look at him. And I saw his back going down the street—and for some reason I felt very sad. I couldn't know, of course, that this would be the last time I'd see him, but I always remembered him fading into the distance as he walked away.

And I thought about the fire in his office, and his various business problems. How sad, I thought—such a marvelous man, and this is how it has turned out for him.

One of the biggest bookings for Hurok Concerts in the 1973–74 season was a comeback tour by two of the century's greatest opera stars: Giuseppe di Stefano and Maria Callas. Now fifty years old, Callas had retired from the stage in 1965, although her legions of fans remained as demented and hopeful as ever. Hurok had great admiration for Callas's remarkable dramatic presence and astounding box office draw, a phenomenon he had witnessed with delight in the course of their collaborations in the past. In 1958, at the height of her fame, she had made a highly successful (and highly profitable) American concert tour under his auspices. In 1959, Hurok organized her appearances in St. Louis and Philadelphia. So it was entirely logical that he should present them once again in America when Callas and di Stefano, her former partner and lover, decided to embark on a worldwide tour beginning in England in late 1973.

Even before the duo reached America, critics had gone on record almost unanimously in describing the tour as the greatest artistic disaster of her career. But even in ruins, Callas's voice—joined with her nearly mythological status in the world of opera and her dramatically tragic love life—was still more than enough to attract the same sort of hysterical crowds drawn to the spectacle of Judy Garland or Edith Piaf in their declining days. More than an hour of the two-hour concerts was taken up by ovations. The tour was less about music than about personality—a quality Hurok valued above all others.

Callas opened the American leg of her tour—which to many observers seemed more like a desperate search for love—in Philadelphia on February 11, 1974. She was scheduled to sing at Carnegie Hall on February 17, her first public appearance in New York in nine years. It was to be a benefit for the Metropolitan Opera Guild. The night before the concert, according to Callas's biographer Arianna Stassinopoulos, the singer "went on taking one sleeping tablet after another, without counting, hardly knowing what she was doing." Not surprisingly, she was unable to sing the next day. Well accustomed to the whims of aging divas, Hurok smoothed things over and the concert was postponed two weeks, to March 5.

Hurok began that day, a Tuesday, in his office with consultations about having his portrait painted by a Canadian artist. He was being sketched and photographed when Lee Lamont, Sheldon Gold's secretary, came in and told the artist and photographer that Hurok was too busy now. They should come back to finish the job the next morning, she told them. "Tomorrow morning will be too late," said Simon Semenoff offhandedly. Hurok then lunched with his old friend and client Andrés Segovia, who had celebrated his eightieth birthday two weeks before. The purpose of the lunch was to try to persuade the guitarist to do a concert cruise with Jan Peerce.

After lunch, Hurok had a meeting scheduled with his longtime acquaintance David Rockefeller, president of the Chase Manhattan Bank. (Hurok had been a large depositor at Chase Manhattan for forty years.) Because the costs of presenting dance companies at the Met had become nearly prohibitive, Hurok wanted to talk with Rockefeller about using Radio City Music Hall as a venue for a new attraction he was developing with Nureyev—*Nureyev and Friends.*

But Hurok never made it to his next meeting. When he arrived at the bank's offices at One New York Plaza at two-thirty, he was informed by the receptionist that Rockefeller's office was in a different building at One Chase Manhattan Plaza, a few blocks away. In reply, Hurok mumbled something unintelligible and suddenly slumped to the floor, unconscious. Three Chase Manhattan employees immediately began to administer external heart massage. Responding to an emergency call, a doctor and two nurses arrived a few minutes later. When they were unable to revive Hurok, he was taken to Beekman Downtown Hospital, where several further attempts at cardiopulmonary resuscitation failed. He was pronounced dead of a massive heart attack. At four P.M., just after the news had been relayed to the Hurok office, Nureyev showed up there for a planned discussion of Rockefeller's reaction to the *Nureyev and Friends* idea.

Within hours, the entire New York entertainment community knew that Hurok had died, and just as theatrically as he had lived— between high art and big business. Maria Callas was in her hotel room preparing for the postponed recital with di Stefano at Carnegie Hall when she heard the news. In her highly excitable and vulnerable condition, she took the death of her old acquaintance and tour manager as a bad omen. It meant that everything she would try would now fail, she believed.

For a while the concert's sponsor, Dario Soria, director of the Metropolitan Opera Guild, wasn't sure he could persuade Callas to go on, but at last she consented. Between anticipation of her appearance and grief at Hurok's sudden death, the atmosphere in the hall was supercharged. Soria escorted the two singers onstage and announced that the concert was dedicated to Hurok's memory. Callas asked the audience to "please bear with us" and admitted that she was suffering from "emotion and fatigue."

In such a context, her badly sung program of Italian and French operatic solos and duets was almost beside the point. The entire evening was a massive exercise in musical group therapy. At the concert's end, her hypersensitive nerves rubbed raw, Callas had what many observers considered to be a near-nervous breakdown. Using Hurok's death as an excuse to lose control, and seizing the stage as a personal podium, she launched into a long, wandering, and (perhaps fortunately) barely audible monologue on her many artistic and personal grievances. The audience, which included most of the members of the Met establishment and many leading opera stars, listened in stunned silence as Callas bitterly attacked opera management for not giving her the conditions she needed for her work. With this sad but undeniably majestic tirade on the night that Hurok died, this Clytemnestra of the operatic stage brought to an unforgettable close her last appearance in New York, the city that had so idolized and, as she believed, humiliated her in the past.

On her way out the stage door, she tossed the roses Hurok had sent her to hundreds of waiting fans. It was a farewell not only to two careers, but also to an era.

CHAPTER TWENTY-FOUR

An Empty Box

"Hurok taught me that sometimes you just have to say 'What the fuck.'"—*Peter Hyams*

SOL HUROK NEVER PLANNED ON DYING. Even though many of his friends and artists had long ago departed this life, he treated their passing as proof of his own apparent immortality rather than as evidence of his own approach to the Stygian shore. "But Hurok is still here!" he would proclaim with childish glee as he surveyed the photos of his deceased associates displayed on his office walls. Like many great egotists used to controlling every aspect of their lives, he refused to talk or think about death, perhaps believing that he could avoid the final reality by the sheer force of the willpower that had so often triumphed over seemingly impossible obstacles in the past. "Hurok had a real phobia about death," observed Isaac Stern.

After he dropped dead suddenly while searching for David Rockefeller's office, therefore, Hurok's family members and colleagues were not completely surprised to discover that he had made no arrangements at all concerning his funeral or burial. "He expected to live forever," explained his son-in-law, Arthur Lief.

Still in shock at the suddenness of his death, Lief and his wife Ruth were suddenly confronted with organizing a fitting tribute to a man who belonged more to his public than to his kin. Their task was made even more difficult by the fact that Hurok had never developed a lasting relationship with any church of any denomination. He was known to have attended two Manhattan synagogues (the Conservative B'Nair Jeshurun and the Temple Emanu-El) over the years, but only infrequently and indifferently. When Walter Prude called both synagogues to ask if they would be willing to handle Hurok's funeral, they declined, explaining that he had developed no affiliation with them. Such services were performed only for members, they explained, and never for outsiders—not even for Sol Hurok.

In need of suggestions, Prude called Jan Peerce. Widely known for his performances as a cantor, Peerce had many connections in the New York Jewish establishment. (He was so deeply religious that he had even disowned his son Larry, a film director, for marrying a gentile woman with two children.) But the tenor knew that no rabbi would be willing to change the rules of his synagogue to accommodate a Jew who had failed to make plans for "when the day comes for him to bid farewell."

So Peerce proposed another, much more suitable venue for Hurok's funeral, a place where they would be more than happy to have him: Carnegie Hall. The idea appealed so strongly to Prude that he tried to improve upon it by suggesting Lincoln Center. "Too ostentatious," objected Peerce. He knew that the current president of Carnegie Hall, Isaac Stern, as well as its manager, Julius Bloom, another friend of Hurok's, could not say no to such a request. After all, Carnegie Hall might not even still be standing if not for Hurok's efforts to save it from destruction in the late 1950s. He belonged there. It was his church and temple, where he had worshiped the spirit of music with reverence and devotion—and not only on Saturdays and Sundays.

Hurok's daughter and grandchildren, none of them particularly religious, were more than happy to entrust the organization of the service to Peerce. He persuaded Dr. Bernard Mandelbaum, former president of the Jewish Theological Seminary and a member of the board of directors of the America-Israel Cultural Foundation, to preside, and invited several of Hurok's artists to participate.

On Friday, March 9, 1974, three days after Hurok's death, more than twenty-six hundred people nearly filled Carnegie Hall for the last glamorous performance of the impresario's life. Limousines pulled up to the stage door, unloading opera stars, ballerinas, musicians, conductors, and stage and film personalities eager to pay tribute to the man who had launched and shaped many of their careers. Those most closely associated professionally with Hurok sat in the center section of the orchestra and in the first tier of boxes. Among them were Leonard Bernstein, Agnes de Mille, Alexandra Danilova, Van Cliburn, Roberta Peters, Renata Tebaldi, Montserrat Caballe, Sir Rudolf Bing, Andrés Segovia and Yakov Malik, the Soviet delegate to the United Nations. Hurok's immediate family sat in the front row at the left: Ruth and Arthur Lief; Ruth's two children by Barry Hyams, her first husband, Peter and Nessa; and Hurok's stepsons, George and Edward Perper.

On this important occasion as on so many others, Hurok's chronically indisposed wife, Emma, did not appear. She would die herself not long afterward, having stubbornly outlasted the husband she had so enjoyed belittling.

The service didn't last long. The stage was empty except for a podium and four chairs, with the coffin in the center, heaped high with hundreds of deep red roses. Rabbi Mandelbaum read from the Bible, including the passage describing how young David played the harp for King Saul. Isaac Stern distilled the emotion of the silent audience in his performance of Bach's B-minor Partita. Then he walked over to the coffin and gently touched it. The eulogy was delivered by Marian Anderson, whose rich deep voice and obvious conviction gave her carefully chosen words an intense spiritual power. She called Hurok a king with a "wise and understanding heart," comparing him to his biblical namesake King Solomon.

"He launched hundreds of careers—he magnified thousands of others, and in the process he brought joy and a larger life to millions," she said. "He made not ripples, but waves, even beyond his own shores, and what is one to say of the man who guided one's life for nigh on to forty years? He was more than the supreme impresario. He was teacher, counsel, friend and even more than that, he was the 'we' in all of us."

Jan Peerce then brought tears to the few dry eyes left in the house by asking the audience to rise while he sang a Jewish hymn. Because the service fell on the feast of Purim, one of the most joyful holidays in the Jewish calendar, he sang a composition of psalms rather than the kaddish, the traditional Jewish prayer for the dead. When the service was over, eight pallbearers came out onto the stage and wheeled the coffin away as a white stage curtain slowly descended.

As funerals go, it was simple but sensational—dignified, theatrical, and performed by a high-powered cast in the best hall around. Many journalists came, and the reviews were good. The only thing Hurok might have regretted is that no admission was charged.

The total value of Hurok's estate at the time of his death was just over $3 million. Most of that amount had come from the 1969 sale to Transcontinental Investing Corporation. Approximately one-half of the sum was held in stocks in such companies as AT&T, Chrysler, Exxon, GE, GM, IT&T, U.S. Steel, and Hurok Concerts. Hurok also held over $1 million in bonds. He had never been interested in real estate and owned, besides Emma's apartment on Central Park West and his apartment on Park Avenue, only a share of some property in Oklahoma purchased for its mineral interests. In his apartment he had assembled a small collection of paintings, mostly by French and Russian artists: several Pissaros (in Hurok's accent, this came out "Pierce-Arrows"), some ballet and stage designs by Alexander Benois, two landscapes by Isaac Levitan, and works by Eugène Boudin and André Dunoyer de Segonzac. At the time of his death, the collection was valued at $129,200. On his many trips to Russia, he had also accumulated numerous pieces of religious and applied art, including icons, silver, vases, malachite candle holders, and porcelain. Altogether, the contents of his apartment were worth about $212,000.

In his will, which was drawn up by Vinson C. Aronson of the firm Lieberman, Aronson, and Rosenberg, Hurok provided first for Emma, their longtime difficulties notwithstanding. "My wife, Emma Hurok, and I have been living separate and apart for many years. I have supported her financially and have made it possible for her to live in comfort, and it is my desire to enable her to continue to live in comfort for the balance of her life." To this end, he left her the sum of $10,000 plus "at least $20,000 annually." In all, Emma received one-third of the "net estate," and his daughter, Ruth, received one-quarter of the "residuary estate." After Emma's death, the remaining principal of the trust was to go in equal shares to Brandeis University, Albert Einstein College of Medicine of Yeshiva University, Columbia University, New York University, and the Juilliard School. At each institution, the money was to be used to establish a Hurok Loan Fund, to provide noninterest-bearing loans for worthy students.

"I firmly believe that an education enriches a person's life intellectually and benefits him materially and that all who desire an education should be given an opportunity to have it," Hurok stated in his will. "I also believe that those who have been assisted financially to obtain an education have a moral obligation to extend similar opportunities to others and that, in most instances, they are in a position to do so within a reasonable time after their graduation." Hurok preferred to establish a loan fund rather than scholarships because a greater number of students would benefit.

Hurok also left money to his grandchildren and to a variety of Jewish charitable organizations, including the United Jewish Appeal of Greater New York, Mt. Sinai Hospital, the Federation of Jewish Philanthropies of New York, and the American Committee for the Weizman Institute of Science. Surprisingly, only one performing arts organization was included in Hurok's will: the Musicians Emergency Fund, Inc. Numerous sources have claimed that in drawing up his will (an exercise for which he had little passion or interest), Hurok relied excessively on his old legal cronies, who persuaded him to give his money to their favorite causes.

Notably overlooked in Hurok's will were his longtime office associates. Martin Feinstein, Walter Prude, and George Perper received no mention—not even any mementos. This led to hurt, even bitter, feelings (especially on the part of Prude's wife, Agnes de Mille) and seemed again to prove that Hurok always thought of Hurok Concerts as his business and his alone.

Similarly, Hurok's failure to use his estate to create a lasting monument to the performing arts (in the form of an endowment fund or contribution or building) suggests that he was a thorough theater person in his insistence on living in the present. When the show was over, it was over, and there was no bringing it back. Hurok was a grasshopper rather than an ant and found it difficult to imagine any future enterprise in which he would not be directly involved. His contribution was himself.

▪ ▪ ▪

Many of the newspaper and magazine accounts of Hurok's death were filled with speculation on the future of Hurok Concerts, Inc. Could it survive intact without Hurok at the helm? Who would replace him at the top of the organization? Not a few observers predicted the company's rapid decline. Rumors also circulated that General Electric was eager to unload its leaderless subsidiary. "Anyone buying Hurok Concerts without Sol Hurok may be buying an empty box," warned one Manhattan manager.

Within two weeks of the funeral, Tomorrow Entertainment and GE answered one question by announcing that for the time being, Hurok Concerts would be ruled by a troika of executive vice presidents with equal power: George Perper, Walter Prude, and Sheldon Gold. Thomas Moore, president of Tomorrow Entertainment, therefore became the de facto boss. In reaction to this news, Harry Zelser, a Chicago impresario who had booked Hurok attractions for decades, said frankly, "It's the natural and ideal solution. The uniform of field marshal was buried with Sol. Or putting it another way, the Hurok concerto could not be taken over by a soloist." Trying to replace Hurok with Perper or Prude or Gold would be like trying to replace the Queen of England with one of her ladies-in-waiting.

This uneasy troika ran the agency for a year, during a very ambitious 1974–75 season that had been booked by Hurok before he died. It included sixteen weeks of performances at the Met, the longest season Hurok Concerts had ever mounted there. First came the Bolshoi Ballet, followed by the Stuttgart Ballet, the long-delayed American debut of the Bolshoi Opera, and finally, three weeks by the National Ballet of Canada with Rudolf Nureyev. Like a star in the heavens, Hurok continued to emit light even after he was gone.

In early April 1975, the administrative situation changed when Sheldon Gold was named president of Hurok Concerts, with Prude and Perper remaining as executive vice presidents. But less than three months later, and the very day before the Bolshoi Opera's oft-delayed gala opening at the Met, it was announced that General Electric had sold Hurok Concerts. The buyer was a newly formed concern called the American Management Corporation. Roger Hall, who had managed several major symphony orchestras, became chairman of "Hurok" (as the papers now called it), pledging to retain the current principal officers as well as the "Hurok traditions."

Hall and his company acquired Hurok Concerts at a time of great financial stress. They had to spend more than $2 million to bring the Bolshoi Opera to New York and eventually lost a sum estimated at between $400,000 and $600,000 on the engagement. Most of the operas the Bolshoi chose to present to New York (particularly Prokofiev's *The Gambler* and *War and Peace*, and Kiril Molchanov's propagandistic *The Dawns Are Quiet Here*) failed to please either critics or audiences. The public reaction to the avant-garde *The Gambler* was so negative that the last performance had to be canceled. If Hurok had been able to preside over the company's American debut, which he had worked so long and hard to obtain, it is unlikely he would have approved of such a repertoire. In reviewing the Met season, critic Clive Barnes called Gold "a bit tighter if not a bit shrewder" than his old friend Hurok, although he congratulated Gold for running the only large-scale arts organization left in America that actually had to turn a profit to survive.

Less than a year after American Management Corporation acquired Hurok Concerts, the relationship between new and old management began to sour. In May 1976, Gold was suddenly ousted as president and replaced with one of the owners, Maynard Goldman. American Management Corporation had decided that it wanted to diversify its entertainment operations, moving beyond solely classical attractions (which attracted a very small market share) into ice shows and the Law Vegas scene.

Almost immediately after his dismissal, Gold was appointed president of ICM Artists, Ltd., a newly formed classical musical and dance subsidiary of Marvin Josephson Associates, which also owned ICM, Inc., a talent agency specializing in actors, writers, and directors. Ten days later, Walter Prude also left Hurok Concerts to join his longtime colleague Gold at ICM Artists. Gold and Prude had built up a strong following among Hurok artists during their many years with the operation, and many of them soon followed their managers to ICM. So many artists deserted the old Hurok Concerts, in fact, that its owners brought a suit against Gold and Prude for breach of contract.

With Gold and Prude gone, the Hurok operation, now in the

hands of relative novices with very little credibility among either artists or presenters, spun rapidly out of control in an increasingly difficult market. Roger Hall resigned as board chairman of Hurok
Concerts in July 1976, leaving the firm in even greater disarray. In
February 1977, American Management Corporation announced
that it was withdrawing from the field of artists' management entirely and that ICM was taking over the operations of Hurok Concerts, Inc. Under the new arrangement, American Management
Corporation dropped its lawsuit and ICM Artists gained the right to
use the Hurok name.

In fact, however, ICM rarely used the Hurok trademark in the
coming years, and it quickly disappeared from marquees, advertisements, and programs. Indeed, after a few years had passed, those
who ran ICM seemed eager to downplay its Hurok origins, almost
as though they feared (rightly) that they could never hope to measure up to the dead impresario. A recent (1993) television documentary film about Isaac Stern, for instance, an ICM artist, neglected
even to mention Hurok's name, despite the fact that Hurok was
single-handedly responsible for giving Stern a big-time career.

Most of what was left of Hurok Concerts, then, ended up at
ICM Artists, where it soon lost its separate name and identity within
a large corporate entity. Some Hurok artists also found their way to
Hurok's former associate Harold Shaw, at his Shaw Concerts, Inc.
After his premature death in 1985, Gold was succeeded as head of
ICM Artists by Lee Lamont, who had worked as his secretary in the
Hurok organization. When she became its president, ICM Artists
was managing about a hundred artists in music and dance.

Many of those who were close to Hurok never believed that his
organization could outlive him and were not surprised when it
didn't. Its success owed too much to his theatrical personality and
outsized ego. "As far as he was concerned, when he went, it all had
to go," said Isaac Stern. "He didn't care if he pulled the house down
with him."

But what of Hurok's influence on the wider arena of the American
performing arts scene beyond his own agency? What legacy did he
leave?

One thing he did *not* leave behind was a theater or concert hall bearing his name. When the old Met was standing empty and abandoned after the opera company's move to Lincoln Center, reports circulated that it would be saved and renamed the Hurok Center for the Arts. Later, there was discussion about renovating the old Manhattan Opera House on 34th Street and naming it after Hurok, who had worshiped the place in his youth.

But neither of these projects materialized, which seems to indicate that Hurok had little appetite for immortality in the form of real estate. In this (as in so many other things) he remained an old-fashioned impresario, more concerned with art than with the structures in which it was presented. Although he adored fine old opera houses like the old Met, the Bolshoi, the Kirov, and Covent Garden, Hurok never considered buildings more important than performers. "There are no bad acoustics for good artists," he once told critic Irving Kolodin. Hurok could also remember the days of touring with Pavlova and the Monte Carlo Ballet Russe, when the fact that the performances were often held in high-school auditoriums and churches did not lower the quality or excitement. Indeed, these performances were often more convincing than many held in more auspicious surroundings.

Hurok always put the performer first—before real estate, before management, before business. Without the performer, there was no art, and without art, there was no magic. Such attitudes demonstrated Hurok's closeness to the European tradition and set him apart from younger American presenters like James Nederlander, who once remarked that he got into the business of presenting dance because he owned a lot of theaters and thought dance would fill them nicely. By the time Hurok died, those who managed and presented the performing arts in the United States were already increasingly producing programming in order to fill buildings rather than to create art. One might compare them to an author more concerned about the book jacket than the words on the pages inside.

Both the economics of presenting classical music and dance and the composition of the audience had changed radically between the time Hurok started out around World War I and the mid-1970s. The new immigrants from Europe who had originally formed the nucleus of the "Hurok audience" in the 1920s were people who related to opera, orchestral music, and instrumental soloists as popular culture and a primary source of entertainment. But growing up in a brash America that was rapidly becoming the technological center of the world, and which had always regarded European "high" culture as effete and effeminate in any case, the children of these immigrants gradually drifted away from such attractions toward film and Broadway shows. The introduction of television on a mass scale in the 1950s further widened the split between "elite" and popular culture. By the mid-1960s, fewer and fewer serious cultural events were being broadcast by the commercial networks.

As the century progressed, the audience for the sort of attractions Hurok presented had become narrower and more socially and economically elite. Simultaneously, ticket prices for opera and ballet and concerts were rising to a point where they were far out of reach of the "masses." Long before the 1970s, the bulk of the Hurok audience had evolved from lower-middle-class immigrants to upper-middle-class professionals and socialites. And fewer students and young adults were attending. In a sense, Hurok and his audience had grown up together and when they died, no one was there to replace them.

A *New Yorker* cartoon that appeared not long before Hurok's death provided an apt characterization of his public. "When S. Hurok presents a happening, *then* I'll go to a happening," states a portly suburban matron to her equally well fed and respectable husband.

Even so, Hurok was so adept at publicity, so shrewd about programming, and had amassed such a loyal, if limited, following that he continued to make money in a business that most people no longer considered economically viable. With the demise of the railroads, sending an orchestra or dance company on tour had become financially prohibitive. Unions that had not existed during the first few decades of Hurok's career demanded higher pay and guarantees for performers and stagehands. Rental fees rose to support the higher cost of running fancy new performing arts centers. The profit margin kept shrinking, especially after the early 1960s. The number of independent managers declined precipitously. Even NCAC, from which Hurok had split in 1957, had fallen on hard times. For more than ten years after Hurok's death, not a single impresario was brave enough to rent the off-season weeks at the Metropolitan

Opera House on a regular long-term basis, as he had done since the 1930s.

The opening of huge performing arts complexes like Lincoln Center in New York, the Kennedy Center in Washington, and the Music Center in Los Angeles in the 1960s and early 1970s also changed the performing arts environment. Controlled by boards of directors and run by salaried executives with large managerial staffs, they did not aim at devising programming that would turn a profit. Indeed, they expected to operate at a deficit that would be made up through contributions from wealthy individuals, corporations, and foundations. The arts in the United States had become institutionalized, and it was impossible for independents—even very talented ones like Hurok—to compete with such monoliths. He had become a dinosaur, the last practitioner of risk capitalism in the arts.

Unfortunately, with institutionalization also comes caution. Hurok never operated with a board of directors; only occasionally (mostly in the days of the Monte Carlo Ballet Russe) did he seek backers of specific attractions. Although he might have asked friends and colleagues for artistic advice, he was free to accept or reject it. In the end, he took the financial risk himself and made his own decisions about whom to present and how to promote them. He had much more freedom than a manager accountable to a board and responsible for filling and maintaining a facility.

"What he taught me," said his grandson Peter Hyams, "was that sometimes you just have to forget caution and take a risk. He taught me that sometimes you just have to say 'What the fuck.' Because 'What the fuck' brings you freedom, and freedom brings opportunity."

Hurok's detractors—and there was no shortage of those— often argued that he did not use this freedom to best advantage. There is universal agreement that Hurok did more than any other single individual in the arts to introduce America to the riches of Soviet/Russian culture, that he played a major role in creating an American audience for ballet and modern dance, and that his pioneering work in bringing the performing arts on tour to the provinces led indirectly to the rise of regional dance and theater companies. But dance critics have faulted Hurok for stressing individual dancers at the expense of choreography and for creating an insatiable appetite for "stars" while minimizing the importance of an artistic ensemble.

Especially in his later years, Hurok did in fact prefer to present familiar titles, but with exciting new stars. This was the case, for example, when he insisted to Ninette de Valois that she and Sadler's Wells bring *Sleeping Beauty* to New York in 1949 with Margot Fonteyn, instead of a program of shorter modern works. Hurok had a great deal to do with increasing the popularity in America of the full-length ballets of Tchaikovsky and of Prokofiev. Remaining true to his Hippodrome roots, he always preferred grandeur and spectacle—the bigger the better. And he adored famous names.

Hurok tread a fine line between following his audience and leading it. Like a successful politician, he knew when to challenge his constituency and when to pander to it. Such behavior left him open to the charge of being inconsistent and unprincipled—and surely he did not have the aristocratic aesthetic convictions of a Diaghilev or a Balanchine. Unlike them, he was ideologically a democrat (and a Democrat).

"Hurok's taste was sometimes very good and sometimes it was very bad," critic George Dorris wrote, "but ultimately it was unreliable, a mixture of what he liked and what he thought would sell." One might add that Hurok's taste was basically quite conservative. As a manager and presenter, he was all-American in his daring and flare for publicity, but as a connoisseur, he was strictly Old World. With a few exceptions (Isadora Duncan, Mary Wigman, Katharine Dunham), he had little use for contemporary music or dance, especially in his later years.

There was one thing that Hurok always insisted upon: star billing for himself. Those who worked for him, and those whom he presented, all knew that the only thing that really angered him was having his name omitted from an advertisement, poster, or marquee. The words "S. Hurok Presents" always appeared *above* the name of the attraction, whether it be Isaac Stern or the Bolshoi Ballet or Maria Callas. Unlike his managerial colleagues, who looked and acted like businessmen fearful of the limelight, Hurok lived and dressed and thought like an artist, with more than enough of the obligatory self-assurance a successful artistic career requires. Because he so completely lived the life of a theater person, most of what he was vanished with him—just as happened with Chaliapin or Pavlova or Nijinsky, whose triumphs on the stage could never be duplicated by other performers or even find adequate description in words, photos, film, or recordings.

Himself one of the greatest of all the Hurok Attractions, Hurok was performing every minute of his life, egged on by the applause and bravos. When death finally brought the curtain down on his long-running one-man show, no other actor could possibly fill the role. He had made sure of that.

APPENDIX
The Ballets Russes Companies:
A Guide to Bewildering Name Changes
■ ■ ■

1. *Ballets Russes de Serge Diaghilev*
The original company, founded in Paris in 1909 by Sergei Diaghilev, based in Monte Carlo and Paris until Diaghilev's death in 1929.

2. *Les Ballets Russes de Monte Carlo*
Founded in Monte Carlo in 1932 by René Blum and Colonel de Basil, with George Balanchine.

3. *Ballets Russes de Monte Carlo*
Basically the same company as No. 2, but without Balanchine. The company performed under this title in London in 1933.

4. *Ballets Russes de Col. W. de Basil* (also known as Col. W. de Basil's Ballets Russes)
Basically the same company as No. 2, but with the addition of Leonide Massine as ballet master. The company performed in London under this title from 1934 through 1937. Blum left the company before the 1935 season.

5. *Monte Carlo Ballet Russe*
The title under which Nos. 3 and 4 appeared in New York from 1933 through 1935.

6. *Col. W. de Basil's Ballets Russes*
The title under which No. 4 (without Blum) performed in New York in 1936 and 1937.

7. *Ballets de Monte Carlo*

Formed in 1936 by René Blum (after his split with de Basil) with Michel Fokine as ballet master.

8. *Ballet Russe de Monte Carlo ("The One and Only")*

Formed in 1938 by Blum with Serge Denham as managing director and Leonide Massine as artistic director. Based in New York. Disbanded in 1962.

9. *Original Ballet Russe*

Formed in 1939 by de Basil. Disbanded in 1951.

NOTES TO THE TEXT

■ ■ ■

Notes are cited by page number in the text and by the first few words of the passage (either in direct quotation or paraphrase) to which they pertain. Informational notes follow the same system. In most cases, I have used commonly accepted spellings for Russian names.

The following abbreviations will be used for frequently cited sources:

JAnderson: Jack Anderson, *The One and Only: The Ballet Russe de Monte Carlo*. New York, 1981.

MAnderson: Marian Anderson, *My Lord, What a Morning*. New York, 1956.

Ashkenazy: Vladimir Ashkenazy with Jasper Parrott, *Beyond Frontiers*. London, 1984.

Bagazh: Nicholas Nabokov, *Bagazh: Memoirs of a Russian Cosmopolitan*. New York, 1975.

Bluebird: Alan Levy, *The Bluebird of Happiness: The Memoirs of Jan Peerce*. New York, 1976.

Borovsky: Victor Borovsky, *Chaliapin: A Critical Biography*. New York, 1988.

BT: Archives on Ballet Theatre (later called American Ballet Theatre) in the NYPL Performing Arts Library at Lincoln Center, Dance Collection.

Buckle: Richard Buckle, *Diaghilev*. London, 1979.

Chaliapin I: Fyodor Chaliapin and E. A. Grosheva, *Feodor Ivanovich Shaliapin, Vol. I, Literaturnoe nasledstvo, pis'ma. N. Shaliapina: Vospominaniia ob otse*. Moscow, 1960.

Chaliapin II: Fyodor Chaliapin and E. A. Grosheva, *Feodor Ivanovich Shaliapin, Vol. II, Stat'i, vyskazyvaniia, vospominaniia o F. I. Shaliapine.* Moscow, 1960.

Chaliapin III: Fyodor Chaliapin, compiled by Yuri Kotliarov and Viktor Garmash, *Letopis' zhizni i tvorchestva F. I. Shaliapina* (Vol. 1). Leningrad, 1989.

Chaliapin IV: *Letopis' zhizni i tvorchestva F. I. Shaliapina* (Vol. 2). Leningrad, 1989.

Chekhov I: Mikhail Chekhov, *Mikhail Chekhov: Literaturnoe nasledie v dvukh tomakh* (Vol. 1). Moscow, 1986.

Chekhov II: *Mikhail Chekhov: Literaturnoe nasledie v dvukh tomakh* (Vol. 2). Moscow, 1986.

Chierichetti: David Chierichetti, *Hollywood Director.* New York, 1973.

Choura: Alexandra Danilova, *Choura: The Memoirs of Alexandra Danilova.* New York, 1986.

Davis II: Ronald Davis, *A History of Music in American Life, Vol. II: the Gilded Years, 1865–1920.* Huntington, NY, 1980.

Davis III: Ronald Davis, *A History of Music in American Life, Vol. III: The Modern Era, 1920–Present.* Huntington, NY, 1981.

Deakin: Archives and letters of Irving Deakin, in the NYPL Performing Arts Library at Lincoln Center, Dance Collection.

Dershowitz: Alan Dershowitz, *The Best Defense.* New York, 1982.

de Valois: Ninette de Valois, *Come Dance With Me: A Memoir 1898–1956.* London, 1959.

Eaton: Quaintance Eaton, *The Miracle of the Met: An Informal History of the Metropolitan Opera 1883–1967.* New York, 1968.

Fonteyn: Margot Fonteyn, *Margot Fonteyn: An Autobiography.* London, 1975.

Fonteyn-Pavlova: Margot Fonteyn, *Pavlova: Portrait of a Dancer.* New York, 1984.

Gabler: Neal Gabler, *An Empire of Their Own: How the Jews Invented Hollywood.* New York, 1988.

Galina: Galina Vishnevskaya, *Galina: A Russian Story.* New York, 1984.

G-Marquez: Vicente Garcia-Marquez, *The Ballets Russes: Colonel de Basil's Ballets Russes de Monte Carlo 1932–1952.* New York, 1990.

Graham: Bill Graham and Robert Greenfield, *Bill Graham Presents: My Life Inside Rock and Out.* New York, 1992.

Haskell: Arnold Haskell, *Balletomania Then and Now.* New York, 1977.

Hayes: Patrick Hayes, *Curtain Calls: A Memoir of the Performing Arts in Washington, D.C.* (unpublished manuscript).

Horowitz: Joseph Horowitz, *The Ivory Trade: Music and the Business of Music at the Van Cliburn International Piano Competition.* New York, 1990.

Howe: Irving Howe, *World of Our Fathers.* New York, 1976.

Iankovskii: Moisei Iankovskii, *Shaliapin.* Leningrad, 1972.

Ickes: Harold Ickes, *The Secret Diary of Harold L. Ickes. Vol. II: The Inside Struggle 1936–1939.* New York, 1954.

Imp: Sol Hurok with Ruth Goode, *Impresario: A Memoir.* New York, 1946.

Irma: Irma Duncan, *Duncan Dancer.* Middletown, CT, 1966.

Kahane: Rabbi Meir Kahane, *The Story of the Jewish Defense League.* Radnor, PA, 1975.

Kerensky: Oleg Kerensky, *Anna Pavlova.* New York, 1977.

Markova: Alicia Markova, *Markova Remembers.* Boston, 1986.

Maska: Fyodor Chaliapin, *Maska i dusha.* Moscow, 1989.

Massine: Leonide Massine, *My Life in Ballet.* New York, 1968.

MCBR: Archives of Monte Carlo Ballet Russe and Serge Denham in the NYPL Performing Arts Library at Lincoln Center, Dance Collection.

McDonagh: Don McDonagh, *Martha Graham: A Biography.* New York, 1973.

McVay: Gordon McVay, *Isadora and Esenin.* Ann Arbor, MI, 1980.

Milstein: Nathan Milstein and Solomon Volkov, *From Russia to the West: The Musical Memoirs and Reminiscences of Nathan Milstein.* New York, 1991.

My Day: Eleanor Roosevelt, edited by Rochelle Chadakoff, *Eleanor Roosevelt's "My Day": Her Acclaimed Columns 1936–1945.* New York, 1989.

NYT: *New York Times*

NYHT: New York *Herald Tribune*

NYPLLC: New York Public Library, Library of the Performing Arts at Lincoln Center.

Obratsov: Sergei Obratsov, *Po stupen'kam pamiati ("Down the Staircase of My Memory").* Moscow, 1987.

Pages: Fyodor Chaliapin, *Pages From My Life: An Autobiography.* Revised, enlarged and edited by Katharine Wright, translated by H. M. Buck. New York, 1927.

Payne: Charles Payne, *American Ballet Theatre.* New York, 1979.

MMY: Arthur Rubinstein, *My Many Years*. New York, 1980.

Sayler: Oliver Sayler, *Inside the Moscow Art Theatre*. New York, 1925.

SHP: Sol Hurok, *S. Hurok Presents: A Memoir of the Dance World*. New York, 1953.

Testimony: Dmitri Shostakovich and Solomon Volkov, *Testimony: The Memoirs of Dmitri Shostakovich*. New York, 1979.

Wigman: Mary Wigman and Walter Sorell, *The Mary Wigman Book*. Middletown, CT, 1975.

Walker: Kathrine Sorley Walker, *De Basil's Ballets Russes*. New York, 1983.

Vehanen: Kosti Vehanen, *Marian Anderson: A Portrait*. New York, 1941.

Zorina: Vera Zorina, *Zorina*. New York, 1986.

After the first complete citation ("HR interview with Van Cliburn"), interviews will be cited in brief (for example, "HR-Van Cliburn").

PART I

Introduction

xiii "This work, it's my vacation": Richard F. Shepard, "Hurok Will Star in Extravaganza," NYT, May 5, 1967.

xviii "Americans who have a passing acquaintance": Arlene Croce, "Making a Mystique," *New Yorker*, August 6, 1990, p. 85.

xix "Today, as we look back": *Muzykal'naia zhizn'*, 1990, No. 2, pp. 26–27.

Chapter One

4 "no such thing as a twice-told tale": HR Interview with Van Cliburn, Fort Worth, Texas, November 10, 1990.

4 "Hurok is the only man I know": *New Yorker*, June 9, 1973, p. 27.

4 "I don't think he was capable":

HR Interview with Agnes de Mille, New York, October 19, 1988.

4 "The main thing": HR Interview with Isaac Stern, New York, May 9, 1990.

4 "a town of no importance": Imp, p. 8.

4 "including pigs": Hurok Interview with Clifton Fadiman, February 15, 1958 (NYPLLC recordings collection).

6 "Hurok knows six languages": HR-Stern.

6 "The first time an automobile": *New Yorker*, June 9, 1973, p. 28.

7 "overflowed with food": Imp, p. 10.

7 "not the shrewdest": *Ibid.*, p. 11.

7 "were well-to-do people": Hurok interview with Bill Moyers, WNET, 1973 (NYPLLC dance collection).

7 "Hurok says he can write": *New York Post*, July 28, 1969.

7 "fairly well off": HR phone inter-

view with Rita Zaitseva, January 13, 1993.

7 "My father was a wise man": *Dance News*, April 1974, p. 11.

8 "the complete deletion": This memo to Darryl Zanuck (dated April 14, 1952) is in the Irving Deakin files, NYPLLC Dance Collection.

8 "fanciful things": HR-Stern.

9 "No. Is mistake": Interview with Peter Hyams, Los Angeles, CA, March 21, 1989.

9 "It's given me a new lease": Stephen E. Rubin, "S. Hurok—Last of the Red Hot Showmen," NYT, May 13, 1973, section 2, p. 1.

10 "In almost Gogolian fashion": Interview with Genrietta Beliaeva, Moscow, April 13, 1988.

11 "our one synagogue": Imp, p. 8.

11 "Christmas was the high": *Ibid.*, p. 10.

11 "Neither stability nor peace": Howe, p. 7.

11 "an inconspicuous figure" and "a stocky man with a long beard": Imp, pp. 13–14.

12 "six or seven instruments": *Ibid.*, p. 12.

12 "If I'd studied the piano": John Chapman, "Impresario," *Daily News*, January 9, 1938.

12 "There was music at night": SHP, p. 15.

13 "Before those domes and steeples": Imp, p. 13.

14 "Back in Pogar": *Ibid.*, p. 14.

14 "When I was about twelve": HR-Hyams.

14 "returned to another small town": Imp, p. 14.

15 "huddled on the hard benches," "when we stepped ashore," and "sleeping in our clothes": Imp, pp. 14–15.

15 "Two weeks within high brick walls": Mary Antin, *From Plotzk to Boston*. Boston, 1899, p. 12.

Chapter Two

18 "immigrants were forced to sleep": Howe, p. 43.

18 "It's important that there be established": Deakin memo to Zanuck; Deakin.

19 "two heavy hampers of clothes," "I had 10 cents left for carfare," and "Wasn't it, after all": Imp, pp. 15–16.

20 "There, I knew, was a freedom": SHP, p. 16.

20 "my relatives' house": Imp, p. 16.

20 "eighteen different jobs in six months": Hurok-Moyers.

20 "I started my job": Tex McCrary and Jinx Falkenburg, "New York Close-Up," NYHT, January 7, 1951.

20 "I got into tragic frame of mind" and "Go, my boy": John Bainbridge, "S. Hurok," *Life*, August 28, 1944, p. 52.

21 "beeg, beeg businessman": McCrary and Falkenburg, NYHT.

21 "People were always getting off at the wrong street": Allan Keller, "And Now, Presenting S. Hurok," New York *World-Telegram*, January 21, 1961.

21 "shabby boys": Imp, p. 16.

21 "heard serious music and appreciated it": Hurok-Moyers.

21 "to see some friends from home": Imp, p. 16.

22 "a cheap slum rooming house": *Cue*, January 20, 1962, p. 9.

22 Hurok's marriage certificate is preserved in the Municipal Archives of New York City at 31 Chambers Street.

23 "By now I was married": Imp, p. 25.

23 "My first wife I never liked": Interview by Joan Kramer with Simon Semenoff, in NYPLLC Dance Collection (Oral History Project).

23 "could live as in the Old Country": Howe, p. 131.

23 "a land of sweatshops": *New York Tribune*, August 30, 1896.

23 "a steaming microcosm": Imp, p. 23.

23 "It was not uncommon for a Jewish worker": Nathan Glazer, *American Judaism*. Chicago, 1972, p. 67.

24 "In meeting rooms above the crowded stores": Imp, p. 24.

24 "Hurok's politics were politics of the heart": HR-Stern.

24 "would hawk silverware": Joseph Roddy, "Impresario Who Booked the Bolshoi," *Life*, June 1, 1959, p. 59.

24 "popular artists of the day": Imp, p. 23.

25 "The fixed rituals": Howe, p. 170.

26 "600 persons and 150 horses": Norman Clarke, *The Mighty Hippodrome*. New York, 1968, p. 28.

26 "picked up more knowledge": *Dancing Times*, May 1936, p. 130.

26 "Hurok told me more than once": *Opera News*, May 1974, p. 15.

28 "short and far from happy stay": Pages, p. 255.

28 "I pity Americans": Davis II, p. 6.

28 "Despite the impact of the sumptuousness": SHP, p. 15.

29 "She looked like an old bubbie": Ruth Hurok Lief interview with Harlow Robinson. I conducted numerous interviews with Ruth Lief on different occasions between 1987 and 1992.

30 "a colossal talent": Boris Schwarz, *Great Masters of the Violin: from Corelli and Vivaldi to Stern, Zuke*. New York, 1983, p. 431.

30 "one of the most worthy of the violinists": NYT, November 13, 1912, p. 15.

30 "in appearance and manner but a boy": NYT, October 14, 1912, p. 15.

30–31 "Destiny, in the person": Philadelphia *Evening Bulletin*, February 28, 1938.

31–32 "This was a moment for me" and "two hundred fifty fervent": Imp, p. 25.

33 "After that I got going": Bainbridge, "S. Hurok," p. 52.

33 "not third, but second class": Imp, p. 26.

Chapter Three

35 "A short fattish man": MMY, p. 147.

35 "could have met at the Grand Hotel": Interview by Joseph Roddy with Fyodor Chaliapin, Jr., 1959.

35 "I will never go to the United States again" and "modest and unnoticed," etc.: Imp, p. 28.

36 "When the evening arrived": James Harding, *Massenet*. New York, 1970, p. 191.

36 "natives of the great country": Pages, p. 255.

37 "bleach away their past," etc.: Howe, pp. 291, 306.

38–39 "He proposed that instead of renting" and "a good strategist": Letter from Marx Lewis to Joseph Roddy, June 22, 1974, private archives of Ruth Lief.

39 " 'Music for the Masses' ": Imp, p. 30.

39 "white elephant with a past": Zander Hollander, ed., *Madison Square Garden*. New York, 1973, p. 9.

40 "The Hippodrome was the place": Imp, p. 30.

40 "to purchase vast quantities": NYT, October 10, 1915.

41 "has done his work with his head full": NYT, October 1, 1915, p. 11.

42 "There was a drug store": Imp, p. 31.

42 "Hurok's ticket booths": Ed Sullivan, "Little Old New York," *Sunday News*, December 13, 1953.

43 "They came by trolley": Imp, p. 32.

43 "In many ways": NYT, June 9, 1973, p. 28.

44 "America, by the strange and

tragic": Henry T. Finck, "In the World's Musical Metropolis," *The Nation*, May 11, 1916, p. 525.

45 "art—particularly music—still connoted" and "cranks and sissies": Davis II, pp. 22, 64.

46 "the interpretation of the ponderous messages": in Fonteyn-Pavlova, p. 51.

46 "Americans still seemed to think of ballet": Massine, pp. 80–81.

47 "How I'd like to take a sock": Mary Jane Matz, *The Many Lives of Otto Kahn*. New York, 1963, p. 112.

47 "According to the frequently nasty Romola Nijinsky": Buckle, p. 311.

47 "With so many glowing notices": Nesta MacDonald, *Diaghilev Observed by Critics in England and the United States 1911–1929*. New York, 1975.

48–49 "slightly confused" and "in a palace courtyard": Clarke, pp. 106–107.

49 "For the first time": New York *Tribune*, January 9, 1916.

50 "Her height was slightly below average": in Fonteyn-Pavlova, p. 55.

50 "to watch and worship": SHP, p. 20.

51 "The words that I would say" and "She sat before her dressing table": Imp, pp. 56–57.

51 "After that I was a frequent visitor": *Ibid.*, p. 59.

53–54 "Even in those early days in Brooklyn": Ruth Lief, *I Remember Papa* (unpublished memoirs); and HR interviews with Ruth Lief.

54–55 "Everyone sat at his table" and "I was walking with my mother and father": Lief, *I Remember Papa*, pp. 1–4.

Chapter Four

56 "Wherever you turned": *Variety*, January 6, 1943.

58 "seemed to be living through a joyful bacchanal": MMY, p. 85.

58 "cast a spell": Boris Schwarz, *Great Masters of the Violin*, p. 435.

58 "There are too many goddamn": MMY, p. 84.

59 "My struggles to establish" and "Perhaps in France": Irma, pp. 185, 165.

59 "an audience of amazingly large size": in Kay Bardsley, "The Duncans at Carnegie Hall," *Ballet Review*, Vol. 19, No. 3 (Fall 1991), p. 94.

60 "It may truthfully be claimed": Irma, p. 169.

60–61 Letter from Augustin Duncan to Harle, *Ibid.*, pp. 203–204.

62 "a spectacular musical play": *Ibid.*, p. 243.

62 "that the latest dances": NYT, November 8, 1919.

63 "There was all the publicity": SHP, p. 97.

64 "in an atmosphere of nostalgic gloom" and "muffed the big chance": SHP, p. 93.

65 "In Boston I began to talk": Imp, p. 60.

65 "Hurok was in love": HR-de Mille.

66 "She had *poi-son-ality*": Undated interview with Hurok by Victoria Huckenpahler ("The Art of Anna Pavlova as Recollected by Sol Hurok," NYPLLC Dance Collection) and Hurok comments used in a 1967 NET special on Pavlova, "The Creative Person."

66 "I want to dance for everybody": Fonteyn-Pavlova, p. 119.

67 "smiled, and you could see": HR Interview with Rudolf Nureyev, Costa Mesa, CA, June 18, 1989.

67 "He never was a great success with the ladies": HR Interview with Lillian Libman, New York, June 23, 1992.

67 "Her face clouded": Kerensky, p. 1.

67 "and made me promise not to tell": Imp, p. 81.

68 "struck many people": Kerensky, p. 131.

68 "Often it meant" Fonteyn-Pavlova, p. 120.

69 "Never mind, Hurokchik": Imp, p. 74.

69 "Little by little": Pages, p. 308.

69 "All these seven years": *Ibid.*, p. 311.

70 "Around his dining-room table": Borovsky, p. 528.

71 "I have received": Iankovskii, p. 324.

71–72 "The day came" and "And so, in August, 1921" Pages, pp. 312–313.

72 "The singer would receive a fee": Iosif Darskii, "Pevets i impressario" ("The Singer and the Impressario"), *Novoe russkoe slovo*, August 28, 1992, p. 27.

72 "Oh, my Irina": Chaliapin I, p. 475.

73 "beginning with Bardush's": Imp, p. 22.

73 "She flung her slender arms": *Ibid.*, p. 39.

73–74 "The Manhattan Opera House was crowded": NYT, November 14, 1921.

74 "I was ill": Pages, p. 323.

74 "continuous and often overwhelming roar" and "25,000 New Yorkers": NYT, November 28, 1921.

74 "acclaimed from his first entrance": NYT, December 10, 1921.

74–75 "most excited and turbulent throngs" etc.: NYT, December 15, 1921.

75 "some changes in what was formerly": NYT, November 6, 1921.

76 "I only realised this": Pages, p. 326.

76 "for a taste of flop-house luxury": Undated clipping, NYPLLC, Dance Collection clipping files.

76 "And once, when we were drying off": NYHT, January 7, 1951.

77–78 "I opened the lid" and "He's running some concerts": MMY, p. 147.

78 "cantata caravan": in Iankovskii, p. 325.

78 "of medium height": Chaliapin I, p. 476.

78–79 "Further acquaintance with him": Pages, p. 324.

79 "In search of talent": Imp, p. 76.

Chapter Five

80 "My husband was a Russian": McVay, p. 242.

80 "in a roseate haze": Imp, p. 135.

80–81 "As his achievements grew": Ruth Lief, *I Remember Papa*, pp. 3–4.

81 "I had got myself divorced": Imp, p. 142.

81 "a legally binding divorce": These documents are in the personal archives of Ruth Hurok Lief.

82 "like all Jewish mothers": HR-Ruth Lief.

82 "Those who couldn't adjust": Gabler, p. 247.

83 "tall, good-looking brunette": Imp, p. 76.

83 "a big scene": HR-Ruth Lief.

83 "They wore a sleek armor": Imp, pp. 77–78.

84 "Chanel Number Five": Interview with Anna Strauss, New York, September 28, 1989.

84 "They gazed with longing": Imp, p. 78.

84 "two stately swans": Fonteyn-Pavlova, p. 70.

85 "anonymous friends": Imp, p. 80.

85 "It took years": *Ibid.*, p. 80.

85 "It was on the originality": *Ibid.*, p. 79.

86 "Marie-Therese even believes": Kerensky, p. 80.

86–87 "I thought she was awful": in

Walter Terry, *Isadora Duncan: Her Life, Her Art, Her Legacy*. New York, 1963, p. 160.

87 "work for the future": McVay, p. 11.

87 "beautiful-depraved face": *Ibid.*, p. 21.

87–88 Telegrams between Duncan and Hurok: McVay, p. 51.

88 "opinions which Miss Duncan": *Musical America*, October 7, 1922.

88 "obliged to remove every stitch": Imp, p. 100.

88–89 "Mr. Hurok protested vigorously": *Musical America*, October 7, 1922.

89 "When the ferry docked": Imp, p. 101.

89 "When we got into our car": McVay, p. 112.

90 "the tall Russian youth": Imp, p. 97.

90 "no different from that of an ordinary": New York *Herald*, October 2, 1922.

90 "woman from Mars": Imp, p. 97.

90 "In every pose and gesture" and "I have given my hand to Russia": New York *Tribune*, October 9, 1922.

91 "tore off her flimsy red tunic": McVay, p. 119.

91 "This—this is beauty!": Imp, p. 105.

91 "My manager tells me": Irma Duncan and Allan Ross Macdougall, *Isadora Duncan's Russian Days and Her Last Years in France*. New York, 1929, pp. 170–171.

92 "Hurok's typically cinematic version of events": Imp, pp. 113–114.

93 "The lurid headlines": *Ibid.*, p. 118.

93 "Hurok officially chartered his operation": MCBR.

93 "considered her art over the heads": Davis, II, p. 75.

94–95 "a big burly man" and "short burlesques": Phyllis Hartnoll, ed., *The Oxford Companion to the Theatre* (3rd ed.). London, 1967, p. 68.

95 "the box-office receipts": Sayler, p. 23.

96 "No dramatic importation": Allen Churchill, *The Theatrical 20's*. New York, 1975, p. 99.

96 "We have never had such a success": in Erica Munk, ed., *Stanislavsky and America: An Anthology from the Tulane Drama Review*. New York, 1966, p. 144.

97 "direct from 1680 successful performances": NYT, January 12, 1925.

97 "to express profoundly the thing": NYT, February 8, 1925.

98–99 "would fill a text book" and "Do you know why I bought": Sayler, p. 22.

Chapter Six

100 "Shakespeare was interested": NYT Magazine, April 2, 1923, p. 7.

103 "A manager does not make an artist": Imp, p. 91.

103 Letter from Hurok to Koussevitsky: dated September 13, 1924. Archives of the Music Library of the Library of Congress, Washington, D.C.

103–105 Quotations from Ekskuzovich about proposed Mariinsky tour come from NYT, June 29, 1923, p. 20.

105 "I read in the papers": Mikhail Fokin, *Protiv echeniia: Vospominaniia baletmeistera (Against the Current: Memoirs of a Balletmaster)*. Leningrad-Moscow, 1962, p. 489.

106 "Though bullets flew": NYT, June 29, 1923.

106 "Roaming around America": Chaliapin I, p. 432.

107 "Salomon, an artist": Imp, pp. 46–47.

107 "all these bloodsucking": Chaliapin I, pp. 433–434.

107–108 "a big, but boring" and "egotistical and extremely cultured": Chaliapin I, pp. 480–481.

108–109 The letter Hurok wrote to Mr. and Mrs. Gershunoff was made available to me by Max Gershunoff.

109 "Ironically, after they had come here" and "You know, Charles Koot was my uncle": HR Interview with Maxim Gershunoff, New York, August 15, 1989.

110 "every week during the season": NYT, July 4, 1925.

110 "would himself invest" and "as Mr. Chaliapin wishes to show": NYT, December 15, 1925.

112 "They wanted to do the same thing": Chaliapin IV, pp. 254–255.

112 "never to shake that man's hand": Darskii, "Pevets i impressario," p. 27.

113 "its curlicues and colors": Joseph H. Mazo, Prime Movers: The Makers of Modern Dance in America. New York, 1977, p. 26.

114 "an interpretative dancer" and "a tired, sick little woman": NYT, October 16 and November 4, 1926.

114 "not one of my proudest": SHP, p. 38.

115 "the world's first ultra-modern publicity machine": Terence Elsberry, Marie of Romania: The Intimate Life of a Twentieth Century Queen. New York, 1927, p. 196.

116 "It told of the monstrous injustice": Oscar G. Brockett and Robert R. Findlay, Century of Innovation: A History of European and American Theatre and Drama Since 1870. Englewood Cliffs, NJ, 1973, p. 334.

116 "ecstatic stylization": Howe, p. 487.

116 "our stage may learn a great deal": NYT, December 14, 1926.

117 "has indeed probably done more" and following: H. I. Brock, "Another Moscow Comes to Broadway,"

NYT Magazine, October 10, 1926, p. 12.

Chapter Seven

120 "ended on their bottoms": Bluebird, p. 144.

120 "inspires confidence": Transcript of bankruptcy hearing on October 2, 1925; the Bankers Trust Co. investigation records are in MCBR files of NYPLLC, Dance Collection.

121 "a new company, Hurok Attractions, Inc.": MCBR.

120–21 "One of the most opulent hostelries" and "I had spent thousands of dollars" and "I was broke": Imp, pp. 142–143.

122 "I had a chance to take stock": Tex McCrary and Jinx Falkenburg, "New York Close-Up," New York Herald Tribune, January 7, 1951.

123 "sumptuous, Junoesque": Eaton, p. 203.

124 "an old-fashioned German hausfrau": Imp, p. 147.

125 "Hurok asserts": NYT, April 22, 1931, p. 28.

126 "That was her hold on him": HR Interview with Nela Rubinstein, New York, January 11, 1989.

126 "She played the piano": Kramer-Semenoff.

127 "have a lot of charm": HR Interview with Edward Perper, Moscow, March 21, 1988.

127 "in order to improve her position": HR-Danilova.

127–28 "I don't know myself why" and "But she knew beauty": HR-Strauss.

128 "a marvelous sad-eyed Russian woman": HR-de Mille.

129 "Many things happened to me in the Thirties": Imp, p. 153.

129 "I don't think even Emma herself": HR-Libman.

129–30 "dancers had brains in their

feet" and "When I was in camp": HR-Ruth Lief.

130 "creatures of a drive": Gabler, p. 246.

131 "Mister Hurok, I'm such heavy artillery": Imp, p. 151.

131–32 "I convinced Glazunov" "It was winter" and "If Hurok hasn't written to me": *Novoe russkoe slovo*, March 26, 1936.

134 "Concert attendance was very low": William Paley, *As It Happened: A Memoir*. Garden City, 1979, p. 330.

135 "He had a contract impossibly favorable": *Variety*, September 25, 1957, p. 70.

136 "He told a Russian newspaper": *Russkii golos*, September 5, 1937.

137 "From the way he spoke": Maska, p. 235.

138 "monopoly right to engage Soviet artists": NYT, August 3, 1930, p. 2.

139 The account of Hurok's reunion with his family in Minsk comes from material provided in a phone interview by Rita Zaitseva (January 13, 1993).

Chapter Eight

141 epigraph: HR-de Mille.

142 "as though she had a premonition" and "She brought sunlight": Imp, p. 125.

142 "Hurok was able to choose": HR-Danilova.

143 "Hurok thought in terms of stars": Haskell, p. 198.

143 "Diaghilev was absolutely determined": *Dance Magazine*, November 1929, p. 17.

143 "Don't you know that I may never": Imp, p. 86.

144 *"woik"* and *"rehoise"*: 1967 NET special, "The Creative Person."

144 "carried on stage in silk tissue paper": Hurok-Huckenpahler.

144 "The Future of the American Ballet," unidentified clipping in Hurok

clipping files, NYPLLC, Dance Collection.

145–46 "He told me I didn't have very good technique," "a peasant and a midget," and "the big managers like Hurok": HR-de Mille.

147 "Does Classical Dancing Pay?" by Joseph Arnold, *Dance Magazine*, June 1929, p. 15.

148–49 "I finally yielded one summer evening" and "I anticipated my coming": Wigman, p. 133.

149 "quite mad": Imp, p. 157.

150 "Occasionally I wondered": *Ibid.*, p. 158.

150 "as if all the journalists" and "whatever you want them to mean": Wigman, p. 138.

150 "just making motions to a piano": NYT, December 22, 1930.

151 "another publicity hyena" and "Raw meat": Wigman, p. 148.

151 "Her ample presence": Margaret Lloyd, *The Borzoi Book of Modern Dance*. New York, 1949, p. 15.

151 "It was a dismal flop": Imp, 161.

151 "one of the most brilliant audiences": NYT, January 18, 1932.

151 "the *Vogue, Vanity Fair*": Imp, p. 163.

152 "one of the most provocative and delightful events": NYT, September 4, 1932.

152 "I never anticipated": *Ibid.*, p. 169.

153 "There are songs": NYT, April 22, 1932.

153 "She had a small role": HR-Danilova.

155 "a mild-mannered man": Jack Anderson, "the Ballets Russes Saga," *Ballet News*, January 1982, p. 11.

155 "a natural propensity": Bernard Taper, *Balanchine: A Biography*. New York, 1984, p. 134.

157 "was too short and trivial": Haskell, p. 198.

158 "financial conditions notwith-

standing" and "American forces to the point": NYT, March 19, 1933.

158 "the outstanding artistic event": Hurok letter to J. F. Phelps Stokes, November 22, 1933, in Bakhmeteff Archives, Columbia University Libraries.

159 "eleven Mamas": Imp, p. 190.

159 "One person would book into an hotel": Markova, p. 78.

159 "big names": Bagazh, p. 190.

159 "Why don't you get rid": Haskell, p. 197.

159 "the first classically trained ballet": NYT, December 31, 1933.

160 "Martin's opinion": NYT, December 23, 1933.

160–61 "Toumanova had been born": Walter Terry, "Baby Ballerinas," Ballet News, June 1981, p. 16.

161 "American reporters wanted": Choura, p. 132.

161 "Allegedly, Hurok": Haskell, p. 198.

161 "the theater was almost empty": HR Interview with Tatania Riabouchinska, Los Angeles, March 21, 1989.

162 "were so poor they didn't have a pot to piss in": HR-Edward Perper.

PART II

Chapter Nine

167 "Most American audiences": Choura, p. 133.

167 "The anguish of the Great Depression": Davis III, p. 83.

167 "Good as it was": Arnold Haskell, "Sol Hurok," Dancing Times, January 1959, p. 179.

168 "the incentive for many dinners": Minneapolis Journal, February 11, 1934.

168 "the most brilliant event of the winter": Chicago Daily News, February 17, 1934.

169 "Then ... vai ... not ... try?" and following: Bagazh, p. 191.

170 "He looked at me with surly eyes": Bagazh, p. 194.

171 "a highly amusing piece of work": NYT, April 26, 1934.

172 "homeopathic doses": Bagazh, p. 196.

172 "ended up without a financial grievance": Walker, p. 37.

172–73 "Three years ago I felt": Philadelphia Evening Public Ledger, March 8, 1934.

173 "parade of brilliant artistic successes" and "Everything he did spoke for the present": Lincoln Kirstein, Thirty Years: The New York City Ballet. New York, 1978, pp. 26–27.

174 "such importations could only": Ibid., p. 32.

175–76 "Hurok always thought about selling," "When the talk got down to business," and "Everyone knew that Hurok": HR-Danilova.

176 "there is no better barometer": Chicago Tribune, August 10, 1934.

177–78 "I must begin by saying": Letter from Hurok to Deakin; Deakin.

178 "on a four-walls basis": Variety, November 5, 1947.

180 "I should be ever so much obliged": Deakin to Hurok letter April 7, 1936; Deakin.

180 "the most popular expression of entertainment": G-Marquez, p. 136.

180–81 "swept everything else to the corners" and "Hurok knew stunts": HR-de Mille.

181–82 "one of deadly monotony": Arnold Haskell, In His True Centre. London, 1951, pp. 134–135.

182 "Holy Russia on Tour": Walker, p. 48.

182 "the most chaotic organization I have ever known" and "a small fortune": Choura, p. 134.

182–83 "The natural hauteur" and

"Mme. Hurok was given first obeisance": Zorina, pp. 80–81.

183 "Under the terms of the three-year contract": MCBR, May 22, 1935.

184 "In return for his financial backing": Sevastianov letter to Deakin June 25, 1936; Deakin.

186 "continue and develop the work": December 4, 1936; MCBR.

186 "finally signed a contract" and financial memo: MCBR.

187 "the 'balletic' world . . . is in complete turmoil": Denham to Deakin letter June 29, 1937; Deakin.

Chapter Ten

189 "Mr. Hurok is one of the last": New York *Sun*, October 26, 1938.

190 "I was a child of fourteen": Hurok interview with Joseph Roddy.

190 "was built along generous lines": MAnderson, p. 154.

191 "To his own daughter Ruth, however": This information comes from my various interviews with Ruth Lief.

193 "Because it was first of all considered family": Conversation between George Perper and Ruth Lief (undated); private archives of Ruth Lief.

195 "been unable to recognize": Harold Clurman, *The Fervent Years*. New York, 1969, p. 158.

195 "Our dear Chekhovites": Chekhov II, pp. 521–522.

196 "amazing concerts": Chekhov I, p. 434.

197 "the most amusing and the most amazingly fresh": Imp, p. 172.

197 "the sort of attraction": NYT, December 28, 1935.

198 "the mainstream of American musical life": MAnderson, p. 75.

199 "things were not going too well": *Ibid.*, p. 112.

199 "with a mixture of open-mindedness": *Ibid.*, p. 141.

200 "In Paris one evening": NYHT, January 7, 1951.

200 "Hurok made a sour face": MMY, p. 406.

200 "almost too many offers": Vehanen, p. 118.

201 " 'inadequate' in the presence of this grand impresario": MAnderson, p. 154.

202 "show whatever I was capable of doing": *Ibid.*, p. 168.

202 "let it be said": NYT, December 31, 1935, p. 13.

203 Eleanor Roosevelt's "My Day" column for February 21, 1936, reprinted in Eleanor Roosevelt and Rochelle Chadakoff, ed., *Eleanor Roosevelt's "My Day": Her Acclaimed Columns 1936–1945*. New York, 1989.

203–204 "all artists who have accepted engagements": "Hurok Sees Gloomy Outlook for Jews of Reich After Tour," *Jewish Daily Bulletin*, August 17, 1934.

205 "not set foot in Hitler's Reich": Imp, p. 53.

205–207 "You probably have been mad like hell": Hurok letter to Deakin July 16, 1937; Deakin.

207 "I am now making arrangements with the Soviet government": Letter from Hurok to Elizabeth Sprague Coolidge, Library of Congress Music Division archives.

207–208 "In Russia the theatre, the music" and "The Government has unlimited funds": Ruth McKenney, "Orchids to Russian Stage, Says Solomon Hurok, Home," New York *Post*, August 29, 1936.

209 "an interview with the New York Russian émigré newspaper": "*S. I. Iurok rasskazyvaet o svoikh vpechatleniiakh i planakh*" ("S. I. Hurok Tells about His Impressions and Plans"), *Novoe russkoe slovo*, September 5, 1937.

210–11 "In those days, before the treason trials": Imp, pp. 52–53.

211 "hated the whole style of life" and following: Borovsky, p. 524.

Chapter Eleven

212 epigraph: A. E. Twysden, *Alexandra Danilova*. London, 1945, p. 107.

213 "At Covent Garden": *New Yorker*, July 24, 1937.

213 "not on speaking terms": G-Marquez, p. 176.

214 Danilova on Massine: in Choura, pp. 136–141.

215 "anyone whomsoever to insert": Hurok letter to Denham December 23, 1937; MCBR.

215 "the finest ballet company": Imp, p. 204.

215–16 The conditions of the de Basil-Denham merger: MCBR.

216 "This incident only shows the danger": May 14, 1938, letter; MCBR.

217 "the outstanding figure": Arnold Haskell, *The Bystander*, July 27, 1938.

218 "with such warmth": Markova, p. 75.

218 "a summer of summers": Imp, p. 209.

218 "to gloat over their equally excellent": Walker, p. 86.

219 "Hurok claims that the negotiating process": Imp, p. 212.

219 "anything I do is in the interests": Hurok letter to Denham August 19, 1938; MCBR.

219 "I must take credit to myself": Hurok letter to Deakin August 10, 1938; Deakin.

220 "much more glamorous": Choura, p. 145.

220 "I do not think his music" and "artistically sound": Hurok letter to Denham April 26, 1940; MCBR.

221 "Are you out of your mind?": *New Yorker*, December 26, 1977, p. 34.

221 "I feel like a whore in a church": *Wall Street Journal*, January 7, 1988.

222 "Benny, pale as a ghost": *Downbeat*, February 1938, p. 5.

222 "The huge audience swayed and rocked": NYHT, January 17, 1938, p. 15.

222 "a social and physical phenomenon": NYT, January 17, 1938.

222 "There seems to be no middle group": NYT, January 18, 1938.

222–23 "I think the band I had": *Downbeat*, February 8, 1956, p. 12.

223 "the one that comes to mind": James Lincoln Collier, *Benny Goodman and the Swing Era*. New York, 1989, p. 230.

223 The findings of Denham's financial investigation of Hurok, dated October 7, 1938, are in MCBR.

224 "Don't dance tomorrow night" and following: JAnderson, pp. 29–30.

224 "Don't talk such tommyrot": NYHT, October 23, 1938.

225 "far below the standards": Hurok letter to Fleischmann January 10, 1939; MCBR.

225 "No amount of endowment": Hurok letter to Denham January 16, 1938; MCBR.

225 "Hurok's trick No. 1000" and following: David Libidins letter to Denham January 14, 1939; MCBR.

226 "a slow, ten-day, one-class boat": Denham letter to Hurok December 28, 1938; MCBR.

226 "The standing of the company": Hurok letter to Denham December 30, 1938; MCBR.

226 "oc-TAW-pus": HR-de Mille.

Chapter Twelve

227 epigraph: MAnderson, p. 189.

227 "not to seek dates for Marian": Imp, p. 244.

227–28 "There was dignity": MAnderson, pp. 170–171.

229 "Certainly, I have feelings": Leon Jaroff, "Marian Anderson: Let Freedom Ring," *Memories*, February/March 1989, pp. 3–5.

230 "in an important hall" and "No date will ever be available": Hayes, pp. 15–16.

230–31 "stood with his arms folded": *Ibid.*, 11–12.

231 "The hall really had been booked": Washington *Star*, September 9, 1979.

232 "Of course Hurok revelled": HR Interview with Patrick Hayes, Wilmington, Vermont, August 21, 1991.

233 "The issue was now larger": Hayes, p. 20.

233–34 Eleanor Roosevelt "My Day" column of February 27, 1939, as reprinted in *"My Day,"* p. 113.

234 "one of the most hopeful signs": NYT, February 28, 1939.

234 Telegram to Koussevitsky is preserved in Library of Congress, Music Division archives.

235 "made a fuss about it": NYT, March 19, 1939.

236 "I trusted the management": MAnderson, p. 185.

236 "She's going to sing there if I have to put up a tent": Hayes, p. 21.

236 "sparkplug president": Imp, p. 258.

237 "obtained immediate consent": Hayes, p. 21.

237 "I could see that my significance": MAnderson, p. 189.

237 "Preparations are going ahead": Ickes, p. 612.

237 "This seems to me to be a good use": Jaroff, p. 35.

239 "the weather was cool," "the best speech I have ever made," "a vigorous candidate for President," and "The whole setting was unique": Ickes, pp. 614–616.

239–40 "I felt for a moment" and

"I am overwhelmed": MAnderson, pp. 191–192.

Chapter Thirteen

242 epigraph: Denham letter to Yakov Rubinstein, January 26, 1940; MCBR.

242–43 "In the event of military hostilities": MCBR.

243 "I am here for the third week now" and "I have negotiated": Hurok letter to Deakin August 7, 1939; Deakin.

244–45 "Whenever we talked about the war": NYT, September 19, 1939.

245 "he was afraid of the reaction": Denham memo September 30, 1939; MCBR.

245–46 "the last boat to leave" and "backstage tattle-tale": Kramer-Semenoff.

246 "about as American as": Edward Downes, "Ballet Premieres," Boston *Transcript*, April 19, 1940.

246 "we are being 'gypped' ": Fleischmann memo to Denham November 1939; MCBR.

247 "faulted a stale repertoire": Hurok letter to Denham December 23, 1939; MCBR.

247 "With regard to the future": Denham letter to Rubinstein January 26, 1940; MCBR.

248 "good food, good cigars": in Glenn Plaskin, *Horowitz: A Biography of Vladimir Horowitz*. New York, 1983, p. 123.

248–49 "I might get him an engagement," "the fat and important-looking," and "Let me vorry about it": MMY, p. 404.

249 "And then between the two of us": HR-Nela Rubinstein.

250 " 'galvanic' account": NYT, November 22, 1937.

250 "I played it with my usual freedom" and following and "What is this

'Prince of Pianists' for": MMY, pp. 427–428.

251 "By 1953, Hurok later claimed": Memo to Darryl Zanuck April 14, 1952; Deakin.

251 "Why would I want to take on": HR interviews with Ruth and Arthur Lief.

252 "His managerial flair": MMY, p. 424.

252 "the artist finds": NYT, September 17, 1938.

252 " 'Europe cannot send us pianists' ": MMY, p. 479.

253 "singing over crackling candy wrappers," "ample and easy," and "Toscanini's tenor": Bluebird, p. 121.

253 "almost everybody was kosher": *Ibid.*, p. 13.

254–55 "I would be having my hair cut," "I could read between the lines," "Is that all there is to it?" and "The Broadway people said": *Ibid.*, pp. 142–143.

256 "go home, make *Kiddush*": *Ibid.*, p. 167.

256 "our *Rigoletto*": *Ibid.*, p. 143.

256 "I never really got close": *Ibid.*, p. 145.

258 "a woman with wild temperament": MMY, p. 475.

258 "nobody knew her very well": HR-Nela Rubinstein.

259 "result of the fact": Hurok letter to Denham August 27, 1940; MCBR.

259 "If one of the companies crumbles": *Time*, November 25, 1940, pp. 38–42.

260 "strength and heartiness": NYT, December 1, 1940.

261 "or perhaps, as Denham complained": Denham letter to Hurok November 26, 1940; MCBR.

261 "a lack of judgment" and "a score by Stravinsky": Hurok letter to Denham December 19, 1940; MCBR.

261 "to defame and sink" and "one of his tactics": Letters from Denham to

Watson Washburn January 2 and January 22, 1941; MCBR.

262 "smashing (as Deakin saw it)": Deakin letter to Dolin October 25, 1940; Deakin.

262 "completely losing his *savoir faire*": Deakin letter to Dolin December 2, 1940; Deakin.

263 "Because of de Basil's inability": SHP, p. 144.

264 "as a patriotic duty": Walker, p. 110.

264 "absolutely void of any idealism": Denham memo April 10, 1941; MCBR.

Chapter Fourteen

265 epigraph: Hurok letter to William Fields December 18, 1947; BT.

266 "Here at last": NYHT, January 30, 1940.

267 "Richard Pleasant thought": John Gruen, "Close-Up: Lucia Chase," *Dance* magazine, January 1975, p. 37.

269 "contaminate Ballet Theatre's purity" and "a negotiator and mediator": Payne, pp. 109–110.

271 "the best I have seen": Los Angeles *Examiner*, September 11, 1941.

271 "While we do not consider": Denham letter to Hurok November 22, 1941; MCBR.

271 "chiefly to satisfy": Denham letter to Alexandra Tolstoy March 17, 1942; MCBR.

273 "People were buying not ballet companies": Imp, p. 229.

275–76 "We had the ballet at a halfway point," "Often I think of Papa Hurok," "My weekly salary," and "We brought the curtain down": Antony Tudor conversation with Ruth Lief (undated).

277 "He knew it would be a flop": HR-de Mille.

277 "How do you know?": Agnes de

Mille, *Portrait Gallery*. Boston, 1990, pp. 141–142.

278 "the artistic validity": George Amberg, *Ballet in America: The Emergence of an American Art*. New York, 1983, p. 55.

278 "the era of Russian ballet": in JAnderson, p. 82.

278 "Now It's 'Miss Jones' ": NYT Magazine, October 11, 1942.

278 "would stand at the back of the theatre": HR-de Mille.

278 "Later, in *S. Hurok Presents*": SHP, p. 161.

278 "You should be Hurok artist": HR-de Mille.

279 "For what company?" "I want you should be Hurok attraction" and "I'm an impresario": HR-de Mille.

280 "This is great recognition": Hurok telegram to Sevastianov May 29, 1942; BT.

280 "We must insist": Harry Zuckert letter to Hurok April 1, 1943; BT.

280 "prominent outstanding artists" and "we certainly must have her": Hurok letter to J. Alden Talbot August 24, 1943; BT.

281 "as concerned with weakening": Payne, p. 130.

281 "could be seen at the Russian Tea Room": JAnderson, p. 85.

281 "They feel you are the most important": Deakin letter to Hurok March 9, 1945; Deakin.

282–83 "Hurok would report": Payne, p. 142.

283 "milkmaid who had drawn": Hurok memo to Deakin (undated); Deakin.

284 "In a detailed report" and "We claim that this": BT.

Chapter Fifteen

288 " 'The question,' Stern recalled" and "I honestly don't remember": HR-Stern.

289 "I played seven concerts": Stephen E. Rubin, "Isaac Stern: The Power and the Glory," NYT Magazine, October 14, 1979, p. 62.

289–91 "When I started playing," "I was the only one," and "Hurok would push the fees up": HR-Stern.

291 "As many observers have pointed out": See, for example, Susan Elliott, "Panic in the Streets," *Musical America Directory 1993*, p. 75.

291–92 "He worked very hard," "Certainly I was aware," and "I knew Emma": HR-Stern.

292 "a nice lady": HR-Ruth Lief.

293 "sit on the telephone": HR-de Mille.

293 "make him bow his head" and "He would sit open-mouthed": HR-Strauss.

293 "You know who died": HR Interview with Martin Feinstein, Washington, D.C., December 29, 1988.

295 "He loved it out here": HR Interview with Betty Ferrell, Torrance, CA, September 26, 1988.

295 "gigantic egos": HR-de Mille.

295 "an empire of his own": See Gabler.

296 "All they do is run around": HR-Ruth Lief.

296 "that the Americans were sticking around" and "the costumes are dirty": HR-de Mille.

296 "The Hurok organization" and "As a creative artist": McDonagh, pp. 185–186.

297 "Walter always had to tell": HR-de Mille.

298–300 "I think I had more knowledge" and "You're a bright young man": HR-Feinstein.

300 "the accounts were tallied": *Ballet*, London, December 1916, pp. 19–21.

300 "a morbid spectacle": Edwin Denby, *Looking At the Dance*. New York, 1968, pp. 202–203.

300 "an anxious memo": dated November 4, 1946; Deakin.

301 "the twelve performances there": Statement of finances for spring, 1947; MCBR.

301 "When the 'Colonel' ": SHP, p. 197.

302 "You should have been with us": Deakin letter to Alexander Haas May 29, 1946; Deakin.

303 "We simply cannot go on": Dolin letter to Deakin January 16, 1948; Deakin.

304 "As reported by John Martin": NYT, November 30, 1947.

304 "According to *Variety*": "Hurok Declines to Renew Ballet Lease for Met," *Variety*, November 26, 1947.

305 "no ballet company existing today": Hurok letter to William Fields December 18, 1947; BT.

305 "When you have a foundation": New York *Post*, December 8, 1947.

305 "through with ballet": SHP, p. 11.

Chapter Sixteen

306 epigraph: Fonteyn, p. 111.

306 "city of austerity": SHP, p. 209.

307 "final phase": de Valois, p. 157.

307 "in a completely non-professional": SHP, p. 210.

307 "The overture started": Clive Barnes, "Barnes On . . . ,": *Ballet News*, June 1981, p. 46.

308 "the radiant gaiety": SHP, pp. 211–212.

308 "failed to make any great impression" and following: de Valois, p. 185.

309 "What made the whole business": "Barnes On . . . . ," p. 46.

310 "I have seen a lot": Hurok letter to Deakin July 18, 1947; Deakin.

310 "a flight of 18000 miles": Hurok letter to Deakin September 15, 1947; Deakin.

310 "Paris is full of Americans": John Taras letter to Deakin July 16, 1948; Deakin.

311 "the biggest transatlantic haul": NYT, September 30, 1949, p. 28.

312 "to smile and show" and "about as frightened": Fonteyn, pp. 111–112.

313 "the sound of a gun": Channel 4 documentary on Margot Fonteyn, 1989, Patricia Foy, producer.

313 "a ballerina among ballerinas" and following: NYT, October 10, 1949, p. 20.

314 "In retrospect" and "only to heads of state": Fonteyn, pp. 112–113.

314 "loveability": Fonteyn documentary.

314 "really fabulous success": Deakin letter to Dolin December 9, 1949; Deakin.

315 "the greatest opening of the popular audience": John Martin article for Royal Ballet Twentieth Anniversary Program at the Met, 1969.

315 "Dead and gone": Irving Kolodin article for 1967 Royal Ballet Program at the Met, p. 14.

315 "very human fashion," etc.: de Valois, p. 188.

316 "the greatest *ballerina*": SHP, p. 254.

316–17 "egg-shaped and bald" and "When I came to know him well": Fonteyn, pp. 110–111.

Chapter Seventeen

320 "Even the critic who reviewed": Rosalyn Krokover, "Backstage at the Ballet," NYT Book Review, December 20, 1953.

320 "the contract between Hurok and Fox": Private archives of Ruth Lief.

321 "high-quality picture on a relatively small budget" and "the film came in $100,000 under budget": Chierichetti, p. 296.

321 The memo written by Deakin

for Hurok, and intended for Zanuck and Jessel, is in draft form in the Deakin archives at NYPLLC, Dance Collection. Following excerpts are taken from it.

323 "I didn't want to do it": Joseph Roddy interview with Arthur Rubinstein.

325 "It was very hard to get any reality": Chierichetti, p. 297.

325 "Oscar Karlweis?": HR-Ruth Lief.

331 "At Darryl's last running": Toumanova letter to Hurok August 18, 1952; Deakin.

331 "It really was beautiful": Chierichetti, p. 300.

331 "a topflight musical drama": *Variety*, January 26, 1953.

332 "supposed episodes": Newark *Star-Ledger*, April 16, 1953.

332 "a rambling conglomeration": NYT, February 13, 1953.

332 "Jews in America will be proud": *Jewish Ledger*, February 12, 1953.

332 "noted on cards": *Sunday Daily News*, April 5, 1953.

333 "remembers being awe-struck": HR-Van Cliburn.

Chapter Eighteen

339 "Between 1936 and 1958, not a single American scholar": Yale Richmond, *U.S.-Soviet Cultural Exchanges, 1958–1986: Who Wins?* Boulder, CO, 1987, p. 7.

339 "Stalin didn't give a damn": Testimony, p. 147.

339 "Under Stalin, it was very difficult": Edwin Bolwell, "Hurok Still Tries to Book Russians," NYT, July 27, 1967.

340 "Even a 1945 invitation": Richmond, p. 4.

341 "I had to answer stupid questions": Testimony, p. 148.

342 "great mistake," etc.: Eric Bentley, ed., *Thirty Years of Treason: Excerpts from Hearings Before the House Committee on Un-American Activities 1938–1968.* New York, Viking, p. 634.

342–43 "to teach the Communists": Harrison Salisbury, "U.S. To Set Up Unit on Cultural Ties with Soviet Union," NYT, August 1, 1955, p. 1.

344 "Tickets were impossible to get": Milstein, p. 222.

344 "the best violinist I have ever heard": Viktor Jusefovich, *David Oistrakh: Conversations with Igor Oistrakh.* London, 1977, p. 52.

345 "a great composition and a great performer": Boris Schwarz, *Music and Musical Life in Soviet Russia* (2nd ed.). Bloomington, IN, 1983, p. 290.

346 "Oistrakh was reportedly paid," etc.: HR Interview with Edward Ivanyan, Moscow, March 24, 1988.

346 "just looked up and said": George Perper and Ruth Lief.

347 "told me he liked our company": HR Interview with Igor Moiseyev, Moscow, March 24, 1988.

348 "When he learned that I didn't know," "They were stingy," "not very pleasant to deal with": *Ibid.*

350 "I arrived in New York about one A.M." and "warm and wonderful audiences": HR-Stern.

350 "Don't spout off politically": Bluebird, p. 236.

351 "yelling and stamping": Bluebird, p. 239.

351–52 "At first they weren't impressed" and "I'm not sure what their reasoning was": HR-Ivanyan.

352 "distribute bribes" and "It took someone with Hurok's energy": HR-Moiseyev.

352–53 "He wouldn't agree": HR-Ivanyan.

353 "Fingerprinting is only": NYT, June 19, 1974.

353 "threatened to solve the cold war": NYT, June 28, 1957.

Chapter Nineteen

355 epigraph: HR-Moiseyev.

356 "as a great showman" and following: Robert J. Landry, "Luben Vichey, Baritone-Impresario, Streamlining National Artists Corp," *Variety*, September 25, 1957, p. 70.

357 "The New York *Herald Tribune* was reporting": NYHT, March 13, 1958.

357 "According to Earl L. Packer": Declassified State Department report on Moiseyev tour, May 8, 1958.

358 "I told him I needed": HR-Moiseyev.

358 "Chicago's Elvis Presley fan club": Horowitz, p. 26.

359 "I've never felt so at home": *Ibid.*, p. 23.

359 "I always knew I wanted": HR-Van Cliburn.

359–60 "The implications of the occasion": NYT, April 15, 1948, p. 41.

360 "Martin Feinstein recalled standing" and following: HR-Feinstein.

361 "was an amazing triumph": HR-Moiseyev.

361 "When Moiseyev arrived": HR-Feinstein.

362 "pointed out to Mr. Schang": Declassified State Department memorandum of conversation, May 9, 1958.

362 "He simply refused to have dinner": HR-Moiseyev.

363 "the most popular and interesting" and following: HR-Ivanyan.

363 "was not advisable" and following; *Ibid.*

364–65 "A story about Lief's appearance" and "if he had discussed": Russell Porter, "9 in Show Business Here Balk At Queries on Communist Ties," NYT, June 19, 1958.

365 "He said, 'So you say you're a conductor' ": HR-Ruth Lief.

366 "I don't want him in the theatre": Russell Porter, "9 More in Entertainment World Refuse to Answer on Red Ties," NYT, June 20, 1958.

366 "I did what I wanted to" and following: HR phone interview with Arthur Lief, January 31, 1992.

366 "tried to defuse the situation": NYT, June 20, 1958, p. 12.

368 "I worried that if I did not": Ashkenazy, p. 73.

369 "Hurok knew how to be generous": *Ibid.*, p. 73.

370 "I didn't exactly feel affection": *Ibid.*, p. 122.

371 "I suppose he was entitled": *Ibid.*, p. 76.

371 "insisting that the Bolshoi Theater group": Declassified despatch from U.S. Embassy in Moscow to State Department, March 3, 1959.

372 "Having remained in Moscow" and "had stood his ground": *Ibid.*

373 "I was very pale": HR Interview with Galina Ulanova, Moscow, April 8, 1988.

373 "swamped with blank checks": NYHT, January 28, 1959.

374–75 "and other necessaries" and "So, my dear, you can practice": NYT Magazine, April 26, 1959, p. 16.

375 "Here was dramatic realism": NYT, July 12, 1992, Section II, p. 2.

375 "the greatest collection of dancers": *Saturday Review*, May 23, 1959, p. 23.

376 "We knew so little about the outside world" and "I have to tell you frankly": HR-Ulanova.

377 "His contract with the Ministry of Culture": Various declassified State Department Reports dealing with cultural exchange, 1959.

Chapter Twenty

378 epigraph: Galina, p. 298.

379 "When my competitors hear": *Dancing Times*, May 1965, p. 406.

379 "I tell you": HR-Ferrell.

381 "uncanny ability": HR-Feinstein.

382 "ingrained nobility and royal swagger": *Musical America*, November 1, 1955, p. 6.

382 "just started crying": HR-de Mille.

382 "a goodwill ambassador": NYT, November 21, 1955, p. 28.

383 "His first words were" and following: HR-Libman.

383 "He may have been a left-wing Democrat": George Perper-Ruth Lief.

384 "for Hurok he was dead": HR-de Mille.

384 "hate" and "get rid of the bum" and "the best boy in the world": Kramer-Semenoff.

384 "Hurok's face darkened": Irving Kolodin, "S. Hurok, Adventurer in the Arts," *Saturday Review*, May 30, 1959, p. 35.

385 "They gave us a lecture," "not to breathe a word about it," and "with Hurok you felt protected": Galina, pp. 288, 298.

386 "the full brunt": Declassified State Department report on Moscow State Symphony tour, March 7, 1960, pp. 2–3.

387 "Throughout the tour of the United States," etc.: HR Interview with Nina Dorliak, Moscow, April 1, 1988.

388 "moody pianist from the Soviet": NYT, October 16, 1960, II, p. 11.

390 "I know what will happen": Undated clipping, NYPLLC Dance Collection, Hurok clipping file.

390 "was a hero to us": HR-Nureyev.

391 "He loved the classics" and "You know if one evening": HR Interview with Konstantin Sergeyev, Leningrad, April 22, 1988.

392 "In the end, they reached a compromise": HR Interview with Larissa Netto, Moscow, March 19, 1992.

392 "These days presenters": HR-Sergeyev.

394 "Mr. Hurok, you know": Kramer-Semenoff.

394 "Nureyev also came to New York": *Ibid.*

394 "while still dealing": Ashkenazy, p. 123.

395 "and she actually listened to me": Kramer-Semenoff.

396 "Of course I understood him": HR-Nureyev.

396 "from minority cult": Arlene Croce, "Postscript: Rudolf Nureyev," *New Yorker*, January 18, 1993, p. 80.

396–397 "that all my family and friends" and "I just couldn't understand": Ashkenazy, pp. 122–123.

398 "a short man with an athletic build" and following: Obratsov, pp. 266–267.

Chapter Twenty-one

399 epigraph: HR Interview with Herbert Wasserman, New York, June 21, 1989.

400 "Hurok's success": HR-Stern.

400 "His office was his family": HR Interview with Lee Walter, New York, October 18, 1988.

400 "some sort of family tragedy": HR Interview with Sergei Obratsov, Moscow, April 12, 1988.

400 "He gave the impression": HR-Libman.

401 "He behaved with her": HR-Strauss.

401 "Did you sign up the Mexicans?": HR-Libman.

401 "psych herself up" and following: HR-Strauss.

402 "I'll come next month" and "He loved her to death": *Ibid.*

402 "In a 1973 interview": NYT, May 13, 1973, section 2, p. 1.

402 "Hurok loved George Perper,": HR-Libman.

402 "numerous other sources": Those include Martin Feinstein, Lillian

Libman, Ruth Lief and Alexandra Danilova.

403 "Hurok called Bloom": HR-Ruth Lief.

403–405 "My mother lived in constant awe of him" and following, "All of a sudden," and "Every other word was fuck": HR-Hyams.

405 "Yes, George, get me a dog": George Perper-Ruth Lief.

405 "to provide for the establishment": Hearings before the Special Subcommittee on the Arts of the Committee on Labor and Public Welfare, U.S. Senate, 88th Congress, on S.165 and S.1316. U.S. Government Printing office, title page.

406 "I see little of more importance": Ibid., p. 1.

407–408 "Where is our Bolshoi," "I am an American," and "find there is probably more income": Ibid., p. 277–281.

409 "not a reasonable solution": New York Post, December 8, 1947.

410 "he predicted he would take in" and following: NYT, February 13, 1965, p. 10.

410 "almost a group accomplishment": NYT, February 12, 1965, p. 9.

413 "The Bolshoi rises to an occasion": NYT, May 9, 1966, p. 48.

413 "Barnes jokingly labelled it": NYT, May 10, 1966, p. 50.

414 "Hurok was under intense pressure": see Variety, November 18, 1966, p. 70.

415 "all the disagreements": HR-Netto.

416 "How can our boys and girls": Variety, July 19, 1967, p. 1.

416 "I am a Jew": Edwin Bolwell, "Hurok Still Tries to Book Russians," NYT, July 27, 1967.

417 "All summer long": HR-Walter.

417 "another big ballet story broke": see, for example, "Fonteyn and

Nureyev Arrested Fleeing Hippie Raid," NYT, July 12, 1967, p. 1.

417 "Don't be silly": HR-Nureyev.

418 "no major attractions": Variety, September 27, 1967.

418–19 "At the time": HR-Netto.

420 "Being S. Hurok's grandson": HR-Hyams.

420 "It was just becoming crazy": Ibid.

421 "either $1.7 or $1.8 million": HR-Wasserman.

421 "I'm not getting out" and following: Donal Henahan, "Conglomerate Acquires Hurok Concerts," NYT, February 25, 1969.

422 "There had been rumors": HR-Libman.

422 "But never for a minute": HR-Walter.

Chapter Twenty-two

423 epigraph: Allan Keller, "And Now, Presenting S. Hurok," New York World-Telegram, January 21, 1961.

425 "I was young, just starting out" and following: HR Interview with Alexander Slobodyanik, Moscow, April 5, 1988.

426 "And I told him that his name": HR-Stern.

426–27 "He didn't have the musical understanding": HR-Slobodyanik.

427 "There were people looking over": HR-Feinstein.

427 "Mr. Hurok used to say": HR-Walter.

428 "The basic elements of the JDL credo": Kahane, pp. 153–154.

429–31 "a radical new chapter," "to awaken the American Jew," "who had hit upon the exchange program," "Mr. Hurok knew," and following: Ibid., pp. 1–7.

431 "If I would be in the business": Donald Henahan, "Hurok Plans for

Debut of Bolshoi Opera Here," NYT, August 28, 1970.

432 "So Hurok had to hear": NYT, December 12, 1970, p. 1.

433 "He was so quiet": HR-Slobodyanik.

434 The information on the meeting between Hurok and Bill Graham comes from Graham, pp. 329–331.

437 "tried to ingratiate himself": HR-Gershunoff.

437 "mean and desperate struggle" and "deciding who would come": HR-Netto.

438 "The Columbia people worked well": *Ibid.*

438–39 "He was walking back and forth": *Ibid.*

440 "to expand the field": "Hurok Concerts Bought," *Christian Science Monitor,* July 3, 1971.

440 "our affiliation with Tomorrow Entertainment": *Dance Magazine*, August 1971, p. 4.

440 "Today, there is very little room": NYT, May 13, 1973, section 2, p. 1.

441 "Frankly, nobody, to a person" and following: HR-Wasserman.

441 "I felt the office was changing": HR-Feinstein.

Chapter Twenty-three

443 epigraph: NYT, May 13, 1973, section 2, p. 1.

444 "We put ourselves down": NYT, January 27, 1972, p. 1.

445 "According to Joe Lewis": "Tributes Paid to Showman," Toronto *Star*, March 7, 1974.

445 "rhetoric of violence," "irresponsible criminals," and following: NYT, January 28, 1972, p. 18.

446 Yevtushenko's poem *("Bombami po balalaikam")* was later published in his collection of poems *Doroga nomer odin*, Moscow, 1972.

447 "When it turned out that the orderlies": HR-Wasserman.

447 "probably covered more mileage": Edwin Bolwell, "Entertainment Stars Gather to Pay Tribute to Sol Hurok," NYT, May 16, 1967.

449 "All my life I've catered": NYT, May 22, 1973, p. 48.

449 "age is for the calendar": *Vogue*, May 1973, p. 140.

449 Telegram from Emma Hurok: Private Archives of Ruth Lief.

450 "interview to Stephen Rubin": "S. Hurok—Last of the Red Hot Showmen," NYT, May 13, 1973, section 2, p. 1.

450–51 "shrewd and complicated strategy" and following: see Dershowitz, pp. 3–84.

453–54 "When the Bolshoi comes to New York": NYT, July 8, 1973, p. 16.

454–55 "Hurok met me at the airport": HR-Sergeyev.

456 "went on taking one sleeping tablet": Arianna Stassinopoulos, *Maria Callas: The Woman Behind the Legend.* New York, 1981, p. 329.

456 "Tomorrow morning will be too late": Kramer-Semenoff.

457 "Nureyev showed up there": Kramer-Semenoff.

457 "please bear with us": NYT, March 6, 1974, p. 26.

Chapter Twenty-four

458 epigraph: HR-Hyams.

458 "But Hurok is still here!": Lillian Libman, "S. Hurok—Ad Infinitum," *Variety*, January 9, 1974, p. 166.

458 "Hurok had a real phobia": HR-Stern.

458 "He expected to live": HR-Arthur Lief.

459 "when the day comes," "Too ostentatious," and following: Bluebird, p. 295.

460 "He launched hundreds of careers": Reprinted in Carnegie Hall Program, April 1970, p. 10.

461 Information on Hurok's estate comes from his will, in the private archives of Ruth Lief.

463 "Anyone buying Hurok Concerts": NYT, March 22, 1974, p. 30.

463 "It's the natural and ideal": *Variety*, March 27, 1974, p. 71.

464 "They had to spend more than $2 million": NYT, May 5, 1976, p. 48.

464 "a bit tighter": NYT, August 8, 1975, p. 10.

465 "As far as he was concerned": HR-Stern.

466 "There are no bad acoustics": *Opera News*, May 1974, p. 18.

467 "A *New Yorker* cartoon": Libman, "S. Hurok—Ad Infinitum."

468 "What he taught me": HR-Hyams.

469 "Hurok's taste": George Dorris, "The Legacy of Hurok," *Ballet Review*, Vol. 5, No. 1, p. 83.

SELECTED BIBLIOGRAPHY
■ ■ ■

Amberg, George. *Ballet in America: The Emergence of an American Art.* New York: DaCapo Press, 1983.

Anderson, Jack. *The One and Only: The Ballet Russe de Monte Carlo.* New York: Dance Horizons, 1981.

Anderson, Marian. *My Lord, What a Morning.* New York: Viking, 1956.

Ardoin, John. *The Callas Legacy.* New York: Scribner's, 1977.

Ashkenazy, Vladimir (with Jasper Parrott). *Beyond Frontiers.* London: Collins, 1984.

Balanchine, George. *Balanchine's New Complete Stories of the reat Ballets.* Edited by Francis Mason. New York: Doubleday, 968.

Balanchine, George. *Choreography by George Balanchine: A Catalogue of Works.* New York: Viking, 1984.

Barenboim, Lev. *Emil' Gilel's: Tvorcheskii portret artista.* Moscow: Sovetskii kompozitor, 1990.

Barnes, Clive. *Nureyev.* New York: Helene Obolensky Enterprises, 1982.

Barnum, P. T. *Struggles and Triumphs, or, Forty Years' Recollections.* Buffalo, NY: Courier, 1875.

Beasley, Maurine. *Eleanor Roosevelt and the Media: A Public Quest for Self-Fulfillment.* Urbana and Chicago: University of Illinois Press, 1987.

Benedetti, Jean. *Stanislavski.* London: Methuen, 1988.

Bentley, Eric, ed. *Thirty Years of Treason: Excerpts from Hearings before the House Committee on Un-American Activities 1938–1968.* New York: Viking, 1971.

Beschloss, Michael. *The Crisis Years: Kennedy and Khrushchev 1960–1963.* New York: Edward Burlingame Books, 1991.

Biddle, Livingston. *Our Government and the Arts: A Perspective from the Inside.* New York: ACA Books, 1988.

Borovsky, Victor. *Chaliapin: A Critical Biography.* New York: Knopf, 1988.

Brockett, Oscar, and Findlay, Robert R. *A Century of Innovation: A History of European and American Theatre and Drama Since 1870.* Englewood Cliffs, NJ: Prentice-Hall, 1971.

Buckle, Richard. *Diaghilev.* London: Weidenfeld and Nicolson, 1979.

Chaliapin, Fyodor. *Feodor Ivanovich Shaliapin. Vol. 1: Literaturnoe nasledstvo, pis'ma. N. Shaliapina: Vospominaniia ob otse.* Edited by E. A. Grosheva. Moscow: Iskusstvo, 1960.

———. *Feodor Ivanovich Shaliapin. Vol. 2: Stat'i, vys kazyvaniia, vospominaniia o F.I. Shaliapine.* Edited by E. A. Grosheva. Moscow: Iskusstvo, 1960.

———. *Maska i dusha.* Moscow: Moskovskii rabochii, 1989.

———. *Pages From My Life: An Autobiography.* Revised, enlarged, and edited by Katharine Wright, translated by H. M. Buck. New York: Harper, 1927.

Chasins, Abram (with Villa Stiles). *The Van Cliburn Legend.* Garden City: Doubleday, 1959.

Chekhov, Mikhail. *Mikhail Chekhov: Literaturnoe nasdelie v dvukh tomakh. Tom pervyi: Vospominaniia, pis'ma.* Edited by M. O. Knebel. Moskva: Iskusstvo, 1986.

Chierichetti, David. *Hollywood Director.* New York: Curtis Books, 1973.

Churchill, Allen. *The Theatrical 20's.* New York: McGraw-Hill, 1975.

Clarke, Norman. *The Mighty Hippodrome.* New York: A. S. Barnes, 1968.

Clurman, Harold. *The Fervent Years.* New York: Harvest, 1975.

Collier, James Lincoln. *Benny Goodman and the Swing Era.* New York: Oxford University Press, 1989.

Croce, Arlene. *Afterimages.* New York: Knopf, 1977.

Cron, Theodore O., and Goldblatt, Burt. *Portrait of Carnegie Hall.* New York: Macmillan, 1966.

Danilova, Alexandra. *Choura: The Memoirs of Alexandra Danilova.* New York: Knopf, 1986.

———. *A History of Music in American Life, Vol. 2: The Gilded Years, 1865–1920.* Huntington, NY: Robert Krieger, 1980.

———. *A History of Music in American Life, Vol. 3: The Modern Era, 1920–Present.* Huntington, NY: Robert Krieger, 1981.

de Mille, Agnes. *And Promenade Home.* Boston: Little, Brown, 1956.

———. *Dance to the Piper.* Boston: Little, Brown, 1951.

———. *Portrait Gallery.* Boston: Houghton Mifflin, 1990.

———. *Speak to Me, Dance with Me.* Boston: Little, Brown, 1973.

Dershowitz, Alan. *The Best Defense.* New York: Random House, 1982.

de Valois, Ninette. *Come Dance with Me: A Memoir 1898–1956.* Hamish Hamilton, London: Readers Union, 1959.

Dimont, Max. *The Jews in America: The Roots, History and Destiny of American Jews.* New York: Simon & Schuster, 1978.

Dulles, Foster Rhea. *The United States since 1865.* Ann Arbor, MI: University of Michigan Press, 1969.

Duncan, Irma. *Duncan Dancer.* Middletown, CT: Wesleyan University Press, 1966.

Duncan, Irma, and Macdougall, Allan Ross. *Isadora Duncan's Russian Days and Her Last Years in France.* New York: Covici Friede, 1929.

Duncan, Isadora. *Isadora Speaks.* Edited and introduced by Franklin Rosemont. San Francisco: City Lights Books, 1981.

———. *My Life.* New York: Boni and Liveright, 1927.

Eaton, Quaintance. *The Miracle of the Met: An Informal History of the Metropolitan Opera 1883–1967.* New York: Meredith Press, 1968.

Elsberry, Terence. *Marie of Romania: The Intimate Life of a Twentieth Century Queen.* New York: St. Martin's Press, 1972.

Fokine, Michel. *Fokine: Memoirs of a Ballet Master.* Translated by Vitale Fokine, edited by Chujoy Anatole. Boston: Little, Brown, 1961.

———. *Protiv techeniia: Vospominaniia baletmeistera. Stat'i, pis'ma.* Leningrad-Moscow: Iskusstvo, 1962.

Fonteyn, Margot, *Margot Fonteyn: Autobiography.* London: W. H. Allen, 1975.

———. *Pavlova: Portrait of a Dancer.* New York: Viking, 1984.

Fordin, Hugh. *Getting to Know Him.* New York: Random House, 1977.

Franks, A. H., ed. *Pavlova: A Biography.* London: Burke, 1956.

Gabler, Neal. *An Empire of Their Own: How the Jews Invented Hollywood.* New York: Crown, 1988.

Garcia-Marquez, Vicente. *The Ballet Russes: Colonel de Basil's Ballets Russes de Monte Carlo 1932–1952.* New York: Knopf, 1990.

Gatrell, Peter. *The Tsarist Economy 1850–1917.* London: B. T. Batsford, 1986.

Glazer, Nathan. *American Judaism.* Chicago: University of Chicago Press, 1972.

Goldin, Milton. *The Music Merchants.* New York: Macmillan, 1969.

Goodman, Walter. *The Committee: The Extraordinary Career of the House Committee on Un-American Activities.* New York: Farrar, Straus and Giroux, 1968.

Gorky, Maxim. *Chaliapin: An Autobiography as told to Maxim Gorky.* London: Macdonald, 1967.

Graham, Bill, and Greenfield, Robert. *Bill Graham Presents: My Life Inside Rock and Out.* New York: Doubleday, 1992.

Gruen, John. *The Private World of Ballet.* New York: Viking, 1970.

Harding, James. *Massenet.* New York: St Martin's Press, 1970.

Hareven, Tamara. *Eleanor Roosevelt: An American Conscience.* Chicago: Quadrangle Books, 1968.

Harris, Neil. *Humbug: The Art of P. T. Barnum.* Boston: Little, Brown, 1973.

Hartnoll, Phyllis, ed. *The Oxford Companion to the Theatre.* Oxford University Press, 1967.

Haskell, Arnold. *Balletomane at Large.* London: Heinemann, 1972.

———. *Balletomania Then and Now.* New York: Knopf, 1977.

Hellman, Lillian. *Scoundrel Time.* Boston: Little, Brown, 1976.

Hollander, Zander, ed. *Madison Square Garden.* New York: Hawthorn Books, 1973.

Horwitz, Dawn Lille. *Michel Fokine.* Boston: Twayne, 1985.

Horowitz, Joseph. *The Ivory Trade: Music and the Business of Music at the Van Cliburn International Piano Competition.* New York: Summit Books, 1990.

———. *Understanding Toscanini.* Minneapolis: University of Minnesota Press, 1987.

Howe, Irving. *Socialism and America.* New York: Harcourt Brace Jovanovich, 1985.

———. *World of Our Fathers.* New York: Touchstone, 1976.

Hurok, Sol (in collaboration with Ruth Goode). *Impresario: A Memoir.* New York: Random House, 1946.

———. *S. Hurok Presents: A Memoir of the Dance World.* New York: Hermitage House, 1953.

Iankovskii, Moisei. *Shaliapin*. Leningrad: Iskusstvo, 1972.

Ickes, Harold. *The Secret Diary of Harold L. Ickes. Vol. 2: The Inside Struggle 1936–1939*. New York: Simon & Schuster, 1954.

Johnson, Gerald. *An Honorable Titan: A Bibliographic Study of Adolph S. Ochs*. New York: Harper and Brothers, 1946.

Jusefovich, Viktor. *David Oistrakh: Conversations with Igor Oistrakh*. Translated by Nicholas dePfeiffer. London: Cassell, 1977.

Kahane, Rabbi Meir. *The Story of the Jewish Defense League*. Radnor, PA: Chilton, 1975.

Kendall, Elizabeth. *Where She Danced*. New York: Knopf, 1979.

Kerensky, Oleg. *Anna Pavlova*. New York: Dutton, 1973.

Kolodin, Irving. *The Metropolitan Opera 1883–1939*. New York: Oxford University Press, 1940.

Kotliarov, Iurii, and Garmash, Victor. *Letopis' zhizni i tvorchestva F. I. Shaliapina* (2 volumes). Leningrad: Muzyka, 1989.

Krinsky, Carol Herselle. *Rockefeller Center*. New York: Oxford University Press, 1978.

Levin, Dan. *Stormy Petrel: The Life and Work of Maxim Gorky*. New York: Appleton-Century, 1965.

Levy, Alan. *The Bluebird of Happiness: The Memoirs of Jan Peerce*. New York: Harper & Row, 1976.

Libman, Lillian. *And Music at the Close: Stravinsky's Last Years*. New York: Norton, 1972.

Lloyd, Margaret. *The Borzoi Book of Modern Dance*. New York: Knopf, 1949.

MacDonald, Nesta. *Diaghilev Observed by Critics in England and the United States 1911–1929*. New York: Dance Horizons, 1975.

Markova, Alicia. *Giselle and I*. New York: Vanguard Press, 1960.

———, *Markova Remembers*. Boston: Little, Brown, 1986.

Martin, John. *American Dancing: The Background and Personalities of the Modern Dance*. Brooklyn, NY: Dance Horizons, 1968.

Masefield, John. *A Letter From Pontus and Other Verses*. New York: Macmillan, 1936.

Massine, Leonide. *My Life in Ballet*. New York: St. Martin's Press, 1968.

Matz, Mary Jane. *The Many Lives of Otto Kahn*. New York: Macmillan, 1963.

Mazo, Joseph H. *Prime Movers: The Makers of Modern Dance in America*. New York: Morrow, 1977.

McDonagh, Don. *Martha Graham: A Biography*. New York: Praeger, 1973.

McVay, Gordon. *Isadora and Esenin*. Ann Arbor, MI: Ardis, 1980.

Milstein, Nathan, and Volkov, Solomon. *From Russia to the West: The Musical Memoirs and Reminiscences of Nathan Milstein*. Translated by Antonia W. Bouis. New York: Limelight Editions, 1991.

Munk, Erica, ed. *Stanislavsky and America: An Anthology from the Tulane Drama Review*. New York: Hill and Wang, 1966.

Nabokov, Nicolas. *Bagazh: Memoirs of a Russian Cosmopolitan*. New York: Atheneum, 1975.

Nevins, Allan, and Commager, Henry Steele. *A Short History of the United States* (6th edition). New York: Knopf, 1976.

Nureyev, Rudolph. *Nureyev*. New York: Dutton, 1963.

Obratsov, Sergei. *Po stupen'kam pamiati*. Moscow, 1987.

Osato, Sono. *Distant Dances*. New York: Knopf, 1980.

Paley, William. *As It Happened: A Memoir*. Garden City, NY: Doubleday, 1979.

Panov, Valery (with George Feifer). *To Dance*. New York: Knopf, 1978.

Payne, Charles. *American Ballet Theatre*. New York: Knopf, 1979.

Percival, John. *Nureyev: Aspects of the Dancer*. New York: Putnam's, 1975.

———. *The World of Diaghilev*. New York: Harmony Books, 1971.

Plaskin, Glenn. *Horowitz: A Biography of Vladimir Horowitz*. New York: Morrow, 1983.

Richmond, Yale. *U.S.-Soviet Cultural Exchanges, 1958–1986: Who Wins?* Boulder and London: Westview Press, 1987.

Robinson, Harlow. *Sergei Prokofiev: A Biography*. New York: Viking, 1987.

Roosevelt, Eleanor. *Eleanor Roosevelt's "My Day": Her Acclaimed Columns 1936–1945*. Edited by Rochelle Chadakoff. New York: Pharos Books, 1989.

———. *The White House Press Conferences of Eleanor Roosevelt*. Edited with an introduction by Maurine Beasley. New York: Garland, 1983.

Roslavleva, Natalia. *Era of the Russian Ballet*. New York: Dutton, 1966.

Rubinstein, Arthur. *My Many Years*. New York: Knopf, 1980.

Sayler, Oliver. *Inside the Moscow Art Theatre*. New York: Bretano's, 1925.

Schwarz, Boris. *Great Masters of the Violin: from Corelli and Vivaldi to Stern, Zuke*. New York: Simon & Schuster, 1983.

———. *Music and Musical Life in Soviet Russia* (2nd ed.). Bloomington, IN: Indiana University Press, 1983.

Segovia, Andrés. *Andrés Segovia: An Autobiography of the Years 1893–1920.* Translated by W. F. O'Brien. New York: Macmillan, 1976.

Seroff, Victor. *The Real Isadora.* New York: Dial Press, 1971.

Shickel, Richard. *100 Years of Carnegie Hall.* New York: Julian Messner, 1960.

Shostakovich, Dmitri (as related to and edited by Solomon Volkov). *Testimony: The Memoirs of Dmitri Shostakovich.* New York: Harper & Row, 1979.

Stassinopoulos, Arianna. *Maria Callas: The Woman Behind the Legend.* New York: Simon & Schuster, 1981.

Stravinsky, Igor. *Selected Correspondence (Vols. 1–3).* Edited and with commentaries by Robert Craft. New York: Knopf, 1982, 1984, 1985.

Subtelny, Orest. *Ukraine: A History.* Toronto: University of Toronto Press, 1988.

Syrett, Harold Coffin. *The City of Brooklyn, 1865–1898: A Political History.* New York: Columbia University Press, 1944.

Taper, Bernard. *Balanchine: A Biography.* New York: Times Books, 1984.

Taylor, S. J. *Stalin's Apologist: Walter Duranty, The New York Times Man in Moscow.* New York: Oxford University Press, 1990.

Terry, Walter. *The Dance in America.* New York: Harper and Brothers, 1956.

———. *Isadora Duncan: Her Life, Her Art, Her Legacy.* New York: Dodd, Mead, 1963.

Troyat, Henri. *Gorky.* Translated by Lowell Bair. New York: Crown, 1989.

Vehanen, Kosti. *Marian Anderson: A Portrait.* New York: Whittlesey House, 1941.

Vernadsky, George. *A History of Russia.* New Haven: Yale University Press, 1954.

Vishnevskaya, Galina. *Galina: A Russian Story.* New York: Harcourt Brace Jovanovich, 1984.

Wade, Graham. *Segovia: A Celebration of the Man and his Music.* London: Allison and Busby, 1983.

Walker, Kathrine Sorley. *De Basil's Ballets Russes.* New York: Atheneum, 1983.

Werth, Alexander. *Russia: The Post-War Years.* New York: Taplinger, 1971.

Wigman, Mary, and Sorell, Walter. *The Mary Wigman Book (Her Writings Edited and Translated)*. Middletown, CT: Wesleyan University Press, 1975.

Wolfe, Gerald. *New York: A Guide to the Metropolis*. New York: New York University Press, 1975.

Yevtushenko, Yevgeny. *Doroga nomer odin*. Moscow: Sovremennik, 1972.

Zorina, Vera. *Zorina*. New York: Farrar, Straus, Giroux, 1986.

INDEX

■ ■ ■